ASSESSMENT CENTRES

Unlocking people potential for growth

2nd Updated Edition

Sandra Schlebusch & Gert Roodt

kr
publishing

2020

ENDORSEMENTS

Everything you need to know about assessment centres you will find in this book. It is extremely useful for organisations and consultants who want to use assessment centres, for potential applicants who want to prepare themselves, and for ambitious researchers. This book also deals with ethical issues, international best practices, and concerns specific to South African conditions. I have rarely held such a comprehensive, differentiated, and useful book on assessment centers in my hands – I am convinced it is a great choice for every reader.

Prof. Dr. Martin Kleinmann, University of Zurich, Switzerland

Like the 1st edition, the 2nd is the "go to" book on how to design and implement an assessment center. Schlebusch and Roodt remain on my list of "Best of..." sources. Based on the authors' many years of consulting experience, the book includes proven, practical, and professionally responsible tips for needs analysis, design of simulations and the overall AC, before/during/after the intervention, and evaluation of ACs for diverse purposes. There are chapters on history, multi-culturalism, and ethical considerations. The content is relevant to AC practice in any country.

George C. Thornton III, Emeritus Professor Colorado State University,
Founder and Director Thornton Institute for Assessment Centers

In Southern Africa the need for assessment methods that are reliable, cost effective and robust are essential to enabling individuals to achieve their potential and build the economy. This book is a compilation of chapters from some of the world's most knowledgeable and experienced experts in the field of assessment centres as well as contributions from authors with extensive experience in cultural diversity. The book blends the practical application of assessment centres with sound theoretical concepts.

For anyone who has a professional interest in assisting individuals and organisations to ensure people are correctly appointed to positions that capitalise on their strengths and are developed to maximise their potential, this book is essential reading.

Terry Meyer, Executive Leadership and Strategy Consultant,
Academic, Keynote Speaker, Author

Since its first publication in 2008, *Assessment Centres: Unlocking People Potential for Growth* has introduced numerous emerging practitioners to the world of assessment centres. It has also been a trusted reference guide for seasoned practitioners – a text that was ever so frequently taken off the shelf to confirm certain concepts or processes in the design and mobilisation of centres or stand-alone simulation exercises. Now, more than a decade later, Sandra and Gert are back with a host of local and international AC heavyweights to provide us with a synthesis of how recent AC research and industry developments will affect the future of AC practice. This well-structured text will once again serve as a foundational guide to newcomers, as well as an indispensable practice framework for those well-familiar with the AC method.

Jaco de Jager, Chairperson, SA Assessment Centre Study Group

The second edition of *Assessment Centres: Unlocking People Potential for Growth* contains everything you need to know about assessment centres and more. It comprehensively creates the current and future context for assessment centres and compellingly explains the theoretical principles informing ACs. The book's strength lies in providing clear and practical guidelines for the implementation of the total Assessment Centre Process and all aspects associated with it – even explaining what to consider when purchasing an Assessment Centre! Anyone who would like to enhance their Talent Management Practices by incorporating assessment centres into their talent strategy should use this as a playbook of leading practices.

Dr. Lydia Cillie-Schmidt, Director of The Talent HUB, and past Chairperson of the ACSG

The editors have done a wonderful job in soliciting contributions from a range of Assessment Centre experts and practitioners, with an understandable emphasis on AC practices within South Africa, making this the 'go to' book for anyone wishing to run professional ACs in the region. The book provides valuable insights into all of the relevant issues that need to be considered when designing and running an AC, and not only provides detailed explanations of all of the key principles but, also covers important matters such as ethical considerations, which are often too readily ignored. I strongly recommend this book to anyone wishing to further their AC knowledge with the aim of running professional ACs.

Nigel Povah, MSc, C.Psychol, AFBPsS, former CEO of a&dc

Assessment Centres: Unlocking People Potential for Growth is an encyclopedic coverage of assessment center methodology. It is truly a must-read book for any academic working with assessment centers.

William C. Byham, Ph.D., Executive Chairman, Development Dimensions International, Inc.

This book is an essential resource for those studying, developing, and implementing assessment centres, both in the South African context and beyond. Both local and international scholars and practitioners lend their expertise, providing evidence-based information pertinent to every stage of the assessment centre process. Important considerations are also covered, including the ethics of AC practices; practicalities of using subcontractors; and the importance of job analysis, pilot testing, and validation. A comprehensive guide to all things AC!

Deborah E. Rupp, Professor of Industrial/Organizational Psychology, George Mason University

Building on the success of the previous edition, *Assessment Centres: Unlocking people potential for growth* continues to provide practitioners and scientists alike with a valuable resource regarding the practice of assessment centres. The book unpacks a four-stage design model for assessment centres, with numerous chapters explaining the intricacies of assessment centre practice. All the chapters have been updated or revised to take into consideration the latest best practices and theories. A number of new chapters and topics were included. The importance of ethnoculturalism and its influence on assessment centres is interesting. Guidelines for the procurement of assessment centre services is also of interest. A chapter is now devoted to the importance of the ethical practice of assessment centres. This edition also looks towards the future, with the inputs from international scholars and practitioners. Novices and seasoned practitioners will welcome the style of writing. It remains the only South African go-to-resource for assessment centre practitioners and scholars.

Dr. Petrus Nel, Associate Professor at the University of Johannesburg, past chairman of the ACSG and longest serving ACSG committee member

First published in 2020.

ISBN: 978-1-86922-798-2
eISBN: 978-1-86922-799-9

Published by KR Publishing
P O Box 3954
Randburg
2125
Republic of South Africa

Tel: (011) 706-6009
Fax: (011) 706-1127
E-mail: orders@knowres.co.za
Website: www.kr.co.za

Typesetting, layout and design: Cia Joubert, cia@knowres.co.za
Cover design: Marlene de'Lorme, marlene@knowres.co.za
Editing & proofreading: Jennifer Renton, jenniferrenton@live.co.za
Project management: Cia Joubert, cia@knowres.co.za
Index created with TExtract / www.Texyz.com

TRIBUTE

We want to acknowledge:

George C. Thornton III

For a lifetime's continued commitment to the enhancement of Assessment Centres worldwide, both in terms of research and practice

and

Hermann Spangenberg

For a lifetime's work in the SA Assessment Centre Study Group (ACSG)

TABLE OF CONTENTS

LIST OF FIGURES xv
LIST OF TABLES xvii
SUMMARY OF CHAPTERS AND AUTHORS xix
ABOUT THE EDITORS xx
ABOUT THE CONTRIBUTORS xxi
PREFACE xxv
ACKNOWLEDGEMENTS xxvii

CHAPTER 1: INTRODUCTION TO ASSESSMENT CENTRES by
Sandra Schlebusch and Gert Roodt 1

1. **INTRODUCTION – WHAT ARE ASSESSMENT CENTRES (ACs)?** 1
2. **WHAT IS AN AC?** 1
    2.1 Demarcation of Terminology 2
3. **TYPES OF ACs** 2
    3.1 Traditional ACs 2
    3.2 Assessment ACs 3
    3.3 Diagnostic ACs (DCs) 3
    3.4 Learning ACs 4
    3.5 Development ACs (DACs) 4
    3.6 Collaborative ACs 5
    3.7 Coaching Development Centres (CDCs) 6
    3.8 Functional ACs 6
4. **FEATURES OF ACs** 6
    4.1 Job analysis 6
    4.2 Use of simulations 6
    4.3 Multiple assessments 7
    4.4 Link between AC assessments and the AC focal constructs 7
    4.5 Multiple observers 7
    4.6 Competent observers and role players 7
    4.7 Behavioural observation and noting 8
    4.8 Classifying and evaluating behaviour 8
    4.9 Data integration 8
    4.10 Standardisation 8
    4.11 Feedback 9
    4.12 Deliverables of an AC 10
5. **STAKEHOLDERS OF ACs** 12
    5.1 Stakeholders directly involved in ACs 12
    5.2 Stakeholders indirectly involved in ACs 14
6. **AC APPLICATIONS** 15
    6.1 Selecting in 15

	6.2	Selecting out	15
	6.3	Development	16
	6.4	Diagnostic purposes	16
7.	**THE DESIGN MODEL**		**16**
	7.1	Steps and stages	17
8.	**THE RATIONALE FOR USING A DESIGN MODEL**		**19**
	8.1	Following a systematic approach	19
	8.2	Keeping the focus on the initial design objectives of the AC	19
	8.3	Following an integrated process	19
	8.4	Adding marketing value	19
	8.5	Ensuring validity, reliability and fairness	19
9.	**CONCLUSION**		**20**

CHAPTER 2: ASSESSMENT CENTRES IN SOUTH AFRICAN HISTORY by *Deon Meiring* **21**

1.	**A BRIEF HISTORY OF ASSESSMENT CENTRES (ACs) IN SOUTH AFRICA**		**21**
2.	**FOUNDING OF THE ASSESSMENT CENTRE STUDY GROUP**		**25**
3.	**AIMS AND OBJECTIVES OF THE ACSG**		**29**
4.	**AC GUIDELINES FOR SOUTH AFRICA**		**30**
	4.1	1991 Guidelines	30
	4.2	1999 Guidelines	31
	4.3	2007 Guidelines	31
	4.4	2015 Guidelines	32
5.	**CODE OF ETHICS FOR ASSESSMENT CENTRES IN SOUTH AFRICA**		**33**
6.	**FUTURE CHALLENGES PRESENTED BY ACs IN SOUTH AFRICA**		**34**

CHAPTER 3: MULTICULTURALISM AND THE USE OF ASSESSMENT CENTRES IN SOUTH AFRICA by *Stella Nkomo and Christina Badalani* **40**

1.	**INTRODUCTION**		**40**
2.	**STRUCTURE AND CONTENT OF CHAPTER**		**40**
3.	**CULTURAL DIVERSITY AND ASSESSMENT CENTRES**		**40**
4.	**LEGAL REQUIREMENTS OF ASSESSMENT CENTRES**		**41**
	4.1	Legal and other requirements for the validity of assessment centres	41
	4.2	South African legal and professional requirements	41
5.	**ETHNOCULTURAL DIVERSITY IN SOUTH AFRICA**		**43**
6.	**HISTORICAL AND POLITICAL CONTEXT OF SOUTH AFRICA**		**44**
	6.1	Ethnocultural diversity since 1994	45
7.	**EMPIRICAL RESEARCH ON NATIONAL CULTURE DIFFERENCES IN SOUTH AFRICA**		**46**
8.	**EMPIRICAL RESEARCH ON CULTURAL DIFFERENCES IN PERSONALITY**		**48**
9.	**ETHNOCULTURAL DIVERSITY AND THE ESSENTIAL ELEMENTS OF ASSESSMENT CENTRES**		**51**

9.1   Definition of assessment centres 51

9.2   The Impact of ethnocultural diversity on ACs...51

9.3   Ten essential elements of ACs and recommendations to minimise ethnocultural diversity effects 55

10.   CONCLUSION **58**

CHAPTER 4: ETHICS AND ASSESSMENT CENTRES by *Rodney L. Lowman* **61**

1.   INTRODUCTION... **61**

1.1   Ethical issues in South African assessment centres 61

1.2   ACs in South Africa 62

1.3   Description of ACs...62

1.4   Which Ethics Codes apply to AC Work? 63

2.   THE SOUTH AFRICAN BEST ASSESSMENT CENTRES PRACTICES DOCUMENT.................. **64**

3.   THE SOUTH AFRICAN AC ETHICS INITIATIVE.. **65**

3.1   Principle 1: Respect for Participant Dignity 65

3.2   Principle 2: Respect for Participant Diversity 66

3.3   Principle 3: Respect for Participant Freedom...67

3.4   Principle 4: Respect for the Client and the Client's Organisation.............................68

3.5   Principle 5: Professional AC Competence...69

3.6   Principle 6: Professional Accountability...70

4.   WHO ENFORCES AC ETHICAL STANDARDS AND AGAINST WHOM?........................... **71**

4.1   Other classificatory schema...72

5.   APPLYING ETHICS GUIDANCE TO THE THREE CASES **74**

6.   SUMMARY AND RECOMMENDATIONS **75**

CHAPTER 5: PURCHASING AN ASSESSMENT CENTRE by *Anne Buckett* **77**

1.   INTRODUCTION... **77**

2.   ORGANISATIONAL PERSPECTIVE... **77**

2.1   Business case...78

2.2   Alignment with other people processes 78

2.3   Assessment Centre policy 79

2.4   Approach to Assessment Centre purchase 79

3.   Service Provider Perspective **86**

3.1   AC consultation process 87

3.2   Contracting the AC 90

INTRODUCTION TO STAGE ONE: ANALYSIS... **93**

1.   WHAT THE ANALYSIS STAGE IS ALL ABOUT **93**

2.   THE PURPOSE OF THE ANALYSIS STAGE.. **94**

2.1   Growing a systematic understanding of the organisational context........................94

2.2   Understanding the organisation, its dynamics and its specific needs........................95

	2.3	Having clarity about the job/role and its demands	95
3.		**CRITICAL DELIVERABLES OF THIS STAGE**	**95**
	3.1	Competency profiles and competency/behavioural elements	95
	3.2	Establishing validation criteria	95
4.		**THE INTENDED OUTCOME OF THIS STAGE**	**96**

CHAPTER 6: NEEDS ANALYSIS by *Gert Roodt* **97**

1.		**INTRODUCTION – THE PURPOSE OF A NEEDS ANALYSIS**	**97**
2.		**SOUTH AFRICA'S DISTINCTIVE SOCIAL CONTEXT**	**98**
	2.1	Understanding South Africa's diverse context	98
	2.2	South Africa's unique legal context	99
	2.3	Ethical conduct demands in South Africa	104
3.		**A COMPANY-SPECIFIC NEEDS ANALYSIS**	**108**
	3.1	Sources of information for a needs analysis	108
4.		**ANALYSIS FOR PREPARING AN AC BUSINESS CASE**	**111**
	4.1	Critical assumptions and constraints	112
	4.2	Analysis of available options	112
	4.3	Cost-benefit analysis	113
	4.4	Considerations in respect of the implementation strategy	114
5.		**CREATING THE APPROPRIATE CLIMATE AND CONTEXT**	**116**
	5.1	Participants	117
	5.2	Project sponsors and ambassadors	117
	5.3	Corporate climate and culture	117
6.		**CRITICAL DECISIONS RELATING TO, AND OUTCOMES OF, THIS STEP**	**117**
	6.1	Analysis of the broad business context	117
	6.2	A company-specific needs analysis	118
	6.3	Creating an appropriate climate or context	118
	6.4	Building a business case or project plan	118

CHAPTER 7: ORGANISATIONAL EFFECTIVENESS ANALYSIS by *Gert Roodt* **119**

1.		**INTRODUCTION – THE PURPOSE OF AN ORGANISATIONAL EFFECTIVENESS ANALYSIS**	**119**
2.		**DIFFERENT VIEWS ON ORGANISATIONAL EFFECTIVENESS**	**120**
	2.1	The effectiveness criteria model	121
	2.2	The goal model	121
	2.3	The multiple-constituency model	122
	2.4	The balanced-scorecard model	123
3.		**MANAGEMENT DEFINED**	**124**
	3.1	Different management levels and management functions	126
	3.2	Key functions and deliverables of each management level	127
	3.3	ACs are designed for different management levels	130

4.	**EXAMPLES OF "GENERIC" MANAGEMENT COMPETENCY PROFILES**	....	**130**
	4.1	Generic management competencies	130
	4.2	Competency elements	134
5.	**ESTABLISHING VALID EFFECTIVENESS CRITERIA**	....	**135**
	5.1	The difficulty in selecting valid criteria	135
	5.2	What to look for in selecting a criterion	136
	5.3	Developing valid criteria	137
6.	**CRITICAL DECISIONS RELATING TO, AND OUTCOMES OF, THIS STEP**	....	**138**
	6.1	Identify and develop appropriate competencies	138
	6.2	Identify and develop evaluation criteria	138

CHAPTER 8: JOB ANALYSIS by *Sandra Schlebusch* **139**

1.	**INTRODUCTION – WHERE DOES JOB ANALYSIS FIT IN?**	....	**139**
2.	**THE AC DESIGN TEAM**	....	**140**
3.	**THE PURPOSE OF A JOB ANALYSIS**	....	**140**
	3.1	What is the target job all about and what is needed to perform the job?	141
	3.2	How does job analysis differ from competency modelling?	142
	3.3	What are the critical competencies leading to success?	144
4.	**JOB ANALYSIS APPROACH**	....	**145**
	4.1	Shelf information	146
	4.2	Process mapping	147
	4.3	Interviews	148
	4.4	Focus-group discussions	150
	4.5	Questionnaires and surveys	150
	4.6	Critical incidents	151
	4.7	Observation	152
	4.8	Competency profile instruments	152
	4.9	Combined techniques	154
	4.10	Information gathered during the job analysis	158
5.	**JOB ANALYSIS DELIVERABLES TO THE AC DESIGN TEAM: DETAILED INFORMATION ON FOCAL CONSTRUCTS**	....	**159**
	5.1	Dimension profiles	159
	5.2	Competency profiles	159
	5.3	Situations as focal constructs (task competencies)	162
	5.4	Situations to use as simulations	163
	5.5	Organisational and industry contexts	163
6.	**SUMMARY OF THE PROCESS OF JOB ANALYSIS FOR AC DESIGN PURPOSES**	......	**163**
7.	**HINTS FOR CONDUCTING A JOB ANALYSIS FOR AC DESIGN PURPOSES**	....	**166**
	7.1	Collect data for two time frames	166
	7.2	Use multiple sources of information	166
	7.3	Use a representative sample	166
	7.4	Obtain sign-off from those involved with the job analysis techniques	167

7.5   Document everything 167

7.6   Get the steering committee's sign-off 167

8.   CRITICAL DECISIONS RELATING TO, AND OUTCOMES OF, THIS STEP **167**

8.1   Dimension/competency profiles per job level 167

8.2   Clear dimension or competency definitions 168

8.3   Dimension or competency (behaviour) elements 168

8.4   Situations that the target job incumbent is exposed to 169

8.5   Understanding the target job context and organisational trends 169

SYNTHESIS OF STAGE ONE: ANALYSIS **173**

1.   THE PURPOSE OF THE ANALYSIS STAGE **173**

1.1   Growing a systematic understanding of the organisational context 173

1.2   Understanding the organisation, its dynamics and its specific needs 173

1.3   Having clarity about the job/role and its demands 173

2.   CRITICAL DELIVERABLES OF THIS STAGE **173**

2.1   Competency profiles, or other focal constructs, and competency/ behavioural
elements 174

2.2   Establishing criteria for validation and evaluation 174

3.   THE FINAL OUTCOME OF THIS STAGE **174**

INTRODUCTION TO STAGE TWO: DESIGN AND DEVELOPMENT **175**

1.   WHAT THE DESIGN AND DEVELOPMENT STAGE IS ALL ABOUT **175**

2.   PURPOSE OF THE DESIGN AND DEVELOPMENT STAGE **176**

2.1   To translate the information from the analysis stage into an operational AC
Blueprint that will guide simulation and AC development 176

2.2   To develop simulations and the support documentation that allow observers to
make valid and reliable assessments of the behaviour 177

2.3   To design an AC process that effectively combines the various simulations 177

2.4   To design an AC that is ready for implementation 177

3.   CRITICAL DELIVERABLES OF THIS STAGE **177**

3.1   An AC manual 177

3.2   A technical AC manual 177

4.   THE INTENDED OUTCOME OF THIS STAGE **178**

**CHAPTER 9: THEORETICAL PRINCIPLES RELEVANT TO ASSESSMENT CENTRE
DESIGN AND IMPLEMENTATION** by *George C. Thornton III* and *Filip Lievens* **179**

1.   INTRODUCTION **179**

2.   BACKGROUND **180**

3.   THEORIES RELATED TO THE OVERALL AC METHOD **180**

3.1   Behavioural consistency 180

3.2	Interactionist theory	181
3.3	Realistic accuracy model	182
3.4	Psychometric theories	183
3.5	Heterogeneous domain sampling model	185
3.6	Gamification	186
4.	**THEORIES RELATED TO ELEMENTS OF THE AC METHOD**	**187**
4.1	Multiple methods of defining the domain	187
4.2	Taxonomy of competencies	187
4.3	Taxonomy of situations	188
4.4	Trait Activation Theory	189
4.5	Taxonomy of aspects of fidelity	191
4.6	Judgmental and statistical integration	192
5.	**CASE STUDY**	**193**
6.	**SUMMARY**	**194**

CHAPTER 10: THE AC BLUEPRINT by *Sandra Schlebusch* **197**

1.	**INTRODUCTION – THE AC BLUEPRINT**	**197**
2.	**PURPOSE OF THE AC BLUEPRINT**	**198**
3.	**AC CONTENT**	**199**
3.1	General simulated setting/context	199
3.2	Simulation specifications	199
3.3	Participant's role	199
4.	**AC OPERATIONAL ASPECTS**	**200**
4.1	AC duration	200
4.2	Number of participants per AC	200
4.3	Observer to participant ratio	200
4.4	AC logistics	200
5.	**AC APPROACH**	**201**
5.1	AC purpose	201
5.2	Dimension-based AC (DBAC), Task-based AC (TBAC), or Mixed-Model AC	202
5.3	AC's focal constructs	202
5.4	AC process	203
5.5	Data driven classification and evaluation, or checklists	203
5.6	Point of assessment	204
5.7	Presentation of AC results to the client	204
5.8	Rating scale	205
5.9	Data integration	206
5.10	Separate or integrated simulations	207
5.11	Use of technology	207
5.12	Purchasing an off-the-shelf AC or custom-made AC	208
5.13	Simulations	208

6.	**APPROVAL OF THE AC BLUEPRINT**	**214**
7.	**EXAMPLE OF AN AC BLUEPRINT**	**214**
8.	**AC BLUEPRINT CHECKLIST**	**218**

CHAPTER 11: DEVELOP SIMULATIONS I by *Sandra Schlebusch* **219**

1.	**INTRODUCTION – SIMULATION DEVELOPMENT**	**219**
2.	**SIMULATION DEFINED**	**220**
3.	**TYPES OF SIMULATIONS**	**220**
	3.1 Typical simulations	221
	3.2 Limitless types of simulations	229
4.	**SIMULATION DESIGN HINTS**	**230**
	4.1 Create a sufficiently complex fictitious organisation/context	230
	4.2 Trait activation theory (TAT) in action	230
	4.3 Simulation modularity	231
	4.4 Instruction clarity	231
	4.5 Neutrality of the setting (context)	231
	4.6 Appropriate language	232
	4.7 Gender neutral names	232
	4.8 Follow a systematic process	232
	4.9 Start with developing the context or setting	233
5.	**SIMULATION DOCUMENTATION**	**234**
	5.1 Participant	234
	5.2 Observer	236
	5.3 Role player	248
	5.4 Simulation administration manual	251
6.	**CONCLUDING REMARKS**	**251**

CHAPTER 12: DEVELOP SIMULATIONS II by *Sandra Schlebusch* **253**

1.	**INTRODUCTION**	**253**
2.	**PRE-PILOT (TRIALLING)**	**253**
3.	**THE SPECIAL CASE OF PARALLEL SIMULATIONS**	**255**
4.	**THE USE OF INFORMATION TECHNOLOGY**	**256**
	4.1 Software development life cycle	257
	4.2 Aspects to consider	259
5.	**IMPORTANT VALIDITY CONSIDERATIONS**	**261**
	5.1 Possible sources of error variance	262
	5.2 Reliability	264
	5.3 Validity	264
6.	**CRITICAL DECISIONS RELATING TO, AND OUTCOMES OF, THIS STEP**	**265**
	6.1 Simulations that elicit enough behaviour linked to the focal constructs being evaluated	265

6.2   Simulation documentation that is easy to use, clear and comprehensive 265

6.3   Simulation administration guidelines that will ensure the simulation is administered in a standard format 266

CHAPTER 13: DEVELOP CENTRE by *Sandra Schlebusch* **267**

1.   **INTRODUCTION – THE PURPOSE OF DEVELOPING A CENTRE** **267**
2.   **AC DESIGN HINTS** **268**
     2.1   AC duration 268
     2.2   Observer participant ratio 268
     2.3   Simulation sequence during the AC 268
     2.4   Participant career discussion 269
     2.5   Orientation 269
     2.6   AC debrief(s) 270
3.   **CENTRE PROCESS ACCORDING TO CENTRE PURPOSE** **270**
4.   **VARIOUS PROGRAMMES** **275**
     4.1   Participant programme 276
     4.2   Observer programme 277
     4.3   Administrator programme 278
5.   **THE ADMINISTRATOR (ALSO KNOWN AS THE CENTRE MANAGER)** **278**
     5.1   Role of the AC administrator 278
     5.2   Specific functions 278
     5.3   Administrator documentation 280
6.   **ADDITIONAL DOCUMENTATION** **282**
     6.1   Final report for an AC for selection purposes 283
     6.2   DAC participant final report 283
     6.3   Development plans 287
     6.4   Hand-outs 288
     6.5   Pre-AC documents 288
     6.6   Participants and observers: AC evaluation form 288
     6.7   Spreadsheets and other data-capturing forms 289
7.   **AC MANUAL AND BUDGET** **289**
8.   **CRITICAL DECISIONS RELATING TO THIS STEP AND THE OUTCOMES THEREOF** **289**
     8.1   A logical, cost- and time-effective AC 289
     8.2   An AC where everyone performs optimally 290
     8.3   An easy-to-use AC manual 290

CHAPTER 14: PILOT CENTRE by *Sandra Schlebusch* **295**

1.   **INTRODUCTION – PILOT THE AC** **295**
2.   **PURPOSE OF PILOTING AN AC** **295**
     2.1   Double-check 296
     2.2   Test the AC 296

3. **IMPORTANT CONTENT AND FACE VALIDITY CONSIDERATIONS** 296
    3.1 AC participant feedback 297
    3.2 AC process owners' feedback 297
4. **SELECTION CRITERIA IN RESPECT OF PEOPLE ATTENDING THE AC PILOT** 297
    4.1 Observers and role players 297
    4.2 Participants 298
5. **IMPORTANT ASPECTS TO CONSIDER** 298
    5.1 Aspects before the AC pilot 300
    5.2 Aspects during the pilot 300
    5.3 Aspects at the end of the pilot 300
    5.4 Aspects after the AC pilot 301
6. **HINTS ON IMPROVING THE AC PILOT'S EFFECTIVENESS** 301
7. **CRITICAL DECISIONS RELATING TO, AND OUTCOMES OF, THIS STEP** 302

SYNTHESIS OF STAGE TWO: DESIGN AND DEVELOPMENT 303

1. **THE PURPOSE OF THE DESIGN AND DEVELOPMENT STAGE** 303
    1.1 Transforming the information from the analysis stage into an operational AC blueprint 303
    1.2 Developing simulations that comply with the specifications set out in the AC blueprint 303
    1.3 Designing an AC that effectively sequences the various AC actions 303
2. **CRITICAL DELIVERABLES OF THIS STAGE** 304
    2.1 An AC manual 304
    2.2 An AC technical manual 304
3. **THE FINAL OUTCOME OF THIS STAGE** 304

INTRODUCTION TO STAGE THREE: IMPLEMENTATION 306

1. **WHAT THE IMPLEMENTATION STAGE IS ALL ABOUT** 306
2. **CRITICAL DELIVERABLES OF THIS STAGE** 307
    2.1 A pool of readily available, competent process owners 307
    2.2 An AC practice that adheres to the AC manual 307
    2.3 Post-AC processes that ensure positive action and a sustained AC process 308
3. **THE INTENDED OUTCOME OF THIS STAGE** 308
    3.1 An AC that is part of the client organisation's culture 308
    3.2 An AC system, process and practice that ensure a reliable and valid AC 308

CHAPTER 15: BEFORE THE CENTRE by *Sandra Schlebusch* 309

1. **INTRODUCTION – PURPOSE OF THIS STEP** 309
2. **OBSERVER** 310
    2.1 Role of the observer 310
    2.2 Selecting internal or external observers 310
    2.3 Observers' background 312

2.4	Observer selection criteria and competencies	313
2.5	Observer training	318
2.6	Content of the online and lecture room training	323
2.7	Continued training	332
3.	**ROLE PLAYER**	**334**
3.1	Role of the role player	334
3.2	Role player selection criteria and competence	334
3.3	Role player training process	335
4.	**ADMINISTRATOR TRAINING**	**339**
4.1	The changing role of the administrator	339
4.2	Training content	339
5.	**POSSIBLE SPECIALIST CAREER PATH IN ACs**	**343**
6.	**TRAINING OF DECISION-MAKERS AND OTHER AC STAFF**	**344**
7.	**LOGISTICS AND AC PAPERWORK**	**345**
8.	**PARTICIPANT AND OBSERVER PRE-AC WORK**	**346**
9.	**CRITICAL DECISIONS RELATING TO THIS STEP AND ITS OUTCOMES**	**347**
9.1	Competent AC process owners	347
9.2	Effective logistical, material, venue and equipment arrangements	347
9.3	Participants informed and ready to participate in the AC	347

CHAPTER 16: DURING THE CENTRE by *Sandra Schlebusch* 349

1.	**INTRODUCTION – PURPOSE OF THIS STEP**	**349**
2.	**CONDUCTING AN EFFECTIVE CENTRE**	**349**
3.	**ORIENTATION SESSIONS**	**350**
3.1	Participant orientation session	350
3.2	Observer and role player orientation session	350
4.	**PER-SIMULATION DEBRIEFINGS**	**351**
5.	**AC PROCESS FLOW FROM AN OBSERVER PERSPECTIVE**	**352**
6.	**DATA INTEGRATION (WASH-UP)**	**353**
6.1	Statistical (mechanical) integration	353
6.2	Judgemental (clinical) integration	354
6.3	Combination approach to data integration	357
7.	**INTEGRATING OTHER ASSESSMENT RESULTS WITH SIMULATION RESULTS**	**357**
7.1	The hurdles approach	357
7.2	Parallel processing of results approach	358
7.3	Serial processing of results approach	358
8.	**PITFALLS TO AVOID DURING AN AC**	**359**
8.1	Cutting time on the programme	359
8.2	Observers are in a rush to finish	359
8.3	Not conducting debriefings owing to time pressure	359
8.4	Participants not openly sharing their experiences during debriefing sessions	360

9.   **PRACTICAL HINTS** **360**
    9.1   Ensure that the AC programme is followed 360
    9.2   Ensure that all documents are completed correctly, comprehensively and on time 360
    9.3   The administrator must assist observers where possible 361
    9.4   Where possible, all the process owners must interact socially with participants 361
    9.5   Note any deviation from the programme and any incident at the AC 361
    9.6   All process owners must model the behaviour, "Walk the talk" 361
    9.7   Arrange the feedback discussion with the participants while still at the AC 362
10.   **CRITICAL DECISIONS RELATING TO THIS STEP, AND THE OUTCOMES THEREOF** **365**
    10.1 Valid and reliable participant profiles 365
    10.2 AC participants are positive towards the AC 365
    10.3 The ACs are conducted consistently according to the AC Manual 365

CHAPTER 17: AFTER THE CENTRE by *Sandra Schlebusch* **367**

1.   **INTRODUCTION – PURPOSE OF THIS STEP** **367**
2.   **POST-AC PROCESSES RELATED TO THE PARTICIPANT** **368**
    2.1   Feedback 369
    2.2   Development plan 385
    2.3   Growth framework and related human capital processes 385
3.   **POST-AC PROCESSES RELATED TO THE FUTURE AND MAINTENANCE OF THE AC** **392**
    3.1   Data capturing 392
    3.2   Storing the participants' simulations and other AC information 393
    3.3   Reconciliation of all costs 394
    3.4   Maintaining the AC 394
4.   **CRITICAL DECISIONS RELATING TO THIS STEP, AND THE OUTCOMES THEREOF** **395**
    4.1   Insight into participants' AC performance 395
    4.2   Comprehensive development plans 395
    4.3   Supportive processes 395
    4.4   An AC that is relevant to the current needs of the organisation 396

SYNTHESIS OF STAGE THREE: IMPLEMENTATION **397**

1.   **PURPOSE OF THE IMPLEMENTATION STAGE** **397**
    1.1   Train process owners and prepare for the AC 397
    1.2   Conduct ACs 397
    1.3   Give post-AC feedback 397
    1.4   Implement processes to ensure future ACs 397
2.   **CRITICAL DELIVERABLES OF THIS STAGE** **398**
    2.1   A pool of competent AC process owners 398
    2.2   ACs conducted in a consistent manner 398
    2.3   AC results accepted by the various stakeholders 398
    2.4   DC and DAC participants actively developing the identified development areas 398

2.5   Data sets for research purposes 398

2.6   AC information and material safely stored 398

2.7   The AC maintained 399

3.   THE FINAL OUTCOME OF THIS STAGE **399**

INTRODUCTION TO STAGE FOUR: EVALUATION AND VALIDATION **400**

1.   WHAT THE EVALUATION AND VALIDATION STAGE IS ALL ABOUT **400**

1.1   The content-evaluation step 401

1.2   The reliability and validity evaluation step 401

2.   CRITICAL DELIVERABLES OF THIS STAGE **401**

2.1   A content-valid AC programme and process 401

2.2   A reliable and valid AC programme and process 402

3.   INTENDED OUTCOME OF THIS STAGE **402**

CHAPTER 18: DESCRIPTIVE (CONTENT) ANALYSIS by *Gert Roodt* 403

1.   INTRODUCTION – THE PURPOSE OF A CONTENT ANALYSIS **403**

2.   THE AC PROCESS OWNERS' EVALUATIONS AND INPUT **406**

2.1   Ensuring content relevance 406

2.2   Ensuring process rigour 407

2.3   In conclusion 408

3.   PARTICIPANTS' EVALUATIONS AND INPUT **409**

3.1   Experience of the content 409

3.2   Experience of the process 410

3.3   In conclusion 411

4.   SUBORDINATES' PRE- AND POST-AC OBSERVATIONS **411**

4.1   Pre- and post-evaluations of manager behaviours in respect of content 411

4.2   Pre- and post-evaluations of managers' behaviours in respect of process 412

4.3   In conclusion 412

5.   MANAGERS' EVALUATIONS AND INPUT **413**

5.1   Strategic relevance of the content 413

5.2   Strategic relevance of the process 414

5.3   In conclusion 414

6.   HUMAN CAPITAL SPECIALISTS' EVALUATIONS AND INPUT **415**

6.1   A critical competency perspective on content 415

6.2   A critical compliance perspective on the process 416

6.3   In conclusion 417

7.   OTHER SOURCES OF INFORMATION **418**

7.1   Contextual and company needs analyses 418

7.2   Job and job-family analyses 418

8. CRITICAL DECISIONS RELATING TO THIS STEP, AND THE OUTCOMES THEREOF 418

CHAPTER 19: RELIABILITY AND VALIDITY ANALYSES by *Gert Roodt* 421

1. INTRODUCTION – THE PURPOSE OF RELIABILITY AND VALIDITY ANALYSES 421
2. WHAT RELIABILITY AND VALIDITY ARE ALL ABOUT 423
3. BASIC STATISTICAL CONCEPTS FOR UNDERSTANDING AND INTERPRETING RELIABILITY AND VALIDITY CONSTRUCTS 423
    3.1   Measure of central tendency (location) 424
    3.2   Measures of variability 425
    3.3   Measures of association 425
4. OPTIONS FOR CALCULATING THE RELIABILITY OF AC RATINGS 426
    4.1   Test–retest reliability 427
    4.2   Equivalent-form reliability 428
    4.3   Split-half reliabilities 428
    4.4   Kuder-Richardson and Coefficient Alpha reliabilities 428
    4.5   Inter-rater and intra-rater reliabilities 432
    4.6   The Standard Error of Measurement (SEM) 432
    4.7   Potential sources of error variance 433
5. OPTIONS FOR CALCULATING THE VALIDITY OF AC RATINGS 435
    5.1   Content (description) validity 435
    5.2   Construct (identification) validity 436
    5.3   Criterion (prediction) validity 437
    5.4   Unitary validity 438
    5.5   Threats to the validity of a measure 439
6. AC RATINGS 439
    6.1   Raw ratings 439
    6.2   Final (integrated) ratings 440
7. SPECIAL CASES AND ISSUES 440
    7.1   Exercise effects 440
    7.2   Rating distributions 440
    7.3   Cross-cultural issues 441
    7.4   Competency redundancies 441
8. CRITICAL OUTCOMES OF, AND DECISIONS RELATING TO, THIS STEP 442
    8.1   A reliable AC 442
    8.2   A content-valid AC 442
    8.3   A construct-valid AC 443
    8.4   A predictive-valid AC 443

CHAPTER 20: INTERNATIONAL PERSPECTIVE – CURRENT PRACTICES AND FUTURE CHALLENGES by *Nigel Povah, Philippa Riley* and *Jordon Jones*.......................... 451

1.	**INTRODUCTION**..	**451**
	1.1 Setting the scene...	451
	1.2 Approach..	452
	1.3 Methodology...	452
2.	**DEMAND/POPULARITY OF ACs**..	**453**
3.	**TECHNOLOGY**..	**454**
4.	**CONSTRUCTS**..	**456**
5.	**CANDIDATE/PARTICIPANT EXPERIENCE**..	**459**
6.	**DIVERSITY AND INCLUSION**..	**460**
7.	**DATA MANAGEMENT**..	**462**
	7.1 Data protection...	462
	7.2 People analytics..	464
8.	**SUMMARY/CONCLUSIONS**..	**465**
9.	**ACKNOWLEDGEMENTS**..	**467**

EPILOGUE: THE FUTURE OF ACs IN SA by *Sandra Schlebusch & Gert Roodt*.............. **468**
GLOSSARY **472**
REFERENCES **479**
INDEX **501**

LIST OF FIGURES

Figure 1.1: The basic design model.. 17
Figure 1.2: The AC design model.. 18
Figure 5.1: Key steps to consider when purchasing an AC 78
Figure 5.2: Key steps to consider when selling an AC.. 87
Figure S1.1: The steps in, and stages of, the design model.. 93
Figure 6.1: The needs analysis step in the analysis stage 97
Figure 7.1: The organisational effective analysis step in the analysis stage............... 119
Figure 7.2: Organisational goals at different time intervals 122
Figure 7.3: The strategic alignment of balanced-scorecard measures with strategic objectives 123
Figure 7.4: An integrated model of management functions on different levels 129
Figure 7.5: Critical behavioural elements for different competencies in a competency set 134
Figure 8.1: The job analysis step in the analysis stage 139
Figure 8.2: Drilling down a section of a process.. 147
Figure 8.3: Eight steps in the job analysis step of the AC design model..................... 164
Figure 8.4: Checklist for the AC Design Team 169
Figure S2.1: Steps in, and stages of, the AC Design Model.. 175
Figure 11.1: The develop simulation step in the design stage..................................... 219
Figure 12.1: Software Development Life Cycle 257

Figure 13.1: The design centre step in the design and development stage 267

Figure 13.2: Process as experienced by the participants during a Selection AC 271

Figure 13.3: Example of a Process at a Diagnostic Centre 272

Figure 13.4: Example of a Process at a Development Assessment Centre 273

Figure 13.5: Example of the Micro-Process at a Collaborative Centre 274

Figure 13.6: Example of the Micro-Process at a Coaching Centre 275

Figure 13.7: Example of a page from the data-integration administrator notes 281

*Figure 13.8: Example of a final report where reporting back takes place per competency,
     per simulation* 284

*Figure 13.9: Example of a final report where reporting back takes place per simulation,
     per competency* 285

Figure 14.1: The pilot centre step in the design stage 295

Figure S3.1: The steps in, and stages of, the AC Design Model 306

Figure 15.1: The step, before the centre, in the implementation stage 309

Figure 15.2: Proposed Observer Training Process 322

Figure 15.3: Role Player Training Process 335

Figure 15.4: AC Administrator Training Content 339

Figure 15.5: Possible career path in ACs 344

Figure 16.1: The step, during the centre, in the implementation stage 349

Figure 16.2: AC process flow 352

Figure 16.3: Example of the Hurdles Approach 357

Figure 16.4: Example of the Parallel Processing of Results Approach 358

Figure 16.5: Example of the Serial Processing of Results Approach 359

Figure 17.1: The step, After the Centre, in the implementation stage 367

Figure 17.2: Post-DC / DAC development process 368

Figure 17.3: Information shared during feedback 372

Figure 17.4: The growth framework 386

Figure 17.5: SPP2 Process 389

Figure S4.1: The steps in, and stages of, the AC Design Model 400

Figure 18.1: The steps in, and stages of, the design model 403

Figure 18.2: Prominent stakeholders in the AC process 404

Figure 19.1: The steps in, and stages of, the design model 421

Figure 19.2: The distribution of recorded weights 424

Figure 19.3: Potential sources of error variance that may affect operational reliability 433

Figure 19.4: Skewed competency rating and internal consistency reliability 434

Figure 19.5: Less skewed competency rating and internal consistency reliability 434

*Figure 20.1: To what extent are different participant facing technology features currently
     being used, and which features are likely to be introduced in the next two years?* 454

*Figure 20.2: To what extent are different assessor, AC manager and administrator technology
     features currently being used, and which features are likely to be introduced in the next
     two years?* 455

Figure 20.3: To what extent are each of these competencies assessed? 458

Figure 20.4: Ratings of the importance of 'employee experience' across regions. 459

LIST OF TABLES

Table 1.1: A typical development plan...11

Table 2.1: International speakers at ACSG conferences (1980-2020) 26

Table 2.2: ACSG chairpersons (1981-2019)...29

Table 3.1: Ethnocultural Diversity and Ten Essential Elements of assessment centres............56

Table 4.1: AC Ethical Challenges Themes 72

Table 5.1: Advantages and disadvantages of off-the-shelf simulation exercises.............81

Table 5.2: Advantages and disadvantages of off-the-shelf virtual ACs.............................82

Table 5.3: Advantages and disadvantages of customised simulation exercises...............82

Table 5.4: Comparison of insourcing versus outsourcing an AC..84

Table 6.1: AC participants' rights and the manner of observance of such rights during an AC 105

Table 6.2: A comparison of alternative assessment methods with ACs..........................112

Table 7.1: Effectiveness criteria and their respective frequency of use in 17 organisational effectiveness models 121

Table 7.2: Key stakeholders and their objectives, and the measurement criteria in respect of such objectives 122

Table 7.3: Management tasks and functions on different management levels.................127

Table 7.4: Key deliverables on each management level..128

Table 7.5: Types and quality of information at different management levels 128

Table 7.6: Technical/functional and generic people skills for different management levels..........130

Table 7.7: Generic management competencies required of top and middle managers......131

Table 7.8: Definitions of generic competency sets and competency dimensions.............131

Table 8.1: Elements of focus during a job analysis 141

Table 8:2: Differences between job analysis and competency modelling 143

Table 9.1: Practical implications of theories relevant to assessment centre design and implementation 195

Table 10.1: Acronyms related to the point of assessment 204

Table 10.2: Example of a focal construct/context matrix..211

Table 10.3: Example of a simulation/context matrix 212

Table 10.4: Example of a focal construct/simulation matrix...213

Table 10.5: AC Detail 214

Table 10.6: Assessor – Competency Assessment Matrix...215

Table 10.7: Assessment Instrument Descriptions 216

Table 10.8: Rating Scale..216

Table 10.9: AC Characteristics 217

Table 11.1: Examples of Gender Neutral Names..232

Table 11.2: Example of participant instructions issued for a group meeting 235

Table 11:3 Example of BARS...237

Table 11.4: Example of a BARS norm table for a competency with six elements/indicators 237

Table 11.5: Example of a BOS 239

Table 11.6: Example of a BOS norm table for a competency with six elements..............239

Table 11.7: Example of a page from an observer report form using an adapted BOS..................241

Table 11.8: Example of a Behaviour Checklist...242

Table 11.9: Example of a Task List used during a TBAC 243

Table 11.10: Example of Observer Guidelines per Simulation (Source: Used with permission
    from Vitatalent (PTY) Ltd)...**246**

Table 11.11: Example of a norm table for a DAC...248

Table 11.12: Example of role player guidelines 250

Table 12.1: Pre-pilot checklist..254

Table 12.2: Compliance Checklist for using Technology during an AC 261

Table 13.1: Individual participant programme for a collaborative DAC......................................276

Table 13.2: Observer programme for a collaborative DAC...277

Table 13.3: Data-integration grid...280

Table 13.4: Competency summary form...282

Table 13.5: Example of a ticked check list..286

Table 14.1: List of concrete AC aspects regarding which feedback is needed 298

Table 14.2: "Moments-of-truth" feedback list..299

Table 15.1: The Basic Observation Task when Following the Behaviour Observation approach 310

Table 15.2: Internal versus External Observers...311

Table 15.3: Advantages and Disadvantages of Observers with Different Backgrounds 312

Table 15.4: List of Possible Observer Competencies 313

Table 15.5: List of Competencies for a CDC observer-coach..317

Table 15.6: Systematic Errors in Behaviour Observation..326

Table 15.7: Potential Problems when Noting Behaviour 326

Table 15.8: Example of Classifying Behaviour in Notes Taken During a Simulation.....................327

Table 15.9: Potential Problems when Classifying Behaviour...328

Table 15.10: Common Rating Errors...328

Table 15.11: Potential Selection Criteria for Role players During an AC......................................334

Table 17.1: Examples of the Various Learning Activities...390

Table 17.2: Comparison of Final Ratings 391

Table 19.1: Reliabilities of 14 interpersonal competency ratings obtained by means of structured,
    competency-rating interviews 429

Table 19.2: Correlation matrix between exercise ratings and final competency ratings, including
    competency and exercise reliability coefficients..431

SUMMARY OF CHAPTERS AND AUTHORS

Chapter Number	Chapter Title	Author(s)
1	Introduction to assessment centres	Sandra Schlebusch and Gert Roodt
2	Assessment centres' South African History	Deon Meiring
3	Multi-Culturism in South-Africa and the Impact on assessment centres	Stella Nkomo and Christina Badalani
4	Ethics and assessment centres	Rodney L. Lowman
5	Purchasing assessment centres	Anne Buckett
6	Needs Analysis	Gert Roodt
7	Organisational Effectiveness	Gert Roodt
8	Job Analysis	Sandra Schlebusch
9	Theoretical Principles to Assessment Centre Design and Implementation	George C. Thornton and Filip Lievens
10	Assessment Centre Blueprint	Sandra Schlebusch
11	Develop Simulations I	Sandra Schlebusch
12	Develop Simulations II	Sandra Schlebusch
13	Develop Centre	Sandra Schlebusch
14	Pilot Centre	Sandra Schlebusch
15	Before the Centre	Sandra Schlebusch
16	During the Centre	Sandra Schlebusch
17	After the Centre	Sandra Schlebusch
18	Descriptive Analysis	Gert Roodt
19	Reliability and Validity Analyses	Gert Roodt
20	International Perspective - Current Practices and Future Challenges	Nigel Povah, Philippa Riley and Jordon Jones
	Epilogue	Sandra Schlebusch and Gert Roodt

ABOUT THE EDITORS

Sandra Schlebusch

Sandra Schlebusch is the managing director of LEMASA (Pty) LTD and the owner of LeCouSa Consulting cc. Sandra obtained a BCom Honours degree in Industrial Psychology at the Potchefstroom University for Christian Higher Education. She continued her studies in business and management-leadership and obtained an MBA during May 2004 at the University of the Northwest, Potchefstroom Campus. She is a registered Psychometrist at the Health Professions Council of South Africa, as well as a practising life, business and executive coach. Sandra's additional memberships includes COMENSA and ICF, and she has extensive work experience in the chemical, transport, broadcasting and telecommunications industries. Her experience covers the whole spectrum of human and organisational development.

Sandra's passion is using simulations and assessment centres for developmental purposes. Her active involvement in assessment centre design, implementation and evaluation started at the end of 1987 and continues today. She received an award for *Recognition for Continuous Contribution to the field of Assessment Centres in South Africa* in 2007 from the Assessment Centre Study Group (ACSG), is a previous chairman of the ACSG, and was awarded Honorary Membership of the ACSG in 2012. Sandra co-established the AC Academy as part of the ACSG in 2012, with the aim of educating and upskilling potential assessment centre users. She has co-authored a published peer-reviewed journal article, is a study supervisor and examiner from time to time for Master's degree students whose research studies are in the field of assessment centres, and is a guest lecturer at universities on the subject of assessment centres. Sandra can be contacted at: Sandra@lemasa.co.za

Gert Roodt

Gerhard (Gert) Roodt (DAdmin) is a licensed psychologist and a registered personnel practitioner, as well as an author/co-author of more than 100 peer-reviewed journal articles, approximately 70 conference proceeding papers, 15 technical reports, 17 books, 70 book chapters and several articles in non-research based journals. He has also presented/co-presented approximately 135 peer-reviewed papers at national and international academic conferences. Gert was the Vice Dean: Research in the Faculty of Management at the University of Johannesburg, South Africa, and is the former head of the Centre for Work Performance in the Department of Industrial Psychology and People Management. He is also a former chair of the Society for Industrial Psychology (1995–1997). Gert serves on the review/editorial boards of nine local and international scholarly journals. Gert retired from academia in 2018, and can be contacted at: roodtg@gmail.com

ABOUT THE CONTRIBUTORS

Christina Badalani

Christina Badalani completed a Bachelor of Arts General in 2000 at the University of Zimbabwe, after which she was an English teacher in Zimbabwe for three years. In 2010 she started studying a BCom in Industrial Psychology with UNISA, graduating cum laude in 2013. Christina completed her honours through UNISA in 2014 and graduated in 2015. She recently completed an MCom in Industrial Psychology at the University of Pretoria. Christina has worked as a research assistant for Professor Stella Nkomo, and is currently working for Re a Dirha Consultants as an Industrial Psychologist intern. She sat for her Industrial Psychology Board Examinations in June 2019. Christina can be contacted at: christinamachingambi@gmail.com

Anne Buckett

Anne Buckett (PhD) is an Industrial Psychologist and Managing Director of Precision ACS, which provides a wide range of clients with support in the area of competency-based assessment and development. Her main focus and passion is assessment and development centres, and she has 20 years' experience in this area. Anne has also worked with several large international consulting firms during her career, acquiring experience across a number of specialised HR interventions. She has served on various industry committees, including the Assessment Centre Study Group of South Africa (ACSG), People Assessment in Industry (PAI), and the Society for Industrial and Organisational Psychology of South Africa (SIOPSA). She has contributed to book chapters and published several articles on assessment centres in the past decade. Anne was part of the task team committee responsible for revising best practice guidelines for assessment centres in South Africa in 2007 and 2015 (co-Chair). Her most recent publication is: Buckett, A., Becker, J. R., & Roodt, G. (2017). General performance factors and group differences in assessment center ratings. *Journal of Managerial Psychology*, *32*(4), 298-313, https://doi.org/10.1108/JMP-08-2016-0264. Anne can be contacted at: anne@precisionacs.co.za

Jordon Jones

Jordon Jones is an Organisational Psychologist. He graduated with first-class honours from his BSc in Psychology at the University of Surrey (UK) and began his career working in schools for children with autism spectrum conditions. He returned to Surrey to complete an MSc in Occupational Psychology.

In his consulting roles with a&dc and later PSI, Jordon led projects for a geographically diverse list of international clients from many industries, including non-profit, retail, pharmaceutical and manufacturing. His solution experience includes the design and delivery of competency frameworks, psychometric tests, assessment centre activities (paper and virtual) and development programmes for all levels of participant. Jordon now occupies the position of Talent Manager in PSI's Human Capital division, managing many of PSI's own internal recruitment, onboarding and development initiatives.

Jordon also has strong relationships with associations such as the British Psychological Society (BPS), the Association of Business Psychologists (ABP), the Chartered Institute of Personnel and Development (CIPD) and the Society for Human Resource Management (SHRM), having frequently delivered presentations, webinars and workshops for them over the years. Jordon can be contacted at: jordonjones@psionline. com

Filip Lievens

Filip Lievens is Lee Kong Chian Professor of Human Resources at the Lee Kong Chian School of Business of Singapore Management University. He is also an Honorary Professor at the University of Cape Town and a visiting professor at Ghent University, Belgium. In 1999, Filip obtained his PhD at Ghent University, Belgium. His main interests deal with talent acquisition, talent assessment, and adaptability. As an internationally recognised scholar, Filip has published over 45 papers in top-tier journals, including the Annual Review of Psychology, Journal of Applied Psychology, Personnel Psychology, Journal of Management, Organizational Behavior and Human Decision Processes, Intelligence, and Organizational Research Methods. Filip serves on the editorial board of the Journal of Applied Psychology and Personnel Psychology, and was the first European winner of the Distinguished Early Career Award of the Society for Industrial and Organizational Psychology. He is also a winner of the Jeanneret Award and the Douglas Bray and Ann Howard Award, which recognize outstanding contributions in the assessment domain. He was a recipient of the Friedrich Wilhelm Bessel-Forschungspreis of the Alexander von Humboldt-Foundation and is laureate of the Royal Flemish Academy of Sciences and Arts, an award that values substantial contributions in any discipline in social sciences. Filip is a fellow of the Society for Industrial and Organizational Psychology (SIOP), the American Psychological Association (APA), the Association for Psychological Science (APS), and the International Association of Applied Psychology (IAAP). Filip can be contacted at: filiplievens@smu.edu.sg

Rodney L. Lowman

Rodney Lowman (PhD, ABAP) is Distinguished Professor Emeritus and Past Program Director and Dean, Organizational Psychology Programs, California School of Professional Psychology, and Provost/VPAA and Acting President of Alliant International University. He is also President of Lowman & Richardson/ Consulting Psychologists, based in San Diego, which provides career counselling and coaching. Rodney, a licensed psychologist, is the author or editor of 12 books and monographs, has published over 130 peer-reviewed articles and chapters, and has made hundreds of professional presentations all over the world. He is a Fellow of the American Psychological Association's Divisions 1 (General Psychology), 12 (Society of Clinical Psychology), 13 (Society of Consulting Psychology), 14 (Society for Industrial and Organizational Psychology), 17 (Society of Counselling Psychology) and 52 (International). His books include: *The Ethical Practice of Consulting Psychology* (with Stewart Cooper); *An Introduction to Consulting Psychology: Working with Individuals, Groups, and Organizations, Internationalizing Multiculturalism: Expanding Professional Competencies in a Globalized World; The Ethical Practice of Psychology in Organizations* (2nd ed.), *Handbook of Organizational Consulting Psychology, The Clinical Practice of Career Assessment: Interests, Abilities, Personality*, and *Counseling & Psychotherapy of Work Dysfunctions*. He has won a number of professional awards and recognitions. Rodney can be contacted at: rlowman1@gmail.com

Deon Meiring

The late Deon Meiring was a full professor in the Department of Human Resources Management at the University of Pretoria. He was registered as an Industrial Psychologist with the HPCSA in 1995 and received his PhD from Tilburg University in the Netherlands in 2007. His field of specialisation was advance assessment practice, and he had extensive experience in assessment and development assessment centres' designs as well as cross-cultural personality test construction (www.sapiproject.co.za). In 2010, Deon received an honorary membership from the Assessment Centre Study Group (ACSG) for his work in the Assessment Centre field in South Africa. In 2018 he received a special recognition award for his contribution to the science and practice of assessment centres in South Africa from the ACSG. He was instrumental in the development and publication of the *Best Practice Guidelines for the use of the Assessment Centre Method in South Africa* (5th ed.), in collaboration with the ACSG Taskforce on assessment centres in South Africa. He also contributed to the development of the Code of Ethics for Assessment Center Practice in South Africa.

Stella M. Nkomo

Stella Nkomo is currently a Strategic Professor in the Department of Human Resource Management at the University of Pretoria, South Africa. She holds a PhD in Business Administration from the University of Massachusetts (USA) and an MBA from the University of Rhode Island (USA). Her internationally acclaimed research on race and gender in organisations, leadership, and managing diversity and management in Africa has been published in numerous journals and books.

Stella is co-author of the critically acclaimed Harvard Business School Press book, *Our Separate Ways: Black and White Women and the Struggle for Professional Identity* and *Courageous Conversations: A Collection of Interviews and Reflections on Responsible Leadership by South African Captains of Industry.* She serves on the editorial board of several management journals and is a South African National Research Foundation A-rated researcher.

Stella is also the recipient of numerous awards, including the *Distinguished Woman Scholar in the Social Sciences Award* from the Department of Science and Technology (South Africa). Two of her most recent awards are the International Leadership Association Lifetime Achievement Award and the Academy of Management Distinguished Service Award. Stella can be contacted at: stella.nkomo@up.ac.za

Nigel Povah

Nigel Povah (MSc, C.Psychol, AFBPsS) was, until his recent retirement, a Chartered Occupational Psychologist and an Associate Fellow of the British Psychological Society. He was also a Founder Member of the Association of Business Psychologists. He has a degree in Psychology from the University of Leeds and a Masters in Occupational Psychology from Birkbeck College, University of London.

Prior to his retirement Nigel was the CEO and founder of Assessment and Development Consultants Ltd (a&dc), which was one of the UK's leading firms of occupational psychologists and is now part of PSI.

During his 30 years with a&dc he established the company as one of the best-known names in the assessment centre field, in which Nigel is widely regarded as one of the UK's leading experts, having designed and run many hundreds of assessment and development centres ranging in duration and format.

Nigel is the co-author of *Assessment & Development Centres* with Iain Ballantyne and *Succeeding at Assessment Centres for Dummies* with his daughter Lucy Povah. He is also the co-editor with George Thornton of *Assessment Centres and Global Talent Management*. Nigel can be contacted at: nigel.povah52@gmail.com

Philippa Riley

Philippa Riley (MSc, CPsychol, AFBPsS) is a Chartered Occupational Psychologist and Associate Fellow of the British Psychological Society, who was Director of Global Assessment Products at PSI. Philippa completed her undergraduate degree at the University of Durham, and her MSc in Occupational Psychology at the Institute of Work Psychology at the University of Sheffield. She is a committee member of the UK Assessment Centre Group (UK-ACG) and a member of SIOP.

During her career to date, Philippa has worked as a consultant with a wide variety of public and private sector organisations, starting her career working at QinetiQ Ltd, a defence and security consultancy. More recently, she has focused on the development of assessment products, initially at Assessment and Development Consultants (a&dc) and then at PSI. Philippa's team delivered products which combined leading technology with psychological science, notably VirtualAC (a virtual assessment centre platform), as well as a range of psychometric tools and situational judgement tests.

Philippa was a contributing author to Povah and Thornton's book, *Assessment Centres and Global Talent Management*, and has published articles and presented at conferences on a wide variety of topics, most recently on the role of artificial intelligence and machine learning in assessment. Philippa can be contacted at: phillyriley@yahoo.co.uk.

George C. Thornton III

George C. Thornton III is Professor Emeritus of Psychology at Colorado State University. He earned his PhD from Purdue University in 1966 and is a Fellow of the Society for I/O Psychology. He received the Distinguished Alumni Award from Purdue University, a Legacy Lifetime Award from the South African Assessment Centre Study Group (ACSG), and a Lifetime Achievement Award from the AC User Group. George specialises in the AC method having advanced theory, research and practice in using ACs to assess and develop leadership competencies in public and commercial organisations. The author of six books, including *Assessment Center Perspectives for Talent Management Strategies* and *Developing Organizational Simulations: A Guide for Practitioners, Students, and Researchers*, George has published scores of publications and made presentations on leadership assessment and development throughout the Americas, Europe, Middle East, Asia and South Africa. George can be contacted at: george.thornton@colostate.edu

PREFACE

Until the first edition of this book was published in 2008, no South African book provided a detailed overview of the design and development, implementation and evaluation of assessment centres (ACs). Sandra and I therefore decided 12 years ago that the time was ripe for taking on the project of writing a book on the development and use of ACs. Since then new research and practice has appeared, leading us to publish this second edition of the book. The content of the book is mainly a product of our own writing, but we have also requested six other authors to make contributions. They in turn solicited the input of four additional authors, but more about them and their contributions further down.

The target audience

The intended target audience for this book is AC scholars, practitioners and service providers; in other words, those people who are exposed to ACs on a frequent basis. The book is thus supposed to serve as a practical "how-to" guide for people involved in the development and use of ACs. But this does not mean that the book is unscientific – it is still based on scientific principles and research-based evidence. It can thus equally well be used to introduce students to the development and use of ACs. In writing the book, we made the following assumptions about our readers:

1. They do not necessarily have to be AC experts or practitioners to grasp the content of the book.
2. Persons or scholars who wish to learn more about ACs will be able to follow the content of the book.

A glossary of terms is also included for those readers who are not familiar with AC concepts, but who would like to learn more about them. We have tried our best not to clutter the book with unnecessary citations or references in order to make it practically accessible.

Objectives of this book

The objectives that we have formulated with regard to this book are thus to:

1. provide a fairly comprehensive overview of the practice of ACs, with specific reference to the analysis, design and development, implementation and evaluation stages of the AC process;
2. present a practice framework or model against which AC practitioners or service providers can evaluate their own practices; and
3. provide a sound scientific or theoretical base for the processes and practices that we propose.

The structure of the book

The plan and layout of the book are simple and easy to follow. The book is in essence structured into three parts: the introduction, the body and a concluding overview.

The introduction: Chapters 1 to 5
The body: Chapters 6 to 19
The concluding overview: Chapter 20 and the Epilogue

The introductory part consists of the first five chapters. Chapter 1 provides an introduction to ACs and explains some key concepts and principles thereof. Chapter 2 by Deon Meiring provides a historical overview of the development and use of ACs in South Africa, and will also introduce readers to some of the main players with regard to ACs in South Africa, including the Assessment Centre Study Group (ACSG). In Deon's chapter he introduces the *Guidelines* for the use of ACs as well as the recently developed *Code of Ethics for Assessment Centres in South Africa*. The introductory part of the book continues with Chapter 3 by Stella Nkomo and Christina Badalani. In this chapter we are introduced to the concept of ethnoculturism and how this potentially impacts operational assessment centres – a new field for assessment centre research. Chapter 4 by Rodney Lowman focuses on ethics and assessment centres, again a field with scarce research. The introductory part of the book concludes with Chapter 5 by Anne Buckett - purchasing assessment centres.

The body of the book consists of Chapters 6 to 19. The body is structured around two sets of guiding principles, namely a design model (borrowed from the training literature) and programme evaluation principles. The design model basically refers to four different stages, namely the analysis, design and development, implementation, and evaluation and validation stages. Each stage starts with an introductory section and provides a flow chart of the section content. Each stage is then concluded with a synthesis and emphasis on some key outcomes of the stage. The programme evaluation principles referred to earlier are included by way of a checklist. AC practitioners and designers can use these checklists to ensure that something important in each stage did not slip their minds. Thirteen of the 14 chapters in the body cover these different stages in a systematic manner. The exception is Chapter 9, written by George Thornton and Filip Lievens. In this chapter we are introduced to the theoretical underpinnings of assessment centres.

The concluding overview consists of the remaining chapter and an epilogue. Chapter 20 by Nigel Povah, Philippa Riley and Jordan Jones covers AC practices globally, highlighting trends and challenges. The epilogue highlights the crucial role that ACs must play in South Africa.

ACKNOWLEDGEMENTS

Sandra and I would like to thank the following people who were directly and indirectly involved in the development of the original idea of an AC book, as well as in the development of the final product. The publication of a book is never the work of one or two people – it is always a team effort:

- **Hermann Spangenberg** – for many years the centrifugal force in the ACSG! We would like to acknowledge your moral support and thank you for the initial supportive comments when we first introduced the design model at a previous ACSG conference. That created the spark for embarking on this journey.
- **Anne Buckett** – a former chairman of the ACSG. Thank you for your willingness to contribute to this edition of the book.
- **Christina Badalani** – on request of Stella Nkomo, Christina agreed to contribute to the book. Christina, thank you for being willing to contribute and thank you for your valuable contribution.
- **The late Deon Meiring** – another former Chairman of the ACSG. Thank you Deon for writing a critical chapter on the historical development of ACs in South Africa.
- **Filip Lievens** – a well-known and esteemed researcher in the field of assessment centres and a well-known presenter at the ACSG. Thank you Filip for being willing to share your research with us in the chapter that you and George contributed.
- **George Thornton III** – for many years now an old friend of the ACSG and an internationally recognised expert on ACs. Thank you for your willingness to contribute the chapter and soliciting Filip Lievens to assist in writing the chapter. It is indeed an honour for us to have your contribution in our book.
- **Nigel Povah** – the retired CEO of a&dc, a company that specialised in assessment centres based in the United Kingdom. Thank you Nigel for being prepared to bring an international perspective about assessment centres to the book. Also thank you for bringing Philippa Riley and Jordan Jones on board.
- **Philippa Riley and Jordan Jones** – thank you for agreeing to contribute to the book and for the valuable contributions you made. We know that it is always a challenge to research and write a chapter for publication.
- **Rodney Lowman** – an internationally recognised authority in the field of IO Psychology and ethics. A huge thank you for writing the chapter about assessment centres and ethics. In addition, thank you for your contribution in compiling the *Code of Ethics for Assessment Centres in South Africa*.
- **Stella Nkomo** – an esteemed researcher and publisher in the field of multiculturism. Stella, thank you for immediately agreeing to contribute to this book and thank you for bringing Christina Badalani on board. Your contribution has definitely opened a field of research in Assessment Centres in South Africa.
- **Wilhelm Crous** – last, but not least, thank you for your trust, support and your willingness to publish this second edition of the book. We know that you share our enthusiasm about ACs. Thank you for providing us with the competent publishing team that helped to make this book a reality. A book can never become great without a good publisher!

And, finally, a special word of thanks to you, the reader, for acquiring this book! We trust that you will start to share our enthusiasm and excitement about ACs as you proceed through the different chapters. Or, if you are presently unfamiliar with this field, we trust that this book will help you in developing an appreciation for ACs and their use.

Sandra and Gert

CHAPTER 1

INTRODUCTION TO ASSESSMENT CENTRES

Sandra Schlebusch and Gert Roodt

1. INTRODUCTION – WHAT ARE ASSESSMENT CENTRES?

The Assessment Centre (AC) technique is a well-known and widely used assessment technique for selecting persons for particular positions or programmes and identifying developmental needs. This technique was first used by the German army during the Second World War. Subsequently, the technique was used by the British War Officer Selection Boards (WOSBs) for selecting officers during that war, and by the United States Office of Secret Service (OSS) to select undercover agents.[1] AT&T was the first private company to apply this technology in industry.

This chapter will introduce the concept of ACs and explain the basic assessment process followed when using the AC technique.

Excluding the introduction and the conclusion, this chapter consists of seven sections. Each of these sections deals with a particular facet of ACs:

- The first section introduces the concept of ACs and explains what they are.
- The second section explains the different types of ACs most commonly found in practice.
- The third section explains the features of ACs.
- The fourth section introduces the different stakeholders of ACs.
- The fifth section briefly explains the different applications of ACs.
- The sixth section introduces the design model that will be applied in this book.
- The last section explains the rationale for employing the design model.

2. WHAT IS AN AC?

The *International Guidelines for ACs*[2] define an AC as consisting of:

> "a standardized evaluation of behavior based on multiple inputs. Any single assessment center consists of multiple components, which include behavioural simulation exercises, within which multiple trained assessors observe and record behaviors, classify them according to the behavioral constructs of interest, and (either individually or collectively) rate (either individual or pooled) behaviors. Using either a consensus meeting among assessors or statistical aggregation, assessment scores are derived that represent an assessee's standing on the behavioral constructs and/or an aggregated overall assessment rating (OAR)".

---

1   Highouse & Nolan, 2011

2   International Taskforce on Assessment Center Guidelines, 2015: 5

For the purposes of this book, the authors will define ACs as a simulation-based process employing multiple assessment techniques and multiple assessors (observers) to produce judgements regarding the extent to which a participant displays selected competencies or other focal constructs required to perform a job effectively. ACs are usually employed either for selection or development purposes. Several variations exist within these two broad categories.

Confusion exists amongst South Africans as to whether the Sectoral Education and Training Authorities' (SETAs') assessments are the same as traditional or conventional ACs, however there is a distinct difference between the SETA assessments and the conventional ACs referred to in this book. Right from the onset, we wish to clearly demarcate the specific meanings attached to assessment in these two contexts.

2.1   Demarcation of terminology

The assessments used by the SETAs refer to selected work samples that people must be able to produce under certain controlled conditions. For example, a person should be able to write a formal business report in English. The assessor(s) will have been trained to accurately assess the outcome of such test in order to declare the person competent or not yet competent according to the established test criteria. The correct term to use in this context would thus be **work-/task-sample assessments** and not ACs.

The Traditional AC is a structured process in which individual and group simulations are used to determine a participant's current level of competence in relation to certain specified focal construct criteria. The assessment of the participant's behaviour is conducted by different observers during simulations where the participant is required to perform specified tasks. The behaviour of the participant is observed, noted, classified and evaluated by qualified observers. Feedback is then given to the participant, the organisation, or both. Feedback is in the form of a written document as well as a discussion.

A focal construct can be a competency, a dimension, or a task. In this book we will use "competency" and "dimension" interchangeably, i.e. when we use "competency" we also mean "dimension" and vice versa. Some ACs use tasks and not competencies to evaluate participant behaviour. When we use the term "focal construct" it can therefore mean dimension, competency or task.

3.   **TYPES OF ACS**

Different types of ACs exist, ranging from Traditional ACs to Learning ACs, Collaborative ACs, and even Functional ACs. However, there is a major distinction between an AC used for selection purposes, called an AC, and an AC used for development purposes, called a Development AC (DAC). We also find Diagnostic ACs (DCs). We will briefly discuss all types of ACs in the subsections below.

3.1   Traditional ACs

During a Traditional AC, participants attend the AC without receiving feedback on their performance during the AC. The participants will, for example, first do an in-box, followed by a counselling discussion, then a group discussion. Finally, they will hand in their assignment on the analysis exercise.

Sometimes, the participants will attend a debriefing session at the end of the AC to ensure that all their questions are answered. During this session, the participants might also be given certain insights into how their behaviour was observed, noted, classified and evaluated.

Participants will receive feedback on their performance only a couple of weeks after attending the AC. This lag is caused by the time it takes for the multiple observers to integrate the collected data on each participant, to reach consensus on the final rating per focal construct assessed, and to write the actual feedback report. Although the feedback is still valuable to the participant, part of its possible impact is lost owing to the length of time that elapses from the time of the simulation to the actual receipt of feedback. Traditional ACs can be used both for selection purposes and to identify development needs.

3.2 Assessment ACs

The purpose of an Assessment AC is to select the most appropriate person to be appointed to a position or programme.[3] Although the same simulations may be used as when a DAC is conducted, the participants must understand that the results of the AC will be used to influence a selection decision.

Feedback on the participants' behaviour during the AC is given to the organisation that initiated the AC, however it is strongly recommended that feedback also be given to the various participants individually. This will assist them in better understanding the decision taken by the organisation, and it will also enable them to learn from the experience.

The results from an AC may also be used to draw up individual development plans for the participants in an AC.

Some of the benefits of using an AC as part of a selection process are that the selection decision is based on results from a culturally neutral scientific process. This minimises subjectivity and the chances of unfair discrimination. Since the focal constructs evaluated during the AC are the focal constructs required of the incumbent of the position, the AC adheres to the selection requirements stipulated in the Employment Equity Act[4] (if the AC has been designed, administered and maintained according to certain principles).

3.3 Diagnostic ACs (DCs)

The purpose of a Diagnostic AC (DC) is to determine a profile of the strengths and development needs of a participant so that a tailored development plan can be designed for the specific participant.[5] The process of a DC is similar to the process followed during an Assessment AC, with the participants receiving feedback about their performance after the DC. The development planning usually takes place after the assessment. The results of a DC may only be used for the purpose(s) that the participant consented to.

---

3   International Taskforce on Assessment Center Guidelines, 2015

4   Employment Equity Act., (Act No. 55 of 1998)

5   Thornton, Rupp & Hofmann, 2015; International Taskforce on Assessment Center Guidelines, 2015; Meiring & Buckett, 2016

The objectives of a DC are to identify development needs and to undertake development planning – for the individual and for the organisation as a whole. This results in each participant having a unique development plan that is tailored to his or her current development needs. When the participant has implemented the development plan, he/she should be more effective in the target role that the AC was aimed at. Cost-effective training and development can take place, since only needs-driven training is conducted. When Workplace Skills Plans (in terms of the Skills Levies Act[6]) are drawn up, these can accurately reflect the needs of the organisation's employees. Moreover, skills levies can be claimed back more easily, since the training is reflected in the Workplace Skills Plans and is truly needs driven.

3.4 Learning ACs

Learning ACs are similar to DCs, but participants attending Learning ACs attend a debriefing session after each simulation. Theoretical inputs are also given during the debriefing sessions.

The objectives of a Learning AC are similar to those of a DC. In addition, learning can also take place during the centre. During the debriefing sessions, participants receive generic feedback on the simulation used, as well as theoretical input that they can apply during the next simulation. Participants have better insight into their performance during a simulation and are therefore more open to accepting development recommendations.

3.5 Development ACs (DACs)

The purpose of a DAC is to determine areas of strength and development needs, and to provide the opportunity to learn while at the DAC itself.[7] The results from a DAC may not be used for any selection decision. Using the results to influence a selection decision will constitute an unfair practice.

A debriefing session on the various simulations used during the DAC is held at various points during the DAC. Participants who attend a DAC also receive individual feedback on their performance at various points during the DAC and start to set development goals and objectives. Participants then have the opportunity to practice new behaviours during further simulations. These further simulations are usually parallel simulations at the same level of complexity as the first group of simulations that the participant received feedback on. At the end of the DAC the participant again receives feedback and further development recommendations. The tangible deliverable of a DAC is individual development plans.

A DAC can take various forms. It can be presented in the form described above, as a Collaborative AC, or as a Coaching Development Centre. What is common to all such forms is that the participant receives feedback aimed at further development and the opportunity to practice new behaviours while at the centre.

---

6   Skills Development Levies Act., (Act No. 9 of 1999)

7   International Taskforce on Assessment Center Guidelines, 2015; Thornton, Rupp & Hoffman, 2015

3.6 Collaborative ACs

A Collaborative AC is a specific variation of a DAC. Collaborative DACs are based on the principles of experiential learning and continuous feedback, using AC methodology.

The typical process followed during a Collaborative DAC is as follows:[8]
- The participant participates in a simulation.
- The participant and his/her facilitator discuss and collaboratively assess the participant's performance during the simulation.
- The facilitator counsels the participant regarding the identified development areas in an environment in which trust and confidentiality are guaranteed.
- The participant participates in the next simulation so as to explore the new behavioural skills that have been acquired.
- The participant, with the assistance of the facilitator, writes a report reflecting the individual strengths and development areas of the participant. In addition, the participant, with the assistance of the facilitator, formulates a development plan.

Variations on the above process exist. For example, instead of one facilitator giving feedback to one participant, all of the other participants can give feedback to the participant concerned according to certain guidelines and after a group discussion.[9] The danger inherent in this approach is that the feedback might not always be given sensitively and could possibly adversely affect the relevant participant's self-esteem. A further concern is that the participants might consider it to be very "dangerous" to have their development areas exposed, especially if the environment concerned is a cut-throat, high-performance one.

During a Collaborative DAC, facilitators effectively counsel participants on the principles underlying the competencies being assessed. Participants gain insight into their own behaviour and the consequences thereof. This results in buy-in and an understanding of the development needs of the participants. During a Collaborative DAC, participants also have an opportunity to experiment with new behaviour in a safe environment and receive objective feedback.

A Collaborative DAC provides each participant with immediate feedback regarding their performance. Participants receive intensive individual attention and are afforded the opportunity to practice the new skill(s). This results in increased commitment to own development and a greater acceptance of strengths and development areas by the participant.

Prerequisites for conducting an effective Collaborative DAC are that the facilitators must be highly skilled observers with extensive experience, and that all documentation must be as comprehensive as possible (e.g. must provide behaviour anchors, examples, weights and norm tables). The integrity of the whole AC design process must therefore be very high. (See Chapter 13 for more information about DACs.)

---

8   Griffiths & Allen, 1987

9   Griffiths & Allen, 1987

3.7 Coaching Development Centres (CDCs)

A CDC is a further refinement of a Collaborative DC, i.e. the same process is followed during the CDC as during a Collaborative DC, however the observers are competent coaches. The participant receives coaching instead of just feedback and counselling after every simulation. (See Chapter 13 for more information about CDCs.)

3.8 Functional ACs

Functional ACs use AC methodology in a functional context. The purpose of a Functional AC may be either selection **or** development. Examples of Functional ACs are ACs for human capital practitioners, sales executives or accountants.

The simulations used during a Functional AC will differ from typical AC simulations as the focal constructs being assessed will dictate what simulations to use.

The observers at a Functional AC must, in addition to being competent observers, be functional experts.

4. FEATURES OF ACS

There are several features an AC should display before it can be called an AC. The Assessment Centre Study Group (ACSG) of South Africa has created guidelines for ACs.[10] In these guidelines, an extensive list of the features of an AC is provided. Some of the most important features are a job analysis, use of simulations, multiple assessments, a link between focal constructs and assessments, multiple observers, competent observers and role players, observing and recording of behaviour, behaviour classification and evaluation, data integration and standardisation. In addition we will briefly discuss feedback.

4.1 Job analysis

A job analysis should be conducted to determine the focal constructs that are important for job success. Even if the job does not currently exist, an analysis should be conducted to determine the competencies or other focal constructs needed for success in the proposed job. The job analysis will also indicate the type of simulations to be used so that such simulations are not foreign to the job. (See Chapter 8 for a detailed discussion about job analysis.)

4.2 Use of simulations

An AC is made up of several assessments that include simulations. A sufficient number of job-related simulations must be used to observe the participant's behaviour in relation to the focal constructs being assessed in more than one setting. As an example, a competency should be evaluated in a paper situation as well as an interactive situation, or, if applicable, in a project-related situation versus a day-to-day situation, or a strategic situation versus a day-to-day situation, or an individual situation versus a group situation.

---

10   Meiring & Buckett, 2016

A simulation is a typical situation to which a job incumbent is exposed. The simulation is designed to elicit behaviours on the part of the participant that are related to the focal constructs being assessed in the AC. The same type of situational stimuli as the participant would be exposed to in the job are given to him or her to respond to behaviourally. The stimuli contained in a simulation, although provided in a different setting, should resemble the stimuli in the work situation.[11]

Simulations may be presented by way of video-based or virtual simulations delivered via computer, video, the Internet or an intranet.

A simulation assesses to what extent a participant displays a particular focal construct and differs from a knowledge-based test. During a knowledge-based test, a participant must know theoretically exactly what needs to be done. However, during a simulation, he or she must not only know theoretically what should be done, but should also demonstrate that he or she is able to do the required action – the difference between describing how to ride a bicycle (knowledge test) and physically riding the bicycle (simulation). (See Chapters 11 and 12 for a detailed discussion about simulations.)

4.3 Multiple assessments

The AC focal constructs must be assessed at least twice during the AC. Various data collection points should exist so that a more holistic perspective of the AC participant's ability to show behaviour related to the focal constructs is obtained. Assessment instruments other than simulations may also be used in conjunction with simulations, namely questionnaires, interviews and psychometric tests.

4.4 Link between AC assessments and the AC focal constructs

The job analysis will indicate the competencies, dimensions and tasks that a successful job incumbent should display or perform. Simulations and other assessment techniques should be identified that would elicit participant behaviour related to the focal constructs identified by the job analysis. An assessment matrix should be drawn-up indicating which construct is assessed during which simulation.

4.5 Multiple observers

The same AC participant must be observed by different observers during the various simulations at the AC. For example, if observer A observes participant Z during simulation D, then observer B must observe participant Z during simulation E. The results of their observations will be pooled during the data-integration session. Having multiple observers ensures that a participant's behaviour that is linked to a specific focal construct is evaluated objectively during an AC.

4.6 Competent observers and role players

Only well-trained and competent people can function as observers at an AC. Being a registered psychologist does not automatically qualify a person as an observer. Very specific training on behaviour

---

11 International Taskforce on Assessment Center Guidelines, 2015

observation, the focal constructs being assessed and the simulations being used must be completed successfully before any person can function as an observer at an AC.

The role players playing the roles during the interactive simulations must also be well trained in the character(s) they will portray, in the focal constructs regarding which they need to elicit behaviour, and in the content of the simulations. (Chapter 15 provides more detail about observer and role player training.)

4.7   Behavioural observation and noting

Behaviour, and not any psychological construct, is observed during an AC. Behaviour is what the participant is saying or doing during simulations. The behaviour of a participant during the AC, and not outside the simulations, is observed and noted.[12]

Observers must use a systematic procedure to note participant behaviour. This can be done by writing verbatim what the participant is saying during a simulation, or by recording a simulation and transcribing the behaviour afterwards.

4.8   Classifying and evaluating behaviour

The participant behaviour must be classified into meaningful categories such as dimensions, competencies, tasks, skills, abilities and knowledge. Again, observers must use a systematic procedure to classify and evaluate behaviour accurately. This can take the form of handwritten notes that are transferred onto structured observer report forms and then assessed according to certain criteria.

4.9   Data integration

At the end of the AC, the observers pool their information on each participant in order to obtain final ratings per focal construct, per participant. This session is chaired by the AC administrator.

The data integration can take the form of a discussion during which each observer presents the other observers with his or her ratings and the behaviour to support such ratings. The team of observers, including the AC administrator, must reach a consensus decision on each rating.

The integration session can also include a statistical integration process that is validated according to certain standards. (See Chapter 16 for a discussion about data integration.)

4.10 Standardisation

The execution of an AC must take place in a standardised manner according to the AC administration manual. This means that all participants must participate in the AC under the same conditions. Standardisation refers to time limits, the way instructions are given, the use of resources, the way

---

12 International Taskforce on Assessment Center Guidelines, 2015

in which simulation stimuli are presented, questions that are asked to participants, the way in which role players fulfil their roles, the number of participants in a group discussion, the sequence in which assessments are administered, the physical conditions under which the AC is administered, and the scoring procedures.

4.11 Feedback

Once an AC has been completed, feedback must be given to certain stakeholders. In broad terms, the stakeholders are the organisation that initiated the AC, the participant and the participant's line manager. The type of AC, namely AC, DC or DAC, will determine who will receive feedback. Who will receive feedback should be agreed upon before embarking on the AC process. The type of AC will also dictate the content of the feedback given. (See Chapter 17 for a more detailed discussion about feedback.)

4.11.1 Client organisations

The client organisation will need feedback on each participant's performance during the AC. This feedback, which can assume the form of either a written report or a verbal feedback report, will then be used in the process of selecting the participant in or out.

Where a DC or DAC has been presented, the organisation's feedback can be in the form of general trends identified, with recommendations as to how to harness the trends or how to address the trends. Sometimes the organisation will also require detailed feedback on each participant.

Care must be taken as to who receives the feedback in the organisation and how the results of the AC are interpreted and used. Again, it must be stressed that the results of a DAC must be used only for development purposes and never for selection purposes. The recipients of the feedback must also know how to interpret the results.

4.11.2 AC participants

The feedback that a participant in a DAC receives is very detailed. The participant needs to know how he or she performed in relation to the focal construct criteria, as well as how he or she could behave differently. The feedback takes the form of a written report as well as a discussion.

It is highly recommended that a participant also receive feedback after attending an AC. Although the feedback is not as detailed as for a DAC, the participant still needs to know how he or she performed in relation to each focal construct assessed during the AC. The feedback can be either in a written or verbal format.

4.11.3 Line managers

The line manager who requested the AC, or the line manager of the participant attending the DC or DAC, also needs to receive feedback.

The feedback can take place at the same time as that given to the participant in a DAC. The purpose of giving feedback to the line manager of a participant in a DC or DAC is to obtain the buy-in of that manager to the participant's development.

4.12 Deliverables of an AC

A few deliverables are necessary upon completion of any AC, namely written reports, feedback discussions and development plans. The absence of, for example, giving feedback in whatever format to the AC participants may result in negative perceptions about the specific AC, but also ACs in general, leading to what can be termed "dysfunctional ACs".[13] It is thus recommended that if at all feasible, AC participants, irrespective of the AC purpose, receive a feedback report, discussion and development plan/suggestions.[14]

4.12.1 Reports

The individual report that each participant receives is a summary of his or her behaviour during the AC. It indicates what he or she has done well in relation to the focal constructs assessed, as well as what the development areas are. A well-written report should also indicate development suggestions to the participant.

The purpose of the report is to serve as a document to which the participant can refer in future in order to assist him or her in his or her development.

A combined report, which is usually submitted to the organisation in written form after an AC, is a summary of each of the AC participants' current strengths and current areas needing further development in relation to the focal constructs. It may also include a ranking of the participants. (See Chapter 17 for more information about written reports.)

4.12.2 Feedback discussions

A verbal feedback discussion should take place. The type of AC will determine who will be present during the discussion.

The purpose of the discussion is to provide insight into what has taken place during the AC and to indicate the consequences if this behaviour takes place in the work situation. It is also an opportunity for everyone present to ask questions. If this is a discussion where the participant is present, a development plan, or at least development action, should be agreed upon. (See Chapter 17 for more information about feedback discussions.)

---

13 Dewberry & Jackson, 2016

14 SA Assessment Centre Study Group, 2018

4.12.3 Development plans

Another deliverable of an AC, especially a DC or DAC, is that each participant receive a comprehensive development plan that will become his or her roadmap for further development. This plan should ideally be drawn-up with the full support of the direct line manager. No action should be included in the plan if the participant does not agree to it.

Typically, a development plan should include the focal construct needing development, the specific behavioural element needing development, on-the-job development, as well as training programmes to attend, books to read, videos to watch and even projects to be involved in.

The plan could look as follows:

Table 1.1: A typical development plan

Competency	Element	On-the-job development	Training programme	Other
Information gathering	• To be able to gather additional information	• Draw up a check list to ensure that answers are gathered regarding who, what, where, when and why. • Remember to gather information from all parties.	Programme: Creative Problem Solving	Book: *Who has done it* – Jo Soap

- **Best practices regarding feedback**

Today it is generally accepted that the minimum deliverable after an AC is a report. After a DC or DAC, the participant should receive a written report, a feedback discussion should take place, and his or her development plan should be drawn-up during the discussion. Only focal constructs that the participant commits to developing should be included in the development plan. If the participant does not commit to the development intervention, no real development will take place and the organisation's resources will have been wasted.

Although not compulsory, it is advisable that participants also receive feedback after attending an AC.[15] This will probably have a positive influence on the participant's experience of the AC.

---

15 SA Assessment Centre Study Group, 2018

5. STAKEHOLDERS OF ACS

Various stakeholders are involved in making an AC a reality. Each of these stakeholder's needs and interests ought to be considered in the process, from the initial design through to the implementation and validation stages. (The roles of these stakeholders are discussed in more depth in Chapter 18.) The stakeholders can be divided into those directly involved in ACs and those indirectly involved.

Those directly involved in an AC are the AC administrator; the AC observers, facilitators or coaches; the simulation role players (all of whom may be referred to as "the process owners"); the AC participants; the participants' direct line managers; and the participants' direct subordinates.

The stakeholders that are indirectly involved are the human capital department, senior management, and unions or organised employee organisations. Each of these stakeholders will be discussed below.

5.1 Stakeholders directly involved in ACs

The stakeholders involved in each AC are the administrator; the observers, facilitators or coaches; the role players; the participants; the participants' direct line managers; and the participants' direct subordinates.

5.1.1 The AC administrator

The AC administrator is accountable for the smooth running of the whole AC. This includes the planning of the AC, the execution of the AC and all the post-AC work.

The AC administrator must schedule the AC, ensure that all venues are booked and that venue requirements are met, see to it that all the participants are invited and arrive, and prepare all paperwork. The AC administrator is also accountable for ensuring that only competent observers/facilitators are involved in the AC.

During the AC, the AC administrator oversees the functioning of the observers/facilitators. He or she is accountable for ensuring that all behaviour is accurately observed, noted, classified and evaluated. If any one of the observers experiences problems, the AC administrator must be able to take over his or her role for the remainder of the AC.

The AC administrator is also accountable for the correct administration of all the simulations, including the role plays. The AC administrator interacts with all participants by answering every question and by ensuring that all their needs are met as far as possible.

The AC administrator is also the person who will present the debriefing sessions for the participants and chairs the data-integration sessions with the observers. In most cases, it will also be the AC administrator who writes the feedback reports and who actually conducts the feedback discussions. (See Chapter 15 for a more detailed discussion about the administrator.)

5.1.2   Observers/facilitators/coaches

The observers involved in an AC are the people who physically observe and note the participant's behaviour during simulations. After the simulation, they will classify the behaviour according to the AC focal constructs and evaluate the behaviour according to the relevant norms. They will then write some form of report that they can present at the data-integration session.

The observers during a Collaborative DAC are called facilitators. Although they also observe, note, classify and evaluate behaviour, they additionally fulfil the role of learning facilitator and mentor during the AC. The facilitators usually work with a participant in a one-on-one setting after each simulation in order to collaboratively evaluate the participant's behaviour. They then counsel the participant in terms of the focal constructs and how he or she can adapt his or her behaviour to more closely resemble the required behaviour. Apart from being competent observers, facilitators should have excellent people skills.

The observers during a Coaching Development Centre are called coaches. In addition to being competent observers, they are also competent coaches who work with participants after every simulation, coaching them about the simulation they have just participated in as well as the focal constructs. They assist the participant in preparing for subsequent simulations.

5.1.3   Role players

Simulation role players are the people who play the various characters with whom the participants have to interact during the interactive simulations. The purpose of the role players is to ensure that an opportunity is created for the participants to display the behaviour that is linked to the focal constructs being evaluated during the simulation. The role play opportunity is not an opportunity for the role player to impress everyone with his or her acting ability.

The role players must therefore understand the characters that they portray so as to ensure that they always remain in-character. In addition, they need to know the focal constructs being assessed, as well as what the behaviour linked to these focal constructs looks like. In addition, they need to know how to elicit the required behaviour and how to use the various behavioural prompts.

5.1.4   Participants

Participants are the people who actually attend the AC. They are the ones who perform the simulations so that their behaviour can be observed, noted, classified and evaluated. Usually, a person attending an AC for selection purposes is called a candidate and a person attending a DC or DAC is called a delegate.

Participants attending a DC or DAC may either already be functioning in the work situation at the level of the AC, or they may be one level lower than the AC and aspire to develop to the AC level. Participants attending an AC for selection purposes are usually at a lower organisational level than the AC, but are ready to be appointed to the higher level.

Usually, participation in an AC is voluntary. However, some organisations explicitly state that appointments at certain levels in the organisation will take place only after the candidate has attended an AC. Some organisations, for organisation development purposes, also compel their employees to attend an AC.

5.1.5 Line managers

The line managers of AC participants have a vested interest in the AC, in that they have to support the participants in their further development. Such managers thus need insight into the performance of the participants at the AC and into how participants can harness their strengths and develop areas needing attention. The line manager thus becomes the person who, on the job, needs to encourage appropriate behaviour and discourage unwanted behaviour.

A line manager can either be a friendly AC ally or an eternal AC enemy who will sabotage the development of his or her subordinates.

5.1.6 Subordinates

A sometimes forgotten stakeholder in the AC process is the participant's direct subordinates. In fact, these are the people who experience first-hand the change in the participant's behaviour. In some cases, it would be ideal to get them on board as soon as possible so that they can support the desired behaviour of the participant and make the participant aware of unwanted behaviour the moment it happens.

5.2 Stakeholders indirectly involved in ACs

All ACs have parties that are not represented at each AC, but who are definitely interested in the AC outcomes. These parties are the human capital department, senior management, unions and other employee organisations.

5.2.1 Human capital department

The human capital department is usually the custodian of the AC. Although it will seldom physically present an AC itself, it will be involved in the process of sourcing AC service providers, analysing the need, designing the AC, implementation and roll-out, as well as validation research.

The human capital department is also the department that ensures that the development processes are in place for the AC participants to develop the focal constructs needing further development.

In most cases, this department is also the department that is accountable for the AC results being stored confidentially and being used only for the purposes intended.

5.2.2 Senior managers

The organisation's senior management should take an interest in the trends emerging from the AC results, as these may give an indication of a possible strength that can be used as a competitive advantage.

Since ACs are an expensive intervention, senior management should take cognisance of whether the organisation is getting value for money. Senior management should hold the human capital department accountable for answering questions regarding return on investment as well as on the ethical use of the results.

Senior management should be the AC sponsors and marketers within the organisation. As such, it should be kept involved and informed every step of the way.

5.2.3 Unions and other employee organisations

Since it is employees who attend ACs, it is advisable to involve all organised employee organisations in the process of the AC needs analysis, design and implementation, as well as in validation research. These organisations are powerful influencers within an organisation and can therefore play an important role in creating a positive AC perception.

6. AC APPLICATIONS

As previously mentioned, ACs can be used either for selection purposes or for developmental purposes. Results from a DAC may never be used for selection purposes, however results from an AC can also be used for developmental purposes.

A selection decision may involve selecting someone into a position or programme, or selecting a person out of a process. Development, on the other hand, may involve developing competence so that a person can perform more effectively in his or her current job, or developing so that he or she is able to perform a future job. A brief discussion of each AC use follows.

6.1 Selecting in

In this selection scenario, a short list of preferred candidates has already been drawn up. The AC is then used to obtain additional information on each candidate so as to influence the final selection decision as to who will be appointed to the position or programme.

6.2 Selecting out

During a process of selecting out, the AC is used to determine who will not progress to the next selection round. In this scenario, the AC is administered to quite a few candidates, not just the short-listed few.

6.3 Development

Participants can attend a DC or DAC at the same level and for the same positions in which they are currently employed. The purpose of their attendance would then be to obtain a snapshot in time of their current levels of competence so that their development plans can assist them in being more effective in their current roles. The focus is therefore on the current situation.

When a participant attends a DC or DAC at a higher level than that at which he or she is employed, the purpose is to assist him or her in developing his or her competence to that level so that he or she can be appointed to such higher level. The focus is therefore on the future.

An organisation can also design an AC that assesses focal constructs in relation to what it will require in future. In such a case, individual development areas are identified in preparation for the organisation as a whole to respond to future challenges.

6.4 Diagnostic purposes

Another application of ACs is for diagnostics. ACs are sometimes employed to assess the current level of functioning of managers or functional specialists. The outcome of this assessment enables the AC practitioner to make an informed judgement about the managers' level of competence or the company's managerial competence. Recommendations can then be made for those managers in terms of specific developmental areas, or in terms of future required focal constructs.

7. THE DESIGN MODEL

The design model has been borrowed from the training literature.[16] The typical process followed in the design model is a four-stage process that consists of the analysis, design, implementation and evaluation stages. The design model thus follows an established methodology in the development of a training or a development intervention. The methodology of the design model will be applied in this book as the design logic and organising principle for developing ACs. The design model will be superimposed on programme evaluation principles[17] in order to assess whether a specific stage has achieved the stated design objectives. Programme evaluation is an established methodology that is also encountered in disciplines such as educational psychology, developmental psychology, political science and sociology. Programme evaluation methodology is used for assessing the impact or effectiveness of development programmes or interventions. Typical programme evaluation questions will therefore be posed at the end of each stage of the AC process.[18]

---

16 Camp et al., 1986; Mager & Pipe, 1979; Michalak & Yager, 1979

17 Lipsey, 2005; Rossi et al., 2004

18 Edwards et al., 2003

7.1   Steps and stages

The four stages of the design model follow one another logically and in a sequential manner, as is depicted in Figure 1.1. The different stages are also interconnected by means of different feedback loops.

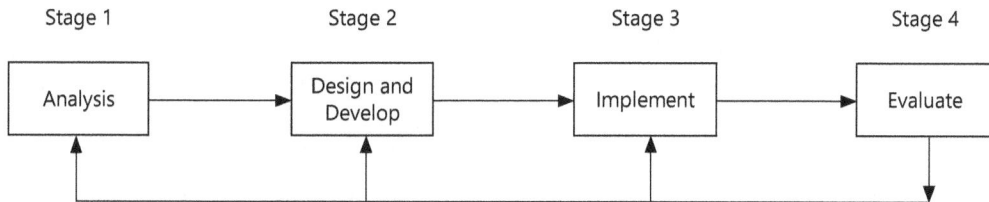

Figure 1.1: The basic design model

In the following subsections, brief descriptions of each of these stages are provided. Every stage can be subdivided into different steps that cumulatively result in a stage outcome.

7.1.1   Stage 1: Analysis

The purpose of the analysis stage is to conduct a proper analysis of the task or job of the organisation and of the organisational context so that the AC design team is clear about what the organisation wants to achieve and about what focal constructs are required by the job incumbent to achieve these business objectives. The AC programme thus serves two objectives, namely yielding competent participants and improving the effectiveness of the organisation. This stage will result in a job and a competency profile that serves to guide the AC design team in assessing or developing the relevant competencies.

7.1.2   Stage 2: Design and develop

The objective of the design and develop stage is to design and develop a programme that will achieve the stated objectives of the programme. Careful formulation of the exact purpose of the programme is of utmost importance, since such formulation will serve as a compass to guide the AC design team regarding the specific content of the AC programme. Trial-and-error test runs will inform the design team as to what is, and is not, feasible. The outcome of the second stage is to provide a Functional AC, that is, the different elements necessary to establish a Functional AC. A Functional AC in this context refers to an AC consisting of different functional components that are not yet fully operational.

7.1.3   Stage 3: Implement

The purpose of the implementation stage is to conduct the programme in its entirety. The implementation stage is a valuable source of information for the AC design team, in that it allows the team to observe the programme as a whole in order to determine whether there are any process and procedural glitches. This information is then used to take corrective action. The outcome of this stage will be an Operational AC. An Operational AC in this context refers to a fully Operational AC that operates according to established and consistent processes and procedures.

7.1.4 Stage 4: Evaluate

Broadly, the objective of the evaluation stage is twofold: first, it serves to determine whether the AC has had the desired impact or effect on the organisation, and second, it serves to determine whether the programme has succeeded in achieving the assessment objectives of the programme[19], that is, of selecting or developing suitable candidates. In other words, has the AC programme achieved its objectives of finding or developing suitable candidates, thereby improving the effectiveness of the organisation? The outcome of this stage will be a validated AC, in other words, an AC that is fair, unbiased and valid.

The overall design model in the AC context can be depicted as comprising different stages and steps (see Figure 1.2).

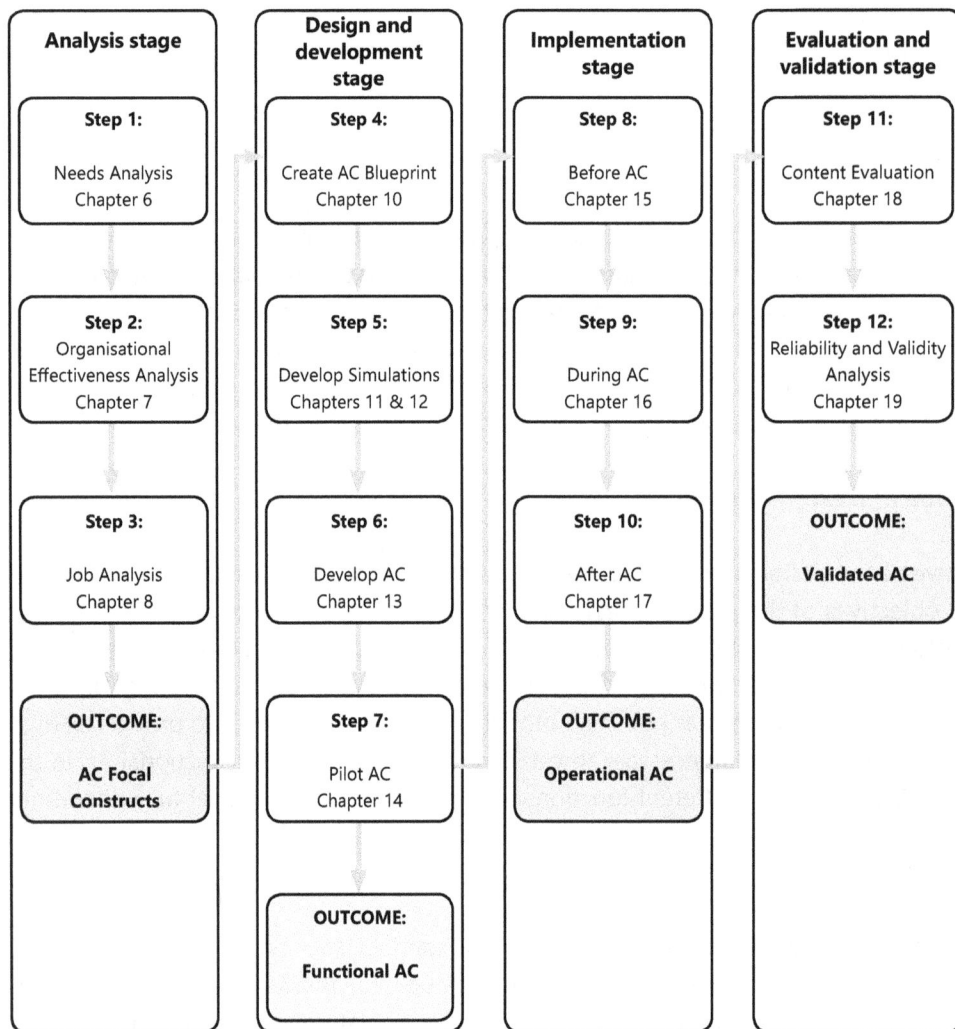

Analysis stage	Design and development stage	Implementation stage	Evaluation and validation stage
Step 1: Needs Analysis Chapter 6	**Step 4:** Create AC Blueprint Chapter 10	**Step 8:** Before AC Chapter 15	**Step 11:** Content Evaluation Chapter 18
Step 2: Organisational Effectiveness Analysis Chapter 7	**Step 5:** Develop Simulations Chapters 11 & 12	**Step 9:** During AC Chapter 16	**Step 12:** Reliability and Validity Analysis Chapter 19
Step 3: Job Analysis Chapter 8	**Step 6:** Develop AC Chapter 13	**Step 10:** After AC Chapter 17	**OUTCOME:** **Validated AC**
OUTCOME: **AC Focal Constructs**	**Step 7:** Pilot AC Chapter 14	**OUTCOME:** **Operational AC**	
	OUTCOME: **Functional AC**		

Figure 1.2: The AC design model

---

19 Rupp et al., 2006

8. THE RATIONALE FOR USING A DESIGN MODEL

There are a number of different reasons for following the logic of the design model in designing and developing ACs:

8.1 Following a systematic approach

The design model is based on an established methodology that follows a logical and systematic process. Every stage has its own objectives (from a design perspective) and predefined outcomes, which enables the AC design team to constantly match the stage and steps against these stated design criteria. The design model framework thus forces the AC design team to follow a disciplined and systematic approach so that no critical elements are omitted in the design process.

8.2 Keeping the focus on the initial design objectives of the AC

The objectives of each stage, as well as the sub-objectives of each step, need to be carefully formulated and thereafter adhered to. The design model then forces the AC design team to keep a constant eye on the objectives of the AC programme during the design process. This design methodology adds tremendous value from a programme evaluation perspective, where the outcomes of each stage are carefully evaluated against predetermined effectiveness criteria.

8.3 Following an integrated process

A further reason for (and benefit of) following the design model is to ensure an integrated AC programme and process in which the different subcomponents form an integrated and logical whole. The overall AC programme objectives serve as an important guiding principle in keeping the whole programme integrated and the components aligned. However, the AC exercises also need to portray a particular climate and culture of the company or business that one wants to simulate. The business and contextual analyses provide valuable information and cues in this regard.

8.4 Adding marketing value

AC practitioners and service providers will definitely benefit if they follow this rigorous and systematic design approach and methodology, while the underlying scientific principles will enhance the validity and reliability of the AC programme and process. A fair and unbiased AC programme that is valid and reliable potentially has a large amount of marketing value, purely based on the fact that this rigorous design methodology will result in a more valid and reliable outcome as opposed to those situations in which such an approach is not followed.

8.5 Ensuring validity, reliability and fairness

The systematic design process ensures a valid and reliable outcome. The systematic and careful design approach forces the AC design team to constantly match the multiple design criteria of both the design model and the programme evaluation approach, of which effectiveness, validity, reliability and fairness are some of the important ones. Only if these criteria are systematically applied will a more valid, reliable and fair assessment process emerge.

9. CONCLUSION

In this chapter, we first introduced the AC concept by explaining what an AC is. Thereafter, the different types of ACs most typically encountered in industry were explained. The features of ACs were also described in order to enable the reader to distinguish the AC from other assessment techniques. Following this, the different applications of an AC were described so as to demonstrate the application potential of this technique in selecting individuals and in developing individuals and organisations.

A further part of this chapter specifically introduced the design model and provided a rationale for following this approach. This design model will be superimposed on programme evaluation principles that form the organising framework for presenting the largest part of the contents of this book.

The next chapter provides an overview of the historical development of ACs and the Assessment Centre Study Group (ACSG) in South Africa.

CHAPTER 2

ASSESSMENT CENTRES IN SOUTH AFRICAN HISTORY

Deon Meiring

1. A BRIEF HISTORY OF ASSESSMENT CENTRES (ACS) IN SOUTH AFRICA

When writing about the history of ACs in South Africa, one needs to reflect on the pioneering work of Prof Hermann Spangenberg, who established the Assessment Centre Study Group (ACSG) in South Africa. In the 1980s, Hermann went on a study tour to the USA and Canada with the specific purpose of learning more about developmental follow-up strategies from top American companies and academics. He also attended the International Congress on AC Methods (ICACM), where he met some of the top practitioners and academics in the field, including Doug Bray, Anne Howard, George Thornton and Bill Byham. These and other North American experts were to play a key role by sharing their expertise during the formative years of the establishment of ACs in South Africa. The implementation of ACs in South Africa during the 1970s and 1980s was, according to Hermann[1] (2018), characterised by some distinct features:

- From the beginning, the main aims of AC application were both assessment and development. The follow-up development of participants was taken seriously. Large organisations, therefore, had competent management development officers and well-equipped development facilities.
- The introduction of ACs was complemented by a thorough, one-week, experiential observer training session in which all AC participants participated. This allowed for the availability of observers, in spite of difficult schedules.
- The reason why the overwhelming number of organisations that introduced ACs did it so effectively is probably due to the top-down approach that was followed. This approach created the understanding and buy-in on the part of senior management that is essential for effective management-leadership training and development. It also enabled competent AC administrators and a core of well-trained observers to deliver according to expectations.

The first accounts of ACs in South Africa can be traced back to the 1970s.[2] The first AC in South Africa was developed in 1971 by the Edgars group. Bill Byham from DDI[3] and Sydney Press, the chairman of Edgars, were brave enough to implement the first assessment centre used to identify the potential of Black employees for managerial positions at Edgars. Other large South African organisations soon followed suit, such as Old Mutual, Transport Services (South African Railway Services), Stellenbosch

---

1   Spangenberg, 2018

2   Meiring & van der Westhuizen, 2011

3   Meiring & van der Westhuizen, 2011

Farmers Winery (SFW) (now part of Distell), the Department of Post and Telecommunication Services (Telkom), Nasionale Pers (Naspers), the South African Army, the South African Police (now SAPS) and SASOL. Most of these organisations were heavily influenced by practices in the USA, and specifically, the methodologies and simulation exercises of DDI.

ACs were introduced into the Old Mutual group in 1973, the second institution to make use of AC technology in South Africa. This was due to Bill Byham, who met the Old Mutual Chairman, Jan van der Horst, and convinced him of the value of ACs. A few personnel and line managers at Old Mutual were sent to DDI to be trained in Byham's behaviour modelling, which was called interaction management. Willie Marais later joined the human resources department of Old Mutual in 1977, where he worked with ACs. The Byham model and competencies were phased out and Old Mutual started to develop its own competencies, which were adopted across Old Mutual's major functional divisions. Five different ACs for sales, back office, intermediary adopted property management, specialists and professionals were developed, making use of case studies and simulations. Old Mutual pioneered the AC by first introducing post-development or competency-based skills development after the completion of the AC. As the organisation's skills profile changed, the AC was adapted and new competencies were assessed, from where skills development took place. Later on, ACs were used more strategically to bring about culture change within Old Mutual. Simulations were used to imitate the future state of the organisation, which was determined by the new strategy of Old Mutual. Managers were assessed on these future-state competencies and received feedback on their behaviours as well as on how they performed against these future-state competencies. Old Mutual also implemented ACs in its offshore companies (e.g. in countries like Zimbabwe, England, Thailand, Malaysia and Hong Kong) during the 1980s. These ACs were locally researched and developed on the basis of specific local jobs, unique business cultures and business-specific content. They were then used for assessment, promotion, transfer and development.

Old Mutual introduced the AC concept to the Transport Services as part of a service agreement concluded in 1975. Piet Brits from the Transport Services was part of a task group that visited the USA that year on a fact-finding mission to determine how companies like AT&T and IBM identified potential and fast-tracked their talent. The Transport Services initially trained a core group of 35 line managers to become observers. From 1976 to 1979, it assessed 670 managers and rolled out its AC as a selection and development tool in the organisation. In 1982, it reassessed the 670 managers as part of the very first validation studies to be conducted in South Africa.

In the late 1970s, Hermann Spangenberg introduced ACs at SFW with the assistance of his colleague, Piet Brand, and consultants, Piet Britz and Adrie de Bod. The SFW AC was implemented as part of a top-down development process starting with directors and senior managers. Using intensive job and organisational analyses, they later developed and implemented a Middle Management Assessment Centre (MMDC) for current and aspiring middle managers. Development was strongly emphasised with, for example, learning points for leadership development serving as scoring criteria in interactive exercises. Line managers serving as observers received intensive observer training.

Piet Britz, Adrie de Bod and Court Schilbach introduced the AC into the Department of Post and Telecommunication Services in 1978. The DDI model was used along with five simulation exercises and was referred to as the "Bosse" in those days (an acronym for *bestuursontwikkelingsentrums* (management development centres)). Over the years, Ben Meyer headed up the AC sections in the Department (later Telkom) and implemented five different management ACs covering levels from pre-supervisory to executive. The results of the ACs, together with the participants' biographical details, achievements and aspirations, constituted important inputs to the succession management systems in these organisations. On 1 October 1991, Telkom was established and a new generation of ACs was introduced. In striving to become a world-class organisation, Telkom started to focus on high-performance leadership competencies, and used the work done by Harold Schroder at Princeton University and the University of South Florida to assess and develop managers at Telkom.

In 1979, Naspers also introduced the traditional AC of Doug Bray and Bill Byham with the intention of identifying senior management with potential in the organisation. In 1983, the company made changes to its AC and started to use it more as a Diagnostic Centre (DC) for identifying senior management potential and development needs, as well as for developing action plans for managers. Coetzee (1995) indicated that, in 1992, Naspers embarked on changing its corporate culture, resulting in the emergence of new needs, particularly regarding the required management competencies that would steer Naspers into the future. The need for a "new" AC and development tool focusing on strategic transformation was evident. The methodology Naspers used to determine key competencies was guided by the repertory grid, a significant technique introduced in South Africa by Valerie Stewart from the United Kingdom (UK). The Collaborative Development Centre (a version of a Development Assessment Centre) was seen at that stage as a more appropriate vehicle for promoting cultural and strategic changes in Naspers (see Chapter 13 for a discussion of DCs and DACs).

In 1978, the Military Psychological Institute (MPI) introduced the AC into the then South African Defence Force. According to Colonel Albert Jansen, the Institute used a standard AC comprising an administrator and several observers, and participants who were assessed and received feedback. The AC was primarily used for selection and development. From 1980 to 1990, special ACs were developed for the selection of Antarctica expedition personnel, military attachés and hostage negotiators. The traditional AC was phased out in 1994 with the amalgamation of the seven defence forces. In 1996, Cora van Wyk, the chief administrator of the AC at the time, introduced the SHL Learning AC into the Army.

The SA Army again identified the need for leadership assessments and development in the early 2000s, and as a consequence, the SA Army Assessment Centre was reconstituted as a joint venture between the SA Army and the SA Military Health Services. In 2009, psychologists working under Johnny O'Neil, the department head from the MPI, were placed at the SA Army College, where the initial focus was on the establishment of a leadership assessment service. From 2009 to 2014, special ACs were developed for the selection of Junior Leaders, Warrant Officers, Unit Commanders, Defence Attachés and Brigadier Generals in the SA Army. The Centre focused on following a construct-oriented psychological assessment approach that included the use of psychometry, role plays, interviews, in-baskets, planning and problem-solving simulation exercises, and practical leadership exercises where candidates were observed by observers. These observers included psychologists and SA Army officers who were specifically selected and trained in behaviour observation. Candidates were assessed for both selection and development purposes and all received feedback reports.

From 2014 onwards the focus shifted from only assessments to include development. This change in focus also included a change in the approach used by the psychologists. More emphasis was placed on the empowerment and development of SA Army personnel (Directing Staff and Instructors) who would facilitate the development of generic development areas such as leadership, adaptability, problem-solving, teamwork and communication, as identified during assessments. The psychologists would focus on the development of "psychologically sensitive" areas such as self-awareness, critical thinking skills, cognitive development, conflict management, influencing skills and performance enhancement.

Furthermore, SA Army personnel were empowered to conduct their own preliminary assessments before they attended the AC at the SA Army Assessment Centre. It is still too early to make final comments on the effectiveness of this new strategy, but the early results seem promising.

The South African Police also made use of ACs in the late 1980s. Court Schilbach introduced the "Bosse" to the Police, where it was administered by the then Institute for Behavioural Sciences (now Psychological Services) during middle and senior management courses. The AC results were used for development, promotion and succession planning. As with the South African Army, the AC was phased out in 1994 with the amalgamation of 11 police agencies into the new South African Police Service (SAPS). It was only in 2000 that the SAPS reintroduced the AC concept in the form of the Emerging Leadership Programme to identify emerging previously disadvantaged leaders in the SAPS. In 2003, the National Commissioner, Jackie Selebi, implemented the AC as a selection tool for choosing senior managers in the SAPS. In 2006, a DC for middle-level managers was developed by Deon Meiring of Psychological Services, which was implemented in 2007. The SAPS have also built an AC facility at their head office in Pretoria, which simulates a senior official's workspace in SAPS. The facility consists of various breakaway rooms, i.e. observers' rooms with one-way mirrors, control rooms with recording equipment and smaller meeting rooms. The AC is currently still being used to select senior managers in the SAPS.

SASOL started to implement development centres (DCs) in 1982 with the completion of its new SASOL III plant in Secunda. SASOL III uses a world-leading technology for the commercial production of synthetic fuels and chemical products. According to Gideon Visagie (G.J. Visagie, personal communication, 27 September 2018), the focus was on designing and implementing DCs to accelerate the development of managerial competence at both the middle and senior levels within the new SASOL III. The DC concentrated on identifying and developing managerial competencies which included problem solving, general management, interpersonal relations and communication. SASOL contracted an American organisation, Assessment Design Incorporated (ADI), which was headed-up by Fred Frank, Stephen Cohen and Cabott Jaffee, to assist them in developing the senior manager DC. This DC included an in-basket exercise (Caustig chemicals), an analysis exercise (Consumer Council), a leaderless group exercise and individual interview simulations. The DC for middle managers was designed in-house by a SASOL task team. The middle managers' DC consisted of a 30-item industry specific in-basket, an analysis exercise (an off-the-shelf purchase), and interactive simulations. Although the dimensions were similar to the senior DC, fewer dimensions were assessed during the middle manager DC. Attending the DC was part of a manager's annual development plan and managers were marked down during their performance appraisals if they did not attend the DC. Managers were also sent for special management training and development courses to enhance their skills as identified in the DC. During 1989 another DC was developed that was aimed at the supervisory level, however SASOL stopped presenting in-house DCs when the demand for DCs decreased due to a stable workforce. A few "DCs" were presented afterwards by the leadership development department where the participants scored their own simulations and wrote their own reports and development plans.

Since 1990 a number of consulting firms (Deloitte, Evelex, Experttech, LEMASA, Precision Assessment Centre Solutions, The Talent Group and Top Talent Solutions (TTS)) have provided professional AC services to various industries in South Africa and abroad.

2. FOUNDING OF THE ASSESSMENT CENTRE STUDY GROUP

At the end of the 1970s, Hermann Spangenberg identified a need to establish the Assessment Centre Study Group (ACSG). At that time, only a few organisations used AC technology. He recalls how colleagues at SFW, practitioners from other organisations and he himself shared ideas on how to run ACs more effectively, particularly regarding how to improve the leadership and managerial effectiveness of their organisations' managers. This need, as well as support from a number of major South African organisations, prompted the creation of the ACSG as a formal forum where practitioners could exchange ideas. Hermann's extensive study tour to the USA and Canada in 1980, during which he met the top AC practitioners and academics, played an important role in that it convinced him of North American support.

At the beginning of the 1980s, the Institute of Personnel Management (IPM) was one of the strongest professional bodies in South Africa, with the dynamic Wilhelm Crous (now the Managing Director (MD) of Knowledge Resources) as its Executive Director. With active branches throughout South Africa and a highly respected IPM journal, the IPM was the ideal organisation to host the ACSG. Wilhelm Crous was, in fact, the Chairperson at the inaugural meeting held in Johannesburg. The meeting was held just before the Annual IPM Convention and was well attended by human resource (HR) practitioners. Hermann Spangenberg was selected as the first Chairperson of the ACSG in 1981. Although part of the IPM, the ACSG operated fairly independently, only drawing on the infrastructure of the IPM when required. Combined with support from Piet Rossouw, HR Director of SFW, particularly with regard to facilities (De Oude Libertas) for presenting the annual conferences, the ACSG was built on a firm infrastructure. Its growing independence over the years led to a break from the IPM in the late 1980s. Over the years, the ACSG presented an annual conference in the Stellenbosch region, where practitioners exchanged research, insights and information related to the science, practice and teaching of ACs. In 2017 a decision was made by the Exco of the ACSG, based on numerous requests by ACSG members, to alternate the hosting of the conference between the Western Cape and Gauteng provinces.

Gert Roodt presenting a lifetime award to Hermann Spangenberg at the 2008 ACSG conference

The main aim of the ACSG conference has always been to create a forum where practitioners can come together to share, discuss and learn more about the AC method. Sharing cutting-edge information and developments in a pleasant atmosphere has been a hallmark of the ACSG ever since its inception. One of the most important considerations for the ACSG has always been to attract some of the best local and international speakers to the annual conference, who share knowledge and the latest research with delegates. Table 2.1 indicates some of the international speakers who have been invited over the years as keynote speakers at the ACSG conferences.

Table 2.1: International speakers at ACSG conferences (1980-2020)

Year	International speaker	Affiliation
1980	Hermann Spangenberg	Establishment of Assessment Centre Study Group
1981	Len Slivinski	Industrial Psychological Services, Canadian Public Service
1982	Jim Huck	Consultant, San Diego (ex AT&T)
1983	Frank Landy	Pennsylvania State University, USA
1984	Cabot Jaffee	Cabot Jaffee & Associates, USA
1985	Lois Crooks	Education Testing Services (ETS), USA
1986	George Thornton	Colorado State University, USA
1987	No International Speaker	
1988	Doug Bray Anne Howard	AT&T, DDI International

Year	International speaker	Affiliation
1989	Wayne Cascio	University of Colorado at Denver and Health Sciences Center, USA
1990	Valerie Stewart	Macmillan, Stewart & Partners, consultant industrial psychologists
1991	Wayne Cascio	University of Colorado at Denver and Health Sciences Center, USA
1992	Frank Landy	Pennsylvania State University, USA
1993	Valerie Stewart	Macmillan, Stewart & Partners, consultant industrial psychologists
1994	Otto van Veen Jeroen Seegers	Nijenrode University, The Netherlands Assessment & development consultant, The Netherlands
1995	George Thornton	Colorado State University, USA
1996	Seymour Adler	Consultant, New York, USA
1997	Harold Schroder	University of South Florida, Tampa, USA
1998	Herman Gillian Peter Saville	GC Consulting Group, UK SHL, UK
1999	Rabindra Kanungo Frank Landy	McGill University, Montreal, Canada Pennsylvania State University, USA
2000	Fareed Jaubocus James Outtz	Partner at De Chazal Du Mee, Mauritius Outtz & Associates, USA
2001	Wayne Casio Fillip Lievens	University of Colorado, USA University of Ghent, Belgium
2002	Jeroen Seegers Mark de Graaf	Assessment & development consultant, The Netherlands Global Alliance for Performance Improvement, The Netherlands
2003	Helen Baron	Independent consultant, UK
2004	Paul Sackett	University of Minnesota, USA
2005	Niel Anderson Marise Born	University of Amsterdam, The Netherlands University of Erasmus, Rotterdam, The Netherlands
2006	Filip Lievens Marise Born Ian Williamson	University of Ghent, Belgium University of Erasmus, Rotterdam, The Netherlands Robert H Smith School of Business, University of Maryland, USA
2007	George Thornton Deborah Rupp Beverly Alimo-Metcalfe	University of Colorado, USA University of Illinois at Urbana-Champaign, USA Real World Group
2008	Deniz Ones Stephan Dilchert Eva Bergvall	University of Minnesota, USA University of Minnesota, USA Municipality in the City of Gothenburg, Sweden

Year	International speaker	Affiliation
2009	Sandra Hartog Anne Howard	Fenestra, USA DDI, USA
2010	Diana Krause Kevin Murphey	University of Paderborn, Germany Pennsylvania State University, USA
2011	Martin Lanik Subrata Pandey	Global Assessor Pool, USA CCMC, India
2012	Martin Kleinmann Filip Lievens	University of Zürich, Switzerland University of Ghent, Belgium
2013 (ICACM combined with ACSG)	Bill Byham Brian Hoffmann Alyssa Gibbons Dan Hughes	DDI, USA University of Georgia, USA Colorado State University, USA a&dc, UK
2014	Duncan Jackson Dan Putke	University of East London, UK HumBRO, Alexandria, USA
2015	Diana Krause Klaus Melcher	Alpen-Adria University, Austria Ulm University, Germany
2016	Marise Born	Erasmus University, The Netherlands
2017	Filip Lievens	University of Ghent, Belgium
2018	Christine Ute-Klehe	Justus-Liebig University, Germany
2019	Martin Kleinmann	University of Zürich, Switzerland
2020	Nathan Kuncel	University of Minnesota, USA

Since its inception 39 years ago, the ACSG has offered pre-conference workshops, and of late expanded its range of services to include AC Academy training workshops, best practice guidelines for AC practices[4], and a code of ethics for ACs in South Africa.[5] The AC Academy has been very prominent, with a clear aim to establish competence and skills amongst AC practitioners in designing, delivering and researching ACs according to best practices and ethical guidelines.

Various chairpersons from different public, private and academic institutions have led the ACSG, as per Table 2.2.

---

4   Meiring & Buckett, 2016

5   SA Assessment Centre Study Group, 2018

Table 2.2: ACSG chairpersons (1981-2019)

Year	Chairperson	Company
1981-1984	Hermann Spangenberg	Stellenbosch Farmers Winery (SFW)
1985	Albert van der Merwe	Sasol
1986-1987	Hermann Spangenberg	Stellenbosch Farmers Winery (SFW)
1988-1995	George Coetzee	Naspers
1996-2001	Hennie Kriek	SHL, South Africa
2002-2003	Willie Marais	Old Mutual
2004-2005	Charmaine Swanevelder	SHL, South Africa
2006-2007	Deon Meiring	South African Police Service
2008-2009	Anne Buckett	Precision HR
2010- 2011	Sandra Schlebusch	LEMASA
2012- 2013	Lydia Cillié-Schmidt	The Talent Hub
2014-2015	David Bischoff	Deloitte
2016-2017	Petrus Nel	University of Free State
2018-2020	Jaco de Jager	TTS

3. AIMS AND OBJECTIVES OF THE ACSG

The SA Assessment Centre Study Group NPC (ACSG) is a special interest group of practitioners in South Africa, which presents an annual conference on Assessment Centre (AC) research, methodology and practice. The ACSG functions independently, both professionally and financially. It is run by an elected committee of volunteers and governed by its own constitution. The ACSG has the following broad and specific objectives:

Broad objectives:
- To promote the professional use of the AC technique.
- To facilitate the exchange of experience, views, opinions and skills of the AC technique.
- To stimulate research about the development and application of the AC technique.
- To ensure that the AC technique is applied in an ethical and professional manner by its practitioners.
- To ensure that the application of the AC technique in South Africa keeps pace with global development in the field.
- To stimulate transformation in the profession by making the ACSG more demographically representative in terms of conference attendees, conference speakers and committee members.

Specific objectives:
- The hosting of an annual ACSG conference.
- The presentation of workshops to improve and maintain practitioners' expertise and skills.
- The establishment and maintenance of a dedicated website on the activities of the ACSG. (The website will provide information to practitioners regarding the activities of the ACSG and other related information which could be of interest to them.)
- The establishment of a bursary/study aid scheme in support of AC-focused research.
- The promotion and facilitation of the publication of articles of a high professional standard in recognised professional and career publications.
- The development of AC and Development Centre guidelines for the South African context.
- The continual liaison and establishment of affiliations with local and global academic and professional organisations/institutions for the promotion of expertise and application of the AC technique in South Africa.
- The promotion and development of ACs among practitioners from all parts of South African society.
- The continuous development and application of an ethical code for AC practitioners in South Africa. The ACSG committee shall manage/be instrumental in any revisions to the South African Guidelines for Assessment and Development Centres.

In striving to achieve these objectives, the ACSG provides a forum where practitioners and individuals can interact and exchange knowledge, best practices and experiences concerning the use of ACs in South Africa.

4.   AC GUIDELINES FOR SOUTH AFRICA

Just as the International Congress on AC Methods established a task force to develop Guidelines and Ethical Considerations for AC Operations, so did the ACSG in South Africa. Over the years (1991-2015), the South African guidelines (available from: https://www.acsg.co.za/south-african-ac-guidelines) have been developed along very similar lines to the international guidelines.

In the mid-1980s, the ACSG started playing an active role with regard to the professional and ethical aspects of ACs, and began reflecting on the application of AC practices in organisations. First, appropriate legislation to regulate the use of personnel assessment techniques was lacking, and secondly, consultants and HR practitioners who were not qualified to implement AC methodology were exposed. These issues were considered to be serious, and at an executive meeting held in June 1987 by the ACSG, it was decided to adapt the 1979 International Guidelines to conform to South African legal requirements. It was furthermore decided to publish a document in the IPM's journal containing the amended guidelines and indicating the role of the ACSG in monitoring AC applications.

4.1   1991 Guidelines

The endorsement of the new International Guidelines by participants at the 17th International Congress on the AC Method in May 1989 in Pittsburgh, Pennsylvania, USA, prompted the South African AC fraternity to follow suit. The guidelines were adapted and subsequently presented to the 11th Annual

ACSG Conference in Stellenbosch in March 1991 by Hermann Spangenberg, the Convenor of the project. Copies were circulated to delegates and the Guidelines were discussed and endorsed unanimously during the Annual General Meeting.

At the same conference, the role of the ACSG Executive with regard to the application of the Guidelines was discussed. Of special interest was the advisory role that Executive Committee members could play during the construction of an AC. However, in order to safeguard committee members from possible litigation, it was decided that such members could not officially be called upon to approve procedures or steps in the construction process. Committee members, who were usually experienced AC practitioners, could, however, be consulted informally. In fact, this was common practice at that time. Although the endorsed guidelines would have no formal legal status, they could play an important role in litigation, in as much as they would be considered the opinions of experts in the field.

4.2 1999 Guidelines

During the 1998 ACSG conference in Stellenbosch, it was decided to revise the 1991 South African Guidelines so that they would be better aligned to legal and social developments in South Africa. In addition, the Guidelines needed to meet the requirements of the new labour legislation as well as rigorous validity procedures. As part of its strategy for revising the Guidelines, the Executive Committee took the following steps:
- Relevant stakeholders were consulted, that is, the members as well as representatives of the Department of Labour and the South African Qualifications Authority (SAQA).
- The draft copy of the Guidelines was also distributed at two sessions of the Psychological Assessment Initiative (PAI), an interest group of the Society of Industrial and Organisational Psychology of South Africa (SIOPSA), and members were asked to give comments on the Guidelines.

The following step-by-step process was then followed:
- Inputs from stakeholders were obtained.
- A task team consisting of members of the ACSG Management Committee integrated the information and developed a draft proposal.
- The final proposal was submitted for endorsement at the March 1999 Annual ACSG Conference.

4.3 2007 Guidelines

During the 2006 Annual ACSG Conference in Stellenbosch, it was decided to revise the 1999 Guidelines so that the South African Guidelines were aligned with the 2000 International Guidelines, and so that they incorporated the 2006 Professional Guidelines for global ACs. One of the key features of the 2007 Guidelines was the incorporation of DACs as part of the Guidelines, at the same time focusing on the cross-cultural application of ACs and DACs in South Africa.

The following steps were taken:
- Various stakeholders, especially in the consulting domain of ACs, were consulted.
- The latest information available on AC guidelines was collected and studied.

- A task team comprising members of the ACSG facilitated a work session at which a broad structure for the 2007 Guidelines was proposed.
- A draft version of the 2007 Guidelines was introduced at the 27th Annual ACSG Conference held in March 2007 in Stellenbosch.

4.4 2015 Guidelines

The 5th edition of the *Assessment Centre Guidelines for South Africa* was compiled by a taskforce under the auspices of the ACSG of South Africa in 2015. The revised 5th edition Guidelines represented an update of the 2007 4th edition Guidelines and took the latest international developments, AC design, implementation and evaluation of ACs in the workplace in South Africa into consideration. In addition, the revised guidelines took into account the many scientific advancements in the AC domain since the publication of the 4th edition. Furthermore, it was necessary to make specific allowance in the 5th edition for the impact of technology, legislation, validation strategies and cultural considerations.

The following steps were taken:
- A taskforce was compiled consisting of previous members of the revision process (4th edition), academics, consultants and emerging AC practitioners.
- Following a structured project management approach, the taskforce members were allocated specific sections of the 4th edition Guidelines to review and amend.
- The suggestions were collated and the taskforce held a half-day workshop to review all comments and suggestions in order to arrive at a majority position on controversial issues.
- Specific attention was given to technology, legislation, ethics, cultural considerations, and the technicalities/practicalities of AC design and validation.
- In particular, the taskforce debated and arrived at a position statement on ACs concerning alterations to the Employment Equity Amendment Act (Act No. 47 of 2013, Section 8, clause d) pertaining to the classification of ACs in accordance with the Act.
- The taskforce further advocated for a stronger alignment to the International Guidelines in terms of structure and content, albeit customised to the South African context, to enhance consistency and standardisation.
- The revised South African AC Guidelines were circulated to ACSG members and delegates prior to the 35th annual ACSG conference.

Taskforce members at the 5th edition of Assessment Centre Guidelines workshop

A copy of the Best Practice Guidelines for the use of the Assessment Centre Method in South Africa (5th ed.)[6] can be downloaded at: http://dx.doi.org/10.4102/sajip.v42i1.1298.

5. CODE OF ETHICS FOR ASSESSMENT CENTRES IN SOUTH AFRICA

Doing what is good for self and what is good for others remains a challenge in AC practice, especially when confronted with the demands of clients, time frames and expectations. Muleya, Fourie and Schlebusch[7] found that despite best practice AC guidelines[8], unethical AC practices are still common in the South African work context. Dewberry and Jackson[9] found that dysfunctional ACs (as experienced by assessors, designers and participants) can stem from poor AC design, inadequate AC implementation, insufficient assessor related training and a lack of consideration for the AC participants.

In 2016, the ACSG embarked on developing a Code of Ethics for ACs in South Africa (available from: https://www.acsg.co.za/sites/default/files/Code-of-Ethics-for-ACs-inSA-Final-15-March-2018-ACSG-AcceptedVersion.pdf).[10] The Code was intended to supplement the legal environment in which ACs take place in South Africa, as well as the voluntary *Best Practice Guidelines for the use of the Assessment Centre Method in South Africa* (5th ed.).[11] The Code was intended to be aspirational, guiding the "how" of behaviour, especially when faced with ethical dilemmas in ACs.

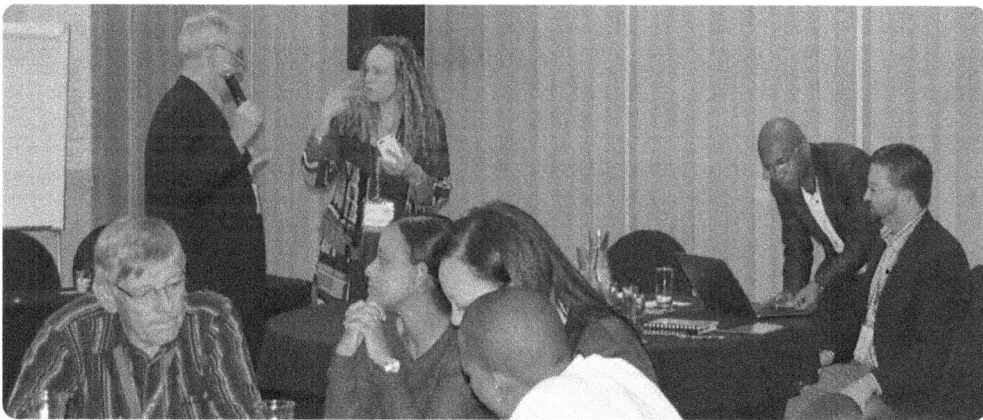

ASCG delegates in 2016 at the Code of Ethics plenary session giving inputs on the development of the Code

The Code was developed to guide AC practitioners in their everyday conduct, thinking and planning, as well as in the resolution of ethical dilemmas, that is, it advocates for the use of both proactive and reactive ethics in AC practice. In addition, the principles and values focus on specific standards that are unique to

---

6   Meiring & Buckett, 2016

7   Muleya et al., 2014

8   Meiring & Buckett, 2016

9   Dewberry & Jackson, 2016

10 Schlebusch et al. 2017; Meiring et al., 2018

11 Meiring & Buckett, 2016

the field of AC practice (see Chapter 4). The Code provides an ethical framework for determining whether the complaint is of enough concern, either at the level of the individual AC practitioner or at the level of the profession as a whole, to warrant action. In determining corrective action for an individual AC practitioner, one of the judgments the adjudicating body (e.g. ACSG, HPCSA or SABPP) needs to make is whether an individual conscientiously engaged in an ethical decision making process and acted in good faith, or whether there was a negligent or wilful disregard of ethical principles. The responsibility for ethical action depends foremost on the integrity of each AC practitioner's commitment to behave as ethically as possible.

Three years in the making (2016-2018), the Code of Ethics for AC Practice in South Africa was presented, accepted and approved at the 38th Annual ACSG conference in March 2018. A collaborative process was followed in identifying the values and clarifying the six principles (respect for participant dignity, respect for participant diversity, respect for participant freedom, respect for the client, respect for the client's organisation, and professional accountability) espoused in the Code, resulting in 43 aspirational and directional standards.

A copy of the Code of Ethics for AC Practice in South Africa can be downloaded at: https://www.acsg.co.za/sites/default/files/Code-of-Ethics-for-ACs-inSA-15-March-2018-ACSG.pdf

6. FUTURE CHALLENGES PRESENTED BY ACS IN SOUTH AFRICA

ACs have come of age in South Africa and are following international trends. In the first period (from the 1970s onwards), ACs were pioneered in South Africa by way of the introduction of the traditional Bray and Byham AC model. Soon, an adapted version of the AC, namely a DC, was introduced that focused on the development of employees. Later, DACs were used as a transformational vehicle in organisations in order to bring about culture change. The second period (1994-1996) focused on the application of the AC method in a newly democratic society. Issues of fairness, culture appropriateness and the role that the AC could play in organisational transformation and change were prominent. In the third period (1997-1999), there was a new awareness of the competence and competencies that the AC measured. Issues of cost-effectiveness (e.g. utility) and using both ACs and DCs for affirmative action initiatives came to the fore. In the fourth period (2000-2005), the focus was on vision and how the AC practitioner could become a strategic partner in organisations. Issues of how we align ACs, competencies and exercises to the strategic direction of the organisation attracted attention. The fifth period (2001-2007) focused on the identification of leadership and organisational talent (e.g. the organisation's talent pipeline), while the sixth period (2008 – 2012) focused on the introduction of new technologies in AC practices. A clear shift away from paper-based ACs towards digital platforms (e.g. email, internet, video, webinar) and format applications was seen at this time. The seventh period (2013-2018) focused on bridging the gap in emerging markets, with ACs providing added value, returns on investments to organisations and personal benefits to individuals.

Adaptation to the disruption in the workplace has seen the introduction of new game-based technologies (e.g. gamification and virtual reality) to the AC space. In terms of the future, we have seen dramatic changes in the world of work. The environment in which organisations must function is uncertain, with serious competition coming from new entrants to the market.[12] Innovative AC technologies are needed for a "new flat world", with a clear focus on decreasing costs, increasing speed and improving the quality of ACs. According to Howard[13], experience has shown that ACs have readily adapted and transformed over different generations and time periods. The new industrial revolution 4.0, with machine learning, artificial intelligence and innovations in technology and the digital field, is set to completely change the world as we know it.[14] According to Schlebusch[15], adaptation to the new disruption in the workplace will require challenging adjustments from AC practices in South Africa:

- AC designers need to re-conceptualise the centres' focal constructs – the competencies, type of simulations and simulation content. The centre participants might not be full-time employees and the focus might be on teams working together per project instead of with individual participants.
- ACs need to incorporate new advancements in technology, for instance increased computational power enables the use of different statistical calculations that reveal different perspectives about issues such as the validity and reliability of ACs (e.g. Bayesian method). Through the use of technology, participants' micro-behaviours such as eye movements, perspiration levels and movement between items when dealing with issues, can be captured and analysed. With the use of algorithms and Big Data, assessment results can be assimilated and feedback reports generated within hours of completing an AC.
- Through Virtual Assessment Centres (VACs), participants and assessors can be dispersed around the globe, be within different time zones and still participate in the same centre. Given technological advancements that enable voice and visuals to be captured in real-time, live role plays can also form part of a VAC. Virtual reality (VR), where a participant is represented by a self-created avatar, has already been used in assessment centres, while successful experiments using artificial intelligence (AI) within an assessment centre have taken place.

According to Schlebusch[16], the potential advantages of all these new technological advances are many. The accuracy of assessments can potentially increase through the combination of many data points; the speed at which assessment results are available can increase; the richness of feedback can increase; and ACs have become scale-able. ACs can also be performed anywhere, anytime, for any number of participants.

Schlebusch[17] indicated that despite new changes in the work environment and new technological enhancements, humans will still be central to the process of AC design, administration, scoring, data integration, report writing and giving feedback. She asked the following questions relating to AC practitioners' future skill sets:

---

12 Schlebusch, 2018

13 Howard, 2016

14 Taylor, 2018

15 Schlebusch, 2018

16 Schlebusch, 2018

17 Schlebusch, 2018

- If we would still need humans, what would their required skill levels be? As an example, would an AC designer need to have software computing skills (coding), or just require skills to articulate the need to a software developer? What are the new skills required of a VAC assessor and role player? How would a participant experience the use of technology in an AC, or how would a future participant experience an AC that does not use technology?

Schlebusch concluded that a future assessment centre would "be a centre that allows agile delivery, that is based on solid science and that adds value to a client organization".[18] Thornton[19] indicated that the long, rich history of ACs is due to the interface of science and practice, and at the same time AC application in the field is an exemplar of "evidence-based management". He concluded that continued cooperation between science and practice is needed to meet the current challenges.

The ACSG has been in existence in South Africa for the past 39 years, and, after the International Congress on AC Methods, it is the second-oldest movement in the world that focuses on AC practice. The latest addition to the AC movement (in which the ACSG has been instrumental) is the UK - Assessment Center Group, which was established in 2015 (www.uk-acg.com).

The ACSG has matured over the last 39 years and has served the science and practice of ACs in South Africa well. The ACSG has been transformed from a small study group of individuals into a study group of more than 200 members who attend the annual conferences in the Western Cape and Gauteng. The ACSG has a well-developed infrastructure and, in 2017, launched its second revamped official website (www.ascg.co.za) along with a new logo.

In 2017, the ACSG had its second strategic session since its inception (first session 2010) in Pretoria. A critical analysis was made of its history, of what is changing in the AC environment, and of the implications of the changes on the ACSG. Key questions were asked regarding the ACSG value-add to stakeholders, the key offering to stakeholders and the strategic priorities for the future.

As to its value-add, the following values emerged for ACSG key stakeholders:
- **AC practitioners:**
  - Cutting-edge knowledge.
  - General promotion of ACs.
  - Networking – Assessor database / Whistle blowing facility / Quality assurance.
  - Business case for using ACs.
  - International alignment.
  - AC related training.
  - Knowledge generators.
  - AC research – students, etc.
  - Inclusivity.
  - Draw-in the "next generation".
  - Exposure to practice – internships to students.

18 Schlebusch, 2018
19 Thornton, 2011

- **Universities (IOP, HR, Business Schools)**:
  - Modules to include in material for programmes.
  - Resources to universities to present AC modules as part of university programmes.
  - Data and research opportunities.
  - Student research opportunities.
  - Connect research institutions.
  - The AC research agenda.
- **Organisations:**
  - Evidence-based selection methods.
  - Ethical selection practices.
  - Cost-effective selection practices.
  - BEE and EE compliant selection practices.
  - Future skills.
  - Selection and development of a global workforce.
  - Staff engagement.
  - Participants feel good about the organisation.
  - Talent pipeline.
  - Valid job previews / valid job performance predictions.
  - Knowledgeable AC practitioners.
  - Best practice guidelines.
  - Resources to enable ethical ACs within organisations.
  - Opportunities to share knowledge and AC practice.
- **International community:**
  - Collaboration and sharing of resources.
  - Information and knowledge dissemination.
  - Laboratories and experience.
  - Benchmarking.
  - Opportunities for visiting students / practitioners.
  - Access to Africa.
- **Candidates/Participants:**
  - Information about ACs, such as AC process information.
  - Whistle blowing opportunities.
  - Practice opportunity prior to doing a full-blown AC.
  - An understanding of what an AC is.
- **General society:**
  - Outreach programmes.

As to key offerings for current and future stakeholders, the ACSG provides the following:
- Assessor database.
- AC service provider database (web page advertisers).
- Obtaining CPD points:
  - Attending conferences.
  - Attending AC Academy training programmes.
  - Studying research articles and doing assignments – e-CPD.

- Research opportunities and learnings from research.
- Bursaries for AC students.
- Networking and Centre Of Practice (knowledge hub).
- Quality assurance - Guidelines to Professional Practice.
- International networks.
- Stakeholder engagement on topical issues.
- Knowledge generation and dissemination.
- Promotion, development and growth of AC profession.
- Practice in AC field (e.g. opportunities for interns to obtain AC experience as part of their internships).
- **Annual conference:**
  - High profile and high quality speakers.
  - New global speakers.
  - Emotional "feel good" experience.
  - Add value to AC profession and conference attendees.
  - Financially affordable – value for money.
  - Speakers available to interact with delegates during the conference.
  - The conference is an opportunity for the exhibiters to meet potential clients.
  - Conference programme: AC user / corporate stream; AC research stream.
  - Conference target: consultants; practitioners; academics; corporate users.
  - Value-adding workshops.
- **AC Academy:**
  - Constant enrolment of potential new AC practitioners.
  - Responds to stakeholder requests.
  - Need to provide content in multiple learning modes.
  - Work towards international standing.
  - Continuously define new modules and courses - constant new products and services.
  - Clarify the governance and management structure.
  - Create a visible AC Academy brand.
- **Research:**
  - Promote constant research output and publishing articles in peer review magazines.
  - Share research on various media.
  - Expand the research focus area – not only USA, but also other universities.
  - Facilitate funding for AC research.
  - Facilitate faculty engagement.
  - Advance the science of ACs nationally and internationally.
  - Be a clearing house for research and a research database, connecting researchers with data.
  - Provide bursaries for AC-related research.
- **Networking and Centre of Practice:**
  - Global network of practitioners.
  - Constantly increase engagement of stakeholders.
  - ACSG to participate at other conferences.
  - Redesign ACSG website – sexy, interactive, etc.
  - ACSG to be active on various social media platforms.
  - Webinars (e.g. every quarter).

- **Professional practice:**
  - ○ Enhance the reading and application of the Best Practice Guidelines.
  - ○ Enhance the adoption of the Ethical Code of AC practice – read and apply.
  - ○ Provide an effective CPD point system.
  - ○ Provide an AC accreditation system that is used.
- **International networking:**
  - ○ Attract more international delegates.
  - ○ ACSG members to speak at international AC conferences (e.g. SIOP; ICACM; UK-ACG; etc.).
  - ○ ACSG members to participate on international AC committees.
  - ○ Create key strategic network alliances.

- **As to strategic priorities for the future:**
  - ○ Increase number of ACSG conference attendees: reposition ACSG; back-to-basics value-add; strong marketing drive; AC research and practice focus.
  - ○ Additional services to ACSG members: e-CPD; AC Academy training programmes; AC accreditation; webinars throughout the year.
  - ○ Additional income streams to fund AC research (bursaries, etc.).
  - ○ Market the value and use of ACs within the business and academic world.
  - ○ Attract younger generation AC practitioners.

CHAPTER 3

MULTICULTURALISM AND THE USE OF ASSESSMENT CENTRES IN SOUTH AFRICA

Stella Nkomo and Christina Badalani

1. INTRODUCTION

The purpose of this chapter is to provide knowledge about how South Africa's multicultural and multilingual society impacts the use of Assessment Centres (ACs) for selection and promotion decisions in the workplace. It is not a topic that has been covered extensively in the literature on assessment centres. Most of the literature on culture and ACs focuses on cross-cultural issues emanating from organisations operating across national borders.[1] Instead, the focus of this chapter is on within-country cultural diversity and the challenge it presents for AC usage in South Africa. ACs have become an important tool for predicting the performance of prospective job candidates. For example, meta-analysis of the predictive validity of ACs across a number of research studies indicates that ACs can predict candidates' future job performance, training performance, and promotion in several occupations, sectors and countries.[2] However, it is important to be aware of how a multicultural context such as that of South Africa may affect the design and implementation of ACs.

2. STRUCTURE AND CONTENT OF CHAPTER

With the above in mind, this chapter is organised as follows:
- Cultural Diversity and Assessment Centres
- Legal Requirements for Assessment Centres in South Africa
- Ethnocultural Diversity in South Africa
- Historical and Political Context of South Africa
- Empirical Research on National Culture Differences
- Empirical Research on Cultural Differences in Personality
- Ethnocultural Diversity and the Essential Elements of Assessment Centres
- Conclusion
- Case Study

3. CULTURAL DIVERSITY AND ASSESSMENT CENTRES

The question of whether cultural diversity has an influence on ACs as a tool for human resource decisions became more important as they spread across the globe. The original usage was concentrated in the United States, followed by the United Kingdom, Germany and the Netherlands.[3] South Africa was

---

1   Lievens & Thornton, 2005

2   Hermelin et al., 2007; Meriac et al., 2008

3   Povah & Thornton, 2011

one of the early adopters in Africa[4] and is today described as the third largest user among the 82 countries making use of ACs.[5] The globalisation of ACs has led to greater sensitivity to the potential effects of cultural diversity on their usage in respect to questions of validity and reliability of selection decisions. Several international surveys and research studies suggest cultural diversity may influence the appropriateness as well as the reliability and validity of ACs.[6] These studies indicate that cultural diversity may influence the design of ACs, choice of dimensions, and the nature and format of the feedback process. For example, a global survey of international AC practices that sampled 443 HR professionals, occupational psychologists and AC practitioners across 43 countries and five continents found differences in the importance of behavioural dimensions assessed. The survey[7] found Africa placed lower emphasis on Persuasive Oral Communication compared to all other continents, while the Asian continent ascribed less importance to Planning and Organizing. According to the survey, the Americas were the only continents that gave Problem Analysis low importance. Researchers speculated that cultural differences may explain the findings but called for further research.

Another important comprehensive survey reported data that included South Africa.[8] The researcher found a number of differences in AC practices compared to Western Europe and North America. The study suggested that AC practices in South Africa are influenced by legal, economic, political and socio-cultural factors.[9] This suggests that it is necessary to understand the legal requirements of ACs within the socio-historical political context as well as the cultural diversity of the population. The next section provides an overview of the legal requirements for ACs, followed by a discussion of the history of cultural diversity in South Africa.

4. LEGAL REQUIREMENTS OF ASSESSMENT CENTRES

4.1 Legal and Other Requirements for the Validity of Assessment Centres

Like all methods used to assess job candidates, ACs are subject to laws and regulations promulgated at the national level. In addition, there may also be professional requirements established by non-governmental bodies like professional associations. For example, in the United States, Title 7 of the 1964 Civil Rights Act contains requirements for personnel decisions that involve the use of tests or other methods of selecting candidates for employment and promotion. However, legislative requirements also have to be considered in light of the outcomes of court cases. These outcomes are important because they provide a precedent for how the courts interpret and apply legal requirements.

4.2 South African Legal and Professional Requirements

Since 1994, there have been a number of legal efforts to overcome the oppression and subjugation of South Africa's majority population. The 1996 Constitution is the foundational document ensuring

---

4   Krause et al., 2011

5   Mulder & Taylor, 2015

6   Povah, 2011

7   Povah 2011

8   Krause, 2011

9   Krause, 2011

equal rights and equity to all citizens.[10] In addition, the revised Labour Relations Act of 1995 prohibits discrimination in the workplace. The specific law applicable to the use and administration of Assessment Centres is the Employment Equity Act of 1998.[11] One of the priorities of the new democratic government elected in 1994 was to put into place interventions and laws to redress the effects apartheid had on the employment status of the majority African, Coloured and Indian population. The Employment Equity Act was promulgated in 1998 to specifically address equity in the workplace.[12] The Act specifies that employment equity is achieved in two ways: (a) promoting equal opportunity and fair treatment in employment through the elimination of unfair discrimination; and (b) implementing affirmative action to redress the disadvantages in employment experienced by designated groups (Africans, Coloureds, Indians, persons with disabilities, and women), in order to ensure their equitable representation in all occupational categories and levels in the workplace.[13]

Thus, the Act has two intentions. One is to ensure equal opportunity and non-discrimination, while the other is to redress demographic disparities in the workplace emanating from the practice of Apartheid. This requirement is reflected in Section 42 of the Act which states, "In determining whether a designated employer is implementing employment equity in compliance with this Act, the Director-General or any person or body applying this Act must in addition to the factors stated in section 15 take into account all of the following: (a) The extent to which suitably qualified people from and amongst the different designated groups are equitably represented within each occupational category and level in that employer's workforce in relation to the (i) demographic profile of the national and regional economically active population; (ii) pool of suitably qualified people from designated groups from which the employer may reasonably be expected to promote or appoint employees; (iii) economic and financial factors relevant to the sector in which the employer operates; (iv) present and anticipated economic and financial circumstances of the employer; and (v) the number of present and planned vacancies that exist in the various categories and levels, and the employer's labour turnover".[14] These provisions are included to ensure that Africans, Coloureds, Indians, women and people with disabilities are equitably represented at all occupational levels.

The Employment Equity Act applies to all employers, workers and job applicants, but not members of the:
- National Defence Force;
- National Intelligence Agency; and
- South African Secret Service.

The provisions for affirmative action apply to:
- employers with 50 or more workers, or whose annual income is more than the amount specified in Schedule 4 of the Act;
- municipalities;
- organs of State;
- employers ordered to comply by a bargaining council agreement; and
- any employers who volunteer to comply.

---

10 The Constitution of the Republic of South Africa, Act No 108 of 1996

11 Employment Equity Act (No 55 of 1998)

12 Van de Vijver & Rothman, 2004

13 Employment Equity Act (No 55 of 1998): 12

14 Employment Equity Act (No 55 of 1998): 36

Chapter II makes provisions pertinent to the use of Assessment Centres although they are not referred to directly. According to the provisions, "every employer must take steps to promote equal opportunity in the workplace by eliminating unfair discrimination in any employment policy or practice".[15] It further states that, "psychological testing and other assessments of an employee are prohibited unless the test or assessment being used: (a) has been scientifically shown to be valid and reliable; (b) can be applied fairly to all employees; and (c) is not biased against any group".[16]

Amendments to the Employment Equity Act in 2013 led to confusion about how assessments should be shown to be valid, reliable, fair and non-biased.[17] The amendment of the Employment Equity Act of 1998, known as Act. No. 47 of 2013, updated the section on psychological testing by adding the requirement that assessments had to be "certified by the Health Professions Council of South Africa, as established by section 2 of the Health Professions Act (Health Profession Act, No. 56 of 1974, as amended by Act 29 of 2007), or any other body which may be authorised by law to certify those tests or assessments".[18] The inclusion of a certification requirement seems to imply that other forms of assessments, including ACs, were covered by the Act.[19] Consequently, the change raised concerns among AC users and industrial psychologists about the feasibility of bodies like the Health Professions Council of South Africa to regulate psychological assessments of all types.

A successful legal challenge to the amendment by the Association of Test Publishers of South Africa culminated in a court decision that "Section 8(d) of Act. No. 47 (2013) was null and void and of no force and effect".[20] In the decision, judges in the high court pointed to the lack of a feasible operational regulatory system to implement the requirements of Section 8(d).[21] Nevertheless, ACs, like all assessments, are subject to the universal principles of demonstrating validity, reliability, and non-bias towards any group or individual. The requirement that assessment tools be valid and reliable, applied fairly and unbiased can be a significant challenge given the cultural diversity of South Africa. A significant aspect of the challenge is identifying the exact nature and extent of cultural differences within the population of South Africa.

5. ETHNOCULTURAL DIVERSITY IN SOUTH AFRICA

The population of South Africa has been described as one of the most complicated and diversified in the world.[22] Capturing South Africa's diversity requires recognition of ethnicity, race and culture, that is, South Africa's population contains both ethnic and race groups. Defining ethnicity versus race has long been a difficult undertaking in social psychology. Some scholars use race and ethnicity interchangeably (in the sense that a group can be both racial and ethnic). For example, this idea has been captured in the term 'racioethnic', which is used in some organisation behaviour and human resource management

---

15 Employment Equity Act (No 55 of 1998): 14

16 Employment Equity Act (No 55 of 1998): 16

17 Muleya et al., (2017)

18 Employment Equity Amendment Act No 47 of 2013: 6

19 Muleya et al., 2017

20 Association of Test Publishers vs President of the Republic of South Africa (May, 2017): 15

21 Association of Test Publishers vs President of the Republic of South Africa (May, 2017): 8-9

22 Jackson et al., 2013

literature.[23] Others argue that there is no such thing as race because of biological evidence to the contrary, and prefer the concept be replaced with ethnicity. Ethnicity is viewed as a broader concept because it embraces cultural differentiation and the idea of shared understandings among members of an ethnic group.[24] The term ethnocultural diversity is used throughout this chapter, as it is the term used most in the published research on culture and personality research in South Africa. However, given the prominence of race in South Africa's history, reference to racial differences cannot be omitted in the discussion of its ethnocultural diversity.

South Africa's population reflects a diverse nation comprised of close to 57 million people representing a number of cultural groups.[25] The population is grouped into four broad categories: Africans (79.2%), Coloureds (8.9%), Whites (8.9%), and Indian or Asian (2.5%).[26] There is small percentage designated as other (.5%). In terms of religion, Christianity is the dominant religion, but Islam, Hinduism, traditional African religions and Judaism are also present.

However, the broad population groupings do not capture the diversity within each category. For example, the African population includes many different ethnic groups. Major ethnic groups include the Zulu, Xhosa, Basotho (South Sotho), Bapedi (North Sotho), Venda, Tswana, Tsonga, Swazi and Ndebele. The White group consists of English and Afrikaans speakers. The Indian/Asian grouping includes Indians who are the descendants of those who came from the Indian subcontinent during the mid-1800s either as indentured labour to work in the sugarcane fields in Kwa-Zulu Natal province or as passenger Indians who were allowed to set up businesses and professional services.[27] Asians consist primarily of descendants of slaves brought by the British from present-day Java, Bali, Timor, Malaysia, Madagascar and China.[28] The Coloured population consists of people of mixed descent. Their mixed ancestry includes the indigenous KhoiKhoi and San people, as well as European settlers and Africans.

Over the years, immigrants from Portugal and other regions of Europe have also settled in South Africa. Recent years have seen an influx of immigrants from Zimbabwe, Somalia and other conflict ridden countries in Africa.

6. HISTORICAL AND POLITICAL CONTEXT OF SOUTH AFRICA

The complexity of South Africa's ethnocultural diversity is further complicated by its history. Throughout South Africa's early history, there were different levels of conflict between indigenous peoples and colonisers and its two colonial powers, the British and Dutch. The latter conflict is particularly important because of its effects on the eventual rise of Apartheid as a system of government.[29] The British colonised the Cape in 1795 until 1802. There was a brief return to Dutch rule, but the British reclaimed the Cape in 1806. Representative governments were granted to the Cape Colony and to the Boer Republic of the Orange Free State in 1854. In 1860, gold and diamonds were discovered in the newly

---

23 Cox, 1993

24 Barth, 1969

25 Statistics South Africa, 2017: 2

26 Statistics South Africa, 2017: 2

27 Maharaj, 1995; Radhakrishnan, 2005

28 Booysen & van Wyk, 2007: 434-439

29 Frederikse, 1990

established Boer Republic. The discovery of mineral wealth led to a British invasion which led to war with the Dutch settlers (i.e. Boers) in 1899. A peace treaty was negotiated and signed in May of 1902, ending the war. In 1910, the Cape and Natal colonies united to form the Union of South Africa. Africans were excluded from this new Union and began to organise politically by establishing the South African Native National Congress in 1912, which became the predecessor of the African National Congress. A number of oppressive laws were enacted by the Union of South Africa including the Natives' Land Act of 1913. The Act appropriated 87% of land to the minority White population and confined the African majority to the remaining 13%.[30]

However, it was the election of the National Party in 1948 that ushered in the formidable political and economic power of Whites, particularly that of the Afrikaner population group. Thereafter, a battery of legislation was passed that entrenched segregation and the oppression of the country's non-White majority population. Apartheid was a system of interconnected social, political and economic structures that systematically oppressed Africans, Indians and Coloureds, while privileging Whites. One's status and access to political rights as well as economic resources were linked to a racial hierarchy that placed Whites at the top, followed by Asians, Coloured and Africans at the very bottom. During the almost 50 years of National Party rule, the best and highest paid jobs in the economy, including management and professional positions, were exclusively reserved for White men. Throughout its reign, the government faced resistance from the majority population as well as condemnation and sanctions from the international community. After years of struggle, democratic elections were held in 1994 which resulted in the election of the African National Congress under the leadership of Nelson Mandela.

The new government promised to build a non-racial and non-sexist society. South Africa's new Constitution established equality and human rights as core values of the new democratic nation. Clause 9 (p. 7) of Chapter 2 makes specific reference to non-discrimination on the basis of race, gender, sex, pregnancy, marital status, ethnic or social origin, colour, sexual orientation, age, disability, religion, conscience, beliefs, culture, language and birth. However, the Constitution does allow for discrimination if it is fair and aimed towards improving the status of disadvantaged individuals. Equality within the South African Constitution means substantive rather than formal equality (i.e. equality of outcome rather than equality of opportunity). This basic principle of equality recognises that attaining equality for previously disadvantaged population groups might require differential treatment and interventions. Subsequent employment legislation reflects this view of equality and has significant implications for the use of Assessment Centres in South Africa.

6.1 Ethnocultural Diversity Since 1994

The new government's aspiration for non-racialism, eloquently expressed in the preamble of the Constitution, "*We, the people of South Africa, recognise the injustices of the past; honour those who have worked for justice and freedom in our land; respect those who have worked to build and develop our country, and believe that South Africa belongs to all who live in it, united in our diversity...*"[31], led to a number of efforts to create a multicultural nation. Among these was the recognition of 11 official languages: Afrikaans, English, isiNdebele, isiXhosa, isiZulu, Sepedi, Sesotho, Setswana, siSwati, Tshivenda and Xitsonga. Additionally, the new national anthem is an amalgamation of three of the eleven official languages. In the early years of the new democratic nation, the term "rainbow nation" was quite popular;

---

30 Booysen & van Wyk, 2007: 434-439

31 The Constitution of the Republic of South Africa, Act No 108 of 1996

it represented the idea of a unified country with diverse population groups who co-exist in harmony. Yet scholars have cautioned that non-racialism is not simply about the idea of the country's racial and ethnic groups living together, but also encompasses establishing equality among racial groups to overcome the effects of Apartheid.[32] Balancing non-racialism with what is referred to as transformation (i.e. changing the demographics of economic and social privilege) continues to create conflict and tensions. The government's emphasis on rectifying the negative effects of Apartheid on previously disadvantaged groups continues to clash with the ideal of a rainbow nation united in its diversity.[33]

While it is accurate to describe South Africa as a multicultural nation, it is more difficult to declare it has achieved multiculturalism. Although there are many nuances to the meaning of multiculturalism, it is generally described as a value system which emphasises the acceptance of different cultural groups along with practices that give equal attention to such groups in a particular setting.[34] Twenty-four years after the end of apartheid, the lingering effects of South Africa's segregated past are reflected in employment figures, where historically disadvantaged groups continue to lag behind Whites in management and professional jobs.[35] This has led to continued concerns about the fairness of human resource practices, particularly in terms of the use of assessments, selection of job candidates and promotions across cultural groups.

Although South Africa is a multicultural nation, there is less clarity about specific cultural differences that exist among ethnocultural groups. The empirical research that provides knowledge about cultural differences in South Africa has either focused on national culture differences or cultural differences in personality. The topic of cultural differences in personality is perhaps the most relevant to whether assessment centres can be used in a culturally unbiased manner in employment decisions.

7. EMPIRICAL RESEARCH ON NATIONAL CULTURE DIFFERENCES IN SOUTH AFRICA

There have been a number of studies on the question of whether South Africa has a distinctive national culture and whether there are cultural and/or racial differences in national culture. In his classic research, Geert Hofstede defined culture as, "the collective programming of the mind which distinguishes the members of one group or category of people from another".[36] Hofstede emphasised that national culture is conditioned by the same education and life experiences or shared reality. To the extent that ethnocultural groups, in particular racial groups, have had different life experiences, largely due to different cultural traditions as well as the effects of Apartheid on life experiences, researchers have expected to find differences in national culture within South Africa.

However, empirical examinations based on Hofstede's model of national culture have found mixed results. For example, a few studies have examined racial and ethnic differences in national culture using Hofstede's four dimensions of national culture. A study of practicing managers[37] found no national

---

32 Nkomo, 2011

33 Habib & Bentley, 2008

34 Arasaratnam, 2013

35 Department of Labour, 2017

36 Hofstede, 1991: 5

37 Thomas & Bendixen, 2000

culture differences among the managers in their study. Despite the managers' identification with their ethnic groups, there was a common national culture at the managerial level. Likewise, a study of South African Defence Force officers found no significant differences in the individualism-collectivism factor between White, Coloured and Black officers.[38] In contrast, the Globe Research Study[39], which expanded Hofstede's dimensions, found among its Black African sample high power distance, high collectivism, high uncertainty avoidance, and high humane orientation, which was markedly different from Anglo countries in the study. Another study[40] using Hofstede's national culture model also reported higher scores for Africans on collectiveness, humane orientation, and gender egalitarianism compared to their White counterparts. A study of university students found African language speakers produced more interdependent and concrete descriptions of self-concept than did English speakers. The authors argued that the findings confirmed individualism-collectivism theory's predication that collectivist cultures (Black African) may have more concrete and interdependent self-concepts than do people from individualistic cultures (Whites).[41]

The finding of higher scores on collectivism among Black ethnocultural groups compared to Whites has led some researchers to focus on the concept of *Ubuntu* as a distinguishing value within the culture of African groups in South Africa.[42] There are debates[43] about the exact meaning of *Ubuntu*, but generally it has been defined as: "humaneness--a pervasive spirit of caring and community, harmony and hospitality, respect and responsiveness--that individuals and groups display for one another. *Ubuntu* is the foundation for the basic values that manifest themselves in the ways African people think and behave towards each other and everyone else they encounter."[44]

Proponents assert that as a value, *Ubuntu* affects the perceptions and ultimately the behaviour of African ethnocultural groups in South Africa. However, it is difficult to find empirical research that has examined the effects of *Ubuntu* on actual behaviour, which would be most relevant to the use of ACs. Further, most of the research is prescriptive in the sense of imploring leaders and managers to practice *Ubuntu* in leading and managing people in their organisations.[45] A recent comprehensive examination of the extent to which leaders in sub-Saharan Africa use *Ubuntu* values in leadership suggests it is more an aspirational cultural value than a reality. In a comprehensive study of leadership in sub-Saharan Africa, researchers found the managerial leadership behaviour preferences of Black and White South Africans to be very similar, with evidence of general acceptance of what they labelled "Western" attitudes toward business leadership.[46] Yet, it is possible that *Ubuntu* is more present among the general population than leaders and managers, many of whom have received a management education based on Western cultural values and knowledge.

Reaching a conclusion about whether *Ubuntu* is a distinct cultural value among Black South African ethnocultural groups is rather difficult based on the empirical evidence. However, South Africa is the only

---

38 Van Dyk & de Kock, 2004

39 House et al., 2004

40 Booysen, 2001

41 Eaton & Louw, 2000

42 Karsten & Illa, 2005; Khoza, 2006; van den Heuvel, 2008; Mbigi & Maree, 1995

43 Gade, 2012

44 Mangaliso, 2001: 24

45 Booysen, 2016

46 Littrell et al., 2013

country in the world where the legal authorities claim that *Ubuntu* is foundational to the constitutional order.[47] The concept appears in the post-amble of the South African Constitution, and according to the highest court in the land, it is a concept that permeates the Constitution generally.[48] Judges have also referred to *Ubuntu* in adjudicated cases. For example, the following statement appeared in a 2005 court judgement: "The spirit of *Ubuntu*, part of a deep cultural heritage of the majority of the population, suffuses the whole constitutional order."[49]

Further, a contrast is typically drawn between the cultures of Black and White South Africans in the cross-cultural psychological literature. The culture of Black South Africans is described as collectivist, while individualism is attributed to the culture of Whites South Africans (people of English and Dutch descent). Black South Africans are generally described as holding a relational view of the self, as expressed in the phrase: "*A person is a person through other persons.*" People in collectivist cultures are said to value group customs and traditions more than individualistic ones. On the other hand, the research suggests that within individualistic cultures, one's self-concept centres on the individual rather than being part of a group. A few cross-cultural studies have confirmed these beliefs. For instance, in a study of the personality profiles of 26 countries, the profiles of Africans were closer to more collectivist countries like Hong Kong and Taiwan.[50] In contrast, the scores of Whites placed them closer to individualistic countries like Austria and Switzerland. South African research reported that general personality descriptions offered by Black groups included dimensions like relationship harmony, whereas those of Whites more often referred to agentic concepts like extraversion.[51]

Research has also been conducted in South Africa that found deference to one's elders to be an important cultural value among Black ethnocultural groups.[52] The research discovered that young African graduate trainees found it disrespectful to question or show authority over an elder. The same study pointed out that in South African Black communities, a proper greeting of another individual is an important social norm, and is seen as very important to the principle of *Ubuntu* and relationship harmony.

While national cultural differences are relevant to ACs, it is also important to explore the research on cultural differences in personality, because it features prominently in the literature on assessments and selection.

8. EMPIRICAL RESEARCH ON CULTURAL DIFFERENCES IN PERSONALITY

In recent years, there has been an emergence of research that explores ethnocultural differences in personality in South Africa. This research has proceeded along two paths. One path focuses on developing a culture-free personality instrument that can be used across South Africa's multiple cultural

---

47 Gade, 2012: 487

48 Gade, 2012: 487

49 Port Elizabeth Municipality v Various Occupiers, 2004: 37

50 Eaton & Louw, 2000; Allik & McCrae, 2004

51 Valchev et al., 2013

52 Dunne & Bosch, 2015: 311

groups. In response to the observation that personality across cultures is predominantly assessed using models and instruments of Western origin with little attention to culture specific manifestations of universal concepts, a group of scholars initiated the development of the South African Personality Inventory (SAPI).[53] The concern was that dominant personality instruments developed with American or Western samples could result in bias if used in South Africa.

Prior to the SAPI research, the prevailing practice in personality research and selection assessment in South Africa was to use imported or adapted Western personality instruments.[54] The goal of the SAPI research was thus to limit the potential of bias by developing an indigenous personality model and an instrument for its assessment that could be used across ethnic groups in South Africa.[55] The development of SAPI was also motivated by the requirement in the Employment Equity Act of 1998 that instruments for psychological assessment be shown to be valid, reliable, fair and free of bias across groups. The research methodology was comprised of a qualitative stage of conceptual model development and a quantitative stage of instrument development.

The researchers were able to develop a model that represented the different ethnocultural groups within South Africa, resulting in a personality measure that is applicable to all major groups. The model comprises six factors: extraversion, conscientiousness, openness, a positive and a negative social relational factor, and neuroticism. Based on the model, the researchers went further to develop an inventory to measure personality that is applicable across groups.[56] For example, the researchers argued that although the notion of *Ubuntu* (referring to the inherently interpersonal aspects of humanity) has been typically attributed to one specific subgroup (the Nguni)[57], the inventory captures a shared meaning system across groups because of the broad social-relational domain covered.[58] The SAPI project has gone a long way in developing a tool to measure personality across South African cultural groups, which may overcome the problem of potential bias of non-culture specific measures.

A second research path examined whether personality can predict real, everyday behaviour[59], that is, what is the predictive validity of SAPI? It is this line of research that is perhaps most relevant to the theme of this chapter as it provides insights into the possible ways personality differences across cultural groups might shape actual behaviour. Since Assessment Centres are used to assess the behaviour of job applicants, differences in the predictive validity of SAPI are potentially important. Researchers pursuing this line of research work from the premise that human behaviour in collectivist cultures is interpreted primarily with reference to social roles and the situation within which actors are embedded. That is, context is important in how collectivist cultures interpret behaviour. Consequently, behaviours of members of collectivistic cultures should be more variable across situations and less predictable from personality than in individualistic cultures.[60] This argument is consistent with the

---

53 Valchev et al., 2013

54 Fetvadjiev et al., 2017: 142; van Eeden et al., 2013

55 Fetvadjiev et al., 2015: 2

56 Fetvadjiev et al., 2015

57 Nel et al., 2012

58 Fetvadjiev et al., 2015: 9

59 Fetvadjiev et al., 2018

60 Fetvadjiev et al. 2018: 2

work that distinguishes high context cultures from low context cultures.[61] In high context cultures, the spoken word carries only part of the meaning of a communication, and the environment and situation are essential to full interpretation. In contrast, in low context cultures, the spoken word carries the meaning, with less importance attached to the environment or situation.

In one of the few empirical studies conducted on the personality and behaviour of South Africans, few cultural differences were actually found. In a multiple phase study, the researchers examined the predictability and consistency in participants from collectivistic Black ethnocultural groups and the more individualistic White group in South Africa.[62] Previous research had suggested that in more collectivistic cultures like those in African countries, context may be a more powerful determinant of behaviour than internal predispositions (i.e. personality).[63] In addition to believing that context would be an important differentiator, the researchers also pointed to previous South African research that found when Africans were asked to describe people they knew well, they used fewer traits and more specific behaviours, preferences and perceptions, as well as more contextualised descriptions embedded in specific situations, compared to Whites.[64] However, the results of the multiphase study indicated that behaviour was predicted by personality on average equally well among Africans and Whites in their sample.[65] They concluded that personality can predict certain aspects of behaviour. The few cultural differences found in situational variability were not aligned with individualism and collectivism as hypothesised. This led the researchers to conclude overall that there are more similarities than differences in the power of personality to predict the behaviour of what is believed to be two culturally distinct groups in South Africa.[66] Given the nascent stage of this research, the researchers called for more detailed research into personality and behaviour prediction.

In total, the published research on cultural differences within South African ethnocultural groups does not provide a definitive answer to the extent and exact nature of cultural differences among groups. While the empirical evidence is mixed[67], there appears to be a general view that African ethnocultural groups have the cultural characteristic of collectivism, while the White group displays a more individualistic cultural orientation. The culture of South Africa's Coloured and Indian populations are also said to be collectivist, as they place great importance on the family with an extended conception of its composition.[68]

However, as noted by several cross-cultural psychologists, including those leading the SAPI project, while beliefs and perceptions of self and behaviour vary systematically across cultures, there may be less cultural variation in the predictability and consistency of displayed behaviour.[69] That is, cultural differences may be more present in socially constructed phenomena such as beliefs and perceptions,

---

61 Hall, 1989

62 Fetvadjiev et al., 2018: 1

63 Rossier, Dahourou & McCrae, 2005

64 Fetvadjiev et al., 2018: 4

65 Fetvadjiev et al., 2018

66 Fetvadjiev et al., 2018: 13

67 Adams et al., 2012

68 Adams et al., 2016

69 Fetvadjiev et al., 2018: 14

than in the actual links between personality and behaviour.[70] The important question is: What does this all mean for the use of Assessment Centres in South Africa? This suggests that while there may be individual deviations from group cultural orientations, the possibility of cultural differences in terms of collectivism vs. individualism, perceptions of personality, and the importance of the situational context should be considered in the design and implementation of ACs. The last section of this chapter focuses on this possibility and offers some recommendations for the use of ACs in South Africa's multicultural context.

9. ETHNOCULTURAL DIVERSITY AND THE ESSENTIAL ELEMENTS OF ASSESSMENT CENTRES

9.1 Definition of Assessment Centres

The following definition of ACs is used to consider the potential effects of South Africa's ethnocultural diversity on their design and implementation:

> *A simulation-based process employing multiple assessment techniques and multiple assessors to produce judgements regarding the extent to which a participant displays selected competencies required to perform a job effectively. ACs are usually employed either for selection or development purposes.*[71]

This definition reflects the view of ACs as an alternative to psychometric tests because it is an effective approach for the measurement of several different candidate attributes at the same time. For example, ACs can be designed to measure interpersonal skills and personality. The definition also indicates the role of judgement in ACs. Although a number of guidelines have been developed to increase objectivity in ACs over the years, research suggests it is important to be aware of the inherent subjectivity of judgemental processes.[72]

9.2 The Impact of Ethnocultural Diversity on ACs

Table 3.1 contains a list of the ten essential elements of ACs described in *Best Practice Guidelines for the Use of the Assessment Centre Method in South Africa* (5th ed.).[73] Table 3.1 also includes the possible effects of ethnocultural diversity for each of the ten essential elements of ACs and recommendations to address them.

However, there are some general concerns that have been identified in different studies. The first general concern is whether ACs have a negative effect (i.e. adverse impact) on different ethnocultural groups. There is some research data from the United States and other countries which suggest a need for attention to the potential negative effects of ACs on certain population groups. A study conducted in the US using meta-analysis data concluded that assessment centres may be associated with more negative outcomes for Africans than is portrayed in the literature, but they may be more "diversity

---

70 Fetvadjiev et al., 2018: 15

71 Schlebusch & Roodt, 2008

72 Kuncel & Highhouse, 2011

73 Meiring & Buckett, 2016

friendly" for Hispanics and females.[74] A study conducted in Israel reported negative effects on Arab candidates.[75] In South Africa, a few studies of this nature were conducted in the 1980s when assessment centres were introduced in the country. A study published in 1994 based on a sample of 317 White and disadvantaged Black and Coloured males found the assessment centre predicted job performance of both the advantaged group (Whites) and the disadvantaged group (Africans and Coloureds).[76] A 2017 South African study of the extent of general performance factors in assessment centre exercises and dimensions found dimensions that are more cognitively loaded, such as problem solving, strategic thinking and business acumen, seem to produce the largest ethnic group differences.[77]

In the employment selection literature, negative effects of selection tools can occur through disparate treatment and adverse impact. Disparate treatment occurs when different standards are applied to different groups[78], while adverse impact occurs when different groups (e.g. within ethnic/cultural, gender, age groups) score on average differently on assessments or experience differential hiring rates.[79] It is important to note that disparate treatment and adverse impact have most often been associated with psychometric tests (e.g. measures of cognitive ability). In fact, research indicates that interviews and assessment centres generally demonstrate lower racial and ethnic subgroup differences.[80] Researchers caution that race and ethnic subgroup differences in assessment centres vary as a function of the amount of cognitive content (i.e. degree of cognitive loading) in a given exercise.[81] Further, it is important to point out that subgroup differences in scores do not automatically indicate bias or unfair discrimination[82], i.e. there could be true differences on a particular attribute of subgroups that explains score differences. A recent multilevel empirical study of adverse impact conducted in the USA found weak evidence of leniency toward White assessees and similar-to-me bias among non-White assessee-assessor pairs.[83] However, these effects did not have a 'trickle up' effect to result in adverse impacts for women and Africans.[84] Rather than guessing the reason for subgroup differences, organisations in South Africa should conduct predictive validation studies because an adverse impact of ACs on historically disadvantaged groups could be challenged legally under the Employment Equity Act of 1998.

Second, research suggests it is important to be aware of the potential impact of bias in the use of ACs. Research literature has generally shown a decrease in what is referred to as overt discrimination or explicit bias[85], however a number of psychological studies have demonstrated the continuing effect of what is known as implicit bias and modern racism. Implicit bias, unlike overt bias, is unconscious. Implicit bias suggests that actors do not always have conscious, intentional control over the processes of social

---

74 Dean et al., 2008

75 Falk & Fox, 2014

76 Hurst & Charoux, 1994: 21

77 Buckett et al., 2017

78 Gatewood & Field, 2001

79 Hough et al., 2001: 152

80 Ployhart & Holtz, 2008

81 Goldstein et al., 2001

82 Thornton et al., 2014: 271

83 Thornton et al., 2019: 13

84 Thornton et al., 2019: 14

85 Brief et al., 2000

perception, impression formation and judgment that motivate their behaviours.[86] According to modern racism theory, the nature of prejudice and bias has changed from old-fashioned and blatant forms to today's modern and subtle forms.[87] That is, prejudiced individuals do not define their own beliefs and attitudes as racist, but instead act in ways to protect a non-prejudiced self-image by evoking a non-prejudiced reason for what could be perceived as prejudice or biased actions.[88]

Research conducted in South Africa has also examined implicit bias. A study of the discourse of employees in a training workshop found that while South Africans had changed their language on race, their assumptions about racial asymmetry persisted in more subtle and implicit forms.[89] A 2011 study of historical trends in racial attitudes paints a complicated picture for South Africa[90] that echoes elements of modern racism theory. The researchers concluded that although South African society remains a society obsessed by race, the social situation has changed dramatically from the days when there was social pressure toward expressing prejudice among Whites. They found that current norms work in the opposite direction as Whites struggle against the stigma of being viewed as prejudiced.[91] However, the study also found that these pressures do not seem to apply to the Black respondents in their sample, where accusations of White racism are common and can potentially serve as grounds for pre-judgement against Whites.[92] However, a 2016 field survey reported improving racial attitudes in South African society. The survey found that more than half (54%) of citizens feel race relations have improved since 1994.[93]

A third concern suggested from research is the potential effect of ethnocentrism on ACs. Ethnocentrism is defined as a basic attitude expressing the belief that one's own ethnic group or one's own culture is superior to other ethnic groups or cultures, and that one's cultural standards can be applied in a universal manner.[94] Accordingly, the attitudes and behaviours of an ethnocentric person are biased in favour of the in-group (their own culture) at the expense of the out-group (another culture). Ethnocentrism is generally depicted as a negative attitude in the psychological literature.[95] A counter perspective argues that it can be viewed as positive in the sense that favouritism to one's own group is important to solidarity, survival, loyalty and group effectiveness.[96] Research studies have demonstrated that ethnocentrism can emerge in interpersonal, group, and organisational environments where persons of different cultural backgrounds interact.[97] For example, ethnocentric attitudes were shown to be negatively correlated with perceptions of physical, social and task attitudes, as well as competence.[98] Ethnocentrism can result in the negative stereotyping of a group, which can impact one's judgment of behaviour.

---

86 Greenwald & Krieger, 2006: 946

87 Brief et al., 2000: 74

88 McConahay, 1986: 93

89 Franchi, 2003: 157

90 Durrheim et al., 2011

91 Durrheim et al., 2011: 276

92 Durrheim et al., 2011: 276

93 News24, 2016-02-29 (online)

94 Hooghe, 2008: 11

95 Hewstone & Ward, 1985

96 Sharma et al., 1994

97 Neuliep et al., 2005

98 Neulipe et al., 2005: 42

In sum, the validity and reliability of ACs in a culturally diverse context may be affected by adverse treatment, adverse impact, implicit bias or ethnocentrism. The most important point is awareness and understanding that threats to validity and reliability can be minimised by paying careful attention to how they may manifest in terms of the ten essential elements of ACs and by taking appropriate actions in their design and implementation.[99] Most recently, scholars have called for research to understand how cultural differences affect participant behaviours, observers' perceptions of the performance of culturally diverse participants, and resulting ratings.[100]

Table 3.1: Ethnocultural diversity and ten essential elements of assessment centres

Essential Element	Possible Ethnocultural Diversity Effects	Recommendations
Job-related behavioural competencies	Universal behavioural competencies may not be transferable across cultures. Implicit bias in assessing the performance of historically disadvantaged ethnocultural groups on competencies.	Ensure validity of behavioural competencies across cultures. Use emic approach to establish behavioural competencies as well as unique cultural and contextual factors. Demonstrate sensitivity to the impact of cultural background on candidate performance.
Relationships between behavioural competencies and AC techniques	Bias in assessing the performance of historically disadvantaged ethnocultural groups on competencies.	Ensure AC techniques are culturally sensitive. Consider possible language barriers when selecting AC techniques.
Multiple assessment techniques	Lack of cultural sensitivity to assessment tools used. Use of assessment tools with greater risk of bias or adverse impact on particular ethnocultural groups (i.e. psychometric tests, interviews).	Ensure validity and reliability of assessment tools through pre-tests. Use a diverse set of tasks in order to limit the specific biases associated with each exercise. Check for adverse impact of different ethnocultural groups.
Simulation exercises	Lack of awareness of the impact of social context on how candidates may interpret the simulation situation. What is deemed appropriate behaviour may differ based on cultural norms. The content of the exercises may include stereotypes of ethnocultural groups or place such groups in stereotypical roles in exercises.	Make sure contextualisation of exercise is not confined to work context only. Consider social and cultural contexts of candidates. Pilot test and audit exercises. Make sure characters in simulation exercise match the participant population.

---

99 Thornton et al., 2019: 15

100 Kleinmann & Ingold, 2019

Essential Element	Possible Ethnocultural Diversity Effects	Recommendations
Observers	Use of homogenous group of observers (i.e. from a single ethnocultural group) may foster misinterpretations, implicit bias and similarity bias towards other groups.	Use a diverse group of observers.
Observer training	Observers not trained about potential ethnocultural effects in ACs.	Include the topic of ethnocultural diversity and ACs in observer training (e.g. awareness of stereotypes and their influence on judgements and scoring).
Observing and recording behaviour	Implicit bias in observations and interpretation of behaviours. Ethnocentrism clouds observations.	Conduct appropriate observer training as noted above. Use audio and/or video recordings for post-hoc review if necessary. Use multiple observers and check interrater reliability for different ethnocultural groups.
Classifying and evaluating behaviours	Implicit bias in interpretation and evaluation of behaviours in within exercise scoring or across exercise scoring of participants could result in adverse impact and treatment. Disparate treatment of a particular ethnocultural group (i.e. applying standards differently with a negative outcome for a group). Ethnocentrism clouds evaluation.	Conduct appropriate observer training as noted above. Use audio and/or video recordings for post-hoc reviews if necessary. Use multiple observers and check interrater reliability for different ethnocultural groups.
Data integration	Implicit bias in integrating data across behavioural simulations. Assigning different weights to particular simulations for different ethnocultural groups.	Consistency in rating each participant's performance across all simulation exercises. Check interrater reliability. Perform criterion-related post-hoc validation studies for different ethnocultural groups.
Standardisation	Favouritism (or bias) towards certain groups in the AC administration (e.g. instructions, time limits, facilities and scoring procedures).	Display procedural fairness in AC administration for all participants.

Source: Meiring & Buckett[101]

9.3 Ten Essential Elements of ACs and Recommendations to Minimise Ethnocultural Diversity Effects[102]

9.3.1 Job-Related Behavioural Competencies

There are two potential effects of ethnocultural diversity in the identification of job-related behavioural competencies. First, developers and users must recognise that universal behavioural competencies may

---

101 Meiring & Buckett, 2016

102 Meiring & Buckett, 2016

not be transferable across ethnocultural groups.[103] For example, a competency like 'aggressiveness', which on the surface appears to be neutral, may lead to negative evaluations of candidates who are members of cultures where aggressiveness is not valued.[104] Second, implicit bias can occur in the assessment of the performance of historically disadvantaged ethnocultural groups in respect to behavioural competencies. It is thus important to ensure the validity of behavioural competencies across cultures. Researchers advocate an emic approach to establish behavioural competencies as well as recognition of unique cultural and contextual factors in their selection. Finally, developers and observers should demonstrate sensitivity to the potential impact of culture and race on candidate performance. This is very important given research that has examined whether race is perceived to be part of the business leader prototype and if it influences the evaluations of White and non-White leaders.[105] Relying upon leadership categorisation theory, researchers in a study conducted in the United States argued that over time, individuals develop a set of beliefs about the behavioural characteristics and competencies of leaders — a leader prototype. To the extent that a particular group has dominated leadership positions, members of that group can be perceived to better fit the leader prototype compared to others. The results of the study found that being White is an attribute of the business leader prototype.[106] South Africa's history of excluding non-Whites from leadership positions makes awareness of the leader prototype phenomenon very important when developing job-related behavioural competencies.

9.3.2 Relationship Between Behavioural Competencies and AC Techniques

The major threat here is implicit bias in rating the performance of historically disadvantaged ethnocultural groups on competencies and adverse impact of AC techniques. Two solutions should mitigate these effects. Again, developers should ensure AC techniques are culturally sensitive. It is also important to consider language barriers when selecting AC techniques. Finally, developers should monitor for adverse impact of AC techniques on the different ethnocultural groups.

9.3.3 Multiple Assessment Techniques

While the use of multiple assessment techniques generally increases the validity and reliability of ACs, in an ethnoculturally diverse context there are potential threats; a lack of awareness of how culture may interact with different assessment tools may increase the risk of adverse impact from an assessment tool. For example, role plays and interviews may be less valid for one group compared to another because they require the demonstration of strong verbal skills that may be impacted by language. The best strategy to limit potential problems is to ensure the validity and reliability of assessment techniques through pre-tests to check for adverse impact on different ethnocultural groups.

9.3.4 Simulation Exercises

The major danger with the use of simulation exercises is a lack of awareness of social context on how candidates from different ethnocultural groups may interpret the simulation situation. Developers should make sure that the contextualisation of exercises is not confined to the work context only,

---

103 Woodruffe, 2011

104 Woodruffe, 2011

105 Rosette et al., 2008: 758

106 Rosette et al., 2008: 762

but should also include the social context, especially relationships among actors in the simulation.[107] As noted earlier in this chapter, research in South Africa found that when Africans were asked to describe people they knew well, they used fewer traits and more specific behaviours, preferences and perceptions, as well as more contextualised descriptions embedded in specific situations, than Whites.[108] Another study of Africans, Whites, Indians and Coloureds found that the African group's self-descriptions contained more explicit relational orientation (i.e. more interdependence with others) and more preference description responses than the self-descriptions of the other groups.[109]

9.3.5 Observers

The use of a homogenous group of observers (i.e. from a single ethnocultural group) may foster misinterpretation or even implicit bias towards non-familiar ethnocultural groups. The best recommendation to avoid this threat is to use a heterogeneous (diverse) group of observers.

9.3.6 Observer Training

A risk here is to exclude content on ethnocultural diversity and its effects on ACs in the training of observers. Standard observer training should include the topic of ethnocultural diversity and potential impact on ACs.

9.3.7 Observing and Recording Behaviour

In observing and recording behaviour, there is the danger of implicit bias in observations and interpretation of behaviours of participants. Appropriate observer training as described above is important. Additionally, audio and video recordings of AC exercises can be used for post-hoc review to assess the validity of observations and recording of behaviours by observers. Finally, the use of multiple observers allows for interrater reliability checks.

9.3.8 Classifying and Recording Behaviour

Ethnocultural diversity can have similar effects as indicated for the observation and recording of behaviour. Implicit bias in the interpretation and evaluation could result in adverse impact. Again, the strategies to mitigate problems include observer training, audio and video recording, and the use of multiple observers.

9.3.9 Data Integration

The general guidelines provided for data integration stress that observers must rate each participant's performance across the various exercises independently against the selected competencies before the data integration. Following this guideline should go a long way to minimise bias in data integration and adverse impact. Additionally, an effort should be made to check interrater reliability. Over time, organisations may want to perform criterion-related, post-hoc validation studies for different ethnocultural groups (i.e. how well performance in the ACs predicted actual job performance).

---

107 Brouwers & Van de Vijver, 2015

108 Fetvadjiev et al., 2018: 4

109 Adams et al., 2012: 385

9.3.10 Standardisation

Standardisation requires that procedures used to administer the AC should ensure all participants have the same opportunity to demonstrate the identified behavioural competencies. A major threat here is favouritism (or bias) towards certain groups in the procedures used (i.e. instructions, time limits, facilities, and scoring procedures). It is important to ensure procedural fairness in AC administration for all participants.

In summary, Table 3.1 highlights the potential effects of ethnocultural diversity on the design and administration of ACs. It also indicates that corrective actions may be needed by developers and users of ACs beyond adherence to the *Best Practice Guidelines* issued in 2016 to minimise negative effects on participants because of South Africa's ethnocultural diversity.

10. CONCLUSION

The purpose of this chapter was to provide an overview of the impact of South Africa's ethnocultural diversity on the use of ACs in employment. Research bearing directly on the topic is sparse, however there is some research that provides information on cultural differences among South Africa's ethnocultural groups. As noted in the chapter, much has been written about the individualism-collectivism cultural distinction between African and White ethnocultural groups. Despite mixed results from research studies, collectivist values are most often attributed to African groups, while individualism is believed to be more prevalent in White groups. At the same time, because race remains a prominent feature in South African society, it tends to overshadow attention to cultural differences.[110] The chapter also discussed the substantial body of research on culture and personality. This literature provides insight into personality differences and their relationship to behaviour.

The lack of conclusive evidence of cultural differences among South Africa's main ethnocultural groups poses a major challenge to offering conclusions about their effect on ACs. However, the legal requirement for assessments in the Employment Equity Act of 1998 makes it imperative that organisations using ACs are sensitive to the possible ways in which ethnocultural diversity may affect the validity and reliability of ACs. The socio-political context of South Africa, characterised by continuing tensions between ethnocultural groups attributed to the lingering effects of Apartheid, underscores the need for vigilance in the design and administration of ACs. What is clear from South African and international research is that ACs are less susceptible to bias compared to traditional paper-and-pencil cognitive tests because they are based on real job behavioural competencies.

The chapter also provides a summary of the potential influence of ethnocultural diversity and makes recommendations of how to mitigate negative effects. Alignment of AC design with the *Best Practice Guidelines* with the recommendations in Table 3.1 should hopefully minimise the exposure of ACs to claims of unfairness and bias. Organisations that make regular use of ACs are strongly advised to invest in predictive validation studies to rule out adverse impacts on ethnocultural subgroups. In the end, there is also the fundamental business case for ensuring cultural sensitivity and fairness in the use of ACs. Selecting the right candidate and achieving diversity in the South African workplace is key to effective talent management in today's competitive environment.

---

110 Donald, Thatcher & Milner, 2014.

11. CASE STUDY

Case Study: Gemma Manufacturing. Are you considering SA's multiculturism?

Background

Gemma Manufacturing is a mid-size company located in Gauteng that uses an Assessment Centre (AC) to select candidates for the first-level management position of Production Shift Supervisor. Production Shift Supervisors are responsible for daily production planning on all machines and management of employees in terms of quality, efficiency and workload. The AC measures five behavioural competency dimensions:
- Problem solving.
- Team leadership.
- Driving results through others.
- Motivating others.
- Organising and planning.

The competencies were developed through a job analysis exercise. The duration of the AC is 1.5 hours and the same group of observers are used throughout. Prior to the AC, candidates complete the Supervisory Skills Test (SST), which is a 48-item objective test that measures a candidate's understanding of management and supervisory principles, practices and behaviours. The test carries a weight of 40% while the AC accounts for the remaining 60%.

Along with other exercises, the Assessment Centre includes two simulation exercises described below.

Instructions

Read each of the following AC exercise descriptions and identify any issues that may arise for participants in respect to the ethnocultural diversity of South Africa.

1. Role Play Exercise Participant Instructions

You are a newly appointed shift supervisor in a mid-sized manufacturing firm. Five employees report to you currently. The employees have an average of 15 years' experience. Two of your employees are over 55 years of age. You have risen rapidly to your current position of Production Supervisor despite your young age because of your outstanding performance and the completion of your B.com degree in business management.

Today you have to conduct a performance review with Themba Masekela who is 58 years old. His performance has been poor during the last year and you have rated his performance as unsatisfactory. You will have ten minutes to think through how you will conduct the face-to-face performance review. Thereafter, you will engage in a 25 minute role play of the performance review. You will be observed by an assessor as you conduct the interview.

2. Leaderless Group Discussion Participant Instructions

You, along with four others, have crash landed in a remote part of Northwest Namibia. The group will be provided with a list of items salvaged from the wreckage of the small plane carrying the group to a company retreat. As a group, you have decided to walk to the nearest town before night fall and can only carry a few items with you.

The task is twofold. First, each member of the group must individually rank the most important items to take. Second, the group must discuss and determine a group ranking of the items to take from the most essential to essential.

Observers will be viewing your group as you make your rankings, especially how each group member behaves. Each observer has been assigned to observe the behaviour of a specific group member. Experts in desert survival have provided a best solution for the ranking of the items. You will be rated on your individual contribution and not how well the group performs on the ranking of the items.

Discussion about the issues that may arise for participants in respect to the ethnocultural diversity of South Africa

The scenario and exercise raise a number of potential issues from an ethnocultural perspective. First, the weight provided for the assessment should be reconsidered as there is room for unintended bias because of the nature of the two exercises. Because the exercises will be subjectively scored, poor performance could affect the selection outcome. The race of the observers is not provided but it would be important that they are diverse (heterogenous).

Role-play exercise

In the role play exercise, the age difference between the supervisor and the employee may pose a problem, particularly for African applicants as there is great deference for older people in many of the cultural groups within South Africa.

The way African participants may approach the exercise may differ from other groups. Research has shown that Coloured and African applicants may be more sensitive to the social context of the situation described. For example, the conditions under which the poor performance occurred would be an important factor in how participants perform the role play.

The exercise may have to be altered to remove the age difference between the supervisor and the employee, as well as provide more contextual information about the poor performance. Additionally, there should be sensitivity among the observers in how they score the participant as the communication styles of some cultures would be less direct in providing negative feedback.

Leaderless group discussion

The leaderless group discussion also raises some sensitive ethnocultural issues. African cultures have been shown to be collective, however the exercise asks individuals to rank the items individually and indicates that they will be scored as individuals. African participants may show a preference for a group approach in terms of making decisions about how to survive.

Other cultures may also have different communication styles based on how they have been socialised to communicate with others. For example, some cultures may have taught children that you never interrupt another individual or to only speak when asked to engage in the conversation.

As you reflect upon the two exercises, think about how your culture may influence your behaviour if you were a candidate participating in the assessment.

CHAPTER 4

ETHICS AND ASSESSMENT CENTRES

Rodney L. Lowman

1. INTRODUCTION

1.1 Ethical Issues in South African Assessment Centres

Case 1: An assessment centre (hereafter referred to as AC/ACs) is contracted for a mining company in a rural area of South Africa. The HR manager of the company had attended a seminar in which ACs were described as an assessment approach that is usually well received by those who participate in them. The manager had discussed the plan with the company's CEO who had approved it prior to commencing the project. The initial AC was staffed by a consulting group located in Europe that specialises in ACs and other selection approaches. The plan was to assess all the senior managers to provide a base line for the strengths and weaknesses of the management team as a whole, to be followed by assessments of each succeeding level of management, down to the first line supervisors. A major contract had been signed for the work. The company brought in a well-trained and experienced team that had never worked in Africa. No local staff were contracted for the initial assessment. When the senior management team was introduced to the assessment idea, they quickly raised a number of objections to the project and waged an active campaign not to pursue it. Due to the strength of the objections the project was cancelled and the contract bought out.

Case 2: The bargaining unit (union) for a group of employees agreed to management's wish to conduct an AC to evaluate and choose employees within the company to staff a new facility that would consist of semi-autonomous work teams. They agreed to it only after the company threatened to hire outside employees, which, since it was a new facility, management could do under the provisions of the union contract. All employees meeting the minimal requirements that had been stipulated were allowed to participate in the AC. A combination of exercises and standardised assessments were used. One employee who had had performed very well in the assessments was opposed by a number of other people going through the AC. They found him to be so difficult to get along with that they threatened to drop out of the process if he was chosen. Ultimately, the assessment team recommended he not be selected despite his strong performance in the AC. The individual was not selected and filed a grievance and a complaint of discrimination with a government agency.

Case 3: When AC group exercises were begun in a not-for-profit organisation, all the participants signed an agreement that they would keep the content of the simulations confidential. Certain participants nevertheless posted the exact content of some the AC components anonymously on the internet. This meant that those who had not yet gone through the process had a comparative advantage over those who had not received the advance information. The AC leaders proceeded as planned with the same exercises and instrumentation on the grounds that it would have adversely affected the validity of the process if different methods were used mid-stream. Those who went through the process after the internet postings were selected at a higher rate than those who had gone through the process earlier.

These cases, which will be discussed in more detail later in the chapter, illustrate some of the ethical issues that can arise when implementing ACs. In this chapter I also discuss issues associated with the ethical conduct of ACs in South Africa, note the current absence of an enforceable AC ethics code specific to South Africa (but comment on the one that was created by the Assessment Centre Study Group), discuss the major ethical standards that apply to this kind of work, and illustrate with case material sample ethical dilemmas.

In the interests of disclosure and contextualising this chapter, I should begin by noting that although I have spent time in South Africa, have addressed the South African Assessment Centre Study Group's (ACSG) conference[1] on ethical issues and have been part of the study group developing the Code of Ethics for ACs in South Africa, I am not a resident of South Africa and am by no means an expert on all issues related to AC practices there. My focus will thus be primarily on identifying ethical issues that may be relevant in the South African context and, as appropriate, to suggest what may be needed to professionalise the field.

1.2 ACs in South Africa

ACs have had a long and expansive history in South Africa.[2] For example, the ACSG, a professional association specifically for AC professionals, was founded in 1981 and held its 39th conference in 2019. Yet, although there has been an international set of AC guidelines for a number of years, i.e. the *Guidelines and Ethical Considerations for AC Operations*[3], only in 2018 did a code of ethics specific to the professional practice of ACs receive the approval of the ACSG. This is not unique to South Africa by any means, but it does raise issues not only about ethical behaviour, but also about whether ethical codes are solely aspirational if they cannot be enforced.

1.3 Description of ACs

The *Guidelines and Ethical Considerations* succinctly define ACs as consisting of: "...a standardized evaluation of behavior based on multiple inputs."[4] They go on to describe the components of an AC as follows:

"Any single AC consists of multiple components, which include behavioural simulation exercises, within which multiple trained assessors observe and record behaviours, classify them according to the behavioural constructs of interest, and (either individually or collectively) rate (either individual or pooled) behaviours... Using either a consensus meeting among assessors or statistical aggregation,

---

1   Lowman, 2016

2   Krause et al., 2011

3   International Taskforce on Assessment Center Guidelines, 2015

4   International Taskforce on Assessment Center Guidelines, 2015: 1248

assessment scores are derived that represent an assessee's standing on the behavioral constructs and/ or an aggregated overall assessment rating (OAR)."[5]

Because ACs often include simulations that are representative of actual job performance, they are typically received favourably. Although they do not necessarily have predictive validity coefficients higher than other predictors (such as general intelligence[6]), participant acceptance of assessment methods is a factor that needs to be considered in selection applications.

1.4 Which Ethics Codes Apply to AC Work?

A number of standards have been promulgated that are widely accepted internationally for the technical aspects of assessments, which have implications for ACs. Of particular importance are the American *Standards for Educational and Psychological Testing*[7], which was jointly promulgated by the American Educational Research Association (AER), the American Psychological Association (APA) and the National Council on Measurement in Education (NCME). Additionally, the ethics standards of the American Psychological Association[8], the basis for many codes of ethics for psychologists around the world, including in South Africa, contain a number of ethical standards related to assessment. Few such ethics standards offer specific guidance related to ACs, however. There are also a number of publications directed to ethical issues in organisational psychology and personnel selection.[9]

The *Guidelines and Ethical Considerations*[10] focus primarily on best practices in ACs, but they also identify a few ethical/legal "considerations", which are essentially recommendations without any apparent enforcement body or mechanism.[i]

These include:

1. ***Informed Participation*** – The organisation is obligated to make an announcement prior to the assessment so that assessees will be fully informed about the programme. This information should be made available in writing prior to assessment events.[11]
2. ***Assessee Rights*** – Noting that AC activities generate considerable data about an individual, this ethical consideration specifies the rights of the assessee to receive feedback on AC performance and any recommendations made (including for members of an organisation employing the AC) to read formal summaries, written reports and recommendations; to access the AC rationale and

---

[i] The *Guidelines* do identify as one of their purposes as being to provide "information for relevant legal bodies on what are considered standard professional practices in this area".

---

5 International Taskforce on Assessment Center Guidelines, 2015: 1248

6 Viswesvaran & Ones, 2018

7 American Educational Research Association, American Psychological Association & National Council on Measurement in Education, 2014

8 American Psychological Association (APA), 2017

9 Newman et al., 2002; Lefkowitz, 2017; Lefkowitz & Lowman, 2017; Lowman, 2018a

10 International Taskforce on Assessment Center Guidelines, 2015

11 International Taskforce on Assessment Center Guidelines, 2015: 1263

validity; to consent to further uses of the assessment data beyond the original purposes; to consent to recordings; and to be provided information about the records and data being collected and how those will be "maintained, used, and disseminated".[12]

3. **Copyrights and Intellectual Property** – Respect for copyrights and the intellectual property of others must be maintained under all circumstances.[13]

4. **Data Protection** – The AC programme must also comply with any relevant data protection laws governing the regions in which assessment is being carried out (e.g., the UK Data Protection Act; the U.S. Freedom of Information Act; the European Union Directive on Data Protection; South Africa's Protection of Personal Information Bill; The U.S. Safe Harbor Privacy Principles; and the General Data Protection Regulations (GDPR)).[14]

5. **Compliance with Relevant Employment Laws and Regulations** – AC design, validation, implementation and documentation must be carried out in compliance with laws and statutes existing both in an organisation's/agency's home locale, state, province or nation, as well as in the locale, state, province, or nation where the AC programme is delivered. This includes preventing unfair discrimination against protected groups (such as native/aboriginal people, racial groups, religious groups, and those protected on the basis of age, gender, disability, sexual orientation, etc.).[15]

Although not framed as ethical considerations, the *Guidelines* also include a section (XII) called "Conducting ACs Across Cultural Contexts" that addresses important multicultural issues.[16]

2. THE SOUTH AFRICAN BEST ASSESSMENT CENTRES PRACTICES DOCUMENT

South Africa's *Best Practice Guidelines for the Use of the Assessment Centre Method in South Africa*[17] also addresses ethical issues. It identified the following as ethical concerns (although some of these may represent suggestions for specific best practices rather than moral concerns):

1. **Informed consent** – Participants have the right to agree to the proposed ACs with advance knowledge of the specific ground rules (including about data collection, storage and use) and should be able to disclose conditions that might affect their performance.

2. **Participant rights** – Rights are noted to include receiving feedback, being informed on procedures and uses, consenting to new uses of obtained data, and other information that is suggested as desirable to provide.

3. **Reassessment** – Specifies concerns about time between repeat assessments.

4. **Dealing with disabilities** – Assuring reasonable accommodations for people with disabilities, assessing a disability's relationship to job performance on an individual basis, and complying with the relevant laws.

---

12 International Taskforce on Assessment Center Guidelines, 2015: 1263-1264

13 International Taskforce on Assessment Center Guidelines, 2015: 1264

14 International Taskforce on Assessment Center Guidelines, 2015: 1264

15 International Taskforce on Assessment Center Guidelines, 2015: 1264

16 International Taskforce on Assessment Center Guidelines, 2015: 1264-1266

17 Meiring & Buckett, 2016

5. **Copyright** – Avoiding violations or misuse of copyright-protected information.
6. **Assessment integrity** – Preserving the confidentiality of assessment materials.
7. **Portraying an AC as delivering results that it was not designed to deliver** – Not representing the AC as delivering results that are not supported by credible evidence.
8. **Using AC results for things other than its intended purpose** – ACs need to be designed for a specific purpose. Their results cannot subsequently be used for different assessment purposes.
9. **Using one AC across different contexts** – Using the same AC when it is not matched to the specific levels and duties of the job.
10. **Repeated exposure** – Assessees should not participate in the identical AC if it occurs within a 12-month period. Those who have been assessors should not complete the same AC that they were assessors in.
11. **Assessors who know participants** – Ensuring that objectivity applies and avoiding conflicts of interests or roles.
12. **Compromising professional conduct** – AC practitioners must not behave unprofessionally when faced with organisational demands to do so.
13. **Social responsibility** – Developmental ACs can help people improve but should not be confused with ones done for high stakes assessments.[18]

3. THE SOUTH AFRICAN AC ETHICS INITIATIVE

South Africa appears to be one of the only countries in which an ethics code has been developed to guide professional practice related to ACs. This initiative was sponsored by the ACSG.

The ACSG's ethics code is organised around six ethical principles. These, in turn, encompass a statement of relevant values and of specific ethical standards. The principles, standards, and substandards are discussed below:

3.1 Principle 1: Respect for Participant Dignity[19]

Standards: In adhering to the principle of respect for the dignity of participants in the AC, AC practitioners will treat participants with:

3.1.1 Integrity:
- By ensuring that the same assessment conditions and norms apply to all AC participants and are impartial.
- By using the AC results solely for the purpose agreed with the AC participants.

3.1.2 Honesty:
- By honestly and fully communicating the purpose of the AC and the use of the AC results to the AC participants as was agreed with the AC client.

---

18 Meiring & Buckett, 2016: 11-12

19 SA Assessment Centre Study Group, 2018

3.1.3 Respectfulness:
- By treating all AC participants with respect and dignity throughout the AC process.

3.1.4 Sensitivity:
- By making reasonable accommodations to all the AC participants so they can fully and fairly participate in the AC process.
- By willingly and professionally answering AC-related questions asked by AC participants, within their scope of practice.
- By endeavouring to create a relaxed atmosphere as far as is professionally possible.

3.1.5 Privacy:
- By treating all information of AC participants with care and restricting access to it in accordance with best practice guidelines and South African legislation.
- By taking appropriate reasonable action to enable the discussions with or about AC participants during the AC process to take place in private.

3.1.6 Confidentiality:
- By taking appropriate, reasonable technical and organisational measures to secure the confidentiality of all AC participant information.

3.1.7 Dignity:
- By taking reasonable steps to ensure that all AC participants are treated with dignity by all assessors and AC staff throughout the process.

3.2   Principle 2: Respect for Participant Diversity

Ethical standards: In adhering to the principle of respect for participant diversity of persons, AC practitioners and assessors will provide:

3.2.1 Procedural fairness:
- By ensuring that the AC is standardised and complies with AC best practice guidelines. This includes ensuring standardised administration, scoring, interpretation and use of AC results.

3.2.2 Interactional fairness:
- By treating all AC participants with courtesy, acknowledging participants and encouraging the feeling of being part of the AC process.
- By ensuring that a code of conduct is followed by all AC stakeholders contributing to interactional fairness.

3.2.3 Distributive fairness:
- By taking into account moderating factors arising from participants' social, political, economic and cultural contexts (e.g. linguistic factors) impacting on AC participants that may have affected AC performance.

- By taking reasonable precautions to ensure that the AC does not discriminate against any group of AC participants, and that participants are evaluated fairly based on objective AC criteria.

3.2.4 Equal opportunity:
- By taking reasonable actions to ensure that all AC participants have equal opportunities to experience, benefit and learn from the AC process.
- By taking reasonable actions to ensure that all AC participants have an equal opportunity to obtain AC outcomes.

3.2.5 Equal treatment:
- By ensuring that all AC participants are treated impartially and without prejudice by AC staff.

3.2.6 Objectivity:
- By ensuring that proper AC scoring mechanisms and norms and their competent use by AC staff contribute to assessment objectivity.

3.2.7 Acceptance of diversity:
- By ensuring that diversity related issues are accepted as important and relevant and are appropriately considered in the AC process.

3.3 Principle 3: Respect for Participant Freedom

Ethical standards: In adhering to the principle of respect for participant freedom, AC practitioners will ensure that participants:

3.3.1 Are clearly informed and the process is transparent:
- By explaining the process and criteria that will be used in the AC so that AC participants know what to expect during the AC process.
- By honestly and fully communicating to AC participants the full purpose of the AC and the intended use(s) of the AC results.
- By including information about who will have access to the AC results and for what purpose(s) and for what period of time they will have access.
- By including information about how long the AC results will be stored and considered to be valid.

3.3.2 Participate freely:
- By giving AC participants the right to choose to participate in the AC process after the purpose of the AC and the consequences of participation have been explained.

3.3.3 Provide/Withhold informed consent:
- AC participants may decide to provide/withhold consent to participate in the AC process after the AC practitioner has explained the consequences of doing so.
- AC participants must give written consent to participate in the AC process and for the AC results to be used for the intended purpose (including future research). If a participant does not provide

informed consent, the AC practitioner may decline the participant's opportunity to participate in the AC.

3.3.4 Are free to withdraw from the process:

* By allowing AC participants to withdraw from the AC process at any time after the consequences of withdrawing have been explained by the AC practitioner.

3.3.5 Receive feedback upon request after the process:

* By providing valid, reliable and constructive feedback about their performance during the AC upon request after the process has been finalised. The responsibility for paying for the costs of the feedback will be clarified at the start of the AC process.
* By considering requests for specific personal follow-up feedback from the AC practitioner after receiving the initial feedback. The AC participant will have to pay for this additional feedback service.

3.3.6 Have access to own information:

* By providing AC participants with access to own AC information in a contextualised format upon request after the process has been finalised. The AC practitioner will ensure that no raw, non-interpreted or non-contextualised data be shared with the AC participant. The AC participant may not have access to material that may compromise the intellectual property of the AC practitioner and/or the AC client.

3.4   Principle 4: Respect for the Client and the Client's Organisation

Ethical Standards: In adhering to the principle of respect for the client and the client's organisation, AC practitioners will:

3.4.1 Deliver effective ACs:

* By ensuring that ACs adhere to the best practices for ACs including reliance on appropriate evidence for the validity and reliability of the AC methods used.

3.4.2 Deliver value-adding ACs:

* By assuring at the outset that an AC is the preferred assessment method given the specific client requirements.

3.4.3 Deliver what was marketed and contracted:

* By only marketing to the client and contracting with the client what the specific AC has been designed to deliver.

3.4.4 Deliver fit-for-purpose ACs:

* By using an AC only for the purpose(s) for which it was designed, e.g., for selection, diagnosis or development.

3.4.5 Deliver practical ACs (fitting into organisational processes):

- By assisting the client to position the specific AC within the client organisation's processes (e.g. talent management; succession planning; learning and development).
- By assisting the client to establish, implement and maintain an AC policy within the client organisation.

3.4.6 Deliver context-focused ACs:

- By doing contextual adaption to the AC based on job analysis in terms of economic, social, political, institutional, linguistic and cultural differences.
- By implementing an AC appropriate to organisational level, industry trends and technology use.

3.4.7 Deliver cost-effective ACs:

- By contracting up-front all foreseeable costs related to the AC for the client's account.
- By agreeing up-front with the client how return on investment for the client will be determined.
- By being transparent with the client about all AC-related costs.
- By endeavouring to deliver a cost-effective AC from the perspective of the client.

3.4.8 Provide appropriate feedback:

- By ensuring that constructive and appropriate feedback is provided to the AC stakeholders, e.g., AC participant, client or line-manager, as per the agreement.

3.5   Principle 5: Professional AC Competence

Ethical standards: In adhering to the principle of professional AC competence, AC practitioners are expected to:

3.5.1 Be knowledgeable about AC design and implementation:

- By ensuring their own competence in AC design and implementation according to the current best practices for ACs.
- By providing support for claims about AC design and implementation competence.
- By demonstrating an effective track record in the design and practical application of ACs in different environments.

3.5.2. Design ACs with scientific rigour:

- By designing ACs according to scientifically sound knowledge.
- Providing support for claims about the evidence-based foundation on which the AC has been designed.
- Documenting the AC design process and the final AC Administration Manual and AC Technical Manual.

3.5.3 Acknowledge own AC skill level:

- By being open and honest about their own AC skill level and contracting or consulting other more experienced AC practitioners when necessary to assure that the proper skill sets are available in the AC application.

3.5.4 Ensure competent AC staff:

- By ensuring that all AC staff are competent for their specific AC roles and duties as assessors, role players, AC administrators, feedback givers and data management staff.
- By providing initial and ongoing training and oversight to all AC staff and re-accrediting staff to work on a specific AC.

3.5.5 Ensure continual AC-related development:

- By regularly attending AC-related professional training and attending AC conferences to uphold AC competence.
- By accepting the ethical obligation to stay abreast of the relevant scientific and professional practice literature, and to update professional practices as needed, based on that literature.
- By adhering to the best practices such as those set-out in the current *Best Practice Guidelines for the Use of the Assessment Centre Method in South Africa* and the *Guidelines and Ethical Considerations for Assessment Center Operations.*
- By accepting the professional responsibility to reflect on their overall AC practices, to learn from mistakes, to capitalise on strengths to improve the AC's future success and to adapt future ACs accordingly.

3.6   Principle 6: Professional Accountability

In adhering to the principle of professional accountability in the AC, AC practitioners will:

3.6.1. Maintain professional standards:

- By always exercising the appropriate level of care, diligence and skill.

3.6.2 Accept accountability:

- By being answerable for AC-related actions and decisions.

3.6.3 Maintain professional conduct and integrity:

- By behaving professionally and with integrity at all times during the entire AC process, even when experiencing pressures from the client or any other stakeholder.

3.6.4 Respect AC governance:

- By adhering to the appropriate processes for making and implementing decisions about all aspects of an AC from the contracting phase to project closure.

3.6.5 Comply with AC design and implementation:

- By following due-diligence in AC design and implementation even when pressured by stakeholders to take unscientific short-cuts.

3.6.6 Maintain AC standardisation:

- By addressing any reasonable exceptions to standardisation in a manner consistent with professional standards and knowledge.

3.6.7 Protect AC use:

- By taking reasonable pro-active action to ensure the objective and appropriate application of AC results by all stakeholders.

3.6.8 Control AC data management:

- By applying appropriate AC data management practices for the safekeeping of AC material and results.

3.6.9 Ensure proper protection of intellectual property:

- By only using AC material for which they hold the intellectual property rights, or have obtained documented permission to use.[20]

4. WHO ENFORCES AC ETHICAL STANDARDS AND AGAINST WHOM?

South Africa has some of the strongest laws in the world for the control and regulation of psychometric testing. For example, the Employment Equity Act, No. 55 of 1998[21] states that psychometric testing "or other similar assessments of an employee" (presumably including ACs) were prohibited to be used unless:

> ...the test or other assessment - a) has been scientifically shown to be valid and reliable; (b) can be fairly applied to employees; and (c) is not biased against any employee or group".[22]

That such an approach seems to impute characteristics of validity and reliability to inherent properties of the test rather than to the particular uses to which it is put (see, for example, AERA, APA and NMCE[23]) is not the major issue here. This law was an effort to control which tests could be used and, by implication at least, who could use them. But how they apply to the subcomponents of ACs and to non-recognised professionals authorised to use psychometric tests, or to electronically delivered ACs in which South African participants may be tested by vendors not even located in the country, is unclear.

Best practices, in any case, according to the *Guidelines and Ethical Considerations*[24], require that ACs always be validated for their intended inferences (typically, employee selection or development). Still, the enforcement mechanisms can become ambiguous when ACs or their components are delivered in South Africa by persons without professional qualifications. According to South Africa's Professional Board for Psychology[25], "Psychometric tests may be administered only by registered persons, e.g. psychologists, psychometrics and registered counsellors."

---

20 SA Assessment Centre Study Group, 2018: 10-19

21 Employment Equity Act., (Act No. 55 of 1998)

22 Employment Equity Act., (Act No. 55 of 1998)

23 American Educational Research Association, American Psychological Association, & National Council on Measurement in Education, 2014"

24 Meiring & Buckett, 2016

25 Professional Board of Psychology, 2010: 10

Because ACs are often cross-disciplinary and may make use of non-professional employees, or they may be contracted for by corporations rather than individually licensed professionals, the ability to control this assessment modality by current legislation is not clear.

Because many individuals without professional credentials are involved in AC administration and planning, an issue that must be addressed before ethical standards have any teeth is how they apply to non-professionals who have been part of AC work. Unless the South African government was to pass laws requiring a set of prescribed (and proscribed) ethical behaviours, regardless of the professional qualifications of those conducting ACs, then a licensing board under current laws would have to go after someone violating a code for improper use of assessment measures rather than for violating a law that did not cover them because they were not professionally licensed under it.

Enforcement concerns similarly arise concerning the AC Ethics Code promulgated by the South African AC Study Group. This is not to suggest such work is wasted (professional consensus on what constitutes ethical and unethical behaviour is of value in and of itself), but to make the point that without enforcement power, ethics codes are less impactful than they may need to be.

4.1 Other classificatory schema

Muleya, Fourie and Schlebusch[26] classified ethical case data into 10 themes related to ethical challenges in ACs in South Africa (see Table 1). The qualitative data were obtained from a sample of 96 professionals who attended an AC conference and completed a short exploratory survey. A focus group of 16 AC professionals subsequently validated and enriched the data through a process of triangulation.

Table 4.1: AC ethical challenges themes

Theme	Examples
Theme 1: Universal ethical values	Morality, justice, equality, honesty, trust, respect, 'no harm', 'doing good', universal human rights, notion of fairness.
Theme 2: Assessor competence, personal characteristics, moral character and ethical intent	Integrity and ethical intent; cognitive, behavioural, managerial and ethical competence; desirable personality characteristics; and awareness of bias and prejudice, cultural sensitivity, leadership.
Theme 3: Psychometric properties of an AC	Reliability and consistency; face, construct and content validity; fit-for-purpose, clear and measurable focal constructs and criteria; good quality exercises and tools; proper scoring mechanisms; appropriate norms.
Theme 4: Bias and prejudice	Cultural, language, gender and racial bias; discrimination; favouritism and nepotism; bias (also bias towards extroverts); prejudice; different points of view or interpretations; preconceived ideas; tendency towards cloning.
Theme 5: Governance of AC process	Robust process; competent administrators; responsibility and accountability; transparency and openness; confidentiality; informed consent; valid, honest and constructive feedback; adequate data management processes; return-on-investment considerations.

---

26 Muleya et al., 2017

Theme	Examples
Theme 6: Ethical culture of the employer organisation	Strategic integration of ethics; openness to consideration of ethics by management versus deception, manipulation, dishonesty and ill intent; organisational or professional conflict and dilemmas.
Theme 7: Participant characteristics	Moral character of participants; social desirability, faking good; exaggeration; dishonesty; resistance.
Theme 8: Multicultural global context	Multicultural and global differences; need for cultural sensitivity; differences in terms of morality; need for sensitivity related to religion; South African socio-political-historical context, including specifically employment equity.
Theme 9: Evasive nature of ethics as a concept	Can you assess ethics? How would you do it?
Theme 10: Regulatory-legal framework for ACs)	Status of ACs as a psychological act; involvement of non-psychologists; intellectual property issues related to ACs; central regulatory body for ACs.

Source: Muleya, Fourie & Schlebusch[27]

In this model, a classification emerges from looking at empirical evidence of what those involved in AC work consider to be problematic, and could be used to work backward to ask whether a promulgated code would cover all these situations.

In a more theoretical approach, Lefkowitz[28] identified five ethical paradigms under which he believed almost all ethical cases can be fitted:

The opportunity to prevent harm: Awareness or anticipation of someone else being harmed or wronged by a third person.

Temptation: Contemplating an action in accordance with some self-serving motive, goal or ambition that would be unjust deceitful or harmful to another.

Role conflict: Facing competing obligations or responsibilities (sometimes to two or more persons), such that fulfilling one means failing to meet the other(s).

Values conflict: Facing important but conflicting personal values so that expressing one entails denying the other(s) expression.

Coercion: Being pressured to violate ethical standards.[29]

These areas of ethical problems are somewhat abstract, but potentially provide a conceptual check list to ensure that ethical standards are encompassing most major types of ethical transgressions, translated, of course, into the specific domain of AC practice.

---

27 Muleya et al., 2017: 9

28 Lefkowitz, 2017

29 Lefkowitz, 2017: 179 – 180

5. APPLYING ETHICS GUIDANCE TO THE THREE CASES

We will complete this chapter where we began, with the same cases now analysed using some of the ethics standards, principles, and "considerations" summarised above.

Case 1 concerned an AC that was implemented on the authority of the HR manager and CEO of a mining company without the agreement or support of the persons to be assessed. The vendor was not from South Africa and not well versed in its culture.

These issues are addressed to some degree in the 'Compliance with Relevant Employment Laws and Regulations' ethical issue raised in the *Guidelines and Ethical Considerations* and the (non-ethics) section of that document on 'Conducting ACs Across Cultural Contexts'.[30] The ethics section of the ACSG "best practices" document include informed consent (item 3) and another one (9) called 'Using one AC across different contexts'[31], which could be interpreted as applying to some of the facts of this case.

The ACSG ethics code includes 'Principle 3, Participant Freedom'. In that principle's related ethics standards, it requires that AC participants be "clearly informed" about the "full purpose of the AC and the intended use(s) of the AC results", and states that participants have the right to choose to, or not to, participate. In this case, the company erred by not explaining the purpose of the AC and obtaining the assent of the would-be participants before launching the programme. This requirement was also a concern of the "Informed Participation" ethical issue raised in the *Guidelines and Ethical Considerations*[32] document.

Additionally, the AC vendor did not appear to be adequately versed in the cultural issues in South Africa and appeared, from the case description, to have done little to have become trained in these issues or to have hired qualified local professionals with relevant expertise. The ACSG draft ethical standards include this requirement:

Ethical Standards: In adhering to the principle of respect for the client and the client's organisation, AC practitioners will ***...deliver context-focused ACs...*** by doing contextual adaption to the AC based on job analysis in terms of economic, social, political, institutional, linguistic and cultural differences...[33]

Case 2 concerned the rejection of an otherwise qualified AC candidate because of behaviour not identified in the AC but known to various would-be co-workers. The applicable ethical standards and considerations need to be considered in the context of the accuracy of the concerns raised. The job description clearly specified requirements to persons selected to work effectively in a team. If behavioural evidence provided persuasive evidence of disinterest in others or aggressiveness that would reasonably cause team dysfunction, this information would be relevant. If, however, the allegations of behavioural difficulties were not substantiated or were simply efforts to impugn the integrity of another candidate, then consideration of such behaviour would be problematic.

---

30 International Taskforce on Assessment Center Guidelines, 2015: 1264

31 Meiring & Buckett, 2016: 11-12

32 International Taskforce on Assessment Center Guidelines, 2015: 1263

33 SA Assessment Centre Study Group, 2018: 13

Assuming that the allegations of team-compromising behaviour were accurate and that the person had been properly rejected as being too large a risk to team development, the participant would nonetheless ethically be required to receive accurate feedback of the basis for the rejection and how that fitted in to the purposes of the AC (Assessee Rights;[34] Participant Rights[35]; Provide Appropriate Feedback[36]). If the assessors relied on unvalidated information to make the rejection decision, however, other ethical standards or principles would apply.

Case 3: In this case there were compromises made to the integrity of the assessment exercises that advantaged some participants and disadvantaged others. Rather than address these issues when they became known to those overseeing the AC, they were ignored with real consequences. The ethics codes *Guidelines and Ethical Considerations*[37] include an item on copyright, intellectual property and participants' rights that are relevant here (even if not precisely covering this particular situation). Similarly, the most recent ACSG "best practices" document[38] includes an ethical issue (6) on assessment integrity having to do with preserving the confidentiality of assessment materials and, like the international "best practices", one on copyright protection (3**). The ACSG ethics code is the most specific, with the requirement of "ensuring that the same assessment conditions and norms apply to all AC participants...", as well as a standard related to copyright "avoiding violations or misuse of copyright-protected information". Additionally, the document includes a standard (B.2.1) on Procedural Fairness specifiying the ethical mandate of those offering ACs in South Africa to ensure "that the AC ensures "standardised administration, scoring, interpretation and use of AC results".[39]

Conclusion: In examining three approaches to ethical issues to case material, each provided some helpful considerations in attempting to understand and adjudicate the cases. However, and understandably since it was the only effort at a full ethics code, the ACSG document was the most useful due to its much more extensive elaboration of ethical standards.

6. SUMMARY AND RECOMMENDATIONS

This chapter considered ethical issues and standards in the practice of AC work in South Africa. All issues and considerations cannot be addressed in a chapter of this length, so three approaches to ethics were considered: those of the international best practices document[40], the ethics sections of the ACSG's "best practices" document[41], and the ACSG ethics code for AC practice in SA.[42]
The following recommendations are made:

---

34 International Taskforce on Assessment Center Guidelines, 2015: 1263-1264

35 Meiring & Buckett, 2016: 11

36 SA Assessment Centre Study Group, 2018: 14

37 International Taskforce on Assessment Center Guidelines, 2015

38 Meiring & Buckett, 2016: 11-12

39 SA Assessment Centre Study Group, 2018

40 International Taskforce on Assessment Center Guidelines, 2015

41 Meiring & Buckett, 2016

42 SA Assessment Centre Study Group, 2018

1. There was considerable overlap of the three documents considered, but the most helpful and most elaborated document was the ACSG ethics code. Of course any such document must be elaborately reviewed, tweaked and modified as consensus develops about some of the covered issues, but I recommend that the AC code be the starting point since the other two approaches are mostly incorporated in the more elaborate code.

2. Ethics standards need enforcement mechanisms or they will remain aspirational documents. The South African legal context needs to consider whether such a code be incorporated into law and if so, to identify which groups (among the many involved in AC work) would be covered. This would require rethinking the current control model's use in SA, as too many of those involved in AC work would appear not to be covered by legal regulations and laws in the current approach.

3. An immediate enforcement mechanism that would be a start would be for ACSG members to be covered by the adopted code. This would require developing a mechanism to address how complaints against members will be processed and adjudicated in a fair and just manner.

4. Ethics codes are often both aspirational and enforceable. The ACSG code will benefit from wide circulation beyond the ACSG members to get input on how its standards are working in practice and to identify what is working well and what is not.

5. Ethics standards need to change over time to adapt to new situations and issues. The ACSG should consider how to create a mechanism for the regular review of the code, once adopted, against actual experience.

6. An important but complicated issue is how, if at all, the code would apply to online ACs, both those administered from other countries on SA residents and those AC purveyors who deliver their services electronically into other jurisdictions.[43]

7. The goal of having a full and enforceable code of ethics for AC work is a noble one. Much work has been done – but much remains to be done – to fully professionalise AC work. But as Nelson Mandela put it, "It always seems impossible until it's done".[44]

---

43 see Lowman, 2018a

44 BrainyQuote, nd

CHAPTER 5

PURCHASING AN ASSESSMENT CENTRE

Anne Buckett

1. INTRODUCTION

Most organisations today use assessments to make selection and/or development decisions about current and prospective employees. When it comes to choosing a standardised assessment, the decision is made easier when the assessment has a proven track record of validity and reliability. In this way, organisations are able to objectively evaluate the merits of available assessments in terms of cost, administration time, ease of scoring and interpretation, available norm groups, and the intended purpose of the assessment.

Furthermore, in countries like South Africa, legislation directs how assessments should be chosen and used by organisations to ensure fairness. However, when it comes to purchasing an assessment centre (AC) the decision is less straightforward. This is because each AC is unique and there is currently no standardised AC that can be applied uniformly across different organisations, organisational levels or even countries. For this reason, it is important for organisations to follow a logical process when it comes to purchasing an AC.

In this chapter, two points of view will be considered when it comes to purchasing an AC. First, the perspective of the organisation will be discussed and practical guidelines will be given to assist organisations to make informed decisions. This will be the main focus of the chapter. Second, the perspective of the service provider will be discussed and guidelines will be provided to improve the level of support that is given to organisations during this process.

2. ORGANISATIONAL PERSPECTIVE

Congratulations! You've decided to purchase an AC for your organisation. While this process may seem daunting and the availability of options overwhelming, establishing criteria upfront and covering critical aspects in the decision making process will ensure that the best AC solution is chosen for your organisation.

The three key steps in the organisational perspective section are depicted in Figure 5.1.

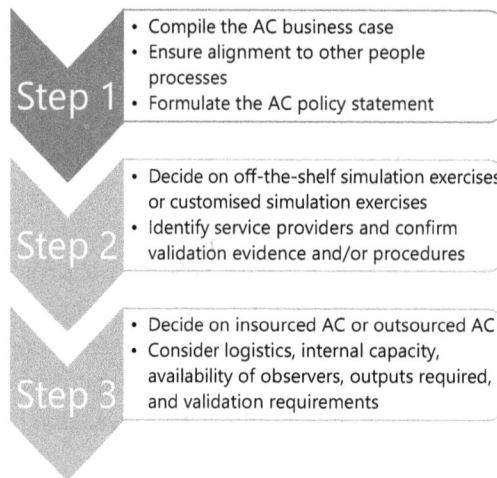

Step 1
- Compile the AC business case
- Ensure alignment to other people processes
- Formulate the AC policy statement

Step 2
- Decide on off-the-shelf simulation exercises or customised simulation exercises
- Identify service providers and confirm validation evidence and/or procedures

Step 3
- Decide on insourced AC or outsourced AC
- Consider logistics, internal capacity, availability of observers, outputs required, and validation requirements

Figure 5.1: Key steps to consider when purchasing an AC

The key steps will now be explained in more detail to help you make an informed decision.

2.1 Business Case

Although it may be tempting to go ahead and purchase the AC without a business case, the organisation runs the risk of making a bad decision in the absence of a clearly drafted rationale. The business case serves as the foundation document for the AC and includes: identifying and clearly defining the need for the AC[1], weighing up the pros and cons of the AC versus other standardised assessments, and identifying where the AC fits in with other talent management processes. The business case also provides the rationale and motivation for the AC, which is then used to secure the required budget and buy-in from stakeholders (see Chapter 6 – Needs Analysis – for more information about the business case).

2.2 Alignment with other People Processes

Once the decision has been made to purchase an AC it is important to consider how the AC fits in with other people processes in the organisation.[2] For this reason, the organisation needs to determine where the AC fits in the employment life cycle. Typically, the AC can be used for the selection of managers at different levels in the organisation, for key positions in the organisation that require scarce skills, for development at various stages in the employee's career with the organisation, or to address a diagnostic need (see Chapter 1 – Introduction to ACs – for more information about AC applications). Another consideration concerns the participant's experience of the AC. When used for selection, a well-designed and implemented AC adds to the positive reputation and brand of the organisation; it

---

1   The British Psychological Society, 2015

2   SA Assessment Centre Study Group, 2018

will leave participants with a positive impression and experience of the organisation. When used for development, the AC adds a richness to the employee's learning and development experience.

2.3 Assessment Centre Policy

As an extension to the above point, the AC should form part of an integrated talent management system, therefore an AC policy statement should be prepared for the organisation for approval. In line with best practice guidelines[3,4], the policy statement should include detailed information on the following aspects:

2.3.1. Purpose of the AC
2.3.2. Frequency of review and updates to the AC
2.3.3. Information on the participants including rights, notification, and process
2.3.4. Conditions for re-assessment
2.3.5. How data will be collected, used and stored
2.3.6. Feedback and reporting requirements
2.3.7. Information on the observers, including how they are selected, what experience and qualifications are needed, and the nature of observer training
2.3.8. Qualifications of the AC designer
2.3.9. Description of the validation model and validation strategy
2.3.10. Legislative requirements
2.3.11. Use of technology

Mini-Case Study 1: No Business Case or AC Policy

The HR department of an organisation decides that it needs an AC. It contracts a service provider to design and implement the AC on an outsourced basis for a period of one year. Within six months of implementation they notice that the various departments are either not using the AC or disregarding the AC results. When they ask the hiring managers why they are not using the AC, the response they get is that they prefer to use psychometric assessment results and that they cannot see the value of the AC results because they often contradict the participants' interviews. The HR department made the mistake at the start of the project of not putting together a business case for the AC, so they did not get initial buy-in and support for the AC from the organisation. Furthermore, they did not update the organisation's assessment policy to include an AC policy. Given the resistance to the AC from the hiring managers, the organisation is considering doing away with the AC altogether, even though they are contractually bound to pay the service provider for another six months.

2.4 Approach to Assessment Centre Purchase

The kind of AC that the organisation chooses is largely a function of capacity, time and cost. There are furthermore a number of decisions that an organisation must make when looking to purchase an AC. Organisations can decide to use off-the-shelf simulation exercises or virtual ACs, or customise their own simulation exercises when designing the overall AC programme. Organisations will also need to decide if the AC will be managed internally or whether the AC will be outsourced.

---

3   International Taskforce Guidelines on Assessment Center Guidelines, 2015

4   Meiring & Buckett, 2016

2.4.1. Off-the-Shelf Simulation Exercises and Virtual ACs

There are a number of service providers that have a catalogue of simulation exercises available for purchase or who provide virtual ACs on a consulting basis. This is a convenient option when an organisation does not have the time or budget to design its own simulation exercises. In addition, well designed simulation exercises and virtual ACs that are validated in context will support valid decision making (note, however, that organisation-specific validation would still need to be done at some stage). In the case of simulation exercises, these are usually sold as consumables, meaning that they are valid for one use only. The organisation will have to re-order simulation exercise materials for each participant every time the AC is run. In the case of virtual ACs, this service is usually delivered and managed by a service provider and invoiced per person. In both instances the intellectual property of the product remains with the service provider/product owner.[5]

However, it is not always easy to know which simulation exercise(s) or virtual AC will work in a particular context. Organisations should take note of the cross-cultural considerations listed in the South African AC guidelines[6] to inform their selection. Service providers may have to tailor exercises to meet specific organisation criteria.[7] In particular, simulation exercise content should be tailored to reflect South African terminology (e.g. place names, prices, distance indicators etc.) and structured rating forms should be designed to factor in organisational culture and context.

Below is a list of questions to help the organisation choose the best off-the-shelf product(s) to form part of the AC:

1. Who is responsible internally to choose the simulation exercise(s)?
2. Is the individual/team suitably skilled to choose the simulation exercise(s)?
3. Is job analysis information available for the targeted job/job family/role/level?
4. What dimensions need to be measured in the simulation exercise(s)?
5. What is the intended organisational level of the simulation exercise(s)?
6. How many simulation exercises are required for the AC?
7. Are there suitable supporting documents, for example, rating forms, guidelines for observers and administration instructions?
8. What are the once-off costs for each simulation exercise?
9. What are the recurring costs for each simulation exercise?
10. To what extent can imported simulation exercises be tailored for the local context?
11. What is the cost of localising the content of imported simulation exercises?

---

5   Pritchard & Riley, 2011

6   Meiring & Buckett, 2016

7   Pritchard & Riley, 2011

12. Is training provided in the use, administration, scoring and interpretation of simulation exercises?

13. What is the cost of training on the simulation exercises?

14. Are technical manuals available for the catalogue of simulation exercises, with a specific focus on how the products were developed and validated?[8]

Below is a list of questions to help the organisation choose the most appropriate virtual AC:

1. Does the service provider have a local footprint/presence?

2. What dimensions are measured in the virtual AC?

3. What is the intended organisational level of the virtual AC?

4. What types of simulation exercises are included in the virtual AC?

5. How does scoring, interpretation and feedback take place?

6. What are the costs of the virtual AC?

7. To what extent can the virtual AC be customised for the local context?

8. Are technical manuals available for the virtual AC, with a specific focus on how the products were developed and validated for the specific target group?

Table 5.1 below lists the advantages and disadvantages of off-the-shelf simulation exercises.

Table 5.1: Advantages and disadvantages of off-the-shelf simulation exercises

Advantages	Disadvantages
Large catalogue and choice of simulation exercises.	Simulation exercises are not designed specifically for the organisation.
Content already designed for different management levels.	Simulation exercises may be imported and therefore content may not accurately reflect the demographics of the organisation.
Quick and easy to order.	Costs incurred with each re-order; discounts on bulk orders tend not to apply to simulation exercises.

Table 5.2 below lists the advantages and disadvantages of off-the-shelf virtual ACs.

---

8   The British Psychological Society, 2015

Table 5.2: Advantages and disadvantages of off-the-shelf virtual ACs

Advantages	Disadvantages
Use technology as delivery format which is more representative of the world of work.	Can be seen as expensive.
Convenient and easy to use.	Usually the organisation cannot customise content.
Outputs are standardised and reputable service providers will be able to provide evidence of validation.	May not yet be validated in country or organisational context.

2.4.2. Custom-made Simulation Exercises

Custom-made simulation exercises allow the organisation to develop simulation exercises that are closely aligned to the target job/job families/roles, intended organisational level, and organisational culture and strategy, which reflect the unique challenges facing managers and/or professionals in the organisation.[9] The initial time and cost involved to design unique simulation exercises can seem expensive but, in the long-run, the benefits associated with this process quickly outweigh the initial capital investment. Organisations can design their own simulation exercises if they have sufficient internal capacity and skill, or they can secure the services of a suitably qualified external service provider. Regardless of who designs the simulation exercises, the stages and steps in the AC design model should be followed (see Chapters 6 – 19 for more information).

Table 5.3 below lists the advantages and disadvantages of customised products.

Table 5.3: Advantages and disadvantages of customised simulation exercises

Advantages	Disadvantages
Exercises can be tailored specifically for the organisation's context, culture, objectives and strategy.	Organisation may not have sufficient time to develop own simulation exercises.
Adds to the brand and reputation of the organisation, thereby enhancing the overall candidate experience.	Requires the services of a skilled AC designer and initial costs will be expensive if sourced externally.
Allows for accurate measurement and evaluation of targeted dimensions unique to the organisation.	Needs commitment and buy-in from the organisation for successful implementation.

The decision to appoint an external service provider to design simulation exercises and to consult on the overall AC programme should not be taken lightly. As with everything in business, you get what you pay

---

9   Pritchard & Riley, 2011

for. It may be tempting to go for the flashiest presentation or sales pitch, or the person who claims to be able to deliver an end-to-end product in one week, or to only look at the costs, yet although these are important aspects, it must be remembered that AC design is a specialised skill that is built on two essential elements: practice and science. An AC designer cannot have one element without the other.

Below are four additional points to consider when evaluating different AC service providers:

- What is the experience and track record of the service provider in designing simulation exercises? (For example, number of years' design experience, number and type of AC projects, client references.)[10]
- What is the approach of the service provider when designing simulation exercises? (That is, evidence-based versus practice, methodology, principles, consultation model, AC-specific design practices employed.)
- How will the service provider determine the validity and reliability of the final product(s)?[11]
- Who retains the intellectual property and copyright of the simulation exercises? (Note: for exclusive use of the designed product the AC designer will charge a higher tariff to offset future revenue loses for not being able to use the product in a different setting.)

2.4.3. Deciding between Off-the-Shelf Simulation Exercises and Custom-made Simulation Exercises

To assist organisations with the decision of whether to use off-the-shelf simulation exercises or custom-made simulation exercises, additional considerations are presented below.

2.4.3.1. Coverage of the Targeted Dimensions

It is important to consider the overall AC programme. By looking at the bigger picture, the organisation can determine how many simulation exercises are required to provide adequate coverage of the targeted dimensions. This will also include the relationship to other measures, such as psychometric assessments, that form part of the overall AC. When considering off-the-shelf simulation exercises, the organisation will need to determine whether the exercise content is able to adequately cover the targeted dimensions.

2.4.3.2. Duration and Frequency of the AC

The organisation should also have a clear idea of the ideal duration of the AC. Adding more simulation exercises and/or psychometric assessments will make the overall AC longer. Therefore, it is important to consider the impact on participants, observers and associated costs when compiling the AC programme. The frequency of the AC is another factor. If the AC is used for selection, the organisation should anticipate how often an AC will be needed and at what stage in the selection process the AC will take place. If the AC is used for development it will be important to establish when, why and how the AC takes place and to ensure alignment with existing talent management processes.

---

10 SA Assessment Centre Study Group, 2018; Meiring & Buckett, 2016; The British Psychological Society, 2015

11 Meiring & Buckett, 2016; The British Psychological Society, 2015

2.4.3.3. Operational Considerations

A number of practical considerations could affect the decision to use off-the-shelf simulation exercises or custom-made exercises in the AC. These include defining the purpose of the AC; establishing the criticality of the role; whether the participants are internal or external to the organisation; how specialised the role is; establishing the relative importance of job knowledge and job performance as part of the AC outcomes; volume of participants expected to attend the AC in a year; the likelihood that the AC provides participants with a realistic job preview; expected shelf-life of the simulation exercise; the importance of ownership of simulation exercises to the organisation; availability of suitable resources to develop simulation exercises; the legal framework around assessments in general; and how technology will be used in the AC.[12]

For example, if the role concerns a critical skill and risk of non-performance has a large financial impact on the organisation, where job knowledge and performance is essential to succeed, and the environment is subject to lawsuits, then the organisation should opt for custom-made simulation exercises.

2.4.4. Insourcing or Outsourcing the Assessment Centre

Organisations will also need to decide whether the AC will be run internally by suitably trained internal staff (i.e. insourcing) or whether the AC will be outsourced to a suitably experienced external service provider. This decision is most often purely practical. The AC is a resource-hungry process and if the organisation does not have sufficient internal capacity (that is, venues, observers etc.), the decision to outsource will be the most likely outcome. There are, however, advantages and disadvantages associated with each option. A decision in this regard will generally require careful consideration on the part of the organisation.

Table 5.4. provides a comparison of insourcing or outsourcing the AC.

Table 5.4: Comparison of insourcing versus outsourcing an AC

	Insourcing	**Outsourcing**
Venue	Using one's own facilities makes it easier to manage the process and create an integrated candidate experience.	Using the facilities of a service provider removes the hassle of on-site management and provides a neutral setting for the participants.
Running Costs	The organisation can manage the costs associated with the implementation of the AC in terms of venue hire, catering, securing observers, and printing of materials (when required).	The service provider takes responsibility for the logistics involved in running the AC on the behalf of the organisation in terms of venue hire, catering, securing observers, and printing of materials (when required).

---

12 Pritchard & Riley, 2011

84

	Insourcing	Outsourcing
Observers	The organisation manages the pool of available observers and takes responsibility for identifying, training and accrediting observers, as well as defining expected standards of performance in terms of scoring, interpretation, reporting and feedback.	The service provider utilises their own trained pool of observers along with ensuring the necessary training and accreditation of the observers.[13]

2.4.4.1. Outputs Required

Information gathered by the AC provides the organisation with a rich source of data about participants' expected performance in line with targeted dimensions for the intended professional/managerial role. The organisation should decide on the level of detail required in terms of feedback and report writing. In a selection context, overall dimension scores for each exercise should be captured. A rank list can be used to display participants' overall performance relative to other applicants. In a development context more detail is typically required and could include a written report and verbal feedback. It is important to put in place a process for capturing scores, collating data and storing information, as this becomes the information used in validation research.

Mini-Case Study 2: (Mis)clarification of Outputs

An organisation has contracted a new service provider to custom-make an AC for senior manager selection. The service provider will also manage the AC 'end-to-end' for the organisation for the next two years. The internal HR project team is familiar with ACs, having previously worked with a different service provider for a once-off middle management Development Centre. All phases of the project are budgeted, approved and signed off. The first senior manager AC is held and the HR project team is surprised to receive a collated one-page summary for the short-listed senior manager applicants in table and bullet point format. When they request more detail, the service provider indicates that individual, detailed candidate reports and feedback to the hiring manager is not provided unless directly contracted, and is subject to additional costs. The organisation mistakenly assumed that, given their previous AC experience in a development context, feedback and detailed reports would be standard outputs. The organisation ends up paying for detailed reports and feedback for two years, of which both expenses were unbudgeted.

Below is a list of questions to help organisations determine whether to insource or outsource the AC.

---

1. How many simulation exercises does the AC include?
2. Are psychometric assessments part of the AC? (Note: certain assessments require specific professional qualifications and additional training/certification.)
3. How long is the AC?

---

13 The British Psychological Society, 2015

4. How frequently will the AC be administered?

5. Does the organisation have a dedicated venue (with several breakaway rooms) to run all the simulation exercises and/or administer the psychometric assessments?

6. Who are the observers? (Note: this can be psychologists, HR professionals, and line managers. In unionised work environments this may include a union representative.)

7. What is the availability of the observers?

8. What training is required by/given to observers?

9. How will feedback and reporting take place?

10. What are the responsibilities of observers before, during and after the AC?

11. Where will participant information and paperwork be stored?

12. Who is responsible for capturing individual participant scores and data?

13. Who is responsible for validation of the AC?[14]

Based on a review of responses to the above questions, the organisation will be able to decide whether to insource or outsource the AC. This decision will always be specific to the organisation. There is no correct decision in this regard; there are as many organisations with sufficient internal capacity to run the AC as there are those that prefer to outsource the AC to a suitably qualified service provider.

Mini-Case Study 3: Creating an Unnecessary Dependency

An organisation contracts a service provider to design and implement an AC with the medium-term goal to take over this function from the service provider. However, after almost one year, no effort has been made by the service provider to transfer knowledge or upskill the organisation's designated internal staff to take over the management of the AC. The organisation is also keen to conduct a validation study on the 150+ participants assessed to date. A meeting is called to discuss these two issues. During the meeting, the service provider informs them that the inclusion of psychometric questionnaires as part of the full AC precludes any of the organisation's current staff from being able to independently manage the AC without the supervision of the service provider. Furthermore, they have not captured any AC data for any participant. They view validation as an 'academic' exercise and indicate that the organisation can justify their selection decisions by citing the Employment Equity Act (1998) so research is pointless. Upset that the service provider has created an unnecessary dependency on their services and does not seem interested in doing any research, the organisation seeks legal advice to terminate the contract.

---

3. SERVICE PROVIDER PERSPECTIVE

You may already be working successfully in ACs both in terms of design and implementation. This section aims to provide useful and relevant information as part of contracting an AC design with organisations as a way to enhance the level of support and service you give to new and existing customers. There are two processes that are considered when selling an AC to an organisation. The first pertains to the AC consultation process and the second pertains to contracting the work.

---

14 The British Psychological Society, 2015

The three key steps in the AC consultation process in the service provider perspective section are depicted in Figure 5.2.

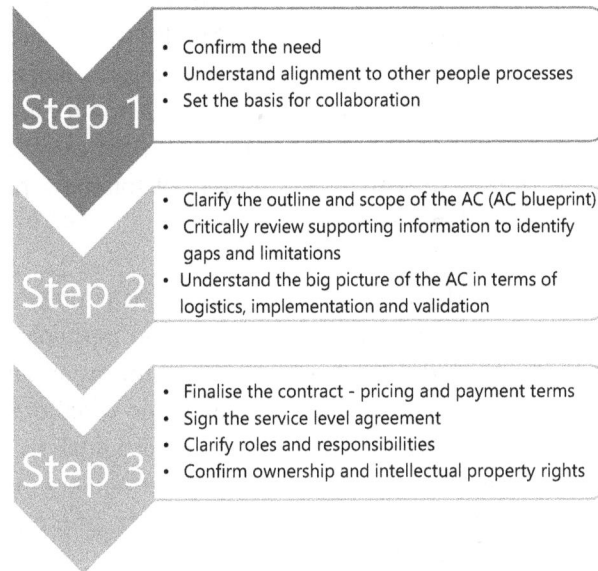

Step 1
- Confirm the need
- Understand alignment to other people processes
- Set the basis for collaboration

Step 2
- Clarify the outline and scope of the AC (AC blueprint)
- Critically review supporting information to identify gaps and limitations
- Understand the big picture of the AC in terms of logistics, implementation and validation

Step 3
- Finalise the contract - pricing and payment terms
- Sign the service level agreement
- Clarify roles and responsibilities
- Confirm ownership and intellectual property rights

Figure 5.2: Key steps to consider when selling an AC

3.1 AC Consultation Process

3.1.1. Establishing the Need

The fact that you focus on ACs probably already means that you understand the value of ACs as part of talent management and see the benefits of using the method for selection and development in applied settings. Many organisations are also likely to understand the value of using ACs to enhance decisions about their employees. However, many organisations do not always make the time to put together a business case (refer to Section 2.1 in this chapter). The business case is an important first step for both the organisation and the service provider. This document clearly establishes the need for the AC and sets the basis for AC design and implementation.

3.1.2. Linking the AC to Organisational Processes

The business case clearly sets out where the AC fits in relation to other organisational processes.[15] It may be tempting for the service provider to offer to write the business case but this document should come from the organisation, at least in draft form. The service provider can assist and guide the organisation in this process. In the absence of a business case, issues may arise later in the process regarding assumptions, constraints, and the division of roles and responsibilities between the organisation and service provider. The worst case scenario would be a situation where the work is cancelled because there is no buy-in from key stakeholders in the business.

---

15 SA Assessment Centre Study Group, 2018

3.1.3. Collaborative Consultation

Organisations may occasionally have unrealistic expectations about the time, cost and application of the AC. The service provider relationship with the organisation therefore becomes crucial to the overall success of the AC. Keeping open communication channels, addressing issues and concerns in a timely manner, and meeting regularly with the organisation to track and monitor progress are key elements in the process.[16] By following the AC design phases, the service provider can strengthen the collaborative relationship with the organisation. Furthermore, it is important for the service provider to follow an evidence-based approach to simulation exercise design.[17]

A critical aspect here is that the AC designer must have, as far as is practically possible, easy access to subject matter experts (SMEs) in order to gather information pertaining to the target job/level/organisational context. A thorough understanding of the job and organisational context lends itself to comprehensive and accurate simulation exercise design. Open collaboration is thus an important prerequisite to this step (see Chapter 8) for a discussion about job analysis. From a practical point of view, it is difficult to work through a third party or internal intermediary indefinitely for a discussion about job analysis. This difficulty may be further compounded if the appointed intermediary does not have a practical understanding of the AC design process.

3.1.4. Outlining and Scoping the AC

It is important to understand the scope of the work required by the organisation. During this process the service provider gathers as much information as possible from the organisation to clearly outline and scope the AC. This will enable the service provider to provide an accurate cost and time estimate for the work.

3.1.4.1. Supporting Information

There may be several consultations with the organisation prior to providing a quote for the work. The service provider needs to know that the AC business case has been compiled and the need for the AC is clearly established. Furthermore, supporting information needs to be reviewed such as job descriptions, competency frameworks or the organisational strategy. If this information is outdated or missing, the AC cannot be designed effectively (see Chapters 6 - 8). An operational AC blueprint will need to be drawn up, approved and signed off by the client to outline the design plan for the AC (see Chapter 10).

3.1.4.2. View of the Overall AC Programme

The service provider requires a big picture view of what the final AC should look like. Discussions here will focus on clarifying the type of AC the organisation wants or needs. Depending on the type of AC required, the service provider may need to design one or several ACs. An overall picture of what the organisation envisages will enable the scope and extent of the work to be clearly delineated.

---

16 SA Assessment Centre Study Group, 2018

17 The British Psychological Society, 2015

3.1.4.3. Logistics

This will be a critical aspect when implementing the AC. Typically, a dedicated venue is required to run the AC with several smaller rooms for interactive activities. Logistical support is also required when communicating with participants and to prepare the AC materials prior to the AC. Roles and responsibilities can be divided between the organisation and the service provider. For example, the organisation can contact participants to confirm arrangements while the service provider provides the venue and manages on-site logistics. This aspect will also be dependent on the nature of the relationship, that is, whether the organisation follows an insourced or outsourced approach.

3.1.4.4. Ownership of the AC

This is an important part of the scoping phase as it has a direct impact on pricing. Many service providers have an existing range of simulation exercises that can be used for different organisations, purposes and contexts. The organisation may, however, choose to design products that are unique to them. In this case, the service provider will design simulation exercises for a particular organisation and these products can become the property of the organisation (depending on what is agreed).[18] The service provider will then need to weigh up the cost of design and transfer of ownership in relation to the impact on future lost revenues when handing over ownership of the product(s) to the organisation.

3.1.4.5. Deliverables

Finally, the service provider will be expected to deliver the product and/or service as contracted. At a minimum, the service provider can be reasonably expected to provide[19]:

- an end-to-end AC and/or custom-made/tailored simulation exercise materials, including instructions for participants, observer score sheets, guidelines for observers, and competent observers;
- a technical manual and relevant documentation supporting the validity of the approach;
- timely input and guidance on any ethical, legal and professional issues that arise during the course of the contract; and
- clear guidelines on the validation approach to be followed.

Mini-Case Study 4: A Win-Win Outcome

An organisation really wants a custom-made AC instead of a standard off-the-shelf AC. Unfortunately, the quote for a custom-made AC is expensive. The service provider is willing to work within the organisation's budget. They indicate that they can still custom-make an AC for the organisation so long as the service provider retains the intellectual property for the designed AC. The organisation is happy with this arrangement as it falls within the allocated budget.

---

18 Pritchard & Riley, 2011

19 The British Psychological Society, 2015

It is clear to see that scoping the AC is a lengthy and complex process. Proper consultation is therefore required so that the service provider can meet its commercial objectives while, at the same time, adding value to the organisation and protecting the working relationship.

Below are some questions to cover during the scoping phase:

1. Has the need for an AC been clearly established?
2. What supporting documentation is available from the organisation to inform the scope of work required?
3. What type of AC is required? (Selection, development, diagnostic, customised versus generic, insourced versus outsourced.)
4. What does the overall AC programme look like? (Simulations only or including other measures such as psychometric assessments and/or interviews.)
5. What is the organisational level of the AC?
6. Will the AC cover jobs/job families/roles at the same organisational level?
7. Is there an existing competency framework?
8. Is the existing competency framework current?
9. How many simulation exercises are required for the AC? (Note that it is only practical to determine the type of simulation exercises after a job analysis has been completed.)
10. What is the scope and extent of the outsourcing agreement? (That is, will the organisation be involved with some of the AC design components or will the service provider be solely responsible for designing the AC?)
11. Will the completed product(s) be transferred to the organisation for implementation?
12. Will the service provider be required to implement and manage the AC for the organisation?
13. What is the nature and type of feedback required from AC data? (Note: this is important as it informs the simulation exercise, rating form and feedback template design.)
14. How and when will feedback take place once the AC is operational?
15. What is the service provider's role and responsibility in relation to reporting and feedback?
16. What are the expected deliverables? (For example, what is the role of the service provider regarding sourcing observers, training observers and other AC users, designing simulations and producing all related documentation?)[20]
17. Who will manage the logistics of the AC?
18. Who retains the intellectual property and copyright of the simulation exercises?
19. What are the procedures for monitoring, evaluating and validating the AC?[21]

3.2 Contracting the AC

There are two elements in this section. First, the specific details to be included or covered in the contract, and second, the technical elements.

---

20 The British Psychological Society, 2015

21 The British Psychological Society, 2015

3.2.1. Contract Specifics

It is unlikely that any work will proceed without a signed contract and service level agreement. The contract is an important legal document that regulates the relationship between the organisation and the service provider. It should include details on roles and responsibilities of both parties, processes for dealing with disputes and conditions for payment. It may be necessary for each party's legal representative to handle negotiations around contract terms and conditions. The service provider may need to obtain a purchase order number prior to beginning the work in order to receive payment.

3.2.2. Technical Specifics

The elements covered in 3.1 in this chapter will form the basis of the contract. The service provider should provide a detailed breakdown on pricing. This will ensure that there are no hidden costs for the organisation and no unnecessary out-of-scope expenses for the service provider. Furthermore, a detailed breakdown on the project phases involved to complete the work should be provided. Other important elements include a clear description on ownership and intellectual property, and validation procedures.

Below are some questions to answer when finalising the contract:

> - What must be contracted with the organisation?
> - What pricing model should be included in the contract?
> - How will payment occur?
> - Who owns the final product(s)?
> - Who does the validation?

Underpinning the legal and technical elements of the contracting phase is the service provider's ethical interaction with the organisation at every stage of the AC design and delivery process. The newly promulgated Code of Ethics for ACs[22] provides a number of ethical standards for AC designers and practitioners. Specifically, the eight ethical standards listed under Principle 4 (Respect for the Client and the Client's Organisation) state that AC practitioners will: 1) deliver effective ACs, 2) deliver value-adding ACs, 3) deliver what was marketed and contracted, 4) deliver fit-for-purpose ACs, 5) deliver practical ACs (fitting into organisational processes), 6) deliver context-focused ACs, 7) deliver cost-effective ACs, and 8) provide appropriate feedback (see Chapter 4 for a discussion about ACs and ethics).

---

22 SA Assessment Centre Study Group, 2018: 15

Mini-Case Study 5: Unclear Expectations

An AC service provider was awarded the contract to design a custom-made AC for an organisation. During the outline and scoping of the work, the organisation indicated that a competency profile for the AC needed to be established in line with new strategic organisational objectives. The service provider accepted this information at face value and did not explore the matter further. Once the work commenced the service provider and organisation quickly began to disagree on the competency profile for the AC. The organisation wanted the competency profile to be designed to include the entire career path for the targeted job, and insisted that the AC must be designed to give them information for all the mapped career paths. The service provider indicated that the nature of the work is part of organisational development and is out-of-scope of the current contract. The service provider further indicated that it is not possible to design one AC to measure several career paths at once. Locked in a dispute, the organisation agreed to do this competency mapping but insisted that the service provider is contractually bound to design the AC in line with their expectations. The service provider does so despite indicating that the AC will not be valid.

ANALYSIS

1.   WHAT THE ANALYSIS STAGE IS ALL ABOUT

With reference to the AC design model that was introduced in the first chapter, the following section of the book will focus on the analysis stage highlighted in Figure S1.1.

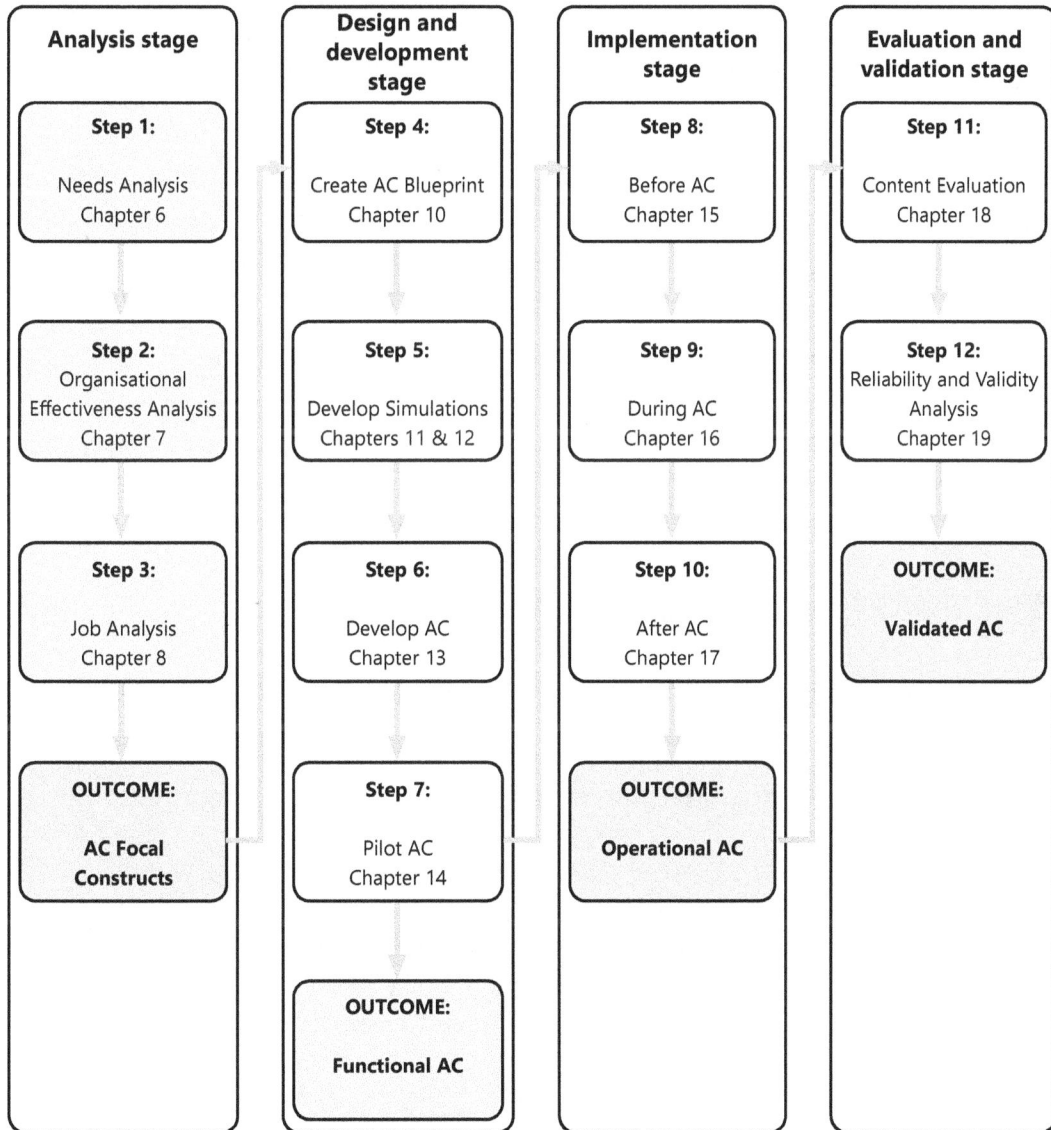

Analysis stage	Design and development stage	Implementation stage	Evaluation and validation stage
Step 1: Needs Analysis Chapter 6	**Step 4:** Create AC Blueprint Chapter 10	**Step 8:** Before AC Chapter 15	**Step 11:** Content Evaluation Chapter 18
Step 2: Organisational Effectiveness Analysis Chapter 7	**Step 5:** Develop Simulations Chapters 11 & 12	**Step 9:** During AC Chapter 16	**Step 12:** Reliability and Validity Analysis Chapter 19
Step 3: Job Analysis Chapter 8	**Step 6:** Develop AC Chapter 13	**Step 10:** After AC Chapter 17	**OUTCOME:** **Validated AC**
OUTCOME: **AC Focal Constructs**	**Step 7:** Pilot AC Chapter 14	**OUTCOME:** **Operational AC**	
	OUTCOME: **Functional AC**		

Figure S1.1: The steps in, and stages of, the design model

It is clear from Figure 1 that the analysis stage consists of different steps. Having obtained clarity about the focus and exact purpose of a specific type of AC (the types of ACs were explicated in Chapter 1, section 3), ACs should be designed in such a way that they address organisation-specific objectives and the specific needs of the various management-leadership levels. This section of the book will thus focus on the systematic analysis of organisation-specific objectives and on the specific needs in relation to the various management-leadership levels. The following chapters in this section will each deal with a specific step in the analysis stage, starting with a wider organisational contextual analysis and then moving to a more specific organisational effectiveness focus, followed by a focus on job-specific analyses.

In Chapter 6, needs analyses will be introduced and systematically covered. This chapter will deal with a contextual analysis and a company-specific analysis before moving on to explain different company-specific approaches to needs analyses. Thereafter, alternatives to ACs are introduced and the utility value of ACs is explained. Before the chapter concludes, the creation of a conducive context for ACs is explained.

In Chapter 7, an organisational effectiveness analysis will be introduced and explained. This chapter will also introduce different approaches to organisational effectiveness and the process of establishing valid effectiveness criteria. Thereafter, the topic of management-leadership levels and management level outcomes is addressed. Before the chapter is concluded, a generic model of management competencies is introduced.

Chapter 8 deals with job analyses. Attention in this chapter is focused on the target job, as it needs to be established exactly what the target job is all about and how the target job differs from those jobs around it. This understanding is gained during the job analysis step in the analysis stage of the design model.

2. THE PURPOSE OF THE ANALYSIS STAGE

The purpose of the analysis stage is threefold and these specific purposes are each covered in a separate paragraph below:

2.1 Growing a systematic understanding of the organisational context

Organisations are often linked to a specific industry that distinguishes them from other organisations in different industries. It is also true that different industries operate in the same country or context that compels them to face similar challenges. Some of these distinctive South African contextual factors across industries and organisations will be systematically covered in Chapter 6, where it will be explained why these contextual factors have to be considered when designing an AC.

2.2 Understanding the organisation, its dynamics and its specific needs

Despite the fact that, on the one hand, organisations share a lot of similar characteristics, each is, in a certain sense, also unique. The purpose of an organisational analysis or a business-case analysis is to gain a better understanding of an organisation, its strategies and objectives, its unique characteristics and processes (these aspects will be partly covered in Chapters 6 and 7), and its specific needs. The analysis will explain why these unique factors should be considered when designing an AC for an organisation.

2.3 Having clarity about the job/role and its demands

People working in organisations have to fulfil various roles or role sets, each of which in turn has its own unique demands. Before designing an AC, one should have a clear understanding of the job descriptions and job specifications (job analysis will be discussed in more depth in Chapter 8). A job analysis is the tool or technique that will enable one to systematically gather this type of information about the job in the first instance (job descriptions and job specifications), as well as for establishing the required competency profile of the job incumbent. Job analysis is therefore explained in more detail in Chapter 8 and it is indicated why this information is required for designing an effective AC.

3. CRITICAL DELIVERABLES OF THIS STAGE

There are two critical outcomes or deliverables in the analysis stage.

3.1 Competency profiles and competency/behavioural elements

Based on the information gained from job analyses, one should have a clear understanding of the competency requirements (job specifications) for a specific managerial-leadership level of the current available competency levels, as well as of the current competency deficiencies for that level in the organisation. A systematic approach to job analysis will enable one to systematically collect information on the job specifications, the required competency profiles of the incumbents, and the current competency deficiencies. This systematic process will not only identify the required competencies, but it will also identify the required behavioural elements that constitute a competency. This information will be of critical importance for the AC design team when collating the different elements under each competency in the process of designing an AC.

3.2 Establishing validation criteria

Having information on company-specific needs analyses, specific job performance outcomes and company performance criteria enables one to specify performance or effectiveness criteria against which the effect of the AC can be evaluated. This information is of critical importance when conducting validation studies on ACs. See the discussion about reliability and validity analyses in chapter 19.

4.   THE INTENDED OUTCOME OF THIS STAGE

A design model for ACs is proposed in this book, which facilitates the application of a programme evaluation approach and principles. The programme evaluation approach enables one to assess each stage of the design process according to specific programme evaluation criteria, but also, in the final instance, to evaluate the impact of the AC on the overall management-leadership effectiveness or management-leadership performance in the organisation. This perspective of the evaluation process therefore focuses more on the impact or effect of ACs as training or developmental interventions as opposed to the assessment process.

The first chapter in this section, Chapter 6, will partly focus on the contextual analysis as well as the company-specific analysis.

CHAPTER 6

NEEDS ANALYSIS

Gert Roodt

1. INTRODUCTION – THE PURPOSE OF A NEEDS ANALYSIS

This chapter will provide an overview of a needs analysis within the larger context of designing an AC. As such, the chapter will also cover the initial step of the first (analysis) stage of the design model proposed in this book. Figure 6.1 depicts the needs analysis step in the analysis stage of the design model.

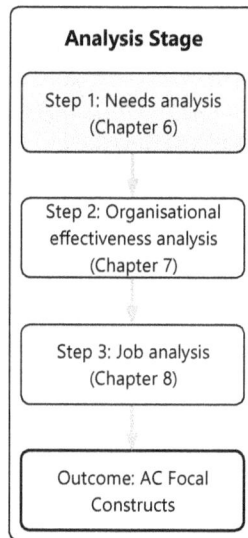

Analysis Stage

Step 1: Needs analysis
(Chapter 6)

Step 2: Organisational
effectiveness analysis
(Chapter 7)

Step 3: Job analysis
(Chapter 8)

Outcome: AC Focal
Constructs

Figure 6.1: The needs analysis step in the analysis stage

A funnel approach will be followed in structuring this chapter (and the following chapters dealing with the analysis stage). This funnel approach entails starting off with a broad, contextual needs analysis of the business context in which South African organisations function (which is covered in Section 2 of this chapter). A business context analysis serves the purpose of sensitising the AC design team to the issues that have to be addressed in the initial conceptualisation of an AC and its design. Specific aspects that will be covered in this section are South Africa's unique diversity context and its unique legal context, as well as the special ethical demands arising from these two contexts that need to be considered.

Zooming in on a specific organisation level, the focus then shifts to the organisation-specific aspects of a needs analysis (dealt with in Section 3 of this chapter). This section will focus on specific organisational characteristics, processes and aspects that are required for systematically gaining an understanding of the specific organisation with which an AC design team is dealing.

The fourth section of the chapter deals with a range of possible alternatives to ACs. These alternatives are listed and, by means of an illustrative cost-benefit analysis, the value of ACs is demonstrated.

The penultimate section deals with how the information obtained can be used to effectively integrate and strategically position the AC within a larger organisational context and within the context of specific human capital systems.

Introductory case study: Abuse of psychometric assessments

The following article appeared in *Rapport*[1] and an abbreviated version was loosely translated as follows:

Hundreds of reservists (i.e. voluntary workers who conduct police work for free) in the SA Police Service may possibly not continue their work after they were found to be unfit to serve in the police service. In cases of smaller police stations, reservists present up to 50% of the workforce. On a station level, the police force cannot function optimally without reservists.

Bryan Mennie, a police reservist in Cape Town, mentioned that 150 reservists in the Western Cape had to complete psychometric tests. He wore the uniform for 18 years before becoming a reservist, but 'failed' his psychometric test. They were informed upfront by an officer that he would see to it that they 'fail' (own quotes) the test. They were informed afterwards by SMS that they were unsuccessful. They were not allowed to see their test papers. The SA Police did not respond to any of the questions directed to them in this regard.

This article raises a number of concerns: (i) How were these tests compiled? (ii) Against which competency or psychometric profiles were these tests compiled? (iii) Were these tests conducted by a registered industrial psychologist or under the supervision of industrial psychologists? (iv) How does this case match 'best practice' guidelines on how to conduct psychometric assessments? (v) Did the assessments serve in the best interests of all the candidates? (vi) Can the employer provide grounds that their decision is equitable and fair?

The diversity background and the legislative background provided in this chapter will help you to determine how many ethical and legal transgressions were committed in the case described above, but most importantly, it will equip you with the knowledge and skills to prevent a repetition of this unfortunate event.

---

2.   SOUTH AFRICA'S DISTINCTIVE SOCIAL CONTEXT

Like any country, South Africa has a unique social context, yet South Africa's population differs in respect of a number of aspects. This creates unique challenges in a range of different arenas, including the workplace. For the purpose of this discussion, the focus will fall specifically on aspects that have a bearing on the design of an AC.

2.1   Understanding South Africa's diverse context

South Africa has what is termed a diverse population. This is evident from the 2016 census, which found that the 56 million people can be divided into a black grouping (45,1 million – 81%), a white grouping (4,5 million - 8%), a coloured grouping (4,9 million - 9%) and Indian/Asian groups (1,4 million

---

1   Gibson, 2017

- 2,5%).[2] The country's diverse context is further emphasised by the fact that there are at least 11 major indigenous language groups and a host of other smaller language groups. These facts certainly pose specific challenges concerning fairness in employment and selection practices.

The question that immediately comes to mind is whether AC practices are perceived by all AC participants (from diverse backgrounds) as being equitable and fair. Chapter 3 in this book takes a closer look at this issue. From a design perspective, special efforts have to be made to ensure that any AC assessments are not perceived as biased (i.e. that no systematic, unfair discrimination is inherent in the assessment process), and that AC practices or processes are not perceived as unfair (i.e. there must be a perception of procedural justice or fairness based on subjective experiences of AC practices or processes). The AC design team should therefore, from the onset, consider all bias and fairness issues in order to ensure that the AC does not have any adverse impact on any specific language, ethnic or gender group, or on any other significant group in the workplace.

2.2 South Africa's unique legal context

South Africa's diverse population context provides the basis for legislation that regulates the relationships between groups and prevents any group from discriminating against any other group. In this respect, South Africa has a well-developed legislative system. A number of different Acts have a bearing on AC practices, specifically those employed when making any employment decision, such as decisions relating to selection, deselection, promotion or demotion. The following Acts have specific relevance in this regard:

2.2.1   The Constitution of the Republic of South Africa[3]

The Bill of Rights of the Constitution (Subsection 9(4)) prohibits a person from directly or indirectly discriminating against anyone on the grounds set out in Subsection 9(3), which includes: "race, gender, sex, pregnancy, marital status, ethnic or social origin, colour, sexual orientation, age, disability, religion, conscience, belief, culture, language and birth."

ACs have to be designed in such a way that they do not discriminate against any of these groups. Furthermore, the Bill of Rights paves the way for other more specific legislation, such as the following:

2.2.2   Promotion of Equality and Prevention of Unfair Discrimination Act4[4]

Subsections 13(1) and (2) of the Act state the following:

2   Statistics SA, 2016

3   The Constitution of the Republic of South Africa, Act No 108 of 1996

4   Promotion of Equality and Prevention of Unfair Discrimination Act. (No 4 of 2000)

(1) If the complainant makes out a prima facie case of discrimination –
    (a) the respondent must prove, on the facts before the court, that the discrimination did not take place as alleged; or
    (b) the respondent must prove that the conduct is not based on one or more of the prohibited grounds.

(2) If the discrimination did take place –
    (a) on a ground in paragraph (a) of the definition of "prohibited grounds" then it is unfair, unless the respondent proves that the discrimination is fair;
    (b) on a ground in paragraph (b) of the definition of "prohibited grounds" then it is unfair –
        i) if one or more of the conditions set out in paragraph (b) of the definition of "prohibited grounds" is established; and
        ii) unless the respondent proves that the discrimination is fair.

Under this Act, the burden of proof rests with the respondent. It is presently not clear what constitutes a "prima facie case". In the case of alleged discrimination, the respondent must show that the discrimination was in fact fair and was not based on any of the prohibited grounds.[i] Theron[5] argues that there is no agreement on these two issues in the South African legal fraternity. In a nutshell, this means that: (a) as a preventative measure, the AC practitioner must ensure that all employment decisions based on AC outcomes are made on the basis of valid evidence (i.e., can be substantiated with appropriate data); and (b) in the case of a potential discrimination lawsuit, the AC practitioner must be able to defend himself/herself in court and must be able to provide valid evidence disproving discrimination. These two points emphasise the need to keep sound assessment records.

2.2.3   The Employment Equity Act[6]

The provisions of subsection 6(1) of the Act correspond with the grounds listed in subsection 9(3) of the Bill of Rights of the Constitution (see above). However, in the case of this Act, HIV status has been added to the list of grounds. Subsections 6(2) and (3) further stipulate as follows:

(2) It is not unfair discrimination to –
    (a) take affirmative action measures consistent with the purpose of the Act; or
    (b) distinguish, exclude or prefer any person on the basis of an inherent requirement of a job.

(3) Harassment of an employee is a form of unfair discrimination and is prohibited on any one, or a combination of grounds of unfair discrimination listed in subsection (1).

The above Subsection 6(2) allows managers to make employment decisions based on the inherent requirements of a job. This underscores the fact that the requirements of the job should be clear and specified upfront.

---

i.   Prohibited grounds are: (a) those referred to in the Bill of Rights of the Constitution as discussed earlier; or (b) any other grounds where discrimination is based on grounds that – (i) cause systemic disadvantage; (ii) undermine human dignity; or (iii) adversely affect the equal enjoyment of a person's rights and freedoms.

---

5   Theron, 2007

6   Employment Equity Act., (Act No. 55 of 1998)

Section 8 of the Act refers to psychological tests and assessments specifically, and states as follows:

> (8) *Psychological testing and other similar forms of assessments of an employee are prohibited unless the test or assessment being used:*
> (a) *has been scientifically shown to be valid and reliable;*
> (b) *can be applied fairly to all employees;*
> (c) *is not biased against any employee or group.*

Foxcroft, Roodt and Abrahams[7] argue that these aforementioned grounds of the Employment Equity Act have major implications for assessment practitioners in South Africa. Assessment practitioners (including AC practitioners) will thus specifically be called upon to demonstrate that their particular assessment measures do not discriminate against particular groups of people. Lopes, Roodt and Mauer[8] suggested that it may be useful to certify measures as "Employment Equity Act-compliant", but bias and fairness go beyond the measure itself, because they also refer to assessment practices. Some kind of certification process in respect of assessment practitioners would therefore assist organisations and managers in selecting and using AC practitioners who conduct unbiased and fair assessments.

Section 11 of the Act specifies the following:

Whenever unfair discrimination is alleged in terms of this Act, the employer against whom the allegation is made must establish that it is fair.

This section clearly places the burden of proof on the employer. The unavoidable consequence of this is that AC practitioners will have to start gathering and collating research evidence on their assessment dimensions and assessment exercises, and, where possible, on related performance or outcomes measures. AC practitioners should therefore be able to prove that they conduct their assessments in an unbiased and fair manner so that no person or group can accuse the practitioner of any procedural injustice or unfair discrimination. ACs thus have to be designed in such a manner as to enable and promote validation research on ACs.

2.2.4 *The Basic Conditions of Employment Act[9]*

The rights of employees are specified in Subsections 78(1) and (2) of the Act. Briefly, these rights include the right to complain to a union representative about work conditions, to discuss conditions with a fellow employee, to refuse to comply with an instruction that is contrary to the Act, to inspect any record kept in terms of the Act, and to participate in proceedings in terms of the Act.

An individual's rights are protected in terms of Subsections 79(1)-(3) of the Act:

---

7   Foxcroft et al., 2005

8   Lopes et al., 2001

9   Basic Conditions of Employment Act. (Act No. 75 of 1997)

(1) In this section, "employee" includes a former employee or an applicant for employment.

(2) No person may discriminate against an employee for exercising a right conferred by this Part and no person may do, or threaten to do, any of the following:

    (a) require an employee not to exercise a right conferred by this Part;

    (b) prevent an employee from exercising a right conferred by this Part; or

    (c) prejudice an employee because of a past, present or anticipated –

        (i) failure or refusal to do anything that an employer may not lawfully permit or require an employee to do;

        (ii) disclosure of information that the employee is lawfully entitled or required to give to another person; or

        (iii) exercise a right conferred by this Part.

(3) No person may favour, or promise to favour, an employee in exchange for the employee not exercising a right conferred by this Part. However, nothing in this section precludes the parties to a dispute from concluding an agreement to settle the dispute.

It is clear from this section that, under the Act, an employee enjoys specific rights regarding employment conditions. No person may therefore be discriminated against on the grounds of the exercise of these rights. In terms of Subsection (2)(c)(i) and (ii), this Act may also imply that an employee has the right to refuse to participate in an AC (or any other assessment for that matter) in respect of which reliability and validity evidence is not available. An employee could, for instance, argue that by participating in the assessment, he/she may be transgressing Section 8 of Act 55 of 1998.

2.2.5 The Labour Relations Act[10]

Section 4 of this Act specifies the rights of individuals to join unions, participate in their activities, and to be office bearers in a union or union federation. Section 5 specifically refers to the protection of union members' rights in this regard:

5. Protection of employees and persons seeking employment

(1) No person may discriminate against an employee for exercising any right conferred by this Act.

(2) Without limiting the general protection conferred by subsection (1), no person may do, or threaten to do, any of the following –

    (a) require an employee or a person seeking employment –

        (i) not to be a member of a trade union or workplace forum;

        (ii) not to become a member of a trade union or workplace forum; or

        (iii) to give up membership of a trade union or workplace forum; (b) prevent an employee or a person seeking employment from exercising any right conferred by this Act or from participating in any proceedings in terms of this Act; or

    (b) prejudice an employee or a person seeking employment because of past, present or anticipated –

---

10 Labour Relations Act. (Act No. 66 of 1995) as amended

> (i) *membership of a trade union or workplace forum;*
>
> (ii) *participation in forming a trade union or federation of trade unions or establishing a workplace forum;*
>
> (iii) *participation in the lawful activities of a trade union, federation of trade unions or workplace forum;*
>
> (iv) *failure or refusal to do something that an employer may not lawfully permit or require an employee to do;*
>
> (v) *disclosure of information that the employee is lawfully entitled or required to give to another person;*
>
> (vi) *exercise of any right conferred by this Act; or*
>
> (vii) *participation in any proceedings in terms of this Act.*

(3) No person may advantage, or promise to advantage, an employee or a person seeking employment in exchange for that person not exercising any right conferred by this Act or not participating in any proceedings in terms of this Act. However, nothing in this section precludes the parties to a dispute from concluding an agreement to settle that dispute.

The Act thus clearly specifies that no discrimination may take place against any employee or any person seeking employment based on the grounds that such employee or person belongs to a union, participates in union activities, belongs to a union federation, participates in the activities of such union or union federation, or is an office bearer in such union or union federation.

AC practitioners should therefore ensure that their assessment practices do not discriminate against any employee who is a union member.

2.2.6 The Skills Development Act[11]

Sections 16 and 17 of the Act provide for the following:

16. Learnerships

A SETA (Sectoral Education and Training Authority) may establish a learnership if –

(a) the learnership consists of a structured learning component;

(b) the learnership includes practical work experience of a specified nature and duration;

(c) the learnership would lead to a qualification registered by the South African Qualifications Authority and related to an occupation; and

(d) the intended learnership is registered with the Director-General in the prescribed manner.

17. Learnership agreements

(1) For the purposes of this Chapter, a "learnership agreement" means an agreement entered into for a specific period between –

---

11 Basic Conditions of Employment Act. (Act No. 75 of 1997)

     (a) a learner;

     (b) an employer or a group of employers (in this section referred to as "the employer"); and

     (c) a training provider accredited by a body contemplated in section 5(1)(a)(ii)(bb) of the South African Qualifications Authority Act or group of such training providers.

  (2) The terms of the learnership agreement must oblige –

     (a) the employer to –

        (i)   employ the learner for the period specified in the agreement;

        (ii) provide the learner with the specified practical work experience; and

        (iii) release the learner to attend the education and training specified in the agreement;

     (b) the learner to –

        (i)   work for the employer;

        (ii) attend the specified education and training; and

     (c) the training provider to provide –

        (i)   the education and training specified in the agreement; and

        (ii) the learner support specified in the agreement.

The Act provides AC service providers with a potential opportunity to establish learnerships and learnership agreements with companies and management training candidates (learners) in terms of which the latter undergo a systematic management training programme. ACs can, in this instance, be used to systematically assess delegates' management potential as well as their management competency deficiencies. Structured management training programmes can then be provided to address these deficiencies. The potential of the Act in providing a source of trained management candidates has not yet been fully explored.

2.2.7   The Skills Development Levies Act[12]

This Act has specific relevance for the design teams of Development ACs. In terms of the Act, management training can be provided by a registered service provider (the Development AC practitioner) and service providers can be compensated for their training services rendered in terms of the Act. Given the fact that, currently, the number of suitably trained and experienced managers in certain management categories is inadequate, the facility provided by the Act is at present clearly not being fully utilised by AC service providers. ACs are probably the best-suited management training programmes to fulfil relevant training needs.

2.3   Ethical conduct demands in South Africa

The first of the foregoing subsections referred to South Africa's diverse context and the second to relevant South African legislation. These two aspects set the scene for a third aspect that AC practitioners have to consider, namely that of ethical conduct. The ACSG has developed a set of guidelines to promote the correct and ethical use of ACs. A number of ethical issues are addressed in these guidelines.

---

12   Skills Development Levies Act. (Act No. 9 of 1998)

Ethical conduct in an AC context has many dimensions and perspectives[13], with the particular perspective adopted depending on who is considering such conduct (e.g. the process owner, the participant or the employer). The most important dimension or perspective is that of the AC participant. Maldé[14], however, challenges AC practitioners to assert unequivocally that the AC participant is indeed always the most important dimension and that an after-care service is in fact provided for participants. Since the participant is the primary recipient of the assessment, this places him or her in the middle of the assessment process. The best question to ask from the point of view of ethical considerations is thus: "Will this (a specific action) serve the best interest of the AC participant?" The AC design team thus has to take a number of ethical considerations into account.

AC practitioners can, when conducting an AC, easily be seduced by their position of expertise and/or authority, thereby losing sight of the rights of the participants. Grieve[15] argues that professionals have to consider the rights of the participants as part of their professional accountability. These rights are indicated in Table 6.1.

Table 6.1: AC participants' rights and the manner of observance of such rights during an AC

Participants have the right to:	Manner of observance of right during an AC
Respect and dignity	Such non-negotiable right must be respected in all exercises.
Fairness	Assessments and the use of ratings must be unbiased.
Informed consent	There must be agreement to participate in the AC, and a clear understanding of its purpose, process and content. The participant also has the right to refuse to participate.
An explanation of test results and their use	The different report formats, and their use and method of safekeeping, must be clearly explained.
Confidentiality	There must be a guarantee that the assessment results will not be made available to others without the participant's express permission.
Restricted access to results	There must be clarity as to who will have access to AC report formats, and under what conditions.
The exercise of professional competence	Assessment practitioners (observers, administrators) must be well trained.
The exercise of professional accountability	There must be professionally qualified persons who can accept final responsibility for the safekeeping and use of assessment records.
Avoid being labelled	Category descriptions must not be negative or offensive.

---

13   SA Assessment Centre Study Group, 2018

14   Maldé, 2006

15   Grieve, 2005

Participants have the right to:	Manner of observance of right during an AC
Be respected if members of a linguistic minority	Language ability should not compromise assessment results.
Be respected if disabled in some or other way	Disability should not compromise assessment results. (People who are hearing- or speech-impaired will probably be adversely impacted.)

Source: Adapted from Grieve[16] and International Guidelines[17]

During the orientation of participants regarding the AC's nature, objectives and process prior to commencement of the AC, they should be clearly informed about their rights and privileges in respect of the assessment process, format and outcome. The ethical principle of informed consent is of crucial importance here.

AC results are normally disseminated to different target groups. Three ethical principles are at stake here, namely those of confidentiality, restricted access and professional accountability. The different observers write or consolidate their observations on their observer report forms and then consolidate their reports with their respective administrators. These observer report forms should not be distributed or shared further than the AC administrator, because they contain unedited or subjective information from the perspective of a single observer. Consequently, the observer report forms must be treated as restricted and confidential information. The commissioning organisation (direct manager) also has the right to access integrated AC reports and outcomes in the predetermined and agreed-upon format. However, the commissioning organisation (direct manager or Human Capital manager) does not have any access to any of the observation reports, nor is it allowed to solicit "unofficial" reports or personal tales from the grapevine, or from observers or role players.

2.3.1 A case of an ethical dilemma

Given South Africa's diversity context and legislative background, the following case illustrates some key transgressions of the aforesaid principles or guidelines:

Ingrid is the manager of a manufacturing company's marketing division. She is concerned about the available management competencies in her own division. After discussing this matter with Daniel, the company's HR manager, and assisted by an external consultant, Sipho, they decide to put all managers in the marketing division through a diagnostic AC. Ingrid decides to withdraw from the AC after being confronted with the fact that she might receive a lower competency rating than some of her managers. Jerry, a junior manager on the production side, and Daniel also participate in the AC.

In the week following the AC, Jerry is invited to Daniel's office to reflect, by way of an informal discussion, on the past week's AC events. Information is solicited from Jerry about some delegates' comments, about issues

---

16 Grieve, 2005

17 International Taskforce on Assessment Center Guidelines, 2015

relating to Ingrid's management style and about the fact that sentiments regarding Ingrid were generally negative. Daniel concurs that these comments were in fact made by the delegates. Sipho then wants to know exactly who said what.

After another week has passed, Jerry receives a phone call from a highly upset John, a marketing manager who participated in the AC. John has been directly confronted by Ingrid concerning the things he supposedly said about her and her management style. Ingrid also confessed that Sipho was her information source. John blames a disillusioned Jerry for being a telltale. John resigns shortly after this incident.

What ethical principles regarding ACs were violated in the above case?

The AC administrator normally generates two reports, one for the organisation (direct manager) and one for the participant. The participant report provides reasons for awarding the ratings on the assessment dimensions. This report is normally accompanied by a personal development plan designed to address the different development areas of the participant, and also contains suggested sources that can assist the participant in this respect. The participant receives personal feedback on the report. During the course of this feedback, the different competency ratings and how they were arrived at are explained.

Anderson and Goltsi[18] reported some negative psychological effects (NPEs) on candidates who are not selected. They therefore suggest that applied psychologists and Human Capital managers should be able to demonstrate that assessment methods do not have NPEs. Research (see Abraham Morrison & Burnett[19]) also indicates that participants who perform poorly in a Development AC are less likely to initiate a process allowing feedback than those who receive positive feedback.

The second report (which is similar to the participant report) is the company report, which is normally submitted to the direct manager. This report also reflects the participants' scores on the different, predefined assessment dimensions, as well as the reasons for awarding the ratings. The report is furthermore accompanied by a personal development plan for each participant. The company (direct manager) receives personal feedback on the participant's ratings and the reasons for awarding them. In the case where there is a suitably qualified Human Capital practitioner (e.g. a registered industrial psychologist), a third report may be submitted to the Human Capital division for record-keeping purposes. This practice is to be endorsed only if there is a professional person who can take personal, professional accountability for the safekeeping and use of these reports. Otherwise, the records should be kept by the AC practitioner.

The organisation has no access to other information relating to the AC. It would be considered unethical to divulge any other scores, ratings or reports, such as individual observer report forms, to the organisation. Distribution of such ratings or scores to the immediate supervisor, the Human Capital manager, or any other party in the organisation, is considered equally unacceptable. It is also deemed unacceptable where a report is submitted only to the participant, without any feedback being given to the organisation.

---

18   Anderson & Goltsi, 2006

19   Abraham et al., 2006

3. A COMPANY-SPECIFIC NEEDS ANALYSIS

This section of the needs analysis will focus more closely on company-specific aspects in order to customise the AC according to organisation-specific needs.

It should be quite apparent by this stage that, in designing an AC, different approaches can be employed with regard to the needs analysis. Among other things, a more generic design approach can be followed that is based on the assumption that there is little or no difference in management functions across different organisations. In the present chapter, however, we will be adopting the stance that organisations are unique and that these unique differences should be accommodated in the design of an AC for a specific company.

3.1 Sources of information for a needs analysis

In conducting a company-specific needs analysis, a number of different sources can be tapped into in order to generate useful information about management competency needs in the organisation. This information will enable the AC design team to include these unique features in the AC design. The following aspects are the most important and frequently encountered ones that come to mind when conducting a company-specific needs analysis.

3.1.1 National government policy priorities

The policy priorities of the national government create important parameters within which companies have to operate and with which they often have to comply. Good examples in this instance are the government's policy on equal employment. This means that companies either have to source the required skills outside the company or have to develop them within the company. Companies also have to periodically submit an employment equity audit to demonstrate their progress in this regard. In this case, the design and development of Development ACs may offer a feasible option for developing the relevant scarce skills and competencies, or, alternatively, the AC could assess how managers develop these skills and competencies in people from designated groups.

3.1.2 The company strategy

Companies function in different industries (e.g. in the information technology, mining or automotive industries) and, depending on the size and scope of their operations, also in different countries, regions or even continents. This, to a large extent, adds to the complexity level of a company's strategy, practices and policies, which, in turn, has a profound effect on the complexity levels of the different management competencies required. Some scholars in the field of stratified systems thinking and complexity (see Jacques[20]) therefore argue that the complexity levels of management competencies are hugely different for managers based in a local company operating in a single region or province when compared with managers in a multinational company with operations in different regions and continents.

---

20   Jacques, 1996

The company strategy is a good starting point for gaining an understanding of what exactly the company wants to achieve (for a more comprehensive discussion on company strategy and strategic planning, refer to Miles & Snow[21]). These strategic objectives can then be translated back into competency profiles on different management-leadership levels. Stated differently, it can be asked: "Which competencies are required on different management-leadership levels in order to achieve these strategic objectives?" The AC design team can determine what the current competency levels are and whether there is a competency deficiency or a performance gap in achieving the stated strategic objectives. These required competencies should then be included in the newly developed AC.

3.1.3 The company culture

Scholars of organisation theory (OT) (see Hatch[22] and Robbins)[23] and organisation behaviour (OB) (see Ivancevich & Matteson[24] and Robbins, Judge, Odendaal & Roodt[25]) acknowledge the fact that organisations have unique characteristics and processes, which are collectively referred to as organisational culture or organisational climate. Without going into too much detail on the differences between these concepts, one can conclude that "climate" refers to the general "look and feel" of a company (see Litwin & Stringer[26]). "Culture", on the other hand, refers to the invisible aspects (values, beliefs or assumptions) of a company, that is, the things below the surface (see Hellriegel, Slocum & Woodman[27]). The following questions relate to a company's culture: Who are the "heroes" and the "villains" in the company and what caused them to be given these labels? What are the tales and the myths about these people, and why are they told/mentioned? What are the company symbols and what is their unique meaning? What are the established traditions and taboos? The information gathered regarding these questions serves as a useful background against which the role plays and the case studies for use in a new AC can be designed.

3.1.4 Human Capital planning

A company's overall Human Capital plan (for a more comprehensive discussion on workforce planning, refer to Cascio & Aguinis[28] and Gerber, Nel & Van Dyk[29]) provides a useful source of information for the AC design team. This plan should reflect the supply of human resources, as well as future human resource demands. Or, stated differently, what are the current competency profiles in use and what competency profiles will be required in the short, medium and long term? The required competency profiles could then be included in the design of the AC so that such design will address future competency

21   Miles & Snow, 1984

22   Hatch, 1997

23   Robbins, 1990

24   Ivancevich & Mattteson, 2002

25   Robbins et al., 2016

26   Litwin & Stringer, 1968

27   Hellriegel et al., 1998

28   Cascio & Aguinis, 2019

29   Gerber et al., 1987

requirements. Needless to say, this exercise should be conducted for the different management-leadership levels at which the newly designed AC is aiming.

3.1.5   Succession planning

Closely related to the company's overall Human Capital plan and strategy is the company's succession plan (see Gerber, Nel & Van Dyk).[30] The succession plan looks at the available talent pool in the company and identifies possible successors for key positions in the company. If suitable successors are not available within the company, they will have to be found outside the company. Obviously, the required competency profiles for positions on different levels need to be drafted. The AC design team should take into consideration what these required competency profiles are and this should be reflected in the AC design.

3.1.6   Management information systems (MIS)

A carefully designed management information system (MIS) is a most useful source of information for tracking management performance deficiencies in organisations. Such a system has the potential to uncover a range of management performance deficiencies, such as those relating to strategic planning competencies, budgeting competencies, operationalising competencies, computer-application skills or even management control competencies. These management performance deficiencies should then be included in the newly designed AC in order to address future management competencies.

3.1.7   Performance management systems

Another useful source of information is the company's performance management system. If the performance evaluations of manager-leaders on different levels are more closely scrutinised, what are the emerging trends? What is the general pattern emerging regarding the lack of skills, competencies or knowledge on different management levels? The AC design team should collate information relating to managers' performance gaps or performance deficiencies in terms of knowledge, skills or competencies. This information then serves as a useful pointer in the design of new ACs for different management levels.

3.1.8   Critical incidents

Critical incidents in a business' history (often cited in business reports or sometimes even in the media) can also serve as a useful source of information on management's performance regarding the application of company policies and procedures. How many incidents were recorded where company policies and regulations were breached? How many incidents of unethical conduct by managers were recorded? How many incidents of unsafe behaviour or of accidents were recorded? The answers to these questions will provide pointers in relation to required management knowledge, skills or competencies. These aspects can then be included in the newly designed ACs in order to address the performance deficiencies.

---

30   Gerber et al., 1987

3.1.9 Image in the media

Closely related to the critical incidents mentioned above is the company's image in the media regarding a particular issue. Often, companies' names appear in the media concerning a particular issue such as safety, accidents, negligence, corruption or fraud. In each case, the names of a few companies or organisations will come to mind. This information can guide the AC design team in addressing these potential management skill deficiencies.

3.1.10 Job analysis

Job analyses allow one to gain a better understanding of what a person is supposed to be doing in his or her job. The outcomes of job analyses are job descriptions and job specifications. A job description provides a broad and systematic description of a task and of the people requirements in respect of a job (a group of positions), while a job specification provides a systematic account of what behaviours, aptitudes, skills and abilities the job requires of a person to perform that job effectively (see Cascio & Aguinis).[31] Job analyses also provide us with information about the current competencies of incumbents relative to what competencies will be required in future. The information yielded by means of job analyses serves as an important source of information in designing an AC. This process of job analysis is described more closely in Chapter 8.

Once the required needs analyses information has been generated by way of a systematic contextual needs analysis, a company needs analysis and a job analysis, the next step is to develop a sound business case or a project plan for the design and execution of the AC programme.

4. ANALYSIS FOR PREPARING AN AC BUSINESS CASE

The design and implementation of an AC programme should be viewed and treated as an organisation development (OD) intervention. The underlying foundational and guiding principles, as listed by Roodt and Van Tonder[32], warrant careful consideration and analysis in the AC design process. The most important OD foundational and guiding principles are, amongst others, that OD involves multiple stakeholders, that the OD process is managed according to project management principles and that OD is about empowering and developing participants. Within the AC context, these principles need to be clarified and the following questions answered: Who are the important stakeholders? What are the most important project management principles? How can the participants be optimally empowered and developed?

Before proceeding with the development of an AC intervention project plan, the following four aspects at least need to be carefully considered and debated within the AC design team, and should be made visible in the team's final project or business proposal.

---

31 Cascio & Aguinis, 2019

32 Roodt & Van Tonder, 2008

4.1   Critical assumptions and constraints

Critical assumptions on which the AC intervention is based should be articulated clearly and made visible. This process will stimulate an open debate and/or discourse in the company regarding the relevant issues and will provide the much-needed basis for acceptance and final approval. Assumptions that are typically discussed are the following: what the exact focus of the AC programme should be; whether there is a management competency deficiency; what the exact management competency discrepancies are; and whether the AC intervention is best suited for addressing the identified management competency discrepancies.

The critical constraints that need to be discussed and considered are aspects such as the available time horizon for developing the competencies, the available budget, the number of candidates to be assessed or developed, and the availability of assessors and administrators to conduct the AC programme.

4.2   Analysis of available options

This aspect addresses the issue of plausible alternatives to an AC programme. If the purposes or objectives of the AC programme are clearly defined, then what other alternatives are available that would yield similar results? Thornton, Rupp and Hoffman[33] have identified a number of alternative assessment methods, such as individual and multi-source performance feedback, cognitive ability tests and personality tests, and behavioural interviews and/or situational interviews. However, each one of these alternatives has its own particular limitations. The limitations of these alternative assessments, as compared with the AC method, are presented in Table 6.2.

Table 6.2: A comparison of alternative assessment methods with ACs

Alternative assessment techniques	AC method
Single and multisource (360°) assessments: • A subjective judgement is made. • Assessment is conducted by one person. • One person is assessed at a time. • Raters have little or no training. • Feedback is only in written format. • Multiple raters are used, e.g. supervisors, peers, subordinates, customers.	• Subjective observations are collated into the final rating. • Standardised procedures are used for collating ratings. • Multiple observers/assessors are used. • Multiple participants are observed at the same time. • Trained assessors are used. • Feedback is both oral and written. • Consistency of rating procedures.

---

33   Thornton et al., 2015

Alternative assessment techniques	AC method
Assessment interviews: • Can easily be faked. • Self-reflection and reporting on past behaviour. • Difficult to verify correctness of responses.	• Observation of current behaviour. • Difficult to fake. • Difficult to anticipate correct behaviour.
Situational tests or video-based simulations: • Can produce high-fidelity simulations. • Highly consistent, with no variation in presentations. • May elicit restricted range of behaviours.	• Can also involve situational tests or vignettes. • Multiple measurements. • Elicits behaviours across different settings. • Provides different simulations of the work situation. • Uses different assessment techniques across exercises.
Psychometric tests – personality questionnaires and cognitive ability tests: • Abstract problems are assigned. • Abilities are inferred from item responses. • May be biased and show adverse impact. • Self-description. • Easy to fake. • Measures stable traits. • Low face validity.	• Concrete, work-related problems are presented. • Visible behaviour is observed. • Little or no bias. • High face validity and fairness. • Hard to fake. • Behaviour description by assessors. • Can measure stable traits and competency deficiencies. • Good face validity and high procedural fairness

Source: Adapted from Thornton, Rupp & Hoffman[34]

If the AC is designed for specific diagnostic purposes, then what other techniques would yield similar information on the management competency deficiencies? A training needs analysis may yield similar results, but how long will it take? What will the costs be? And will it yield comparable (equally valid) information for the different management-leadership levels? Will psychometric tests yield comparable information?

4.3 Cost-benefit analysis

Once the alternatives have been identified, a proper cost-benefit analysis (also called a utility analysis) needs to be conducted in respect of each of the alternatives in order to determine which alternative will be the most cost-effective. Cascio[35] defined the utility of a selection device as "the degree to which its use improves the quality of the individuals selected beyond what would have occurred had that device not been used". Cascio[36] provides a simple equation for testing the utility value of a measure:

---

34 Thornton et al., 2015

35 Cascio, 1982: 221

36 Cascio, 1989: 211

Formula 3.1

$$\Delta U = n\, t\, r_{xy}\, SD_y\, Z$$
Where:

ΔU	=	increase in productivity as a monetary value
n	=	number of persons hired
t	=	average job tenure in years of those hired
r_{xy}	=	the validity coefficient representing the correlation between the predictor and job performance in the applicant population
SD_y	=	the standard deviation of job performance as a monetary value (roughly 40% of the annual wage)
Z	=	the average predictor score of those selected in the applicant population, expressed in terms of standard scores

Thornton and Rupp[37] made slight adjustments to the above equation and proposed the following equation for comparing other assessments with the AC method:

Formula 3.2

$$U = t\, N_s\, (r_1 - r_2)\, SD_y\, L\, /\, SR - N_s\, (c_1 - c_2)\, /\, SR$$
Where:

U	=	utility of the new measure
t	=	average tenure of the selected people
N_s	=	number of people selected
r_1	=	validity of the alternative procedure
r_2	=	validity of the AC procedure
SD_y	=	unrestricted standard deviation in performance in monetary value terms
L	=	ordinate of the normal curve at the selection ratio
SR	=	selection ratio (ratio of people hired to the number of applicants)
c_1	=	cost of the alternative method
c_2	=	cost of the AC method

For the less mathematically minded, an alternative method of comparison would be to create a detailed balance sheet for each of the alternatives by listing the direct (tangible) and the indirect (intangible) costs and benefits. This information will enable the design team to provide the commissioning organisation with a clear picture of all the available alternatives so that such organisation will be able to make an informed decision.

4.4 Considerations in respect of the implementation strategy

The implementation strategy itself entails a number of different considerations that should be covered in a systematic manner in the presentation of the project proposal. The most important aspects to be listed, and which need careful consideration and clarification, are the following.

---

37   Thornton & Rupp, 2006: 259

4.4.1 AC policy statement

The AC policy statement serves as the framework for planning and scoping the AC project. First of all, it defines the nature of the AC – whether it is an AC or a DAC – and which functions and levels are being targeted. Secondly, it specifies who the key role players are and defines and delineates their respective roles and responsibilities. Thirdly, it specifies the criteria for the selection and/or nomination of participants in the AC process. Finally, it sets the deadlines by which the deliverables of the project should be executed (see Chapter 5 for a list of topics to be covered in an AC policy).

4.4.2 Constitution of the AC design team

A specific group of role players constitutes the AC design team, which is responsible for the initial analysis and design of the AC. The project plan should make specific reference to the roles and responsibilities of these role players in the AC design and development process.

4.4.3 Project sponsor

Who in top management will be finally accountable for the project from a management perspective? This person is normally a member of the top management team and will have the final say in terms of the project scope, the project leadership and the project budget. The AC design team needs to develop a close relationship with this person in order to facilitate the project development and proposal stage of the AC programme.

4.4.4 Project ambassadors

The project ambassadors are those persons in key management positions in the organisation who have gone through an AC programme themselves and who can make informed decisions about the value and contribution of the AC process. These ambassadors can make a valuable contribution to the initial organisational debates and discourses that are conducted to test critical assumptions and constraints in respect of the AC project. Needless to say, they play a key role in establishing the right climate for an AC solution.

4.4.5 Project leader

The project leader and his or her project team will be appointed by the project sponsor. The project leader will be finally responsible for the development and execution of the project plan.

4.4.6 Project steering committee

The project leader is assisted by a project team or a project steering committee. Each member of the steering committee takes responsibility for a different aspect of the development and execution of the project plan, such as the budget, the physical facilities needed, internal communication in the organisation, the selection of participants, and so forth.

4.4.7   Resource plan and approval

The project team is responsible for developing a resource plan that will cover the total scope of the project in terms of budget needs, human capital needs, physical facilities (studios and offices), video- and audio-recording facilities, computer facilities, availability of suitably trained assessors and administrators, and suitable participants or candidates. The entire project plan needs to be submitted to, and signed off by, the project sponsor.

4.4.8   Union approval

The project team needs to involve the relevant unions right from the onset. Union representatives need to be involved in the overall AC process and must be informed about such process, as well as about the different practices and procedures within that process. Union representatives can eventually become some of the best ambassadors for the implementation of an AC programme.

4.4.9   Agreement on the project scope and time frame

Once the project plan, the project scope (number of participants to be assessed) and the time frame have been developed, these need to be approved and signed off by the project sponsor.

4.4.10 Final approval from the top

Final approval for the project needs to be obtained from top management, which needs to have a clear picture of the project scope, the dedicated human resources and the budget, that is, of the resources it will be committing to this project.

4.4.11 Project communication plan

The project communication plan is the final and critical step in the operationalisation of the AC project. In this plan, the initial introduction of the AC project to the organisation should be systematically covered and the further implementation of the AC project should be systematically explained and unpacked. In the final instance, all organisational members should have clarity regarding the objectives of the project, who the key role players are, and what everyone's involvement and responsibilities will be.

Before final implementation of the project plan, the AC design team must ensure that the most conducive context and climate for the implementation of the AC are created.

5.   CREATING THE APPROPRIATE CLIMATE AND CONTEXT

The following can contribute to the creation of a positive climate and context for conducting ACs.

5.1 Participants

Participants should be informed about the AC purpose, process and outcome. It is a generally known fact that unfamiliarity breeds anxiety and fear, however if participants are informed about the purpose, process and outcome of the programme, this will largely diminish the levels of anxiety and fear about the programme.

The degree of "openness" in selecting and appointing participants for the AC programme will also contribute to creating a conducive climate and context. The criteria for selection should be stated publicly so that there is no uncertainty about how and why people have been nominated or selected to participate.

5.2 Project sponsors and ambassadors

The involvement of key persons such as project sponsors and project ambassadors in the assessment process can, as was explained earlier, make a huge difference in an organisation. Their involvement in promoting the AC concept in the organisation can be helpful in creating a positive climate or setting for establishing the AC programme.

5.3 Corporate climate and culture

The creation of a positive culture and climate regarding assessment and evaluation in general in the organisation can contribute to favourable attitudes to, and a general acceptance of, AC programmes in such organisation. For this climate and culture to be positive, they should be consciously managed by all managers in the organisation. As role models, managers, together with project ambassadors, can play an important role in setting the tone and climate in organisations.

6. CRITICAL DECISIONS RELATING TO, AND OUTCOMES OF, THIS STEP

The following critical outcomes are achieved, and the following decisions need consideration, during this step.

6.1 Analysis of the broad business context

The first outcome is a thorough analysis of the broad business context in which South African organisations are functioning. Three important facets of this context were specifically analysed, namely the population diversity context and the legislative context, both of which have a profound impact on the creation of the ethical context. It was argued that the population diversity context sets the scene for a specific legislative context that has to be equitable and fair to all people in the country. These diversity and legislative imperatives, in turn, dictate the ethical considerations that will govern the behaviour of assessment practitioners and specialists. It is therefore advisable that AC practitioners take careful stock of their own assessment practices in order to ensure that such practices are reliable and valid. Data on the validity, reliability and non-discriminatory nature of the assessment should be kept for evidentiary purposes. AC practitioners should also have a thorough knowledge of the relevant legislation that governs the work context, and specifically assessment practices. The overall AC procedure needs to be implemented in such a manner that it is considered equitable and fair by all participants. Adhering to a strict set of ethical rules and guidelines will be helpful in this regard. All these considerations (the "rules that govern the game") need to be kept in mind by the AC design team.

6.2   A company-specific needs analysis

The second outcome of this step is a company-specific needs analysis. A range of different information sources can be used that will provide useful information on the competency deficiencies of managers. These sources will also provide useful information about the climate and culture of a specific company. This latter information is important when the exercises are designed, for it is helpful in creating a real and authentic context. A systematic analysis of all the different sources (including a job analysis) will enable the design team to determine on which level the management-leadership competency deficiencies are, what the exact nature of these competencies are or what competencies are required in future, and what behavioural elements they each consist of on the different management-leadership levels. Overall, the design team should know exactly what the company needs are. Only then can an AC be designed that targets the specified management competencies.

6.3   Creating an appropriate climate or context

Besides the AC practitioners, line managers, the project sponsor and the project ambassadors have perhaps the most important impact on the creation of a conducive climate in organisations. The process relating to how candidates are selected for, and introduced to, the AC programme also plays a major role in how the programme is received, perceived and evaluated. Conscious decisions should therefore be taken as to who the AC champions are and as to how the programme should be introduced in the company. A clearly communicated process should also exist regarding how participants are selected for, and are introduced to, the programme. A situation where the perception exists that there are no clear criteria, or that managers have favourites, should be avoided at all costs.

6.4   Building a business case and project plan

The last outcome in the analysis step is to carefully build a business case and project plan before commencing with implementation. The design team needs to critically consider some key assumptions and constraints, as well as take different, available alternatives into consideration. Are other available options perhaps less time-consuming and less expensive? Will the AC solution address the specified company needs in the best way, compared with other alternative methods? In this instance, a utility analysis can be conducted to compare the different alternatives with an AC programme in order to provide valid information for making these decisions. Where management-leadership development is at stake, the golden rule is: "There are no quick fixes and cheap solutions." The reason is that arrogance, quick fixes and cheap solutions only get you deeper into trouble, more quickly! The more serious side of this is the situation where a lack of knowledge, or even ignorance (or arrogance), prevents you from realising that you are in trouble.

CHAPTER 7

ORGANISATIONAL EFFECTIVENESS ANALYSIS

Gert Roodt

1. INTRODUCTION – THE PURPOSE OF AN ORGANISATIONAL EFFECTIVENESS ANALYSIS

Against the background of the general and the contextual needs analyses discussed in the previous chapter, this chapter deals with an organisational effectiveness analysis as the second step in the analysis stage of our design model. The second step of the analysis stage is depicted in Figure 7.1.

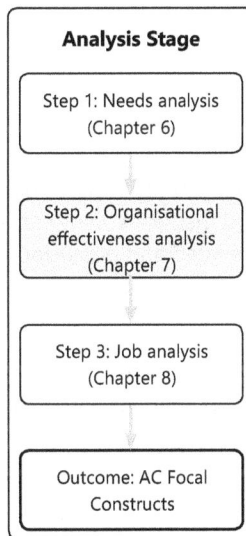

Analysis Stage

Step 1: Needs analysis
(Chapter 6)

Step 2: Organisational
effectiveness analysis
(Chapter 7)

Step 3: Job analysis
(Chapter 8)

Outcome: AC Focal
Constructs

Figure 7.1: The organisational effective analysis step in the analysis stage

The first section of this chapter will focus on organisational effectiveness *per se*, and on the different approaches that are most frequently used in organisations to assess or measure effectiveness. Against the background of a myriad different models and approaches to organisational effectiveness, we will (in the first section of the chapter) consider the effectiveness criteria, the goal, the multiple-constituency model and the balanced-scorecard model. Implications for the design of ACs will be emphasised when dealing with each of the models.

Since a lot of ACs are aimed at management-leadership, the second section of the chapter will focus more closely on what exactly management is, on the different management levels, on the different management functions on the different levels, as well as on the deliverables of these different tiers.

In the third section, we will present and discuss a "generic" management competency model and framework across different management levels. Special attention will be given to generic competencies as well as to specific elements within each of these competencies.

Against the complex background of the different models and approaches in respect of effectiveness, and against the background of the different management levels, we will, in the fourth section of the chapter, take a closer look at the establishment of effectiveness criteria. Topics that will be addressed in this section are, first, the difficulties in selecting valid criteria for assessing AC outcomes, and, secondly, the considerations one should keep in mind when selecting a criterion. The third part of the section will then focus on the development of valid criteria.

Introductory case study: 'Stepping up' to the AC challenge

Frank is one of manufacturing firm A's crack, newly introduced first level supervisors. Frank has succeeded Benjamin, who was promoted to a middle management position. Despite Frank's lack of experience, he is performing exceptionally well – he achieves or even exceeds all set production targets, he has very low turnover in his team, and his team members like him and are fairly satisfied with their work setting and arrangements.

The division manager, Linda, for whom Frank is working, decides to send him (Frank) on the newly introduced AC for middle level managers. Although Linda has not experienced an AC for middle managers herself, she feels that this is the next career development challenge for the 'new star' Frank. The AC was developed according to generic management competencies.

After the AC, the evaluation reports were submitted to Linda and Frank, but the results did not exactly reflect what they were expecting. Assessments on most dimensions were indicated in the category 'needs development'. Both Linda and Frank were extremely disappointed and disillusioned with the reports, as well as with the idea of introducing ACs to the organisation.

What is described above happens frequently in South African organisations. Talented people are often nominated for attending ACs, yet their experience of ACs is negative and they feel disillusioned when receiving feedback. How could this have been dealt with differently, resulting in more positive outcomes for the organisation and for Frank?

This chapter will tell you more about ACs and how and for what purpose they are constituted.

2. DIFFERENT VIEWS ON ORGANISATIONAL EFFECTIVENESS

Organisational effectiveness is frequently loosely defined as a situation "when organisations achieve their objectives". A more cautious approach is a multivariate definition in which organisational effectiveness is defined "as an organisation's capacity to acquire and utilize its scarce and valued resources as expeditiously as possible in the pursuit of its operative and operational goals".[1] From this perspective, organisational effectiveness includes multiple variables or dimensions of effectiveness.

---

1   Zey-Ferrell, 1979: 328

2.1 The effectiveness criteria model

Steers[2] listed a number of effectiveness criteria that are often cited in organisational effectiveness models and also indicated the frequency of their use in such models. These criteria and their frequencies are listed in Table 7.1.

Table 7.1: Effectiveness criteria and their respective frequency of use in 17 organisational effectiveness models

Effectiveness criteria	Frequency of use
Adaptability-flexibility	10
Productivity	6
Satisfaction	5
Profitability	3
Resource acquisition	3
Absence of strain	2
Control over environment	2
Development	2
Efficiency	2
Employee retention	2
Growth	2
Integration	2
Open communications	2
Survival	2
Other criteria	1

Source: Adapted from Steers[3]

Although all these listed criteria are highly relevant, the problem is that most organisations cannot keep an eye on all these performance measures at the same time. Multiple criteria possess the potential to open up a futile debate on which criteria are more important than others. The emphasis should rather be on whether these criteria are appropriate for measuring the organisation's specific goal achievement in a specific context.

The goal model is therefore introduced and discussed in the next section.

2.2 The goal model

Ivancevich and Matteson[4] presented a model that focuses on different organisational objectives at different time intervals. The model thus focuses on different goals or objectives in the short, medium and long term that specify a number of measurement criteria for these different time intervals. The

---

2   Steers, 1975

3   Steers, 1975

4   Ivancevich & Matteson, 2002: 28

model also illustrates the principle that criteria or goals can be grouped or categorised – an organising principle that becomes useful later on in this chapter.

Short-term goals	Medium-term goals	Long-term goals
Quality	Quality	Quality
Productivity	Adaptability	Survival
Efficiency	Development	
Satisfaction		

Figure 7.2: Organisational goals at different time intervals
Source: Adapted from Ivancevich & Matteson[5]

Managers should have the skills to formulate goals that are appropriate to their respective management levels, and should also be able to develop criteria for measuring the achievement of these goals. From a design perspective, ACs should be designed in such a way that they are able to measure whether or not these management skills are present.

The multiple-constituency model is discussed in the next section.

2.3   The multiple-constituency model

The multiple-constituency model is based on the assumption that the organisation serves multiple constituencies, such as shareholders, managers, employees, unions, suppliers, consumers and the immediate community in which it functions. All these stakeholders pursue different objectives that, in most instances, may contradict the objectives of the organisation. The challenge for the organisation (especially management) is therefore to "juggle" the interests of the different stakeholders so that the organisation serves the interests of all its stakeholders. According to this model, an organisation can define its goals and specify such goals' respective measurement criteria in terms of these different stakeholders. Table 7.2 provides an illustrative example.

Table 7.2: Key stakeholders and their objectives, and the measurement criteria in respect of such objectives

Key stakeholders	Objectives	Measurement criteria
Shareholders	Maximising ROI Growth	ROI % growth
Managers	Organisational effectiveness Efficiency	% growth in share value Ratios
Employees	Satisfaction Safety	Survey outcome Accident reports
Unions	Conflict Accidents	Conflict incidents % decline
Suppliers	Sustainable partnerships	Profitability of partnership

---

5   Ivancevich & Matteson, 2002: 28

Key stakeholders	Objectives	Measurement criteria
Consumers	Quality Affordability	% complaints Growth in market share
Community	Stability Sustainability	Number of community incidents, amount of noise, number of spills, amount of pollution, etc

The relevance of this model for the AC design team is that managers should have the skills to identify objectives, develop concomitant measurement criteria and be able to manage the interests of different and often competing stakeholders within the same organisation.

2.4 The balanced-scorecard model[6]

The setting of only business objectives eventually results in a skewed picture. To counter this, Kaplan and Norton propose a four-dimensional approach that includes a financial perspective, a customer perspective, an internal business process perspective, and an innovation and learning perspective integrated by the strategic focus of the company. Objectives and measures are then formulated for each of the dimensions.

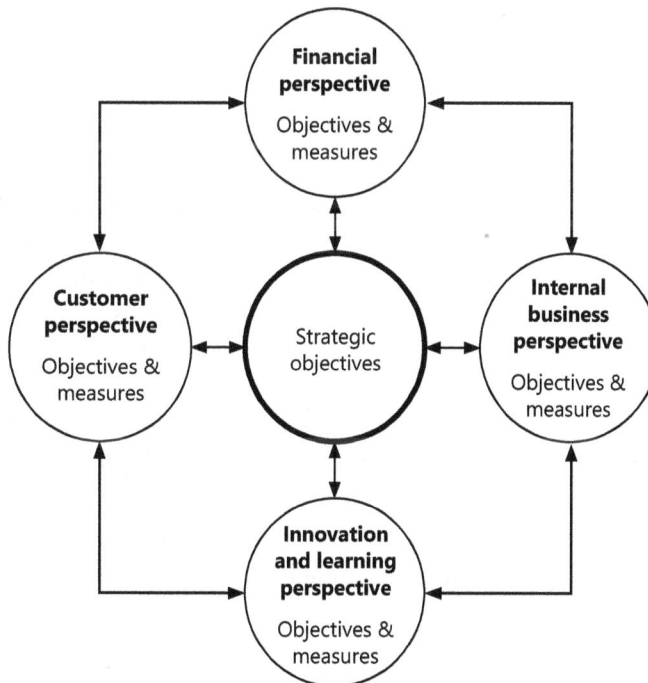

Figure 7.3: The strategic alignment of balanced-scorecard measures with strategic objectives
Source: Adapted from Kaplan & Norton[7]

---

6   Kaplan & Norton, 1992

7   Kaplan & Norton, 1992

From the point of view of an AC design perspective, managers should have the ability to translate strategic objectives into business or operational level objectives for each of these four dimensions, and they should also be able to develop measures to track the degree of goal attainment regarding these respective objectives. This should be possible on all three management levels.

A further complicating factor is that goals and objectives exist on different management levels of the organisation. The next section of the chapter therefore first examines the concept of management and then considers these different management levels.

3.   MANAGEMENT DEFINED

The logical starting point in management-leadership training and development is to define exactly what management is. A clear conceptualisation of what management is will then enable the management trainers and developers to equip participants with the required skills, knowledge and attitudes. This principle also holds for ACs. A seemingly straightforward definition of management therefore appears to be that "the nature of management is conceptualized in terms of what it is thought that managers need to know".[8] Yet this definition directs us only to the question: What is it that managers ought to know?

Townley[9], however, was of the opinion that "definitions of management, unfortunately, suffer from conceptual obscurity", while Reed[10] argued that there is a "need for a substantial reconsideration of the conceptual equipment through which we approach the theoretical, methodological, empirical and evaluative issues which crystallize in the general theme of 'management'".

In a similar vein, the writers of a number of articles have questioned the approaches taken in the study of management.[11] Willmott[12] pointed out that, in view of the central importance of management, it could have been expected of academics to take a serious interest in its study, which has not happened. Astley[13], meanwhile, argued that there is a clear lack of awareness as to what constitutes the field's (managerial science's) core knowledge. Stewart[14] emphasised that management is rarely precisely defined, because the terms "managerial work", "managerial jobs" and "managerial behaviours" are often used interchangeably. The author also noted that management is all too often portrayed as a static entity and universally similar activity that is prone to the development of lists.

There is an ever-present danger that 'management' may lose its status as a theoretical concept in favour of a view that it should be treated as a natural entity.[15] What this means is that the traditional

---

8   Stewart, 1984: 324

9   Townley, 1993: 222

10   Reed, 1984: 279

11   Townley, 1993: 222

12   Willmott, 1984

13   Astley, 1984

14   Stewart, 1989

15   Townley, 1993: 222

categories of management (planning, organising, leading and control) (compare Carroll & Gillen)[16] are often unquestionably accepted as if they were natural entities. In view of this, Reed[17] asked for a fundamental re-evaluation of the management concept so that management can be fully understood on theoretical, methodological and empirical grounds. Townley[18] concurred by stating that "conceptual clarity is important because it forces the recognition that 'management' has the status of a conceptual object, an abstraction".

Koontz[19] identified no less than six different schools of management theory. In doing so, he demonstrated that management can be studied as an abstract concept from different vantage points (based on sound theoretical, methodological and empirical grounds), while also highlighting some of the most important features of management studies. According to the schools identified by Koontz[20]:

- Management can be viewed as a goal-directed process consisting of different functions and of different activities within such functions. Management can therefore be simultaneously viewed as an activity and as a process (**Process School**).
- Management is empirically derived from the best practices of successful managers, that is, from what they do and how they do it (**Empirical School**).
- Management involves getting things done with, and through, other people, and therefore relies on the interpersonal relations and behaviours of managers (**Human Behaviour School**).
- Management is strongly based on the conception of organisations as socially constructed, context-specific realities or organisms consisting of power coalitions, social systems (such as formal and informal groups, in-groups and out-groups), as well as related culture concepts (**Social System School**).
- Management is viewed as a rational decision making process, thereby emphasising the predictability of outcomes. From this perspective, several rational decision making or budgeting processes and aids are studied (**Decision Theory School**).
- Management is viewed as a system of mathematical models or processes. This is an approach rather than a school of thought, and these mathematical models rather serve as management aids (**Mathematical School**).

What emerges from these different management theory schools is, according to Roodt[21], the following:

- First, management takes place in a **social context**[22] with and through people, but also in a socially constructed reality, referred to as "organisations".
- Secondly, management is, at the same time, an **activity and a process**.[23] The process view of management has emerged as a counter reaction to the obvious limitations of the structural view of management.

---

16 Carrol & Gillen, 1996
17 Reed, 1984: 279
18 Townley, 1993: 222
19 Koontz, 1996
20 Koontz, 1996
21 Roodt, 1999
22 Reed, 1984: 279
23 Reed, 1984: 279

- Thirdly, the **political** dimension[24] of management is emphasised by indicating the similarities with power-related concepts such as authority, leadership, influence and decision making. Power coalitions do exist within organisations that systematically study power sources, their leverage potential and the required political skills to reach desired conclusions.[25]
- Fourthly, management has a **unique** dimension that is determined by the distinct role players in a specific situation and by the unique situation or context. This perspective emphasises the contextual aspect of management, which is often overlooked by proponents of the Universal Management School.

Based on the above, management can be studied either from a generic (universal) process perspective or from the perspective of a context-specific set of activities, but it can also be conceptualised as a science and as a discipline that is an integrated, multi-dimensional field of study involving different disciplines in its explanation and prediction. This definition, inferred from Roodt,[26] suggests that management exists on different levels of abstraction and can therefore be studied (explained) in either specific or generic terms from different disciplinary perspectives.

3.1 Different management levels and management functions

Most management scholars are in agreement that organisations have at least three management levels, namely top, middle and lower management levels. The subsections that follow will focus more closely on these three levels and their functions.

3.1.1 Top (strategic) management

Managers on this level are often referred to as top, senior or strategic management. Top managers on the strategic management level are primarily involved in the process of deciding on the mission and objectives of the organisation, on the resources to be used in attaining these objectives, and on the strategic guidelines and policies that will guide and govern the management and the planning process.[27] This management level is thus primarily involved in an organisation's strategic planning process.

3.1.2 Middle (tactical) management

Managers on this level are often referred to as middle, line, tactical or business managers. Middle managers are primarily responsible for the development of business plans that will ensure the procurement of resources, and for the development of plans that relate to the effective utilisation of these resources in the execution of business objectives in the different functional areas of the organisation.[28] This management level is thus primarily involved in the organisation's business planning and control process.

---

24 Townley, 1993: 222

25 Reed, 1984: 279

26 Roodt, 1999

27 Schutte, 1991

28 Schutte, 1991

3.1.3   Lower (operational/technical) management

Managers on the lower level of organisations are often referred to as operational, technical, lower or supervisory managers. Lower level managers on the operational level are primarily responsible for the:

- execution of specific tasks;
- specification of efficiency standards;
- measurement of performance;
- identification of variances from these efficiency standards; and
- initiation of corrective actions.[29]

Managers on this level are thus more concerned with operational execution and control.

3.2   Key functions and deliverables of each management level

If managers on different management levels have different management responsibilities, then what are they mainly responsible for? Table 7.3 addresses this question.

Table 7.3: Management tasks and functions on different management levels

Management level	Tasks and functions
Strategic planning Top and senior management levels	• Deciding on the company's vision and mission. • Specifying the company's objectives. • Reframing any changes in these objectives. • Allocating resources to support the execution of business objectives. • Determining guidelines and policies to govern the execution of business objectives.
Management planning and control Middle management level	• Developing plans for the acquisition and distribution of resources. • Developing plans for the effective utilisation of resources within different functional areas. • Determining policies and procedures regarding the utilisation of resources.
Operational control Operations management and supervisory levels	• Clearly delineating the tasks to be performed. • Establishing clear performance procedures. • Establishing clear performance standards. • Measuring actual performance. • Identifying variances in performance standards. • Initiating corrective actions.

Source: Adapted from Schutte[30]

It should be noted that the task of top management is focused primarily on strategic planning, while middle management is involved in business planning and control, and lower management with

---

29 Schutte, 1991: 6

30 Schutte, 1991

operational execution and control. It is clear that all these management functions have to be planned, organised and executed, and that some control measures have to be implemented on all levels to ensure that the plans are indeed executed. The key deliverables for each of the management functions are presented in Table 7.4.

Table 7.4: Key deliverables on each management level

Management level	Key deliverables
Top management	• A strategic plan • A vision and mission • Clearly formulated strategic objectives • A resource allocation strategy • Policies and guidelines on business planning • Policies and guidelines on business governance
Middle management	• An overall business execution plan • A business execution plan as per function • A resource acquisition plan as per function • A resource utilisation plan as per function • Policies and procedures on operational execution and control
Lower management	• An operations execution plan • A task execution plan • Task specifications and procedures • Specification of standards • Performance measurements • Policy on deviance from standards • Policy on corrective actions

Source: Adapted from Schutte[31]

In order to achieve these key deliverables, managers should be able to deal with the management information for the different levels as indicated in Table 7.5. It should be clear that the ability to handle the different types of information effectively requires different competencies on these different managerial levels.

Table 7.5: Types and quality of information at different management levels

Management level		Information characteristics	
	Complexity	Source of information	Degree of structure
Strategic planning Top and senior management levels	Highly complex; innovative and analytical; long time horizon	Different sources; mostly external – from political, economic and financial sources	Highly unstructured

---

31 Schutte, 1991

Management level	Information characteristics		
	Complexity	Source of information	Degree of structure
Business planning and control Middle management level	Medium complexity; creative and judgemental; medium time horizon	Mostly internal – from MIS and hierarchy (up and down); integrated	Fair degree of structure
Operational execution and control Operations management and supervisory levels	Low complexity – execution of policies; follow rules; high complexity – execution of technical tasks; creative and innovative; short time horizon	From internal sources – project management information system; MIS; from external sources – customers	Internal – structured; external – unstructured

Source: Roodt[32]

Against the background of Table 7.5, the information processing skills necessary to perform a management task effectively require specific competencies. The required competencies are further complicated by the fact that some companies operate in different geographical regions, or even across national boundaries or on different continents. Figure 7.4 provides an integrated picture of the competencies on different management levels.

Table 7.6 provides a more precise overview of the specialised technical/functional competencies, as well as the required people skills, at the different management levels. The table also provides the background to the formulation of specific "generic" managerial competencies at the different management levels.

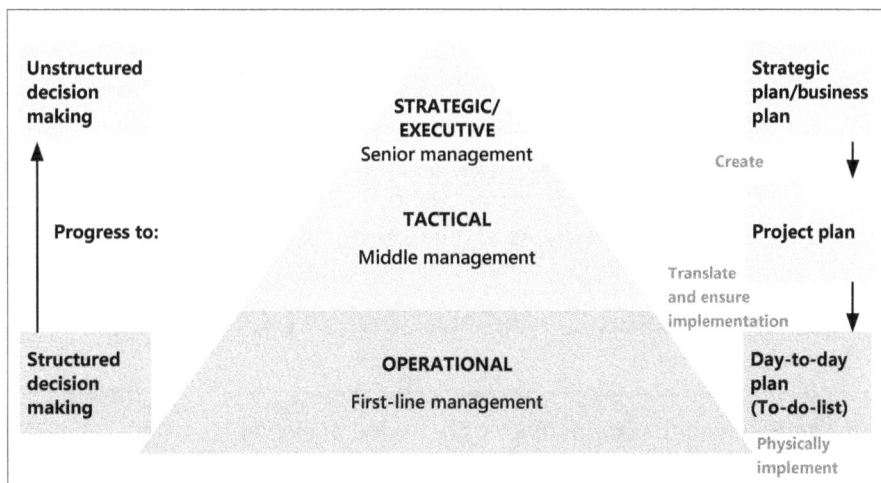

Figure 7.4: An integrated model of management functions on different levels
Source: Obtained from, and used with the permission of, LEMASA

---

32 Roodt, 2006

Table 7.6: Technical/functional and generic people skills for different management levels

Management level	Required technical/functional competencies	Generic people skills
Strategic planning Top and senior management levels	• Strategic planning and execution skills • Systems thinking skills • Ability to deal with different, complex issues in an integrated manner • Governance	• Leadership skills • Communication skills • Problem-solving/decision making skills • Conflict/negotiation skills
Management planning and control Middle management level	• Business planning and execution skills • Organising skills • Budgeting and financial management skills • Management control	• Leadership skills • Communication skills • Problem-solving/decision making skills • Conflict/negotiation skills
Operational execution and control Operations management and supervisory levels	• Task planning and execution skills • Project management skills • Setting performance standards • Measuring performance • Performance management	• Leadership skills • Communication skills • Problem-solving/decision making skills • Conflict/negotiation skills

Because different competency levels are required to perform the different management functions on these respective levels, different ACs have been developed to take these competency differences into account.

3.3 ACs are designed for different management levels

Is there a single AC for assessing competencies on all management levels? This is a question that has puzzled AC design teams for a long time. Experienced AC design teams soon realised that a one-size-fits-all approach for all management levels is an unrealistic ideal, so it was decided to differentiate the ACs according to different management levels, resulting in a top management, a middle management and a lower management AC. The required competencies were then specified for each of the different management levels, based on careful analyses of the relevant jobs on these levels.

4. EXAMPLES OF "GENERIC" MANAGEMENT COMPETENCY PROFILES

The following two sections respectively describe generic competency sets and their definitions, as well as the process for determining the competency or behavioural elements.

4.1 Generic management competencies

It is fairly generally accepted that the generic competencies indicated in Table 7.7 are required to competently perform management functions on the top and middle management levels.

Table 7.7: Generic management competencies required of top and middle managers

Competency factors or competency sets	Competency dimensions
Leading and deciding	Deciding on and initiating action Providing leadership and supervision
Supporting and cooperating	Teamwork and support Serving customers and clients
Interacting and presenting	Relating and networking Persuading and influencing Communicating and presenting
Analysing and interpreting	Writing and reporting Applying expertise and technology Problem solving
Creating and conceptualising	Learning and researching Creating and innovating Forming strategies and concepts
Organising and executing	Planning and organising Delivering quality Complying and persevering
Adapting and coping	Adapting and responding to change Coping with pressures and setbacks
Enterprising and performing	Achieving results and developing career Enterprising and commercial thinking

Source: © SHL Group[33] (Reproduced with permission) (see also Robertson, Callinan & Bartram[34])

The competency factors or sets in Table 7.7 are fairly generally applied in the competency assessments of middle and top management levels. In Table 7.8, the definitions of the eight competency sets and their respective competency dimensions are provided.

Table 7.8: Definitions of generic competency sets and competency dimensions

COMPETENCY SET AND DIMENSIONS	DEFINITIONS
FACTOR 1: LEADING AND DECIDING	**Takes control and exercises leadership. Initiates action, gives direction and takes responsibility.**
1.1 Deciding on and initiating action	Making effective decisions (even in difficult circumstances), taking responsibility and showing initiative.
1.2 Leading and supervising	Providing others with clear direction, establishing standards of behaviour for others, and motivating and empowering individuals.

---

33 SHL, 2004

34 Robertson et al., 2002

COMPETENCY SET AND DIMENSIONS	DEFINITIONS
FACTOR 2: SUPPORTING AND COOPERATING	**Supports others and shows respect and positive regard for them in social situations. Puts people first, working effectively with individuals and teams, clients and staff. Behaves consistently, with clear personal values which complement those of the organisation.**
2.1 Working with people	Demonstrating interest in others, working effectively in teams, building team spirit, and showing care and consideration for individuals.
2.2 Adhering to principles and values	Upholding ethics and values, acting with integrity and promoting equal opportunities.
FACTOR 3: INTERACTING AND PRESENTING	**Communicates and networks effectively. Successfully persuades and influences others. Relates to others in a confident and relaxed manner.**
3.1 Relating and networking	Establishing effective relationships with customers and staff, networking effectively within and outside the organisation, and relating well to individuals at all levels.
3.2 Persuading and influencing	Making a strong impression on others, gaining agreement and commitment through persuasion and negotiation, and managing conflict.
3.3 Presenting and communicating information	Speaking clearly and fluently, expressing opinions and arguments clearly and convincingly, and making presentations with confidence.
FACTOR 4: ANALYSING AND INTERPRETING	**Shows evidence of clear analytical thinking. Gets to the heart of complex problems and issues. Applies own expertise effectively. Quickly takes on new technology. Communicates well in writing.**
4.1 Writing and reporting	Writing clearly and succinctly in an interesting and convincing manner and structuring information in a logical manner to facilitate the understanding of the intended audience.
4.2 Applying expertise and technology	Applying specialist technical expertise, developing job knowledge and expertise, and sharing knowledge with others.
4.3 Analysing	Analysing data of a verbal and numerical nature and other sources of information, breaking information down into components, probing for further information, and generating workable solutions to problems.
FACTOR 5: CREATING AND CONCEPTUALISING	**Works well in situations requiring openness to new ideas and experiences. Seeks out learning opportunities. Handles situations and problems with innovation and creativity. Thinks broadly and strategically. Supports and drives organisational change.**
5.1 Learning and researching	Learning new tasks quickly, remembering information, and gathering data for effective decision making.
5.2 Creating and innovating	Producing new ideas and insights, creating innovative products and solutions, and seeking opportunities for organisational change and improvement.
5.3 Formulating strategies and concepts	Working strategically to attain organisational goals, developing strategies, and taking account of a wide range of issues that impact on the organisation.

COMPETENCY SET AND DIMENSIONS	DEFINITIONS
FACTOR 6: ORGANISING AND EXECUTING	**Plans ahead and works in a systematic and organised way. Follows directions and procedures. Focuses on customer satisfaction and delivers a quality service or product to the agreed standards.**
6.1 Planning and organising	Setting clear objectives, planning activities well in advance, and managing time effectively.
6.2 Delivering results and meeting customer expectations	Focusing on customer needs and satisfaction, setting high standards for quality and quantity, and consistently achieving set goals.
6.3 Following instructions and procedures	Following instructions and procedures, adhering to schedules, and demonstrating commitment to the organisation.
FACTOR 7: ADAPTING AND COPING	**Adapts and responds well to change. Manages pressure effectively and copes well with setbacks.**
7.1 Adapting and responding to change	Adapting to changing circumstances, embracing change, being open to new ideas, and dealing effectively with ambiguity.
7.2 Coping with pressure and setbacks	Working productively in a stressful environment, controlling emotions in difficult situations, and handling criticism effectively.
FACTOR 8: ENTERPRISING AND PERFORMING	**Focuses on results and achieving personal work objectives. Works best when work is related closely to results and the impact of personal efforts is obvious. Shows an understanding of business, commerce and finance. Seeks opportunities for self-development and career advancement.**
8.1 Achieving personal work goals and objectives	Accepting and tackling demanding goals, working longer hours when necessary, and identifying opportunities for progressing to more challenging roles.
8.2 Entrepreneurial and commercial thinking	Keeping up to date with competitor information and market trends, identifying business opportunities, and demonstrating financial awareness.

Source: SHL Group.[35] Universal Competency Framework (UCF20™). © SHL Group (Reproduced with permission.)

The above-mentioned generic competencies, or some variations thereof (see Rupp, Gibbons, Runnels, Anderson & Thornton[36]), are used when ACs are developed (also see Chapter 9 for a discussion about competencies assessed during ACs). If one examines what competencies are assessed by different AC service providers, it becomes clear that not all AC developers are in agreement on what these generic competency sets are.

Factors that may contribute to this situation are the exact purpose for which an AC is designed (as discussed in Chapter 1), the management level at which the AC is aimed, and whether the AC is specifically designed for addressing company in-house needs or a "generic" management competency set.

---

35 Schutte, 1991

36 Rupp et al., 2003

4.2 Competency elements

At this stage it should be clear that different competency sets, together with their accompanying competencies, require specific competency elements or critical behavioural elements (also referred to as behavioural indicators). These behavioural elements should be based on the required abilities, knowledge and skills identified in the different needs and job analyses as described above. The different behavioural elements can range from relevant (+), to neutral (?) to counterproductive (-). These behaviours can be depicted in the manner indicated in Figure 7.5 for each competency in a competency set:

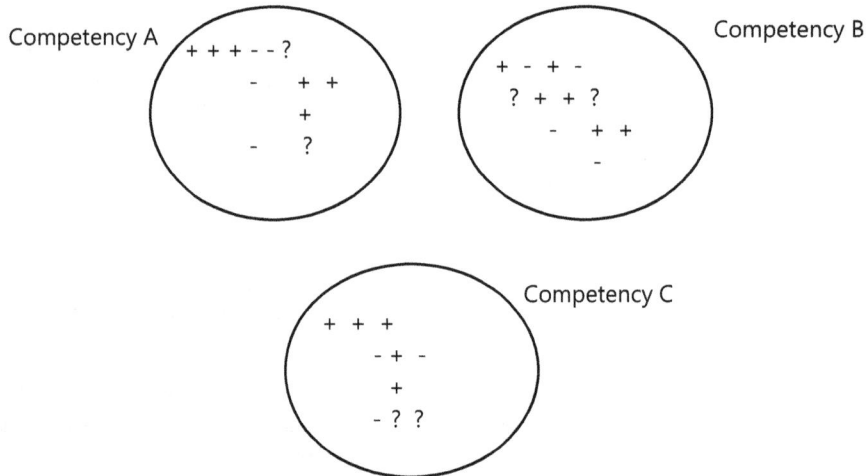

Figure 7.5: Critical behavioural elements for different competencies in a competency set
Source: Adapted from Byham[37; 38; 39]

The AC design team needs to identify the range of critical, observable behaviours within each competency. A range of clearly formulated examples should exist in each case so that observers will have no doubt regarding the characteristics by means of which they can recognise these applicable behavioural elements or any other non-relevant behaviours (see Chapter 8 for a discussion about behavioural elements).

Once the different competencies and their elements have been identified, the next step will be to develop criteria for evaluating the effectiveness of managers. This will enable the AC practitioners to collect data, enabling them to correlate the competency evaluations and the actual performance or effectiveness of managers. This data are important for validation purposes and for programme evaluation purposes.

The following section of this chapter will deal with the identification of managerial effectiveness criteria.

---

37 Byham, 1981

38 Byham, 1982a

39 Byham, 1982b

5. ESTABLISHING VALID EFFECTIVENESS CRITERIA

Effectiveness criteria are identified for two reasons: first, for validation purposes and, secondly, for programme evaluation purposes. The establishment of external evaluation criteria (also known as performance measures or effectiveness criteria) is not an easy matter – in fact, it sounds a lot easier than it actually is in practice.

The following subsection will deal with some of the problems and challenges that the AC design team may encounter in the identification and development of effectiveness criteria.

5.1 The difficulty in selecting valid criteria

In the process of selecting an external effectiveness criterion, several issues come to mind that may compromise the measure itself or may play a confounding role in the interpretation of the relationship using the competency ratings obtained. Let's take a closer look at these issues.

5.1.1 Different management levels

Selected effectiveness criteria should have a direct link with the management level in question. For instance, it would not make any sense to link the degree of strategy achievement of a company to the competency scores of supervisors. In the case of strategy achievement, the performance of the company in terms of goal achievement or financial performance would be a more appropriate criterion. Stated differently, effectiveness criteria that are directly related to the specific management level would be more appropriate.

5.1.2 Different outcome levels

Outcomes are often multi-determined by nature; in other words, outcomes may have different causes. One should therefore be careful to select criteria that may have a host of different causes. Performance criteria of top managers are often also the result of actions by middle and lower-level managers.

5.1.3 The cause-effect relationship

In order to prove a cause-effect relationship, the cause must precede the effect in time. One should therefore select criterion measures for a specific management level that are only clear consequences of their specific management actions.

5.1.4 A poorly defined criterion

The precise criterion definition is of utmost importance. The exact definition, and consequently a well-developed criterion construct, will ease the work of AC practitioners. One is often tempted to use some or other performance rating of a specific individual, however performance ratings are normally subjective in nature and, most of the time, are generated by people who are not professionally trained observers of human behaviour. A specific performance outcome, such as a productivity figure, would therefore be more appropriate.

5.1.5   Error variance in criterion measures

Closely related to the above-mentioned issue is the degree of error variance in a subjective measure (the predictor or the criterion), which is often increased by multi-source ratings. Any multi-source measure consists of some degree of true variance and some error variance that constitutes the total variance of that measure. If the exact nature of error variance cannot be determined, the precise interpretation of the criterion measure will prove difficult.

5.1.6   Criterion relevance

The criterion relevance issue raises the question, "Does it (the criterion) matter?" The selected criteria should be an important consequence to a specific management level. If the outcome is totally unrelated to management action, do not even bother to measure it. The importance of job analysis information will guide the AC design team in selecting job-relevant criteria.

The few pointers provided above will sensitise any AC design team in the selection of some effectiveness or performance criteria.

The next subsection provides some guidance on selection of the appropriate criteria.

5.2   What to look for in selecting a criterion

A common sense and logical approach to the selection of an external criterion will often help one in the selection and development of appropriate evaluation criteria. A number of criteria (standards) that a good criterion should meet are: reliable, realistic, representative, related to other criteria, acceptable to the job analyst, acceptable to management, consistent from one situation to another, predictable, inexpensive, understandable, measurable, relevant, uncontaminated and bias-free, as well as sensitive.[40] The following criteria will be helpful in guiding the criteria-selection process.

5.2.1   Clearly conceptualised and defined

It is almost unnecessary to state that the criterion should be clearly conceptualised and defined. If management competence on a supervisory level is assessed, what then will reflect the manager's competent performance in his or her job? If you can arrive at a clear answer to this question, you are already halfway there. The other half consists of precisely measuring this performance outcome.

---

40   Muchinsky et al., 1998

5.2.2   Reliable and valid

As with any other measure, the criterion should also meet the requirement of reliability and validity. Repeated measures of the criterion should yield consistent results that covary with the actual performance of the manager in question. The measure should also accurately reflect the manager's performance in the exact domain of the management competency in question. The measure should further meet other requirements of reliability and validity. The criterion should not be biased towards any group on such grounds as gender, age, race or home language.

5.2.3   Covariance within the measure

The selected criterion should yield scores that covary according to the difference in managers' performance. This requirement implies two things, namely that the criterion should be related to (covary with) the predictor, and that it should provide a sound range (distribution) of scores. A measure that will yield the same scores for all managers in a group will thus not suffice. This criterion measure will exhibit no variance and will not reflect differences in managers' performance.

5.2.4   Economical

The selected criterion should be economically obtainable and measurable. One may sometimes identify the most wonderful criteria, yet they are too costly to measure, e.g. they may be too costly to generate the data, or to develop a system that will capture the data effectively.

5.2.5   Practical and accessible

Another consideration when selecting a criterion is practicality and accessibility, i.e. it should be easy and practical to collect the data. The question is: "Why reinvent the wheel if the data already exist?" It is therefore important to scrutinise management information systems, performance management systems or even HR information systems for existing data that can effectively serve as a management performance criterion.

5.3   Developing valid criteria

In the preceding two subsections, several important aspects that influence the selection and development of a criterion were identified. The challenge, therefore, is on the one hand to avoid those aspects that will negatively impact the validity and reliability of a criterion. On the other hand, it is to promote those aspects that will enhance the establishment of valid criteria.

Muchinsky, Kriek & Schreuder[41] listed a number of possible objective criteria that meet the standards described above. These are production figures, sales figures, tenure or turnover figures, absenteeism figures, accident figures, and incidences of theft. These figures need to be interpreted in relation to some standard or norm that is applicable to the group in question (such as averages).

---

41 Muchinsky et al., 1998

6. CRITICAL DECISIONS RELATING TO, AND OUTCOMES OF, THIS STEP

The following are the critical decisions relating to, and outcomes of, this step:

6.1 Identify and develop appropriate competencies

The first outcome of this chapter was to identify and develop appropriate competencies for the specific management level on which the AC is focusing. Design teams should, however, keep the purpose of the AC in mind when deciding on the specific competencies. Critical decisions have to be taken concerning the following questions: is the AC being designed for assessment, development or diagnostic purposes? Should the competencies focus on generic skills or specific company in-house skills? The answers to these questions will guide the AC design team in its choices and regarding the exact focus of the AC.

6.2 Identify and develop evaluation criteria

The second outcome of this chapter was to identify and develop concomitant criteria for evaluating and validating the AC, the competency dimensions and the AC exercises. Again, the AC design team should keep the purpose of the AC in mind. First, the design team needs to reflect on the following critical questions: Does the competency reflect the critical management behaviour as determined in the needs and job analyses? Which management behaviours have the greatest impact on the selected performance criteria? Is the selected criterion appropriate for validating the management competency set? Can the design team provide evidence to show that the AC did, in fact, contribute to improved company performance? The answers to the first two questions will guide the design team in terms of validation issues, while the answer to the last question will guide the team in terms of programme evaluation issues.

CHAPTER 8

JOB ANALYSIS

Sandra Schlebusch

1.   INTRODUCTION – WHERE DOES JOB ANALYSIS FIT IN?

Against the backdrop of knowing that there is a definite need in the organisation for an AC (see Chapter 6), what organisational influences impact on what will be assessed during the AC (see Chapter 7), and what criteria to use for the validation studies, attention should now be focused on the target job. It is necessary to establish exactly what the target job is all about and how it differs from those jobs around it. This understanding is gained during the job analysis step in the analysis stage of the design model.

The AC design team will use the job information, together with the information gathered during the needs analysis and the organisational effectiveness analysis steps, to inform the AC focal constructs. The information will form the basis for identifying the dimensions, competencies or tasks that need to be assessed during the AC, the most appropriate simulations to use, the trends in the industry and organisations to simulate, and the AC process itself (Stage Two – the design stage). The greater the accuracy of the job analysis, the more valid the focal constructs will be, and the design of the simulations and the AC as a whole will be more realistic.[1] The third and last step in the analysis stage is depicted in Figure 8.1.

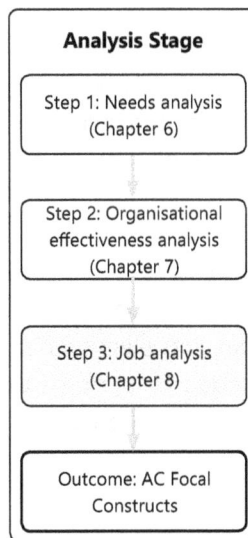

```
┌─────────────────────────────┐
│       Analysis Stage        │
│  ┌───────────────────────┐  │
│  │ Step 1: Needs analysis │  │
│  │     (Chapter 6)        │  │
│  └───────────────────────┘  │
│             │               │
│  ┌───────────────────────┐  │
│  │ Step 2: Organisational │  │
│  │ effectiveness analysis │  │
│  │     (Chapter 7)        │  │
│  └───────────────────────┘  │
│             │               │
│  ┌───────────────────────┐  │
│  │  Step 3: Job analysis  │  │
│  │     (Chapter 8)        │  │
│  └───────────────────────┘  │
│             │               │
│  ┌───────────────────────┐  │
│  │ Outcome: AC Focal      │  │
│  │     Constructs         │  │
│  └───────────────────────┘  │
└─────────────────────────────┘
```

Figure 8.1: The job analysis step in the analysis stage

---

1   Koch et al., 2012

This chapter starts with a brief discussion about the AC design team. The chapter continues by providing an overview of the purpose of a job analysis when designing an AC, indicates some of the job analysis techniques that exist, provides hints on conducting a job analysis, offers a summary of the process of job analysis that supports AC design, and sets out the critical decisions relating to, and the outcomes of, this step in the design model.

2. THE AC DESIGN TEAM

The job analysis for the AC design will probably be conducted by the AC design team, which is the team of people who will design the AC in its totality. This group of people is usually involved in the analysis and design stages of the design model. They might oversee stage three – the implementation stage – but are definitely actively involved again during step four, that is, during the evaluation and validation stage. Only if the AC is shown to be valid is the work of the current design team finished.[2]

The AC design team should be composed of seasoned behaviour analysts. Ideally, it should be made up of people who have been involved previously in simulation and AC design. These people might not be readily available inside the target organisation and might therefore have to be specialists who are contracted to the project. The team should also be composed of people who are knowledgeable about the organisation. Typically, this means senior line managers or specialists who know the organisation functionally, and who also know the target organisation's culture and current climate. It is also strongly recommended that representatives from the human resources department, and specifically the organisational design section, be part of the AC design team.

3. THE PURPOSE OF A JOB ANALYSIS

Job analysis is a systematic process of gaining an understanding of the target job.[3] In the AC design context, it indicates what the target job is all about, what the roles and accountabilities in respect of the job are, what competencies are needed for the incumbent to perform effectively in the job, what resources the incumbent uses to perform the job, and what typical situations the incumbent is faced with.

A job analysis, according to Cascio and Aguinis[4], is about defining a job, identifying what behaviours are needed to perform it, and identifying the personal characteristics necessary to demonstrate these behaviours. Job analysis is therefore about two elements: specifying what the job is all about (task requirements) and specifying what is needed to perform the job (people requirements). However, Sanchez and Levine[5] argued that a third element should be added, namely the work context in which the job is performed.[6]

---

2   SA Assessment Centre Study Group, 2018

3   Sanchez & Levine, 2012

4   Cascio & Aguinis, 2005: 213

5   Sanchez & Levine, 2012

6   Cascio & Aguinis, 2019

Table 8.1: Elements of focus during a job analysis

Element of Focus	Description
Work Activities/Task Requirements	• Tasks/duties/function/responsibility/work activities • Tools, information and technology
Worker Attributes/People Requirements	• Abilities • Interests, values, work styles • Skills, knowledge, education • Experience, licenses, certificates, registrations
Work Context	• Physical and social factors influencing work

The job analysis should clearly indicate to an AC design team the uniqueness of the target job, as the design team needs to know exactly what differentiates the target job from other jobs. For example, if the AC is focused on a management job, the design team should know how the first line manager's job differs from the middle manager's job and the senior manager's job.

The AC design team would use a job analysis to answer the question: "What is the target job all about and what is needed to perform the job?" Another question needing an answer is: "What are the critical competencies leading to success?" The answers to these questions will be discussed in the following subsections of this chapter.

3.1 What is the target job all about and what is needed to perform the job?

The typical question that the AC design team will ask is: "What is the purpose of the target job and what is the job incumbent accountable for?" A follow-up question is: "What does the incumbent use (resources or input) to produce that for which she or he is accountable?" These questions are answered during a job analysis.

The written document in which job information is typically included is called a job description. The job description indicates what the incumbent actually does, how she or he does it, and why. This is indicated as follows in a job description:[7]
- Job title – what the position is called.
- Job activities and procedures – the tasks performed, the equipment used, the interaction with other positions and the extent of supervision given or received.
- Working conditions and physical environment – the situation in which the tasks are performed, for example lighting, heat, indoor/outdoor, hazardous conditions, physical location, etc.
- Social environment – the amount of interpersonal interaction required and the number of positions in the work group or team.
- Conditions of employment – for example, hours of work, place in the formal organisation.

---

7   Cascio & Aguinis, 2019

The above is typically the information that is included in a task-based job description. Some organisations prefer a more behavioural-based job description, for example instead of stating that the incumbent must compile formal letters in English by typing them on a computer using Microsoft Word, the description might state that the incumbent must communicate effectively in writing using English. An advantage of the more behavioural-based description is that it describes only the required behaviour and not the method of delivery. Over time, the behaviour remains the same, although the method of delivering the behaviour depends on the current technology in use. The behaviour-based description thus remains valid for longer periods.

Job descriptions are valid to the extent that they accurately represent the job content, environment and conditions of employment.[8] Although the job description as described above might give a good indication of the tasks expected of the incumbent, it still lacks a description of the knowledge, skills, abilities and other attributes (KSAO) necessary to perform the job. Knowledge is job-related conceptual, factual and procedural information held by an incumbent.[9] Skills are proficiencies required to execute the tasks, and abilities are capacities that enable task completion.

The KSAO are described in the job specifications, which indicate the minimally acceptable standards for selection and later performance.[10] They identify the personal characteristics (educational background, experience, training) that are valid for screening, selection and placement. Job descriptions are valid to the extent that people who possess the personal characteristics stipulated in the job specification do in fact perform more effectively in their jobs than people lacking such personal characteristics.[11]

The job description, together with the job specification, allows one to understand the content of the job, as well as the context in which the job must be performed. This information might be sufficient if a work-sample test is to be designed. However, to design an AC, additional information is needed, for example information on the organisation's culture, climate, vision and strategy. Although some of this information will already have been gathered during step one (needs analysis) and step two (organisational effectiveness analysis) of the analysis stage of the design model, additional information still needs to be collected to support the AC design. This additional information will be collected during the job analysis step by using various job analysis techniques in conjunction with one another.

3.2 How does job analysis differ from competency modelling?

Following the UK approach (as opposed to the US approach) to competency description, a competency is a group of related behaviours that will assist in enabling a job outcome[12]; it is an employee-focused job analysis process that identifies broader characteristics of individuals. The alternative US approach to describing a competency focuses on the full range of KSAOs (motives, traits, attitudes, personality

---

8   Cascio & Aguinis, 2019

9   Thornton et al., 2015

10   Cascio & Aguinis, 2019

11   Cascio & Aguinis, 2019

12   Venter, 2017

characteristics) needed for effective performance in respect of the target-job level.[13] The competencies also characterise high performers on the target-job level. Bergh and Theron[14] stated that competencies may also relate to various aspects of being competent in a job. They may refer to input characteristics (i.e. the genetic or acquired characteristics of the incumbent), process characteristics (i.e. how the incumbent carries out the work tasks), and output characteristics (i.e. the results of the tasks being carried out). An organisational competency model is a list of competencies seen as desirable within the organisation.[15]

A quick description of the differences between job analysis and competency modelling will be given since there is often confusion about the differences[16]:

Table 8:2: Differences between job analysis and competency modelling

	Job Analysis	Competency Modelling
Purpose	To provide an objective description of the essential elements of the job as it is currently; it describes the Knowledge, Skills, Attributes, and Other characteristics (KSAOs) that on average are required to perform the job.	To provide a description of the role as it should ideally carry out work activities; it describes how the job should be interpreted and carried out.
	Describes the minimum that the job holder needs to perform to earn the associated salary – ideally suited for use in the areas of selection, training, job evaluation, etc.	Describes behavioural themes required to realise performance excellence aligned to organisational strategy – ideally suited as an instrument to assist strategy execution.
	Provides lists of unique activities and (KSAOs) (job descriptors) for job performance.	Provides a set of competencies, representing behavioural themes aligned to company strategy.
	Job descriptors are unique to jobs.	The same set of competencies cuts across jobs and organisational levels, indicating how the same competency is performed at the different organisational levels.
	It is a data collection process with the aim of understanding the unique jobs that ensure current organisational performance.	It is often an organisational development intervention with the aim of organisational change.
Focus	It is focused on the specific job, its purpose and its contribution to the organisation.	It typically includes an understanding of the organisation's business context and competitive strategy. There is usually a direct line of sight between individual competency requirements and the broader goals of the organisation.

---

13   Venter, 2017; Cascio & Aguinis, 2019

14   Bergh & Theron, 2003

15   Markus et al., 2005

16   Sanchez & Levine, 2009; Campion et al., 2011; Thornton et al., 2015

	Job Analysis	Competency Modelling
Time Orientation	It indicates past and current job performance – it is descriptive of how the job in its current format is performed.	It indicates how the job should be performed in future – it is prescriptive, often indicating future job requirements.
Indicated Performance Levels	It focuses on how the job is performed on average, indicating typical job performance.	It focuses on how top role performers should be performing, indicating ideal job performance.
Approach to Compile	The process of job analysis involves job incumbents, their line managers and subject matter experts (SMEs) – it is typically a bottom-up approach.	The process of competency modelling involves identifying competencies aligned to the organisation's strategy and cascading them down to all roles within an organisation – it is typically a top-down approach.

From Table 8.2 above, it is clear that only following one or the other approach is not going to deliver the required information to design an AC. Although a competency modelling approach will provide information about what is required to prepare the organisation for the future, it does not provide relevant information about the inherent job requirements for current job performance. It is a requirement of the Employment Equity Act[17] that all assessments linked to selection are based on inherent job requirements.[18] Only using information about the current job performance in turn ignores what is required to enable the organisation's envisioned future. During the job analysis step in the design model, a process that combines traditional job analysis with competency modelling is needed.

3.3 What are the critical competencies leading to success?

The information gathered during the traditional job analysis describes what the job incumbent does, as well as what the minimum KSAOs are for performance in the job. However, the AC design team is also interested in what separates the mediocre incumbent from the exceptional incumbent. In addition, the AC design team would like to link this information to the bigger picture of the organisation – the organisation's strategy, vision and future. This link is important to the AC design team in order to get top management's initial, but also continued, support for the design and running of the AC.

Although the information from the more traditional job analysis is needed, it is recommended that this be enhanced with an organisation-wide competency framework. This framework might indicate what will be valued and rewarded in the future in the organisation, and may also indicate what competencies will be needed to create a future for the organisation.

The challenge for the AC design team is to clearly establish the link between the information gathered from the more traditional job analysis (the individual job on the target-job level) and the needs of the organisation as a whole (its vision, strategic objectives, and current and future climate). This challenge is met by using various techniques to conduct a job analysis and to identify competency profiles per job category or organisation level.

---

17 Employment Equity Act., (Act No. 55 of 1998)

18 Thornton et al., 2015

The various job analysis techniques will be discussed in the next section.

4. JOB ANALYSIS APPROACH

Various job analysis approaches exist. The choice of approach, or combination of approaches, will depend on the purpose of the job analysis. For example, a different approach will be used when information is being collected to design a hierarchy of jobs in a pay structure (to conduct a job evaluation) than when information is needed to redesign a person–machine interface.[19] Cascio and Aguinis mentioned eight different choices confronting the job analyst:

- Work activities (task focused) or worker attributes (worker requirements focused)? Some job analysis techniques focus solely on the tasks that get done (i.e. they are task-oriented), while others focus solely on how the tasks get done (i.e. KSAO). Other techniques also include a process linking the two (so called hybrid methods). The AC design team would be interested in a method combining what gets done, as well as how it gets done.
- General work activities (GWA) or specific/detailed work activities (DWA)? This refers to the level of detail needed in the analysis. The AC design team would need enough detail to fully understand the job.
- Qualitative or quantitative? Qualitative analysis entails describing the job in a narrative form, while a quantitative analysis includes describing the job by means of numeric evaluations based on a fixed set of scales (time, frequency, importance, criticality, consequences, etc.). The AC design team would again prefer a combination that narratively describes a task or requirement and a quantitative description indicating, for example, the complexity of the target job relative to other jobs in the organisation.
- Taxonomy-based or blank-slate? A taxonomy-based job analysis uses general work activities or worker behaviours that apply to a broad range of jobs. For example, the Position Analysis Questionnaire (PAQ) and O*NET are taxonomy-based approaches.[20] The alternative approach (blank-slate approach) would be for trained observers or job incumbents and other subject matter experts (SMEs) to develop lists of job activities or attributes that apply to specific jobs or job families. This approach can potentially provide greater detail than taxonomy-based approaches. Both these approaches are useful to the AC design team, however the blank-slate approach perhaps allows for more of the work context to be documented, for example climate and typical organisational challenges.
- Observers or incumbent and line managers (SMEs)? Trained observers observe the incumbent at work and then write up the quantitative or qualitative descriptions of the work. Alternatively, the incumbent and his or her line manager may be asked to identify tasks. Observing jobs becomes difficult when the job entails deliverables that are not easily noted, such as deliverables where mental activities are involved (e.g. providing a legal opinion). It would be easier for the incumbent(s) of the job to document these aspects. If the AC design team has to choose between these two approaches, more information can potentially be collected when the incumbents and their line managers themselves identify the tasks.

19 Cascio & Aguinis, 2019
20 Morgeson, 2017; O*NET Resource Center, 2019

- Knowledge, skills and attitudes or other personal characteristics added? The additional personal characteristics allow a wider range of attributes to be included in the analysis. These other characteristics might include traits, values and attitudes. The AC design team would definitely prefer the additional information to be included.
- Single-job or multi-job analysis? At times, the analysis might be in respect of a single job, such as when developing a functional AC for sales executives. At other times, the focus is on documenting similarities and differences across jobs. This would be the case where an AC is designed for middle managers in an organisation.
- Descriptive or prescriptive? When the job analysis is about a job that already exists, the analysis describes the current job, however sometimes a job analysis is conducted concerning a job that will come into existence in the future. This is called a prescriptive job analysis. When the job analysis forms part of a change intervention, it might also include competencies that are not currently part of the specific job. However, these additional competencies might be deemed crucial for success in the future, based on changed technology, market requirements or other strategic needs.

In considering the choices mentioned, the AC design team will decide on a combination of approaches and techniques to gather the information that will describe the target job adequately enough for the team to identify valid competency profiles and, subsequent to that, simulations that accurately reflect the target job. Some of the techniques will now be discussed.

4.1 Shelf information

Possibly the easiest way to learn about a job is to study all existing information that is usually stored somewhere. This "shelf information" normally includes a task-based job description and a traditional job specification. Existing performance appraisal forms can also be scrutinised.[21] Although an understanding of the job is obtained by studying this material, it is still in a "vacuum". This information needs to be brought to life by analysing the context inside the organisation in which this job functions. Documents that can assist with this are annual reports, strategic and business plans, recent organisational surveys, policy and procedure documents, training material, equipment specification documents[22] and any other document related to the target job and the future of the job. The organisation might also have an existing competency profile/model for the target job that can be studied. Another source of information is information readily available on the internet, for example organisations' official websites, organisations' official social media platforms and the Occupational Information Network (O*NET).[23] The O*NET is a job analysis system designed and maintained by the US Department of Labour that has information on a large number of jobs, including various industries and sectors. It provides information on worker characteristics, worker requirements, experience requirements, occupational requirements, workforce characteristics and occupation-specific information. Although not all information available on O*NET is applicable in the South African context, it still provides valuable information as a starting point.

---

21   Morgeson, 2017

22   Thornton et al., 2015

23   O*NET Resource Center, 2019

However, studying shelf information on its own will seldom provide enough information for the AC design team to design an AC. Other job analysis techniques need to be used to augment the knowledge gleaned from the shelf information.

4.2 Process mapping

Process mapping is not a traditional job analysis technique, however it is an excellent technique for obtaining an understanding of where the target job fits into the bigger picture of the organisation. When used in conjunction with the more traditional job analysis techniques, a complete understanding of the internal business context of the target job is obtained. Through process mapping, an understanding is obtained of where in a process the job fits, the role of the job, the inputs received by the job, the value that is added to the inputs by the job incumbent, and the outputs delivered by the job.

A process is a method by means of which inputs are transformed into outputs, while process mapping is a technique whereby processes within an organisation are broken down into their constituent elements and are displayed visually.[24] Each section of a process is a smaller process. In turn, the sections of that process form another process, and so on. This is called "drilling down" into the various processes that combine to form the overall business process of the organisation. In the case of process mapping, a high-level map of the overall business process will first be drawn. A section of this overall map will then be chosen to "drill down".[25]

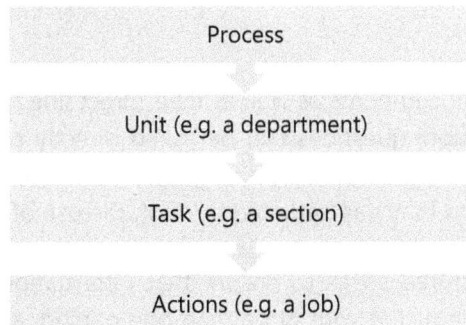

Process

Unit (e.g. a department)

Task (e.g. a section)

Actions (e.g. a job)

Figure 8.2: Drilling down a section of a process

The first subsection of a process is called a unit. A unit can be a location (branch office, head office), a type of work (testing, installation, research), a stage of work (preparing, assembly, quality control), or any other logical breakpoint. Each unit, in turn, is a small process – input is transformed into output that becomes the input for the next unit.

Each unit can be broken into tasks. Again, each task is a smaller process that uses the output of the previous task to produce the input of the next task. Each task can be broken down into various actions. How each action is completed is documented in organisational procedures.[26]

---

24 Jacka & Keller, 2002

25 Jacka & Keller, 2002: 16

26 Jacka & Keller, 2002

A process can stretch across departments in an organisation, a unit within the process can be a specific department in the organisation, and the tasks in the unit can each be sections within the greater department. The actions within the unit can be the various jobs within each section and one, or a group, of these jobs can be the job analysed. The overall business process has thus been drilled down to the target job being analysed. A review of this drilled-down process reveals where the target job fits into the wider business process. The impact of this job on the organisation as a whole then becomes apparent. If the target job has a great impact on the overall business process it will strengthen the business case for using an AC for the selection of job incumbents or a DAC for the development of incumbents.

Probably the biggest advantage of using this technique during job analysis is that the AC design team obtains a holistic view of where the target job fits into the overall business. Additional advantages include the fact that the incumbent(s) of the target job, as well as the incumbents of the positions around the target job, feel involved in the process of job analysis. This creates a sense of ownership of, and buy-in into, the process of job analysis, but also of and into the eventual design of the AC.

To reap the full benefit of process mapping, the AC design team should provide the process owners and the other people involved in the mapping process with feedback regarding the final result of the mapping process. The process owners, job incumbent(s) and other people who were involved should sign off the final maps (the visual representation of the process(es)). It is recommended that those involved be shown how the process map(s) will be used in the AC design.

4.3 Interviews

Conducting interviews with job incumbents as well as their direct line managers is another technique that is used to gather information; questions can be asked directly of job incumbents. This allows information to be gathered that might be difficult to gather in any other way.[27] It also allows the AC design team to verify information that was gathered through the use of other techniques.

The interviews should be structured so as to ensure that information is gathered in a systematic way. Since interviews will be conducted with more than one person, a structure ensures that similar information is covered during all the interviews.

Questions should be carefully chosen so as to ensure that the information gathered is really applicable to the target job and is not the consequence of the interviewer influencing the interviewee's answer. The choice of words, the way the question is phrased, the response of the interviewer to the answer given, and even how the answer is noted, can all potentially influence the outcome of the interview. For this reason, the AC design team should select questions to be asked during the interview that[28]:

- are related to the purpose of the analysis;
- are clear and unambiguous; and
- do not presuppose any answer.

---

27   Cascio & Aguinis, 2019

28   Cascio & Aguinis 2019

The interviewer should also be thoroughly trained in asking the questions, as well as in listening to and correctly noting the answer to each question. He or she should be able to ask follow-up questions to ensure that there is clarity regarding the answers given by the interviewee. It is recommended that, as soon as possible after the interview, the interviewer review the notes he or she made during the interview to ensure that the answers are accurately captured.

By conducting interviews with more than one job incumbent and more than one direct line manager, one is able to ensure that a comprehensive picture is created of what the job entails. If the job occurs in diverse sections of the organisation, care should be taken to ensure that interviews are conducted with a representative sample of all the sections in the organisation. This will help to guard against a picture being created of the job that might be true only of incumbents in one section of the organisation. For example, if the target job being analysed is that of sales executive and the organisation has sales executives who function in different regions of the country, interviews should be conducted with a representative sample of sales executives from all the different regions.

It could also be a good idea to conduct interviews with the subordinates of the target job. This will probably add another perspective to what outputs are expected from the target job, as well as what constitutes effective behaviour. Care should be taken in choosing the subordinates who will be interviewed so that personal prejudice does not influence the picture created. Another approach would be to include the clients/customers of the target job. Again, care should be taken to ensure that information is gathered on the target job and not only on the overall service of the organisation or the specific incumbent.

The timing of the interviews can influence the information received, for example if the interviews are conducted during a period of wage negotiations or any labour action, a distorted picture might be created. Also, if the job incumbents are under more pressure than usual, the quality of information gathered might be negatively affected. For example, if the target job is that of financial manager and the interviews are conducted during the financial year-end period, the incumbents might be too busy to give their full attention to the interview. The interviewer should therefore be sensitive to what is going on in the organisation.

The interview also gives the AC design team the opportunity to gather information on general trends in the organisation. Information can be gathered on the typical, current challenges with which the job incumbent is faced and how these differ from the challenges of two years ago. For example, 10 years ago most incumbents in managerial positions in South African organisations were faced with implementing the Codes of Practice relating to Broad-Based Economic Empowerment. Today, the implementation of the codes is a given and in some instances remains a challenge. A bigger challenge currently, however, is ensuring ethical and transparent business practices throughout organisations.

A variation on the interview is the visionary interview. This is an interview that is conducted – usually with senior people in the organisation – about the future needs of the organisation. Typically, technological changes will be filtered into the picture when the interviewees are asked to describe what the expectations in respect of the target job will be in future. The results of this type of interview are competencies that might not currently be needed by job incumbents to function effectively, but which are needed in order to be effective in the future.

4.4 Focus-group discussions

A focus group usually consists of SMEs, also known as job content experts (JCEs).[29] An SME is a person who is/was an incumbent of the target job, a line manager of the target job, or a colleague who has worked closely with the target job or proposed job. Cascio and Aguinis[30] stated that approximately six to ten SMEs are generally included in each focus group discussion. The total group of SMEs involved in the various focus group discussions should be representative of 10 to 20 percent of the target job incumbents and their direct line managers.[31] This group should also be representative of race, gender, location and any other variable applicable to the target job. An important variable that should be represented in the SME sample is experience. A distorted picture could be created if a broad cross section of experience is not included in a sample of the SMEs.[32]

The group is prompted to provide information on the content of the job as well as on what distinguishes high job performers from mediocre and below-par job performers. The facilitator of the focus group discussion should ensure that disagreements concerning answers are openly discussed and that consensus is reached regarding the answers. This requires that the focus group facilitator be well trained in facilitation skills. It is recommended that two facilitators be present during every focus group discussion. While the one facilitator is focusing on the group process, the other facilitator can note the decisions taken. This will assist in accurately and reliably capturing the information provided by the SMEs.

It is again recommended that feedback be given to all participants in focus group discussions. This will not only ensure their buy-in into the competencies that will eventually be assessed during the AC, but also leaves them with a sense of completion.

Future scenario workshops are a variation on a focus group discussion, wherein the SMEs are presented with various realistic situations that the organisation might find itself in. They discuss how the organisation will react to the unforeseen situations and what competencies the employees would need to successfully operate in the situations.[33]

4.5 Questionnaires and surveys

Questionnaires can be drawn up and distributed to job incumbents and their direct line managers for the purpose of collecting job analysis information. This is a relatively cheap and quick approach to gathering this information. A large number of people can be included in the job analysis process by using standardised questionnaires.

29 Thoresen & Thoresen, 2012

30 Cascio & Aguinis, 2019

31 Cascio & Aguinis, 2019

32 Cascio & Aguinis, 2019

33 Thornton et al., 2015

A problem in using questionnaires is that any misunderstanding of questions by the respondents usually goes unnoticed, which negatively influences the quality of information collected. Designing a questionnaire might also be time consuming. Since it is difficult to follow up on the information gathered through the use of questionnaires, it is recommended that questionnaires be used during the job analysis process when the information can be supported by additional information gathered during the use of an interactive technique. For example, a questionnaire is useful when shelf information is not available and a broad idea of what the job is all about needs to be created. The information gathered in this way should then be verified and augmented with information gathered during interviews and focus group discussions.

The types of questions asked in questionnaires can vary from open-ended questions that will gather more qualitative information, to questions that merely require the respondent to choose between certain answers. The advantage of using open-ended questions is that the quality of information gathered might be greater, but the disadvantage is that it takes longer to process the collected information. The advantage of only asking questions that can be answered by choosing between answers is that the processing of the answers is quicker, however the compilation of such a questionnaire takes longer. Moreover, it requires the compiler to already have some idea as to the content of the target job and it limits the respondent in his or her answer. This, in turn, might influence the quality of the information gathered.

Surveys are similar to questionnaires in that they can be administered to a large group of people. In the job analysis context, surveys are used to obtain quantitative information[34] about predetermined tasks, attributes, situations or other work context elements. As an example, for the question: "How often does the incumbent perform the task of...?", a scale can be presented that the respondent can chose an applicable rating from, such as a five point scale where 1 is never and 5 is always. Surveys can be administered verbally or in written format. SurveyMonkey[35] is a useful platform to use if an organisation does not have an internal electronic platform to administer the survey.

An advantage of using a survey is that a large number of people can be involved in the process to assist with obtaining input from a representative sample within the organisation. However, information obtained through a survey must be augmented by information obtained from other job analysis techniques.

4.6 Critical incidents

The critical incident technique refers to the collection of anecdotes on job behaviour that describe effective and ineffective job performance.[36] The situations described are crucial for achieving the target job's purpose and objectives.[37] Each anecdote describes what led to the incident, as well as the context of the incident, what the job incumbent did that was effective or ineffective, the perceived

---

34 Mouton, 2008

35 SurveyMonkey, 2019

36 Cascio & Aguinis, 2019

37 Koch et al., 2012

consequences of the behaviour[38], and whether the consequences were within the incumbent's control. Alternatives to what the incumbent did are also identified.

Critical incident information can be gathered from the job incumbents, from their direct line managers, from their subordinates, or from any other person who is familiar with the job. The information can be collected via the use of a questionnaire or an interview, or both.

Critical incidents provide valuable information for understanding both the dynamic and static elements of the target job. They are also a rich source of ideas for the AC design team to use when designing simulations.

4.7 Observation

The AC design team can observe an incumbent performing the target job[39] in-person, or via recordings. The observer needs to note carefully what is observed, as well as the consequences of the activity. Observation as a technique to obtain job analysis information is not very effective for jobs that are not physical in nature, such as management-leadership positions where it is difficult to "see" what the incumbent is busy doing.[40] However, when a functional AC is designed, observation could add valuable information, such as details of activities, sequence of activities, or context/situational variables.

4.8 Competency profile instruments

The AC design team can also decide to use one of the competency profile instruments that are on the market. These are instruments that analyse a job in terms of predetermined competencies (taxonomy of competencies), which are a wide range of generic competencies that can be found in certain job categories. Typically, the instrument will be used to select competencies from the range applicable to the type of job being analysed.

The advantage of using such an instrument is that these are usually valid and reliable. They are also normally already standardised in a format suitable for use in South Africa. The distributors of these instruments generally distribute other instruments that can be used in conjunction with the competency-profiling instruments.

A possible disadvantage of using such an instrument is that some yield a too-generic profile of the target job. The AC design team will thus not be able to use only such an instrument to fully understand exactly what the target job is all about, however when the instrument is used in conjunction with other job analysis techniques, valuable information is collected.

---

38   Sanchez & Levine, 2012

39   Thornton et al., 2015

40   Cascio & Aguinis, 2019

4.8.1   Work-profiling system (WPS)

The WPS is an integrated job analysis system that describes both the job's and the incumbent's characteristics. The purpose of the job, the functions of the job, the objectives set to achieve the purpose, the tasks needed to be executed to meet the objectives, and the competencies required of the incumbent to perform the job are identified during an analysis session. SMEs in respect of the target job, and frequently their managers, attend the analysis session.

The analysis questionnaires are administered either via an online platform, a personal computer, or by using questionnaire booklets and machine-readable answer sheets. The information is imported into the WPS software database, the responses are analysed by the computer, and a job analysis report is produced (© SHL Group Limited).

4.8.2 Online Competency Profiler (OCP)

The OCP is a standardised online competency profiling tool that provides a systematic approach to identifying the essential competency requirements for a job. Similar to the WPS, the purpose of the job and key job objectives are identified in an analysis session by SMEs (current job incumbents and their managers), providing the context of the job and organisational requirements. The SMEs then work through a series of paired comparisons to rank order the set of competencies in terms of the relative importance of each competency in achieving the job objectives and purpose.

The OCP is administered via an online platform, which analyses the responses automatically upon completion of the questionnaire. The resultant competency profile can be displayed immediately to the SMEs, allowing the job analyst to facilitate a validation discussion before finalising the profile (© SHL Group Limited).

4.8.3 tts-define Success and Competency Profiling Software Platform

This is an online platform that enables multiple subject matter experts to simultaneously participate in a job analysis and competency profiling process, by employing a drag-and-drop interface to create job profiles aligned to measurable competencies. This results in comprehensive, validated profiles that define job-specific success factors such as the relevant job purpose and objectives, contextual variables, as well as the required incumbent experience, knowledge, skills, abilities and behavioural characteristics (@ Top Talent Solution).

4.8.4 JvR Africa Role Competency Survey

The JvR Africa Role Competency Survey[41] is a competency profiling tool that enables clients to identify the six to ten critical and important behavioural competencies for a specific role. The participant is required to rate behavioural statements in terms of how important the tasks are to function in the job, as well as how frequently the specific actions need to be displayed. The output provides a list of the competencies in the JvR Africa competency framework identified as critical, important and less important for the role.

---

41 JvR Africa Group, 2018

4.8.5 Hogan JET[42]

Being a job analysis system, the Job Evaluation Tool (JET) is designed to identify personal characteristics and competencies required by jobs. Professionals are provided with a systematic way to describe a job and compare it to other jobs. The results from the JET can be used for a variety of professional purposes, including matching people to jobs and defining the personal characteristics needed for future jobs.

4.9 Combined Techniques

Using only one technique is not going to deliver adequate (and legally defensible) information for the AC design team to design the AC[43], thus a combination of techniques should always be used. Two examples of combined techniques will be described briefly.

4.9.1 Task Analysis[44]

With the method called Task Analysis, tasks related to the target job are identified and information about the tasks collected. A task has a clear beginning and end and is aimed at achieving job objectives.[45] A task is a collection of activities executed closely in time. There are four steps in this method:

Step 1: Develop a comprehensive list of tasks related to the target job
SMEs are requested to compile the list of tasks. This can be done through individual brainstorming, focus group discussions, questionnaires or interviews. The AC design team can also observe incumbents performing the job or certain aspects of the job, and consult shelf information. Task statements are developed, which are generally formatted as: a verb that describes what the incumbent does; how the task is done; to whom or what the task is done; and why the task is done.

Step 2: Developing a job analysis survey
During step 1, qualitative data are collected. The purpose of designing and administering a survey is to augment the qualitative data with quantitative data. Tasks are grouped into duties. Multiple types of job related data can be collected with the survey, for example:
- Is the task performed by the respondent as part of his/her job?
- How much time is spent on the task?
- How difficult is the task to perform?
- How frequently is the task performed?
- How critical is the task to the job?
- How serious are the consequences of performing the task incorrectly?

An important consideration is the response scale(s) that will be used in the survey, which should deliver the required information in an effective manner.

---

42 Hogan Assessment Systems, 2009

43 Thornton et al., 2015

44 Morgeson, 2017

45 Morgeson, 2017

Step 3: Administering the survey
The survey respondents should be familiar with the target job; usually current incumbents and their line managers complete the survey. It is important that a representative sample of the incumbent pool participates in the survey. As such, demographic information should also be collected: age, gender, work experience, education, ethnicity, location of work (e.g. head office, region, finance, marketing, etc.).

Step 4: Developing a summary report
The results from the survey need to be reported in a user-friendly format. Means and standard deviations per task can be reported, as well as per duty.

The information from a task analysis can provide the AC team with information that indicates which tasks to include in the AC (e.g. critical tasks/duties), as well as the complexity that needs to be simulated in the various simulations.

4.9.2 Combination Job Analysis Method (C-JAM)[46]

The C-JAM is a hybrid job analysis method, which combines a work-oriented job analysis with a worker-oriented job analysis. With this method, task statements are developed and rated in terms of importance. In addition, the knowledge, skills, attributes and other worker characteristics (KSAOs) required to perform the tasks are identified and rated for importance to job performance. The method has seven steps:

Step 1: Task Generation Meeting
A group of SMEs attend the meeting away from the work-site. Each participant, on their own, generates a list of tasks for the target job (approximately 50 tasks). Copies of each participant's list are handed to all other participants and an overall list of tasks is compiled. The AC design team will edit the final list.

Step 2: Task Rating Meeting
Another group of SMEs attend the task rating meeting. The facilitator goes over each task one-by-one with the group, allowing changes to be made to the list. Once the list has been finalised, the group rates each task according to: 1) task difficulty (1 = easy; 7 = most difficult); and 2) task criticality (1 = consequences of error are not too important; 7 = consequences of error are extremely important).

Step 3: Calculate Final Task Values
The mean of all ratings are used to derive the final values. A task's importance is determined by combining the task's difficulty rating and the task's criticality rating.

Step 4: KSAO Generation Meeting
The final copies of the task list are handed to another meeting of SMEs. This group considers the sensory and motor requirements of the target job, as well as the KSAOs required to complete each task.

---

46 Morgeson et al., 2019

Step 5: KSAO Rating Meeting

The group of SMEs individually rate each identified KSAO on the below:

- Is the KSAO required of a new incumbent? Yes/No
- Is the KSAO practical to expect? Yes/No
- Is trouble likely if the specific KSAO is ignored? 1 (no trouble); 7 (trouble is a given)
- To what level does the KSAO distinguish superior performers? 1 (not at all); 5 (clear distinction)

Step 6: Calculate Final KSAO Ratings

The average rating across all SME ratings is calculated per KSAO.

Step 7: Verification

The final list of tasks and KSAOs is verified by again presenting it to a group of SMEs.

Case Study:

How did the Canadian Armed Forces decide on their Assessment Centre (AC) Competencies?[47]

The Canadian Armed Forces (CAF) is a large organisation with almost 100,000 employees (approximately 68,000 regular force and 27,000 reserve force). The CAF has over 100 occupations across three environments – Army, Navy and Air Force – and enrols approximately 4,000 to 5,000 people each year. The CAF has a long history of using ACs, starting from World War II, but ACs were discontinued in 1967. ACs were again used from 1982 (by the Combat Arms Selection Board) and 1984 (Naval Officer Selection Board). However, due to cost and minimal benefit, the ACs were discontinued in 1989.

During 2016 it was decided to re-introduce ACs as part of the Combat Arms Officer selection process. The reasons for the re-introduction were four-fold. Firstly, there were high attrition rates between enrolment and graduation of candidate officers. Secondly, there were inefficiencies identified in the selection system. The system relied on a "selection through training" approach which was inefficient, compared to a system that selected earlier in the process, because resources were spent on training many members who would not ultimately be successful. It would be more efficient to identify more of the successful ones earlier in the process before training resources were spent. This was a concern for leadership within the Combat Arms, as well as personnel researchers. Thirdly, there was a concern that the necessary competencies were not being measured. Combat Arms' leadership was concerned that the necessary competencies were not being measured because of the high failure rates and also because a "selection through training" approach would focus more on the technical competencies necessary for the job, but not necessarily on some of the more soft competencies necessary for the job. Fourthly, there was a need to provide candidates with a realistic job preview of the occupations.

The Combat Arms consists of three occupations that participate in tactical ground combat, namely Infantry, Armour and Artillery. The Combat Arms Officers command and lead the Combat Arms troops. The challenge was to identify the appropriate AC competencies applicable to all three occupations.

The job analysis methodology used by the Director General Military Personnel Research and Analysis is the Combined Job Analysis Method (C-JAM). An adapted version of the C-Jam was used to identify this AC's competencies.

---

47   Myslicki et al., 2018

Three focus groups were conducted, one each from Armour, Artillery and Infantry:

Occupation	Number of SMEs per Group	SME Gender
Armour	6	1 Female; 5 Males
Artillery	6	0 Females; 6 Males
Infantry	10	0 Females; 10 Males

The focus groups were asked to identify Outputs; Tasks and Knowledge, Skills, Abilities and Other Attributes (KSOAs) for the specific occupation (officer level).

The following results were obtained:

Occupation	Number of Outputs	Number of Tasks	Number of KSAOs
Armour	3	111	203
Artillery	4	118	141
Infantry	3	183	347

The identified tasks and KSAOs were used to compile a field survey for each occupation. In the field survey, the tasks were rated on: 1) difficulty to perform; and 2) criticality (consequences of error) of the task. A 7-point Likert-type scale ranging from 1 (this task is one of the easiest) to 7 (this task is one of the most difficult) was used for both scales. Tasks that had an average rating of 4.0 (adding ratings from both scales and dividing by two) or higher were retained as critical tasks.

The KSAOs were rated on: 1) the necessity for the candidate to possess it prior to training; 2) practicality to expect it in the candidate pool; 3) trouble likely if ignored during the selection process; and 4) ability to distinguish between average and superior performers.

Questions 1 and 2 were answered on a dichotomous yes/no scale. Question 3 used a 5-point Likert-type scale ranging from 1 (not at all) to 5 (trouble definitely likely if ignored in selection). Question 4 also used a 5-point scale ranging from 1 (not at all) to 5 (definitely distinguishes superior from average candidates).

KSAOs were retained if questions 1 and 2 were answered "yes" by at least 75% of respondents, they had an average rating of 3.0 or higher on question 3, and there was an acceptable r_{wg} value based on the number of raters on Q3. If a KSAO had an average rating of 2.0 or higher on question 4, it would be used as a selection criteria. For a value of 2.0 or less, it would be used for screening.

The retained KSAOs were combined by SMEs into overarching competencies. The results were as follows:

Occupation	Number of Raters	Number of Tasks	Number of KSAOs	Number of Competencies
Armour	377	81	48	12
Artillery	280	81	35	11
Infantry	376	104	34	11

The results from the three job analyses (three occupations, which already had considerable overlap) were grouped using a rational sorting approach. This resulted in 13 competencies:

1. Adaptability (adapt to changing situation)
2. Analytical Thinking (information processing, problem analysis, decision making, etc.)
3. Communication (written and spoken)
4. Developing Self and Others (learn from situation, give/accept feedback, etc.)
5. Industrious (maintain focus, hardworking and disciplined, detail-oriented)
6. Interpersonal Skills (tact and teamwork)
7. Leadership (assertive, influence others, delegate)
8. Personal Effectiveness (Integrity/Honesty)
9. Physical Fitness
10. Plan and Organise (time management)
11. Resilience (cope with stress, self-confidence, positive mindset)
12. Spatial Ability (spatial orientation, navigation, mental rotation)
13. Working Memory.

In summary:
- Subject Matter Experts (SMEs) were used during the job analysis process.
- All currently serving Combat Arms officers had an opportunity to participate in the process.
- Task statements and KSAOs were generated by individuals currently performing the role.
- Tasks and KSAOs were evaluated in a field survey.
- Competencies were derived through an analysis of the KSAO ratings and can be directly linked to the required tasks and outputs.

Source: Case study used with permission from the Canadian Armed Forces

4.10 Information gathered during the job analysis

Once the process of gathering all the available job information is finished, the AC design team should have a comprehensive understanding of the target job. The team should have clarity regarding the target job's roles, accountabilities, outputs, interactions with other jobs and processes; the job's specific context; and the job's impact on the organisation as a whole. The AC team should know the KSAOs that the incumbent needs in order to perform effectively in the job. It should also know what high performance in the job looks like; what the incumbent should do to achieve high performance; what low job performance looks like; what a typical "day in the life of" the job incumbent looks like; and what will be expected of the incumbent within cycles of 6 months, 12 months, 18 months, etc.

In addition, the team should have an understanding of the typical challenges facing the target job incumbents. These challenges will, in all likelihood, change over time, but are relevant currently. An example of a challenge might be that the incumbents need to penetrate a new market segment with the organisation's current product offering. The design team should have an understanding of the trends within the organisation, for example, the organisation might be busy promoting project management as a way of running the business.

The organisation's culture should be clear. Does the organisation might have an unwritten rule that states: "Deliver, no matter what"? It might also be a high-stress environment, or it might be an environment where a slower pace is maintained. The current climate within the organisation should be known, for example employees might be unsure about their own future within the organisation due to rumours of a possible merger with another company.

5. JOB ANALYSIS DELIVERABLES TO THE AC DESIGN TEAM: DETAILED INFORMATION ON FOCAL CONSTRUCTS

The AC design team needs to have enough information to design a legally defensible AC that will be valid. Although a lot of ACs use competencies as focal constructs, some ACs have dimensions as focal constructs and others have situations or tasks as focal constructs.[48]

5.1 Dimension Profiles

A dimension is a "logically homogeneous cluster of observable behaviour".[49] Different ACs will focus on different dimensions depending on the industry, organisation, job and level of the target job. The labels and descriptions of the dimensions might be specific to an organisation, or they might be similar to dimensions published in articles and other sources, for example: "Oral communication – the extent to which an individual communicates fluently and effectively in an individual and group situation." Dimension elements (behavioural elements or indicators) will be indicated per dimension. These elements will be used in the AC's observer report forms to assess a participant's ability to visibly show the behaviour linked to a dimension.

A profile of dimensions consists of a list of dimensions required for job performance per target job.

5.2 Competency Profiles

An alternative focal construct is a competency. Although a dimension is in some instances called a competency, there is a difference, i.e. a competency is a group of related behaviours that can be linked to the organisation's strategic intent. A competency is usually derived from a competency modelling process, or, as is the recommendation for AC design, a combination of a job analysis and a competency modelling process.

---

48 Thornton et al., 2015
49 Thornton et al., 2015: 45

A competency profile is a group of competencies that the job incumbent needs to perform effectively in the target job. If the AC is designed for a target management job on a specific organisational level, the design team might find it useful to also compile competency profiles for the other management levels within the organisation (supervisory level, middle management level, senior management level). Typically, the list of competencies can be grouped into areas such as achievement competencies, decision making competencies, leadership competencies, communication competencies, management competencies and even functional competencies (see Chapters 7 and 9 for discussions about competencies).

When defining each competency, the AC design team can choose from predefined competencies, such as the SHL's Universal Competencies, or it could formulate its own definitions (see Chapter 7 for the Universal Competencies). When formulating its own competency definitions, the design team can choose between defining singular competencies or using a combined definition, or even defining a situation. These approaches will be discussed briefly.

5.2.1   Singular competencies

A singular competency describes a specific group of behaviour required of the target job incumbent, for example "the ability to delegate decision making power to the most suitable person". This can be the definition of a competency called "delegation". The competency "delegation" can be assessed during the AC by way of various simulations. These simulations can be paper-based or interactive; day-to-day or strategically focused; an individual or group simulation; or any other type of simulation that depicts typical situations to which the incumbent is exposed (see Chapter 11 for a discussion about typical simulations).

The advantage of defining competencies in this way is that a clear picture is gained of the AC participant's ability to perform according to that specific competency. The possible disadvantage of this approach to defining competencies is that a perception might be created that the consequence of a participant's behaviour in the work situation will be effective when in fact other competencies also need to be effective in order to achieve job results. For example, when "delegation" receives an effective rating, the deduction might be made that the participant will achieve results in the work situation when he or she delegates tasks to subordinates. This might, however, not be the case, since the effectiveness of the subordinate's behaviour is also influenced by other competencies such as the AC participant's guidelines with which he or she provides the subordinate (providing direction), as well his or her style of interacting with the subordinate (interpersonal sensitivity).

An alternative to defining singular competencies is to combine individual competencies into combined competencies.

5.2.2   Combined competencies (broad competencies)

Combined competencies refer to a situation where more than one specific group of behaviours are combined to constitute the competency. An example of this would be "the ability to adopt an effective interpersonal style when directing or leading individuals to task completion or problem solving". This competency, called "individual leadership", combines the competencies of "delegation", "providing direction" and "interpersonal sensitivity". The competency specifies the context in which the behaviour should be demonstrated, namely an individual context.

The advantage of this approach to defining competencies is that an effective evaluation of the competency does imply that the AC participant's behaviour in the work situation will lead to effective consequences, since most influencing factors are included in the competency.

A possible disadvantage of the approach might be that important elements of the competency could already be at an effective level or need development, but do not get adequate recognition. As a consequence, the development actions recommended in order to improve the competency might not be effective, since they might address elements already in place or neglect important elements. This possible disadvantage can be overcome by adequately reporting the elements already at an effective level and those needing further development.

Another possible disadvantage of this approach might be that the list of elements loading onto the competency might be very long. This complicates the assessments, the reporting and, eventually, the design of development interventions intended to develop the competency.

5.2.3   Competency levels

When deciding on competency profiles, it is also necessary to distinguish between different levels within the organisation, as each level will have its own competency profile. The competency profile indicates, per level, the competency requirements for effective functioning on that level. For example, as was mentioned earlier, when an AC is designed for a management position, it is necessary to distinguish between management at supervisory level, middle management level and senior management level. Each level has a specific role and specific deliverables (see Chapter 7 for a discussion about the differing deliverables per level). Although each level will have competencies specific to the level, some of the competencies might be needed on all three levels within the organisation.

Control is an example of a competency that might be required on all the various levels within an organisation. Although the principles underpinning the competency on all three levels remain the same, the competency is applied with more complexity (more variables to consider, less structure to assist in choosing options, a longer time before the impact of actions becomes visible) at each progressive management level. Control on a supervisory level is usually control of the employee's own behaviour as well as control over tasks that are delegated and require completion and feedback in the short term. At a senior management level, control is still exercised with regard to the employee's own behaviour, however the control over tasks that are delegated usually requires completion and feedback over the longer term.

The AC design team needs clarity as to what behaviour looks like at each level per competency before the design of the simulations and AC can start.

5.2.4 Dimension/competency elements (behavioural indicators)

With the dimensions and competencies clearly identified and defined, the behavioural elements, or indicators, linked to each dimension or competency need to be identified.[50] Whereas the dimension or competency definition describes the cluster of behaviours in concrete and job related words, each element describes an aspect of the specific dimension or competency; the elements should cover the breadth and depth of the specific dimension or competency. To ease construct validity (see Chapter 19 for a discussion about construct validity). It is recommended that a minimum of six and a maximum of 12 elements per dimension or competency be identified.[51]

The following are aspects to keep in mind when writing the elements:[52]
- Include only one theme/aspect of the dimension or competency per element, for example "Asking investigative questions".
- Use clear (only one meaning) and concise wording.
- Avoid using negative expressions, for example, "Not keeping appropriate eye contact".

A rule of thumb when choosing behavioural elements to include in the dimension or competency description is to ask: "How will we observe the behaviour in the AC/simulation?" When it is difficult to envision how the element will be observed, reconsider its inclusion.

5.2.5 Hints on designing dimension and competency definitions and elements

When deciding on the definition of a dimension or competency, it is advisable to ensure that the dimensions or competencies within the profile do not contaminate one another; in other words, the definitions should ensure that clarity exists regarding the behaviour elements associated with each competency or dimension. The behaviour elements associated with a specific dimension or competency should also not be associated with another dimension or competency. If the same behaviour element can be associated with more than one dimension or competency, it is called "contamination between dimensions or competencies".

Dimension or competency contamination can lead to a situation where a skewed picture of the AC participant's competence level is created. This happens because the same behaviour element is assessed more than once and thus influences the rating of more than one dimension or competency.

5.3 Situations as focal constructs (task competencies)

This approach describes behaviour that is needed for the effective handling of a situation, for example, "The ability to conduct a discussion with a subordinate that will motivate the subordinate to improve his or her job performance so that everyone benefits". This refers to a "counselling discussion". This approach can also describe a specific task, for example, "The ability to solve a problem during an inter-active situation", referring to "problem solving".

---

50 Cascio & Aguinis, 2019

51 Lievens, 1998

52 Foxcroft & Roodt, 2004

A list of required behaviours is identified to deal effectively with the situation or task. This list is then used in the AC observer report forms to assess the participant's ability to deal with the situation or task.[53]

An argument that supports this approach to defining AC focal constructs is that the situation that the participant finds himself or herself in determines whether effective behaviour is demonstrated. A participant might receive effective ratings on some of the dimensions or competencies measured during a counselling discussion simulation, but could also receive ratings of "development needed" on the same dimensions or competencies measured during a group discussion. During the counselling discussion simulation, the participant shows that he or she is capable of demonstrating the required behaviour, but in a different situation, namely the group situation, he or she cannot demonstrate the same level of competence in respect of the same competencies. It is therefore not necessarily the dimensions or competencies that need development, but the participant's ability to perform in a different situation. This indicates that the performance of the participant is situational.

A compromise in deciding which approach to AC focal constructs to use might be to assess both dimensions or competencies and tasks or situations (mixed approach). This will allow a picture to be formed of exactly where development is needed – regarding the input dimensions or competencies (the building blocks), or dealing with the specific situation or task.

5.4 Situations to use as simulations

The AC design team needs clarity on which situations to simulate during the AC. The situations should be typical situations that the target job incumbent is exposed to, or critical situations for the target job. A critical situation is a situation that has critical consequences for the organisation and therefore requires effective job incumbent performance. The design team needs to understand how complex and difficult these situations are, what triggers the situations, what resources the target job incumbent has to address the situations, who else is involved in the situations, the frequency of the situations occurring, the duration of the situations, and what the deliverables or desired outcomes of the situations are.

5.5 Organisational and industry contexts

To be able to design an AC that is face and content valid, the design team needs to understand the trends and characteristics of the organisation and industry of the target job. This understanding will assist in designing a fictitious organisation in which all AC simulations simulate the important aspects of the client organisation's operating environment (see Chapters 11 and 12 for discussions about simulation development).

---

53   Thoresen & Thoresen, 2012; Thornton et al., 2015

6. SUMMARY OF THE PROCESS OF JOB ANALYSIS FOR AC DESIGN PURPOSES

As a summary of the job analysis step, eight sub-steps can be identified. Some of these steps can take place simultaneously, although these are indicated as separate steps in the figure that follows.

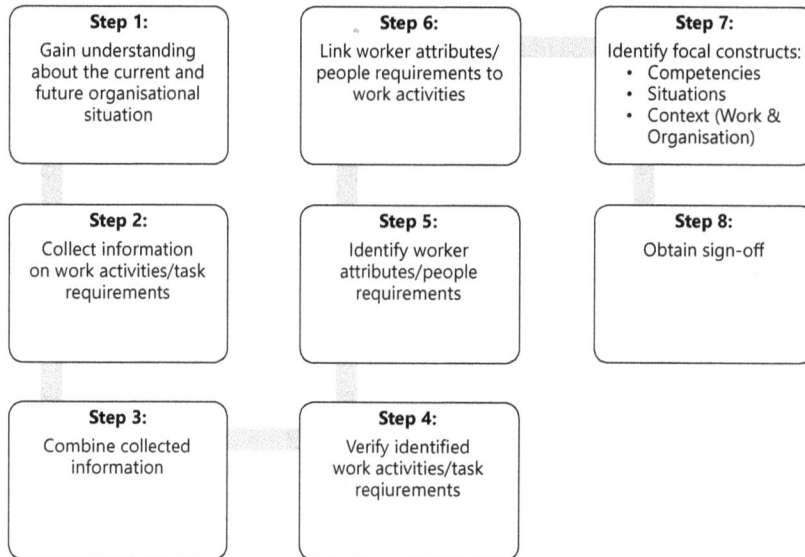

Step 1:
Gain understanding about the current and future organisational situation

Step 6:
Link worker attributes/people requirements to work activities

Step 7:
Identify focal constructs:
- Competencies
- Situations
- Context (Work & Organisation)

Step 2:
Collect information on work activities/task requirements

Step 5:
Identify worker attributes/people requirements

Step 8:
Obtain sign-off

Step 3:
Combine collected information

Step 4:
Verify identified work activities/task requirements

Figure 8.3: Eight steps in the job analysis step of the AC design model

The steps will briefly be discussed:

Step 1: Gain an understanding of the current and future organisational situation

Step one is about understanding the organisation's vision, mission, values, strategic objectives, current and future performance, and operating environment and challenges. Key questions for the AC design team are: What is the impact on the AC and to what extent does the AC need to simulate these?

Step 2: Collect information on work activities/task requirements

The AC design team needs to obtain a comprehensive understanding of the tasks and activities of the specific target job. This is obtained through using various job analysis techniques. What is the target job all about and what makes the job unique are two key questions that need answers.

Step 3: Combine collected information

Since various sources of data during steps one and two will be used, all data need to be integrated into a comprehensive and logical whole. The AC design team can use various techniques such as content analysis and various statistical procedures to assist them in identifying groups of activities and requirements. Various themes or constructs can also emerge from the gathered data.

Step 4: Verify identified work activities/task requirements

The combined information about the target job needs to be verified by the SMEs who participated in the data collection process. In addition, a separate group of SMEs who did not participate in the process can be used to verify the combined information. This could positively contribute to both the face and content validity of the envisioned AC, since two independent groups of SMEs verified the identified activities and requirements.

Step 5: Identify worker attributes/people requirements
Once the work activities have been verified, the KSAOs required to perform the target job need to be identified. Again, the AC design team will involve a group of SMEs to identify the KSAOs.

Step 6: Link worker attributes/people requirements to work activities[54]
This often overlooked step is crucial to ensure the legal defensibility of the focal constructs of the AC. Each KSAO needs to be linked to an identified and verified work activity or task. Again, it is recommended that a group of SMEs verify the links between the people requirements and work activities. A separate group of SMEs could, in addition, be given the list of work activities/task requirements, as well as the list of identified KSAOs, and be asked to match the KSAOs with the work activities/task requirements. This is called retranslation and is advisable when constructing workplace assessments that might impact employees' futures.[55]

Step 7: Identify potential AC focal constructs: competencies, situations, context and their behavioural elements/indicators
The AC design team uses the verified information from the preceding steps to identify the dimensions, competencies, tasks and/or situations that describe the target job. In addition, each dimension, competency or task's/situation's behavioural elements/indicators need to be identified. A process like the following can be used:
- The AC design team, together with a group of SMEs, identifies the initial list of dimensions, competencies or tasks/situations, as well as the definition of each.
- The same team identifies the behavioural elements/indicators linked to each dimension, competency, or task/situation.
- Another group of SMEs is provided with the list of the identified dimensions, competencies, or tasks/situations, as well as the verified information that the previous group of SMEs worked with, and is asked to match the verified information with the dimension, competency, or task/situation.
- This second group of SMEs is also asked to match the identified behavioural elements/indicators with the dimensions, competencies or tasks/situations.

Step 8: Obtain sign-off
The final document summarising the potential AC focal constructs for the target job needs to be signed-off by the AC project steering committee. Typically this document will consist of the following headings: Title page; Executive summary; Project overview and scope; Methodology (description and rationale, alternative methods considered, data sources); Results/Outcomes; References; and Appendices that contain the detailed information.[56]

---

54 Robinson-Morral et al., 2018

55 Cascio & Aguinis, 2019

56 Stetz & Chmielewsla, 2015

7. HINTS FOR CONDUCTING A JOB ANALYSIS FOR AC DESIGN PURPOSES

The purpose of this chapter is not to provide an exhaustive discussion on conducting an effective job analysis, but rather to provide the AC design team with guidelines that will enable it to gather the required information to allow it to design an AC that will be reliable and valid. With this in mind, a few practical hints are discussed below.

7.1 Collect data for two time frames[57]

Focus the job analysis process on gaining information about the target job in the present (as is). This will assist in showing the link between what will be assessed during the AC and inherent job requirements, as is legally required.[58] In addition, collect information about what will be expected of the job in the future. This more strategic perspective of the job will assist with the AC's focal constructs remaining relevant for a period of time. Both time perspectives contribute unique information to the job analysis process and should therefore be part of the process.[59]

7.2 Use multiple sources of information[60]

Include both incumbents, as well as line managers of the target job, as SMEs in the process of data collection. Both groups of SMEs contribute unique information about the job and the inclusion of both groups will probably assist in minimising inaccuracies in the data collected.[61] It is further recommended that more than one person per group be included in the process to collect comprehensive job information.

7.3 Use a representative sample

When a job analysis is conducted, use a representative sample of the incumbents of the target job as participants in the various job analysis techniques. Ensure that all variables are represented, including gender, qualifications, experience, age and race. Also ensure that all variables within the job itself are included in the job analysis techniques, such as the use of technology in performing the job, the location of the job (office-based, home office-based or virtual office; head office versus regional jobs), the number of subordinates, multiple reporting lines, and so on.

Not only will the information gathered during the job analysis be more valid, but the face validity of the information will be higher when a representative sample is used.

---

57 Koch et al., 2012

58 Employment Equity Act., (Act No. 55 of 1998)

59 Koch et al., 2012

60 Koch et al., 2012

61 Koch et al., 2012

7.4 Obtain sign-off from those involved with the job analysis techniques

The principle to adhere to is that every person who "touched" the process should receive feedback on the output of the process. Each person should also confirm, in writing, that he or she agrees with the output, that is, they should sign-off on it.

This serves as evidence of the comprehensiveness and transparency of the process followed, as well as the inclusivity of the process. On a personal level, it also provides completion for those who participated, and hopefully a willingness to participate in a similar project in future.

7.5 Document everything

The information gathered during the job analysis step, together with the information gathered from the organisational effectiveness step (Chapter 7) and the needs analysis step (Chapter 6), will be used to design the simulations and the AC process itself. Since this information forms the basis of the AC, it is necessary to document everything so that future reference to the information will be facilitated. It is necessary to document who participated and on what dates, the data collected, the resulting conclusions, and the feedback from the participants on the conclusions and final outcomes. Create a paper trail of every step within the whole analysis stage.

This documented information should be stored in a safe place so that it can be referred to in the future if it becomes necessary to show the reliability and validity of the AC.

7.6 Get the steering committee's sign-off

A very important group that needs to sign-off on the information gathered and the resulting potential focal constructs is the steering committee for the AC project. The steering committee needs to be informed how the job analysis and the organisational effectiveness analysis were conducted, as well as about the information gathered and the final output of this stage.

Only once the steering committee has given its sign-off (i.e. has agreed to the potential focal constructs) can the AC design team continue with the next stage of the design model, namely the design stage.

8. CRITICAL DECISIONS RELATING TO, AND OUTCOMES OF, THIS STEP

The following are the critical decisions relating to, and outcomes of, the job analysis step.

8.1 Dimension/competency profiles per job level

The first outcome of this step in the analysis stage of the design model is a dimension or competency profile that can be used during the design stage. If the target job is a management job, then the outcome is competency (dimension) profiles – a profile for the supervisory level, another for the middle management level and one for the senior management level within the organisation. These profiles should be the result of a process where the uniqueness of the target job has been analysed in all its detail. The resulting profiles should capture the competencies needed to effectively deliver the uniqueness of the target job.

A golden thread should run through all three of the profiles, clearly indicating what is needed for effective functioning at each level within the organisation, but also indicating the growth in competence needed to perform effectively at each progressive level.

Although the profiles will possibly be used for the AC design, they should also be used to inform the performance management process and the other talent management processes in the organisation.

8.2   Clear dimension or competency definitions

Each dimension or competency within the profiles should be described in clear, simple words. The sentence construction should include only one major idea per sentence, as this will improve the readability of the definition. In addition, it will facilitate understanding of the dimension or competency. This ease of understanding the dimension or competency will assist during observer training when it is necessary to ensure that all observers have the same understanding of the dimension or competency. Clear, understandable definitions will further facilitate the process of giving feedback to AC stakeholders. During the feedback discussion, the feedback recipient needs to understand the dimension or competency before meaningful feedback on performance can be given.

When reading the definition, one should also be able to gain an idea as to whether it is a singular dimension or competency, or a combined dimension or competency.

Although dimension or competency elements will explicitly be indicated for each dimension or competency, they must also be evident when reading the dimension or competency definition. When a clear, comprehensive definition is read, a trained observer will probably be able to identify the elements that will be assessed under the dimension or competency.

8.3   Dimension or competency (behaviour) elements

Each dimension or competency should be broken down into elements that reflect the various visible behaviours that are associated with the specific dimension or competency. For example, the competency, "information gathering", can be broken down into elements such as asking investigative questions, probing issues, linking related information and identifying facts.

The elements associated with each dimension or competency will be used in the observer report forms referred to during the simulation design step in the design stage of the design model (see Chapter 11).

8.4 Situations that the target job incumbent is exposed to

Another outcome of the job analysis is a description of the typical, as well as the critical, situations that the target job incumbent is exposed to. These situations will guide the simulations that can possibly be designed for the AC. Designing simulations that relate to the situations that the job incumbent is exposed to assists in improving the face and content validity of the AC. As an example, even though competency planning and organising might be important to function effectively as a train driver, and an in-box is a good simulation to elicit behaviour linked to planning and organising, designing an in-box to be administered to train drivers to assess planning and organising will be inappropriate, as they are usually not expected to deal with an in-box type situation in their work situation.

8.5 Understanding the target job context and organisational trends

At the end of the job analysis, the AC design team needs to have a clear understanding of the context within which the incumbent of the target job is functioning. For example, who does the job incumbent interact with and what type of supervision is he or she exposed to? The team also needs to understand the organisation's culture, climate, trends and challenges. This understanding assists with deciding what type of situational triggers to build into the simulations. When the situational triggers presented to the participant during the simulation are not a reflection of the triggers experienced by job incumbents, the validity of the AC might again be compromised.

Checklist for the AC Design Team

The design team needs answers to the following questions from two time frames at the end of the job analysis:

1. What is the purpose of the target job?
2. What is the job incumbent accountable for?
3. How does the target job differ from other jobs in the organisation?
4. What differentiates exceptional job performance from mediocre job performance in the target job?
5. What does a typical "day-in-the-life" of the target job incumbent look like?
6. What is the target job incumbent expected to deliver in cycles of 6 months, 12 months, and 18 months?
7. What dimensions or competencies relate to the target job?
8. What are the dimension or competency elements?
9. What situations is the job incumbent exposed to?
10. What outcomes need to be achieved with the various situations?
11. Who does the job incumbent interact with?
12. What is the nature of the interactions with other people?
13. What is the level of complexity that the target job incumbent deals with?
14. What are the job contexts that the job incumbent encounters?
15. What are the characteristics and trends in the organisation and industry?
16. To what extent does the job incumbent use technology?
17. What type of technology does the job incumbent use?

Figure 8.4: Checklist for the AC Design Team

Case Study 2:[62]
What does the new role of a Private Banker entail?

A leading South African bank decided to use simulations as a final assessment after a new learning programme for private bankers. The purpose of the assessment centre (AC) was to determine whether the learners could practically implement what they had learnt during the programme.

As the AC's simulations had to focus on the actual business requirements and deliverables of the role of private banker, it was necessary to do a thorough job analysis of exactly what the current and future role entailed, as well as the business processes, policies and business rules involved.

The following methods were used to get a thorough understanding of the role of the private banker:

Method	Examples of information gathered
Document reviews (**shelf information**)	• Private banker role profile. • Private banker's assistant role profile. • Scorecards. • Organisational structure. • Company strategy and value proposition. • Client segmentation documentation, and many more.
Review of functional criteria (**shelf information**)	• Operational procedures. • Forms. • Business requirement specifications. • Systems manuals/System training manuals. • Reports. • Training material and presentations. • Screen dumps from systems. • System demonstrations.
Presentations by stakeholder teams (for example the L&D team, business intelligence team, client experience team, fiduciary team, etc.)	Examples of questions asked during these presentations: • How does their function impact on the role of the private banker? • How do they help the private banker to achieve their objectives? • What do they expect from the private banker regarding their process? • What are the private bankers currently doing that is working well? • What would they like the private bankers to do differently or better? • What knowledge should the private bankers have regarding their process/function? • What tools do they have to assist the private banker?

---

62   Cillié-Schmidt, 2018

Method	Examples of information gathered
Interviews with line managers (SMEs)	Examples of questions asked during these interviews: • Describe the purpose of the role of the private banker. • How does this role differ from the role of the private banker's assistant? • What does a private banker do? • What makes the difference between a good private banker and others? • How do you measure the performance of the private bankers? • What knowledge and skills do private bankers need? • What systems do private bankers use? • What will your expectations of private bankers be in the future? • What would you like private bankers to do differently or better?
Interviews with private bankers (SMEs)	Examples of questions during these interviews: • Describe the purpose of your role. • Describe what you do during a typical day/week/month/year. • What systems/processes/documents do you use to do your work? • What reports do you have to submit as part of your role? • What planning do you need to do? • Describe the different stakeholders that you interact with and why. • What makes you successful in your role? • What type of training did you receive to prepare you for your role? • What will assist you in making your job easier?
Observing the private banker while they were dealing with clients. In this case samples of good, average and poor performers were observed	The following aspects were noted during the observations: • Process followed. • Behaviour displayed during interaction. • Language used. • Knowledge components of interaction. • Impact on the client.

The upfront analysis provided an in-depth understanding of the role of private banker, as well as an understanding of the processes used by a private banker. The AC design team realised that the role was that of an Advisor, with the following broad processes: new account acquisition, existing account development and retention, client services and support (fulfilment), self-management and portfolio management. In each of these broad processes certain foundation competencies were used, for example product knowledge, relationship building, solution creation, etc.

The final Private Banker Assessment Centre consisted of the following simulations:
• Simulation One: Strategic portfolio planning and management
• Simulation Two: First telephonic contact with a lead
• Simulation Three: First face-to-face meeting with a prospective client
• Simulation Four: Client review (review of an existing client)
• Simulation Five: The private banker's inbox

The value of doing a comprehensive analysis upfront was further realised by drafting behavioural checklists, which were used in the AC's observer report forms. The checklists ensured that the behaviour measured during the simulations related to the functional requirements of the role of the private banker, as well as the related foundational competencies.

ANALYSIS

1. THE PURPOSE OF THE ANALYSIS STAGE

As the name of this stage suggests, it is all about analysis and gaining a systematic understanding of the organisational context, the company's specific needs, and what specific competencies are required in the job. At the beginning of the stage, the purpose of the stage was formulated as being a threefold one:

1.1 Growing a systematic understanding of the organisational context

The organisational context was systematically analysed in Chapter 6 with special reference to the diverse social context in South Africa, the South African legislative context, and the ethical context. In this step, a company-specific needs analysis is conducted with specific reference to information sources that may inform the AC design team of company-specific needs. Thereafter, a specific business case is developed for the implementation of the AC process. Alternatives are considered and a procedure for conducting a utility analysis is provided.

1.2 Understanding the organisation, its dynamics and its specific needs

The organisational effectiveness analysis was covered in Chapter 7. Different views on organisational effectiveness were briefly covered, after which management was introduced as a construct. The different management levels in organisations were introduced with specific reference to the management functions, deliverables and required competencies for each level. A generic competency profile was then suggested for each level.

1.3 Having clarity about the job/role and its demands

The job/role analysis was covered in Chapter 8. During step three of the analysis stage – the job analysis step – attention is focused on understanding the uniqueness of the target job. Understanding is also created of the context in which the job functions. The deliverable of this step is a competency profile(s) that includes behavioural elements and situational triggers. This output will form the input for Stage Two – the design and development stage.

2. CRITICAL DELIVERABLES OF THIS STAGE

The analysis stage focuses on two key deliverables that have to provide the following information in a clear and concise manner:

2.1 Competency profiles, or other focal constructs, and competency/behavioural elements

This stage needs to provide clearly defined competency profiles, or other focal constructs, for each organisational level that will match all the organisational needs as specifically reflected by the organisational needs analysis, the organisational effectiveness analysis and the job analyses. The profiles of focal constructs should consist of clearly defined behavioural elements.

2.2 Establishing criteria for validation and evaluation

This stage should also provide clearly defined and well-developed criteria for the validation and evaluation of the different competency dimensions, but also for the overall AC rating. In order to achieve this, clear overall AC processes, practices and policies need to be established in order to ensure the consistent application thereof.

3. THE FINAL OUTCOME OF THIS STAGE

In the final instance, the organisational context, the company-specific needs analysis and the job analysis should yield a competency profile or a profile of other focal constructs and corresponding assessments that are content valid, as well as the identification of validation criteria that can serve as the basis for validating and evaluating the AC in order to meet current and future organisational needs.

After completing the analysis stage, can you confirm the following?

- That you know the exact nature of the management or functional performance problem you wish to address.
- That you know how a contextual needs analysis will inform the required nature of a company's competencies.
- That you know the exact nature and scope of the company's current and future competency needs.
- That you know what a company's exact competency needs are from the perspective of employees on different levels.
- That you know exactly which behavioural elements are included in each of the competencies.
- That you know which criteria will inform you that these competencies are being successfully executed.
- That you know how you will be assessing the competencies on the different organisational levels.
- That you know which alternatives are available for assessing the competency levels.
- That you know which option is the best in terms of a cost-benefit analysis.

If you can respond positively to all of the above questions, you will have successfully completed the analysis stage.

DESIGN AND DEVELOPMENT

1. WHAT THE DESIGN AND DEVELOPMENT STAGE IS ALL ABOUT

The second stage in the AC design model, which is discussed in the next section of the book, is the design and development stage. This stage is highlighted in Figure S2.1.

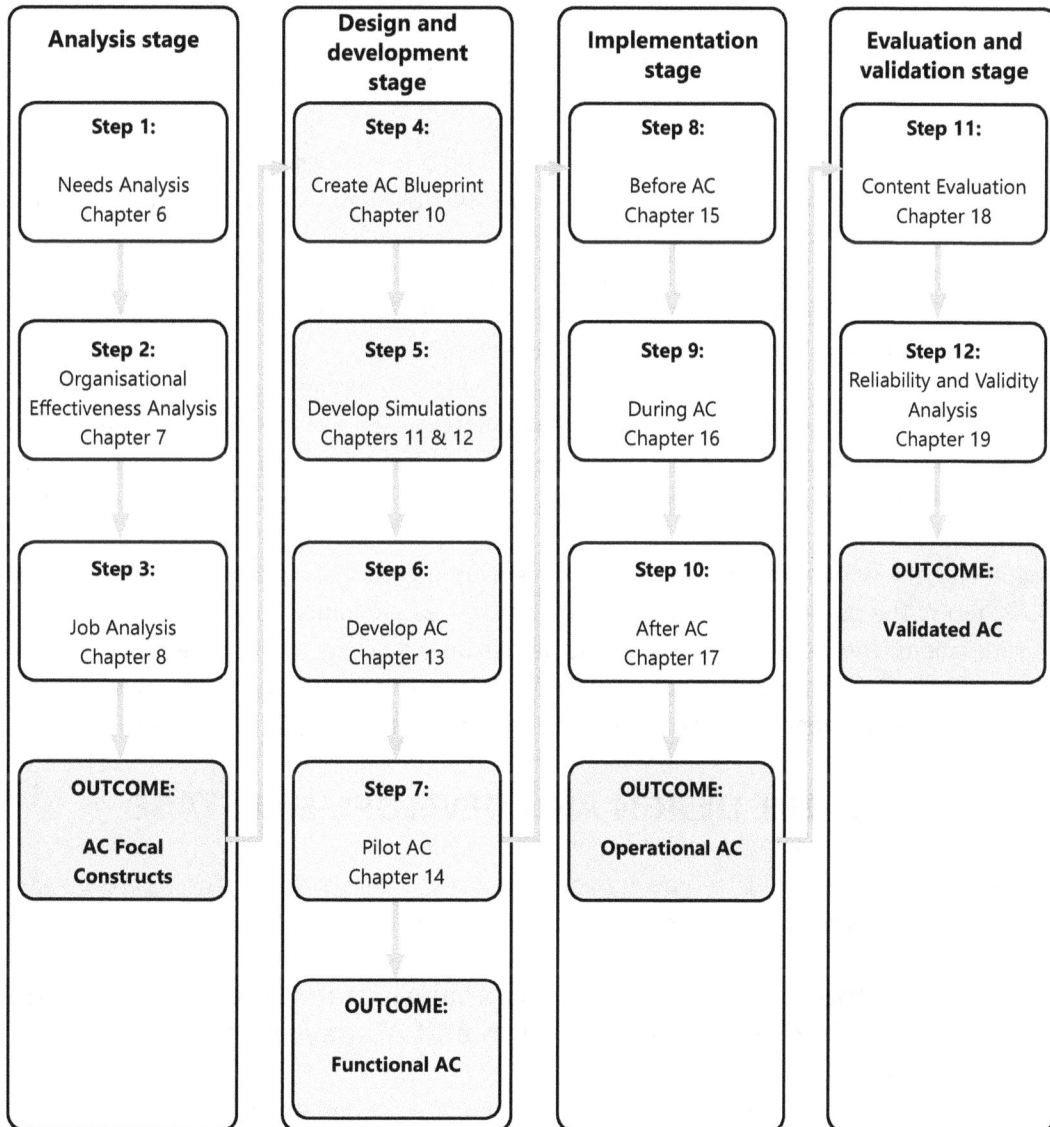

Analysis stage	Design and development stage	Implementation stage	Evaluation and validation stage
Step 1: Needs Analysis Chapter 6	**Step 4:** Create AC Blueprint Chapter 10	**Step 8:** Before AC Chapter 15	**Step 11:** Content Evaluation Chapter 18
Step 2: Organisational Effectiveness Analysis Chapter 7	**Step 5:** Develop Simulations Chapters 11 & 12	**Step 9:** During AC Chapter 16	**Step 12:** Reliability and Validity Analysis Chapter 19
Step 3: Job Analysis Chapter 8	**Step 6:** Develop AC Chapter 13	**Step 10:** After AC Chapter 17	**OUTCOME:** **Validated AC**
OUTCOME: **AC Focal Constructs**	**Step 7:** Pilot AC Chapter 14	**OUTCOME:** **Operational AC**	
	OUTCOME: **Functional AC**		

Figure S2.1: Steps in, and stages of, the AC Design Model

The design and development stage takes the analysis stage's output and turns it into the reality of a functional AC. The stage consists of four steps, each of which uses the output of the previous step and transforms it into a deliverable that brings us closer to a functional AC. The first step in the stage uses the competency profiles or other focal construct profiles, as well as the organisational trends identified during the analysis stage, as the basis on which the AC Blueprint is designed. The second step in this stage develops simulations according to the specifications set-out in the AC Blueprint. The simulations are sequenced to form an AC, the third step in this stage. The AC is piloted during the last step of this stage.

The layout of the next section is as follows:

- Before the design and development of the AC is discussed, Chapter 9 introduces the theories on which ACs rest.
- Chapter 10 highlights a critical step in the whole design process, i.e. the AC Blueprint, which takes the output of the analysis stage and designs a plan to inform the development of the AC (Step 4 in the design model).
- Chapter 11 deals with simulation development – Step 5 in the design model. The chapter starts by providing an operational definition of a simulation, followed by an introduction to typical AC simulations. The rating scales are then discussed, followed by design hints and the documentation that needs to be developed. The special case of parallel simulations, as well as the use of information technology in the development of simulations receive attention, before the chapter concludes by stating the critical decisions and outcomes of the step.
- Chapter 12 deals with the development of the AC – Step 6. The chapter starts with AC design hints, followed by an introduction to the various programmes needed at an AC. This chapter introduces the AC administrator and describes the additional documentation needed at an AC. The AC manual is briefly discussed before the chapter concludes with the critical decisions and outcomes of the step.
- Chapter 13, the last chapter in the design and development stage, deals with administering a pilot AC – Step 7. The purpose of the AC pilot is discussed, as are important content and face validity considerations. The selection criteria for the people attending the AC pilot are highlighted before other important considerations are introduced. Hints on conducting an effective AC pilot are shared and the chapter concludes with the critical decisions relating to, and outcomes of, the step.

2. PURPOSE OF THE DESIGN AND DEVELOPMENT STAGE

The purpose of the design and development stage is to deliver a functional AC. This is brought about by achieving the following incremental purposes leading to the overall purpose:

2.1 To translate the information from the analysis stage into an operational AC Blueprint that will guide simulation and AC development

The information obtained during the analysis stage should be translated into a document that can guide the simulation and, eventually, the AC design. This document is called the AC Blueprint.

2.2 To develop simulations and the support documentation that allow observers to make valid and reliable assessments of the behaviour

A simulation should be designed with the purpose of eliciting visible behaviour from the participant that can be associated with the focal constructs being evaluated in the simulation. The information gained during Stage One of the design model (Chapters 6 to 8) dictates the specifications and parameters that the simulation should adhere to. The final simulation should therefore be designed in such a way that it adheres to the specifications, falls within the parameters, elicits the required behaviour and does not elicit unwanted behaviour. The visible behaviour of participants during a simulation is observed, noted, classified and evaluated (ONCE) by observers. The simulation design should facilitate this process of observation and evaluation. If the participant behaviour cannot be ONCEd, the simulation is not fulfilling its purpose.

2.3 To design an AC process that effectively combines the various simulations

The various simulations intended for use during the AC should be sequenced in such a way that they are most effective in terms of time, cost and participant/observer/role player/administrator performance.

2.4 To design an AC that is ready for implementation

At the end of Stage Two, all the simulations, documentation, processes and programmes should be developed and tested, and perhaps adapted, so that they adhere to all the requirements set during Stage One of the design model.

3. CRITICAL DELIVERABLES OF THIS STAGE

The following are the critical deliverables of Stage Two:

3.1 An AC manual

All documentation related to the various simulations and the AC as a whole should be compiled into a single document called the AC manual. This manual contains all the participant and process owner documentation needed during the AC.

3.2 A technical AC manual

The technical AC manual documents everything related to the AC pilot. The purpose of the manual is to provide an audit trail for use during the implementation and validation stage of the design model.

4. THE INTENDED OUTCOME OF THIS STAGE

A functional AC that is ready for implementation is the intended outcome of this stage. All the simulations, documentation, programmes and processes should have been designed, tested and sequenced in such a way as to allow optimal performance of everyone at the AC. The functional AC now becomes the input for the next stage in the design model, namely the implementation stage.

CHAPTER 9

THEORETICAL PRINCIPLES RELEVANT TO ASSESSMENT CENTRE DESIGN AND IMPLEMENTATION

George C. Thornton III and Filip Lievens

"There is nothing so practical as a good theory."[1]

1. INTRODUCTION

Decades ago, ACs originated by applying the best available evidence and theory to the assessment of managerial performance dimensions.[2] The objectives of this chapter are to take stock of these existing theoretical principles, present additional theoretical principles that have emerged in recent times, and describe the practical implications of these principles for effective AC design and implementation. Thus, while all ACs include several essential elements, developing and implementing a specific AC involves a complicated set of choices. This chapter shows how these choices can be guided by theories relevant to the AC method as a whole and to each of its essential elements. The chapter is quite timely because of recent research findings questioning the validity and fairness of ACs and practical pressures to streamline the process. Furthermore, the chapter is the first to explicate the applications of these several theories in one place.

The practical implications of the theories cited in this chapter are to a large extent compatible with guidance from several other valuable sources:
- Guidelines and ethical considerations for assessment center operations, including international[3] and South African guidelines.[4]
- Laws and regulations governing psychological testing and assessment, specifically ACs.
- Research findings from empirical studies.[5]
- Benchmarking provided by surveys of AC practices around the world.

These principles generalise reasonably well across the different types of ACs, even though some might become more important than others depending on the type and purpose of the AC. For example, standardisation may be essential for many high-stakes ACs used for promotion in civil service organisations, but somewhat less relevant for diagnosing strengths and developing high-potential executives.

---

1   Lewin, 1951

2   Bray & Grant, 1966

3   International Taskforce on Assessment Center Guidelines, 2015

4   http://www.ACsg.co.za/ac_information/guidelines

5   Thornton et al., 2015

2. BACKGROUND

The AC method has evolved over the years. Starting in a few large business organisations in industrialised countries to make high-stakes promotions, it has spread to governmental and educational organisations of all sizes across continents to facilitate a wide array of talent management activities. Whereas the method was for many years conducted in quite similar ways, now all of its elements have been adapted to meet different objectives and local needs.

In this chapter we present a series of relevant theoretical principles that provide practical implications for the construction and implementation of ACs. In addition, we give a description of each theoretical principle and their implications for building effective ACs. Table 9.1 summarises the key points in the chapter.[6]

3. THEORIES RELATED TO THE OVERALL AC METHOD

This section deals with theories related to the overall AC method, which are relevant to more than one essential AC element. The next section deals with theories related to specific elements of the AC method. The reader will see that the theories often overlap and are usually compatible, and in the end they reinforce each other to buttress the AC as a whole. We acknowledge that the implications of the theories in the two sections often overlap and strengthen one another. Throughout the chapter we initially present each theory separately as though it operates independently of other theories, as we believe that this clarifies the unique contribution of each. We further point out connections between multiple theories.

3.1 Behavioural consistency

Behavioural consistency is a basic principle of the AC method[7] that assumes that participants' behaviour in a selection process will be consistent with their behaviour on the job. In ACs, it means that the behaviours displayed in simulations mirror work behaviour. A related, and more concrete, principle is point-to-point correspondence.[8] This suggests that simulations should be built to reflect key tasks of the job and to elicit specific behaviours in the exercises that correspond with specific behaviours required on the job.

The principle of behaviour consistency helps to clarify the difference between high-fidelity and low-fidelity simulations. High-fidelity simulations such as work samples and AC simulations call for participants to demonstrate overt behaviour mirroring work behaviour. By contrast, low-fidelity simulations such as situational judgment tests capture behavioural intentions and procedural knowledge of appropriate behaviour, but not actual overt behaviour. While overt behaviours are central to both work samples

---

6 Portions of the text and table in this chapter have been published in Thornton, Mueller-Hanson & Rupp, 2017. So as not to burden the presentation with frequent citations, we acknowledge this source in the following sections: 3.2, 3.3, 3.4.1, 3.5, 4.2, 4.3, 4.4, 4.5, 6 and Table 7.1.

7 Wernimont & Campbell, 1968

8 Schmitt & Ostroff, 1986

and simulations, these two methods differ. Whereas work samples are often exact replicas of discrete tasks on the job, simulations call for performance in situations similar to the job. ACs can thus assess competencies even though the person does not have direct work experience.

3.2 Interactionist theory

Interactionist theory[9] states that behaviour is a function of both the person and environment. The theory is expressed as a simple formula: $B = f (P \times E)$. The assumption is that behaviour will be affected by both person variables (that is, there are individual differences in performance levels) and characteristics of the environment. Thus, for behavioural consistency to yield an accurate assessment, both relevant performance dimensions and high-fidelity simulations must be chosen, as described in subsequent sections of this chapter.

Note the "x" in the formula. This means that there is an *interaction* between the characteristics of the person and the situation, not just an addition of the two. In other words, the theory assumes both person and situation variables are in a dynamic interaction, and they affect each other in different ways. For example, an AC participant may be an effective leader in coaching a single staff member, but not so effective in leading a group of peers.

One implication of this theory is that at the design stage of ACs, both multiple diverse competencies being assessed and multiple diverse situations depicted in the simulation should be clearly specified and different from each other. The AC developer should keep in mind that if the competencies are very similar to one another, it is unlikely that they will provide unique diagnostic information. The same is true for situations depicted in the simulations. Extensive similarities among competencies or simulations could mean not accounting for the full performance domain if the purpose of the assessment is prediction/selection, or not being able to produce a profile of strengths and developmental needs if the purpose is diagnosis/development.

An extension of this implication is that the difficulty of assessment should be set at a level which results in individual differences among participants in behaviour and differences in performance across diverse situations for any one participant. To be useful for either selection or development, the scores should vary across situations.

A second implication is that the scoring and reporting should consider:
- overall ratings for each competency (across situations);
- overall ratings for each situation or exercise (across competencies); and
- for each competency, a person's *pattern* of proficiency across situations (i.e. how consistent he or she is across situations[10]).

---

9   Lewin, 1951; Mischel & Shoda, 1995

10   Gibbons & Rupp, 2009

3.3 Realistic accuracy model

The AC method calls for multiple observers to observe, classify and rate behaviours in multiple simulation exercises. Several steps are taken to ensure the accuracy of ratings, including careful choice and training of observers, and use of rating aids to support the observers' judgments. Funder's Realistic Accuracy Model is relevant to the AC process because it describes what must happen for a perceiver to provide accurate judgments about a person's traits.[11] The process includes four steps:

1. The person must show in some way behaviour relevant to the trait being judged.
2. Behaviours relevant to the trait must be available/observable to the perceiver.
3. The perceiver must detect/know what behaviours are relevant to the trait.
4. The perceiver must utilise and interpret the behaviours correctly.

These steps of the Realistic Accuracy Model have direct application to ACs. In particular, in a first step, the simulation must be designed to elicit behaviours relevant to the dimension being assessed. Design features that can elicit relevant behaviours include instructions, case material, questions by role players, follow-up questions by observers, etc. Second, the participant in the simulation must have the opportunity to display relevant behaviours, for example, all participants in a group discussion simulation must have the opportunity to participate fully. The assessment situation must be arranged so the observer assigned to observe a particular participant can see that participant display or omit dimension-relevant behaviours. While a simulation is unfolding, observers must be close enough (physically or virtually) to see and hear what participants are doing and saying. A lack of opportunity to observe may occur in complex group simulations where participants move around a great deal. Video technology could thus be used to rewind specific participant interventions and actions. Third, observers must be trained to know what dimension-relevant behaviours to watch for. During observer training, clear definitions of the dimensions (including detailed behavioural examples of various levels of proficiency on the dimensions) must be provided. Fourth, after the observers observe participant behaviours, they must know how to evaluate the effectiveness of the behaviours for the dimensions being assessed.

The principles embedded in the Realistic Accuracy Model encompass and further articulate both the behaviour-driven and schema-driven theories of perception of social interactions.[12] The Model assumes observers can carefully observe and use specific behavioural cues. It also assumes that observation and judgment will be guided and improved by providing observers with clearly defined performance dimensions. Furthermore, the Model undergirds the processes of frame-of-reference training.[13]

According to Funder, this stepwise process is more likely to result in accurate personality judgments when four conditions are present. These four conditions are seen as moderators of the above steps and accurate judgments. The first moderator is a "good target", that is, the person is easy to figure out. Some people are more transparent and provide more, and more consistent, behaviours. For example,

11 Funder, 2012

12 Lievens, 2001; Thornton & Rupp, 2006

13 Schleicher et al., 2002

some people are more open in their expressions. To the extent possible, participants in ACs should be encouraged to be open and cooperative in demonstrating behaviours relevant to the dimensions being assessed. If the participants are reticent and even evasive, assessments may be more difficult.

The second moderator is "good traits". Traits such as extraversion and agreeableness are easier to judge than traits such as values and deceptiveness, i.e. some dimensions are more "assessable" than others. For example, it is much easier to obtain accurate assessments of dimensions such as Oral Communication and Interpersonal Effectiveness than Career Ambition in a standard AC simulation.[14]

Third is the factor: "good information". This means accuracy will be greater when high quality information is available to the perceiver. The trait activation principle of designing moderately strong simulations (see below) that elicit dimension-relevant behaviour is relevant here. In addition, the simulation must also provide multiple cues for participants to demonstrate several behaviours relevant to the dimensions. This implication is also related to the psychometric principle that more observations enhance reliability ("law of aggregation", see below).

Fourth, "good judges" should be available. In the case of ACs, this refers to carefully selected, conscientious and well-trained observers who, apart from being skilled in observation and evaluation, should also create a comfortable atmosphere for participants to be as open and expressive as possible. Observers must be trained to make the participants feel comfortable and not threatened. In short, the accuracy of observations and evaluations of behaviour are central to any form and application of the AC method.

Funder's Realistic Accuracy Model suggests various ways to optimise assessment using organisational simulations. Suggestions apply to both simulation design (so as to improve trait expression) and observers (so as to improve the observation/evaluation process). Recent research also attests to the importance of the interplay between these aspects. In particular, in a series of studies, Lievens, Schollaert and Keen found that when trait-relevant behaviour was elicited and observer training was employed, behaviours were more observable and ratings were more accurate, reliable, and valid.[15] So, to improve the elicitation of behaviours relevant to the dimensions being assessed, role players should be trained to provide cues that prompt participants to demonstrate dimension-relevant behaviours. In addition, to improve the evaluation of behaviours, observers should be trained on the behavioural cues designed into the simulation (for example, specific role player behaviours). This will lead the observer to watch for behaviours relevant to the dimensions being assessed.

3.4 Psychometric theories

Psychometric theories provide guidance for the construction of all psychological measurement tools, including the AC method. Below we focus on principles related to standardisation, aggregation and heterogeneous domain sampling.

---

14 Bowler & Woehr, 2006

15 Lievens et al., 2015

3.4.1 Standardisation

Standardisation refers to the consistency of administration and scoring. A measure is standardised if all participants are presented with the same questions, testing conditions, and response options. Standardisation is important because it has direct implications for the outcomes of an assessment, including reliability and validity.[16] Standardisation is particularly challenging for complex and interactive simulations, where it includes uniformity in:

- instructions;
- materials;
- time allowances;
- interactions with administrators, role players and observers;
- methods of observing, recording, and classifying behavioural responses; and
- standards of judgment by observers.

Standardisation is essential when the purpose of the AC is to provide information for high-stakes decision making. The results of an assessment will be fair to all participants for selection or promotion only if everyone is treated the same. When the results will be used for diagnosis or development, standardisation is still important but perhaps less critical. For example, observers may ask different questions of participants in a programme where individualised assessment is pivotal to provide recommendations for differentially important follow-up interventions.

The practical implications are to establish and follow prescribed procedures for all aspects of the AC method, including orientation, instructions, assessment situation, behaviour of role players in interaction simulations, follow-up questions by observers, time provided, and scoring.

Standardisation, reliability, and validity are related, but not necessarily in ways that are readily apparent. At the surface, it may typically be the case that standard conditions will enhance reliability and validity. For example, if all observers are required to ask only the same standard questions of all participants after the completion of a role play simulation, this will eliminate biases that might influence evaluations. On the other hand, if observers are allowed to follow up with unique questions for different participants, a more in-depth understanding of each individual may increase the scope and thus the validity of the assessment. Similarly, a forced inter-observer agreement may preclude unique insights into a participant's full set of true abilities. The old adage is apt here: people touching the trunk, tusk, tail and leg of an elephant will surely provide different, and accurate, descriptions of an elephant. After all, perfect agreement may be reliable but not fully valid. If observers show perfect agreement, why have more than one observer?

3.4.2 Aggregation

The principle of aggregation implies that a measure which includes an increasing number of questions or observations will provide a more stable measurement.[17] Any individual test item includes some

---

16 Ghiselli et al., 1981

17 Epstein, 1979

error of measurement, however an average over several items reduces the error of measurement of the aggregation. In general, a longer test will be more reliable than a one-item test. This principle undergirds many essential features of the AC method: multiple dimensions, assessment techniques, simulations, observations, and observers. For example, because many simulations call for observers to make judgments about behaviour, inter-rater reliability/agreement is particularly important, and can be improved with multiple, well-trained observers.

Several practical implications for ACs flow from this principle. Ask multiple observers to make multiple ratings of multiple dimensions based on multiple observations of behaviour in multiple simulation exercises; the reliability of dimension ratings and the overall assessment rating will be enhanced following this principle.

3.5 Heterogeneous domain sampling model

A number of related theories argue for heterogeneous methods. Cronbach and Meehl reasoned that construct validity is established by a series of studies, including investigation of the internal structure of the test, to determine if it matches the hypothesised structure of the construct to be measured, which may be quite complex such as job performance.[18] Classical psychometric theory says that a measure will have construct and predictive validity if it has diverse content which matches the complexity in the criterion being predicted.[19] The heterogeneous domain sampling model states that a predictor will correlate with a complex criterion if it is composed of a set of measures known to be related to the criterion.[20] For example, a measure of emotional intelligence was found to be related to supervisory-related job performance because it is composed of measures of a heterogeneous sample of seven components, such as cognitive ability, emotional stability and conscientiousness.[21]

The heterogeneous domain sampling model implies that a diverse set of measurement methods, including tests, questionnaires and multi-source (360 degree) ratings, along with behavioural observations in simulation exercises, will enhance the accuracy of an AC. Such diversity was common in early ACs[22], and in recent years there has been a move to again include a wide variety of other assessment techniques, especially to assess executives and high potentials for top leadership positions.[23] By implication, the principle argues for using a diverse set of types of simulations; it is better to have three different types of exercises (for example, a group discussion, case, and interview simulation) rather than three of only one type (say, three group discussions).

---

18 Cronbach & Meehl, 1955

19 Nunnally & Bernstein, 1994

20 Joseph et al., 2015

21 Kunnanatt, 2004

22 Thornton & Byham, 1982

23 Thornton et al., 2016

3.6 Gamification

Gamification refers to applying game mechanics and dynamics to non-game situations for the purpose of enhancing participant motivation and engagement. The key distinction between games and gamification is that games are for the sole purpose of entertaining the players, whereas gamification is applied to non-entertainment contexts for the purpose of achieving some other goal, for example, deepen assessment, change behaviour, develop a new skill, drive innovation.[24]

No concise and widely accepted theory of gamification has emerged, however a comprehensive list of nine widely mentioned elements of gamification was provided by Bedwell, Pavlas, Heyne, Lazzara and Salas[25], which includes action language (how the player communicates with the system), assessment (feedback given the player), conflict/challenge (the difficulty, problems, and uncertainty presented), control (the degree of interaction and agency the player has), environment (presentation of the physical surroundings), game fiction (fantasy and mystery in the story and world), human interaction (human-to-human contact), immersion (player's perception of immediacy and salience), and rules/goals (clear rules to attain goals). Mechanisms to employ gamification include earning and accumulating points, achieving levels of advancement, badges showing awards, and leader boards showing which players have top scores or ranks.

In many ways, organisational simulations in ACs are already "gamified", that is, they have always employed elements of gamification such as challenge, immersion and fiction, but not other elements such as fantasy, immediate feedback and leaderboards.

There appears to be different potential for building elements of gamification into simulations used for different purposes, for example simulations used for high-stakes assessment might include different forms for action language and control. Simulations used for training/development, however, might include letting participants try multiple solutions to a problem; providing feedback at multiple points in the AC; and focusing on the ability to learn from mistakes and do better in subsequent trials.

Recommendations for the application of gamification concepts for the AC include:
- being clear about the purpose of gamification and making sure it is appropriate to the situation, i.e. do not pursue gamification for entertainment's sake or simply to give the experience more surface "frills";
- ensuring you have a deep understanding of the business' and players' goals. Use gamification which helps both the organisation and participants achieve their goals, for example, assess participant skills plus give participants a realistic preview of work so they can make an informed decision about whether the organisation is right for them;
- designing the experience to engage target audiences (for example, millennials, experienced managers) at a relevant emotional level; and
- doing a careful analysis of whether the costs of technological advances needed to employ gamification are worth the benefits.

---

24 Landers et al., 2015

25 Bedwell et al., 2012

The disadvantages of gamified assessments in work settings is that they may appear silly and irrelevant, and may contaminate the assessment of relevant competencies among some participants.

4. THEORIES RELATED TO ELEMENTS OF THE AC METHOD

In this section we describe the practical implications of theories related to individual essential elements of the AC method, i.e. analysis of the performance domain; definitions of competencies to be measured; features of situations in the simulation exercises; multiple assessment methods; simulation exercises; overt behavioural responses and observations; multiple, trained observers; and systematic integration of multiple sources of information.

4.1 Multiple methods of defining the domain

Understanding the performance domain and providing guidance for assessment involves multiple methods, ranging from in-depth job analyses of current performance on individual jobs, to broader competency modeling of current and future organisational strategic goals. Analytical methods include the study of existing job descriptions, questionnaires, on-the-job observations, examination of an organisation's goals and objectives, expert opinions, and interviews and focus groups with incumbents, managers and executives. The results of such methods include the identification of attributes to be assessed, tasks to be accomplished, the industry and setting to be built into simulations, or the roles carried out by incumbents in the target organisation.

A key practical implication is to use multiple methods to analyse the job and its requirements; there is no one best way. In addition, the AC developer should study the target job in the current organisation – do not rely only on job information from existing sources. Furthermore, these methods should be conducted before the subsequent steps in AC development. Finally, contemporaneously document all these methods to provide a defence of the AC.

4.2 Taxonomy of competencies

A large number of human characteristics such as knowledge, skills, abilities, and other personality variables have been found to affect job performance, and can be evaluated with diverse predictor measures. The distinction between predictors (predictor constructs) and criteria (criterion constructs) is important. In this section we focus on predictor constructs, and note that past theory and research have shown that these characteristics can be clustered into a manageable number of competencies.

Shore, Thornton and Shore identified two broad categories of dimensions in a single large AC: performance style (e.g. originality and work orientation) and interpersonal style (e.g. orientation to people and impact).[26] Arthur, Day, McNelly and Edens identified 168 dimensions from 34 empirical AC research studies. These dimensions were systematically collapsed into seven competencies: organising and planning, problem solving, drive, communication, consideration/awareness, influencing

---

26   Shore et al., 1990

others, and tolerance for stress/uncertainty. The seven dimensions were further collapsed into three categories (administrative, drive and relational dimensions) derived from the leadership literature.[27] Meriac, Hoffman and Woehr factor-analysed numerous sets of AC dimensions and confirmed a model including administrative skills, relational skills and drive.[28]

These frameworks provide useful bases for ACs, as a designer need not "reinvent the wheel". These competencies can be adopted and adapted to fit new applications and programmes, as long as the analysis phase shows evidence of their job relevance, and as long as they are defined according to the context of the focal organisation and job. The definition of these competencies provided in the sources cited can be adapted and supplemented by terminology in specific organisations. For example, while leadership may be defined simply as the "ability to influence others", it will help to describe the behaviours for the type and style of leadership deemed appropriate in a specific organisation.

A second implication is that it is not necessary or feasible to assess a long list of dimensions. In many applications, organisations have tried to assess more dimensions than observers can handle. Recent research indicated that observers are capable of assessing no more than four to six different dimensions[29], thus the AC developer can look to the taxonomies described above to winnow the list of dimensions to a manageable number.

4.3 Taxonomy of situations

In comparison with the several well developed taxonomies of human characteristics forming the bases for AC dimensions, there are few widely accepted taxonomies of situational characteristics to provide guidance in constructing the content of organisational simulations. This can be frustrating because the number of potential situational characteristics to consider probably surpasses the number of human characteristics.

Recently, four taxonomies provided frameworks for constructing the situations in AC exercises. First, VUCA originated in US military educational settings to describe military challenges[30] and is now being used to provide a description of the general business environment.[31] VUCA means *Volatility, Uncertainty, Complexity* and *Ambiguity*. Consulting organisations are using this framework to design assessment tools. Second, DIAMONDS provides a taxonomy of eight dimensions of psychologically meaningful situational characteristics. People perceive the situation to call for *Duty* when something needs to be done. *Intellect* is salient when the situation presents intellectual challenges and deep thinking is required. *Adversity* is present when the situation contains threats and conflicts. *Mating* is salient in many social situations but is probably not one that will commonly be depicted in AC exercises. *pOsitivity* means the situation is approachable, pleasant and fun. *Negativity* means the situation is frustrating, tense and can cause negative feelings. If there are issues of mistrust, lying and betrayal permeating the

27 Arthur et al., 2003

28 Meriac et al., 2014

29 Thornton et al., 2015

30 Steihm & Townsend, 2002; Whiteman, 1998

31 Bennett & Lemoine, 2014

situation, *Deception* is present.[32] Finally, *Sociality* is a situation in which social interactions are present and important. Third, Hoffman, Kennedy, LoPilato, Monahan and Lance used a taxonomy of five exercise characteristics to study the validity of AC exercises: *Complexity*: information processing is required for effective task completion; *Interdependence*: cooperation is required for effective task performance; *Structure*: the task is well-defined and unambiguous; *Interpersonal*: interaction among participants is required; and *Fidelity*: the exercise is consistent with the job context.[33] (In a following section, the notion of fidelity is expanded.) Fourth, the basis for developing new simulations may come from taxonomies of psychological situations such as the features of CAPTION: Complexity, Adversity, Positive Valence, Typicality, Importance, humor, and Negative Valence.[34]

There is both commonality (for example, complexity, positivity vs. negativity/adversity, ambiguity vs. structure, sociability/interdependence) and uniqueness (for example, volatility, deception) among the features in these models relevant to ACs. More theoretical development and analyses are needed to compare and contrast the characteristics in these models to whittle them down to a common core of situational variables. In the meantime, the lists provide practical suggestions for AC developers to select impactful and representative situations in AC exercises.

What these perspectives suggest for simulation developers is that, during the analysis stage, effort should be taken to identify the core situational characteristics of the focal job, as well as the organisational and industry contexts. These existing taxonomies can provide guidance on the types of characteristics to look for. Once identified, the most job-relevant situational characteristics can be built into the simulation. These elements might serve as situational cues of dimension-relevant behaviour, or as units of assessment in and of themselves (i.e. where exercise proficiency is measured in addition to dimensional proficiency).

4.4 Trait Activation Theory (TAT)

As noted in Section 3. 2, social scientists have long recognised that a person's behaviour is "caused" by both characteristics of the individual (for example, personality and ability) and characteristics of the situation. Trait Activation Theory (TAT) is an example of an interactionist theory that has emerged in recent years as an important framework in the AC field for better understanding trait expression.[35] Building on early works by Murray and Allport[36], TAT addresses how individual traits come to be expressed as behaviour in response to trait-relevant situational demands. Two factors are posited to be of central importance. The first factor is *situation-trait relevance*, i.e. a situation is considered relevant to a trait if it provides cues for the expression of trait relevant behaviour.[37] Thus, situation trait relevance is a qualitative feature of situations that is essentially trait specific; it is informative with regard to which cues are present to elicit behaviour for a given latent trait. Such cues are considered to fall into three

32 Rauthmann et al., 2014

33 Hoffman et al., 2015

34 Parrigon, Woo, Tay & Wang, 2017

35 Lievens et al., 2009; Tett & Burnett, 2003; Tett & Guterman, 2000

36 Murray, 1938; Allport, 1951

37 Tett & Guterman, 2000

broad and interrelated categories: task/individual, social/group, and the organisation. For example, the need for autonomy may be activated by arbitrarily structured tasks, rule-driven bosses, and/or protracted dealings with bureaucratic organisations. In this example, the common theme linking these situations is restriction in behaviour options, which is relevant to the trait of need for autonomy.

The second factor in TAT, *situation strength,* refers to the clarity and imperative nature of situational cues. A *strong* situation produces similar behavioural responses from virtually all individuals, whereas responses vary considerably in *weak* situations. Strong situations are thus situations that are so powerful that they suppress individual differences, while weak situations have few normative expectations for behaviour, therefore individual differences in personality are readily observable. For example, a casual social gathering can be considered a rather weak situation; some people will be outgoing and gregarious, while others will tend to be quiet and reserved. Although Mischel was the first to distinguish between strong and weak situations[38], Meyer, Dalal and Hermida delineated four conditions that have to be present for situations to be called strong situations.[39] These are that they should be: (1) consistent, (2) clear, (3) have important positive or negative social consequences, and (4) appropriate responses fall within narrow ranges.

The two factors (relevance and strength) outlined in TAT have direct relevance to designing simulations. In terms of situational trait relevance, the situation must allow for the trait to be expressed. In other words, an individual must be able to demonstrate a particular personality trait through his or her behaviour. In terms of situational strength, the developer must take care to ensure that the situation in the simulation is weak enough to allow individual differences to shine through, but not so weak that behaviours relevant to a trait will not be elicited. Furthermore, simulations should be generally designed to assess how individuals differ along several dimensions (for example, leadership, communication skills, interpersonal sensitivity).

More concretely, AC designers have various options to put these two principles into practice by taking them into account when designing the exercise as a whole. For example, if an organisation wishes to assess oral communication, participants will be more or less able to demonstrate this proficiency depending on how the simulation is structured. For example, if the simulation is a group discussion with non-assigned roles, observers may or may not have a chance to observe behaviours relevant to oral communication skills. If the group contains a few very aggressive and talkative individuals, these participants may dominate the conversation, allowing very few opportunities to observe the communication skills of the quieter group members. Instead of eliciting oral communication, the simulation in this example has elicited dominance. The simulation could be redesigned to elicit oral communication by simply instructing the group members to each make a five-minute presentation to the group, stating their position before the discussion ensues. Therefore, after the desired dimensions have been identified, the simulation developer must carefully design the simulation so that behaviours relevant to these dimensions will be elicited. The simulation must be structured so that it provides cues to elicit the dimensions, for example, instructions may ask participants why they chose a course of action as a prompt for decision making behaviours.

---

38 Mischel, 1973

39 Meyer et al., 2010

In addition, AC designers can train role players to use specific predetermined cues for eliciting trait-relevant behaviour (aka prompts). For example, role player cues triggering interpersonal sensitivity might vary from a momentarily distressed facial expression in someone present to overt sobbing. An early and well-known example of how to design a simulation with role players to elicit dimension-relevant leadership behaviours is the construction exercise in the process of assessing espionage agents for the Office of Strategic Services in World War II.[40] Participants were asked to supervise two role player assistants, Kippy and Buster, to build a structure out of poles and blocks. Kippy was passive and sluggish; he did nothing without specific instructions. Buster was aggressive, too ready with impractical suggestions, and critical of the participant. The actions they displayed are examples of "cues" designed to elicit behaviour relevant to Leadership, Emotional Stability, Energy, and Initiative, that is dimensions relevant to the service as espionage agents. Observers were trained to observe how the participants responded to these cues. In more recent times, AC designers have relied on technology to plant cues into assessment centre exercises. Examples are incoming emails, sudden obstacles, or an influx of additional information in online in-baskets/boxes. Research shows that the use of such predetermined cues to elicit trait-related behaviour are generally effective in terms of increasing observability, inter-rater reliability, and discriminant validity, especially when observers are familiar with these cues.[41]

Another set of cues comes from the instructions for a simulation. If the group members are told that their oral communication skills will be evaluated and that they should participate actively in the discussion, they are more likely to do so. Research has demonstrated that merely providing more information about the dimensions upon which one will be assessed increases the display of dimension-relevant behaviours.[42] However, more information might also reduce criterion-related validity, so it is important not to create situations which are not too strong.

4.5 Taxonomy of aspects of fidelity

Simulations have relatively high fidelity to the job or performance domain of interest to the practitioner or researcher. Here, we discuss the notion of fidelity in a bit more depth, as the concept is actually quite complex. To say a simulation has fidelity could mean that many different aspects of the simulation emulate aspects of the job. Theory and research in this area have suggested that, in order to successfully build valid simulations, the following types of fidelity should be considered:

- Fidelity of the *stimuli* presented to the participant, including the medium, problems and instructions. For example, how does a supervisor/participant get information from subordinates (for example, in writing, verbally)?
- Fidelity of the *responses* called for by the participant, including the behaviours he/she must display and the products he/she must produce. For example, how is the participant's decision communicated (for example, electronically, handwritten)?
- Fidelity of the *content*, including the substance of the problems. For example, the simulation of a sales job could include problems of dealing with irate customers and preparing a marketing plan, or more general challenges in retail sales.

---

40 Office of Strategic Services Assessment Staff (OSS), 1948

41 Lievens et al., 2015; Schollaert & Lievens, 2012; Oliver et al., 2016

42 Kleinmann et al., 1996

- Fidelity to the *level of difficulty* presented by the challenges in the situation. For example, does the complexity of the simulated issues align with the complexity of the situations faced on the job?
- Fidelity of the organisational and environmental *context*, including the industry, organisation climate, and country culture. For example, if the target job is a sales job in the life insurance industry, the simulation might portray life insurance sales, or sales in a similar domain.
- Fidelity of the *constructs* being assessed. For example, while the job may require leadership, the simulation could require generally accepted leadership behaviours or particular leadership behaviours appropriate for the challenges posed in the organisational setting of interest.[43]

In building a simulation, each of these features must be considered individually and in combination with each other. In any given simulation, any one of the features can have low, moderate, or high fidelity. For example, stimulus fidelity can be high, but response fidelity low. Such an arrangement may be appropriate if cost constraints call for multiple choice responses rather than constructed free written or oral responses. In contrast, stimulus and response fidelity may be high, but the context may be a company and industry that are quite different from the target job. This arrangement may be appropriate if participants have different amounts of exposure to the target job.

4.6 Judgmental and statistical integration

Different theoretical perspectives have guided the two most common ways in which multiple sources of AC information have been integrated: consensus discussion and statistical aggregation. The two can be used jointly. The first perspective has been called "judgmental", "clinical", "wash-up" or "integration session". In this method, observers conduct some portion of the assessment process (for example they observe one or more exercises, conduct an interview, or review some test results), and then enter into a discussion. Here they share observations, possibly provide preliminary ratings on performance dimensions, and come to an agreement on ratings. This is the traditional method used by early AC adopters. The theoretical basis for the method is that judgment provided by multiple observers provides the best holistic and individualised assessment of each unique participant. This method provides valid and useful behavioural insights into each individual personal profile of strengths and developmental needs, and thus is most useful for giving behavioural feedback and prescribing a plan for behavioural change.

The second process, statistical aggregation, also called mechanical data combination, involves arithmetically combining the ratings of multiple observers on multiple dimensions across exercises, and where applicable, other sources of assessment (for example, test scores). The theoretical basis for this method is that it provides the most objective way to combine data, i.e. results are not vulnerable to observers' irrelevant biases. A variety of research evidence supports the superior reliability and validity of a statistical combination of multiple sources of evaluations for making predictions of success criteria in educational and business settings.[44] Currently, applications of artificial intelligence (AI) are being explored, but these are not yet widely validated. Support, albeit mixed, has been found for the predictive accuracy, social validity, and other indicators of success for ACs using judgmental integration when ACs are used for personal development, organisational change and societal change.[45]

---

43 Lievens et al., 2015; Thornton & Kedharnath, 2013

44 Kuncel et al., 2013

45 Thornton et al., 2015

5. CASE STUDY

> ## Case Study: Assessment Centres at a large Civil Service Agency in the USA
>
> The civil service agency of a large city in the United States conducted an AC consisting of a job knowledge test and behavioural simulations for the promotion of police officers into the first-level managerial rank of sergeant. Because of administrative and legal challenges of validity and fairness to prior promotional exams, it was essential that the new process be tightly secured, transparent, valid and fair.
>
> The job analysis and competency modeling identified six performance dimensions that were important for success as a sergeant in the department, which had recently initiated community policing practices including problem solving, conflict resolution, customer service orientation, and leadership. Three simulation exercises (in-box, oral presentation, and tactical analysis) provided highly realistic opportunities for participants to display behaviours relevant to the dimensions. All six dimensions were rated in each simulation.
>
> The observers were second, third, and fourth level managers in comparable cities throughout the US, who were sent preliminary training materials including information about the police department and job descriptions. Two days of on-site training consisted of meetings with the chief and deputies of the department and frame-of-reference training. The process of observation, rating, and integration of scores was described and practiced.
>
> To help the participants be more comfortable, they were required to attend an orientation meeting for the AC process where they were told the dimensions and types of exercises, along with tips on how best to approach the process. During the AC, one exercise was administered on each of three successive days to the 210 participants. Each day, participants were randomly assigned to different waves of approximately 17 participants each. Those in morning waves were kept separate from each other and from participants in the afternoon waves to ensure that the content of each day's exercise could not be shared among the participants. Across days, participants rotated from morning to afternoon waves to reduce the threat of time-of-day and order effects. The assignment of observers to participants was done randomly and followed procedures to ensure observers and participants did not know each other. Race and gender were not taken into account in these assignments, because the civil service department closely adhered to a policy and practice of not making any race- or gender-based decisions within personnel practices. Each observer was paired with a different observer for different sets of waves in the morning and afternoon. Observers who were not assigned a wave were kept on standby in case an on-duty observer faced some kind of emergency and had to leave.
>
> The observers asked three standardised questions in the form of role playing at the end of each simulation exercise. The questions were designed to elicit responses relevant to the performance dimensions. No other interaction was allowed between participants and observers. The observers observed participant behaviour and took written notes. Behaviourally anchored rating scales guided the observers' observations and ratings. After a participant left the examination room, the observers independently (i.e. without conferring with each other) rated each dimension within that exercise on a scale from 1-5, using 0.5 intervals (for example, 3.5). If the two observers differed by more than one point on any dimension in their initial independent ratings, they compared observations of behaviours and were required to come to consensus within one point. No further discussion was allowed. The average of the ratings by the two observers yielded scores on dimensions. Overall assessment ratings were calculated by averaging across dimensions and exercises.

The overall assessment ratings were standardised and weighted (55%), then combined with the standardised and weighted knowledge test scores (45%) to yield the final promotional exam scores. The final promotional exam scores were used to make promotion decisions on a strict top-down basis.

Analyses of the results supported the fairness of the AC process. No same-race or same-gender bias between the race/gender of the observers and participants was present, and final promotions showed no adverse impact against racial or gender sub-groups.[46] Economic utility was demonstrated in that the per-participant dollar return from selecting better sergeants ($1,995) far exceeded the per-participant cost ($764) of developing and implementing the AC.[47] A survey of participants revealed satisfaction with the relevance and administrative fairness of the process. No protests or legal challenges were levied against the process.

After all the promotional decisions were made, the participants were offered the opportunity to receive feedback. Staff in the training section of the human resource division met with individual participants and went over information accumulated in his or her assessment portfolio (including test scores and observer notes and ratings) and discussed follow-up actions.

6. SUMMARY

Theories of psychology, observation, judgment and measurement provide valuable insights into the processes of constructing and implementing simulations. Table 9.1 provides several practical tips resulting from these theories. The AC developer will benefit from referring regularly to these recommendations.

The takeaways of the chapter include the following:
- Behaviour is a function of both the person and the situation.
- The AC method assumes participants' behaviour in simulations is consistent with work behaviour, thus simulations should be built to reflect key tasks of the job.
- Person characteristics can be summarised by a taxonomy of competencies.
- Situational characteristics can be summarised by a taxonomy of features of situations built in simulation exercises.
- Several distinguishable aspects of fidelity of simulations guide the structure and context of simulation exercises.
- Principles of social perception and judgment help train observers to follow a systematic process of observing, recording, classifying, and rating behaviour.
- Following the psychometric principles of standardisation, aggregation, and domain sampling heterogeneity in the many complex elements of the AC method ensures that ACs yield reliable and valid results.

---

46 Thornton et al., 2019

47 Thornton & Potemra, 2010

Table 9.1: Practical implications of theories relevant to assessment centre design and implementation

Theory	Key Points	Practical Implications
1. Theories Relevant to the Overall Assessment Method		
1.1 Behavioural Consistency	Behaviours in the assessment will be consistent with behaviours on the job.	Design the AC method to elicit and evaluate overt behaviours reflecting effective job performance.
1.2 Interactionist Theory	Behaviour is a function of characteristics of both the person and environment, and their interactions. B = f (P x E)	Clearly specify both multiple diverse competencies of the person and characteristics of the situation. Report evaluations of competencies, performance in exercises, and profiles of competencies in multiple exercises.
1.3 Realistic Accuracy Model	A rating process involves (a) eliciting and displaying behaviour (by participants), and (b) observing, classifying, and rating behaviour (by observers).	Build simulations to elicit behaviours relevant to observable competencies. Set up the AC so relevant behaviour is displayed and is observable to the observers. Train role players to provide cues to prompt dimension-relevant behaviours. Use the frame-of-reference method to train observers to observe, record and classify behaviours, and use the behaviours to make performance ratings. Do not overload observers.
1.4 Psychometric Theories		
1.4.1 Standardisation	Ensuring that all elements of the assessment are the same for all participants leads to accurate results. Increasing numbers of items yields more reliability.	Establish and follow prescribed procedures for instructions, conditions, timing, and scoring.
1.4.2 Aggregation		Call for multiple observations and ratings on multiple behaviours in multiple simulations by multiple observers.
1.4.3 Heterogeneous domain sampling model	Additional unique items leads to validity.	Use different assessment methods, unique simulations, diverse observers.
1.5 Gamification	Game elements heighten participant involvement.	Make the simulation media rich and competitive, if appropriate. As appropriate, provide participants immediate feedback. For developmental ACs, provide multiple feedback.

Theory	Key Points	Practical Implications
2. Theories Relevant to Essential Elements of the ACs		
2.1 Multiple Methods of Defining Domains	There is no single method of analysing a performance domain.	Use multiple methods ranging from top-down competency modeling to bottom-up task analyses. Do not rely solely on marketed lists of competencies.
2.2 Taxonomy of Competencies	Behaviours indicating performance effectiveness can be clustered into a small number of competencies.	Adopt and adapt a set of commonly accepted competencies. Define competencies in the language of the organisation. It is necessary to assess only a small number of competencies, for example, 4 – 6.
2.3 Taxonomy of Situations	The infinite number of situational characteristics can be clustered into a manageable set.	Adopt and adapt a commonly accepted set of situational characteristics. Build simulations to reflect key situational characteristics. Place the simulation in a setting acceptable to the organisation.
2.4 Trait Activation Theory	Behaviour related to a trait will be demonstrated if it is elicited by a situation calling for that trait.	Design simulation stimuli, including instructions, case material, role player prompts and follow-up questions, to elicit behaviours relevant to the dimensions assessed. Set the strength of the stimuli to accomplish the objectives of the simulation, i.e. clear but not too strong.
2.5 Taxonomy of Aspects of Fidelity	Distinguishable aspects of fidelity include: stimulus, response, difficulty level, context, and psychological.	Specify the level of each aspect of fidelity appropriate for the purpose of the AC.
2.6 Judgmental and Statistical Integration	Systematic procedures for combining information improve reliability and validity.	Use statistical integration to make predictions. Use judgmental integrations to enrich feedback for developmental ACs. Use both procedures.

CHAPTER 10

THE AC BLUEPRINT

Sandra Schlebusch

1. INTRODUCTION – THE AC BLUEPRINT

The first step in the design and develop stage – step four of the design model – is about drawing-up the AC blueprint. The information derived from Stage One – the analysis stage – informs the type of simulations to be designed, the complexity and difficulty level of the simulations, as well as the technology to be used when administering and responding to the simulations. In addition, Stage One provides guidelines for the setting (context) of the simulations.[1] The information from the analysis stage of the design model thus needs to be converted into information that will guide the development of the AC. This converted information is contained in the AC blueprint. Step four – the AC blueprint – is depicted in Figure 10.1.

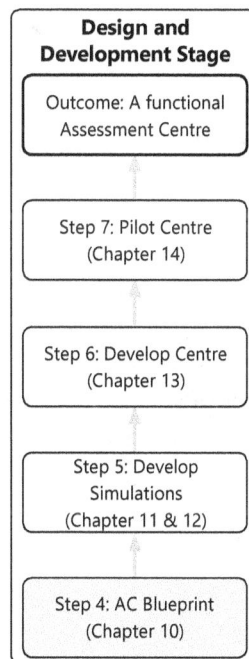

Figure 10.1: The AC blueprint step in the design and development stage

This chapter discusses the purpose and the content of the AC blueprint. The first section explains the content of the AC in order to clarify the participant's role when completing the AC, the trends that will be simulated in the AC's fictitious organisation, as well as the simulation specifications. The second section, AC operational aspects, explains the logistical requirements to execute the envisioned AC,

---

1   Thornton et al., 2015

as well as the observer – participant ratio. The third section, AC approach, clarifies all the "technical" decisions that have to be taken before the AC development can start. The chapter continues with a short discussion about the AC blueprint approval and an example of an AC blueprint, before ending with a checklist to use when designing a blueprint to ensure that all aspects are covered.

2. PURPOSE OF THE AC BLUEPRINT

The AC blueprint is a design document that specifies *what* needs to be developed, the *rationale* for deciding what needs to be developed, and all the *specifications* of what needs to be developed. The AC blueprint can be compared to the building plan of a house, which contains all the specifications according to which the house needs to be built. The builder uses the blueprint to build the house exactly according to the plan that was approved by the client. Likewise, an AC must be developed exactly according to the blueprint that was approved by the client.

The AC blueprint serves three purposes. Firstly, it synthesises the information obtained during Stage One of the design model and converts it into a plan according to which the AC will be developed. At the end of the analysis stage, the AC design team is presented with possible AC focal constructs that include a competency profile or profiles, the behavioural elements comprising the competencies, the tasks or situations that the incumbent of the target job is exposed to, as well as the target job's context inside the organisation. Some organisational trends are also indicated. The first task of the AC design team upon receiving this information is to decide on an AC blueprint based on this information. The simulations and other assessments will be developed according to the specifications set out in the AC blueprint once the development of the AC starts (step 5).

Secondly, the AC blueprint is used by the design team to obtain the client's approval of the concept before the development starts. Mutual expectations about the AC can be clarified upfront during the AC blueprint discussion between the client and the AC design team. Possible misunderstandings about the AC setting, AC duration, number of simulations, number of observers per centre and other AC aspects might be avoided by having a rigorous discussion about what will be developed before the development starts. This blueprint and discussion will assist the AC design team to deliver a context-focused and cost-effective AC, as stipulated in the *Code of Ethics for Assessment Centres in South Africa*[2] (see Chapter 4 for a discussion about the Code of Ethics).

Thirdly, the AC blueprint assists with the AC validation process. The blueprint will indicate how the information obtained during the analysis stage was converted into the operational AC, which is the outcome of the third stage in the design model. With the approval of the client, the AC blueprint can indicate that the client agreed to the AC's focal constructs and other aspects of the AC. This can form part of the evidence collected to indicate content validity during the last stage of AC development, namely the evaluation and validation stage.

---

2   SA Assessment Centre Study Group, 2018

3. **AC CONTENT**

The first category in the AC blueprint is the AC content, which refers to the detail about the specific AC's content that will be developed. It indicates the specifics that the AC design team will adhere to during the simulation and AC development process.

3.1 General simulated setting/context

The general simulated setting refers to the fictitious organisation that will be created. If an integrated simulation approach is followed, all the simulations will take place within this fictitious organisation. Care must be taken to simulate the characteristics and trends identified in the organisation and industry during the analysis stage (see Chapters 6 - 8). These trends and characteristics should be listed in the AC blueprint. It is recommended that the fictitious organisation be similar to, but not an exact replica of, the client organisation. This will assist with assessing the focal constructs of the AC and not unintended issues from the client organisation that are unknown to the AC design team.

3.2 Simulation specifications

All simulations that will be developed need to be specified in the blueprint. The following detail needs to be specified per simulation:

- The type of simulation to be designed, for example one-on-one role play simulation; analysis exercise, etc.
- The reason for including the simulation and the simulation's purpose, for example the link with the type of situation identified during the analysis stage should be indicated, as well as the envisioned deliverable of the simulation.
- A high-level description of the simulation's focal problems and challenges, for example if an in-box will be developed, the number of in-box items and each item's topic needs to be indicated. If a role play will be developed, the AC blueprint should indicate with whom the participant will have the discussion (subordinate, peer, client, line-manager, etc.), as well as the main challenges that need to be addressed during the discussion.
- The time duration of the simulation. This should include the time to give instructions to the participant, the participant's preparation time, as well as the time to execute the simulation.
- The required resources to administer the simulation. This includes the number of role players, the venue and other logistical requirements, and the required equipment.
- The simulation documentation that will be developed, including participant instructions, observer guidelines, role player guidelines, observer report forms, norm tables, etc. (See Chapter 11 for a discussion about the documentation.)

3.3 Participant's role

The role that the participant will fulfil during the simulations and the AC as a whole needs to be specified, for example if the target job is an operational manager in a production environment, the participant's role in the fictitious organisation could be a newly appointed operational manager. It is recommended to provide as much information as possible about the fictitious role and organisation in the AC blueprint, so that the client can form a clear idea as to what will be simulated during the AC. Again, clearly indicate the link with the information identified during the analysis stage.

4. AC OPERATIONAL ASPECTS

The second category in the AC blueprint, the operational aspects of the AC, includes all logistical and resource requirements to execute the specific AC.

4.1 AC duration

The AC blueprint will indicate the total amount of time needed for the AC, which will be broken down into the time frames that each simulation should require. These time frames account for the time each simulation should take from the point of giving instructions to the point where the participant completes the simulation and the observation process is completed by the observers.

These allocated times will serve as a guide to the design team when the AC is being developed. The overall AC duration will be impacted by the organisation's needs and the AC design team will have to fit the proposed simulations into the time duration that the client is prepared to allow.

4.2 Number of participants per AC

The maximum and minimum number of participants that will be accommodated per AC needs to be indicated in the AC blueprint. The number of participants per AC is influenced by the process of the specific AC, as well as the overall time available to conduct the AC and to deliver the results.

4.3 Observer to participant ratio

Using multiple observers to observe and evaluate AC participant behaviour is a core element of the AC method.[3] The number of observers that will be employed per AC needs to be specified in the AC blueprint. Although the ideal ratio would probably be one observer for every participant (so as not to increase the observer's cognitive load), it might not be a cost-effective option. The number of observers per AC will influence the total number of observers to be trained-to-competence on the specific AC and will also impact each AC's cost. A workable compromise is to perhaps work with a ratio of one observer for every two AC participants. With this ratio the observers' workload should be manageable, while the labour cost of the AC should still be reasonable.

4.4 AC logistics

All resources, equipment, venues and any other requirements need to be clearly stated. If the AC will use computer technology and an internet facility, the browser requirements need to be stated. If the AC will be an in-person AC, the number of break-away rooms, as well as the requirements of the rooms, need to be indicated.

---

3   International Taskforce on Assessment Center Guidelines, 2015

5.   **AC APPROACH**

The AC approach refers to "technical" AC decisions that need to be taken about the specific AC.   A lot of the information in this section of the AC blueprint might not be of direct interest to the client, but is critical as a guide to the AC design team.   It is recommended that the information still be included in the AC blueprint so that the AC design process is completely transparent to the AC client, and that expectations are clear to both the client and the AC design team.[4]

The 13 topics covered in this section are:

1. AC Purpose	5. Data Driven vs. Checklists	9. Data Integration	13. Simulations: • Fidelity • Level of Complexity • Maximum vs. Typical Performance • Types of Simulations
2. Dimension-based vs. Task-based AC	6. Point of Assessment	10. Separate vs Integrated Simulations	
3. Focal Constructs	7. Presentation of Results	11. Use of Technology	
4. AC Process	8. Rating Scale	12. Purchase or Custom Build	

Each topic will now be discussed.

5.1   AC purpose

Will the AC be used for selection purposes or for developmental purposes? If the AC will be for developmental purposes, will it be a diagnostic centre (DC) diagnosing a profile of current strengths and development areas, or will it be a development assessment centre (DAC) identifying areas of strength and areas requiring development while also providing training at the same time?   Although this decision will already have been clarified in the AC business case (see Chapter 6 for a discussion about the AC business case), the AC design team needs to reaffirm the purpose.[5]   The answer to this question will influence the choice of focal constructs, the design of the simulations, the design of the AC, the design of the additional documents for the AC, as well as the design of the processes following the AC.

Closely linked to the purpose is the answer to the question: Who are the target participants? Will they be people already in the target job, or people aspiring to the target job?   The answer to this question could influence the process after the AC, which includes the continued support provided to AC participants.

---

4   SA Assessment Centre Study Group, 2018

5   Thornton et al., 2015

5.2   Dimension-based AC (DBAC), Task-based AC (TBAC), or Mixed-Model AC

A decision needs to be taken on whether the AC will follow a dimension-based, task-based, or mixed-model approach. When the AC follows a dimension-based approach, the AC participants' behaviour during simulations is evaluated according to the applicable dimensions or competencies (or other focal constructs such as strategies), and ratings are given per dimension or competency. Feedback to the participants and client is also given according to the dimensions or competencies. See Chapter 11 for a discussion about observer report forms using dimensions or competencies.

With the task-based approach the dimensions and competencies are removed from the simulations and the participants' behaviour is evaluated according to their ability to perform the task(s) in the simulation. Ratings are given per task and the feedback to the participants and client is also given according to the participant's ability to perform the tasks. This approach is based on the premise that in every job the incumbent has to fulfil certain roles and effectively deal with certain situations. The simulations at the TBAC resemble the situations that the incumbent has to deal with while in a specific role. The observers use a task list (checklist) to evaluate the participant's behaviour. The task list is made up of actions that the incumbent has to do to deal effectively with the situation. (See Chapter 11 for an example of a TBAC's task list.)

A third option is to use both dimensions and tasks as the units of measurement. With this approach participants receive feedback about their performance per dimension or competency, as well as their ability to perform the tasks per simulation.

5.3   AC's focal constructs

The AC design team is presented with a list of possible focal constructs resulting from the AC design model's analysis stage, a list of dimensions or competencies, and a list of situations that the target job incumbent is exposed to (see Chapter 8 for a discussion about the job analysis deliverables). The AC design team then has to decide which to include in the AC.

An important aspect to keep in mind is that the more competencies and simulations included in an AC, the longer the duration of the AC, the more the AC will cost, and the bigger the cognitive load placed on the observers at the AC. The increase in observer cognitive load might lead to overloading the observers' mental resources, thus increasing the possibility of observers inaccurately observing, noting, classifying and evaluating participant behaviour.[6] It has been suggested that a maximum of four dimensions or competencies be assessed during a simulation to try and alleviate observer cognitive overload.[7]

The purpose of the AC also impacts the choice of dimensions or competencies in the AC.[8] If the purpose of the AC is selection, the focal constructs should be more stable, i.e. more difficult to develop.

6   Melcher et al., 2010; Thornton et al., 2015

7   Thornton et al., 2015; Thornton et al., 2017

8   Rupp et al., 2006; Thornton et al., 2015; Thornton et al., 2017

ACs for developmental purposes should assess developable focal constructs[9] that can be improved in a relatively short period of time, with reasonable effort. If the organisation cannot (or will not) provide the resources for a participant to develop a focal construct, it is best to not include that focal construct in the diagnostic centre (DC) or development assessment centre (DAC). In addition, the focal constructs assessed during a DAC should be developable during the centre itself, or during follow-up interventions.

The focal constructs assessed during a DC and a DAC should also be perceived by the participants as developable.[10] If participants perceive a focal construct as not being developable, chances are that they would not "waste their energy" in trying to develop the focal construct.

The implication of the above is that the AC design team might draw up two lists of AC focal constructs, namely a list for an AC for selection purposes, and a list of focal constructs for a DC and/or a DAC. (See Chapter 9 for a discussion about the taxonomies of competencies and situations to possibly include in an AC.)

The AC design team needs to take note that initial research on South African AC data indicated that cognitively loaded dimensions and competencies such as problem solving, strategic thinking and business acumen seem to produce large ethnic group differences.[11] The design team thus needs to carefully consider the importance of these dimensions and competencies, as indicated in the job analysis information, before deciding to include these dimensions and competencies as focal constructs for the AC.

5.4 AC process

The process of an AC for selection purposes and the process for a DC are different from the process followed during a DAC. The proposed process therefore needs to be briefly described in the AC blueprint. (See Chapter 13 for a discussion about the process followed during centres.)

5.5 Data driven classification and evaluation, or checklists

There are two approaches to classifying and evaluating participant behaviour during simulations. The first approach is a "data driven" approach, in which observers observe and note participant behaviour, which is then classified according to the focal constructs. Finally, the behaviour is evaluated according to the applicable norm. Both the quantity and quality of the behaviour are considered when evaluation takes place.

The second approach is one where participant behaviour is observed and noted, before being evaluated according to a checklist.[12]

---

9   Rupp, et al., 2006; Thornton et al., 2015; Thornton et al., 2017

10   Rupp et al., 2006

11   Buckett, Becker & Roodt., 2017

12   Thornton et al., 2015

Whichever approach will be followed during the AC needs to be mentioned in the AC blueprint, as it will impact the design of the observer report forms (see Chapter 11 for a discussion about observer report forms).

5.6 Point of assessment

There are two approaches to when an assessment can take place when dimensions or competencies are evaluated, i.e. after every simulation (post-exercise dimension rating (PEDR)), or at the end of the AC across simulations (AEDR). When it is a task-based AC, an overall assessment per simulation or task is made (OER). The following table is a summary of the approaches and the applicable acronym.

Table 10.1: Acronyms related to the point of assessment[13]

Acronym	Description	Comment
WEDR	Within-exercise dimension ratings	The dimension or competency is evaluated and rated after every simulation.
AEDR	Across exercise dimension ratings	The dimension or competency is evaluated and rated after considering the evidence of behaviour linked to the dimension or competency displayed by the participant during all simulations
OER	Overall exercise rating	The participant's behaviour in a simulation or task is evaluated after considering the checklist items.

The approach that will be followed needs to be indicated in the AC blueprint.

5.7 Presentation of AC results to the client

It should be clarified in the AC blueprint whether or not an overall assessment rating (OAR) will be calculated. An OAR is a rating of a participant's overall performance during an AC.[14] When it is an AC for selection the results can be indicated as an OAR per candidate, the candidates can be ranked according to certain agreed criteria, or each candidate's results can be presented for the client to take decisions on. It should further be indicated whether a report per candidate will be compiled, or an overall integrated report containing all candidate's results will be delivered to the hiring manager.

There will not be an OAR when a DC or DAC is presented, as participants' results are indicated in profiles of areas of strength and areas for development. A report per participant will usually be compiled to assist with the feedback process, as well as a personal development plan (PDP).[15]

The AC blueprint should further indicate with whom feedback discussions will take place. Again, the purpose of the AC is important. If the AC is for selection, feedback is given to the hiring manager. It

13 Adapted from Thornton et al., 2015: 99

14 Thornton et al., 2015

15 Woo et al., 2008

is also recommended that feedback be given to each AC participant.[16] Detailed and comprehensive feedback should be given to each participant if the AC's purpose is development. When the purpose of the AC is development, the type of feedback given to the client organisation should be indicated in the AC blueprint.

5.8 Rating scale

Before embarking on the process of simulation development, the AC design team needs to decide on an appropriate rating scale to use during the AC. When deciding on a scale, the purpose of the AC is again of importance. If the AC is a DAC, a limited rating scale can be used, however for an AC designed for selection purposes, a broader rating scale might be needed.

There are a few criteria to consider when choosing a rating scale: the scale must facilitate the validation studies during the evaluation and validation stage of the design model; the rating scale should be easy to understand as far as the observers, participants and any other feedback recipients are concerned; and the rating scale must be easy to use during behaviour evaluation.

The rating of behaviour is against the norm of the AC; the norm used at a particular AC is the behaviour of an effective incumbent of the target job.

5.8.1 Rating scale for a DAC

The recommended rating scale for a DAC is a four-point rating scale. Behaviour is highly effective (HE), effective (E), needs rounding-off (R), or needs development (ND).

If a focal construct is rated as HE, it means that the participant displayed behaviour linked to the focal construct that is better than expected of an effective incumbent of the target job. If the same behaviour is displayed in the work situation, it will in all probability lead to positive consequences. If a focal construct received a rating of E, the participant displayed behaviour linked to the focal construct that is as expected of an effective incumbent in the target job. A rating of R means that the participant displayed the behaviour linked to the focal construct to the extent that is expected of the incumbent of the target job. However, here there is a specific element of behaviour relating to the focal construct that needs the participant's attention. For example, where the participant displays the behaviour linked to most of the focal construct elements, but neglects to display a specific element's behaviour, a rating of R can be given to that focal construct in the simulation. When a participant receives a rating of ND on a focal construct, it means that the elements in the focal construct need development.

Although the feedback given to the participant and to any other party who receives feedback on the participant's performance at the DAC will be in terms of ND, R, E or HE per focal construct, these ratings need to be converted to a numerical value. This is necessary for the statistical analysis during the evaluation and validation stage. For example, the following numerical values could depict the ratings: ND = 1; R = 2; E = 3; and HE = 4.

---

16 SA Assessment Centre Study Group, 2018

A final overall rating per focal construct in a dimension-based DC or DAC can also be in the form of a split rating, as example HE/ND. A split rating indicates that the participant's behaviour was at an HE level during one type of simulation, but needed development during the other type of simulation. This indicates that the participant's development should rather be focused on improving the focal construct in a specific type of situation.[17]

5.8.2 Rating scale for an AC used for selection purposes

Using a four-point rating scale might be too limiting when the AC is used for selection purposes. A scale with a greater range might therefore be more useful, for instance using a five-point scale where 1 indicates a clear development area, 2 indicates that some development is needed, 3 indicates that the participant's behaviour is at an acceptable level, 4 indicates that the behaviour is at a more than acceptable level, and 5 indicates that there is absolutely nothing that the participant can improve on regarding the competency.

The same rating scale should be used during all the AC simulations[18] (see Chapter 11 for a more comprehensive discussion about rating scales).

The proposed rating scale and the rationale for deciding on the rating scale should be indicated in the AC blueprint.

5.9 Data integration

How the AC data from the various simulations will be integrated needs to be specified in the AC blueprint. There are three options:
- The data can be integrated during a consensus discussion between the observers.
- A statistical formula can be used to integrate the data.
- A combination can be used where certain data are integrated statistically, and others are integrated through the consensus discussion.[19]

The purpose of the AC will influence the choice of data integration method. The consensus discussion option provides rich information about a participant that can be valuable in the process of giving feedback and designing a personal development plan during a DC or DAC. It appears that the statistical approach to data integration provides more valid and reliable ratings, making this approach possibly more suited for ACs for selection purposes. (See Chapter 16 for a more comprehensive discussion on the AC data integration process.)

---

17 Thornton et al., 2015

18 The British Psychological Society's Division of Occupational Psychology, 2015

19 Thornton et al., 2015

5.10 Separate or integrated simulations

The AC blueprint will also indicate whether all the simulations will take place in terms of one scenario, with the participant in the same role throughout the AC. This is called an integrated simulation AC. In the case of this approach, a single set of background information about a fictitious organisation is created and used for all the simulations during the AC. This is also called a "day-in-the life" approach. A possible advantage of this approach is that the participants might experience it as being more realistic, thus increasing the possible face validity of the AC as a whole.[20] Another possible advantage is that time might be saved during the AC since participants only need to be oriented towards the fictitious organisation once. Unintentional cognitive load and stress is also not placed on the participants, who only need to orientate themselves towards one scenario instead of several scenarios. A potential disadvantage is that behaviour during previous simulations might influence participant behaviour during later simulations.

An alternative approach is that each simulation takes place in terms of a different scenario, with the participant in different roles. This is called a separate simulation AC. Each simulation contains all the information that the participant needs to execute the simulation. This approach requires different sets of background information for the fictitious organisation(s) for each simulation. The advantage of this approach is that the simulations can take place in any sequence during the AC, since all the information that the participant needs to complete the simulation is contained in the simulation itself.[21] A possible disadvantage is that the participant might become confused by the different sets of information.

The AC design team will decide on an approach (i.e., either integrated simulations or separate simulations) based on the purpose of the AC, the effectiveness of each approach in the organisation's specific situation, and the information obtained during the analysis stage of the design model.

5.11 Use of technology

The overall use of technology during the AC needs to be indicated in the AC blueprint, as technology could be used to facilitate certain aspects of an AC. These ACs are called Technology Enhanced Centres (TEACs). Technology can be used as follows during an AC[22]:
- To schedule participants, role players and observers.
- To deliver the simulation stimuli (e.g. instructions, etc.).
- To capture participant behaviour during the simulation (e.g. recording of voices, typed and other data).
- To capture observer ratings and integrate data.
- To generate reports.

When an AC relies almost entirely on software technology, the AC is referred to as a Virtual Assessment Centre (VAC).

---

20 Thornton et al., 2015

21 Thornton et al., 2015

22 Thornton et al., 2015; Scott et al., 2018

The level of technology integration into the administration of the AC will depend on the target job incumbent's use of these technologies in the work environment. For example, it should be simulated at the AC if the incumbent is expected to lead discussions with delegates to a meeting who are connected to the discussion via videoconferencing facilities. Another example of the use of technology is where the participant is put in a simulated office, complete with Internet and intranet access. The flip side of this situation is one where the participant is placed in a conference room with only basic stationery to assist him or her.

The level of technology integration on the observation side will perhaps depend on logistical constraints and challenges, the cost of using the technology, and the level of customisation required to adhere to the requirements that emerged from the analysis stage. The more an AC relies on technology, the more limited the amount of customisation possible within a reasonable time frame and cost, if an off-the-shelf AC is purchased. However, travel costs can be saved if the participants and the observers are not at the same location while the simulation is taking place. Technology can be used to record and relay the behaviour of the participants in real time to the observer(s) via webcasting. Since certain hardware and software are required, a cost-benefit analysis should be conducted to decide on the level of technology used by the observers.

If the AC will be using any form of technology, the browser and other IT related requirements or constraints need to be indicated in the AC blueprint. A clear business case for the use of IT needs to be drawn-up, weighing-up the development and maintenance costs with the needs to be addressed, as well as the potential benefits to be gained.[23]

5.12 Purchase an off-the-shelf AC or custom-made AC

The AC design team has options on how to develop the AC, which can be purchased off-the-shelf from a third party (the off-the-shelf simulations can be adapted to suit the specific organisational needs) or custom designed based on the exact needs of the organisation. Whichever option is decided upon, the rationale for choosing the option must be indicated in the AC blueprint. (See Chapter 5 for a discussion about the options.)

5.13 Simulations

The AC blueprint needs to indicate which type of simulation will be developed, as well as the simulation specifications and characteristics. Thornton et al.[24] posited that simulations can be described according to six characteristics, namely:
* complexity – the extent that information processing by the participant is required;
* technology – the extent to which the participants and observers will use computer technology;
* interpersonal – the extent to which the participant will interact with people from a higher level, peers, subordinates, and people external to the fictitious organisation;

---

23 Scott et al., 2018
24 Thornton et al., 2015

- interdependence – the extent to which the participant has to rely on the cooperation of others (role players and/or other participants) to achieve success in the simulation;
- structure – the extent to which that the task is clearly explained to the participant; and
- fidelity – the extent to which the simulation resembles the target job.

Simulation fidelity, level of complexity and whether the simulations will evaluate maximum participant performance will briefly be discussed before attention is paid to the various required matrices.

5.13.1 Simulation fidelity

When drawing up the AC blueprint, it is appropriate for the AC design team to decide to what extent the simulations will resemble the actual target job. (See Chapter 9 for a discussion on the types of fidelity.)

When an AC is designed for selection purposes, it will be fairer to all the participants if the simulations take place in an organisation and industry different from those in which the target job is performed. If it is a DAC that is being developed, more similarities to the target job may occur, however it is recommended that, even for a DAC, the organisation and the industry differ from the target job's. This will ensure that the intended AC's focal constructs are evaluated and not other organisational and job constructs.

Similarity to the target job in terms of the content of the problems presented to the participant should be present in the simulation. For example, if the target job incumbent needs to resolve conflicting work schedules, this type of problem should be presented. It is also advisable that the medium in which the situation stimuli are presented, as well as the expected simulation deliverables, are the same as in the target job. In addition, the simulation should resemble the typical trends current in the organisation in which the target job is performed. If the organisation is busy expanding into China, this trend of international expansion should somehow be simulated. If at all feasible, the participant should also respond to the simulation stimuli using the same resources as in the target job. For example, if the incumbent of the target job finds himself or herself mostly in interactive situations, most of the AC simulation stimuli should be presented interactively.

The similarities between the various AC simulations and the actual target job should be clearly indicated in the AC blueprint.

5.13.2 Level of complexity and difficulty

The level of difficulty or complexity of the overall AC and each simulation should be stated. If the AC is a manager–leader AC, "level" refers to whether the AC is at a supervisory or first-line management level, at a middle management level, or at a senior or executive management level within the client organisation. If the AC is a functional AC (an AC aimed at a specific discipline, for example an HR business partner), "level" refers to whether the target job is at entry level, intermediate level, or specialist level. Again, the level of difficulty and complexity that needs to be simulated will be informed by the AC business case (see Chapter 6) and other information gathered during the analysis stage of the design model.

The level of difficulty and complexity are impacted by aspects such as the number of pages that the participant needs to work with during the simulation, the number and complexity of the challenges presented in the simulation, the diversity of the people that the participant interacts with, the number of interrelated issues in the scenario, the time frames to consider, etc.[25]

5.13.3 *Maximum or typical performance*[26]

Another aspect to include in the AC blueprint is whether or not each simulation will evaluate the participant's maximum performance or the participant's typical performance. "Maximum performance" refers to the peak level of performance at which the participant is able to perform. Usually performance at this level cannot be sustained for long periods, however certain target job environments require job incumbents to be able to perform at peak levels for certain periods. A participant's maximum performance can usually be evaluated during a high-stress simulation at an AC. Maximum performance can be elicited by presenting the participant with a complex scenario leading to high levels of cognitive processing by the participant, limited time to deliver outputs, and "severe" consequences in the simulated environment for non-delivery. Again, if maximum performance will be evaluated during the AC, the link to the information obtained during the analysis stage should be clearly indicated.

"Typical performance" refers to a participant's average level of performance. This is the level of performance that the participant is able to sustain over longer periods. An indication of a participant's typical performance can be obtained by considering how the participant performed during various simulations at the AC.

It should be noted that any AC, whether for selection or development purposes, usually places the participant under stress, possibly impacting "typical" performance levels. A question to consider is whether typical performances can be elicited from participants during an AC that usually takes place under time constraints.

Maximum and typical performance also relates to assessing the participant's abilities or motivation to perform certain tasks.[27] In a typical performance situation, the participant is presented with less structure in the stimuli, leaving it to the participant to decide how to go about delivering the requested outcome. The participant's motivation will have a bigger impact on how he or she decides to go about performing the task in this situation. In a maximum performance situation, the stimuli provides structure in terms of what needs to be delivered, for example, 'Compile a five-page business plan that explains the organisation's five year strategic focus covering marketing, production, talent and innovation'. In this situation, the participant's ability to integrate information and envision a future for the organisation, covering specific areas, is assessed.

---

25 Thornton et al., 2015

26 Cascio & Aguinis, 2019; Thornton et al., 2017

27 Thornton et al., 2017

5.13.4 Types of simulations

An AC should consist of simulations that elicit overt participant behaviour, linked to the focal constructs or the behaviour in the checklists, which can be observed by observers.[28] These simulations should portray situations that the target job incumbent is exposed to. (A more comprehensive discussion about simulations will follow in Chapters 11 – 12.)

When drawing up the AC blueprint, the AC design team needs to ensure that the focal constructs are evaluated in more than one simulation. This is one of the essential elements of ACs.[29] It is also recommended that a focal construct be evaluated in different contexts, for example written versus interactive, group versus individual, strategic versus operational or tactical, and competitive versus cooperative (see the discussion about simulation characteristics). The first two contexts, namely written versus interactive and group versus individual, are determined by the type of simulation. The last two contexts, namely strategic versus operational or tactical and competitive versus cooperative, are determined by the content of the simulation. The various contexts in which the focal construct needs to be evaluated are determined by the various contexts within which the target job incumbent is functioning. This information is gained during the analysis stage (see Chapter 8). As was stated in Chapter 9 by Thornton and Lievens, it is better to have a variety of different simulation types at an AC, rather than multiple versions of the same type of simulation. This allows for the participant to show focal construct related behaviour in the various contexts that the target job incumbent has to function in, thus possibly improving the predictive validity of the AC. Assessing a participant's behaviour on the same focal construct within various contexts indicates whether the person's behaviour is consistent across all contexts and allows for richer feedback about possible developmental focus areas.[30] An example of a focal construct/context matrix appears in Table 10.2.

Table 10.2: Example of a focal construct/context matrix

	Written context	**Interactive context**	**Group context**	**Individual context**	**Strategic context**	**Operational/ tactical context**
Initiative	X	x	x	x	x	x
Information gathering	X	x	x	x	x	x
Judgement	X	x	x	x	x	x
Empowerment	X	x	x	x		x

---

28 International Taskforce on Assessment Center Guidelines, 2015; Thornton et al., 2015

29 International Taskforce on Assessment Center Guidelines, 2015

30 Gibbons & Rupp, 2009; Thornton et al., 2015

	Written context	Interactive context	Group context	Individual context	Strategic context	Operational/ tactical context
Interpersonal sensitivity		x	x	x		x
Task structuring	X	x	x	x	x	x
Persuasiveness		x	x	x		
Written communication	X				x	x
Presentation skills		x		x	x	
Control	X	x	x	x	x	x

Source: LEMASA AC administration documents

The competency *Initiative* will be evaluated in the following contexts: written, interactive, group, individual, strategic and operational/tactical.

Once the various contexts within which the focal constructs should be evaluated have been decided upon, the AC design team needs to decide which specific simulations to develop. The simulations must depict the various contexts. Each simulation will be introduced in the following chapter. It is recommended that the design team again draw up a matrix showing which simulation will be used to represent each context.

An example of a simulation/context matrix of an AC is given in Table 10.3.

Table 10.3: Example of a simulation/context matrix

	Written: individual context	Group: interactive context	Individual: interactive context	Strategic context	Operational/ tactical context	Total
In-Box	x			x	X	3
Constructive dialogue			x		X	2
Group meeting		x			X	2
Analysis exercise	x			x	X	3
Oral presentation			x	x		2
Total	2	1	2	3	4	

Source: LEMASA administration documents

In the above example of a simulation/context matrix, the In-Box simulation is indicated as representing the following contexts: written, strategic and operational/tactical.

When deciding on the various simulations to develop, the AC design team needs to attempt to ensure that focal constructs are preferably evaluated in more than one simulation. A focal construct/simulation matrix should be drawn up that visually displays during which simulation each focal construct will be evaluated.[31]

An example of a focal construct/simulation matrix appears in Table 10.4.

Table 10.4: Example of a focal construct/simulation matrix

	In-Box	Constructive dialogue	Group meeting	Analysis exercise	Total number of evaluations
Initiative	1		2	3	3
Information gathering	1	2	3	4	4
Judgement	1	2	3	4	4
Empowerment	1	2	3		3
Interpersonal sensitivity		1	2		2
Task structuring	1	2	3		3
Persuasiveness		1	2		2
Written communication			1	2	2
Presentation skills			1	2	2
Control	1	2	3	4	4

Source: LEMASA AC administration documents

In the above example of a focal construct/simulation matrix, the competency *Initiative* is evaluated during the In-Box, Group Meeting and Analysis Exercise simulations. That competency is thus evaluated three times during the AC.

After conceptualising the AC and compiling the AC blueprint, the blueprint needs to be presented to the client for approval.

---

31 Thornton et al., 2015

6.   APPROVAL OF THE AC BLUEPRINT

Before the AC design team can continue with the development of each simulation and the AC as a whole, the blueprint needs to be signed-off by the AC project steering committee (the client). It might also be necessary for senior management in the organisation to approve the blueprint. This might assist in maintaining continuous organisational support of the AC.

7.   EXAMPLE OF AN AC BLUEPRINT

Below is an example of an AC blueprint compiled for an AC for selecting assessors to work at an operational AC.

Example of an Assessment Centre Blueprint

1.   **Introduction**

Company X will be using an Assessment Centre (AC) to select the preferred candidates for appointment to newly created AC Assessor positions (4) in the section Assessment Services. The position title, the AC date, the number of candidates to attend the AC, as well as the venue are:

Table 10.5: AC Detail

Position Title	Date	Number of Candidates	Venue
Assessor	24 June 2019	4	Venue A: • 1 Main Room with data projector and flipchart – U-lay-out • 2 Break-away Rooms – round table
Assessor	25 June 2019	4	Venue A: • 1 Main Room with data projector and flipchart – U-lay-out • 2 Break-away Rooms – round table

This document outlines the assessment-competency matrix, the proposed assessments, the rating scale and the proposed AC's characteristics.

2.   **Assessment-Competency Matrices**

Below is the AC's matrix.

Table 10.6: Assessor – Competency Assessment Matrix

	Assessor							
Focal Area	**15FQ+**	**GRT**	**Competency-based Interview**	**Observe & Note Behaviour**	**Classify & Evaluate Behaviour**	**Write a Feedback Report**	**Feedback, Coaching & Compiling a Development Plan**	
Analytical and Strategic Thinking	Yes	Yes		Yes	Yes	Yes	Yes	6
Deciding & Initiating Action	Yes				Yes		Yes	3
Teamwork & Partnering	Yes							1
Communicating Effectively					Yes	Yes	Yes	3
Innovating & Driving Change	Yes		Yes				Yes	3
Observe and Assess Candidates			Yes	Yes	Yes			3
Provide Constructive Feedback, Coaching & Development Planning			Yes			Yes	Yes	3
Functional Knowledge			Yes	Yes	Yes	Yes	Yes	5
Total	4	1	4	3	5	4	6	

3. Simulations and Other Assessments

Below is a short description of each assessment instrument that will be used during the AC.

Table 10.7: Assessment Instrument Descriptions

Assessor	
Personality Questionnaire	15FQ+ • Duration approximately 30 minutes
Reasoning Tests: • Verbal • Numerical • Abstract	Graduate Reasoning Test Battery • Duration approximately 30 minutes
Competency-based Interview	• 60 minutes face-to-face interview • 2 Observers
Written Simulation	Write a candidate feedback report from an integrated assessment matrix, as well as the applicable Observer Report Forms • Duration – 60 minutes
One-on-One Role Play (Interactive)	Facilitate a candidate feedback discussion and the compilation of a personal development plan • Preparation – 30 minutes • Discussion – 30 minutes
Individual ONCE	Observing and noting behaviour during a video-recorded counselling discussion; classifying and evaluating behaviour on an Observer Report Form • Observing and Noting – 30 minutes • Classify and Evaluate – 60 minutes
TOTAL Duration per Candidate	5,5 hours

All simulations are custom designed according to client specifications.

4. Rating Scale and Norm

A five-point Likert type scale will be used. The scale description is as follows:

Table 10.8: Rating Scale

1	2	3	4	5
Not Observed	Needs Development	Needs Rounding-Off	Meets Requirements	Well above Requirements

The norm against which the candidates are evaluated is that of a successful job incumbent.

5. AC Characteristics

The AC will have the following characteristics:

Table 10.9: AC Characteristics

Characteristic	Approach during ACs
Approach to Observation	Data Driven Approach; frame-of-reference alignment will be done prior to the AC's commencement
Observer Report Formats	Adapted Behaviour Observation Scale (BOS)
Point of Evaluation	Post Exercise Dimension Ratings (PEDRS)
Data Integration Approach	Statistical – Unit weighting with qualitative notes
Type of Candidate Performance Assessed	Maximum performance
Approach to simulation design	Separate simulations (not a day-in-the-life of)
Integration of Psychometric Tests	Serial Processing (afterwards)
Observer – Participant Ratio	One observer to every two candidates; each simulation integrated with two observers
Quality Assurance	A third observer to do quality assurance
Candidate's role during AC	Candidates are in the role of an Assessor at an AC
Use of Technology	• The simulations will be administered in a pen-and paper, face-to-face situation • Candidates will use a laptop to prepare for and respond to the simulation stimuli • The 15FQ+ will be done on-line using and internet connection
Fidelity	• Content – candidate is in the role that was applied for, but in a fictitious organisation • Stimuli – the stimuli are presented in the same format as in real life • Responses – the candidates need to respond in formats as would be expected of them as job incumbents • Level of Difficulty – the difficulty is a reflection of what the job incumbent will experience • Constructs – the focal constructs are derived from the listed competencies and situations mentioned in the job effectiveness descriptions, job advertisements, and subject matter interview (11 June 2019)

6. **AC Feedback Reports**

A feedback report per candidate will be compiled. The aspects that will be covered in the reports are:
- Assessment instruments used.
- The candidate's approach to each simulation.
- The candidate's performance per competency, simulation and instrument.
- A profile of the candidate's current areas of strength and areas needing development related to the focal constructs.
- An overall assessment rating (OAR) per candidate.

A feedback discussion will be held with the hiring manager to discuss the outcomes of the AC.

Client accepted the AC Blueprint per email – Date of acceptance

8. AC BLUEPRINT CHECKLIST

AC Blueprint Checklist

The following must be covered in the AC blueprint:

1. The AC purpose.
2. The AC's focal constructs (dimensions, competencies, tasks).
3. The AC process.
4. Approach to classification and evaluation (data driven, checklists).
5. Point where evaluation takes place (PEDR, across simulations).
6. Presentation of AC results (OAR, profile, report(s), personal development plans, feedback discussions).
7. Rating scale.
8. Method of data integration.
9. Will the simulations be integrated or separate simulations?
10. The use of technology.
11. The extent that the simulations resemble the actual target job (fidelity).
12. The difficulty level of the simulations.
13. Will participant maximum or typical performance be evaluated? Will participant abilities or motivation be evaluated?
14. Various matrices (simulation-competencies, simulation-contexts, contexts-competencies).
15. Will the AC and simulations be purchased from a third party or will they be custom designed?
16. The general setting of the simulations (details of the fictitious organisation).
17. Types of simulations.
18. The simulation specifications.
19. The role of the participants during the AC.
20. The AC overall duration.
21. The number of participants per AC.
22. The observer to participant ratio.
23. AC logistics.

CHAPTER 11

DEVELOP SIMULATIONS I

Sandra Schlebusch

1. INTRODUCTION – SIMULATION DEVELOPMENT

The purpose of step five in the design and development stage of the design model is to develop simulations that will elicit visible behaviour from the AC participants. This visible behaviour must be linked to the focal constructs that need to be evaluated during the simulation. The behaviour must be easy to observe by the observers (see Chapter 9 for a discussion about RAM). During this step of the design model, all the documentation directly linked to the various simulations used at the AC needs to be developed and each simulation must be individually tested (trialled) to ensure that the simulation achieves its purpose in the most effective way. Step five – develop simulation – is depicted in Figure 11.1.

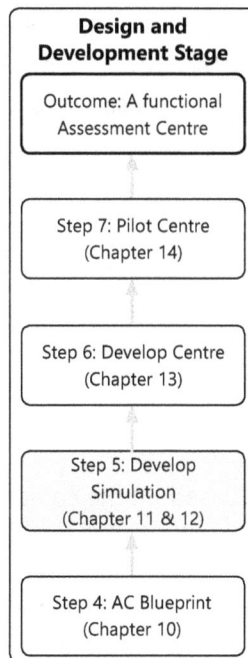

Design and Development Stage

Outcome: A functional Assessment Centre

Step 7: Pilot Centre (Chapter 14)

Step 6: Develop Centre (Chapter 13)

Step 5: Develop Simulation (Chapter 11 & 12)

Step 4: AC Blueprint (Chapter 10)

Figure 11.1: The develop simulation step in the design stage

This chapter proposes a definition of a simulation, followed by an introduction of various types of simulations. Hints to follow when designing and developing simulations are described and the chapter ends with a discussion about the various documents that need to be designed per simulation. The discussion about developing simulations is continued in Chapter 12.

Please note: during this and following chapters, the word "competency" will be used to represent all types of focal constructs such as competencies, dimensions and tasks.

2. SIMULATION DEFINED

A simulation exercise is a situation with which the target job incumbent is faced that is simulated at an AC. The AC participant is presented with certain complex stimuli and is expected to respond with complex visible behaviour.[1] The stimuli that the participant is presented with can be written instructions and other written material, information that a role player or other participants present during the simulation, actions by a role player or other participants, or even answers to questions posed by the participant to a role player or other participants. The participant's visible behaviour is observed by observers, who note and classify the participant's behaviour according to the AC competencies being evaluated in the simulation. The observers evaluate the classified behaviour according to the AC norm. The visible behaviour that participants display can comprise of what they say or do, for example writing a memorandum or giving instructions to another person verbally are examples of what is considered visible behaviour.

The two criteria that an exercise needs to adhere to in order to be called a simulation are that the simulation participants should show *visible behaviour*, and they should *decide on and construct* their response to the stimuli themselves, not merely choose a response from a set of pre-defined responses.[2]

3. TYPES OF SIMULATIONS

Keeping the definition of a simulation in mind, various types of simulations exist. Simulations, as experienced by participants, differ from one another regarding aspects such as whether the simulation is verbal or written, if it reflects a day-to-day situation or a strategic situation that does not occur regularly, if it simulates a group situation or an individual situation, and if it is a competitive situation or a cooperative situation.

Simulations also differ from one another based on the content of the simulation and the technology used in administering the simulation.

Another difference between simulations is the competencies being assessed; both the number of competencies and which competencies are assessed differ from simulation to simulation. Each simulation is designed to elicit behaviour linked to specific competencies.

Simulations are designed based on the variables mentioned above. These variables are derived from the information gathered during the analysis stage and are contained in the AC blueprint. Such variables can be called the specifications to which the simulation design must adhere.

---

1   Thornton et al., 2017

2   Meiring & Buckett, 2016

3.1   Typical simulations

Over time, typical AC simulations have come into being. Most ACs assessing management–leadership competencies will in all probability have one, or all, of the typical simulations. Although the simulations used during an AC may be similar, the content, difficulty level, setting and other variables specified in the AC blueprint will differentiate between the various simulations. Below is a brief discussion about some typical simulations used during an AC.

3.1.1   In-Box

An In-Box is a written exercise that simulates the typical pile of reports/letters/memos/e-mails/voice-mails confronting a person, for example at the start of a working day or after a trip or holiday. It is expected of AC participants to respond to these in the way they think best, for example delegate tasks to subordinates, request information, give instructions etc., within a specified time.

An In-Box consists of various items eliciting visible behaviour from the participant that can be classified under the various competencies assessed during the simulation. The items can be delivered electronically or in paper format, or in a combined way.

An In-Box can be designed to simulate any target job, however the purpose of the exercise during a management–leadership AC is to determine participants' current ability to manage and lead their department's performance in a written context so that the department operates productively and its objectives are met. To achieve this, the participant has to use the competencies that are evaluated during the specific simulation.

At some ACs, the observer will conduct an interview with the participant after the participant has completed the In-Box. The purpose of this interview is to enable the observer to gain clarity on what the participant means by each response, as well as to gain insight into the participant's thinking.

Designing an In-Box can be time-consuming as interrelated problems need to be devised, however administering an In-Box is relatively easy.[3] Having received training, any responsible person should be able to administer an In-Box. The In-Box observer does not have to be present while the AC participant completes the exercise, as the evaluation of In-Box responses takes place only after the participant has completed the In-Box. The evaluation, instead of taking place at the time and venue where the In-Box was administered, can take place at quite a different time and venue.

In-Boxes can be administered to one participant or to many participants simultaneously. This means that all the AC participants can complete the In-Box in one room at the same time if it is a pen and paper In-Box. Since a wide variety of competencies can also be evaluated with an In-Box, it is quite a cost-effective simulation. A word of caution, however; initial research on South African AC results (ACs used for developmental purposes) indicated large between group (Black and White) differences

---

3   Thornton et al., 2017

at team leader level.[4] At middle management level the difference was smaller, possibly indicating that the acculturation of different ethnic groups to an organisational culture reduces group differences.

Typical competencies that can be evaluated during an In-Box are:
- initiative;
- problem analysis;
- decision making;
- planning and organising;
- control;
- written communication; and
- leadership.[5]

3.1.2   One-to-one interaction simulation

During a one-to-one interaction simulation, the participant conducts a discussion with a role player. The participant is usually in charge of the discussion. The role player has been trained and declared competent to play a certain character and to create opportunities during the discussion for the participant to display behaviour linked to the competencies being evaluated during the discussion. The discussion between the participant and the role player is usually recorded verbatim, either through using recording devices and/or the observer noting down the discussion verbatim. After the discussion, the observer will conduct an interview with the role player, and sometimes with the participant.[6] The purpose of this interview is to enable the observer to determine both parties' reactions to the discussion. The participant can also complete a questionnaire afterwards instead of having the interview with the observer.

The participant will receive instructions for the simulation and will probably have time to prepare. The instructions can indicate very specifically what needs to be achieved, or they can be vague, depending on whether abilities or motivation are being evaluated (see Chapter 10 for a discussion about maximum and typical performance).). When the participant is ready, and once the observer has settled into a position from where he or she is able to observe and note all behaviour, the role player will enter (if the discussion is done face-to-face without the use of technology). The simulation is timed from the moment the role player enters the room.

Technology can be used to record the behaviour. A webcam can, for example, be used to record and relay the discussion in real time to the observer, who might be at a different location. The role player and the participant may also be in different locations, linked to each other in real time via webcam and other technology. The role player and participant see and hear each other while technology records the video and sound for later use. Technology can also be used when the observer classifies and evaluates the behaviour. Software programmes can be written to assist the observer in this regard.

---

4   Buckett et al., 2017

5   Thornton et al., 2015

6   Thornton et al., 2017

An example of a one-to-one interaction simulation is a counselling discussion, which is an interactive exercise that simulates a typical situation where a manager notices a subordinate's performance problem. The manager requests a discussion with the subordinate to determine the reason for the performance problem and to ensure that future performance is on par. The AC participant is put in the position of the manager and then has to conduct the discussion with a role player. The role player, in turn, plays the role of the subordinate experiencing performance problems.

The purpose of a counselling discussion exercise is to determine a participant's current ability to conduct a discussion with a subordinate that will motivate the subordinate to improve his or her job performance to the benefit of everyone.

A well-designed one-on-one interaction can be relatively short while still eliciting required behaviour, especially when principles of Trait Activation Theory are used (see Chapter 9 and later in this chapter). This type of simulation may also have high face validity[7], however role players may not play the role consistently, impacting the standardised administration of the simulation. An interactive role play simulation may take longer to design than some of the written simulations, since the role player guidelines and script needs to be designed along with the other simulation material.

A word of caution is called for. One-on-one interaction role plays might be considered culturally alien in some African countries. Manji and Dunford[8] mentioned that managers from Sudan have in the past refused to participate in one-on-one role plays, claiming that "it is for children". Participants from other East African countries asked how they are supposed to behave during the role play and felt it was necessary to refer positively during the simulation to the company conducting the role play. This stresses the importance of adapting simulations to the specific circumstances in the country and organisation[9], and trialling simulations before rolling them out in an operational AC.

Typical competencies that can be evaluated during a one-on-one role play are:
- problem analysis;
- decision making;
- control;
- oral communication;
- negotiation;
- leadership; and
- interpersonal sensitivity.[10]

3.1.3 Group meeting

A group meeting is a discussion between four to six people with the purpose of solving a problem or making a decision within a specified time. Each participant receives instructions on the simulation

---

7   Thornton et al., 2017

8   Manji & Dunford, 2011: 410

9   International Taskforce on Assessment Center Guidelines, 2015

10 Thornton et al., 2015

and is allowed time to prepare. The instructions to the participants can be vague, such as "Arrive at a decision", or very specific, such as "Indicate the amount each project will be allocated". The instructions on how the group should arrive at a decision can again be vague or specific, depending on the competencies being evaluated. The observer, or group of observers, observes and notes the behaviour of the participant(s) during the discussion. After the discussion, the participants may be asked to explain their decision.

Various forms of group meetings exist, including a non-assigned role, leaderless group meeting; an assigned-role, leaderless group meeting; and a true-allocated role group meeting. Each will briefly be discussed.

(a) *Non-assigned role, leaderless group meeting*

During a non-assigned role, leaderless group meeting, four to six participants take part in a discussion to achieve a mutual goal.[11] The meeting participants receive the same information in order to prepare themselves. This is usually background information on the organisation and the specific challenge. The participants have time to prepare for the meeting and, once the meeting has started, they need to achieve the meeting objective within the allocated time. Usually, observers observe two participants' behaviour during the meeting. This type of group meeting is also called a cooperative group meeting. However, if the meeting is part of an AC for selection purposes, the essence of the meeting remains competitive.

(b) *Assigned-role, leaderless group meeting*

During an assigned-role, leaderless group meeting, each participant is assigned a specific role. Again, the participants receive background information on the organisation and the specific challenge, however depending on the role each participant is assigned, the participant receives additional unique information. Once the preparations have been completed, the group meeting starts with each participant aiming to promote their case according to the instructions, but also with a view to achieving the group's overall goal. This is called a competitive group discussion.[12] However, to achieve the overall goal of the group within the allowed time, a certain amount of cooperation is still needed.

An advantage of using a leaderless group discussion during an AC is that time can be saved by involving a few participants in the same simulation. Thornton et al. stated that a leaderless group meeting also allows the assessment of emergent leadership.[13] During a leaderless group meeting it sometimes happens that enough behavioural evidence is gathered only in respect of a few of the participants. This is due to the fact that participants are sometimes under the impression that leadership entails "being heard, no matter what", and they therefore do not give others the opportunity to participate during the meeting. This is a major disadvantage. Another disadvantage is that a leaderless group discussion might favour people who are extroverts[14], and there might be

---

11 Thornton et al., 2017

12 Thornton et al., 2017

13 Thornton et al., 2017

14 De Beer, 2012; Blume et al., 2010

other biases[15] within the simulation such as cultural aspects that impact participants' behaviour (see Chapter 3). For example, Manji and Dunford[16] mentioned that in East Africa female participants are appointed as scribes, while male participants are appointed as chairmen, during leaderless group meetings.

Another concern in using a leaderless group meeting during an AC for selection purposes is the lack of standardisation[17]; every meeting varies since the participants are different and react differently to the instructions and to each other. This creates problems in adhering to one of the essential elements of an AC, as indicated in *The Best Practice Guidelines for the use of the Assessment Centre Method in South Africa*.[18] It also provides a challenge in terms of the Employment Equity Act, Act 55 of 1998, section 8 number b, which states that assessments must be applied fairly to all employees.[19] Since the participants behave according to their own preference and understanding of the instructions, it might create a situation that can be interpreted as being unfair to certain participants.

(c)   A true-allocated role group meeting

During a true-allocated role group meeting, only one AC participant participates at a time. The rest of the group meeting participants are role players, each portraying a specific role and character. Typically, these roles are those of a talkative person, a person who tends to be quiet, and a person who feels passionate about the topic of discussion. The participant is placed in the role of meeting facilitator and needs to prepare as such. He or she is given instructions that include background information on the organisation and on the specific problem needing resolution, as well as background information on who will be attending the meeting.

After the meeting has ended, both the role players and the participant are asked separately about their reaction to the meeting.

Although a true-allocated role group meeting is time consuming when used during an AC, the advantage of this approach might be more important than the time it takes to allow all the AC participants to hold a group meeting. The advantage of this type of group meeting is that the participant is given the opportunity to demonstrate all the behaviours linked to the competencies being evaluated. The various role players play their roles in such a way as to ensure that opportunities are created for the participant to demonstrate the desired behaviour. The role player guidelines could include prompts to elicit behaviour linked to the various competencies being assessed, increasing the chances that the participant will show the required behaviour (see Chapter 9 for a discussion on Trait Activation Theory). This type of discussion can be standardised with regards to the type of stimuli provided to every participant. A potential disadvantage is that the role

---

15 Thornton et al., 2017

16 Manji & Dunford, 2011

17 Thornton et al., 2015; Thornton et al., 2017

18 Meiring & Buckett, 2016

19 Employment Equity Act, (Act 55 of 1998)

players might not play the various roles consistently. Another possible disadvantage is that a true-allocated role group meeting will take longer to design than a leaderless group meeting, as the role player guidelines, scripts and prompts need to be designed.

Typical competencies that can be evaluated during a group meeting are:
- problem analysis;
- decision making;
- facilitation skills;
- leadership;
- interpersonal sensitivity;
- oral communication;
- teamwork[20]; and
- negotiation.

3.1.4 Analysis exercise

An analysis exercise is a written exercise that simulates a situation where a person is required to analyse a problem or potential problem, and then identify strategies and actions that will resolve the problem and turn the situation around.[21] This is also referred to as a strategic exercise.

The AC participants have to conduct a comprehensive analysis, generate solutions and an action plan, and produce a report on their findings and recommendations. Some analysis exercises include a situation where participants make a formal oral presentation on their findings and recommendations to senior management. The senior managers may also sometimes ask the participant questions. If the senior managers (role players) ask questions, it is recommended that these be scripted to ensure standardisation. Sometimes the participants of an AC need to discuss their findings and recommendations during a group meeting.

The information given to a participant includes both quantitative and qualitative information.[22] Since it is a multi-function analysis that is required, the participants receive information covering all the various functions in the organisation – finances, operations, sales, marketing, research, human capital, etc. The participant has to understand this wide variety of information, note trends and patterns in the information, identify the important problems embedded in the information, and recommend solutions. Usually, more data are given to the participant than is actually needed. It might also be required of the participant to search the Internet for useful and applicable information.

The participants prepare their report and presentation on their own. The advantage of this is that the observer only has to be present for the oral presentation and group meeting (when used) and to receive the analysis exercise report. A possible disadvantage is the time it takes to develop an effective analysis exercise as well as the time needed to administer the simulation.

---

20 Thornton et al., 2015

21 Thornton et al., 2017

22 Thornton et al., 2017

Typical competencies that can be evaluated during an analysis exercise are:
- problem analysis;
- decision making;
- planning and organising;
- control; and
- written communication.[23]

3.1.5   Oral presentation

The participants have to prepare for, and deliver, a formal business presentation (a stand-up presentation) in such a way that the audience accepts their message within the allocated time. Not only must the participants prepare the structure of the presentation, but they must also prepare visual resources and then use these resources during their presentation.

A few variations of the oral presentation exist. The presentation can be a pre-AC prepared presentation[24], a presentation prepared at the AC, or a totally unprepared presentation.

In the case of a pre-AC prepared presentation, the participants receive the instructions for the presentation before the AC. They then have to arrive at the AC totally prepared to make the presentation. Sometimes the participants even deliver the presentation before the start of the AC.

Where the presentation is prepared at the AC, the participants receive instructions for the presentation only at the AC. They then have to prepare their presentation, including their visual resources, at the AC. They will also be required to make the presentation at a specified time during the AC.

The third variation is when the participants have to make an unprepared presentation. Typically they receive the instructions for the presentation and then only have a couple of minutes to prepare.

During some ACs, the participants make presentations to an audience comprising both the other AC participants and the observers. At other ACs, the participants make their presentations to an audience comprising the observers only.

Sometimes the oral presentation is used in conjunction with a group discussion. Each participant delivers their presentation at the start of the discussion. During some ACs, the oral presentation forms part of the analysis exercise discussed earlier in this chapter.

Irrespective of what variation of presentation is delivered, the participants hand in copies of their visual resources to the observers. The observers may also ask the participants a few questions based on their presentations. After the presentations, the group of observers may confer on the participants' presentations.

---

23 Thornton et al., 2015

24 Thornton & Mueller-Hanson, 2004

Typical competencies that can be evaluated during an oral presentation are:
- decision making;
- oral communication[25]; and
- presentation skills.

3.1.6   Oral fact-finding exercise

During an oral fact-finding exercise, the participants individually receive information about a situation that has occurred in an organisation or on a decision that has been taken. The participants then have the opportunity to ask questions of a role player who has all the required information. The role player is trained to answer the participants' questions if the questions are asked appropriately. After gathering the additional information, the participants must make recommendations on what should be done and will sometimes even be challenged on the recommendations made. A variation is when the simulation is performed as a group/team.

The exercise is usually conducted verbally. The participants must gather the required information orally and must also present their recommendations orally. The participants must therefore gather additional information orally, must evaluate the various options orally, must make recommendations orally, and must even defend their recommendations orally at the time of the simulation. The participants thus have to be able to "think on their feet".

Usually one of two types of scenario is created.[26] The first scenario is where a problem has occurred and senior management consults the participant on the road ahead. Usually a decision needs to be taken on one of two alternatives. The second scenario is where a person at a lower rank on the organisation chart has made a decision that is being challenged by other stakeholders in the organisation. Senior management now seeks advice as to whether it should support the decision, or whether it should overturn it.

The role player can fulfil two functions during this exercise. First, the role player is the source of information for the participant. The participant needs to ask specific questions to gather the required information from the role player. Once the participant has made their decision and shared their recommendations, the role player can fulfil the second role, namely that of challenging the participant's recommendation. Now the role player may try to get the participant to change their recommendation.

Typical competencies that can be evaluated during an oral fact finding exercise are:
- problem solving; and
- oral communication.[27]

---

25 Thornton et al., 2015

26 Thornton & Mueller Hanson, 2004

27 Thornton et al., 2015

3.1.7 Business game

A business game is a complex group exercise that simulates a wide range of problems in an organisation.[28] Typically, the organisation is faced with various functional problems simultaneously. The game is played with the participants (up to 18 at a time) moving around to perform certain tasks. The game can last from three hours, to a day, to several days, depending on the complexity of the organisation and the problems presented.

Owing to the complex nature of a business game, it is quite taxing to design an effective one. Technology can, however, be used during a business game. Some AC practitioners have designed software programmes that respond to the various decisions made by the participants. This means that the stimuli presented to participants differ from one game to another, depending on the "unique" choices and decisions taken by the participants. The extent of technology used during a business game will depend on the purpose of the game, the costs involved, as well as the geographic dispersion of the participants. For example, a business game can be designed that is played over months with the participants and facilitators being in different locations, making use of avatars to represent them.[29]

Typical competencies that can be evaluated during a business game are:
- problem solving;
- decision making;
- planning and organising; and
- teamwork.[30]

3.2 Limitless types of simulations

Since the type of simulation to be designed depends on the information gathered during the analysis stage of the design model, a limitless number of different types of simulations can be designed. The type of simulation used is limited only by the design team's ability to accurately capture the target job trends and characteristics in such a way that the simulation will elicit the behaviour needing evaluation in the most cost-effective way.

When simulations are designed for a functional AC, such as an AC for accountants, human capital professionals or sales executives, creativity is called for. It might be necessary to design unique simulations, for example, during a sales AC, a group of simulations might be created where the participant must first clarify the exact need of the client during a face-to-face, cold-call meeting. The participant must then prepare a proposal on how to satisfy the identified need. When presenting their proposal to the client, the participants might stumble across new information that totally changes the situation. In this case they will need to adapt their presentation and sell the new solution to the client.

---

28 Thornton & Mueller-Hanson, 2004

29 Howland et al., 2015

30 Thornton et al., 2015

4.   SIMULATION DESIGN HINTS

There are nine hints to keep in mind when designing simulations:

4.1   Create a Sufficiently Complex Fictitious Organisation/Context

When designing simulations, it is recommended that a fictitious organisation be created that is sufficiently complex to allow all the simulations to take place inside the fictitious organisation. Each simulation will still require its own set of background information about the specific scenario and instructions, but the participant will only need to be introduced to one organisation. This will enable the participants to more easily orientate themselves. This is recommended irrespective of whether the AC is a day-in-the-life of, or consists of separate simulations. In addition it is recommended that the names of the organisation, as well as its competitors, be fictitious and not real organisations that can be identified. If an organisation can easily be identified, the risk exists of participants bringing into the simulation additional, unwanted information based on their experience or knowledge of the organisation.

4.2   Trait Activation Theory (TAT) in Action

Situations need to be created that will allow the individual behaviour of participants to come to the fore. This means that the AC design team needs to avoid creating simulation situations that predetermine behaviour, in other words, situations that are too strong. For example, in certain organisational cultures, all instructions coming from the office of the Managing Director will immediately be executed without question. The immediate execution will take place even if it means that a task critical to the company's core business needs to wait. Here, the participants' reaction to the stimulus is predetermined by the organisation's culture. This emphasises the importance of identifying the organisational culture and climate during the analysis stage of AC design. Understanding the culture and climate within the target organisation will thus assist the AC design team to not create scenarios where behaviour is predetermined.

Another hint from TAT is to design prompts for role players to use when the simulation is measuring participants' abilities. Keep in mind that when a role player provides a prompt for competency linked behaviour, the evaluation is no longer about the participants' motivation to show behaviour linked to a competency[31]; it is then probably about the participant's ability to show the behaviour. Also, the use of prompts during a simulation changes the strength of the scenario. Without the prompt the simulation might elicit differing participant behaviour, however with the prompt, the scenario might become too strong to differentiate participant behaviour.

Since there is evidence that shows prompts elicit behaviour linked to interpersonal competencies[32], it is recommended that while designing a simulation, the possible prompts, related to the various

---

31 Lievens, Schollart & Keen, 2015

32 Lievens, Schollart & Keen, 2015

scenarios, be identified for these competencies. An example of a prompt might be that the role player says to the participant, "I might have suggestions about how to handle the situation". This is a strong prompt to elicit behaviour linked to a competency that evaluates a participant's ability to allow other people to solve problems. It is important to ensure that both the role player(s) and the observers are trained on using the prompts during simulations.

4.3 Simulation Modularity

Although a simulation is designed according to an overall theme, e.g. a discussion with a subordinate who has performance problems, one must identify the various mini-scenarios (modules) that will be combined into the overall simulation. Each of these modules presents different social demands[33] that the participant has to deal with and will probably have a different effect on the participant (see Chapter 9 for a discussion about Interactionist Theory). The content of these modules should be dictated by the information obtained during the analysis stage of the design model and should be indicated in the AC blueprint. When the simulation is pre-piloted (see later in this chapter), the effectiveness of the use of each module within a simulation should be examined.

4.4 Instruction clarity

When designing a simulation that needs to evaluate a participant's maximum level of performance, clearly instruct the participant to deliver the required output. Since maximum performance is related to a participant's ability, it is advisable not to leave the participant the choice of deciding whether or not to deliver. When participants can choose whether or not they will execute a specific task, the simulation is evaluating a participant's motivation to perform the task. This evaluation then gives an indication of the participant's typical performance. For example, when there is an item in the In-Box that specifically measures the participant's ability to handle a particular situation that is currently critical to the target organisation, instruct the participant to respond to the item. Where the participant is left to decide if he or she is going to respond to the item within the time constraints of the In-Box, his or her motivation is evaluated (also see Chapter 10 for a discussion on maximum and typical performance).

4.5 Neutrality of the setting (context)

When deciding on simulation settings, rather choose neutral settings that will not unfairly advantage or disadvantage participants. However, when a DAC is designed, it is recommended that a setting within a similar business sector be chosen. For example, where the target organisation is within the production sector, choose a fictitious organisation that is also in the production sector. The same applies to target organisations in the retail sector, the services sector, the finance sector, or any other sector. This increases the face validity of the AC in the eyes of the participants. The higher the face validity to the participants, the more likely they will be to accept the AC results and action the resulting development recommendations.

---

33 Lievens et al., 2015

4.6 Appropriate language

When writing the simulations, special care should be taken to use appropriate language. Do not use language that might be experienced as sexist or offensive, and avoid jargon and acronyms. Use a readability index to determine the readability of the simulation material. The level of reading complexity should be appropriate for the target AC participant.

4.7 Gender neutral names

It is recommended that gender neutral names be used for simulation characters. Any name indicating gender should be avoided when it is the name of a character that will be played during the simulation by a role player. This makes it easier when choosing role players for the various simulations, because the gender of the role player does not matter. In addition, take care not to give gender-specific names to any simulation character who is a so-called 'high or low performer'. Finally, choose names that have no cultural or religious connotations in order not to offend any person unintentionally. Table 11.1 contains examples of gender neutral names.

Table 11.1: Examples of Gender Neutral Names

Pat	Sam	Alex	Terry	Sidney
Chris	Tebogo	Oratile	Mpho	Sandy
Amahle	Neo	Unathi	Sihle	Robin
Dumisile	Simphiwe	Thalente	Zonkizizwe	Thokozile
Anele	Kholwa	Siphesihle	Ayise	Vuyo

4.8 Follow a systematic process

When designing simulations, a generic systematic process is recommended. This process consists of nine steps:[34]
- Step 1: Clarify the competencies and the competency elements that need to be evaluated during the simulation.
- Step 2: Clearly state the purpose of the simulation.
- Step 3: State the type of simulation that will be designed.
- Step 4: Clarify the simulation specifications as signed off in the AC blueprint.
- Step 5: Design the simulation context and content.
- Step 6: Design all simulation documentation.
- Step 7: Specify the resources needed to administer the simulation.
- Step 8: Pre-pilot (trial) the simulation.
- Step 9: Adapt the simulation according to the pre-pilot findings.

---

34 Thornton et al., 2017

4.9 Start with developing the context or setting

Before each simulation can be designed individually, it is necessary to create a fictitious organisation (the setting or context) in which all the simulations can take place. As was mentioned earlier in this chapter, this fictitious organisation needs to be complex enough to allow all the simulations to take place. For example, creating a fictitious organisation that is a conference centre in a rural area might not have the complexity to allow all the simulations of a middle management AC to take place. However, if this conference centre is part of a multinational organisation that uses complex technology to hold conferences where delegates are in different world regions with different time zones, and these conference delegates are world leaders who need 24-hour protection, enough complexity exists to allow simulations to be designed for a middle management AC.

Again, the AC blueprint will indicate how much complexity should be included in the whole AC. The industry and organisational trends and characteristics that need to be considered when creating the fictitious context should be indicated in the AC blueprint (see Chapter 10).

Typically, a document – referred to as the participant orientation document or an on-boarding document – is drawn up. The orientation document contains all the information that new employees will typically receive on their first day in the new job. It contains information on the fictitious organisation itself, on the role the AC participant will fulfil, on the role's accountabilities, and perhaps also information on the people with whom this role interacts. Typical information on the fictitious organisation that is contained in this document is information relating to the history of the organisation, the company's products and services, its annual turnover, its organogram, its vision and mission, its current strategic intent, and its policies.

Once the fictitious organisation has been created, the individual simulations can be designed. It is recommended that the In-Box be designed first. When this is complete, the AC design team can decide whether they will use scenarios or themes from the In-Box to design some of the other simulations. For example, some of the In-Box items might be used as topics of discussion during the counselling discussion or the group meeting. If the AC will be using integrated simulations, certain of the themes from the analysis exercise might be taken from the In-Box items.

When the integrated simulation approach is followed for the AC, the AC design team might find it useful to design the simulations in the sequence that the AC participant will be performing the simulations. This ensures that all the AC themes are developed logically.

Earlier in this chapter, the nine steps in the design of a simulation were mentioned. Although steps 1 to 4 (clarify the competencies and their elements; state the purpose of the simulation; state the type of the simulation; and clarify the simulation specifications) are already stipulated in the AC blueprint, the AC design team needs to double-check all the detail before embarking on step 5, which entails designing the simulation context and content. Step 5 is the creative step in the whole design process. The design team's imagination can be allowed to run free, as long as what the team creates is anchored in the information from the analysis stage. It is recommended that, while designing the simulations, the design team consults with various SMEs to ensure realism regarding the content of the simulation.

For each simulation, enough background information needs to be created so that the participant is at least oriented about the situation/problem/challenge/opportunity. In the case of an analysis exercise and an In-Box, the background information on the organisation should be quite extensive.

Once the context and content of a simulation have been designed, it is necessary to design all the documentation needed.

5. SIMULATION DOCUMENTATION

Every simulation has documentation for the participant and the observer. If the simulation involves a role player, the role player documentation also needs to be designed.

We will discuss each person's documentation in detail.

5.1 Participant

The AC participant is the person who will execute the simulation. His or her behaviour therefore needs to be observed, noted, classified and evaluated during the simulations. To elicit behaviour from the participant, the participant needs to know what to do so that the appropriate behaviour can be demonstrated. The participant thus needs to receive instructions for every simulation.

5.1.1 Participant instructions

The participant needs to receive background information on the particular situation of the simulation. Typically, the presenting symptoms of the situation will be given to the participant in order to sketch what is going on. In addition, the participant needs to be instructed what to deliver and, sometimes, how to arrive at the deliverable. These instructions can be very specific, for example when the participant is instructed: "Decide whether or not the role player will receive money to study and explain the reason for your decision." Alternatively, the instructions can be vague, for example: "Get to know Sam (the name of the fictitious character), understand the problems in his or her section, and jointly decide on the road ahead."

Whether or not the instructions will be specific depends on whether ability or motivation is being evaluated (discussed earlier in this chapter).

Table 11.2 provides an example of a true-allocated role group meeting's instructions to the participant. Remember, apart from the participant, the rest of the meeting delegates are role players trained to elicit specific behaviour linked to the competencies being evaluated.

Table 11.2: Example of participant instructions issued for a group meeting

---

Group meeting
Participant instructions

Shortly before his untimely death, your predecessor and the supervisors concerned established the need for improving cooperation between the different sections in the Operations Department. The issue has obviously not been addressed since then.

You have therefore requested the respective supervisors to prepare inputs on this topic for a formal meeting that you will chair/facilitate. You have made it quite clear that the objective of the meeting is not to identify problem areas (you accept that this was attended to in detail during the first meeting), but to **jointly decide on a method of improving cooperation between the different sections in your department**. You will also prepare your own suggestions and, as you need your team's support in proving yourself in your new position, you will strive to reach consensus on the measures to be taken. You have 30 minutes to prepare for the meeting and 25 minutes for the meeting itself.

Suggestions cannot simply be listed as the solution to the problem. Consensus must be reached on one idea.

Source: LEMASA AC documentation

A requirement in respect of instructions is that clear language be used. The participant must also receive an indication of the time frames involved for every simulation.

5.1.2 Participant report form (After Action Review)

The ideal situation would probably be for the observer to conduct a short interview with every participant directly after each simulation, however this is not a cost-effective option in the case of most ACs. An alternative is to request the participant to complete a participant report form.

The purpose of the report form is to allow the participants to reflect on the simulation, to gain insight about own behaviour[35], and to air their views on the simulation and the role player(s). This forms part of the overall debriefing of the AC participants. Another purpose of the form is for the observer to gain additional information that might not have been forthcoming during the simulation.

The following are examples of instructions/questions contained in a participant report form:
- Describe your approach to responding to the In-Box.
- Which items or problems were given priority? Why?
- What decisions were the most difficult to take? Why?
- Which factors (if any) prevented you from doing your best?
- What was the biggest problem in the organisation?
- Would you handle the In-Box differently if you had the opportunity to redo it? If so, in what way?

---

35 Thornton et al., 2017

The questions above are examples of questions that are used to gain qualitative information reflecting the participants' experience of the simulation. This information can be useful during the evaluation and validation stage of the AC design model. To make it easier to use the information from the participant report form for statistical evaluations, it is recommended that a conversion table be created for use by the observer. For example, the answer to the question, "Which items or problems were given priority?", can be converted to a numerical value as follows: cash flow – 1; marketing – 2; etc.

It is also advisable to obtain quantitative information from the participants. In addition to asking the qualitative questions such as those indicated above, questions that need to be answered in a quantitative manner can also be asked. For example, the participant can be requested to rate, on a scale of 1 to 5, how realistic he or she considered the simulation to be.

By asking both qualitative and quantitative questions, a more holistic picture of the participant's experience can be gained. This will assist in the process of showing the validity of the AC.

5.2 Observer

The observer's role at an AC is to observe, note, classify and evaluate (ONCE) the participant's behaviour during simulations. To allow the observer to fulfil this role effectively, observer documents need to be designed. The documents that the observer will use are notepaper to note the behaviour during an interactive simulation, the simulation's observer report form on which the participant's behaviour is classified under the competencies being evaluated (scoring rubric), and norm tables that assist the observer to evaluate the classified behaviour by converting raw scores to a converted score.

The notepaper used to note the behaviour during an interactive simulation can be paper from an ordinary A4 examination pad, or a specially designed document can be used. Irrespective of whether a specially designed document or an ordinary sheet of paper is used, the observer should have enough space to write verbatim what the participant says and to reflect the role player's comments.

5.2.1 Observer report form (scoring rubric)

The purpose of the observer report form is to guide the observer in classifying the observed behaviour under the simulation competencies. The observer report form should make it as easy as possible for the observer to classify all the participant behaviour under the competencies being evaluated. If it is a well-constructed simulation, all of the participant's behaviour should be classified under the relevant competencies.

To assist the observer, it is recommended that the definitions of the competencies being evaluated during the simulation be given on the observer report form. The specific elements (behaviour indicators/elements) of the competencies that are being evaluated in the simulation should also be listed on the same page as the competency's definition. Behaviour examples of each element should be provided. Space should be allowed next to each behaviour example for the observer to note all of the participant's behaviour that can be classified under the specific element.

The competency elements are identified during the analysis stage and are specified in the AC blueprint (see Chapters 8 and 10). To determine the behavioural examples, the AC design team can ask: "What will behaviour linked to this element look like in this simulation?" In asking itself this question, the design team should also ask this question of the SMEs that were involved during the analysis stage.

5.2.1.1 Observer report formats

There are at least three options of formats, namely Behaviour Anchored Rating Scales (BARS), Behaviour Observation Scales (BOS) and checklists.

Behaviour Anchored Rating Scale (BARS)

BARS uses behaviour statements to illustrate the rating scale levels. A description of behaviour for each rating per competency element/indicator is provided.[36] In the example below, a five-point scale is used to illustrate what the participant behaviour should look like to allocate the specific rating to the observed participant behaviour. The competency element/indicator "Persuades the audience to accept an idea/concept" is evaluated in the example below.

Table 11.3: Example of BARS

Element 1: Persuades the audience to accept an idea/concept					
1 – Little Evidence	2 – Less than Adequate	3 – Adequate	4 – More than Adequate	5 – Excellent	Participant Behaviour
Fails to convince that ideas have any benefits	Presents benefits of ideas, but does not elaborate – is not convincing	Clearly indicates the benefits of the ideas in a convincing way	As for 3, plus indicates how the benefits will be achieved	As for 4, plus indicates how business and personal outcomes will be different	

A norm table converts the raw score per competency into an overall rating for the competency, for example:

Table 11.4: Example of a BARS norm table for a competency with six elements/indicators

Converted Rating	Needs Development	Rounding Off	Proficient	Strength	Superior
Raw Score	6 - 10	11 - 15	16 - 20	21 - 25	26 - 30

---

36 Tziner et al., 2000

An advantage of BARS is the linking of behaviours to each rating, which aims to increase the chances that different observers will interpret and rate behaviours in the same way. In so doing, the inter-rater reliability is hopefully increased (see Chapter 18 for a discussion on operational reliability and Chapter 19 for a discussion on reliability). A possible disadvantage is the time it takes and the difficulty in developing the scale, which lies in ensuring that the rating is measuring the same construct in increasing difficulty or mastery. Another disadvantage of BARS is that it requires the observer to choose a single rating that most closely reflects the observer's assessment, which might lead to a situation where other related behaviours are not reflected in the rating.[37] For example, as per Table 11.3, the participant may clearly indicate the benefits of one idea in a convincing way, but not the other ideas. What rating would be most appropriate to allocate?

Developing BARS for each simulation

Since the applicable competencies and their elements are already identified and indicated in the AC blueprint (see Chapter 10), a process like the following is recommended when developing BARS:

- The AC design team, together with the first group of SMEs, identify likely behavioural examples per competency element/indicator that a simulation participant will display. Behavioural examples for effective behaviour, ineffective behaviour and average behaviour should be identified.
- A second group of SMEs receives a list of behaviours that the first group identified, together with a list of the competencies and their elements/indicators. This second group needs to link the identified behaviour to the applicable competency element/anchor (retranslation).[38] Krippendorff's α (Kalpha) can be used to determine the agreement between the two groups of SMEs. Elements/indicators with a lower than 80% agreement need to be reconsidered.[39]
- A third group of SMEs are tasked with placing scale values to the behaviour per competency element/indicator, and identifying the "missing behaviours". For example, this group allocates the 1, 2, 3, 4, and 5 to behaviour when a five-point scale is being used.
- Again, the first group of SMEs (or a totally different group) is requested to re-allocate the example behaviours to the rating scale from a list of behaviour examples per competency element/indicator (retranslation). Kalpha can again be used to determine the level of agreement, with 80% used as the indicator that the rating allocation should be reconsidered.

Behaviour Observation Scale (BOS)

A BOS gives the observer a behavioural statement (the behavioural element/anchor) as indicated in the AC blueprint (see Chapter 10), and requests the observer to indicate the frequency at which that the participant displayed the behaviour during the simulation.

---

37 Tziner et al., 2000

38 Cascio & Aguinis, 2019; Latham & Wexley, 1994

39 Georganta & Brodbeck, 2018

Table 11.5: Example of a BOS

Analytical Ability							
	1 Never/ Almost Never (0-64%)	2 (65-74%)	3 (75-84%)	4 (85-94%)	5 Almost Always (95-100%)	Behavioural Examples	Participant Behaviour
Speaks with conviction						Participant comes across as though he is committed to own solution.	
Uses convincing arguments to support own idea						There is logic in the arguments; the arguments build a believable business case	
Indicates the benefits of ideas						Benefits to the organisation are indicated; "What's in it for me" (decision makers; employees; etc.) is indicated	

A norm table converts the raw score per competency into an overall rating for the competency, for example:

Table 11.6: Example of a BOS norm table for a competency with six elements

Converted Rating	Needs Development	Rounding Off	Proficient	Strength	Superior
Raw Score	6 - 10	11 - 15	16 - 20	21 - 25	26 - 30

An advantage of BOS is that it requires observers to describe specific participant behaviours that have occurred during the simulation. This allows for rich participant feedback.[40] Since specific behaviours of the participant are noted, it might lead to more specific developmental goals being set during or after the feedback discussion, as the feedback centres around the participant's specific displayed behaviour. A possible disadvantage is that it might take observers longer to use this format, since specific participant behaviour needs to be noted on the observer report form. Another possible drawback is that the schemas that observers have around each element, and the ratings thereof, might differ. This emphasises the importance of the frame-of-reference training for observers to ensure that the scale is implemented in a reliable manner (see Chapter 14).

40 Tziner et al., 2000

Developing BOS for each simulation

Since the applicable competencies and their elements are already identified and indicated in the AC blueprint (see Chapter 10), a process like the following is recommended when developing BOS:

- The AC design team, together with a group of SMEs, identifies the behavioural examples from the simulation linked to every behavioural element/indicator.
- A second group of SMEs is presented with the behavioural elements/indicators, as well as the list of behavioural examples from the simulation identified by the first group of SMEs. The second group is tasked with matching the behaviours to the elements/indicators (retranslation). Kalpha can again be used to determine the level of agreement, with 80% used as the indicator that the behavioural example should be reconsidered. New behavioural examples may be required.

Adapted Behaviour Observation Scale

It might be useful to link each competency element/indicator to a maximum "score". After having written down all the behavioural examples from the simulation, the observer can then allocate a score, out of a maximum score, to that specific element. This allows for not only considering the frequency of behaviour, but also the quality of the behaviour showed by the participant.

The maximum score per competency element/indicator is an indication of the relative importance of that specific element within the overall competency. The maximum score per element/indicator can therefore be seen as a weight. The importance of each behavioural element/anchor (its weight) is derived from the information gathered during the analysis stage, as well as from again consulting SMEs and using the principle of retranslation. A norm table, as is the case with the other formats, would be used to convert the raw scores to a converted rating per competency.

In the following example, the behaviour element/indicator "Asked investigative questions" is the most important element in the competency "Information Gathering", as is indicated with the total rating of 18. This means that the observer can allocate, after considering all participant behaviours linked to the element, a rating of 0 – 18. Once all three elements have been rated, an overall rating out of 25 is obtained as the raw score. This raw score is converted on the norm table to a converted rating for the competency "Information Gathering".

Table 11.7 contains an example of a page from an observer report form using an adapted BOS.

Table 11.7: Example of a page from an observer report form using an adapted BOS

	Competency and competency element	+/-	Max	Examples of behaviour	All relevant participant behaviour
1.	Information gathering			**Final rating:**	
	Actively gathers data from all possible sources; identifies information elements and links related issues.				
	Elements of competence:				
a.	Asked investigative questions.		18	What is causing the big turnover in your department? What is causing the delay in delivering the equipment?	
b.	Asked open-ended questions.		2	What, why, how?	
c.	Established a connection between problems in the department and Alex's management style.		5	1. Alex's task orientation is leading to stressful working conditions. 2. Alex prefers to work on his/her own owing to his/her introvert personality and teamwork is therefore not promoted. 3. Alex's academic approach to business matters, coupled with an autocratic management style, often lead to frustration among his/her staff, mainly because wrong decisions are taken which increase the work pressure. 4. Other	
	TOTAL		25		

Source: LEMASA observer training documents

The advantage of this adapted BOS is that the observer has the opportunity to take the quality of behaviour, together with the frequency, into consideration when evaluating the participant behaviour. This allows for rich feedback discussions and possibly more specific developmental goal setting.[41] The same possible disadvantages as for a BOS might apply.

Checklists

Checklists are lists of activities that a participant should perform in order to complete a task successfully (positive behaviours). The listed activities could also include behaviours that the participant should not have done (negative behaviours) in order to achieve success in the situation. The observer checks (x) a behaviour if the participant displayed the behaviour during the simulation. At the end of the checklist the observer totals the checks and converts the total to a converted rating. The AC blueprint will be the

---

41 Tziner et al., 2000

source document indicating the competencies and the competency elements to use in the checklists (see Chapter 10).

A simple example of an in-basket checklist is provided below. Both positive and negative behaviours are listed. At the end of the example, the norm table indicates the converted rating and the narrative label attached to the conversion.

Table 11.8: Example of a Behaviour Checklist

In-Basket Observer Report Form

Competency: "Dealing with Employees" # of +'s _____ # of –'s _____

Competency Element/Indicator: *Treats People Fairly*

_____+ Highlights disciplinary policy to Joseph (#4)

_____+ Responds fairly to Maria about Nicole's memo (#3)

_____+ Turns down Nicole's request (#5)

_____+ Tells Mpho that performance needs to improve (#6)

_____+ Tells Nicole not to accuse Joseph or to jump to conclusions prematurely (#3)

_____- Gives Nicole Freedom Day Weekend off (#5)

_____- Gives promotion to Joseph (#6)

_____- Assumes wine was stolen by employee (#3)

_____- Takes punitive action against Neo Dlamini (#3)

(Other competency elements/indicators related to the competency were excluded in this example.)

OVERALL SCORING

Subtract the number of Minus (-) items checked from the number of Plus (+) items checked.

Using the guide below, rate the participant's overall performance on the competency "Dealing with Employees".

Norm Table:

Raw Score	Converted Rating	Narrative Label
-7 to -5	1	Needs Development
-4 to -1	2	Rounding Off
0 to +2	3	Proficient
+3 to +5	4	Strength
+6 to +8	5	Superior

An advantage of using a checklist during a simulation is that the participant's behaviour during the simulation can be quickly evaluated. The feedback to the participant can also focus on those behaviours displayed and not displayed, making the behaviour examples "concrete" for the participant. A disadvantage is that the quality and frequency of participant behaviours are not taken into consideration.

Developing a checklist for each simulation

When developing a checklist for a dimension-based AC (DBAC) the competencies and the competency elements/indicators are indicated in the AC blueprint. The following process is recommended:
- The AC design team, together with a group of SMEs, identifies the list of activities per competency element, per simulation.
- A second group of SMEs, independent from the first group, also identifies a list of activities per competency element per simulation.
- The two lists are compared and the common activities are included in the final list. The activities not indicated on both lists are presented to a third group of SMEs to decide upon the inclusion of those activities.
- A fourth and fifth group of SMEs are asked to independently indicate the conversion table. Again, the areas of disagreement are discussed and consensus on the initial conversion table ratings is reached.

Task-based Assessment Centres (TBACs)

Checklists are also used in TBACs. The listed activities would then not be sorted into competencies as is the case in the example above, but would indicate a list of overall activities that the participant should have done (or not done) in order to deal effectively with the situation. The AC blueprint would contain the situations to be simulated, as well as a high-level list of the activities to be evaluated during each simulation. The finer detail of the activity lists would be developed after the actual simulation content has been developed.

Table 11.9: Example of a Task List used during a TBAC

Simulation Task List		No Evidence	Needs Development	Rounding-off	Meets Expectations	Above Expectations
1	Scanned through all items before responding to any of the items					
2	Linked item content to other information					
3	Linked related issues (items) to each other					
4	Allocated time to each item for responding to it and worked according to the time allocated					

		No Evidence	Needs Development	Rounding-off	Meets Expectations	Above Expectations
	**Simulation Task List**						
5	Asked clear questions to obtain specific answers to questions					
6	Put action in place to contain a negative situation					
7	Enabled own team (subordinates) to make decisions and solve problems (Empowerment AND Providing Direction)					
8	Ensured that action is implemented by a certain time/date, going on in and around the Operations Department					
	TOTAL					
	OVERALL TASK SCORE (AVERAGE)					

The process to develop a TBAC checklist is similar to the process followed to develop checklists for DBACs, however the activities are identified per simulation and not per competency.

Observer report form design hints

When designing the observer report form layout, keep in mind that there should be enough space per competency element or activity (in the case of checklists) for the observer to classify all relevant participant behaviour under the appropriate competency or activity.

In addition, keep in mind that the observers will probably be working according to a tight time schedule when they are using the observer report forms, therefore it is advisable to design the forms so that they are as user-friendly as possible. User-friendly documents will not only make the work of the observer easier, but will also increase the possibility that the observer will complete the documents comprehensively and correctly. This, in turn, positively influences the AC's reliability and validity.

If the AC will use Trait Activation Theory during simulations, the observer report form should have space for the observer to indicate which prompt was used (if any) per competency, as well as what behaviour followed the prompt.

5.2.2 Rating Scales

When an observer uses a rating scale, four processes take place, namely: 1) comprehension of the behavioural element and the categories on the scale; 2) retrieval or linking participant behaviour to the element; 3) evaluation of the participant behaviour according to the scale, and 4) allocating the rating or the observer response.[42] This can happen in a "fast and frugal process"[43] or in a slower, more elaborate process.

The challenge for the observer is to express what was observed in such a way that it communicates effectively relative to the norm of the AC and it eases statistical analysis, as was stated in Chapter 10. The probability that observers can accurately express their evaluation through choosing a category on the rating scale depends on how such a rating scale was constructed. Likert type scales are mostly used as rating scales during ACs. The scale can have any number of categories such as 4, 5, 6 or 7. In addition, there is a trade-off that needs to be made: the wider the scale, the more nuanced the evaluation, and the better and the stronger the evaluation of the evaluation will be. This could possibly positively impact the AC's ability to distinguish between participants.[44] However, the wider the scale, the more the cognitive load placed on the observer who has to use the scale while at the AC, increasing the possibility of rater error.

Another decision that the AC design team needs to take is whether the scale will have an even or odd number of categories. Including a midpoint on a scale – using an odd number of categories – has been shown to lead to a decrease in overall extreme response style, i.e. the tendency to use the extreme categories on the scale.[45] However, the inclusion of a midpoint might lead to observers allocating the midpoint rating when they are unsure as to how to rate the behavioural element, resulting in the central tendency.

The third decision is whether to label all the categories on the scale, or just label the extremes and perhaps the midpoint.[46] The recommendation is to fully label all the points on the rating scale.[47]

5.2.3   Observer guidelines

The observer guidelines refer to the document that explains the simulation to the observer. The purpose of this document is to ensure that, each time, the observer is competent to observe participants in the simulation. The document is there to refresh the observer's memory, not replace observer training. Typically, the guidelines will explain the type of simulation and the reason for choosing this type of simulation. The document will also explain the competencies being evaluated in the simulation, as well as the competency elements/indicators.

The guidelines will explain in detail the content of the simulation to the observer. They will highlight important aspects in the content, as well as certain trends in the information – some of which will be obvious and some not so obvious.

The guidelines will explain in detail to the observer how to use the simulation documents. In Table

---

42   Weijters et al., 2010

43   Kleinmann & Ingold, 2019

44   Weijters et al., 2010

45   Weijters et al., 2010

46   Weijters et al., 2010

47   Weijters et al., 2010

11.10, an example of observer guidelines are presented.

Table 11.10: Example of Observer Guidelines per Simulation (Source: Used with permission from Vitatalent (PTY) Ltd)

ASSESSOR FACILITATION AND SCORING GUIDE

THE SCENARIO

- INSURE- ALL, a large insurance company, has tried to incorporate new training and development methodologies based on Global Best Practice and the latest thinking in the field.
- However, efforts to date have not managed to produce the desired results and candidates are now tasked with reviewing the situation and providing recommendations for improvement.

INFORMATION GIVEN TO CANDIDATES TO PREPARE

- Instructions from HR Director on how to complete the challenge.
- Three video examples of Other Large Organisations that have successfully incorporated new Training and Development initiatives to create a Culture of Learning in their respective organisations.
- Hand Out of INSURE-ALL's current Project Plan for incorporating these new methodologies into their existing training services to employees.

EXERCISE STRUCTURE

Classification: Group Discussion Exercise

Group Size: 4

Assessor to Candidate Ratio: 1 Assessors to 2 Candidates

Total Time Allocated to Session: 2 Hours (90 min Facilitation + 30 min for Scoring)

Preparation Time: 20 Min Video Examples & 15 min individual review of Handout

Time Allowed to Record Behaviours: 45 min

Output Required: 10 Minute Presentation

Set Up: Candidates seated in meeting style layout and assessors positioned away from main discussions in a non-intrusive position

OUTPUTS OF 90 MIN SESSION

- 2 x Completed Scoring Sheets from Assessor 1
- 2 x Completed Scoring Sheets from Assessor 2
- Remember: All materials should be returned to the Assessment Centre Administrator at the end of the day.

11 STEP EXERCISE PROCESS

① Check all materials and set up is in place for exercise

② ORIENTATION AND INSTRUCTIONS

Assessor Introduces the Exercise and provides Handouts to candidates — **5 min**

READ INSTRUCTIONS: Welcome to Exercise 1 – Creating a Culture of Learning. I have a video message for you from your HR Director who will be explain in detail what this challenge entails. Please listen carefully to all the instructions and remember to make notes. ("hand out docs for the exercise) This Exercise should take 90 min to complete. Once you have listened to the instructions, I will give you an opportunity to ask questions and clarify any areas you might be uncertain about. Everyone ready? Great let's start.

③ Play Recording of Exercise Instructions — **15-min**

④ Assessor Checks for Understanding on Individual Preparation Instructions, once candidates have read the onscreen instructions

⑤ Candidates Individually Reviews Handout — **15-min**

⑥ Assessor Checks for Understanding on Team Discussion Instructions once candidates have read the onscreen instructions

ASSESSORS START RECORDING BEHAVIOURS

⑦ Team Discussion Commences

Note: The following information will appear on screen during this period. — **30-min**

- A letter from a concerned trainer on new approach.
- An email from aggrieved employees.

NOTE: In the event that candidates seem unsure of what is required when new information appear onscreen, assessors should say the following ". Once you have read and understood the onscreen information you should continue your discussions – The information should remain onscreen for the next 5 minutes"

⑧ Only if required: Assessor Checks for Understanding on Instructions for presentation after it displays onscreen — **15-min**

⑨ ASSESSORS STOP RECORDING BEHAVIOURS

⑩ Candidates Presents Outcomes to Assessors — **10-min**

Assessors Collects all Hand Outs and all note pages before candidates leave the room — **END**

⑪ SCORING OUTCOMES

- **Assessor 1** – Scores Candidate 1 & 2
- **Assessor 2** – Scores Candidate 3 & 4 — **30-min**

TOTAL TIME — **120-min**

EXERCISE MATERIAL REQUIRED

- Schedule: Candidate names, timeslots allocated and venue
- Video Instructions for Exercise 1
- 1 x Scoring Sheet per Candidate
- 4 x Hand Outs on Exercise 1 (1 per candidate)
- Note pages to RECORD behaviours
- Flip chart / whiteboard

INSTRUCTIONS TO CANDIDATES (ON-SCREEN)

INDIVIDUAL PREPARATION (15 MIN)

- Review the INSURE-ALL PROJECT PLAN.
- Identify and list all the problems and inefficiencies with the current project plan and think about how the project plan can be improved?

TEAM DISCUSSION (30 min)

Discuss what are the issues with the CURRENT PROJECT PLAN and how it can be improved.

PREPARATION FOR PRESENTATION (15 MIN)

Candidate are reminded that they should start preparing for the presentation.

GROUP PRESENTATION (10 min)

- 10 min presentation on findings and recommendations

Overall Outcome Required:

- An ACTIONABLE PLAN FOR IMPROVEMENT
- The steps the organisation should take to ensure the project vision is achieved.

NOTES TO ASSESSORS

- Candidates are allowed and should make notes for themselves on the handout provided.
- In the event that candidates seem unsure about what to do, assessors may remind them (for example as new information appears on screen during team discussion).
- Candidates should use the full 15 min to prepare individually. i.e. they may not start team discussions or start collaborating on content before the team discussion instructions display on screen.
- Time needs to be managed carefully to ensure the next exercise can be started on time and as per the assessment centre schedule.

ASSESSOR FACILITATION AND SCORING GUIDE

9 STEP SUMMARY PROCESS FOR SCORING EXERCISE 2

STEP 1
- Remind yourself of what this exercise intends to measure.
- Read through the summary page (page 2) of the scoring sheet.

STEP 2
- Start with the first competency **STRATEGIC OUTLOOK**, and read through description of the behaviourally anchored rating scale for **1 – 5.**

STEP 3
- Read through your notes and label all examples that would serve as evidence of the behaviours specified for **STRATEGIC OUTLOOK.**
- As you find examples in your notes. Label them with the initials **SO (STRATEGIC OUTLOOK)** next to the sentence as per the illustration to the right:

  SO · "local business owners **will** want to get involved if this creates more business opportunities for them"
  SO · "I think we need to focus on the big picture here and not worry about the small problems"
  SO · "two visions might confuse people – lets create one vision for everyone"

STEP 4
Next, decide if this is a **POSITIVE** example of **STRATEGIC OUTLOOK** or a **NEGATIVE** example and put a **+** or **-** sign next to the label.

+ SO · "local business owners will want to get involved if this creates more business opportunities for them "
+ SO · "I think we need to focus on the big picture here and not worry about the small problems"
+ SO · "two visions might confuse people – lets create one vision for everyone"

LIST POSITIVE AND NEGATIVE EVIDENCE BELOW

- local business owners get involved - creates more business opportunities for them
+ Focus on the big picture and not worry about the small problems now
+ two visions - confuse people – create one vision for everyone

STEP 5
Transfer the evidence from your notes to the relevant section in your scoring sheet.

TIP: When transferring the positive and negative evidence from your notes – you can just summarise evidence instead of re-writing the whole sentence in full.

STEP 6
Repeat STEPS 2, 3, 4 and 5 for: COMPETENCIES INNOVATION AND ENGAGING FOR COLLABORATION

1. Read through the description of the behaviourally anchored rating scale for **1 - 5**
2. Label examples in your notes with the initials of the element you are assessing
3. Add +/- sign next to your label to indicate if this is a positive or negative example
4. Transfer the evidence to the relevant section of your scoring sheet
NOTE AT THIS POINT YOU SHOULD HAVE BEHAVIOURAL EVIDENCE FOR ALL COMPETENCIES MEASURED ON THIS EXERCISE

STEP 7

SCORING KEY

SCALE	DEFINITION	DESCRIPTION
1	Poor / Little Evidence	No evidence OR Showed multiple and clear evidence of a low level of competence in the dimensions and no positive evidence
2	Less Than Adequate	Showed more negative evidence of the competence than positive evidence
3	Adequate	Showed more positive evidence of the competence than negative evidence
4	More Than Adequate	Showed clear evidence of competence in the dimension with little negative evidence
5	Excellent	Showed multiple and clear evidence of a high level of competence in the dimension and no negative evidence

STEP 8
Evaluate and **balance both the quality and quantify of evidence** you have for Strategic Outlook and make a judgement. Score this competency on page 1 of your scoring sheet (1-5 score).

STEP 9
Repeat STEP 7 and 8 for: COMPETENCIES - INNOVATION AND ENGAGING FOR COLLABORATION.

247

In the example depicted in Table 11.10, the scenario is explained to the observers, while the information that the participants receive as well as the expected output are mentioned. The 11 steps to administer the simulation are provided and the 9 steps to score the simulation are explained. The advantage of designing such a detailed observer guide is that observers can refer to the guide while they are busy administering and scoring the simulation without having to consult someone else. It also increases the likelihood of standardised simulation administration.

5.2.4   *Norm tables (standards/conversion tables)*

Another important tool for the observer is a norm table. Again, each simulation should have a norm table to assist the observer in deciding on an overall rating per competency. Although the observer decides on a rating per competency based on the norm table, the final rating per competency will be agreed upon only during the data-integration session that takes place towards the end of the AC (see Chapter 16 for a discussion about data integration).

The norm tables are decided upon by the AC design team, together with a group of SMEs. For example, the team may decide that a rating of 65% on a competency equals an effective rating. When the simulation is designed, this table is decided upon by the AC design team together with the SMEs who assisted in the design of the simulation. When the simulation is pre-piloted, the norm is established based on the feedback of everyone concerned. When the AC is piloted, the norm is further refined. Table 11.11 contains an example of a norm table. In the example, the ratings per competency element are calculated as percentages and the percentages are converted to a rating per competency.

Table 11.11: Example of a norm table for a DAC

Norm/Conversion Table In-Box			
	Needing development	**Effective**	**Highly effective**
Initiative	0 – 60%	61 – 80%	81 – 100%
Information gathering	0 – 64%	65 – 84%	85 – 100%
Judgement	0 – 74%	75 – 90%	91 – 100%
Empowerment	0 – 64%	65 – 84%	85 – 100%
Providing direction	0 – 64%	65 – 84%	85 – 100%
Control	0 – 64%	65 – 84%	85 – 100%

5.3   Role player

In the above example, the conversion for the competency 'Judgement' requires higher levels of participant behaviour than the other competencies evaluated during the In-Box. This indicates that 'Judgement' is, in this context, the competency that is most important for effective job performance.

5.3.1 Role player guidelines

The role player is the person who plays a particular character during a simulation and is specifically trained to play the specific role. The purpose of a role player is to create the opportunity for the participant to demonstrate behaviour linked to competencies. In addition to the simulation instructions, the role player provides stimuli to which the participant needs to respond.[48] This means that the role player should be well trained in the content of the simulation, the character, and the competencies being evaluated.

Each role player should ensure that he or she follows the guidelines for each character in a simulation.

The character that the role player portrays should be linked to a character and level of role that the target job incumbent has to interact with.[49] This character is identified during the job analysis and is specified in the AC blueprint. The role player guidelines are set out in a document containing all probable information that the person playing the role of a character during a simulation might need to know. The document contains information on the instructions given to the participants, biographical information about the character, information regarding the personality or disposition of the character, background information on the specific scenario, possible answers that the role player should provide to specific questions, and arguments and possible counterarguments to use during the role play. In addition, the character's attitudes and thoughts about certain pertinent issues are described. Although the guidelines are designed so that most eventualities are covered, the guidelines should provide enough information for the role player to respond to the unforeseen "in character".

The purpose of the role player guidelines is to ensure consistency of the characters among the different role players. For example, the role player needs to respond to the participant's behaviour in a manner consistent with the character and not the role player's own personality. If the character would be offended by something the participant has said, then the role player must act offended, even though the role player would not have been offended in real life. Then again, another role player's own character might be similar to that of the simulation character being portrayed. This role player must also abide by the role player guidelines and not over-respond to the participant's behaviour.

Another purpose of the role player guidelines is to ensure that the same information is given to the various participants. This is very important, especially in the case of an AC following the integrated simulation approach. If the wrong information is given to the participant, the wrong information is carried over to the next simulation and might accordingly lead to wrong information being used throughout the remainder of the AC.

Table 11.12 provides an example of typical background information given in a role player guideline document.

---

48 Thornton et al., 2017

49 The British Psychological Society's Division of Occupational Psychology, 2015

Table 11.12: Example of role player guidelines

Zodwa Dlamini – Sales Manager Role Player Guidelines

You will be Zodwa Dlamini, Sales Manager: Gauteng for Global Training Solutions (GTS).

Background on GTS: Global Training Solutions is a consulting company with its head office in Cape Town. The company is divided into regions, with the Gauteng region being the largest. The company specialises in providing training and development solutions for small, medium and large organisations. The company's motto is: "If you can imagine it, we can train it."

Your background: You are the Sales Manager for the Gauteng region. You were appointed in June last year to this position from your previous employer. You were previously a training consultant.

You are accountable for the total sales function in the region. As such, you have 10 sales executives reporting to you. You report directly to the Regional Manager. The AC participant is in the role of Regional Manager. You have an HR diploma, which you obtained five years ago from Damelin. You have not attended any sales- or management-related training.

Your character: You are a talkative, socially outgoing person who always sees the "bright side of things". You enjoy being in the limelight, but get quite upset when people ignore you or leave you out. You enjoy recognition and, if people do not give you compliments on their own, you will, from time to time, compliment yourself. You become defensive when you feel personally attacked or blamed.

How to play the role: You must start the discussion in a positive manner, thinking that the new Regional Manager wants to meet you because of the important role you fulfil in the region. You are quite shocked at any mention of problems within your section. The few problems (not reaching targets, high turnover of staff, low morale) are due to organisation- and market-related trends. Do not initiate behaviour, but do create opportunities for the participant to demonstrate behaviour linked to all the competencies being evaluated.

Counterarguments regarding problems raised by participant:

Budget overspent – You were not involved in drawing up the budget. You were asked to give your inputs. You gave your inputs, but nothing you recommended was included in the budget. The budget is unrealistic. It is therefore normal management practice to "ignore" the budget and to spend wisely. If prompted, you recommend that, for next year's budget, everyone's input should be considered. The budget should also be more directly linked to the sales target.

Not reaching targets – The targets are also unrealistic. It is common knowledge that, in every industry, there are peaks and valleys, yet it is expected of your team to meet the same money targets every month, irrespective of whether it is December, June or April.

In addition, the whole economy is slowing down. The net effect of this is that companies are cutting back on training and development interventions. Multinational training companies are now the competition. They have a lot of money to spend on marketing and creating brand awareness. GTS does not have that. When asked for suggestions, suggest that more market information be obtained. A whole marketing drive should be embarked on. This drive should coincide with a strong sales drive in which a one-stop training function is offered.

> *High staff turnover in sales section* – Sales executives leave because they are offered better remuneration packages elsewhere. If asked, suggest that a proper salary survey should be conducted in the market and that sales executive packages be adapted to the market norm.

Source: LEMASA observer-training documentation

If the AC is making use of Trait Activation Theory, the prompts per competency that the role player will provide must also be clearly indicated. For example, the role player might say to the participant, "I have prepared suggestions as to how we can resolve the problem", to elicit participant behaviour linked to a behavioural element like: "Ask the role player for their suggestions."

5.4 Simulation administration manual

The simulation administration manual contains all the participant, role player and observer documentation. In addition, it stipulates the resources needed to administer the simulation, as well as the physical venue requirements. For example, the document will stipulate that the room must be one where privacy and confidentiality can be maintained and must be able to accommodate three people at two tables (two at one table and one at another table). The room should be noise-free. The participants should also be given notepaper to use while they are preparing.

6. **CONCLUDING REMARKS**

Thus far in the AC development process, the simulations have been developed according to the specifications set-out and signed-off in the AC blueprint. Although care has been taken to develop simulations that adhere to all requirements, the simulations need to be tried out in a "life" situation called the pre-pilot. The next chapter will explain the pre-pilot in detail.

CHAPTER 12

DEVELOP SIMULATIONS II

Sandra Schlebusch

1. INTRODUCTION

In the previous chapter, simulations were defined and the various types of simulations were described. Design hints were shared and the chapter discussed the various documents that need to be developed per simulation. This chapter continues the discussion about the development of simulations by discussing the pre-pilot of simulations, before discussing how parallel simulations can be developed. Guidance is then provided on incorporating information technology (IT) into a simulation. Important validity considerations are then shared before the chapter ends with a discussion about the critical decisions related to, and outcomes of, step 5 in the design model.

2. PRE-PILOT (TRIALLING)

Every simulation should be tested before it is used as part of an AC. This test is called a pre-pilot, which occurs when the simulation is administered, according to instructions, to a group of participants from the target population.[1]

The purpose of the pre-pilot is to determine whether the simulation elicits the required visible behaviour from the participants. A well-designed simulation should elicit enough behaviour in respect of each competency so that a big enough behaviour sample is obtained to evaluate the participant's behaviour. If a lot of behaviour on the part of the participant is elicited, but this behaviour is not an example of behaviour linked to the competencies being evaluated, the simulation is not effective. The simulation should then be changed.

During the pre-pilot, the wording of the simulation instructions is tested. Are the instructions clear? Are the words simple enough, or perhaps too simple? Are there any words that offend? Is there any terminology or are there any characters that do not fit into the target organisation's culture? Is there perhaps another way of wording the instructions so that they will lead to the desired behaviour on the part of the participants?

The pre-pilot will indicate whether the role player guidelines are comprehensive enough, as they should prepare the role player for most eventualities.

The pre-pilot will also show whether the simulation scenario is one that allows individual behaviour to come to the fore. If the scenario does elicit individual behaviour, the scenario setting is appropriate. However, if the scenario within the organisation's culture predetermines the participants' behaviour (in other words the scenario is too strong), the scenario should be changed.

---

1   The British Psychological Society, 2015; International Taskforce on Assessment Center Guidelines, 2015; Thornton et al., 2017

The pre-pilot provides an opportunity for the AC design team to establish whether the documentation is comprehensive and sufficient. An aspect to pay attention to is how easy it is for the observers to use the documentation. The requirement in respect of the documentation is that all participant behaviour should be noted and then easily classified under the various competencies being evaluated. Are all the competency elements adequately covered in the observer report form? Does the assessment table give a fair rating of the participant's behaviour?

The answers to all of the above questions can only be obtained from the participants in the pre-pilot and from the role players and the observers involved. The AC design team should therefore have an in-depth discussion with each group to obtain the answers to the questions. The participants, role players and observers should also be asked for feedback on any other aspect of the simulation. The AC design team should act on the suggestions given by the participants, role players and observers.

It might be necessary for the simulation to be pre-piloted again. This is a requirement if a lot of changes have to be made to the simulation after the first pre-pilot.

The design of a simulation is not complete until the whole design process has been documented. When the steering committee has signed off on a simulation, the design of the simulation is complete for the moment.

Table 12.1 below is the start of a checklist for use during the pre-pilot.

Table 12.1: Pre-pilot checklist

Pre-pilot checklist

1. **Competencies**
   1.1 Is visible behaviour linked to all the competencies elicited?
   1.2 Is enough visible behaviour elicited?
   1.3 Is behaviour that is not linked to the competencies being elicited ("noise")?
   1.4 Is individual behaviour that is unique to the participant being elicited?

2. **Simulation content**
   2.1 Is the time to prepare for, perform and observe the simulation adequate?
   2.2 Is enough information on the scenario given to the participant before the simulation as well as during the simulation?
   2.3 Is the choice of words appropriate?
   2.4 Are all words simple words (not words with more than one meaning or words not in general use)?
   2.5 Are all sentences easy to understand (not sentences with more than one major idea)?
   2.6 How was the simulation experienced by the participant, role player and observer?

3. **Simulation instructions**
   3.1 Are all the deliverables clearly stated?
   3.2 Are the words simple?
   3.3 Is the choice of words appropriate?
   3.4 How can the wording of the instructions be changed in order to be clearer to the participant?

4. **Documents**
   4.1 Participant documents
      4.1.1 Are all the documents easy to use?
   4.2 Role player documents
      4.2.1 Is enough information about the scenario given to the role player?
      4.2.2 Is enough information about the character given to the role player?
      4.2.3 Is enough information on the arguments and counterarguments given to the role player?
   4.3 Observer documents
      4.3.1 Are all documents easy to use?
      4.3.2 Are enough behavioural examples given per competency element?
      4.3.3 Are all competency elements stated on the observer report form relevant?
      4.3.4 Have any competency elements been left out?
      4.3.5 Is the maximum rating per competency element realistic?
      4.3.6 Are the assessment tables realistic?
      4.3.7 Is there enough space on the observer report form to classify all behaviour?
   4.4 Administration guide
      4.4.1 Are all the required resources clearly stated?
      4.4.2 Are the conditions under which the simulation must take place clearly stated?

3. THE SPECIAL CASE OF PARALLEL SIMULATIONS

From time to time there is a need to use parallel simulations, i.e. simulations with different content, but at the same level of difficulty or complexity as the original simulations. Although it is difficult to develop a parallel simulation that is an exact duplicate of the original simulation, Brummel, Rupp and Spain[2] proposed that a three-step process be used. These steps will be briefly discussed.

Step 1: Design detailed simulation specifications

The original simulation's specifications serve as the reference point, and need to be clarified and augmented with more detail by analysing the simulation. Typically, the following need to be specified for the simulation to be cloned: target population; focal constructs being evaluated; simulation type; difficulty level; setting or context; specific topics covered in the simulation; number of pages that the participant works with; type of material; and the participant's role in the simulation.

Step 2: Develop the alternate simulation

Armed with the detailed simulation specifications, the development of the parallel simulation can start. Again, the context in which the simulation will take place needs to be developed, along with all the documentation required for each simulation. Once "finished" with the development of the simulation, a group of subject matter experts needs to scrutinise the newly designed simulation to determine the extent to which the new simulation is parallel to the original. After making the recommended changes to the new simulation, the simulation is ready to be pre-piloted. Again, changes will probably be made to the simulation based on the outcome of the simulation pilot. The simulation is now ready to be administered as an alternative to the original simulation.

---

2   Brummel et al., 2009: 149

Step 3: Compare sample statistics and compute equating function

Once enough people have participated in the newly developed parallel simulation, the statistical analysis can start. The means and standard deviations across the simulation versions can be determined, and, if there is a significant difference between the two samples, an equating function can be determined to adjust scores in future samples. Sources of variance need to be examined and the relationship between the two simulations needs to be determined (parallel, tau-equivalent, essentially tau-equivalent, congeneric).

The results from the statistical analysis need to be interrogated and it might be necessary to change some aspects of the parallel simulation. Only after the statistical analysis shows that the two versions of the simulation are parallel to each other, can this claim be made about the simulations.

The next section of this chapter discusses how to incorporate information technology into simulation design.

4. THE USE OF INFORMATION TECHNOLOGY

The advancements in information technology (IT) enable the use of technology in various aspects of ACs (see Chapter 10 for a discussion about TEACs and VACs). In addition, an AC should attempt to mimic the world of work as far as possible. Since IT is part of most, if not all, knowledge workers' worlds of work, ACs should also make use of IT. This section will discuss, at a high level, how simulations can be migrated to online delivery.

There are hardware (equipment), software (programmes) and telecommunications components involved when using technology to deliver any aspect of a simulation or an overall AC. The hardware refers to aspects such as the devices that the AC participants, observers, role players or administrators will use to access the simulation or AC (desktop, laptop, or mobile device), as well as the various servers and storage devices to be considered. Software aspects such as internet browsers and firewalls are important and telecommunications aspects such as the bandwidth need to be considered.

When using IT during an AC, the services of an IT provider that already has a functional and safe platform can be obtained (a third party platform), or a platform tailored to the specific simulation or AC's need can be developed. If the decision has been taken that a new platform will be designed it is recommended that an IT team becomes involved in the design process as early as possible. A further recommendation is to ensure that the individual simulation is eliciting the required behaviour (pre-piloted) before starting with the coding to create the virtual simulation. The typical IT team that will be involved in the process are user interface and user experience designers, software engineers, software/ quality assurance testers, business analysts and systems architects.[3]

---

3   Scott et al., 2018

The analysis exercise, or case study, is the simulation that is the easiest to convert to an online simulation. The In-Box is also relatively easy, while the one-to-one role play is more challenging and a group meeting is difficult to convert to an online platform.

4.1 Software Development Life Cycle

The typical process of software development is depicted in the figure below:

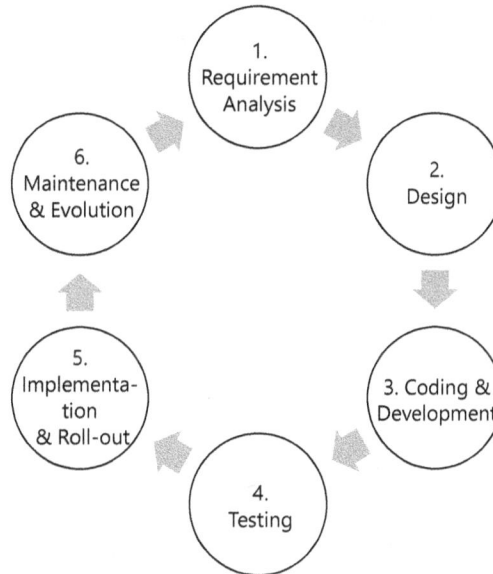

Figure 12.1: Software Development Life Cycle
Source: Adapted from Scott, Bartram & Reynolds[4]

The software development process becomes a project within the total simulation/AC design project. A brief discussion of the various steps will follow.

4.1.1 Step 1: Requirement Analysis

The AC blueprint, as well as detailed discussions between the AC design team and the IT team, are the main sources of information. If the client organisation's IT department is not already part of the IT team, they need to be co-opted so that they can be closely involved in this step to articulate the internal IT architecture of the organisation.

4.1.2 Step 2: Design

From the information gathered during step 1, the design specifications are created. A useful technique during this step is to create user personas.[5] A persona is an imaginary character that personifies the typical user; their behaviours, attitudes, goals and other traits. Personas are built for the back-end

---

4   Scott et al., 2018: 121

5   Scott et al., 2018

user – the AC administrator, and the front-end users – the AC participants, observers and role players. With a clear understanding of the users, the user interface and user experience, designers can design the experience directed at the specific needs of the users. Specific user interface elements that are important are:[6]

- lay-out (alignment, consistency, proximity, button placement, visual hierarchy);
- text (line width, contrast, orientation, case, font, alignment);
- graphics (placement, size, embedded text);
- colour (variety, intensity, relevance); and
- single access point.

It is recommended that prototypes be built – first low-fidelity and then high-fidelity prototypes. Using prototypes allows the IT team to discover which design aspects work and which do not have the desired user reaction.

The design specifications need to be signed off by both the AC design team, as well as the AC steering committee.

4.1.3 Step 3: Coding and development

Once the IT specifications have been signed-off, the software programmers and database designers can start to write code. The quality assurance testers will check the written code for errors in an attempt to eliminate bugs as far as possible.

4.1.4 Step 4: Testing

This step usually takes longer than the time allocated in the project plan. Once the initial software programmers and user experience testers are satisfied that the most obvious problems have been solved in the coding, the code is exercised to specifically identify errors to be fixed. Formal test plans that simulate specific functionality paths through the system can be tested. This process of testing, correcting and retesting continues until the team is satisfied that the programme and platform is ready for implementation. During the Alpha version of the programme, the programme is fully functional as the quality testing begins.[7] Bugs are logged and fixed. With the release of the Beta version, the content is complete and the final quality testing begins to fix the remaining bugs.

4.1.5 Step 5: Implementation and roll-out

The final "product" is considered ready for release when it seems as though the programming is bug-free. Activities included in this step are software packaging, delivery, configuration and user training.

---

6 Scott et al., 2018

7 McNamara et al., 2014

4.1.6 Step 6: Maintenance and evolution

All programmes and systems need to be maintained and updated from time-to-time. This can include perfective maintenance – enhancing existing features; preventative maintenance – anticipating potential problems and accommodating for them before they happen; corrective maintenance – fixing problems as they occur; and user support.[8]

4.2   Aspects to consider

Some of the important aspects to consider when building a simulation or AC on an IT platform are security, standardisation and legal and other guideline considerations. Each will be briefly discussed.

4.2.1 Security

The following are security related aspects to consider:
- Data security – the upload, download and storage of data needs to be secured. The data also needs to be protected against hacking (i.e. encrypted; multiple server configuration – application server, database server, scoring and reporting server; de-identification of data; secure firewalls; active monitoring of intruders).
- The Intellectual Property (IP) of the simulation/AC content, observer report forms, decision rules and algorithms need to be protected. This can be done by disabling options to cut, print, copy, paste, store, use hot keys and the right mouse context menu, as well as installing a test security agent to prevent other applications from copying from the platform/system.[9]
- AC participant verification – there must be a formalised protocol in place that limits cheating and ensures that the participant's identity is confirmed during the simulation/AC administration. This can be done by using a combination of password authorisation; analysing keystroke patterns; fingerprint authorisation; photo authorisation; retinal scanning; and online monitoring through the use of webcams.[10]

4.2.2 Standardisation

The experience of the AC participants need to be standardised, for example the download speed, bandwidth and testing conditions are important. A clear Technical Requirements Manual needs to be drawn up explaining the technical requirements in order for the participant to partake in the simulation/AC. It is recommended that the participants should be able to test whether their IT conditions adhere to the requirements by clicking on a button on the system/platform and receiving immediate feedback from it.

---

8   Scott et al., 2018

9   Naglieri et al., 2004

10 Naglieri et al., 2004

Where the simulation/AC is administered in the participant's own environment, they should take accountability for ensuring that the appropriate test conditions exist. However, these conditions need to be clearly stated upfront to the participant.[11]

4.2.3 Legal and guideline considerations

There are various South African laws to consider when designing and implementing VACs or TEACs. These include the Protection of Personal Information Act (Act 4 of 2013)[12], the Electronic Communications and Transactions Act (Act 25 of 2002)[13], and national and international guidelines about tests in general and ACs delivered over the internet.[14] Below is a list of some of the guidelines that need to be adhered to:
- International Test Commission (2001). Guidelines on Test Use.
- Association of Test Publishers (2002). Guidelines for Computer-Based Testing.
- Society for Industrial and Organizational Psychology (2003). Principles for the Validation and Use of Personnel Selection Procedures.
- Naglieri et al. (2004). Psychological Testing on the Internet: New Problems, Old Issues.
- International Test Commission (2006). Guidelines on Computer-Based and Internet-Delivered Testing.
- ISO/IEC 23988 (2007). Information technology – A Code of Practice for the Use of Information Technology (IT) in the Delivery of Assessments.
- International Test Commission (2010). Test-Takers Guide to Technology-Based Testing.
- ISO 10667 (2011). Assessment Service Delivery – Procedures and Methods to Assess People in Work and Organizational Settings.
- American Psychological Association and others (2014). Standards for Educational and Psychological Testing.
- International Test Commission (2014). Guidelines on Test Security.
- British Psychological Society (2015). Standards in the Design and Delivery of Assessment Centres.
- International Task Force on Assessment Center Guidelines (2015). Guidelines and Ethical Considerations for Assessment Center Operations.
- The Best Practice Guidelines for the Use of Assessment Centre Method in South Africa (5th ed.).[15]
- European Union General Data Protection Regulation (GDPR) (2018).

From the above list it should be clear that it is not as easy as one might think to develop a platform that adheres to all the stringent requirements. Table 12.2 below is a checklist compiled from the mentioned legislation and guidelines to assist in migrating a simulation or AC to an electronic platform.

---

11 Scott et al., 2018

12 Promotion of Access to Information Act, (Act No. 2 of 2000)

13 Electronic Communications and Transactions Act, (Act No. 25 of 2002)

14 Scott et al., 2018

15 Meiring & Buckett, 2016

Table 12.2: Compliance checklist for using technology during an AC

Compliance Checklist for using Technology during an AC[16]

1. Is there equivalence of simulation/AC results across different media (desktop, laptop, mobile device)?
2. Are the accuracy of the decision rules and algorithms backed by scientific rigour when results are integrated electronically?
3. Are the hardware and software requirements compatible?
4. Is the platform/system robust?
5. Has the system been designed to make reasonable adjustments to accommodate simulation/AC participants with special needs?
6. Have various screen design issues been accommodated?
7. Is the participant data automatically saved during administration to ensure retrieval should the administration be interrupted?
8. Have the conditions under which the simulation/AC can be administered specified?
9. Are the end users (AC administrators, observers and role players) competent in the use of the system/platform?
10. Can the identity of the AC participant be confirmed during the administration?
11. Is the intellectual property secured?
12. Is the data secure when transferred over the internet (i.e. encrypted, etc.)?
13. Are the results stored on a server secured and in compliance with data privacy requirements?
14. Have reasonable precautions been taken to physically safeguard the servers?
15. Is there participant informed consent for the use, transfer and storage of results?

The use of technology *is* the future of simulations and ACs. Care should, however, be taken to ensure that technology is used responsibly and that the resulting "product" still adheres to the 10 essential elements to be called an AC (see Chapter 1).

5. IMPORTANT VALIDITY CONSIDERATIONS

When the AC design team embarks on the process of designing simulations, it needs to consider the requirements of the validation and evaluation stage, i.e. Stage Four of the design model. Care should therefore be taken to ensure that the simulations are designed according to the specifications derived during the analysis stage (Stage One), and captured in the AC blueprint. As was the case during the analysis stage, all actions and processes, as well as reactions to and changes in the simulations, need to be documented.[17] Sign-off of the designed simulations must be obtained from the AC project steering committee, as well as from other people involved during the pre-pilot of the simulations.

The various simulation documents should be designed in such a way as to facilitate the capture of information from the documents for research purposes if it is not a VAC. Since the criterion for use during the analysis stage is known (see Chapter 7 for a discussion about effectiveness criteria), aspects from the various documents that need to be captured electronically in order to allow comparison with

---

16 Adapted from Scott et al., 2018

17 Thornton et al., 2017

the criterion must be prominently placed on the documents. This will ensure not only that the observers complete the documents thoroughly, but also that the data capturer sees the information easily.

Care should be taken not to include cultural bias in the content of the simulation (see Chapter 3 for a discussion on the various forms of bias). For example, cultures differ regarding the roles of spouses in marriages. If the scenario created for the simulation includes an interaction between a husband and wife, the behaviour displayed by the participant might be a reflection of the cultural roles assigned to each spouse. This might lead to a situation where the simulation does not elicit the behaviour linked to the competencies being evaluated.

As was mentioned in Chapter 10, the number of competencies being evaluated during a simulation might impact the reliability by which they can be assessed by the observers due to cognitive fatigue. In addition, the more the number of competencies assessed, the more likely it is that the behaviours linked to the various competencies are difficult to distinguish from each other.[18] This might lead to competency contamination, impacting the simulation and AC's construct validity.

During step five of the design model it is important to design the simulations in such a way that:
- they limit the sources of error variance;
- the reliability of the evaluations and the resulting ratings are increased; and
- the chance that the simulations and the whole AC are valid is also increased.

Each of these issues will briefly be discussed.

5.1 Possible sources of error variance

There are several possible sources of error variance, which is unwanted variation that can distort the results.[19] We will briefly discuss six sources that can be found in the circumstances surrounding the administration of an AC.

5.1.1 Physical conditions

The first possible source of error variance is the conditions in which the simulation takes place. Simulations should therefore be administered under standardised conditions.[20] The first aspect that comes to mind is the physical surroundings in which the simulation takes place. Noise, temperature, lighting, distance between the AC venues and access to resources are all examples of physical conditions that may vary from participant to participant or AC to AC. If these vary a lot, they might influence the ratings of the participants on each competency. In turn, this influences the extent to which the various participants' final ratings can be compared with one another. In the guidelines on how to administer the simulation, the physical conditions should be clearly specified, and such specifications must be adhered to during administration.

---

18 Thornton et al., 2015

19 Cascio & Aguinis, 2019

20 Thornton et al., 2017; Thornton et al., 2015; Meiring & Buckett, 2016; SA Assessment Centre Study Group, 2018

5.1.2 Delivery of instructions

Not only are the physical surroundings important, but the way in which the simulation instructions are given to each participant is also key.[21] The second source of error variance is the delivery of the simulation instructions to the participant. Various AC practitioners might not give the instructions in a standardised format, which may influence the participants' behaviour. Using synonyms for words in the instructions, expanding on the instructions and giving examples of the required deliverables that are not indicated in the instructions are all examples of how the simulation instructions could be given differently to the various participants. This may result in the instructions being understood in different ways by the various participants (see Chapter 9 for a discussion about Interactionist Theory and Trait Activation Theory). Writing clear and simple simulation instructions that need to be read verbatim can potentially minimise this source of error variance. Some AC practitioners also record[22] the simulation instructions and play these instructions to the various AC participants.

5.1.3 Content of the instructions

The third source of possible error variance is the content of the simulation instructions. If participant ability is being measured (see Chapter 10 for a discussion on measuring abilities and motivation) the instructions should clearly specify the deliverable expected of the participant. This will help them to understand the purpose of the simulation, as well as what is expected of him or her. In turn, it might increase the construct validity of the simulation.[23]

5.1.4 Observers

A fourth potential source of error variance is the observers. Over time, the same observer might evaluate the same behaviour differently, while different observers might also rate the same behaviour differently.[24] This potential source of error variance can possibly be controlled by designing the simulation documents in such a way that all behaviour examples are noted and chances of correctly classifying behaviour is increased. It is necessary to use behavioural examples and mention the competency definition often in the observer documentation. Using weights, behaviour anchors and norm tables also decrease the possibility of error variance as they increase standardisation. Comprehensive observer training and observer refresher training, including frame-of-reference training, are also needed. Observer training will be discussed during the implementation stage, i.e. Stage Three of the design model (see Chapter 15).

5.1.5 Role players

A fifth possible source of error variance is the simulation role players, i.e. the way the role is played from participant to participant, and from role player to role player, might differ. Adequate role player

21 Thornton et al., 2017
22 Caldwell et al., 2003
23 Thornton et al., 2017
24 Jackson et al., 2005

guidelines and scripts are thus called for.[25] The training of role players will be discussed during the implementation stage of the design model (see Chapter 15).

5.1.6 Other participants

A sixth possible source of error variance is other simulation participants. During a leaderless group discussion, for example, other participants are also involved. The behaviour of the other participants will be the source of creating a non-standardised simulation. Even though the participants receive clear instructions on the deliverables of the simulation, the differences in character and skill of each participant will still create the variance in the stimuli to which the participant is exposed (see Chapter 9 for a discussion about the Interactionist Theory, and Chapter 3 for a discussion about bias).

5.2 Reliability

Reliability is an important aspect to consider. The question is: "Can the observers rate the same behaviour consistently the same over time?"[26] Again, using techniques in the simulation documents such as behaviour anchors, rating scales and norm tables will increase the likelihood of reliable ratings.

Another approach to increase reliability is to operationalise the competencies used during the AC. Not only should each competency be broken down into elements, but each element should be illustrated by way of a behaviour example. Each competency needs to be explained in terms of how behaviour linked to the competency will look during the various simulations. For example, "control" in a paper-based simulation could entail the participant giving due dates for an assignment, while "control" during an interactive simulation could entail the participant asking the role player by what date the assignment will be finished. Reliability is discussed in more detail in Chapter 18.

5.3 Validity

The validity of the simulation results should be shown. Validity refers to the degree a simulation measures what it proposes to measure.[27] Evidence needs to be presented that the required participant performance during the simulation is related to the required job performance of an effective incumbent in the target job. Although the validity of the AC is discussed in detail during the evaluation and validation stage of the design model (see Chapter 18), it is crucial to keep a few aspects in mind when designing the simulations that make up the AC.

Evidence should exist that the simulations are based on the information gathered during the analysis stage, and the trends identified during the analysis stage should be depicted in the content of the simulations. The AC and the simulations should therefore be designed according to the AC blueprint, since the information collected and the trends identified during the analysis stage should be included in the AC blueprint (see Chapter 10). The competencies that are evaluated during each simulation

---

25 Caldwell et al., 2003

26 Cascio & Aguinis, 2019

27 Cascio & Aguinis, 2019

need to be explained by way of behavioural examples, while the observer documentation needs to be designed so that the observers will be able to recognise the behaviour being assessed. The observers themselves need training in how to observe behaviour during a specific simulation (see Chapter 9 for a discussion about RAM). We will discuss observer training during the implementation stage of the design model in Chapter 14.

6. CRITICAL DECISIONS RELATING TO, AND OUTCOMES OF, THIS STEP

The following are the critical decisions relating to, and outcomes of, the design simulation step.

6.1 Simulations that elicit enough behaviour linked to the focal constructs being evaluated

Simulations are designed for the specific purpose of eliciting behaviour from the AC participant that is linked to the competencies being evaluated. The behaviour demonstrated during a simulation involving a participant should also be a large enough sample of behaviour so that a realistic evaluation of the applicable competency can be made.

It is not a desirable situation when the simulation elicits a lot of behaviour that is not linked to the competencies being evaluated. This is called "noise". The simulation content and instructions should be changed so that the noise is eliminated.

The behaviour elicited by the simulation should distinguish between participants; in other words, each participant should react in his or her own unique way to the simulation stimuli. If the same type of behaviour is elicited from all participants, the specific scenario might be dictating the type of behaviour within the target organisation's culture. The simulation scenario should then be changed so that the participants can choose how to react to the stimuli.

6.2 Simulation documentation that is easy to use, clear and comprehensive

All documentation used during a simulation should be designed in such a way that it is easy to use when administering the simulation and when observing, noting, classifying and evaluating the simulation. The easier the documentation is to use, the greater the likelihood that it will be used correctly. Ease of use also increases the chances of the documentation being completed comprehensively. Correct and comprehensive use of the simulation documents contributes to the overall reliability of the simulation results.

If the simulation and the AC are not using technology, the simulation documentation should be designed with the needs of the data capturer in mind, as they will capture certain simulation information electronically after the AC. This electronic information will be used for statistical calculations that form part of the evaluation and validation stage of AC design.

6.3 Simulation administration guidelines that will ensure the simulation is administered in a standard format

A simulation should consistently deliver reliable results. The reliability of these results is influenced by the conditions under which the simulation is administered. To ensure that the conditions remain comparable from one administration to the next, the simulation should be administered according to the conditions described in the simulation administration guide.

The role player guidelines should also be comprehensive so as to ensure that the roles are consistently played in character. The information shared by the role player during the simulation should be the same for all participants.

The guidelines given to the observers should be comprehensive enough to ensure that they observe, note, classify and evaluate behaviour in a consistent manner. The same rating should be awarded to the applicable competency by all the observers when the same behaviour is observed by different observers. The same rating should also be awarded if the same observer observes the behaviour again after a period of time.

CHAPTER 13

DEVELOP CENTRE

Sandra Schlebusch

1. INTRODUCTION – THE PURPOSE OF DEVELOPING A CENTRE

The next part of the design and develop stage of the design model is step six: develop centre. During this step, the simulations that will form part of the AC are sequenced in a logical and time- and cost-effective way. The purpose is to create an AC where the simulations flow logically and are experienced by everyone involved as effective.

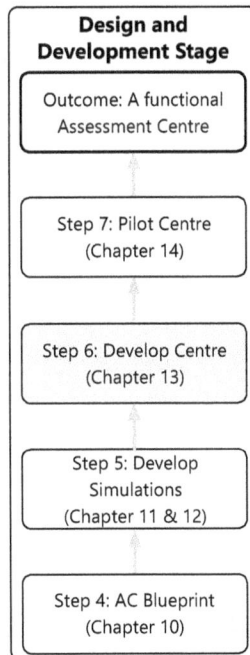

```
┌─────────────────────────────────┐
│       Design and                │
│   Development Stage             │
│  ┌───────────────────────────┐  │
│  │  Outcome: A functional    │  │
│  │  Assessment Centre        │  │
│  └───────────────────────────┘  │
│             ↑                   │
│  ┌───────────────────────────┐  │
│  │  Step 7: Pilot Centre     │  │
│  │  (Chapter 14)             │  │
│  └───────────────────────────┘  │
│             ↑                   │
│  ┌───────────────────────────┐  │
│  │  Step 6: Develop Centre   │  │
│  │  (Chapter 13)             │  │
│  └───────────────────────────┘  │
│             ↑                   │
│  ┌───────────────────────────┐  │
│  │  Step 5: Develop          │  │
│  │  Simulations              │  │
│  │  (Chapter 11 & 12)        │  │
│  └───────────────────────────┘  │
│             ↑                   │
│  ┌───────────────────────────┐  │
│  │  Step 4: AC Blueprint     │  │
│  │  (Chapter 10)             │  │
│  └───────────────────────────┘  │
└─────────────────────────────────┘
```

Figure 13.1: The develop centre step in the design and development stage

During this step, the golden thread running through all the simulations is created. The AC process as a whole is thus created. All the experiences of the participants and observers are consciously placed so that optimum performance by everyone, with the available resources, is created every time the AC is administered. The AC is designed with the requirements of reliability and validity in mind. It is also designed in such a way that the face validity of the AC as a whole is increased. Step six – develop centre – is depicted in Figure 13.1.

This chapter starts with a discussion on AC design hints, followed by an overview of the various centre processes. An introduction to the various programmes that need to be created for the AC is followed by introducing the last of the process owners, namely the centre administrator. The other roles that are embraced by the term "process owners" are those of the role players and observers. Both these roles were introduced in Chapter 11. After discussing the additional documentation that is needed to run an effective AC, the chapter concludes by summarising the outcomes of this step.

2. AC DESIGN HINTS

2.1 AC duration

The biggest challenge for the AC design team during the develop centre step is to schedule all the simulations and AC activities within the overall time allocated to the AC (this is specified in the AC blueprint). Not only must all the simulations take place according to each simulation's time requirements, but the participants and process owners should also not be placed under unnecessary time stress. When they are under unnecessary time stress, fatigue can influence the effectiveness of the AC. Observers should have enough time to effectively observe, note, classify and evaluate (ONCE) participant behaviour post a simulation, and ideally observers should not be expected to work extended hours.[1] If it is a DAC, enough time should be allowed for the participant feedback discussions, as well as the development planning during the DAC.[2] DACs are usually longer than an AC or DC.[3]

2.2 Observer participant ratio

If the decision has not yet been taken (see the AC blueprint), the design team must decide on the observer : participant ratio, which will influence the duration of the AC. When fewer observers are used, the overall time for observation increases because fewer observers must observe more participants. This influences the overall duration of the AC. However, the more observers participate in an AC, the more expensive the AC becomes. A compromise between the AC duration and the observer costs must thus be reached. Another factor to consider is the reliability with which observers can observe multiple participants.[4] It is recommended that an observer : participant ratio of 1:2 be used, i.e. one observer for every two participants.

2.3 Simulation sequence during the AC

When designing the AC process, it is recommended that the simulations be sequenced logically. It is useful to design the AC with the participants' experience of the AC in mind, thus the AC design team should put themselves in the "shoes of the participant". The team should ask the question: With which simulation should the AC process start so that the whole process makes sense? It might be useful to create a story line for the AC. This increases the face validity of the AC and helps the participants to orientate themselves to the AC process. If the AC is aimed at management–leadership, a logical starting point is often the In-Box. By completing an In-Box, the AC participants obtain a holistic view of the

---

1   Thornton et al., 2019; Dewberry & Jackson, 2016

2   Goodge, 1994; Goodge, 1995

3   Griffiths & Allen, 1987

4   Melchers et al., 2010; International Taskforce on Assessment Center Guidelines, 2015

fictitious organisation in a very short time. This knowledge will probably assist the participants when they are preparing for other simulations, especially if the simulations are integrated.

2.4 Participant career discussion

It is recommended that a career discussion be included in the process of a DAC. The purpose of this discussion is to enable the observer to obtain insight into the career objective(s) of the participants, as well as what the participants have already done to prepare themselves to achieve such objective(s).

A career discussion also serves the purpose of clarifying, for the participants, where they are going with their career. It is sometimes a wake-up call for the participants to realise the development options that are available to them that have never been used. If a career discussion forms part of the DAC, it will be easier to link the development recommendations from the DAC to the participants' career objectives. This will increase the chances of the participants committing to the development actions and implementing them after attending the DAC.

2.5 Orientation

Another recommendation is to allow time at the start of the AC to orientate the participants regarding the AC process, its purpose, the focal constructs (competencies and simulations) that will be evaluated, where the AC fits into the client organisation's vision and other organisational processes, and what will happen after the AC. The consequences of participation and non-participation should be explained, as well as who will have access to the results. The length of time that the results will be stored should also be clarified.[5] During this orientation session, the participants have the opportunity to ask questions and share their concerns. This allows for their concerns to be addressed before the start of the AC so that they are able to focus more on the AC itself. After explaining the above and addressing their fears, participants can be requested to sign the informed consent form. A benefit of explaining the competencies being assessed during the AC is that participants' ability to identify criteria (ATIC) is equalised, so that all participants have an opportunity to show competency-relevant behaviour during simulations.[6] This may increase the AC's construct validity[7], however making AC competencies transparent may negatively impact the criterion-related validity of AC results.[8]

The AC process owners should also be orientated at the start of the AC about the specifics of the AC, e.g. the programme, logistics, etc.

---

5   Protection of Personal Information Act, (Act 4 of 2013); ACSG, 2018

6   Kleinmann & Ingold, 2019

7   Kolk et al., 2003

8   Kleinmann & Ingold, 2019; Ingold et al., 2016; Jansen et al., 2013

2.6 AC debrief(s)

Ideally, the participants should receive some theoretical input on the simulations after having completed them. This is usually done during a debriefing session. Depending on whether it is an AC for selection purposes or a DAC, the debriefing sessions can take place during the AC or at the end of the AC. Usually no debriefing session takes place in the case of an AC for selection purposes, thus the AC design team will have to decide if debriefing sessions will take place. If they do, the team needs to decide whether a debriefing session will take place after each simulation, or if only one debriefing session will be held at the end of the AC. If time allows, it is recommended that a debriefing session be held after every simulation at a DAC.

In addition, it is recommended that the AC process owners participate in a separate debrief discussion. This will allow the process owners to provide feedback on how they experienced the AC and make recommendations about possible improvements.

3. CENTRE PROCESS ACCORDING TO CENTRE PURPOSE

The purpose of the AC will determine the process of the AC. The three main purposes of an AC are: selection (Selection AC); diagnosing development needs (Diagnostic Centre – DC); and development (Development Assessment Centre – DAC) (see Chapter 1). Both the focal constructs and the interaction of the process owners with the participants differ.

During an AC for selection purposes, the process owners have minimal interaction with participants. They administer the simulations, observe and note participant behaviour during simulations, and play the roles as required according to the simulation instructions. However, at a DAC the process owners are in continuous interaction with participants since they also fulfil the roles of facilitators and coaches to the participants.

The participants' experience of the whole centre process will therefore also differ. During an AC for selection, the participants will attend a brief introduction and orientation session followed by participation in the AC activities. The participants will then leave the AC and only receive feedback about the outcome of the selection process. This process is depicted in Figure 13.2.

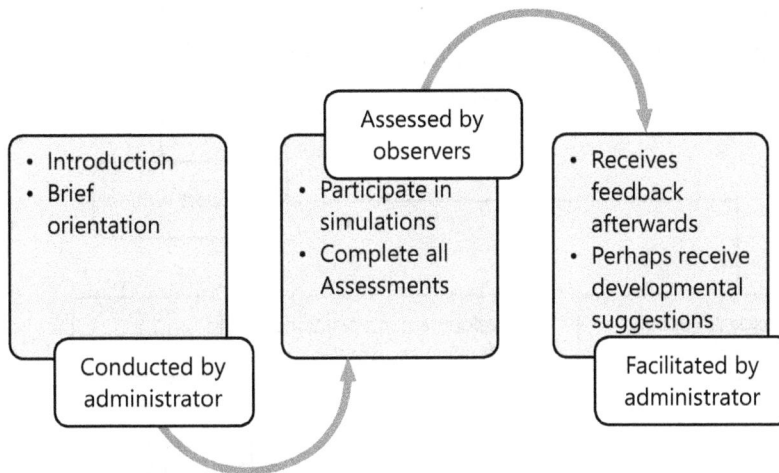

Figure 13.2: Process as experienced by the participants during a Selection AC

As can be seen from Figure 13.2, the interaction of the participants with the AC process owners is limited to simulation administration. The process that DC participants experience is similar to the process experienced by participants of a Selection AC.

In Figure 13.3, an example of the process followed during a DC is depicted. Participants will be invited to attend the centre and attend an orientation session, before participating in the various AC activities. Usually a de-brief session will take place during which participants have the opportunity to share their experience of the whole process and receive some theoretical input about the various centre activities. Usually the observers would participate in the data-integration session concurrently to the de-brief session. After the data-integration session, the participant feedback reports are written. Participants receive feedback about their centre performance either at the end of the centre before they leave, or very soon after attending the centre. During the feedback discussion, development plans addressing the agreed upon issues are drawn-up. During some DCs participants receive initial, brief feedback at the end of the centre, as well as in-depth feedback afterwards once the report has been written. It is also advisable that the participant's line-manager attends the feedback discussion and participates in drawing-up the development plan, as this will potentially increase their support for the developmental activities.[9] Once the development plan has been agreed upon, the participant should receive support from the client organisation to facilitate the implementation of the agreed upon development interventions.[10]

9   Goodge, 1995

10 Thornton et al., 2015

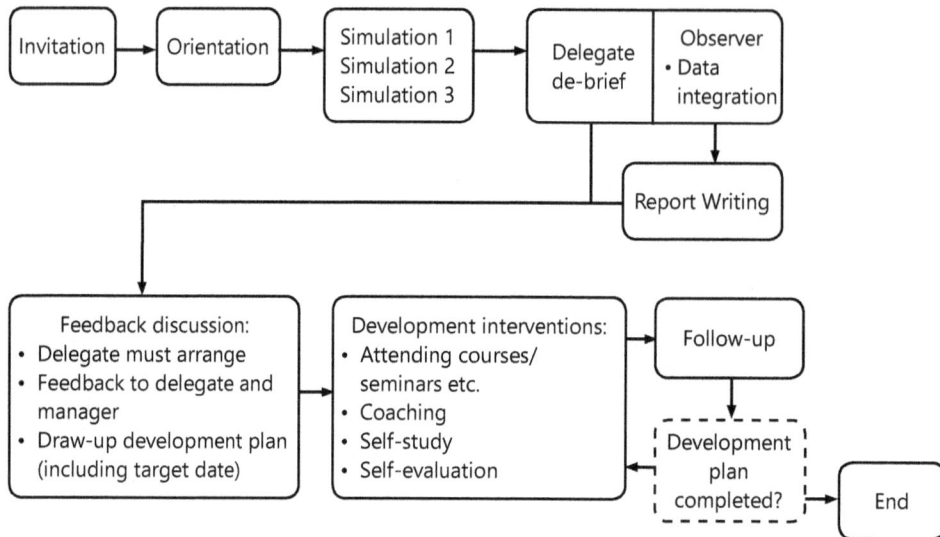

Figure 13.3: Example of a Process at a Diagnostic Centre

In Figure 13.3, regular follow-up on the implementation of the participants' development plans are indicated. Once the plans have been fully implemented the follow-up process comes to an end.

In 1987, Griffiths and Allen proposed that the centre design itself needed to change to accommodate the development needs of both the AC participant and the client organisation.[11] They also argued that participants should be more active in the process and that the observer role should be broadened to include being a learning facilitator.

Changing the centre process to further engage participants resulted in DACs, which are outlined in Figure 13.4.

---

11 Griffiths & Allen, 1987

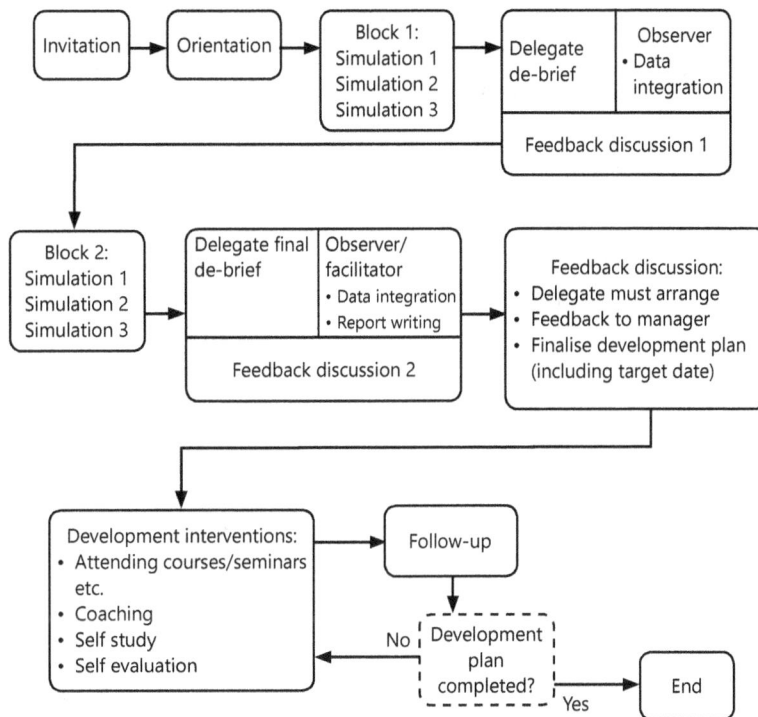

Figure 13.4: Example of a Process at a Development Assessment Centre
Source: Adapted from Thornton, Rupp & Hoffman[12]

As per Figure 13.4, participants attend an orientation session where the focal constructs and the centre process are explained in detail. After the orientation session, the participants participate in the first block of simulations. These simulations might include an In-Box, a one-on-one role play and a group meeting. Participants then attend a de-brief session while the observers share their observations during a data-integration session and compile an initial report. Participants receive detailed feedback about their performance from the first block of simulations, after which they have the opportunity to ask questions to gain an understanding about the focal constructs and their own performance. Improvement objectives are set during the feedback discussion.

Participants have the opportunity to practice the skills that they received feedback on during the second block of parallel simulations. A parallel simulation is a simulation at the same level of difficulty as the original simulation, which assesses the same focal constructs as the original simulation.[13] Again, participants attend a de-brief session while the observers integrate the observed data from the second block of simulations. The participants receive feedback a second time about their performance, as well as the behavioural improvements on the focal constructs. Development planning takes place again, but with a longer term focus this time.[14] It is recommended that a feedback discussion takes place after the DAC with the participant's line manager present. The individual development plan is finally agreed

---

12 Thornton et al., 2015

13 Brummel et al., 2009

14 Thornton et al., 2015

upon by all parties. Regular follow-up on the implementation of the development plan should ideally take place. The process of follow-up ends once the participant has fully implemented the development plan (also see Chapter 17 for a discussion about the growth framework).

A variation on the DAC process is indicated in Figure 13.5. The indicated process is that of a collaborative centre, during which the participants engage in an actual assessment of their own behaviour.[15]

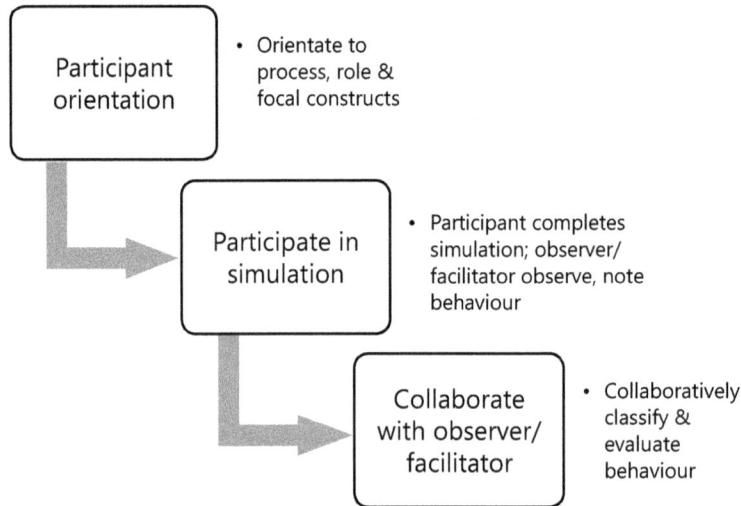

Figure 13.5: Example of the Micro-Process at a Collaborative Centre[16]

During a collaborative centre, observers/facilitators observe and note participant behaviour during a simulation, however they only classify and evaluate the observed behaviour once the participant is with them. This collaborative process of classifying and evaluating participant behaviour increases the participants' understanding of the focal constructs, as well as of the expected behaviour. Since the observer/facilitator and participant teams still use the applicable observer report forms and norms, the reliability of the centre ratings should not be compromised.

A change to the collaborative centre approach is the coaching development centre. During a coaching development centre, the observer also takes on the role of a coach, providing coaching on the focal constructs after the participant behaviour has been collaboratively classified and evaluated.[17] This micro-process of a coaching development centre (CDE) is depicted in Figure 13.6.

---

15 Griffiths & Allen, 1987

16 Adapted from Schlebusch & Gouws, 2013

17 Woodruffe, 1993

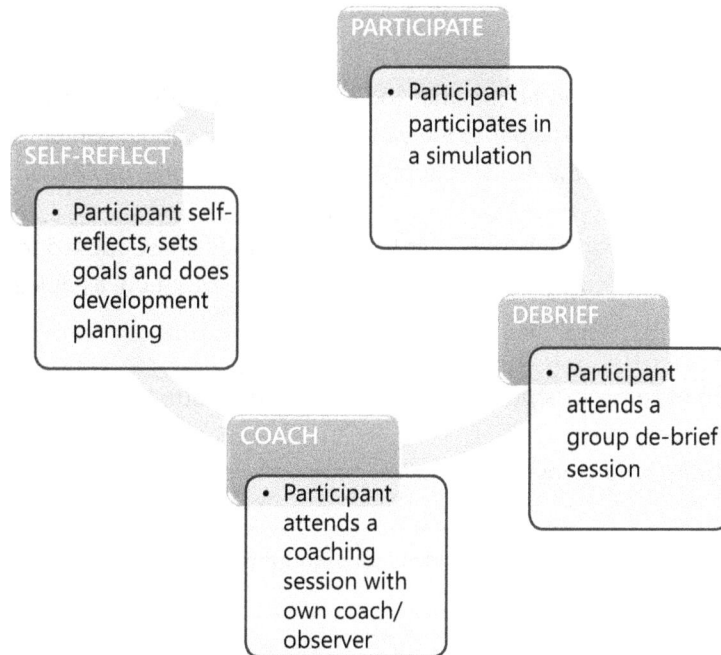

Figure 13.6: Example of the Micro-Process at a Coaching Development Centre[18]

The biggest difference between a collaborative centre and a coaching centre is the actual coaching that takes place. During a collaborative centre the observer/facilitator is the feedback giver and the person assisting the participant to set developmental objectives. During the coaching centre, the observer, who is also a professional coach, coaches the participant following a co-active process. The depth of the discussion and the quality of the participant's learning is at a different level than during a collaborative centre.

4. VARIOUS PROGRAMMES

The process at the AC is documented in the various AC programmes. These programmes are needed to ensure that each AC is conducted in a standardised manner. When the AC process owners (observers, role players and administrators) conduct each AC according to the same format, operational reliability is easier to show. The AC design team should ideally create the overall AC programme so that the observers can classify and evaluate participant behaviour very soon after observing and noting the behaviour during the simulation.[19] The AC programmes should allow time for participants and process owners to move between the various venues and there should be time indicated for breaks.[20]

Every AC has at least three different, although related, programmes – one for the participants, one for the observers and the last for the AC administrator.

---

18 Adapted from Schlebusch & Hoole, 2018

19 Thornton et al., 2015

20 The British Psychological Society, 2015

4.1   Participant programme

Participants should receive a programme that indicates in detail all the activities that they will be involved in during the AC. Each participant's individual programme should contain the following details: time, venue and all activities for the AC. This applies whether it is a one-day AC or a three-day DAC.

Apart from ensuring that the participants always know where they are supposed to be, the programme gives the participants some security in a potentially stressful AC situation, as at least they know where they are supposed to be at what time.

Table 13.1 provides an example of a programme for a participant attending a collaborative DAC.

Table 13.1: Individual participant programme for a collaborative DAC

DAC: Individual programme

Participant 1: _____

Observer 1: _____ (Room 1:_____)

Day 1

TIME	ACTIVITY	VENUE
08:00 – 09:30	General orientation	Main:
09:30 – 10:30	Career and self-development discussion	Room 1:
10:30 – 11:30	Study general instructions	Main:
11:30 – 13:00	In-Box exercise	Main:
13:00 – 13:30	**LUNCH**	
13:30 – 15:00	In-Box: Debriefing	Main:
15:00 – 17:00	In-Box: Evaluation	Room 1:

Day 2

TIME	ACTIVITY	VENUE
08:50 – 09:30	Counselling discussion preparation	Room 1:
09:30 – 10:10	Counselling discussion	Room 3:
10:10 – 12:10	Tool box 1 and 2	Main:
12:10 – 12:30	**LUNCH**	
12:30 – 14:00	Counselling discussion debriefing	Main:
14:00 – 16:00	Counselling discussion evaluation	Room 1:

Source: LEMASA administration documentation

4.2 Observer programme

The observer programme indicates to observers where they must be, and at what time, to observe the participants they are supposed to observe during each simulation. The observer programme does not necessarily indicate to the observer all activities the participants will be busy with during the AC.

The purpose of the observer programme is to ensure that the correct participant is observed by each observer at the time indicated on the programme, and enables the observers to plan their time effectively. The programme will indicate when and where the observer must be to observe participants, but will not necessarily indicate what the observers' own activities should be during the whole AC, for example the most appropriate time to classify and evaluate the participants' behaviour before the start of the next simulation. The observers should therefore plan their own time to ensure that they have finished classifying and evaluating all participants' behaviour in time for the data-integration session to take place. Table 13.2 provides an example of an observer programme for a collaborative DAC.

Table 13.2: Observer programme for a collaborative DAC

DAC — Programme for observers				
DAC no.:_____ **Date:**_____				
Simulations	**Observer/Participant**			
	Observer 1		**Observer 2**	
	Participant 1	**Participant 2**	**Participant 3**	**Participant 4**
Career and self-development discussion Day 1	**Discussion time:** *09:30 – 10:30*	**Discussion time:** *10:30 – 11:30*	**Discussion time:** *09:30 – 10:30*	**Discussion time:** *10:30 – 11:30*
In-Box Day 1 Do simulation: *11-30 – 13:00* Debriefing: *13:30 – 15:00*	**Evaluation time:** **Day 1**: *15:00 – 17:00*	**Evaluation time:** **Day 2**: *07:30 – 09:30*	**Evaluation time:** **Day 1**: *15:00 – 17:00*	**Evaluation time:** **Day 2**: *07:30 – 09:30*
Counselling discussion – Day 2 Counselling discussion debriefing: *12:30 – 14:00*				
Role player	Administrator	Administrator	Administrator	Administrator
Venue	Room 3	Room 3	Room 3	Room 3
Instructions: Room 1	08:50 – 09:30	09:30 – 10:10	10:10 – 10:50	10:50 – 11:30
Do simulation	09:30 – 10:10	10:10 – 10:50	10:50 – 11:30	11:30 – 12:10
Lunch	12:10 – 12:30			
Evaluation	Day 2: 14:00 – 16:00	Day 2: 16:00 – 18:00	Day 2: 14:00 – 16:00	Day 2: 16:00 – 18:00

Source: LEMASA administration documentation

4.3 Administrator programme

The administrator programme is a combined programme indicating all the activities of the AC participants as well as all the activities of the AC observers. The administrator programme will indicate which role player must play the role for each participant during each simulation. In addition, the administrator programme should indicate the resources needed for each simulation.

5. THE ADMINISTRATOR (ALSO KNOWN AS THE CENTRE MANAGER)

5.1 Role of the AC administrator

The AC administrator's role can best be described as that of overseer of the whole process. They are in charge of all AC preparation, all AC activities and all post-AC activities. The administrator is the person who is professionally accountable for the whole AC process.[21]

5.1.1 Accountabilities

The administrator's accountabilities include selecting appropriate observers for each AC, corresponding with the observers and ensuring that the observers will be at the AC. The administrator needs to schedule appropriate role players and ensure that suitable participants are invited to the AC.

The AC administrator's accountabilities also include ensuring that the appropriate venues and other resources are booked and ready for use for the duration of the AC if the AC is not a VAC. This includes arranging meals and other refreshments, as well as accommodation if required.

The AC administrator is the person accountable for ensuring that all AC materials are ready when needed during the AC.

Post-AC, the administrator is accountable for ensuring that all feedback reports are of a professional standard and are ready in time for the feedback to take place. The administrator is accountable for the feedback discussions themselves, as well as for any correspondence, queries and requests about the AC afterwards.

The AC administrator is accountable for ensuring that all the necessary AC information is captured for research purposes. The administrator needs to ensure that the AC results are handled confidentially and stored in a safe place for at least five years.

5.2 Specific functions

At the AC itself, the administrator fulfils specific functions which will be briefly discussed.

---

21 Meiring & Buckett, 2016

5.2.1 Working with the participants

The AC administrator is the person who conducts the orientation session at the start of the AC. In addition, they conduct the debriefing sessions during the AC. The administrator usually gives the simulation instructions, and starts and stops the simulations. It is therefore the responsibility of the administrator to ensure that the simulations are administered under standardised conditions.

The administrator is the point of reference for the participants, that is, the administrator is the person they interact with regarding their needs and questions.

5.2.2 Working with the observers

The administrator can be seen as a "super" observer. As was mentioned earlier, the administrator takes full professional accountability for the AC. This implies that the administrator needs to ensure that the observers take comprehensive notes during simulations, and that they classify and evaluate the participant behaviour correctly. If any of the observers cannot, for whatever reason, continue to observe during the AC, the administrator should be able to stand in until a replacement observer arrives.

The administrator is also the person who will facilitate the data-integration session at the end of the AC.

5.2.3 Facilitating the data-integration session

A data-integration session is a meeting where the observers pool all the information about a participant; a participant's behaviour will have been observed during the different simulations by different observers. The observers individually will have noted and classified each participant's behaviour on the observer report forms. When a post exercise dimension rating (PEDR) approach is followed, the observers will have evaluated such behaviour according to the norm tables. During the data-integration meeting, each observer presents a specific participant's behaviour that he or she observed during the simulation to the rest of the team of observers. The team of observers agrees on a rating per competency, per simulation. Once all the evidence of a participant's behaviour during all the simulations has been presented, the team of observers decides on a final overall rating for the specific competency. The integration session will be discussed in more detail during Chapter 16.

The integration of the ratings can be done qualitatively (also referred to as the judgemental approach) or mathematically (the mechanical approach). When the qualitative option is used, the observers need to reach consensus on the rating that will be allocated. This might lead to a long, though usually fruitful, discussion. When the mathematical option is employed, the various ratings are integrated according to a specific formula decided upon by the AC design team. The two approaches can also be combined.

The administrator will need certain documents to assist him or her during the data-integration session. These documents are discussed below.

5.3 Administrator documentation

The AC administrator will need three documents, namely a data-integration grid, the data-integration administrator notes, and the competency summary form.

5.3.1 Data-integration grid for use with a post exercise dimension rating (PEDR) approach

The data-integration grid is a document in which the initial rating per competency allocated by the observer is indicated, as well as the final, agreed-upon rating per competency, per simulation. There is also space in this document for the final overall rating per competency agreed on by the team of observers.

This document should be visually displayed when the discussion is taking place. Using a data projector for this purpose is therefore convenient.   Table 14.3 contains an example of a completed data-integration grid.

Table 13.3: Data-integration grid

Data-integration grid								
DAC no: VM10/2007 Participant: Joeline Soap								
	In-Box		**Counselling discussion**		**Group meeting**		**Analysis exercise**		**Final rating**
	Obs	Fin	Obs	Fin	Obs	Fin	Obs	Fin	
Initiative	1	1			1	1	2	1	1
Information gathering	2	2	2	2	2	2	1	2	2
Judgement	3	3	4	3	3	3	3	3	3
Empowerment	2	2	3	2	2	2			2
Interpersonal sensitivity			2	2	2	2			2
Task structuring	3	3	3	3	2	2			2
Persuasiveness			2	1	2	2			2
Written communication					3	2	2	2	2
Presentation skills					2	2	3	3	2
Control	2	2	2	2	2	2	2	2	2
Observer	CS		DdT		CdW		PS		

The figures indicated in Table 13.3 in the column "Obs" (Observer) are the initial ratings given to each competency by the observer of that simulation. The second rating, in the column "Fin" (Final), is the final rating per competency, per simulation, that the team of observers agreed upon after discussing the evidence tabled by the specific observer.

5.3.2   Data-integration administrator notes

Apart from the grid, the administrator will need a document to make notes in about the comments and evidence presented per competency, per simulation, during the data-integration session. These notes will be used when the final report on the participant is written. Figure 13.7 is an example of a page from the data-integration administrator notes.

Information gathering

Final rating:

Definition:

Actively gathers data from all possible sources, identifies information elements and links related issues.

Behavioural Elements/Indicators:
- Asked investigative questions
- Asked open-ended questions
- Established relationships between elements
- Identified facts
- Noticed detail

In-Box: Rating:____
(notes)
Counselling discussion: Rating:____
(notes)
Group meeting: Rating:___
(notes)
Analysis exercise: Rating:___
(notes)

Figure 13.7: Example of a page from the data-integration administrator notes
Source: LEMASA administration documents

The administrator can note, per competency and per simulation, any comments that will assist in writing the final report on the participant.

5.3.3   Competency summary form for use with a post exercise dimension rating (PEDR)

Another document that will be used during the data-integration session is the competency summary form. This document is completed during the discussion each time consensus is reached on the final rating per competency. Table 13.4 provides an example of a completed competency summary form.

Table 13.4: Competency summary form

DAC no: VM10/2007

Participant: Joeline Soap

	In-Box	Counselling discussion	Group meeting	Analysis exercise	Final rating
Initiative	ND		ND	ND	ND
Information gathering	R	ND	R	ND	ND
Judgement	E	E	E	E	E
Empowerment	ND	E	E		E/ND
Interpersonal sensitivity		E	E		E
Task structuring		ND	ND		ND
Persuasiveness		ND	ND		ND
Written communication			E	ND	E/ND
Presentation skills			ND	ND	ND
Control		E	E	ND	E/ND

Source: LEMASA administration documents

The document provides a summary of the participant's performance and will probably be included in the final report. The competency summary form will be used by the person who is going to write the final report, together with the data-integration administrator notes.

Note that in the example in Table 13.3, a five-point rating scale is used. This is the rating scale recommended for use at an AC for selection purposes. The rating scale in Table 13.4 is a descriptive, four-point scale recommended for use at a DAC. The split final ratings indicate that the participant's performance as regards that competency in the one context is already at an effective level, i.e. the interactive context. The participant should now focus on transferring this competence to the other context where development is required.

6. ADDITIONAL DOCUMENTATION

During this step, that is, developing the Centre, all the documentation needed to ensure an effective AC must be created. This documentation comprises the documents that will link all the simulations at the AC. The documents referred to are the participant final report, the participant's development plan, all the hand-outs that the participant will receive, and the AC evaluation forms that will be completed at the end of the AC.

6.1   Final report for an AC for selection purposes

The primary recipient of a final report written after an AC for selection purposes is the line management that requested the AC (the hiring manager) and the human capital professional who is accountable for the ethical use of AC results. Since none of these people attend the AC itself, the report needs to be comprehensive enough for them to obtain insight into each participant's behaviour. However, it might not be necessary to provide detailed feedback on every participant in terms of every competency in every simulation. The format of the report needs to be agreed upon before the AC takes place (see Chapter 10 regarding the AC Blueprint).

An approach often followed in writing final reports for an AC for selection purposes is to write a combined report, which provides feedback on each participant per simulation, per competency. An example of this type of reporting was given in Figure 13.4.

6.2   DAC participant final report

The primary recipients of the DAC participants' final reports are the participants themselves. This report is one of two tangible "take-aways" for the participant at a DAC. The other "take-away" is their development plan.

The purpose of the final report is to assist the participants to remember what happened at the AC, to understand the competencies and each competency's elements, to understand the individual ratings per competency, and to understand what they can do to improve their performance.

A secondary recipient of the final report is the line manager of the DAC participant, who will need to be informed about the participant's performance and understand what can be done to improve it. In reality, the line manager needs to support the participant's post-centre development. If he or she does not, the development might never happen. If the line manager is informed about the participant's DAC performance and understands what can be done to improve performance, the chances are greater that the line manager will support the participant's post-centre development.[22]

Another secondary recipient of the final report is the custodian of the DAC final reports in the client organisation's learning and development department. This person is accountable for the safekeeping of the reports and for the confidentiality of the DAC results.

The AC design team not only has to design the layout and content of the final report, but also the guidelines for the report writer. Sentences should be simple and, on average, should not be longer than 20 words (see Chapter 17 for a discussion on report writing).

At the very least, the report should contain the following information: the participant's name and other applicable biographical information; information on the DAC itself (such as the date and number of the DAC, and who the administrator, observers and role players were); the competency definitions; the

---

22 Goodge, 1995; Pollock, Jefferson & Wick, 2015

competency elements; the simulations used; an indication of which competency was evaluated during which simulation; a final rating per competency; and development recommendations.

When deciding how the behaviour will be reported on, the AC design team can decide between reporting back per competency, per simulation, or per simulation, per competency. An example of each approach is given in Figures 13.8 and 13.9 respectively.

Competency: Creative problem solving

Final rating: ND

Definition:

> Identifies the existence of problems, evaluates information and solves problems. Identifies risks and considers all options in making effective decisions.

Discussion:

In-Box – ND
Mr Strydom initiated action for all items in the In-Box. He noticed some important details and asked a number of sound, investigative questions in order to gather more information. He displayed a tendency to introduce preventative systems to solve the root causes of problems as well as proactive measures to take advantage of future opportunities.

Development opportunities:
- Linking related items to identify the underlying problem.
- Using only confirmed information.
- Introducing immediate corrective measures to contain the pressing problem until it can be solved permanently.

Counselling discussion – ND

Mr Strydom asked a few investigative, closed-ended questions. He decided that the problem should be solved through training and EAP assistance.

Development opportunities:
- Asking more open-ended and probing questions.
- Exploring all facets of the situation and making sure that all root causes of problems are identified and agreed upon.
- Identifying risks.

Figure 13.8: Example of a final report where reporting back takes place per competency, per simulation
Source: LEMASA observer training documentation

In Figure 13.9, feedback is given per simulation, per competency.

In-Box

1.1.1 Initiative – ND
Mr Dlamini generated action to address the issues, while he sometimes also tried to prevent problems from recurring. The potential undeniably exists, but it was not demonstrated consistently enough to constitute an established, proactive management style. It is recommended that he not only solve the symptoms of problems, but focus on solving the root causes thereof permanently.

1.1.2 Information gathering – ND
Mr Dlamini once again showed potential. He often observed some of the detail and also asked a few questions to gather additional information. He should, however, focus on consistently asking questions and noticing detail. It is furthermore recommended that he integrate all the related material to identify the underlying problem areas.

1.1.3 Judgement – HE
Mr Dlamini often realised the urgency of matters and carefully weighed and considered the consequences of his actions He consistently involved all interested parties in the process and also acknowledged receipt of correspondence.

1.1.4 Task structuring – R
Mr Dlamini sometimes provided guidelines to stimulate the actions of his subordinates. He should, however, consistently explain the outcomes expected, structure their tasks at hand or include his own thinking on the matter. This will ensure that his subordinates do what is expected of them.

1.1.5 Empowerment – E
Mr Dlamini often delegated tasks and problems to his subordinates, thereby making use of their initiative and judgement. He also sometimes delegated the final decision to them. He furthermore always identified the appropriate person for the job.

1.1.6 Control – ND
Although Mr Dlamini prioritised the tasks at hand and responded to all the problems within the time limit (time management), he applied the more mechanistic elements somewhat inconsistently. He should focus on setting due dates for tasks, on requesting feedback on delegated matters, and on using his diary to control due dates and appointments.

Figure 13.9: Example of a final report where reporting back takes place per simulation, per competency
Source: LEMASA observer training documentation

The AC design team will need to decide which approach will be more useful to the various recipients.

Another decision facing the AC design team is to decide whether the report will be in a narrative format, as for the two examples given above, a ticked checklist, graphical representations, or any other format.

Table 13.5 contains an example of a ticked checklist.

Table 13.5: Example of a ticked check list

Secretarial in-box
Ms Bekkie Kwaam

Competency	Element	Needing development	Effective	Highly effective
Information gathering		ND		
	Linking	ND		
	Seeing detail		E	
	Gathering information	ND		
Judgement			E	
	Consequences of actions		E	
	Informing everyone			HE
Initiative		ND		
	Taking action		E	
	Creativity	ND		
Interpersonal skills				HE
	Tact and courteousness			HE
Control			E	
	Using own diary			HE
	Feedback		E	
	Follow-up		E	
Functional			E	
	Typing speed			HE
	Typing accuracy		E	
	Minuting		E	
	Filing			HE
	Creating slides	ND		
	Diary coordination		E	
	Sending e-mail			HE
	Photocopying		E	

Source: LEMASA observer training material

Again, the AC design team needs to decide on a format that is best suited to the needs of the client organisation.

A further decision that the AC design team needs to take is deciding on who will write the final report. The report can be written by the AC administrator or an observer, or, in the case of a collaborative DAC, the participants themselves.[23]

The advantage of the AC administrator or an observer writing the report is that the report will perhaps be a more accurate and comprehensive description of what has happened at the AC. The disadvantage is that there may be a time-lag between the participant attending the AC and the report being ready.

The alternative in the case of a collaborative DAC is that the participants themselves, with the assistance of their observer/facilitator, write their own final reports. The report is then in the participant's own words, using expressions that have meaning to them. The advantage of this alternative is that the report is immediately ready for the participant to take away after the DAC. In addition, since they wrote it themselves, they were more engaged in the whole DAC process, increasing the probability of them being more committed to the development recommendations contained in the report.[24] The disadvantage of the participant writing the final report is that the report may perhaps not be as professional in terms of wording and may also not be as comprehensive as when it is written by an AC administrator or observer.

The AC design team will have to weigh up the advantages and disadvantages of each approach and then decide which alternative to implement.

6.3 Development plans

The second tangible deliverable that participants at a DAC will take away with them is their personal development plan (PDP). This is a comprehensive document indicating the following: which competencies need to be maintained; which competencies need further development; which elements in the competencies need development; the priorities of the development areas; and the development strategy that will be implemented to develop the specific competency.

The AC design team needs to design a document that is easy to use by the participant, but also by the line manager and the learning and development department. Most client organisations require the development plan to be aligned with their Learning Management System (LMS).

A development plan is sometimes also needed after an AC for selection purposes. Again, the layout and content of the plan need to be agreed upon and designed.

---

23 Goodge, 1994

24 Goodge, 1994

6.4 Hand-outs

During an AC, participants will receive various hand-outs to assist them in understanding the AC process, as well as the competencies being evaluated. It is recommended that the participants receive a hand-out indicating at least the following: the purpose of the AC; the use of the AC results; who will have access to the results; the competencies being evaluated; the elements of the competencies; which competencies will be evaluated during which simulation; how the process of observation, noting, classifying and evaluation works; who the observers and the administrator are; and, perhaps, tips on how to approach the AC.

The AC design team might use the opportunity to give documents to the participants that contain certain theoretical inputs on some important aspect. For example, a hand-out might be created dealing with the various leadership styles.

6.5 Pre-AC documents

Participants at an AC sometimes have to complete documentation prior to the AC. For example, if a career discussion will be held with each AC participant, the participants might have to complete a background information form. This can be done prior to attending the AC. The AC design team has to design this document. Typical information requested in this document is information on the participant's career aspirations and education, training and development courses attended thus far, and career history.

It might also be necessary to design a 360-degree evaluation document. The content of this document will be related to the competencies to be evaluated during the AC. Typically, the AC participant must ensure that this evaluation is completed before the AC starts.

6.6 Participants and observers: AC evaluation form

Final documents that need to be created are the AC evaluation documents. These documents are completed by the participants and the observers at the end of the AC. Both parties are requested to give feedback on aspects such as the venue and accommodation, as well as other logistical arrangements; the orientation and debriefing sessions; the simulations; the role players and observers; and the AC process as a whole.

The feedback can be obtained by way of open-ended questions asked in a questionnaire. The alternative is to use a rating scale for each aspect in respect of which feedback is required. The advantage of using a rating scale is that the information is easy to capture electronically for evaluation and validation research during the evaluation and validation stage of the design model. The possible disadvantage is that the richer, open, qualitative feedback is limited.

6.7   Spreadsheets and other data-capturing forms

To ensure that all the AC data needed during the evaluation and validation stage is captured after every AC, it is recommended that the AC design team at this point already design the electronic spreadsheet(s) if the AC is not a VAC or TEAC. The advantage of designing the spreadsheet(s) during this step of the design model is that the team ensures that all the AC documentation is aligned, comprehensive and easy to use.

It might be necessary to design additional documents for use during the AC so as to capture data for the validation and evaluation stage. For example, participant information such as gender, race, age, number of years' service with the client organisation, formal qualifications, and specific training courses attended might be useful information during the performance of statistical procedures in the validation and evaluation stage. Biographical and other information on the observers is also useful during the validation stage. Documents need to be designed to capture this information during the AC itself.[25]

7.   AC MANUAL AND BUDGET

All the AC material must be combined into an AC manual. This manual, once finalised after the AC pilot, becomes the blueprint for every AC that will be administered within the client organisation.

Having a comprehensive manual that includes all the simulation material, the various programmes and the additional documents will make it easier to show operational reliability, in other words, it will be easier to indicate that the AC is administered in a standardised manner each and every time.

It will now be possible for the AC design team to draw up a draft AC budget. This budget will be finalised after the pilot and adjusted annually to accommodate inflation costs.

This manual – at this stage also in a draft format – must be signed off by the AC steering committee before the AC pilot. Once the AC has been piloted, the necessary changes to the manual will be made and the final manual will be signed-off for implementation.

8.   CRITICAL DECISIONS RELATING TO THIS STEP AND THE OUTCOMES THEREOF

The following are the critical decisions relating to the develop centre step and the outcomes thereof.

8.1   A logical, cost- and time-effective AC

The simulations and all the other AC activities need to follow one another logically during the AC. This will increase the face validity of the AC.

---

25 Thornton et al., 2019; Kleinmann & Ingold, 2019

All the resources at the AC need to be used in the most effective way since an AC is already an expensive intervention. The resources include the participants' time away from work; the money spent on paying the process owners; and the venue, travel, accommodation and refreshment costs. None of the resources should be unnecessarily idle, however none should be double-booked or over-used during the AC.

8.2   An AC where everyone performs optimally

The AC should be designed in such a way that no person at the AC suffers from unintended fatigue. The AC process itself will create stress for the participants, since it is a situation where their behaviour is being evaluated.[26] The observation process is also a very taxing process for the observers and administrator.[27] Everyone at the AC will therefore be tired at the end of the AC, however the design should eliminate unnecessary time pressure on everyone.

The AC process should be designed in such a way that the participants perform the more difficult simulations at times when they are rested. There should be enough time on the AC programme for the observers to finish the observation process effectively before the next simulation starts, or before the data-integration process at the end of the AC starts.

8.3   An easy-to-use AC manual

The AC manual is the document that will be used for as long as the particular AC is administered within the client organisation. Different people will probably use the AC manual. This requires the manual to have a logical layout, a contents page and other reference aids to assist the users.

The AC manual must be comprehensive; all the AC documentation, and even the PowerPoint slides that will be used during the orientation and debriefing sessions, should be included. The AC design team must be able to hand the AC manual to an administrator and team of observers and role players, and they must then be able to present an effective AC by following the instructions in the manual.

Case Study 1

Design and Implementation of a DAC for Training Professionals

During 2009 – 2010, the Total Reward II (TRII) system was implemented within ArcelorMittal South Africa (AMSA). This system was a competency based system where the competencies of the negotiation category employees were linked to their remuneration. The *Functional and Generic Training Academy* would in the future be responsible for the management of the Bargaining Category employees' Position Requirements and Individual Development Programmes. The Academy was accountable to co-ordinate and facilitate the delivery of competency development, competency assessment and competency declaration to meet the business training needs, to grow competencies in the workplace, and to actively drive the Total Reward II process.

---

26 Fletcher et al., 1997

27 Melchers et al., 2010

However, the training team was Not Yet Competent (NYC) to deliver on expectations. The following problems were experienced:

- The training team did not achieve their key performance areas (KPAs) and key performance indicators (KPIs).
- Reactive service delivery (if any) from the training team.
- Client complaints were increasing.
- The lives of the employees were at stake if of the negotiation category employees were NYC to do their jobs.
- There would be legal consequences in the case of accidents and fatalities.

The Academy could not determine current competency levels of individual training staff since NYC staff piggy-backed on others and they covered for each other. There were no personal development plans for the training staff, hence everyone attended all training. Various training sessions were held for the whole team, presented by internal and external training providers. The practice that everyone attended all training programmes wasted time and money and had a negative impact on competent staff who were forced to attend training that did not address a personal need.

AMSA partnered with a reputable AC service provider to develop a custom designed Collaborative Development Centre (CDC) for the training Academy, based on the TRII. The agreed deliverables of the CDC were an individual personal development plan for every staff member, together with individual feedback discussions afterwards based on the outcome of the CDC. A summative report indicating the strengths and development areas of the team was required, as well as regular six-monthly follow-up discussions with each CDC participant to support the continuous development of the training staff.

The AC Design Model was followed to design, develop and implement a competency-based CDC. The following competencies were evaluated during the CDC:

- Analytical Ability.
- Judgement.
- Initiative.
- Building and Maintaining Relationships.
- Oral Communication.
- Persuasiveness.
- Written Communication.
- Presentation Skills.
- Providing Direction.
- Control.

Three simulations were designed: a First Consulting Meeting (one-on-one role play), a Presenting and Facilitation Meeting (a true-allocated role group meeting), and an Analysis Exercise (a written exercise). The CDC observers/facilitators were from the AC service provider.

The design and implementation of the CDC was a partnership between AMSA and the AC Service provider. This partnership necessitated AMSA senior management involvement in the design and implementation process, which included a senior manager opening every CDC and positioning the CDC strategically. The deliverables of the CDC were agreed upfront, and a thorough job and context analysis was conducted. The AC blueprint was agreed upon and signed off by the client. Every simulation was pre-piloted (trialling) before the CDC in totality was piloted. The CDC design team had continuous and full access to the Subject Matter Experts (SMEs) for the duration of the whole project. The SMEs designed the technical content of the Analysis Exercise and an SME, trained on role playing the character, was a role player during the CDCs. An SME also coached the participants individually on the Analysis Exercise during every CDC.

The following reliabilities on the competencies were obtained:

Competency	Cronbach-Alpha
Analytical Ability	0,772
Judgement	0,740
Initiative	0,364
Building and Maintaining Relationships	0,649
Oral Communication	0,905
Persuasiveness	0,697
Written Communication	0,860
Providing Direction	0,506
Control	0,793

The graphs below indicate the differences in the AMSA workforce competency level, as well as the risk areas after implementing the CDC.

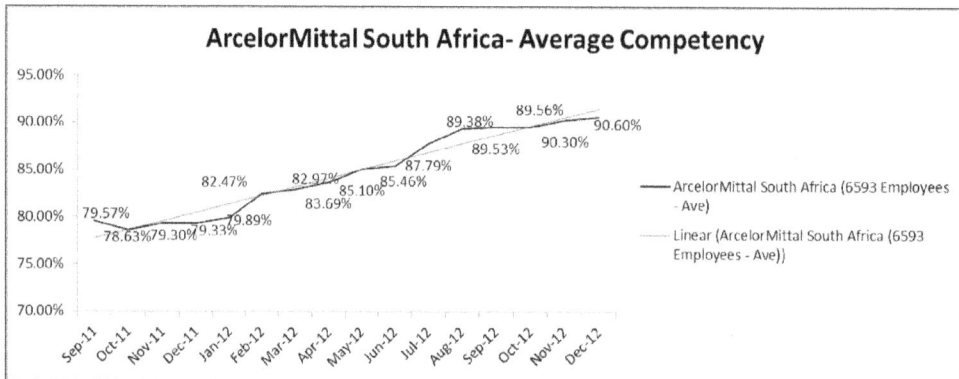

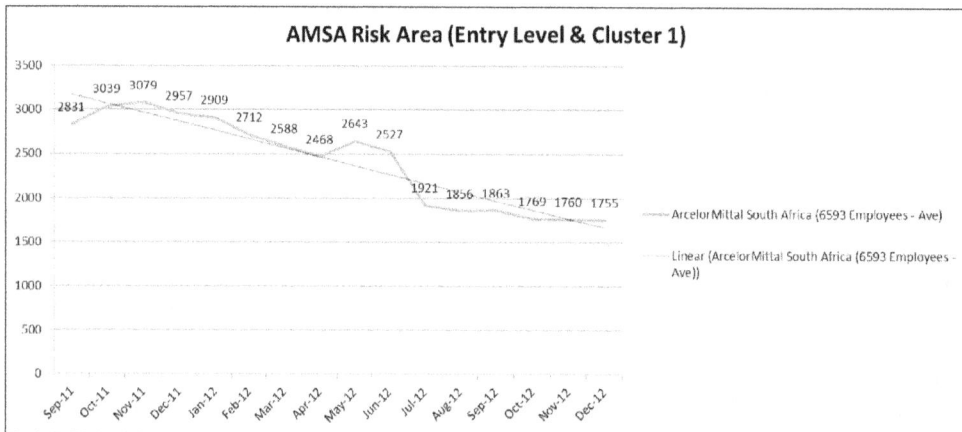

The graphs indicate an overall positive impact on two critical metrics that were directly impacted by the service delivery of the Functional and Generic Training Academy. The management of the Academy contributed the positive change in the metrics to the increase in the knowledge and skill levels of the training team due to attending the CDC. Some of the comments of the training team during a follow-up discussion in February 2013 were:

- "Positive process – started my development and created awareness";
- "Very positive process – I calmed down at work; learned skills";
- "I got to find myself a career – am now sure";
- "I realised I must find out things myself – I must not wait for others";
- "Eye opener"; and
- "Very positive – I applied analytical techniques in my studies – I got a distinction!"

Reflecting on the project, the client and AC service provider had the following to say:

- Partnering works – neither the client, nor the service provider would have been able to design and deliver a CDC that had so much impact on their own.
- Following the rigour of the AC Design Model assisted in creating a very realistic CDC experience for the participants, and assisted in securing AMSA senior management commitment through-out the project.
- High fidelity simulations are excellent learning and development instruments. The whole CDC created a safe environment where participants could be open and honest about their own knowledge and skills levels and learn hands-on from each other and coaches.
- The involvement of the CDC participants in drawing-up their own development plans increased them taking ownership of their development.
- The six-monthly follow-up discussions were also important to allow continuous focus on own competency development for the participants.

CHAPTER 14

PILOT CENTRE

Sandra Schlebusch

1. INTRODUCTION – PILOT THE AC

Step seven in the design model is piloting the AC. This is the fourth and final step in the design and develop stage of the AC design model. During this step, the AC is administered with all the simulations in the proposed sequence and all the AC documentation in use. The AC pilot is attended by participants and process owners. The AC pilot is the last opportunity for the AC design team to ensure that the AC adheres to all the requirements set out in the AC blueprint and business case. However, this is the first opportunity to showcase the new AC to the target organisation. This step is depicted in Figure 14.1.

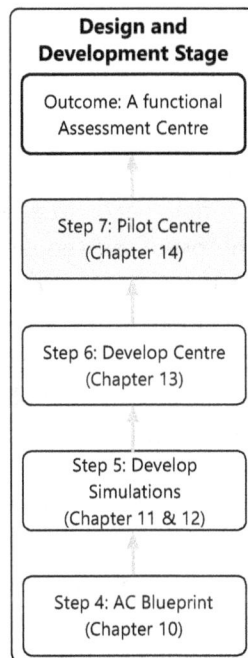

Design and Development Stage

Outcome: A functional Assessment Centre

Step 7: Pilot Centre (Chapter 14)

Step 6: Develop Centre (Chapter 13)

Step 5: Develop Simulations (Chapter 11 & 12)

Step 4: AC Blueprint (Chapter 10)

Figure 14.1: The pilot centre step in the design stage

2. PURPOSE OF PILOTING AN AC

The purpose of the AC pilot is to establish whether the envisaged AC can be practically implemented. When an AC is piloted, the design team wants to know whether the simulations elicit the required behaviour, whether the sequence of simulations is effective, whether all the documentation is easy to use and is comprehensive, and whether any changes to the logistical requirements should be made.[1]

---

1   The British Psychological Society, 2015; Meiring & Buckett, 2016

Specifically, the purpose of the AC pilot is to double-check and test; to double-check what was already tested during the simulation pre-pilots and to test what has not been tested yet, namely administering the simulations in sequence. The design team needs to ensure that the "machinery" of the AC works and can do what it is supposed to do before training and handing the "machine" over to the users, i.e. the process owners.

2.1 Double-check

During a previous step (step 5: develop simulations) all the simulations were individually pre-piloted to ensure that they did in fact elicit the required behaviour and that the documentation was appropriate and comprehensive. When the AC is being piloted, the AC design team has the opportunity to double-check whether the individual simulations work effectively. Each simulation can be scrutinised to determine whether behaviour linked to the competencies evaluated in the simulation is elicited. Is enough behaviour elicited per competency? Again, gaps in the simulation documentation can be identified and filled in before the AC is implemented. The AC pilot tests the norm per competency, per simulation.

2.2 Test the AC

The AC in its entirety is tested during the AC pilot. The AC design team knows that the simulations are effective when administered individually. It now needs to establish whether the simulations produce effective results when administered in the proposed sequence of the AC. The AC pilot results are compared against the AC blueprint. Does the AC elicit the required behaviour as set out in the AC blueprint? Does it effectively cover all the competencies during all the simulations? Is the rating scale appropriate for the AC? Can the same scale be used effectively during all the simulations? Is the AC at the appropriate level of complexity as stipulated in the blueprint? Can the AC potentially fulfil its purpose as set out in the business case and blueprint?

The AC pilot also provides an opportunity to collect information from the participants and process owners on their experience of the AC. The participants should report on their experience of fatigue during the whole AC, as well as on their experience of whether the AC is a reflection of the target job. In turn, the process owners should report on their experience of fatigue. Both the participants and process owners should report on the quality and quantity of information received before, during and after the AC. Feedback should also be given on the time frames for all AC activities.

3. IMPORTANT CONTENT AND FACE VALIDITY CONSIDERATIONS

During the last stage of the design model, namely the evaluation and validation stage, the AC's content and face validity will be determined. The AC pilot provides an opportunity to adjust the design of the AC in such a way that it is deemed content and face valid. The AC pilot therefore serves as preparation for the evaluation and validation stage of the design model.

The two groups of people involved in the AC pilot are the AC participants and the AC process owners. These two groups' of people's feedback on the AC should be obtained on the AC content and the AC process.

3.1   AC Participant feedback

The AC pilot participants should provide feedback on how relevant the AC content is to the target job. This feedback should be given regarding the individual simulations, as well as regarding the fictitious organisation that has been created for the simulations to take place in. The AC content should be relevant and not an exact duplication of the target job. The relevance of the AC content to the target job has a direct impact on whether the actual AC participants will experience the content of the AC as face valid.

Feedback from the AC pilot participants should be gathered on how they experienced the AC process as a whole. Feedback on whether the process is relevant and fair should be obtained. For example, it might be expected of an effective incumbent in the target job to produce an analysis of a business problem, but is it fair to expect AC participants to analyse the business problem within the allocated time frame and with the limited resources available?

3.2   AC process owners' feedback

The AC process owners involved during the pilot should give feedback on the content of the AC. Feedback should be given on the following: the relevance of the competencies being evaluated to the level of the AC, the range of competency elements being evaluated during the individual simulations and the AC as a whole, and the relevance of the simulation stimuli to the target job. The AC process owners should also give feedback on the AC process. The feedback should be provided concerning the structure of the AC, the AC documentation, the evaluation process, and the feedback formats. These aspects will eventually influence the AC's operational validity and reliability; these concepts will be discussed in detail in Chapters 18 and 19.

4.   SELECTION CRITERIA IN RESPECT OF PEOPLE ATTENDING THE AC PILOT

Since the AC pilot plays such an important role in the overall design of an AC, the people invited to the pilot should be carefully chosen. A discussion on the selection criteria follows.

4.1   Observers and role players

The observers invited to an AC pilot should be experienced and competent observers who have enough AC experience to give feedback on the content and process of the AC that is being piloted. They must also be competent enough to be able to observe, note, classify and evaluate the participant behaviour according to the competencies during the simulations, without having received in-depth training regarding the specific AC.

The role players during an AC pilot should also be experienced and competent enough to be able to play the various roles effectively while having received the minimum of training.

4.2 Participants

The participants invited to an AC pilot should come from two main groups of people. The first group of people should comprise current incumbents of the target job, while the second group must comprise the target population from which the AC participants will come. In the case of both groups, a few high performers and a few low performers should be invited to the AC. Typically, it can be expected that the high performers will perform well at the AC and will become the AC ambassadors. Hopefully the rest of the pilot participants will also experience the AC positively and as a result will promote the AC within the client organisation.

The people attending the AC pilot should be well informed regarding the purpose of their attendance. Apart from each person having to fulfil a specific role (participant, observer, role player, administrator), the people attending need to know that they will be requested to give feedback on various issues.

There are a few important considerations in ensuring that the AC pilot will be a success.

5. **IMPORTANT ASPECTS TO CONSIDER**

The AC design team needs to ensure that the AC adheres to the requirements set out in the AC blueprint and the AC business case. In addition, the team must ensure that all the documents are sufficiently comprehensive and detailed to enable the AC participants and process owners to perform during the AC. The AC design team therefore needs to obtain feedback on concrete aspects of the AC, but it also needs feedback on the qualitative experience of the AC. Table 14.1 lists the concrete aspects that the AC design team needs feedback on.

Table 14.1: List of concrete AC aspects regarding which feedback is needed

Feedback from the AC administrator, observers and role players is needed on:	**Feedback from the AC participants is needed on:**
AC manual – layout; content; ease of use; comprehensiveness	Invitation and pre-work
Observer and role player guidelines – comprehensiveness; ease of use	Simulation instructions – clear; comprehensive
Observer report forms – layout; competency elements; behavioural examples; maximum scores; ease of use	Participant report form
Rating scale	Participant programme – timetables
Norm tables	Feedback report – layout; ease of understanding

Feedback from the AC administrator, observers and role players is needed on:	Feedback from the AC participants is needed on:
AC programmes – timetables	Development plan
Simulation content and participant instructions	Hand-outs – layout; usefulness; ease of understanding
Simulation-participant feedback form	AC venue
Feedback report	AC resources
Development plan	
Administrator data-integration grid	
Data-integration administrator notes	
Competency summary form	
Participant hand-outs	
Participant pre-work	
Spreadsheets	
AC venue	
AC resources	

In addition to feedback on the concrete elements, the AC design team needs feedback on the participants' and process owners' experience of the AC, that is, more qualitative feedback. The "moment of truth" approach can be followed. Table 14.2 lists possible "moments of truth" at the AC that feedback can be given on.

Table 14.2: "Moments of truth" feedback list

Moments of truth experienced by the AC administrator, observers and role players:	Moments of truth experienced by the AC participants:
Training as administrator, observer, role player	Invitation and pre-work – explanation of the purpose, content and timetable of the AC; explanation on how to complete the pre-work
AC invitation and pre-work	Arrival at AC
Orientation sessions	AC orientation session
Simulation-observation process	Simulations
Data-integration session and process	Debriefing sessions
Observer debriefing session	Interaction with administrator, observers and role players
Interaction with participants	Interaction with other participants
Interaction with venue personnel	Interaction with venue personnel

Moments of truth experienced by the AC administrator, observers and role players:	Moments of truth experienced by the AC participants:
Meals and refreshments	Meals and refreshments
Social gatherings	Social gatherings
AC closure proceedings	AC closure proceedings
	Feedback discussion

To enable the AC design team to obtain the feedback it requires, the team needs to pay attention to a few aspects before the start of the pilot, during the pilot, towards the end of the pilot, and, lastly, after the pilot.

5.1 Aspects before the AC pilot

All the AC documentation should be ready before the start of the pilot. This includes ensuring that all AC documentation is packed and presented at the AC pilot in the same way as it would be packed and presented to the actual AC participants and process owners. The invitations and pre-work should also reach the parties concerned within the same time frames as the actual AC time frames.

The AC venue for the pilot should meet the same requirements as the venue proposed for administering the actual AC. In fact, it is preferable if the venue could be the same.

Although the training material for the observers and role players will not yet have been developed, they should receive some training in the competencies being evaluated in the AC process and the simulation content. This training should happen well in advance of the AC pilot so that the observers and role players have enough time to study the material. They should also be oriented at the start of the pilot in the same way as will happen when the AC is administered during the implementation stage.

5.2 Aspects during the pilot

The AC design team should note improvement opportunities during the pilot as and when such opportunities become apparent. In fact, the team, or at least a representative of the team (usually the AC administrator), should make notes of the opportunities as they occur. During the pilot, this representative should also note down any comments and suggestions made by the participants and process owners.

5.3 Aspects at the end of the pilot

After the pilot AC has come to an end, the AC design team should hold debriefing sessions with the participants and with the process owners. Ideally, these sessions should be conducted before any person physically leaves the AC venue. Feedback should be obtained on the various elements already mentioned in this chapter. All the comments, observations, experiences and recommendations should be carefully noted.

In addition, debriefing sessions should be conducted with the feedback recipients after the AC feedback has been given to line management or the AC participants (depending on whether it is an AC for selection purposes or a DAC). Not only should comments and recommendations regarding the feedback discussion and feedback report be encouraged, but feedback should be given on the AC itself.

The AC design team should document who the participants and process owners attending the pilot were. This will be useful in the future if there are any queries about the AC during the implementation or evaluation and validation stages.

5.4 Aspects after the AC pilot

The AC design team should consolidate and discuss in detail all the notes taken during the AC and the AC pilot debriefing sessions. Decisions should be taken on whether the recommendations will be implemented and design changes made to the AC. The reasons for not implementing any of the recommendations should be noted.

All the field notes taken during the AC pilot and notes on changes to the AC itself should be included in the AC technical manual. This technical manual will be used and updated during Stage four: the evaluation and validation stage. The AC design team should also update the AC manual.

Sign-off in respect of both manuals should be obtained from the AC steering committee before the AC design team can move on to the next step and stage in the design model – the implementation stage.

6. HINTS ON IMPROVING THE AC PILOT'S EFFECTIVENESS

Since valid feedback needs to be obtained on all aspects of the AC, it is strongly recommended that, during the pilot, all the AC material be used in the sequence proposed for the AC, i.e. no short cuts should be taken.

The pilot should be a live pilot. The participants should actually experience the same benefits by attending the pilot AC as would participants to the AC once it is implemented. The same applies to the process owners.

During the pilot, the AC administrator can be part of the AC design team. However, if this is the case, it is recommended that an extra AC administrator attend the AC pilot. Although this extra administrator will not act as AC administrator, he or she will be useful should any unforeseen circumstances arise. For example, if problems with time frames are experienced during the AC pilot, he or she can make the necessary changes to the programme while the AC administrator himself or herself continues uninterrupted with his or her AC duties. The extra administrator can also make valuable improvement recommendations, since he or she is usually an experienced AC practitioner.

7. CRITICAL DECISIONS RELATING TO, AND OUTCOMES OF, THIS STEP

The most important outcome of this step is an AC that is ready for implementation. All the design work has been done, all the simulation and AC documentation is in place, the AC process works, and clarity exists regarding the resource needs of the AC. The AC design team should also be satisfied that the AC adheres to all the requirements set out in the AC blueprint and business case. The draft budget drawn up at the end of the previous step can be amended and approved by the AC steering committee.

The AC process owners who have attended the pilot must be satisfied that the AC in its current format can be implemented. The AC steering committee now gives the go-ahead for the AC to be implemented.

A comprehensive AC manual exists that can be used during the implementation stage to design training material for the AC administrators, observers and role players.

A comprehensive AC technical manual exists that can be used during the evaluation and validation stage. This manual will then also be updated with the results of that stage.

A successful AC pilot serves as a showcase for the client organisation. It indicates the potential benefits that can be derived from an AC and highlights the potential, future use of ACs within the client organisation.

DESIGN AND DEVELOPMENT

1. THE PURPOSE OF THE DESIGN AND DEVELOPMENT STAGE

The purpose of the design and development stage is to develop an AC that complies with the specifications and addresses the organisational needs identified during the analysis stage. The AC should in its totality elicit the required behaviour from the AC participants in the most effective manner, and the process owners should be able to fulfil their roles in the most useful way. All the documentation should be comprehensive and easy to use. In short, the purpose of the design and development stage is to develop an AC that is ready for implementation.

The purpose of the design and development stage was formulated as follows at the beginning of the stage:

1.1 Transforming the information from the analysis stage into an operational AC blueprint

The information from the analysis stage needs to be transformed into a document that serves as a guideline for the AC simulation development. This document also serves as the guide to designing the AC as a process. The AC blueprint ensures that the simulations, and consequently the AC as a whole, address the intended purpose.

1.2 Developing simulations that comply with the specifications set out in the AC blueprint

The AC blueprint specifies exactly the level of difficulty of the simulation. It also specifies the focal constructs and their behavioural elements needing evaluation during the simulation, as well as other technical requirements. The simulations should be designed in such a way that they elicit enough behaviour in respect of each of the focal constructs, and the least amount of "noise". Each simulation needs to be pre-piloted to ensure that it adheres to the set requirements.

1.3 Designing an AC that effectively sequences the various AC actions

Since a profile of focal constructs needs to be evaluated, one single simulation will not be able to elicit behaviour regarding all the focal constructs. Focal constructs also need to be evaluated in different contexts and in more than one simulation or assessment technique. The various simulations that will elicit the required behaviour in respect of the spectrum of focal constructs need to be sequenced in such a way as to allow the optimal performance of everyone at the AC. The AC should also be designed in such a way as to allow reliable evaluations of the participant's behaviour.

2. CRITICAL DELIVERABLES OF THIS STAGE

The design and development stage focuses on one key deliverable, namely, to deliver a fully functional AC. To achieve this overall deliverable, two other deliverables should be achieved:

2.1 An AC manual

The AC manual contains all the AC documentation needed by the AC participants, observers, role players and administrator. This manual should be so complete that experienced process owners can implement the AC repeatedly in a standardised format and achieve the required results.

2.2 An AC technical manual

The AC technical manual contains the audit trail that will be needed to show that the AC is valid and reliable. The whole AC pilot process should be documented in the manual.

3. THE FINAL OUTCOME OF THIS STAGE

In the final instance, the AC should adhere to all the set requirements from the analysis stage, yet also be able to be implemented effectively during the implementation stage. In addition, the operational AC should be able to withstand close scrutiny during the evaluation and validation stage so that it can be shown to be valid and reliable for the purpose it was designed.

After completing the *design stage*, can you confirm the following?

If you can respond positively to all the statements below, you have successfully completed the design and development stage.

- You have a competent design team that will assist you in the design and development process.
- You know what the exact purpose is of the AC you have designed.
- You know on which organisational level the AC is focused.
- You are clear about which focal constructs need to be assessed.
- You are sure which behavioural elements need to be assessed in each focal construct.
- You know which simulations are best suited for assessing a focal construct.
- You have identified which rating scale format would be best suited for the assessments.
- You have the required documentation (scripts, guidelines, etc.) for the role players.
- You have all the required documentation (norm tables, observer guidelines, observer report forms) for the observers.
- You have all the required documentation (participant report form, participant instructions, reflection forms) for the participants.
- You have conducted a pre-pilot in respect of the different simulation exercises.
- You know whether a chosen simulation will elicit the right frequency of behavioural elements.

- You have identified methods for capturing the criteria data.
- You have considered different feedback formats (rating format and narrative feedback) for use by delegates and observers.
- You have piloted the AC.
- You have identified the correct participants and observers for the pilot.
- You have a written programme for participants and observers.
- You have received a systematic evaluation from all stakeholders on the content and the process of each simulation and on the programme as a whole.

INTRODUCTION TO STAGE THREE

IMPLEMENTATION

1. WHAT THE IMPLEMENTATION STAGE IS ALL ABOUT

The third stage in the AC design model is the implementation stage. The following section of the book will focus on this stage, which is highlighted in Figure S3.1.

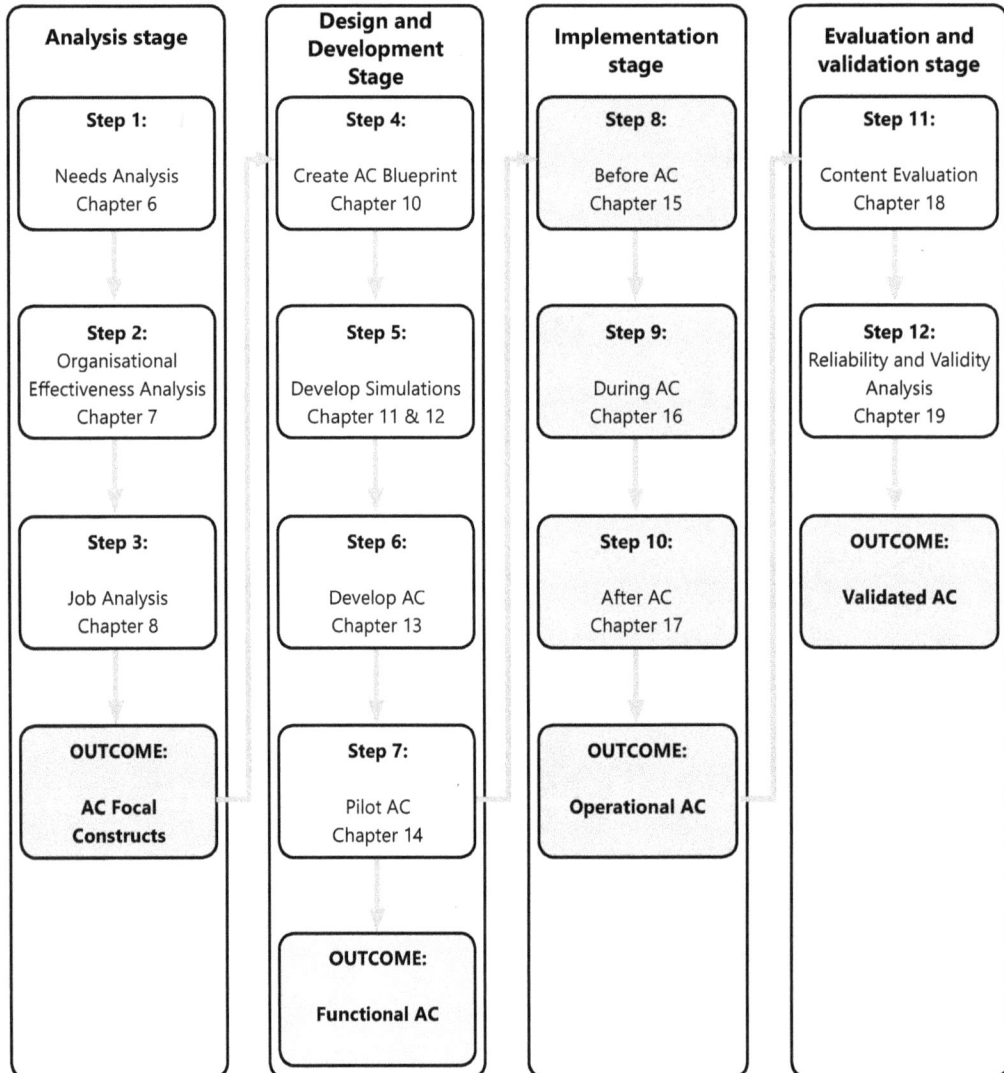

Analysis stage	Design and Development Stage	Implementation stage	Evaluation and validation stage
Step 1: Needs Analysis Chapter 6	**Step 4:** Create AC Blueprint Chapter 10	**Step 8:** Before AC Chapter 15	**Step 11:** Content Evaluation Chapter 18
Step 2: Organisational Effectiveness Analysis Chapter 7	**Step 5:** Develop Simulations Chapter 11 & 12	**Step 9:** During AC Chapter 16	**Step 12:** Reliability and Validity Analysis Chapter 19
Step 3: Job Analysis Chapter 8	**Step 6:** Develop AC Chapter 13	**Step 10:** After AC Chapter 17	**OUTCOME:** **Validated AC**
OUTCOME: **AC Focal Constructs**	**Step 7:** Pilot AC Chapter 14	**OUTCOME:** **Operational AC**	
	OUTCOME: **Functional AC**		

Figure S3.1: The steps in, and stages of, the AC Design Model

During the implementation stage, the AC that was developed and tested during the previous stage is put into practice. The AC is handed from the AC design team to the process owners, who must ensure that the AC is implemented according to the AC manual. If the AC is compared to a machine, one can say that the design engineers (the AC design team) have finished all the design and testing work on the new machine (the AC), and have produced a manual indicating how to use the machine (AC manual). The design engineers will still assist with the installation, but then they will hand the new machine to the production engineers (the AC process owners) for use. The process of installation, handover and use constitutes Stage Three of the design model, namely implementation.

In Chapter 15, the first step in the implementation stage (before the AC) is discussed. The chapter starts with a discussion on the selection and training of the process owners. Attention is given to the content of the training of the observers, the role players and the AC administrator. The required logistical needs are discussed as well as the AC pre-work.

Chapter 16, a short chapter, is about what happens during the AC. Pitfalls to look out for during the AC and practical hints are shared. A discussion on the crucial orientation sessions, the debriefing sessions and the data-integration session is also included in this chapter.

Chapter 17, the last chapter relating to the implementation stage, focuses on the post-AC processes. A crucial activity after each AC is the feedback given to the various interested parties. The feedback process is discussed in detail in this chapter, as well as the development plan and the growth framework. The discussions include information on the data capturing that is required after each AC and on the storage of AC material and information. Attention is also given to the maintenance of the AC.

2.   CRITICAL DELIVERABLES OF THIS STAGE

The following are the critical deliverables of Stage Three:

2.1   A pool of readily available, competent process owners

A machine or process is only as effective as the people using the machine or process. This is also true of an AC. All the process owners, namely the AC administrator, the observers, the role players and the person who gives the feedback after the AC, must be well trained in AC theory and skills in general, and specifically in the AC they will be involved in. The competence of the process owners will have a direct impact on the reliability and validity of the AC. The process owners should be trained and declared competent in the use of the specific AC.

2.2   An AC practice that adheres to the AC manual

The designers of a machine can only guarantee the machine's effectiveness if the machine is used according to the guidelines stipulated in the machine's manual. Likewise, the AC design team can only "guarantee" that the AC will elicit the behaviour linked to the focal constructs being evaluated if all the guidelines stipulated in the AC manual are followed. If the process owners consistently follow these guidelines during consecutive ACs, this will again assist in showing that the AC is reliable and valid during the evaluation and validation stage of the design model.

2.3   Post-AC processes that ensure positive action and a sustained AC process

An AC does not end when all the participants and process owners physically leave the AC. If the AC process is well designed, one process will feed into the next. For example, if a participant attended an entry-level DAC, the post-AC processes should enable such participant to action his or her resulting developmental recommendations. Once actioning of these recommendations has been completed, the post-AC process should allow the participant to attend the next level of DAC. The same applies for an AC used for selection purposes. The participants, whether or not appointed to the target position, should receive feedback that will enable them to be better prepared for the next AC they attend.

3.   THE INTENDED OUTCOME OF THIS STAGE

The intended outcome of this stage can be summarised as an Operational AC. This is an AC that is fully functional and embedded in the client organisation.

The intended outcome is as follows:

3.1   An AC that is part of the client organisation's culture

The AC should be embedded in other organisational processes. For example, the development plan drawn-up for each AC participant should feed into the organisation's workplace skills plan.

Ideally, the AC should be associated with a certain standard that is perceived by line managers as adding value to the operations of the organisation. The AC target population should be eagerly awaiting its turn to attend the AC. In marketing terms, a "pull" in the AC market (the internal target population) should exist. This means that line managers and human capital practitioners should demand the AC.

3.2   An AC system, process and practice that ensure a reliable and valid AC

The integrity of the AC itself can only be guaranteed if the AC is administered over time in a consistent manner, as then it will be possible to interpret the results from each AC in a similar manner. The AC needs to be maintained to remain relevant to the client organisation's need. Moreover, complete sets of data need to be stored accurately so that the validity of the AC can be determined.

CHAPTER 15

BEFORE THE CENTRE

Sandra Schlebusch

1. INTRODUCTION – PURPOSE OF THIS STEP

The purpose of the step, "Before the centre", is to ensure that everything is ready for the AC to take place. The AC in its entirety has been developed and tested, so it is now time to ensure that the AC process owners (observers, role players, and administrators) are ready to take over from the AC design team and that the conditions are such that the AC can be conducted immediately.

This step, overall step 8 in the design model, is depicted in Figure 15.1.

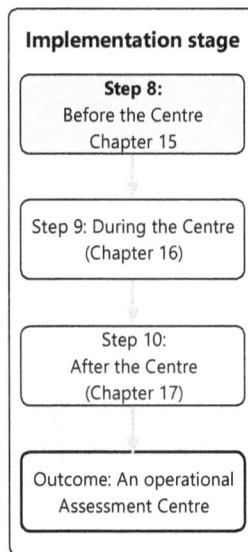

```
┌─────────────────────────────┐
│   Implementation stage       │
│  ┌────────────────────────┐ │
│  │      Step 8:            │ │
│  │  Before the Centre      │ │
│  │    Chapter 15           │ │
│  └────────────────────────┘ │
│              ↓               │
│  ┌────────────────────────┐ │
│  │ Step 9: During the Centre│ │
│  │    (Chapter 16)         │ │
│  └────────────────────────┘ │
│              ↓               │
│  ┌────────────────────────┐ │
│  │      Step 10:           │ │
│  │   After the Centre      │ │
│  │    (Chapter 17)         │ │
│  └────────────────────────┘ │
│              ↓               │
│  ┌────────────────────────┐ │
│  │ Outcome: An operational │ │
│  │   Assessment Centre     │ │
│  └────────────────────────┘ │
└─────────────────────────────┘
```

Figure 15.1: The step, Before the Centre, in the implementation stage

All process owners should be trained to competence and should maintain their competence levels to function in their respective roles during a specific AC for the AC to be considered ethical, reliable and valid.[1]

Chapter 15 starts with a discussion on the selection and training of the process owners and other stakeholders. The possibility of a specialist career path in ACs is discussed, which is followed by a discussion on the logistical arrangements for a traditional face-to-face AC. The pre-AC work that needs to be done by the participants and process owners is discussed before the chapter concludes with a discussion on the critical decisions relating to, and outcomes of, this step.

---

1   SA Assessment Centre Study Group, 2018

2. **OBSERVER**

2.1 Role of the Observer

The group within the AC process owners that can potentially have a great impact on the whole process is the observers. This is the group of people who will observe, note, classify and evaluate (ONCE) the AC participants' behaviour during the various simulations. Table 15.1 describes each of these sequential tasks when a behavioural observation approach is followed:

Table 15.1: The Basic Observation Task when Following the Behaviour Observation approach

Task	Description
Observe	Observing participant behaviour, both verbal and non-verbal, during the simulation. This includes observing the role player and other participants' reactions to the observed participant's behaviour.
Note (Record)	Noting behaviour includes making verbatim notes of the participant's behaviour during the simulation. This might take place in real time, or afterwards when the observer is working with a recording of the participant behaviour.
Classify	Classifying the observed participant behaviour into the various competencies or other AC focal constructs.
Evaluate	After classifying participant behaviour into the AC focal constructs, attaching a rating to the behaviour according to a standardised rating scale and norm is what evaluating is about.

According to Caldwell, Thornton and Gruys[2], two of the most common mistakes made at ACs are using unqualified and poorly trained observers. If the observers are not competent in their role, negative perceptions of the AC might be created, as well as possible legal challenges, and there will be problems with the AC's standardisation, reliability and validity.[3]

Before discussing the training of observers, it is necessary to assess the advantages and disadvantages of using internal or external observers to the client organisation, and the background of the observers. The decisions about the observers should be indicated in the client organisation's AC policy (see Chapter 5). Another important aspect is the selection criteria for the observers.

2.2 Selecting internal or external observers

AC observers can be external to the client organisation or employees. External observers are usually human capital specialists such as psychologists or psychometrists. When the observers are internal, they can be human capital specialists or line managers who are trained as observers.

---

2   Caldwell et al., 2003

3   Thornton et al., 2017

Both approaches have advantages and disadvantages, which are summarised in Table 15.2:[4]

Table 15.2: Internal versus External Observers

AC Observers Internal to Client Organisation		AC Observers External to Client Organisation	
Advantages	**Disadvantages**	**Advantages**	**Disadvantages**
No additional direct cost added to the cost of the AC.	Might be affected by internal organisational politics resulting in additional bias towards participants.	Less influenced by the organisation's internal politics.	Observer fees increase the overall AC cost.
Might be more familiar with the target job requirements.	Since the role of AC observer is not fulfilled regularly, internal observers might not be as competent in ONCE as external observers.	Should have specialist and professional ONCE skills, possibly increasing rating accuracy.	Might not be as familiar with the target job requirements as internal observers.
Might be difficult to find internal observers who are not known to the AC participants.	Might not be readily available to act as an AC observer and might withdraw from the AC due to own work demands.	More likely to be unfamiliar with the AC participants.	Possible contamination of competencies since the observers also work at other client organisations' ACs with other, but similar, competencies.
Familiarity with the client organisation's culture and climate within which the target job functions.	Future working relationships might be negatively impacted if the outcome of the AC is negative for a participant who may have to work together with an AC observer in future.		

The list of advantages and disadvantages in Table 15.2 indicates that the advantages of using one group of observers mostly counter the disadvantages of using the other group. A possible win-win approach could be to use a combination of external and internal observers during an AC. In doing so the advantages of using each group is harnessed, while controlling for the disadvantages of using one group. Irrespective of which group of observers is used at an AC, comprehensive observer training, conducting an observer orientation session at the start of each AC, and giving feedback to observers afterwards about their competence to fulfil the role, are required. The credibility of both groups of observers will increase the face validity of the specific AC, thus it is recommended that the suitability of the observers to fulfil the role be made clear to the AC participants at the start of the AC.

---

4   Thornton et al., 2017

2.3 Observers' background

People from diverse backgrounds can function as observers during an AC, including line managers from various organisational disciplines (e.g. operations, marketing, IT, finance, etc.) and/or psychologists/psychometrists. Table 15.3 summarises the advantages and disadvantages of using each group of observers.

Table 15.3: Advantages and Disadvantages of Observers with Different Backgrounds

Line Managers		Psychologists/Psychometrists	
Advantages	**Disadvantages**	**Advantages**	**Disadvantages**
Line managers are perhaps more able to evaluate participant behaviour in relation to organisation specific norms and values (differential accuracy).[5]	Line managers might find it difficult to link specific behaviours to the specific competencies being evaluated[6], resulting in lower criterion validity.	Psychologists are perhaps better able to classify behaviour according to the AC competencies, resulting in possible higher construct validity.	Psychologists might not be as familiar with the client organisation's norms and values.[7]
Line managers' observer skills transfer to other situations managers are expected to deal with.			

A major advantage of using line managers as observers, as is indicated in Table 15.3, is that they become sensitive to behaviour, as well as to what behaviour linked to the various focal constructs looks like. Since the focal constructs being evaluated during the AC have been derived from an in-depth analysis of the organisation's needs (see Chapter 8 for a discussion on job analysis), they are critical to the future of the organisation. If the line managers know the focal constructs, as well as the behaviours linked to these, they are better able to support employees to show the sought-after behaviour on a day-to-day basis in the work situation. If the same focal constructs are evaluated in the organisation's performance management system, the line managers will be able to make a more valid evaluation of the employees' performance. Line managers trained as observers seem to be able to conduct effective performance appraisals as they are trained in observing and noting specific behaviour[8], and they may be able to conduct more effective performance discussions when they are trained on giving feedback.

A possible disadvantage of using line managers as observers is that their observations might not be as accurate and reliable as those observations made by psychologists. However, this possible disadvantage can be overcome by comprehensive and continued training.

---

5   Lievens, 2001

6   Lievens, 2001

7   Lievens, 2001

8   Macon et al., 2011

Since line managers are perhaps more able to evaluate participant behaviour in relation to organisational values and norms, it is recommended that line managers who are competent and experienced as observers be included on the observer panel when an AC is used for selection purposes.[9]

When an AC is designed to evaluate the functional competence of specialists, it is useful to use a team of observers comprising of line managers and psychologists/psychometrists. The psychologist can observe and note the participant's behaviour during the simulation, and then together with the line manager, classify and evaluate the observed participant behaviour. Following this approach ensures that the behaviour is observed and noted comprehensively, and that functional competence is correctly evaluated. The AC process is also seen by the AC participants as being fairer, since a line manager who "knows the job" was part of the process.

2.4 Observer selection criteria and competencies

Becoming an observer at an AC is a commitment to being a competent observer, as well as to one's own growth and development. Not only must observers learn, on a continuous basis, to use new technology and new simulations during an AC, but they must also be role models of the focal constructs that they evaluate and regarding which they give AC participants feedback. This is a requirement to ensure the credibility of the AC process.

Irrespective of observers' backgrounds and whether they are internal or external to the client organisation, there are certain criteria they need to adhere to.

Thornton, Mueller-Rose and Rupp[10] stated that observers are usually people who are interested in other people and find it easy to engage in conversations. Although there is not a lot of research about the specific competencies required to be an effective observer, it might be stated that observers, at a minimum, need observational skills and an understanding of the selection or development process that the AC forms part of.[11] Table 15.4 lists proposed competencies that observers might need to be effective in their role.

Table 15.4: List of Possible Observer Competencies

	Competency (ability and attitude)	Description
1	Ethics and Integrity	The ability to do what is good for self and good for others[12]; being honest and fair.
2	Sustained high energy and perseverance	The ability to work extended hours and to maintain concentration and focus to complete the task at hand.

---

9   Lievens, 2001; Wirz et al., 2013; Lievens & Thornton, 2005

10 Thornton et al., 2017

11 Patterson et al., 2014; Venter, 2017

12 Rossouw & van Vuuren, 2014

	Competency (ability and attitude)	Description
3	Emotional maturity	The ability to control own emotions, including stress levels, and to respond emotionally appropriately.
4	Openness to feedback	The ability to respond positively to feedback.
5	Continuous learning	The ability to embrace new approaches and to keep own skill levels relevant and at a competent level.
6	Professional conduct	The ability to conduct self in an appropriate manner and to uphold high standards.[13]
7	Detail oriented	The ability to work accurately with detail.
8	Keeping confidentiality	The ability to maintain confidentiality about the AC and participant performance.
9	Team focus	The ability to work well with the AC administrator, other observers and role players.
10	Communication skills	The ability to express ideas in writing and verbally, and to listen actively.[14]
11	Decision making skills	The ability to be confident and decisive; being prepared to support decisions if challenged.
12	Technology savvy (if using a TEAC or VAC)	The ability to comfortably use the applicable information technology.
13	Time management	The ability to work under time pressure, to keep to a time schedule, and to deliver on expectations within specified time frames.

As can be seen from the above list, not all people interested in ACs will be able to become observers. Some of the listed competencies are skills that can be learnt, while others are more inherent characteristics.

2.4.1 Line managers as observers

Apart from the listed competencies, additional requirements apply to line managers fulfilling the role of observer, for example they themselves must have already attended an AC, they should have benefited from the AC process, and they should feel very positively towards an AC. They should thus be openly promoting the AC.

It is recommended that the line managers should be functioning effectively in their current roles and should be seen as role models.[15]

---

13 Patterson et al., 2014

14 Patterson et al., 2014

15 Meiring & Buckett, 2016

Line managers should have insight into their own behaviour and the impact of such behaviour on those around them. They should therefore already, to a degree, be behaviour-sensitive and emotionally mature when selected as potential observers.

Being an observer entails long hours, hard work and being prepared to receive feedback. The position that the line managers are employed in should therefore not be too demanding on their time. They should be able to attend the intensive observer training and be able to attend an AC without being interrupted with work-related issues during the AC.

It is strongly recommended that those who become observers do so voluntarily, however once a line manager is committed to being an observer, it might be a good idea to build this into their annual performance appraisal and discussion. In doing so, the line managers receive additional recognition for their efforts and they might put in extra effort while being an observer.

When line managers are used as observers, they should be employed at a higher organisational level than the target level of the AC. This will increase the observer's objectivity and decrease the possibility of organisational politics being present at the AC; the participant is no threat to the observer, and hopefully vice versa, when the observer line manager is at least two levels higher in the organisation.

2.4.2   Internal human capital specialists as observers

Since the AC process is usually seen as a human capital process, the assumption is sometimes made by the client organisation that the human capital practitioners who act as observers are specialists in observing, however this is not necessarily true. Human capital practitioners, even if they are registered psychologists, need additional knowledge, skills, attitudes and experience to be competent observers. Human capital practitioners acting as observers need not be employed two levels higher in the organisation than the target job. Since human capital is a staff function, human capital employees should already have experience working at senior levels in the organisation when they service their client base. People from the human capital department should actually have a good understanding of the organisation in its entirety.

With human capital practitioners, the person concerned should have an honours or master's degree in a behavioural field. For example, the human capital practitioner should have a minimum qualification of an honours degree in industrial and organisational psychology, or an honours degree in human resource management.

In addition to being behaviour-sensitive, the human capital practitioner should be knowledgeable about, and have an understanding of, business. A diploma in business management, a BCom degree, or having completed a management development programme at a university might enable a human capital practitioner to understand business. It is an advantage if the person has owned his or her own business.

The human capital practitioners should also have management–leadership experience if they will act as observers at management–leadership ACs. The knowledge and insight gained from being a manager–leader themselves, together with the knowledge and insight gained from studying towards a business qualification, will provide a frame of reference for the human capital practitioner so that they can easily understand the focal constructs, and their impact, in the work situation.

Their position in the organisation, as well as the client base they service in the organisation, must not be so demanding that it will not be possible for them to attend an AC without being disturbed by work demands.

2.4.3 External AC specialists as observers

As is the case with human capital practitioners, external AC specialists should have a minimum qualification of an honours degree in the behavioural sciences. It is advisable that they have a business qualification and experience in a senior management–leadership position within an organisation.

Although already a specialist, the external AC specialist should be willing to attend training in the specific AC.

The client organisation should get value for its money when it spends additional money on obtaining the services of an external observer. It is therefore recommended that the organisation ascertain what the external AC specialist's track record is. This can be done by requesting to see the observer's logbook (discussed later in this chapter) and by obtaining feedback from other AC process owners with whom the AC specialist has worked before.

2.4.4 Observers working as Coaches at a coaching development centre (CDC)

Functioning as an observer during a Development Assessment Centre (DAC) requires skills relating to being a learning facilitator, including the ability to give constructive feedback. Being an observer at a CDC requires additional coaching competence. Ideally observers at a CDC should, in addition to being competent in observer skills, be a competent professional coach. Table 15.5 lists the competencies required of an effective observer-coach at a CDC:[16]

---

16 Venter, 2017

Table 15.5: List of Competencies for a CDC observer-coach

		Competency	Description
1		Communication skills	The ability to effectively engage with CDC participants.
2		Empowering behaviour	The ability to motivate participants and to enhance their perceived ability of attaining the desired level of performance.
3		Honesty	The ability to provide specific feedback regarding participants' strengths, development areas, effectiveness and performance levels.
4		Openness to experience	The ability to be attentive towards participants' feelings and encourage dialogue.
5		People orientation	The ability to interact effectively with people.
6		AC knowledge	Knowledge of the competencies being assessed, knowledge of how to ONCE, and other AC relevant knowledge.
7	Core Competencies	CDC specific knowledge	The ability to cope with the unique demands of a CDC, such as: high degree of structure; vast amount of paperwork; the assessment materials; the timeframes; limited available time with participants; ability to endure long hours.
8		Positive regard	The ability to provide basic support and acceptance of the participant, regardless of what the participant says or does.
9		Relational attunement	The ability to encourage conversation and display empathy towards participants.
10		Interpersonal sensitivity	The ability to accurately assess others' behaviour from non-verbal cues.
11		Analytical thinking skills	The ability to visualise, articulate and conceptualise problems by making sensible decisions given the available information.
12		Tactically supportive behaviour	The ability to provide constructive advice and guide participants to achieve developmental goals.
13		Flexibility	The ability to adjust one's behaviour or approach to what is appropriate in a given situation or task.
14		Emotional control	The ability to maintain focus on the task at hand.

		Competency	Description
15	**Secondary Competencies**	Mutual responsiveness	The ability to encourage reflection.
16		Exploratory behaviour	The ability to explore alternative forms of behaviour.
17		Goal orientation	The ability to envision change and to articulate exactly what is needed for change to occur.
18		Objectivity	The ability to not be influenced by subjectivities when interpreting facts.
19		Energy/Drive	The ability to maintain one's strength and vitality.
20		Emotionally supportive behaviour	The ability to display the necessary comfort and sympathy towards participants.
21		Time management skills	The ability to use one's time effectively or productively.
22		Concentration skills	The ability to maintain focus on the task at hand.
23		Cultural self-awareness	The ability to be mindful of the perceptions, mindsets and attitudes that may impede interactions with participants.
24		Conscientiousness	The ability to be thorough, organised, self-disciplined and hard-working with regards to a particular job.
25		Motivational reinforcement	The ability to improve participants' focus and perseverance.
26		Cultural sensitivity	The ability to effectively function in different cultural settings.

The list of competencies for an effective CDC observer-coach in Table 15.5 overlaps with the competencies listed in Table 15.4 for an observer. The additional competencies that are required of a CDC observer-coach centres around being a conduit for the participant to develop and grow while at the CDC. Training to be an observer-coach therefore consists of two development journeys, one journey being an observer at an AC, and the other being a coach.

2.5 Observer Training

Once observers have been selected, it is time to train them to be competent observers.[17] The Realistic Accuracy Model (RAM) discussed in Chapter 9 emphasises the appropriateness of observer training. There are two approaches to observing participant behaviour and therefore training observers. The first approach is the behaviour observation approach where the observers sequentially follow ONCE, also known as the data-driven approach. The second approach is the frame-of-reference approach (FOR) to observing and evaluating behaviour.

---

17 Lievens, 2001; Wirz et al., 2013; Thornton et al., 2017; Thornton et al., 2015; Meiring & Buckett, 2016; International Taskforce on Assessment Center Guidelines, 2015

With the first approach the observers focus on first observing and noting a behaviour, then classifying the behaviour, and lastly evaluating the behaviour. The focus is therefore on observing and noting behaviour, increasing observational accuracy. With this approach, detailed notes on participant behaviour are taken that support rich developmental feedback to participants. With the second approach, FOR, the focus is on the observers being able to rate the observed behaviour according to a shared frame-of-reference (schema) of performance. The observers are therefore trained on being able to recognise the performance level (rating) of the observed behaviour, increasing rating accuracy, inter-rater reliability and perhaps even construct validity.[18] It is recommended that both approaches be used in training observers to fulfil their roles effectively[19], although aspects of FOR training have always been part of training for the behaviour observation or data-driven approach.[20]

2.5.1 Purpose of observer training

The purpose of observer training is to enable potential observers to accurately observe and evaluate participant behaviour during simulations according to the norm so that the ratings correspond to other observer ratings based on the same behaviour. In addition, comprehensive evidence for the rating needs to be captured. Observer training has a direct impact on the accuracy with which observers fulfil their role.[21]

2.5.2 Content of the training process

The international best practice guidelines state that the following must be included in observer training:[22]

"(a) The behavioral constructs to be assessed, including their behavioral definitions
(b) The observation, recording, classification, and evaluation of behaviors relevant to the behavioural constructs to be assessed
(c) The content of the simulation exercises as well as which behavioral constructs are targeted in which simulation exercises, including examples of effective and ineffective performance in each simulation exercise
(d) Awareness of the nature of common observational and rating errors (including how to distinguish behaviors from inferences)
(e) Security/confidentiality, standards of professionalism, and issues of fairness and non-discrimination."

In addition, the following should be included depending on the AC's purpose:[23]

---

18 Lievens, 2001; Roch et al., 2012; Cascio & Aguinis, 2019; Lievens & Thornton, 2005

19 Thornton et al., 2015; Noonan & Sulsky, 2001; Thornton et al., 2017

20 Thornton at al., 2015

21 Wirz et al., 2013

22 International Taskforce on Assessment Center Guidelines, 2015: 13

23 Meiring & Buckett, 2016: 15

"1. Knowledge of the organisation and job/management context being assessed to provide background for accurate assessor judgements.

2. Thorough knowledge and understanding of the competencies, definitions, behavioural indicators and links to job performance.

3. Knowledge of and certification (where applicable) in all assessment techniques to be used in the AC, for example, psychometric tests.

4. Demonstrated competence in observing, recording, classifying and evaluating behaviour as it is associated with the behavioural simulation exercises and structured rating forms. The outcome of which is a certification of proficiency for each assessor.

5. Thorough knowledge and understanding of the evaluation and rating procedures, including how data are integrated.

6. Demonstrated competence in using technology associated with the AC, for example, how to log onto the assessment platform, navigating the assessment platform, how to troubleshoot and resolve technological issues during the AC and how to retrieve participant data when the AC is finished.

7. Thorough knowledge and understanding of the organisation's assessment policy, with an emphasis on how data can be used.

8. Thorough knowledge and understanding of feedback and reporting procedures.

9. Demonstrated ability to give accurate, fair and objective verbal and written behavioural feedback to participants, if applicable.

10. Demonstrated knowledge of the role play exercise (where applicable) and the ability to play the role consistently across different ACs."

The guidelines also state that observers should be declared competent and certified to:[24]

"(a) Observe, record, and rate behavior in a standardized fashion

(b) Classify behaviors according to behavioral constructs

(c) Provide ratings that are calibrated in scale to the assessor team or an expert standard

(d) If applicable, report behavioral construct-relevant behaviors to the administrator or assessor team

(e) If assessors also serve as exercise administrators, administer exercises

(f) If assessors also serve as role players, objectively and consistently perform the role called for in interactive exercises

(g) If assessors are to provide feedback to assessees, deliver positive and negative behavioral feedback with supporting evidence in a manner that conveys concern/empathy and maintains or enhances assessees' self-esteem

(h) If assessors serve in a coaching role, establish clear expectations at the outset of the program (i.e., what behaviors can be expected from the assessor, what behaviors are expected of the assessee), motivate assessees, provide constructive and challenging feedback, and engage in coaching, developmental action planning, and goal setting

(i) If assessors are to provide feedback to line management, deliver clear, unambiguous, and well-constructed feedback on assessees' strengths and developmental needs

---

24 International Taskforce on Assessment Center Guidelines, 2015: 14-15

(j)   If assessors are to write reports for organizational decision making or assessee feedback purposes, deliver reports that are clear, well written, comprehensive, well integrated, and proofread."

The UK Standards suggest that training should also include information about the corporate risks associated with the recommendations and decision making based on the outcomes of the AC, as well as all the stakeholders for the AC outcome.   In the South African context, Nkomo and Badalani (see Chapter 3) strongly recommends that the topic of ethnocultural diversity be included in observer training (e.g. awareness of stereotypes and their influence on judgements and ratings).

2.5.3   Timing of the observer training

The various guidelines[25] state that potential observers should undergo the training prior to acting as an observer, however if six months have passed without acting as an observer, the observer should again attend training.   Although limited research about the time between attending training and acting as an observer exist, Gorman and Rentsch[26] suggest that the competence obtained during training should last for up to two weeks.   As a guideline, observer training can thus be scheduled two weeks prior to acting as an observer.

2.5.4   The training process

The approaches of blended learning, together with experiential learning based on adult learning principles, are recommended.   As such theory needs to be shared, potential observers need hands-on practice of observing and evaluating, as well as feedback about their progress towards competence. This implies that the potential observer will undergo practical exposure, do online learning and pass knowledge tests, attend lectures for BOT and FOR training, and be an observer in training until declared competent.   A suggested process of observer training is depicted in Figure 15.2.

---

25   International Taskforce on Assessment Center Guidelines, 2015; Meiring & Buckett, 2016

26   Gorman & Rentsch, 2017

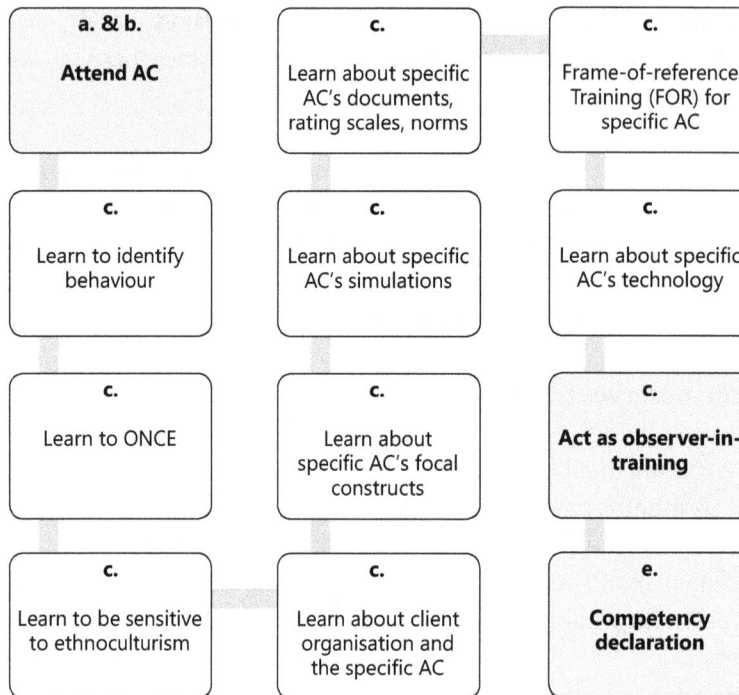

Figure 15.2: Proposed Observer Training Process

The clear blocks in Figure 15.2 indicate the aspects that will be addressed either through attending online modules or lectures, while the shaded blocks indicate the practical work at an operational AC. The distinct steps in the figure will be discussed below.

---

a. Attend the AC part 1: As a participant

A requirement for being an observer is to first attend an AC as a participant. This will ensure that the observer has first-hand knowledge of the simulations as well as of the stress to which participants are exposed. The potential observer participates in all the participant activities just like any other AC participant. This includes the potential observer completing all pre-AC documentation. After the AC, the potential observer will also receive feedback and a development plan.

b. Attend the AC part 2: As part of the observer team

Once potential observers have experienced the AC as participants, it is necessary to provide them with an overview of the total observation process. The potential observers thus attend their second AC, but this time as part of the observer team. Although not participating in any simulation, either as a participant or as an observer, the potential observers attend all the observer activities as a qualified observer would.

It might happen at this stage that some potential observers prefer not to continue with their training.

This might be because they realise how much work and dedication are required of observers who become involved in the process at an AC. It might be that they are not prepared to invest the time or effort, or perhaps they cannot invest such time and effort while still having other commitments to attend to. Either way, the sooner that potential observers decide not to continue with their training, the sooner attention can be given to those who will eventually become observers.

A word of caution though: those potential observers who decide not to continue with their training should still be positive about the AC. The trainer should therefore ensure that the potential observer does not walk away from the training with negative feelings about the training, the other observers, the AC, or any other part of the AC process.

c. Attend online and/or lecture room training

Having obtained an overview of what the observer process involves, it is time for the potential observer to attend the observer training. Such training comprises theoretical input about ACs; observation and evaluating in general; the specific AC; as well as the client organisation. Practical sessions on ONCE and the applicable FOR are also included.

d. Act as assistant observer

On average, the potential observer will need to act as an assistant observer twice. This entails performing all the tasks required of a competent observer, but having a qualified observer shadowing the potential observer. The competent observer remains accountable for ensuring that the observation process adheres to the qualitative standards. The competent observer also gives immediate feedback to the potential observer the moment that a problem is noticed.

e. Competence declaration

Only when the competent observer, the AC administrator and other process owners agree, will the potential observer be declared competent and allowed to function on their own as an observer.

Take note: The South African guidelines on ACs state that each potential observer be declared competent to fulfil the role during the *specific* AC.[27]

2.6 Content of the online and lecture room training

This section starts with a discussion on the training duration, followed by the themes related to the international and South African guidelines to be included in the training, either in the online section of the training or in the physical lecture room contact session.

---

27 Meiring & Buckett, 2016

2.6.1. Duration

The duration of the lecture room training depends on the length of the AC, the complexity of the various assessments and the experience of the observers. The longer the AC, and the more simulations used, the longer the training. The international AC guidelines recommend that two days of training be attended for every one day of assessments for observers with no prior AC experience.[28]

2.6.2 Themes

The themes that the lecture room/online training should cover can be divided into two categories. The first category, category A, is about aspects generic to all ACs, while the second category, category B, is about aspects specific to the AC during which the potential observers will be fulfilling their role. The themes will be discussed according to the categories.

2.6.3 Generic AC Training Content

2.6.3.1 General AC aspects

During the lecture room/online training, aspects such as a description of an AC, the 10 essential elements of an AC, and the history and purposes of ACs (selection, diagnosing, development) need to be discussed. In addition, the potential observers need to be sensitised to the *Guidelines and Ethical Considerations for Assessment Center Operations*[29] and the *Best practice guidelines for the use of the assessment centre method in South Africa (5th ed.).*[30] Attention should be paid to the *Code of Ethics for Assessment Centres in South Africa*[31] so that each observer understands their contribution to ethical ACs. Observers should also be made aware of South African legislation impacting the execution of ACs.

2.6.3.2 Behaviour recognition

A very important aspect to cover during training is the matter of what constitutes behaviour, i.e. what the participant says or does during the simulation. The potential observers need to be able to clearly distinguish between behaviour and someone's interpretation of behaviour, or inferences from observations. These potential observers need to become competent in noting only behaviour and in transferring behavioural examples to the observer report forms. They need to be sensitised not to use generalised statements (e.g. "The participant's attitude was a problem"), interpret behaviour (e.g. "The participant was rude"), or try to describe the participant's underlying personality (e.g. "The participant's introverted behaviour..."). Observers work with visible participant behaviour during simulations.[32]

---

28 International Taskforce on Assessment Center Guidelines, 2015

29 International Taskforce on Assessment Center Guidelines, 2015

30 Meiring & Buckett, 2016

31 SA Assessment Centre Study Group, 2018

32 Thornton & Mueller-Hanson, 2004

2.6.3.3 **ONCE**

When a certain level of competence in recognising behaviour has been achieved, the potential observers need to be introduced to the process of observing behaviour, noting it down, classifying it according to focal constructs, and evaluating it according to a norm; this is the so-called behaviour driven approach to fulfilling the observer role.

2.6.3.4 **Observing and Noting (ON**CE*)*

The potential observers need training in how to observe behaviour and to note behaviour verbatim as it happens. Typically, video vignettes are used to give the potential observers practice. After each practice run of observing and noting down behaviour, the potential observers need feedback on their attempts.

Usually the potential observers need training in how to observe and note the following:[33]
- What the participant says verbatim.
- The nonverbal behaviour of the participant.
- The role player's reaction, and the reactions of the other participants at the group meeting, to the participant's behaviour.
- Changes in participant behaviour.

Although it is initially difficult to note verbatim what the participant has said, the task becomes easier with practice. Writing down verbatim what has been said increases the credibility of the whole AC process, especially if the AC is a collaborative DAC and the participant sees the verbatim notes. The participant is also then more likely to accept the feedback from the simulation.

It is recommended that the observers be trained to take a few minutes directly after each observation and note-taking session to complete their notes. Over time, observers develop their own "shorthand" that they use during note-taking. Using a few minutes after each session allows the observers to complete their notes by also writing out the words where shorthand notes were made. This is important, since the notes should be legible so that other observers are able to use them. This requirement is necessary if the AC is being used for selection purposes and one of the participants queries the AC results. In such a case, it might be necessary to provide the original notes taken by the observer during the simulation, in conjunction with the completed observer report form, as supporting evidence for the rating on the focal constructs.

The potential observers need to be made aware of the possible errors that can occur during behaviour observation. Thornton and Zurich[34] found that training observers on the systematic errors in human judgement[35] assists in avoiding the errors being made during the actual ONCE behaviour observation process. Table 15.6 lists some of the errors relating to behaviour observation:[36]

---

33 Thornton et al., 2017

34 Thornton & Zorich, 1980

35 Campbell, 1958

36 Thornton et al., 2017

Table 15.6: Systematic Errors in Behaviour Observation

Error	Description	Example
Middle message loss	The observer "loses" some of the behaviour halfway through the simulation.	The observer starts to "listen" to the conversation or cannot note fast enough the whole argument presented by the participant, thus focusing on the start and end of the message.
Contamination from prior information	The observer does not observe the actual behaviour presented by the participant during the simulation, but only listens for evidence of pre-conceived ideas about the participant.	Knowing that the participant has a reputation for being able to reason effectively, the observer notes only positive behaviour examples.
Prejudice or stereotyping	The observer consciously or unconsciously specifically listens for participant behaviour that will enforce his or her prejudice.	The observer listens for the female manager to keep quiet after being challenged by the role player to enforce the stereotype that females are afraid of confrontation.

Observers can also make errors in noting apart from the errors listed in Table 15.6. When noting the participant behaviour, the observer should be aware of the following potential problems:

Table 15.7: Potential Problems when Noting Behaviour

Problem	Description	Example
Loss of detail	The observer does not note verbatim what the participant has said.	The observer notes "used various influencing techniques".
General descriptions	The observer notes his or her own description of what the participant did without any specific detail.	"Was rude" [Instead of the actual behaviour – the following question remains unanswered: What did the participant say or do that was rude?]
Conclusions, interpretations, opinions	The observer notes his or her own conclusions, opinions, interpretations of the participant's behaviour.	"Lacks interpersonal sensitivity [the following question remains unanswered: What did the participant say or do that led to that conclusion?]
Vague statements	The observer notes statements, not actual behaviour.	"Is friendly."
Failure to take notes	The observer for whatever reason does not make any notes about the participant's behaviour.	If the behaviour is not observed and noted, it cannot be classified and evaluated.
Noting behaviour of the wrong participant	If a leaderless group discussion is being observed and the discussion is not video recorded, the observer takes notes about the wrong participant.	If the participant's behaviour is not observed and noted, it cannot be classified and evaluated.

2.6.3.5 *Classifying behaviour according to focal constructs* (ONCE)

It is a time-saving habit if, once the observers have completed their notes, they start classifying the behaviour into the various focal constructs. This classification can be indicated by writing the focal construct's name next to each behavioural example. If the simulation has been well designed (i.e. there is no noise), all participant behaviour should be classified into the AC focal constructs. Table 15.8 indicates an example of classifying behaviour on the observer's notes.

Table 15.8: Example of Classifying Behaviour in Notes Taken During a Simulation

Participant	Role Player
Right Alex I would like to have a conversation with you on something that I picked up and it is not an easy discussion for me, but I am not here to tell you what you are doing wrong. I actually want to find out and want to keep track on what you are doing and how I can assist you. *Providing direction*	
	Are you referring to the memos that I have sent you?
I have seen a lot of memos this morning on my desk and there are three topics that I just want to discuss with you if it is fine. *Providing direction*	
	Ok, what topics would you like to discuss?
Ok, Alex, if I can ask you, what are the top five challenges you have in your department? *Information gathering*	

The process of classification has already started when behaviour is labelled as indicated in the example of Table 15.8. Next, the potential observers need to be trained to transfer all the participant behaviour, in behavioural terms, to the observer report form. It is important to transfer all applicable behaviour examples. Some observers have the bad habit of transferring only enough behaviour to justify a specific rating on the focal construct. This becomes problematic when the other observers challenge the rating during the data integration session or when the final rating is challenged by the participant or any other person.

When classifying the participant's behaviour, be aware of the following problems:

Table 15.9: Potential Problems when Classifying Behaviour

Problem	Description	Example
Wrong classification	The observer classifies the behaviour incorrectly.	Participant behaviour that is an example of the competency "Providing Direction" is incorrectly classified as an example of the competency "Empowerment".
Not classifying all behaviour	The observer only classifies a select few examples of behaviour linked to each focal construct instead of classifying all relevant behaviour.	The observer only classifies "enough" behaviour to justify (according to him or her) the rating that he or she allocates to the focal construct.

The problems listed in Table 15.9 should be addressed through effective training.

2.6.3.6 *Evaluating Behaviour* (ON**CE**)

The potential observers should be trained to rate the behaviour transferred to the observer report form according to the specific AC's norm. After rating each behavioural element, an overall rating per focal construct should be allocated according to the norm table (when a within exercise competency rating approach is followed – see Chapter 10). Again, it is advisable to sensitise the potential observers to common rating errors. These errors are as follows:[37]

Table 15.10: Common Rating Errors

Error	Description	Example
Halo effect	The specific focal construct's rating is not based on the performance of the participant regarding the specific focal construct, but rather on the overall impression gained of the participant.	A well-groomed person may be rated higher on focal constructs unrelated to personal physical appearance.
Horns effect	This is the opposite of the halo effect – one negative observation may cloud the ratings of other focal constructs without participant behaviour supporting the lower ratings.	If someone does not greet others they may mistakenly be perceived as unfriendly or withdrawn.

---

37 Thornton et al., 2017

Error	Description	Example
Recency	The rating on a focal construct is not based on all the behavioural evidence, but only on the most recent behaviour of the participant during the simulation.	Throughout the simulation the participant involves the role player in decision making. Only when it comes to the last decision does the participant take a decision on his or her own without involving the role player in the process. Because of this one example, the participant then receives a low rating on the focal construct being evaluated.
Similar to me/ different to me bias	The rating on a competency is not based on the behavioural evidence, but on certain qualities or characteristics of the participant that are similar to or different from those of the observer.	The participant receives a higher or lower rating because the observer has experienced the participant as the same as him or her and he or she knows that his or her own intention in that situation would have been....
Restricting the rating scale – severity, middle tendency, leniency	These three types of errors relate to an observer's propensity to allocate high, middle of the scale or low ratings to the focal construct.	Some observers are especially tempted to allocate high ratings during collaborative DACs where the participant sits next to them and challenges ratings directly.
Overemphasis on the negative or positive	The observer overemphasises one aspect of the participant's behaviour (e.g. one element) relating to a focal construct and does not evaluate the total focal construct according to the norm.	The participant shows a lot of behaviour linked to four of the focal construct's elements, but no behaviour linked to a specific element, and receives a lower rating. The opposite can also happen.
Stereotyping	The observer labels characteristics as typical as a result of the participant belonging to a certain group.	Considering ex-military people as "aggressive".
Projection	The observer pushes his or her own personal view of how behaviour fits together. This leads to preconceptions and inaccuracies.	Assuming that if someone is assertive, they must be "naturally" outgoing.
Illusion	The observer's view is distorted by the context of the simulation.	A moderately talkative participant may be perceived as very talkative in a group of more quiet participants.

2.6.3.7 *Ethnoculturism*

Part of the training of potential observers is training about ethnoculturism, especially in the South African context, which is training about being aware of culture-based stereotypes and their influence on judgements and ratings during an AC. See Chapter 3 for an in-depth discussion on this topic.

2.6.4 *Training specific to the AC*

Since ACs differ from each other in so many ways, all observers must undergo training about the specific AC that they will be working with, as well as about the specific client organisation. The required specific training will now be discussed.

2.6.4.1 **Client organisation and ACs**

During the lecture room training the background of the client organisation should be covered. Background on the actual analysis conducted during Stage One of the AC Design Model, namely the Analysis Stage, should be shared. Specifically, training should focus on a description of the target job and on where the job fits into the larger organisation. The client organisation's policies and procedures about ACs, the use of the AC results, and where and how the AC is embedded in other people processes need to be discussed. The observers need to be knowledgeable about the feedback processes and the process available to participants of objecting to the outcome of the AC results.

2.6.4.2 **AC focal constructs**

Specific, in-depth training must be provided regarding the competencies and/or focal constructs, as well as the specific behavioural elements. The potential observers need to understand the focal constructs and their elements, and also what behaviour linked to these looks like. They need to understand how the behaviour varies from one simulation to another, as well as what behaviour linked to each rating on the assessment scale looks like.

When the principles of Trait Activation Theory (TAT) are used during the AC (see Chapter 9 for a discussion about TAT), observers should, for example, learn to recognise the cues when given to participants and note their responses to those.

2.6.4.3 **Simulation content**

The training should focus on the content of the specific simulations and on the fictitious organisation for the specific AC. The observers should have a thorough understanding of these aspects to enable them to answer possible questions posed by participants and to be able to evaluate the participant behaviour effectively during each simulation.

2.6.4.4 **Documentation specific to the AC**

An AC consists of multiple assessments[38], with each assessment having documentation related to the specific assessment (see Chapters 11 and 12 for a discussion on the documentation required per simulation). If observers will be administering the various assessments, they need to be trained on how to administer these in a standardised manner. Potential observers need training on how and when to complete each document, as well as how to use each document during the process of fulfilling their role. Specific attention should be paid to the rating scale being used, as well as the norm of the AC.

---

38 International Taskforce on Assessment Center Guidelines, 2015; Meiring & Buckett, 2016

2.6.4.5 *Frame-of-Reference (FOR) training*

When the observers are knowledgeable about the AC simulation content, focal constructs and elements, rating scale and documentation, they are ready to undergo FOR training to create the common performance schema for the specific AC. The purpose of frame-of-reference training is to provide the potential observers with a "theory of performance" that they can use during the AC. This "theory" needs to imprint what the behaviour linked to the various focal constructs and elements looks like, as well as what behaviour spread across the rating scale on a specific focal construct and elements looks like.[39]

The potential observers typically observe and note a video recording of a participant during a simulation, before evaluating the behaviour in the video according to the AC's focal constructs as discussed. They also individually rate the behaviour. The group of potential observers then discusses their evaluation of the behaviour while the trainer facilitates the discussion. The trainer will then explain the appropriate evaluation and rating to the potential observers. This process is repeated until there seems to be a mutual understanding (schema) of what behaviour linked to the focal constructs looks like per rating scale category.[40]

2.6.4.6 *Training on a specific AC's technology*

If the AC is a technology enhanced AC (TEAC) or a virtual AC (VAC), the observers need to be trained on the use of the applicable technology. Not only must the observers be comfortable in using the technology, but they also need to be able to do basic troubleshooting if they or the participant experience any technical problems during a simulation.

2.6.5 *Development Assessment Centres (DAC)*

If observers are trained to facilitate at a collaborative DAC, additional training in facilitation skills will have to be provided. Observers functioning as a coach during a coaching development centre should ideally already be a certified coach, however the minimum performance expectations about what a coach should do must be clarified. For example: clarifying mutual expectations with the AC participants at the start of the centre; motivating and building the participant's self-efficacy about the AC's focal constructs; giving constructive and challenging feedback to the participant; providing coaching; and assisting in crafting development action plans and goal setting.[41]

2.6.6 *Training in giving feedback*

Training should be given to the person, or people, who will conduct the feedback discussions after the AC. Again, the training should include theory and practice. The feedback can be given by the observers or the AC administrator, or by a different person specifically trained for the task.

Chapter 17 contains a more detailed discussion on giving feedback.

---

39 Cascio & Aguinis, 2019

40 Cascio & Aguinis, 2019

41 International Taskforce on Assessment Center Guidelines, 2015

2.7 Continued training

Since the competence of the observers influences the validity and reliability of the AC, special care should be taken to ensure that they remain competent. It is therefore advisable that actions be taken to ensure continued competence.

2.7.1 Regularly act as observer

The minimum requirement as indicated by the International Guidelines for ACs[42] is that an observer fulfils the role at least once during two consecutive years. However, it is recommended that observers act as observers more often. Since the demands placed on an observer during an AC are quite extensive, the AC administrator should ensure that observers are not overworked. Care should be taken that observers do not act too frequently as observers at an AC, resulting in "observer fatigue" that could cause the quality of their work to deteriorate.

2.7.2 Attend regular observer refresher training

Since an AC norm is also qualitative in nature, it can happen over time that the different observers start applying the norm with slight differences, in other words, there is a change in the shared performance schema. To counter this, regular refresher training should take place.[43] It is recommended that observers attend refresher training and be re-certified as competent at least twice a year. This will ensure that both the observer skill and the specific AC's norm remain relevant.

AC simulations can also be updated. For example, new technology may be introduced or the AC programme might change. This might require additional observer training which can be carried out during the refresher training.

Since a pool of observers will exist per AC, and as only a limited number from the pool will attend each AC, it might happen that the observers know of one another, but do not know each other. The refresher training is the ideal opportunity for the observers to interact socially.

2.7.3 Attend pre-centre orientation

Every traditional face-to-face AC should be preceded by an observer orientation session. The purpose of the session is to ensure that the observer's knowledge of the simulations, the programme and their role is refreshed. During this session, all possible questions put by the observers should be answered. This session is facilitated by the AC administrator.

During this session the administrator will typically work through every simulation's content, as well as the observer report form and norm. The administrator will give as many examples as possible to ensure that the observers' frames of reference remain the same. Such a session usually takes a few hours and

---

42 International Taskforce on Assessment Center Guidelines, 2015

43 International Taskforce on Assessment Center Guidelines, 2015

is generally held on the day before the AC starts. Attendance of this orientation session is not optional. It is also advisable that the role players, if they will not be part of the observer team, attend this session.

The format and roll-out of a virtual assessment centre (VAC) will determine how the orientation sessions take place.

2.7.4   Attend post-centre feedback

It is recommended that every AC finish off with the administrator giving individual feedback to all the other process owners about their performance during the AC. The administrator should give individual feedback on the note-taking during the interactive simulations; the accuracy and comprehensiveness with which the observer report forms have been completed; the accuracy in using the applicable norm; the quality of the role plays; the contributions during the data-integration session (if applicable); the interaction with the participants and other observers; and any other aspect that might influence the reputation of the AC. The administrator should also share feedback from the AC participants with the other process owners.

It is recommended that the administrator invite feedback from the other process owners on his or her own performance during the AC.

2.7.5   Attend the Assessment Centre Study Group's (ACSG) annual conference

The ACSG (www.acsg.co.za) holds an annual conference that usually takes place during March. During this conference, national and international speakers share their AC-related research and their practical application of AC technology. It is recommended that all AC process owners attend this conference to ensure that they keep up-to-date with the latest trends and developments in the field of ACs. In addition, observers can attend the International Congress on Assessment Centre Methods (ICACM) (www.assessmentcenters.org), which is held annually in different countries.

2.7.6.   Logbook per observer (portfolio of evidence)

It is said that a process is only as good as the people using it. This is true of any AC, as even a well-designed AC can fail if the process owners are not competent. If AC participants are unhappy with the results of the AC, they can challenge the results. Not only must the AC design team then be able to show that they have followed a logical, systematic process in the design of the AC and that the focal constructs are relevant to the target job, but the process owners' competence must also be shown. The process owners should be accountable for providing evidence of their competence, for example by building a portfolio of evidence (POE) of all the work done in the specific process owner capacity.

Typically, observers should indicate in the POE each time they functioned as an observer, each time they were a role player, each time they wrote feedback reports, and even each time they gave feedback. The POE should also contain evidence of membership of an AC design team.

3. ROLE PLAYER

3.1 Role of the Role player

The role player provides the stimuli, in addition to the participant instructions, for a participant to respond to during an interactive simulation. The role player is the person who interacts with the participant during a simulation, either face-to-face, over a phone, or by webcam. The role player is accountable for creating the opportunity during an interactive simulation for a participant to demonstrate behaviour linked to the focal constructs being evaluated.[44] The role players must perform the role through the character they portray by responding to the unique behaviour of the participant. Role players should provide the stimuli in as much of a standardised way as possible, given that they adapt (in character) to the participant.[45] Role players should not overplay or underplay a role so as not to take away an opportunity for the participant to demonstrate behaviour. They should also not provide more than the necessary opportunities for the participant to demonstrate behaviour.

At some ACs observers are also expected to be role players, however the tasks are too complex for a person to be the role player AND observe and note the participant behaviour simultaneously during a simulation.[46] Observers should thus rather be role players during simulations observed by other observers. During some ACs, professional actors are used as role players. This seems to be happening during ACs in the United Kingdom, but not very often during ACs conducted in South Africa.

3.2 Role player selection criteria and competence

There is limited research about the selection criteria and competence of AC role players. In Table 15.11, a list of the potential competencies to select role players on is provided.[47] This list is not meant to be a finite list, but serves as a starting point to identify the required selection criteria.

Table 15.11: Potential Selection Criteria for Role players During an AC

	Competency (ability and attitude)	Description
1	Ethics and integrity	The ability to do what is good for self and good for others[48]; being honest and fair.
2	Sustained high energy and perseverance	The ability to work extended hours and to maintain concentration and focus to complete the task at hand.
3	Emotional maturity	The ability to control own emotions, including stress levels, and to respond emotionally appropriately.

44 Meiring & Buckett, 2016

45 Thornton et al., 2017; International Taskforce on Assessment Center Guidelines, 2015

46 Thornton et al., 2017

47 Patterson et al., 2014

48 Rossouw & van Vuuren, 2014

	Competency (ability and attitude)	Description
4	Openness to feedback	The ability to respond positively to feedback.
5	Continuous learning	The ability to memorise scripts, to embrace new approaches and to keep own skill levels relevant and at a competent level.
6	Professional conduct	The ability to conduct self in an appropriate manner and to uphold high standards.
7	Keeping confidentiality	The ability to maintain confidentiality about the AC and participant performance.
8	Team focus	The ability to work well with the AC administrator, other observers and role players.
9	Communication skills	The ability to express ideas verbally and to listen actively.
10	Technology savvy (if using a TEAC or VAC)	The ability to comfortably use the applicable information technology.
11	Acting	The ability to enter into the role play character, to adopt the character as own character, and to perform the character consistently across participants and time.

Once potential role players have been selected, they must participate in a training process.

3.3 Role player training process

The duration of training will depend on the complexity of the character and on the simulation, as well as on the role player's current skill levels. If the role player is also one of the observers, the training will focus merely on training with regard to the character for the role.

The proposed role player training process is depicted in Figure 15.3.

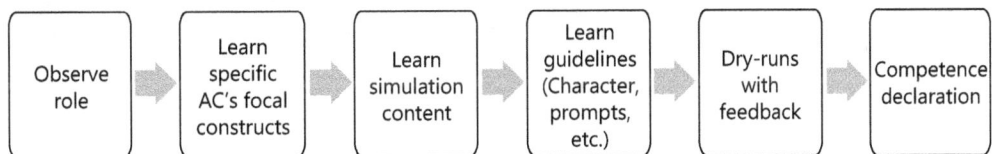

Observe role → Learn specific AC's focal constructs → Learn simulation content → Learn guidelines (Character, prompts, etc.) → Dry-runs with feedback → Competence declaration

Figure 15.3: Role Player Training Process

The process as depicted in Figure 15.3 consists of six distinct focus areas:

3.3.1 Observe the role

The training process starts with the potential role player observing the role being performed by a competent role player. This provides the potential role player with a frame of reference regarding how to portray the character.

3.3.2 Learn the specific AC's focal constructs

To enable role players to fulfil their role, they need training in the focal constructs being evaluated, recognising the behaviour linked to the focal constructs, and the use of the cues related to each focal construct. Attention should be given to train role players in the sequence of giving the cues so that standardisation is enforced.

3.3.3 Learn simulation content

The potential role players need training in the content of the specific simulation(s). Sometimes it will also be necessary for the role player to understand some of the other simulations, especially in the case where the AC follows an integrated simulation approach.

3.3.4 Learn role player guidelines

The training should include theoretical input during which the character is discussed in detail. The potential role players need to learn the character scripts, the character pre-disposition, the character's thoughts about specific aspects, as well as the typical arguments and counter-arguments that the character will use. It is also recommended that role players are trained on ethnoculturism (see Chapter 3)[49] and the potential impact thereof in performing the role.

3.3.5 Participate in dry-runs

Each potential role player should be allowed the opportunity to perform the role and receive immediate feedback on their performance. This should be repeated until a certain level of competence is achieved.

3.3.6 Competence declaration

Only once the potential role players have shown that they can accurately portray the character and elicit the required participant behaviour by using the various cues correctly, should they be declared competent.

---

49 International Taskforce on Assessment Center Guidelines, 2015

Case Study:
Pinsight™ Observer Training[50]

Introduction

Pinsight™ is a virtual company that offers virtual assessment centres (VAC) to clients across various continents. They have different levels of assessment, from junior management to executive leadership, and within these levels there are different VACs. During the three-hour VACs participants receive emails about various issues related to the VACs' fictitious organisation to which they need to respond. Participants also have to create implementation or project plans, and participate in real-time interactive simulations with live role players. After participants complete the VACs, observers classify and evaluate their performance. Pinsight's™ service commitment is to deliver participant reports within 24 hours after the completion of a VAC.

Pinsight™ Observers

Since Pinsight's™ client base is global and spread over different time zones, their observers reflect this diversity and come from different countries, speak different languages and work in different time zones. Currently observers are from:
- United Kingdom, The Netherlands, Slovakia, Belgium
- Israel
- Brazil, Columbia, Costa Rica, Peru, Mexico
- New Zealand
- South Africa
- United States of America
- China

Pinsight™ generally requires their observers to have at minimum a Masters' degree in a relevant field such as organisational psychology, coaching, business, leadership, or Human Resources. For senior level observer roles, considerable relevant experience is also required. In addition, observers are required to be comfortable interacting with people and playing the role play character, have good language skills, and be skilled at observing behaviour.

As Pinsight's™ business grows and it enters new territories, new observers are selected, trained, and accredited as competent. Regular recalibration and recertification training[51] is done in order for the diverse team of observers to classify and evaluate behaviour in a consistent and standardised way so that VAC results are reliable and valid. The recertification training is conducted every six months.

The challenge

The geographical dispersion of the observers in terms of their differing time zones means that real-time discussion and training is not possible. In addition, creating a sense of teamwork and engagement is challenging because observers usually never meet in person.

---

50 Hall, 2019

51 International Taskforce on Assessment Center Guidelines, 2015

Pinsight's™ Solution

All Pinsight™ training solutions are offered online through the Pinsight™ University platform. After completing the VAC as a participant, the new observer invests on average about 14 hours to obtain their Pinsight™ certification. The modules cover the following topics:
- Introduction to Pinsight™
- VAC technology
- Observational techniques and guidelines
- Simulation content, including role player guidelines (per VAC)
- Evaluating behaviour using the applicable BARS (per VAC)
- Coaching/feedback process

At the end of the modules, there are online tests which must be passed with a minimum of 80% in order to become a certified Pinsight™ observer. Thereafter practice role plays are done with Pinsight's™ Head Assessor in order to further prepare observers for role plays with real participants. After certification, observers can revisit the Pinsight™ University modules to refresh and refine their skills further.

Ongoing training

Since the Pinsight™ system records all assessments, quality assurance is conducted on observer role plays and evaluations to ensure accuracy and consistency. Feedback is offered to observers for ongoing learning and development.

After certification, observers are required to participate in recertification exercises every six months to retain their observer status. These recertification exercises assist with a consistent and standardised classification and evaluation of behaviour so as to increase the chances of reliable and valid VAC results.

The recertification exercises are available on the Pinsight™ University platform. Certified observers are notified that the recertification module is available and that it should be completed before a cut-off date. After this date, observers are asked which scoring areas they found difficult and these areas are addressed, as well as general scoring challenges, in the online post-recertification discussion. These discussions are recorded and available afterwards to those observers who were unable to attend.

In addition, regular online recalibration training is offered to address issues raised by observers, for example, tricky scoring areas. These more informal recalibration sessions encourage sharing of experiences and build a sense of teamwork.

The advantages of following a continuous, modular online observer training process are as follows:
- Inter-rater reliability is enhanced since the frame-of-reference of observers is continuously aligned.
- Observer confidence increases knowing that their ratings and interpretation of the BARS are aligned to those of the rest of the team.
- Training efficiency is improved since all observers "hear the same message" and learn the same lessons.
- Clients are assured that all observers are regularly recertified and are competent to conduct and evaluate the VACs.
- The online modules are delivered in a convenient way as observers can work through a module in their own time, with no additional load on Pinsight™ resources.
- The recertification discussions provide the opportunity for observers to discuss tricky situations and evaluation challenges, ensuring ongoing learning.
- The regular recalibration discussions encourage observer interaction and build a sense of engagement and teamwork.

4. ADMINISTRATOR TRAINING

The process owner accountable for the whole AC is the administrator. The administrator takes both administrative and professional accountability for the execution of the AC according to the AC manual. This person therefore needs training in this role.

4.1 The changing role of the Administrator

The administrator's role is impacted by, and made easier with, the use of technology, to such an extent that this role might morph into being the person providing technical support to participants, role players and observers before, during and after a VAC. This role then becomes the person, perhaps assisted by a bot, that is available for live chat during the VAC and who follows up with observers and role players about their on-time delivery on commitments.

Depending on the technological platform, this person might assist in the electronic scheduling of participants and observers, as well as follow-up with participants if their AC pre-work is not done in time for them to participate in the VAC. The participants and other stakeholders might contact this person to assist with accessing the reports following a VAC. Although this person is knowledgeable about every aspect of the VAC, it might not be a requirement for this person to be a competent observer and role player. More important requirements for this person are to be technologically competent and client centred. The training requirements of this role will depend on the specifications of the VAC and will not be discussed further in this chapter.

The training of the administrator that will be discussed further in this chapter is an administrator during a traditional face-to-face AC.

4.2 Training content

The most effective training approach for an administrator in a traditional face-to-face AC is once again to combine theoretical input with practical experience. Figure 15.4 indicates the aspects on which the potential AC administrator needs training.

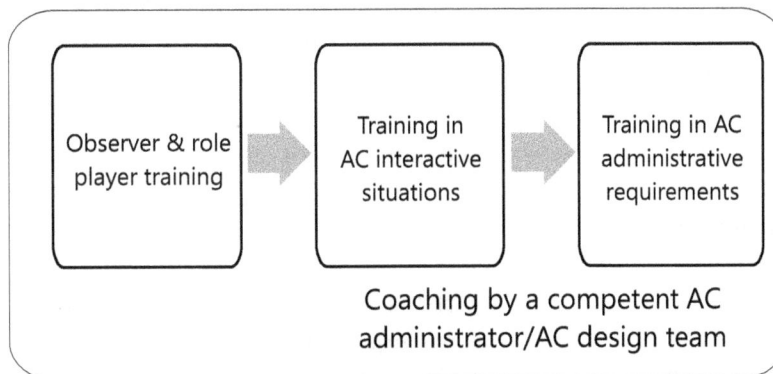

Figure 15.4: AC Administrator Training Content

Throughout the training process, the potential administrator needs to have access to an experienced administrator or an AC design team member who can serve as a coach. The potential administrator needs training in how to conduct the AC according to the AC manual. Specifically, such a potential administrator first needs training in being a competent observer. Thereafter, training is needed in the interactive situations during and post-AC, as well as in administrative requirements.

4.2.1   Observer and role player training

A prerequisite for becoming an administrator is to be a competent observer and role player, as was discussed above.

4.2.2   Training in interactive AC situations

The approach to training should be that potential administrators attend a few of the interactive situations as "observers", having received guidance regarding the principles to follow during the sessions. Thereafter they should be allowed to conduct the sessions themselves with the competent administrator or AC design team member, who acts as a coach. After the sessions, the potential administrators should receive immediate feedback. This process can be repeated as many times as it takes the potential administrators to be comfortable with the role.

(a)   Orientation sessions

The first AC interactive session that the administrator will conduct is the observer as well as the participant orientation sessions. The administrator needs to hold separate orientation sessions with the AC participants and the AC process owners.

The administrator needs training not only in presentation skills, but also in facilitation skills. The presentation skills are applicable during the orientation session held for the AC participants, however the administrator will require all possible facilitation skills (as well as plain savvy) to address some of the AC participant's concerns at the start of the AC. It is crucial that the administrator be able to address and satisfactorily resolve all possible concerns before the AC progresses. If these concerns are not resolved at the start, the specific participant will probably not be as open to the AC experience as is necessary. Not only will that specific participant be affected, but all the other participants might also be negatively influenced.

The skills used during the process-owner orientation sessions are mostly informal facilitation skills.

(b)   Simulation administration

During a lot of ACs, it is the responsibility of the AC administrator to administer the simulations according to the specifications in the AC manual. Again, the administrator must be able to answer all possible questions and address the concerns of the participants as and when these are aired.

(c) Debriefing sessions

The purpose of the debriefing sessions is to allow the AC participants to express their experiences of the simulation(s) or of the AC as a whole. During such sessions, the participants have the opportunity to ask questions about the simulations and even to share ideas with one another regarding such simulations.

The debriefing sessions with the AC participants are a very important "moment of truth". The administrator must be able to deal, in a positive and constructive manner, with all the possible emotions and negativity that might be aired. He or she should ensure that the experience is reframed as a learning opportunity, and if any negativity is present, that it gets aired during the debriefing session(s). If any negativity is not aired during these sessions, it is taken back to the workplace where it has the potential to create a negative perception of the AC.

In addition, the debriefing session(s) provides an opportunity for the administrator to share theoretical input on the simulation and perhaps on how to handle similar situations in the future.

(d) Data integration sessions (wash-up sessions)

The purpose of the data integration session is for the observers to pool all the information about a specific participant that has been gained during the AC. Each observer will have the opportunity to present the participant's behaviour per simulation that he or she observed in detail per focal construct. The rest of the observer team will then consider the evidence presented by the specific observer and reach consensus on a rating for that specific focal construct (depending on the approach followed – see Chapters 10 and 16 for discussions about data integration approaches).

The observers might become defensive about the way that they have completed the observer report form or about the rating that they have allocated to the focal constructs. Since consensus must be reached, it could happen that the administrator will need advanced facilitation skills to ensure such consensus.

(e) Feedback discussions

In the case of a Diagnostic Centre (DC), the feedback session is the session where the participants themselves receive feedback on their performance during the DC. This might be the first time that they have access to the information. Sometimes their line managers will also be present. Every participant reacts differently depending on their personality, the participant-line manager relationship, the organisational culture and climate, as well as the AC's reputation. The reaction will also depend on the feedback skills of the person providing the feedback. The way in which the feedback report has been structured and worded further influences the participant's reaction.

In the case of an AC for selection purposes, the feedback will probably be given to the line manager who requested the AC, and perhaps also to the human capital representative. Not only will the content of this feedback discussion be different from that of the feedback session after a DC, but the content of the feedback report will also differ (see Chapter 17 for a more detailed discussion about giving feedback and report writing).

4.2.3 Training in administrative AC requirements

Since the administrator is professionally accountable for the whole AC process, a potential administrator also needs training in handling AC administrative duties professionally. Again, the recommended training process is for the potential administrator to first "observe" the duties being performed by an experienced administrator, then to receive guidelines regarding such duties. Thereafter, the potential administrator should actually perform the duties under close supervision, receive feedback regarding such performance, and progressively be allowed to perform the duties independently.

(a) Preparation for the AC

The first task is to book suitable venues for the AC if it is a traditional face-to-face AC. Once the venue bookings have been confirmed, the scheduling regarding the AC participants and process owners can start. The administrator needs to invite AC participant nominations according to the AC policy (see Chapter 5 for the content of the AC policy). Once the nominations have been received, the administrator must ensure that the nominated persons meet the requirements in respect of the AC target population. Those potential participants who are eligible to attend the AC need to be invited to the AC. The administrator must provide detailed feedback to the nominators of those who are not eligible for the AC.

The process owners also need to be confirmed. Again, if internal observers are to be used, they need to be at least two levels higher in the organisational structure than the target job level of the AC, and they must not have any relationship with the potential participants.

The administrator also needs to ensure that all the AC paperwork is photocopied, that it is checked for quality, and that it is packed in the required format for easy use during the AC.

The duties described above require the potential administrator to be trained in organisational skills, control, tact and diplomacy.

(b) Report writing

In some ACs it is required of the AC administrator to write final reports. These reports will have different recipients and serve different purposes. Where the report is intended for a participant who attended a DC, the content of the report should be developmentally focused. On the other hand, a report intended for a line manager who requested an AC will be written so as to indicate who performed the best during the AC. The potential administrator needs in-depth training in writing reports that will serve these respective purposes.

(c)   Statistical analysis

The fourth stage in the AC design model is the evaluation and validation stage. The potential administrator needs training in what information needs to be captured before, during and after each AC that will facilitate the statistical calculations during Stage Four. The administrator will also need training in performing some of the calculations and in interpreting the results. The AC design team will assist in the interpretation of the results, as well as in actioning the changes that are required.

5.   POSSIBLE SPECIALIST CAREER PATH IN ACs

Over the years, a possible specialist career path in ACs has emerged, which is for people interested in, and passionate about, ACs. It starts with attending an AC as a participant. After implementing the resulting development plan, training can start for the purpose of becoming an AC observer and role player. Once a person has become a competent observer and role player, the training in becoming an AC administrator can begin. Only after a person has been an AC administrator for a while are they ready to be a member of an AC design team. From there, growth can be into the position of an AC design team leader. If this has been accomplished successfully, it is time to head the whole project relating to AC design and implementation. It must be stated that most people never have the opportunity to be part of an AC design team. Instead, they are trained as observers, and remain very competent observers. A few people are trained to be AC administrators, but even fewer have the opportunity to design an AC.

The possible career path is indicated in Figure 15.5.

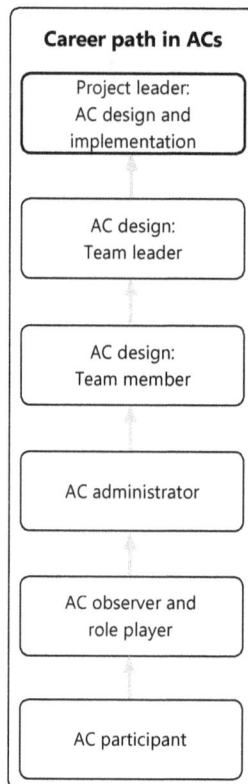

Figure 15.5: Possible career path in ACs

6.   TRAINING OF Decision MAKERS AND OTHER AC STAFF

The accountability of the AC process owners does not stop upon delivery of the AC results to the client organisation's decision makers. How the decision makers use the AC results impact the procedural fairness of the selection or development process and can potentially lead to unfair discrimination.[52] It is thus important that decision makers be trained on the use of AC results. Examples of the training content are:

- what is an AC, including the ten essential elements;
- the various purposes of ACs;
- the benefits of using an AC;
- ACs and the legal context;
- the organisation's AC policy; and
- how to use and interpret the specific AC's results.

Other AC staff need to be trained to fulfil their roles competently, for example the:

---

52 Employment Equity Act, (Act 55 of 1998); International Taskforce on Assessment Center Guidelines, 2015

- AC venue co-ordinator;
- AC data capturer (if not done automatically through an AC platform);
- AC material handler – the person who physically prepares all AC-related material and stores all material and participant exercise material;
- AC report writer (discussed in Chapter 17);
- AC feedback giver (discussed in Chapter 17);
- any other AC administrative and support staff; and
- Learning and Development staff, as well as coaches who will work with AC participants.

7. LOGISTICS AND AC PAPERWORK

Scheduling the appropriate people to attend an AC is very important. Another key aspect is ensuring that the logistical arrangements are made so that every person is where he or she should be on time, and with the necessary equipment and resources.

Since ACs will differ in their logistical needs, it is recommended that a checklist be drawn up to ensure that all arrangements are made in time and that all required resources are available.

As far as special needs relating to the venue of a face-to-face AC are concerned, there must be a main room that is capable of accommodating all the participants and process owners at the same time. Moreover, there must be enough breakaway rooms so that the various role plays can take place in an atmosphere where confidentiality is assured and there will be no disturbances.

When the AC is conducted at a venue where the participants and the process owners sleep over, the rooms must be able to accommodate people working at desks until late in the evening. It is recommended that an AC take place off-site at a venue with sleeping facilities. Mothers with young children in particular find it difficult to do the AC preparation work at home; most find it easier to arrange for someone to look after their children for the duration of the AC.

The equipment needs in respect of the AC will depend on the technology used during the administration of the various simulations. At the very least, the venue should be set up so that there is a data projector and access to enough electric sockets so that all participants can use their laptops. It is also useful if the venue has network coverage so that Internet access is possible.

Special attention should be given to the meal and refreshment requirements of everyone at the AC. Ensure that the venue will be able to serve the meals and refreshments at the times indicated on the AC programmes. Also ensure that the venue will be able to serve halal, kosher, vegan and vegetarian meals, as well as low-salt foods and foods for diabetics. In this regard, it is a good idea to develop a checklist for use by the administrator and venue coordinator.

Another aspect that can potentially lead to many problems is the AC material. The administrator needs to ensure that all the AC material is copied, checked, packed, checked again and ready for use before the AC starts. It is recommended that check lists be drawn up in respect of the material to be photocopied and packed. Sign-off of the material once it is correctly packed for use during the AC and sign-off again when the material is packed after the AC should take place.

An aspect that is usually forgotten is to ensure that a basic first-aid kit is packed for use during the AC. Ensure that there is enough headache medication and medication for indigestion. Plasters are also often used during an AC.

A lot, if not all, of these logistical arrangements and paperwork fall away when technology is used (ether a TEAC or a VAC). The administrator should then just check that all participants and process owners have access to the applicable material on time.

8. PARTICIPANT AND OBSERVER PRE-AC WORK

AC participants usually have pre-AC work. This can take the form of preparing for a simulation (e.g. a pre-AC prepared presentation) or completing personal background documents prior to the AC. Participants to a DC and DAC are sometimes requested to complete a 360-degree evaluation on the focal competencies that will be evaluated at the AC. Depending on the specific 360-degree form, participants have to obtain feedback from subordinates, colleagues and their line manager as to how they experience the participant's behaviour in relation to the focal constructs to be evaluated at the AC. The participants themselves need to complete the questionnaire as well. Apart from using the feedback from the 360-degree feedback questionnaire during the centre, the 360-degree evaluation result can also be used as part of the statistical evaluation and validation studies on the particular AC.

Each participant must consent to participate in the AC, as well as to the use of the AC results prior to the AC commencing. Participation needs to be preceded by informed consent. This means that participants need to know:
- what will be assessed during the AC;
- exactly who will have access to the AC results;
- where the results will be stored and under what conditions;
- for how long the results will be stored; and
- what the AC results will be used for.[53]

This explanation can be given in a document sent out prior to the AC, or the information can be shared during the orientation session at the start of the AC. However, an AC for selection purposes cannot continue unless the participants have handed in their signed consent forms.

The timelines for the pre-AC interaction with the participants can be as follows:
- Long in advance – confirm the participant's booking on the AC.
- Two weeks prior to the AC –send out invitation letters with all the logistical arrangements confirmed and the pre-work attached.
- Four days prior to the AC – send out a reminder indicating the AC times, venue and pre-work.

---

53 Protection of Personal Information Act, (Act 4 of 2013)

- The day before the AC – send out an SMS to all participants confirming the starting time of the AC as well as the venue.

9. CRITICAL DECISIONS RELATING TO THIS STEP AND ITS OUTCOMES

The following are the critical decisions relating to this step and its outcomes.

9.1 Competent AC process owners

A large enough pool of competent observers and role players is needed to ensure that these process owners are always available for every AC. The pool should consist of a wide variety of process owners so that every AC can be attended by a gender and culturally diverse team, reflecting the diversity of the AC participants. Most face-to-face ACs function with two administrators attending, however as mentioned, it would be wise to have other trained administrators available who can attend at short notice.

9.2 Effective logistical, material, venue and equipment arrangements

Even though an AC might be well designed and have the most competent observers and role players on hand, the quality of the whole AC suffers when problems arise with regard to the logistical, venue and equipment arrangements. Moreover, if the AC material is not ready when it is required, the AC cannot take place.

9.3 Participants informed and ready to participate in the AC

Participants must have completed their pre-work and be fully informed about the AC. In addition, they need to have given informed consent to participate in the AC before the AC can commence.

When the above three outcomes have been achieved, the AC can start.

CHAPTER 16

DURING THE CENTRE

Sandra Schlebusch

1. INTRODUCTION – PURPOSE OF THIS STEP

The second step during the implementation stage of the AC design model is the step that takes place during the AC itself. This step entails conducting the AC, according to the AC Manual, for the purpose for which it has been designed.

This step, namely overall step 9: During the centre, is depicted in Figure 16.1.

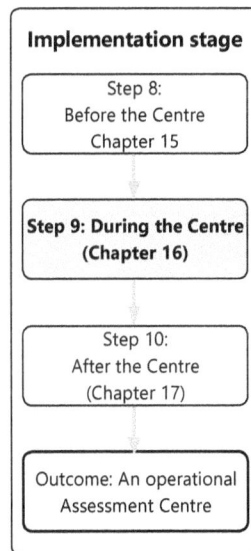

```
┌─────────────────────────────────┐
│      Implementation stage       │
│  ┌───────────────────────────┐  │
│  │          Step 8:          │  │
│  │      Before the Centre    │  │
│  │         Chapter 15        │  │
│  └───────────────────────────┘  │
│                                 │
│  ┌───────────────────────────┐  │
│  │  Step 9: During the Centre│  │
│  │       (Chapter 16)        │  │
│  └───────────────────────────┘  │
│                                 │
│  ┌───────────────────────────┐  │
│  │         Step 10:          │  │
│  │      After the Centre     │  │
│  │       (Chapter 17)        │  │
│  └───────────────────────────┘  │
│                                 │
│  ┌───────────────────────────┐  │
│  │  Outcome: An operational  │  │
│  │     Assessment Centre     │  │
│  └───────────────────────────┘  │
└─────────────────────────────────┘
```

Figure 16.1: The step, During the Centre, in the implementation stage

This chapter deals with conducting an effective AC. Some detail on the various orientation sessions, the debriefing sessions and the data integration session, as well as pitfalls and practical hints, will be shared. The chapter ends with a brief discussion on the critical decisions relating to, and outcomes of, this step.

2. CONDUCTING AN EFFECTIVE CENTRE

The challenge faced by every AC process owner is to conduct an effective AC each and every time one is presented. The AC is mostly perceived by the client organisation as being only as good as the last AC presented. Although the AC might be the process owners' 10th AC in a particular year, it is the first for the AC participant. Attention should therefore be given to ensuring that every detail of the AC goes according to plan. The AC Manual needs to be followed in detail, in large part to ensure that the AC is executed in a standardised manner.[1]

The AC Manual indicates, step by step, how an AC should be conducted. The manual contains the programmes, time schedules, instructions and documentation to be used during the AC.

3. ORIENTATION SESSIONS

Thorough orientation sessions with each group of people should take place at the start of every AC. The AC administrator is responsible for presenting these sessions. The AC Manual contains the information to be shared during the sessions.

3.1 Participant orientation session

The first experience that a participant has at an AC is the participant orientation session. The purpose of this session is to create the appropriate context in which the AC can take place. The possible questions that the participants might have can be answered and the participants' fears and anxieties about the AC can be addressed.

The following are typical topics that need to be addressed during the participant orientation session:
- The history of ACs in general and particularly in the client organisation.
- The purpose of the AC.
- Who will have access to the AC results.
- What an AC is and what simulations are.
- The focal constructs that will be evaluated during the AC.
- Which focal constructs will be evaluated during which simulation.
- The rating scale that will be used.
- The AC programme.
- Who the observers and role players are.
- Post-AC activities and process.
- Any other burning issue that the participants might table.

The AC participants must be fully oriented and prepared for the AC experience after the orientation session.[2]

3.2 Observer and role player orientation session

This session usually takes place the evening before the AC starts, or if two administrators attend the AC, the second administrator conducts the observer orientation session while the participant orientation takes place. The purpose of the session is to affirm the purpose of the AC and to orientate the observers to the client organisation, the target job and the participants.

---

1   Meiring & Buckett, 2016; International Taskforce on Assessment Center Guidelines, 2015
2   SA Assessment Centre Study Group, 2018

The following are typically the topics for the orientation session:
- The AC programme and any changes to the distributed programme.
- Any unusual situation, event or possible problem that the observers need to know about.
- Each observer's role and the participants he or she will observe.
- A discussion of the problems experienced during the previous AC, and how to rectify these.
- Highlighting any changes to the simulations or the AC Manual.
- Working through every simulation's observer report form as well as each competency and behavioural example.
- Confirming the use of the norm tables.
- Confirming that all the observers have the same frame of reference when it comes to the use of the norms.
- Confirming how each role should be played during every interactive simulation.
- Any other burning issue raised by the observers and role players.
- Clarifying that the observers have no relationship with any of the participants.

All the AC process owners must be ready to start and conduct an effective AC after they have attended the orientation session.

4.   PER-SIMULATION DEBRIEFINGS

Once the participants have experienced a simulation, they normally want to discuss their experiences. This can be done during the debriefing session. The purpose of the debriefing session is to allow the participants to share their experiences of the simulation with one another in a controlled environment. The administrator is present to answer questions and to reframe any possible negative experiences the participants might have had. During the debriefing session, the participants are also prepared for the simulation feedback that they will receive. Typically, during a debrief session the administrator will share theoretical input on the focal constructs evaluated during the simulation, as well as hints on how to handle future similar situations.

The type of AC will determine whether or not debriefing sessions will take place, and if so, how many. If it is an AC for selection purposes, a very short debriefing at the end of the last simulation will probably be held.

If the AC was for developmental purposes, a few possibilities exist. At a traditional DC, only one in-depth debriefing session takes place at the end of the last simulation. During this debriefing session, all the simulations are discussed. The advantage of having only one debriefing is that the duration of the AC is shorter for the participants.

During a learning DAC, debriefing sessions take place more often. For example, a debriefing can take place once a day or at the end of every simulation. If it is a collaborative DAC or a coaching DAC, debriefing sessions take place immediately after every simulation. After every debriefing session, the participant sits with a facilitator/coach (an observer) and, on a collaborative basis, evaluates his or her behaviour during the simulation.[3] The participant's learning therefore takes place during the debriefing

---

3   Woodruffe, 1993

sessions and also during the collaborative evaluation sessions with the facilitator/coach. The advantage of this approach is that the participant can implement his or her learning from the debriefing and evaluation discussion immediately during the next simulation.

5. AC PROCESS FLOW FROM AN OBSERVER PERSPECTIVE

The participant executes the simulations while the observers perform their role of observing and evaluating participant behaviour during the AC. The process of observation starts when the observer physically observes the participant in the execution of the simulations (either in-person or a video recording), or when the observer observes the participant's output after executing a simulation, for example In-Box responses. The observer classifies the participant's behaviour according to the AC focal constructs and either then allocates a rating according to the AC norm (PEDR), which he/she will present to the rest of the observer team during the data integration session, or no rating is allocated by the individual observer, who presents the participant's behaviour per focal construct to the team of observers who will allocate a rating per focal construct during the data integration session. Final ratings are allocated and the outcome is reported in either a profile of strengths and development areas, or an overall assessment rating. This process flow is depicted in Figure 16.2.

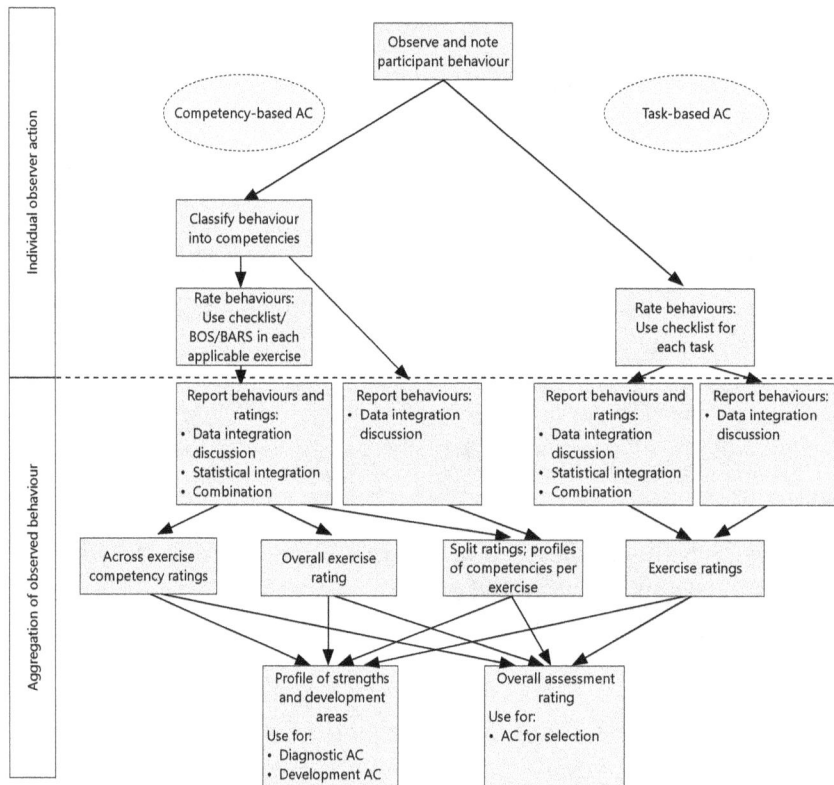

Figure 16.2: AC process flow
Source: Adapted from Thornton, Rupp and Hoffman[4]

---

4   Thornton et al., 2015: 100

In Figure 16.2, the various options of integrating the AC data is shown in the row of blocks underneath the dotted line. The integration can take place during a data integration session, by means of statistical integration, or a combination of the two approaches (these will be discussed in more detail in the following section).

Depending on the AC's approach, the observers either present the participant's behaviour per focal construct without having allocated a rating, or they present the behaviour per focal construct, first indicating their rating followed by the behavioural examples to support their ratings. The integration can take place per focal construct across simulations, or an overall exercise rating can be obtained. Split ratings can be allocated or exercise ratings can be obtained. Depending on the purpose of the AC, an overall assessment rating can be allocated, or a profile of strengths and development areas can be compiled.

6.   DATA INTEGRATION (WASH-UP)

AC participant behaviour linked to the AC focal constructs and observed during the various applicable simulations needs to be combined into ratings per competency, task or simulation, depending on the specific AC's approach. The integration takes place at the end of the AC after the observers finish completing the observer report forms for each participant. The integration can take place at various stages of evaluation, namely:[5]

- when the ratings per behavioural element during a simulation need to be combined into a within exercise dimension rating (WEDR), or an overall exercise rating (OER) needs to be determined;
- when two or more observers observed the behaviour of the same participant during a simulation and their ratings need to be combined;
- when WEDRs need to be combined into across exercise dimension ratings (AEDRs);
- when OERs are combined into an overall assessment rating (OAR); and
- when the results of the AC need to be combined with other ratings from outside the AC.

As was mentioned earlier, there are three approaches to integrating participant data: statistical, judgemental (having a discussion and reaching consensus) or a combination of the two.

6.1   Statistical (mechanical) integration

The statistical integration approach involves using a formula to combine ratings.[6] The ratings that need to be integrated can have equal weightings or differential weightings. When the ratings have equal weighting, the ratings are averaged to obtain the final rating. To avoid the effect that an extreme rating can have on the final rating, the median rather than the average can be used.

When differential weighting is used, the weight attached to each behavioural element, competency or simulation indicates the relative importance. For example:

---

5   Thornton et al., 2015

6   Thornton et al., 2015

OER (Role Play) = (2 x Information Gathering) + (4 x Judgement) + (3 x Empowerment) + (2 x Interpersonal Sensitivity) + Providing Direction

The differential weights in the example indicate that the most important competency in this simulation is Judgement, followed by Empowerment, Information Gathering and Interpersonal Sensitivity, and lastly, Providing Direction.

The differential weights can be based on:[7]
- organisational decision makers, or subject matter experts' opinion about the relative importance;
- job analysis findings; and
- statistical methods.

6.1.1 Advantages and disadvantages of statistical data integration

The advantages of using a statistical approach to integrate AC results are that it saves time and can be accurate if the observers are competent.[8] Some research findings suggest that statistical methods of combining data have more predictive validity (academic success and job performance) than judgemental approaches.[9] The disadvantages are that the accuracy is dependent on the competence of all the observers, and some of the rich information gained during a judgemental approach and used during feedback, is lost.

A recommendation is that the statistical data integration approach be used during an AC used for selection purposes.[10] Each AC will use its own formula. Of importance is that the same formula and the same procedure, rules and guidelines be consistently used from AC to AC, and from participant to participant, when deciding on a final rating per focal construct. This is necessary to ensure the validity of the AC (discussed during Stage Four of the design model). The use of algorithms is useful in this regard.

6.2 Judgemental (clinical) integration

The judgemental data integration session takes place at the end of the AC. The purpose of the session is to enable the observers to pool all the information on a participant and jointly decide on ratings per focal construct. It allows observers to openly discuss possible disagreements about the rating of participant behaviour during the various simulations and to discuss each participant's performance overall during the entire AC.[11]

The data integration session is facilitated by the administrator. The group of observers decides which participant's information will be integrated first. If two administrators attended the face-to-face AC and enough observers as well, it might be possible to split the session into two separate sessions that will take place simultaneously. However, the first participant's information will be integrated while both

---

7   Thornton et al., 2015
8   Thornton et al., 2015
9   Kuncel et al., 2013
10 Thornton et al., 2015; Thornton, 2011
11 Caldwell et al., 2003

administrators and all the observers attend the same session. This session, called the norm session, is held to ensure that all the process owners have the same frame of reference when it comes to the rating scale and norm. Usually, the administrators try to choose the participant who they think will perform the best on the focal constructs evaluated at the AC, as the participant for the norm session. The reason for choosing this participant is to allow the observers to use the full rating scale during the norm session.

Each observer will present the simulation they evaluated to the team of observers. He or she will usually start by giving an overview of the participant's approach to the simulation, before sharing with the group the rating he or she assigned for the focal construct. This is followed by the detailed behaviour evidence per behaviour element and the score he or she allocated per element. Each time the group of observers must confirm or disagree with the score per element and the final rating per focal construct. When the observers disagree, they must share with the group the reasons why they disagree and must suggest a new score or rating. The administrator facilitates this discussion until consensus is achieved.

The group of observers need to decide on a final rating per focal construct once all the individual focal constructs have been rated per simulation. Usually there will be a set of guidelines to guide the decision on the final rating. At a DAC, the rule usually applies that the lowest rating will determine the final rating. For example, if the participant received a 3 for a competency relating to the In-Box, a 2 for the same competency relating to the role play, and a 3 relating to the competency in the group meeting, the final rating will be a 2.

6.2.1 Summary of the discussion process

The process followed during the integration session can be summarised as follows:

a. Each observer classifies and evaluates all focal constructs by completing the observer report forms (ORF).
b. During the discussion:
    1. an observer presents all evidence per focal construct for the simulation he/she evaluated (source: Completed ORF);
    2. all other observers listen critically and evaluate the focal construct on a blank observer report form independently; and
    3. all observers discuss their ratings and reach consensus on a final rating per focal construct.
c. All final ratings per focal constructs are captured and consensus reached on the overall ratings.

6.2.2 Advantages and disadvantages of judgemental data integration

The advantages of this approach to data integration are that rich information is obtained that can improve the quality of feedback given to stakeholders, and the benefit of multiple perspectives is gained.

The disadvantages are that this approach is time consuming and various pitfalls might be experienced. The potential pitfalls are related to the pitfalls of group decision making, namely:[12]
- a verbally dominant observer may unduly influence the group's decisions;
- the most senior observer, or the majority opinion, may be accepted even though the minority proposed a qualitatively better decision;[13] and
- group think may occur, leading to the absence of critically questioning the information presented to the group.

During a discussion, it might happen that an inappropriate weight, not based on empirical information, be assigned to a specific simulation during which the focal construct is evaluated.[14] This could impact the validity of the final ratings. The possibility also exists that additional criteria, not part of the AC's focal constructs, be introduced into the decision making process.[15] For example, although it was not originally part of the AC design, the participant's fit with the organisational culture might be consciously or unconsciously used as criteria. Observers may communicate their general impressions of a participant to other observers and in so doing, might potentially unduly influence the ratings the participant receives on the AC's focal constructs, even though the focal constructs are unrelated to the expressed impression. Lastly, observers themselves complain that there is too much unnecessary and unproductive discussion during these conversations.[16]

6.2.3 Best practice guidelines for judgemental data-integration

Thornton, Rupp and Hoffman[17] suggested the following best practice guidelines for the observer data integration discussion:

a. Explain to the observer team (and adhere to) the data integration steps and procedure.
b. All observers need to take detailed notes of all participant behaviour during simulations.
c. Observers need to present behavioural evidence to support their ratings.
d. All observers first need to independently rate the specific aspect after being presented with all behavioural evidence (effective and ineffective behaviour examples) before the discussion starts.
e. All observers need to have the opportunity to change their initial ratings after hearing all behaviour evidence (allow time for this).
f. Reinforce the performance frame of reference during the integration session.
g. Encourage the observers to think critically and question the ratings and evidence.

In addition, encourage the observers to maintain high levels of work ethic, and ensure that the same team of observers does not always work together as a team during the various ACs to avoid group think. It is also recommended that the observers be kept accountable for effective role performance.

12 Thornton et al., 2015
13 Dewburry, 2011
14 Dewburry, 2011
15 Dewburry & Jackson, 2016
16 Dewberry & Jackson, 2016
17 Thornton et al., 2015

When it is necessary to obtain insight into participants' behaviour, especially tendencies that seem to be opposites of each other, judgemental data integration may be preferred so as to capture all information shared by the various observers about the participant's behaviour, for example, during a centre for developmental purposes.[18]

6.3 Combination approach to data integration

An alternative approach to data integration is to combine the statistical integration approach with the judgemental integration approach. For example, although a mathematical formula is used to integrate the ratings, observers still participate in a discussion to augment the final ratings with relevant behavioural examples. The advantage of this approach is that the potential higher predictive validity of the statistical method is maintained, while information that will enhance the feedback discussion is obtained. The disadvantage is that such an approach takes longer than just the statistical integration approach.

7. INTEGRATING OTHER ASSESSMENT RESULTS WITH SIMULATION RESULTS

Often simulations and other assessment instruments such as psychometric tests, interview results and 360° evaluations are used to evaluate the AC's focal constructs. The results from these instruments need to be integrated with the AC results. There are three approaches to integrating the results, namely the hurdles approach, the parallel processing approach, and the series processing approach.[19]

7.1 The hurdles approach

With this approach, the AC results form just one of multiple hurdles that the participants have to successfully navigate. For example, the results from the other assessment instruments are used to select-out applicants so that the AC is only attended by the shortlisted candidates. Figure 16.3 illustrates this approach.

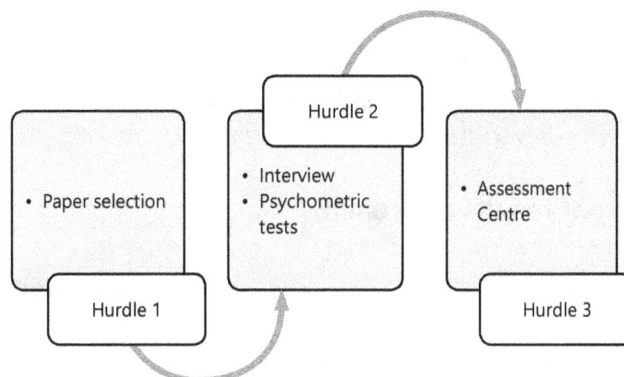

Figure 16.3: Example of the Hurdles Approach

18 Thornton, 2011
19 Thornton et al., 2015

During the selection process depicted in Figure 16.3, the applicants are evaluated according to the selection criteria based on their curriculum vitae and/or their application form. The successful candidates complete the required psychometric tests and participate in a selection interview. Only candidates who are successful during this hurdle will be invited to attend the AC. The advantage of this approach is that the large number of applications is reduced to a number that can cost-effectively participate in an AC. This approach is the typical approach that one of the big South African banks follows during their annual graduate selection process.

7.2 Parallel Processing of Results Approach

In this approach the results from all the assessment instruments are integrated to obtain final ratings per focal construct during the data integration discussion, or with a statistical formula or algorithm. This process is depicted in Figure 16.4.

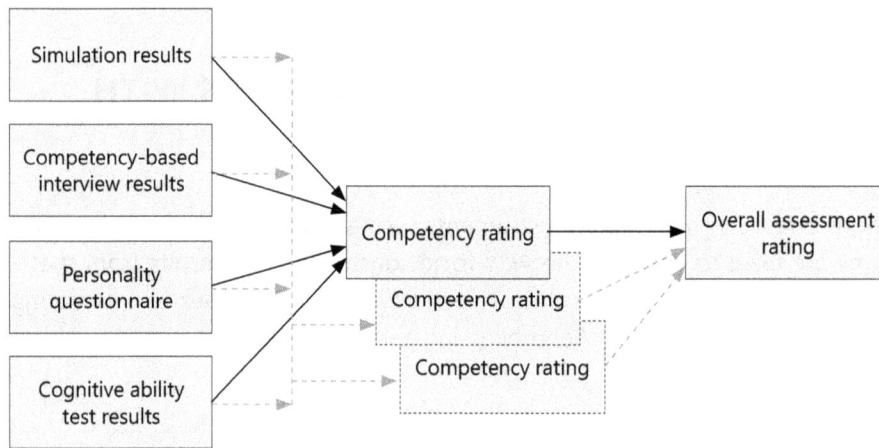

Figure 16.4: Example of the Parallel Processing of Results Approach
Source: Adapted from Thornton, Rupp and Hoffman[20]

The results from the various other assessment instruments are considered by the observer team (or the formula) together with the ratings obtained during the simulations to arrive at a final rating per focal construct. A possible disadvantage of this approach (when a data integration discussion is used) is that the team of observers needs to be knowledgeable about the interpretation of the other instruments' results. The training of the observers thus needs to accommodate this requirement.

7.3 Serial processing of results approach

With this approach the focal constructs are evaluated based on the results from the simulations and the final ratings. Only after the final ratings have been decided upon are the results from other assessments incorporated to determine the overall assessment rating. This can be done using the statistical approach, an algorithm, the data integration discussion, or by someone after the AC. This process is depicted in Figure 16.5.

---

20 Thornton et al., 2015: 142

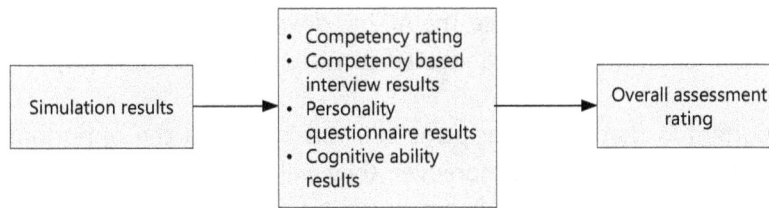

Figure 16.5: Example of the Serial Processing of Results Approach
Source: Adapted from Thornton, Rupp and Hoffman[21]

In the example, the competency ratings are decided upon first before the additional assessment results are considered to arrive at the overall assessment rating.

8. PITFALLS TO AVOID DURING AN AC

There are a few pitfalls to avoid during an AC. These will be discussed briefly.

8.1 Cutting time on the programme

During an AC it might happen that a participant has to withdraw, which creates a gap with regard to programme timelines. While the process owners may be tempted to make last-minute changes to the programme to fill the gap, these changes might affect the other participants' preparation time for simulations. This not only inconveniences the participants, but also impacts the consistency with which the ACs are conducted, since such practice constitutes a deviation from the AC Manual.

8.2 Observers are in a rush to finish[22]

Sometimes the observers are in a rush to finish the AC, so they start to agree to ratings during the data integration session that they would not normally agree to. Consequently, the quality of the AC suffers because the ratings have not been allocated in a consistent manner.

The observers may also be in a rush to finish classifying and evaluating behaviour on the observer report form after a simulation so that they can be on time for the next simulation that they need to observe. Again, the quality of the AC will suffer as not all of the participant's behaviour has been classified and, as a consequence, the ratings that the participant receives are not a true reflection of what transpired during the AC.

8.3 Not conducting debriefings owing to time pressure

It might happen that the AC is behind schedule, so to save some time and catch up on the programme, the process owners might be tempted not to conduct a scheduled debriefing session.

---

21 Thornton et al., 2015: 142

22 Dewberry & Jackson, 2016

If this debriefing session does not take place, the AC has deviated from the AC Manual. As a result, the ACs at the client organisation will not be conducted consistently in the same way.

What is more important is that the participants will not have had the opportunity to share their experiences of the particular simulation. Moreover, they will not have received any theoretical input into the focal constructs or on how to handle future similar situations. When they receive their ratings for a simulation during the feedback discussion, these might be a complete surprise to them, causing them to reject the feedback and not take action concerning any development recommendations.

8.4 Participants not openly sharing their experiences during debriefing sessions

Administrators sometimes interpret it as a good sign when participants do not participate during debriefing sessions, however since participants will have worked through the simulation, they will have experienced the simulation in a particular way. This means that they will have had an emotional reaction to the simulation – either positive or negative. If this emotion is not properly dealt with during the debriefing session, it can build up and surface in a harmful way. It is thus important for the administrator to ensure that all participants actively participate in the debriefing sessions. The participants need to air their views on the AC in an environment where concerns can be addressed constructively.

9. PRACTICAL HINTS

Apart from avoiding the pitfalls, there are also a few practical hints to apply that will contribute to effective ACs.

9.1 Ensure that the AC programme is followed

The AC programme is designed and tested during the design stage of the design model. The programme is accepted and signed off by the AC steering committee. The programme is also part of the AC Manual that will ensure that ACs are conducted in a similar manner over time.

There are reasons for the sequence in which the participants will do the simulations, which were considered when the programme was designed. If the sequence is changed, the integrity of the AC will be affected and, as a result, the validity of the AC.

Improvements to the programme can be made, however the changes must be noted so that subsequent ACs can be conducted accordingly.

9.2 Ensure that all documents are completed correctly, comprehensively and on time

It can be very frustrating when the person who captures the data after the AC discovers that some documents have not been completed correctly and/or comprehensively. This person then has to attempt to obtain the required information. This is not only a waste of time, but all the required information is also seldom collected after an AC. As a result, the data sets needed for the validation and evaluation stage are not complete and can therefore not be used.

The required action is for the process owner to ensure that all documentation is completed comprehensively and on time. The responsibility lies with the observer, but the accountability lies with the administrator to ensure that this is done.

9.3 The administrator must assist observers where possible

The overall professional accountability for the AC lies with the administrator, therefore he or she is also the person who the observers will consult. The administrator should not wait for the observers to ask for assistance, but should rather notice that an observer needs help and then volunteer it. The assistance can be in the form of him or her helping to classify and evaluate a simulation, requesting another observer to help out, or even bringing in a role player to play the roles that the particular observer had to play.

9.4 Where possible, all the process owners must interact socially with participants

In the past, especially during traditional ACs, observers kept to themselves. In some instances, they created the impression among the participants that they were the experts and had all the answers. They were even seen as being unapproachable.

Although the observers at an AC for selection purposes must still guard against unfairly giving hints to participants, they should interact with them as this helps to put the participants at ease. During a DAC, the interaction between the observers and participants will occur even more often and more freely. At a collaborative DAC or a coaching DAC, the facilitators are seen as the coaches and mentors of the participants, and interaction is therefore very frequent.

9.5 Note any deviation from the programme and any incident at the AC

The administrator needs to note any changes to the AC programme, as well as the reasons for the changes. This serves as a paper trail during the evaluation and validation stage. Likewise, if any out-of-the-ordinary incident has taken place at the AC, the administrator should make comprehensive notes of the incident. Not only is this good practice as far as creating an audit trail is concerned, but if any enquiries or queries about the incident are made later, the administrator can consult his or her notes.

Typical incidents to note would be an electricity cut or a participant becoming ill during the AC.

9.6 All process owners must model the behaviour, "Walk the talk"

The face validity and the integrity of the AC can be seriously impaired if the process owners are seen by the participants as behaving in contradiction to the behaviour suggested by the focal constructs being evaluated during the AC. This applies to behaviour both at the AC and outside the AC. For example, if participative management is encouraged at the AC, but one of the observers is a known autocrat in the work situation, the credibility of the AC will have been damaged. The possible message that some participants might get is that it is acceptable to be an autocrat, as long as you verbally indicate the opposite.

9.7 Arrange the feedback discussion with the participants while still at the AC

The feedback discussions should take place as soon as possible after the participant has attended the AC. This applies to both ACs conducted for selection purposes and DACs. The feedback discussion after a DAC is usually with the participant and their line manager. It is ideal to arrange this feedback session with the participants while they are still at the AC, as not only is it convenient for the AC administrator, but it also increases the credibility of the whole process from the participant's point of view as it shows the participant that feedback will take place as was promised.

Case Study: Where is the AC Data?

Background

A reputable South African organisation in the financial sector introduced an annual Assessment Centre as part of their multi-hurdle bursary selection process in 2012. The client organisation employed the services of a consulting firm to design the selection process, as well as the AC. The project allowed three weeks for the design, development and piloting of the whole selection process.

The selection process is as follows:

```
┌──────────────────┐
│ Hurdle 1:        │   • Selection based on information
│ Application      │     obtained from a comprehensive
│ form             │     competency-based application
└──────────────────┘     form
        │
        ▼
    ┌──────────────────┐
    │ Hurdle 2:        │   • Candidates participate in
    │ Interview and    │     an individual presentation
    │ simulation       │     simulation and a competency-
    └──────────────────┘     based interview
            │
            ▼
        ┌──────────────────┐
        │ Hurdle 3:        │   • Candidates
        │ Assessment       │     participate in
        │ Centre           │     2.5 day AC
        └──────────────────┘
```

The AC consists of both psychometric tests (the tests are registered with the HPCSA) and custom-developed simulations. The psychometric tests that are used are an integrity questionnaire and a cognitive ability assessment.

The simulations are two Leaderless Group Discussions (LGDs), one Assigned Leader group exercise and an Individual Analysis Exercise (Case Study) (written activity).

Five dimensions are evaluated during the AC which are deemed important by the organisation's senior management. The Observer Report Forms use a BARS approach and a five-point Likert type scale. Dimensions are rated after every simulation following a Post Exercise Dimension Rating (PEDR) approach. All ratings are combined statistically using an algorithm to obtain an overall assessment rating (OAR) and to rank order all candidates. The final decision to award bursaries is a senior management decision.

AC observers are volunteers from the organisation who attend a one-and-a-half day training programme prior to the AC. Observers work in teams of three with a ratio of one observer for every two candidates.

The AC administrators ensure that all AC materials are collected after every AC and that candidate results are stored securely.

Operationalising the Selection Process

Through active marketing that includes various media campaigns and visits to schools and universities, interest in the organisation is created. Annually approximately 3,000 candidates apply for the bursary, yet only 150 bursaries are awarded. Approximately 300 candidates attend the AC annually. There are normally three separate ACs of 100 candidates each.

The annual ACs usually take place during weekends in holiday season so that the least disruption is caused in the lives of the candidates and observers. The AC programme has tight deadlines leading to the observers working extended hours to be able to finish all evaluations in time for the statistical integration to take place.

Although candidates find the overall experience motivational, they are also busy with activities for extended hours during the AC, leading to them being tired at the end of the AC. Each year activities are included on the candidates' programme that are not related to the selection process. These activities are aimed at building a positive organisational image, as well as activities from which candidates can learn knowledge and skills that might assist them as students. These additional activities differ from year to year.

The Challenge

After conducting the selection process for five years, the organisation identified the need to validate the selection process against academic results achieved at university. The need to validate the process was based on management wanting to establish whether the tools used by the organisation were valid and reliable and whether they showed any form of predictive validity. Management also wanted to perform a qualitative review around its Success Profile methodology. The team wanted to know whether they were on the right track in selecting the right individuals for their programme. Again, the services of a consulting firm, this time specialising in statistics, was enrolled.

Each assessment instrument in the selection process individually, as well as the whole process' reliability, construct and predictive validity, were to be determined. It was decided that Confirmatory Factor Analysis (CFA) as well as regression analysis would be used as statistical methods.

The starting point was to access complete data sets on the bursary holders. This proved to be a challenge since not all candidates' selection processes and other data were captured centrally on a CRM system. There was also the issue of the data for candidates scoring lower not being captured. This meant that before a data file could be handed to the service provider for analysis, the data had to be sourced from the storage company and captured electronically. Not only was this a very laborious and time-consuming task that lasted six months, but it was discovered that not all data per bursary holder was readily available. In addition, the specific

AC observers per candidate, per simulation, were never noted. Further, there was no criterion data available about the candidates not selected as bursary holders. The available AC results were only at dimension level, not at dimension behavioural element level, resulting in the analysis not being done on simulation raw scores.

The Results

A total of three data sets, consisting of 1,120 complete cases, were created. Hurdle 1 – the application form – delivered moderate reliability, but poor construct and predictive validity. The simulation of hurdle 2 delivered moderate reliability, but again, poor validity and a strong exercise effect. The reliability and the construct validity of the psychometric tests used during hurdle 3 – the AC – were not calculated, as the AC was conducted separately to the validation study. One of the tests showed very poor predictive validity, while the four simulations of the AC showed exercise effects, but not construct validity. However, the combined scores of hurdles 2 and 3 showed a 60% correlation with academic success at university.

Based on the validation project's results, the organisation decided on the following:
- Clarify through research the dimensions (the focal constructs) to be evaluated during the selection process.
- Re-design and develop the selection process, as well as the AC.

Lessons Learnt

Going through the whole validation project allowed the organisation to learn the following lessons:
- Base the focal constructs of a selection process on evidence-based data, not the opinion of senior management.
- Follow a process with scientific rigour when designing a selection process.
- Specifically, follow a rigorous process, allowing adequate time, when designing and developing the AC.
- Ensure that all ACs are delivered in a standardised manner. This means that the additional, non-evaluated AC candidate activities need to be standardised for all future ACs.
- Re-design the AC programme to allow enough time for observers to classify and evaluate behaviour.
- Redesign the Observer Report Forms so that observers' biographical details can be captured. This will allow for inter-rater reliabilities to be calculated, as well as the identification of potential rater biases.
- Agree during the design stage what data need to be captured and design all documents to accommodate the data requirements.
- Ensure that all candidate and observer data are captured at behavioural element level directly after each AC. Capturing data at the behavioural element level will assist in calculating construct validity, while capturing data immediately after every AC will ensure that comprehensive and complete data are available on time.
- Include determining content validity in future validation projects.
- Conduct validation studies at regular intervals so that just-in-time adaptions and corrections can be made to the whole selection process.

10. CRITICAL DECISIONS RELATING TO THIS STEP, AND THE OUTCOMES THEREOF

The following are the critical decisions relating to this step, and the outcomes thereof.

10.1 Valid and reliable participant profiles

After every AC, the profiles of the participants should be valid and reliable, as only then will it be possible to compare participant profiles with one another over time. Valid and reliable profiles will only result if the process owners competently fulfil their roles and if the AC Manual is followed consistently during every AC.

10.2 AC participants are positive towards the AC

If the AC participants are positive towards the AC, they will be more likely to implement the development recommendations. Consequently, over time, a positive perception of the AC is created within the client organisation and this helps to assure its future existence. Word of mouth is very powerful from a marketing perspective. If all, or most, AC participants are positive about the AC, they will probably tell their colleagues about it, which could then create a waiting list of people who want to attend.

10.3 The ACs are conducted consistently according to the AC Manual

At the end of the day, the client organisation will want to know whether the AC measures accurately and consistently. To answer these questions, the AC's reliability and validity need to be shown. If the AC process owners consistently conduct the ACs according to the AC Manual, it will be easier for the AC design team to show that the AC evaluates accurately and consistently.

CHAPTER 17

AFTER THE CENTRE

Sandra Schlebusch

1. INTRODUCTION – PURPOSE OF THIS STEP

Step 10, namely After the Centre, is the last step in the implementation stage of the design model. The purpose of this step is to ensure closure concerning all aspects relating to the specific AC, to prepare the data for the evaluation and validation stage, to create safe storage of AC data, and to take action to ensure the future use of the AC. Tasks need to be done to ensure that the participants of a Diagnostic Centre (DC) or Development Assessment Centre (DC) follow a development plan, that the people who requested an AC for selection purposes have the answers they require, that all the required data for research is captured, and to maintain the AC to ensure its continued future in, and relevance to, the client organisation.

This step is depicted in Figure 17.1.

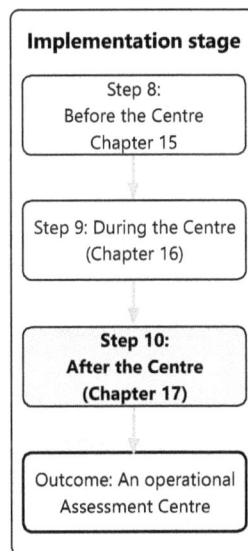

Implementation stage

> Step 8:
> Before the Centre
> Chapter 15

> Step 9: During the Centre
> (Chapter 16)

> **Step 10:**
> **After the Centre**
> **(Chapter 17)**

> Outcome: An operational
> Assessment Centre

Figure 17.1: The step, After the Centre, in the implementation stage

This chapter is divided into two sections. The first section focuses on the processes related to the participant and the people who requested the AC. Aspects like feedback, the development plan, the growth framework and other related human capital processes are discussed. The second section focuses on processes related to the maintenance and future of the AC. The chapter ends with a brief discussion on the critical decisions relating to this step, and the outcomes thereof.

2. POST-AC PROCESSES RELATED TO THE PARTICIPANT

The AC participants are arguably the most important people attending an AC. Their behaviour during the various simulations at the AC is observed and evaluated by the observers. If the AC was for selection purposes, the line manager who requested the AC receives feedback afterwards on the various participants' performance. The feedback will typically be in the form of a feedback discussion and a written report.[1] After attending a Diagnostic Centre (DC) or a Development Assessment Centre (DAC), the process continues with the participants receiving feedback and a development plan to implement.

A personal development plan is drawn up during a DAC, while a development plan is drawn up after a DC. Development plans are optional after an AC for selection purposes. The development process after a DC or DAC is depicted in Figure 17.2.

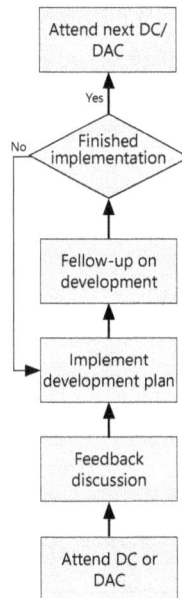

Figure 17.2: Post-DC / DAC development process

A feedback discussion takes place after the participant has attended the DC or DAC, which typically includes the participants and their line managers. During this discussion, the participants' development plans are drawn up or finalised. After the discussion, the participants implement the action agreed upon during the discussion and indicated on the development plan. After approximately six to eight months, a follow-up discussion takes place at which the participant's development is reviewed and the development plan is adapted accordingly. The process of follow-up discussions continues until all the agreed-upon actions on the development plan have been implemented and everyone agrees that the development areas have developed. The participant can then attend another DC or DAC to continue their development journey.

Since feedback forms the bridge between what has happened at the AC and the consequences of the AC, we will discuss the feedback process in detail.

---

1 Thornton et al., 2017

2.1   Feedback

Feedback can be described as sharing the participant's performance related to the AC's focal constructs and norm during the AC, and linking it to consequences and the work situation.[2] It is based on the participant's behaviour during the AC's simulations and other applicable assessment activities. The purpose of the specific feedback depends on the purpose of the AC, as well as the needs of the feedback recipients. However, in general, the purpose of feedback is to provide insight into a participant's behaviour during the AC. The lack of providing feedback to the AC participants is listed by both AC designers and AC participants as an example of a feature of problematic ACs.[3] Since an AC participant has the right to request feedback about their own performance, it is recommended that feedback always be given to them.[4] This may assist in creating positive regard for the specific AC and ACs in general.[5]

The feedback could be in the form of a feedback discussion as well as a written report.[6] A feedback discussion provides an opportunity to discuss the participant's current areas of strength as well as those areas needing further development. The participant's performance on each focal construct during each simulation is discussed. Although an overall picture of performance is created during the feedback discussion, the feedback recipients may not be able to fully comprehend the feedback at the time. The written report therefore provides the documentation that can be studied at a later stage and should assist the participant to fully comprehend the feedback.

The feedback can be given by the AC administrator, the AC observers, or a person specifically trained to give post-AC feedback.[7] However, it is recommended that only people trained and competent in AC methodology, and who are competent observers at the specific AC, give feedback. It is also advisable that only people who attended the specific AC give feedback to the AC feedback recipients.

Several variables influence feedback which will now be discussed in more detail.

2.1.1   Variables influencing feedback

The variables influencing the content and format of the feedback are:[8]
- the purpose of the AC (selection or development);
- the type of development centre (DC or DAC);
- the recipients of the feedback (the AC participants and their line managers, organisational decision makers, and representatives of the human capital department);
- the feedback recipients' knowledge and experience of ACs;

---

2   Thornton et al., 2015; SA Assessment Centre Study Group, 2018

3   Dewburry & Jackson, 2016

4   SA Assessment Centre Study Group, 2018; Meiring & Buckett, 2016, Protection of Personal Information, (Act 4 of 2014)

5   Thornton et al., 2017

6   Abraham et al., 2006; Thornton et al., 2017

7   The British Psychology Society for Organisational Psychology, 2015

8   Schlebusch & De Wet, 2007

- organisational aspects (organisational culture and climate, organisational practice); and
- other people-related processes within the organisation (e.g. succession development programmes).

a) Purpose of the AC

Where the AC was for selection purposes, the feedback may be simplistic[9], indicating the overall assessment rating. The written report can be a combined report where all the AC participants' final ratings per focal construct are provided. In addition, a short discussion on the performance of each participant can be included. However, in a report after a DC or DAC, more detail is given to the participants on their behaviour regarding each focal construct. A DC report, for example, will probably indicate a profile of the AC participant's strengths and development areas. Typically both positive and negative behavioural examples, as well as recommended development activities, are shared during the feedback following a DAC.

b) Type of development centre (DC or DAC)

After a DC, the administrator or one of the DC observers will generally write a detailed report on the participant's behaviour. The participants will only gain insight into their actual performance at the DC during the feedback discussion post DC. The feedback giver will probably fulfil a more directive role during the feedback discussion so as to share the results and explain the reasons for each rating.

However, where the participants have attended a DAC, they might write the final report themselves, with the assistance of an observer, during the DAC.[10] The participants will therefore be fully aware of how they performed during the DAC and they themselves will be able to give feedback during the feedback discussion to their line manager on their performance at the DAC. The feedback giver will probably only fulfil the role of a facilitator during the DAC feedback discussion. S/He will guide the discussion by asking questions from time to time and by answering questions from the participant and line manager.

c) Feedback recipients

Different feedback recipients will in all likelihood have different needs, hence the focus of the feedback will probably differ. Although the overall message will remain the same, the feedback should be adapted to the needs of the recipients. For example, AC participants may want to know how they performed on the focal constructs in relation to the norm, as well as how they can develop or strengthen the required behaviour. AC participants' line managers might, in addition, be interested in how they can support the AC participants' development. The organisational decision makers might want to know who to include on a programme such as succession development, while the representatives from the human capital department might need to know what organisational support they need to provide to the AC participant.

---

9   Thornton et al., 2017
10 Goodge, 1994

d) Feedback recipients' knowledge and experience of ACs

The feedback recipients' experience and knowledge of ACs influence the feedback. If the recipients are unfamiliar with ACs, the danger exists that the feedback recipients might misunderstand the feedback. The feedback giver should therefore ensure that there is clarity regarding exactly what was and was not evaluated, as well as regarding what the results can be used for and how to interpret the AC results. A written report should be given to line managers or inexperienced human capital practitioners only after an in-depth feedback discussion has taken place.

e) Organisational aspects

Organisational aspects might impact the AC participants' initial reaction to the feedback, as well as the implementation of the recommendations from the feedback and possible behavioural changes.[11] The support that the organisation as a whole provides, but specifically the support from the AC participants' direct line managers, are of importance when it comes to behavioural change after receiving feedback. The organisational culture and current climate could be important influencing factors. If, for example, the culture of the client organisation is described as a high-performance culture and this is combined with a climate where development is seen as a last resort in "sorting out below-par performance", participants will probably struggle to accept that any focal construct evaluated during the DC needs further development. Typically the participants may resort to defensive behaviour and even start attacking the AC itself and the process owners.

Another organisational factor that can potentially affect how the feedback is received and actioned is the trust levels between management and the rest of the employees. If the organisation has just been through an amalgamation and rumours of possible retrenchments are doing the rounds, AC participants might be suspicious of how the DC or DAC results will be used. Again, this might lead to defensive behaviour during the feedback discussion.

f) Other people-related processes

Other internal processes that influence the AC feedback are, for example, succession development and the talent pipeline. An AC might be used to select delegates for the organisation's succession programme(s). The AC results will probably be discussed in a forum of line managers and human capital practitioners (the Talent Review Committee) who need to decide on the succession development delegates. Once delegates have been accepted on the programme(s) they might attend a DAC with the purpose of drawing up a development plan to guide their growth while they are part of the succession development programme(s). The feedback from the DAC might then be shared with the Talent Review Committee in addition to the participant's line manager. The feedback will probably be positioned in the context of the programme that the centre forms part of.

---

11 Blume et al., 2010; McCarthy & Garavan, 2006

2.1.2   Information shared during feedback

The kind of feedback provided to AC stakeholders differs from organisation to organisation. An international survey on AC practices identified nine typical kinds of feedback.[12] The feedback in Figure 17.3 distinguishes between the purpose of the AC, namely for selection only; for selection and development; and for development only or primarily.

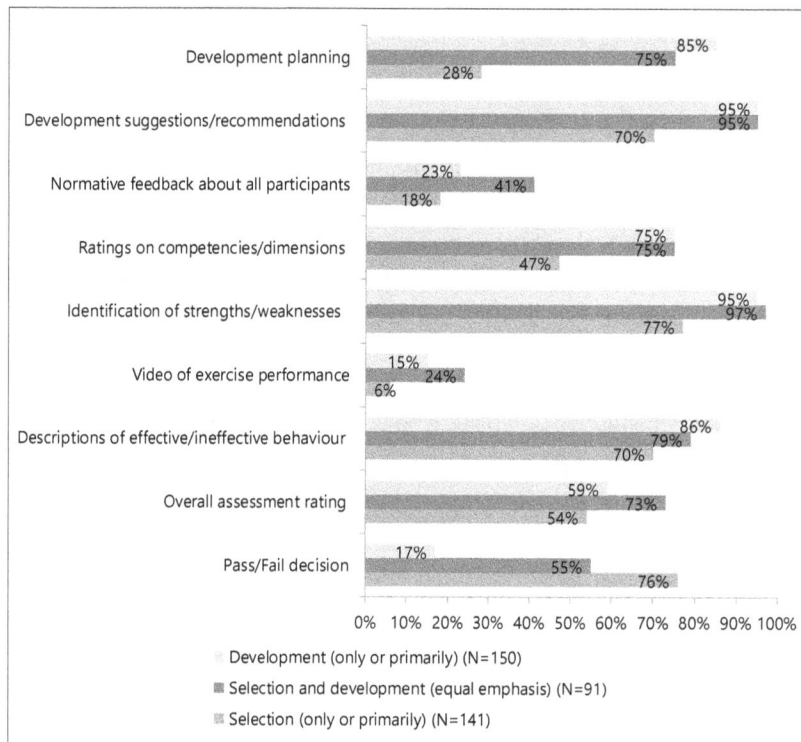

Figure 17.3: Information shared during feedback
Source: Adapted from Hughes, Rilley, Shalfoosan, Gibbons and Thornton[13]

Although 76% of ACs for selection purposes provided a pass/fail decision, only 17% of ACs for development purposes provided this kind of feedback. Development planning usually takes place during/after ACs for developmental purposes, while only 28% of ACs for selection purposes focus on this. It seems that video recordings of participant performance are seldom shared as feedback during all ACs (ACs for development – 15%; ACs for development and selection – 24%; and ACs for selection – 6%). The identification of strengths and weaknesses are shared during feedback related to ACs for all three purposes indicated in Figure 17.3.

Irrespective of the purpose of the AC, the minimum information that needs to be shared during feedback is the focal constructs, the simulations, the norm, the participant's performance, development

---

12   Hughes et al., 2012

13   Hughes et al., 2012, p52

recommendations, the process owners at the specific AC, and the specific needs of the feedback recipients.[14] These will briefly be discussed.

(a) Focal Constructs

First the focal constructs need to be explained[15], then the behavioural elements in each focal construct, and thereafter the behaviour that is linked to each focal construct. If possible, examples should be given of the behaviour.

(b) Simulations

Secondly, all the simulations used during the AC need to be explained. A brief description of each simulation should be given and the role fulfilled by the participant during the simulation needs to be explained. An indication should also be given of which focal constructs were evaluated during the simulation.

(c) Norm

Thirdly, the norm used during the AC should be explained. For example, it could be indicated that the participant's behaviour was evaluated against the behaviour of an effective middle manager in the client organisation.

(d) Participant behaviour

The fourth aspect that should be included in the feedback is the participant's actual behaviour during the AC. This is the participant's behaviour during the simulations that is linked to the focal constructs being evaluated, as well as the final ratings.

(e) Development recommendations

The fifth aspect that needs to be covered during the feedback is the recommendations on how to improve each development area. It is important to relate the recommendations to the work situation and make them practical. For example, an on-the-job activity to improve the competency, "Information Gathering", could entail the participants drawing up a checklist with the questions, "Who, what, where, when and how". They then keep the checklist on their desk to remind themselves to ask these questions every time they are presented with a problem.

(f) AC process owners

It is recommended that the process owners who attended the specific AC also be indicated during the feedback. This can potentially increase the AC's credibility and ease the process of contacting the appropriate people if there are any queries.

---

14 Schlebusch & de Wet, 2007

15 Thornton et al., 2015

(g) Address specific needs

Lastly, apart from the minimum information that needs to be shared during the feedback session, the various feedback recipients will also have specific needs that they will expect to be met during the feedback.

For example, the DC or DAC participants will want to know what they did well and what needs to improve. The participants would probably also like to know what they will need to do more of, or less of, in order to improve their own competence. In addition, the participants will likely have unique questions and fears that they would like answered and addressed. Another need that most DC or DAC participants have is the need to know "the road ahead". The feedback giver must explain, in detail, how the future development will take place, as well as the follow-up process (if any).

The feedback recipients of an AC for selection purposes will need to know how each AC participant performed. In addition, they might want to know which person from among the AC participants they should select or appoint. In this regard it is recommended that the AC participants be ranked during the feedback, but that the final decision be left to the feedback recipients. It is advisable to suggest that the AC results be used in conjunction with other instruments' results in making a final decision.

2.1.3 General principles guiding feedback

There are general principles to abide by when it comes to effective feedback, i.e. it needs to be timely, objective, behaviour-oriented, constructive and supportive, practical, positive, open and honest, as well as balanced.[16] We will briefly discuss these principles.

(a) Timely

Feedback after an AC, whether for selection or developmental purposes, should take place as soon as possible. Since the AC participants who attend a selection AC will have applied for appointment to a specific position or entry into a certain programme, they will probably be experiencing anxiety while waiting for feedback. The people who requested the AC will also be anxious to receive feedback so that they can proceed with the selection process.

The feedback given to the DC or DAC participants also needs to take place as soon as possible after the DC or DAC to allow the participants to receive the feedback while they still remember what happened during the centre. Receiving feedback soon after the centre will further enable the participants to start implementing their development plan as soon as possible.

(b) Objective and behaviour-oriented

Since the behaviour of the AC participant during the various simulations at the centre will have been evaluated, the feedback should focus on the participant's behaviour and not personal characteristics.

---

16 Thornton et al., 2017; The British Psychological Society, 2015; Schlebusch & De Wet, 2007

For example, it should be stated, "It is recommended that Ms Dlamini engage in more openly debating issues during interactive situations", rather than stating, "It is recommended that Ms Dlamini be less of an introvert during interactive situations".

(c) Constructive and supportive

The feedback should be given in a manner that is perceived by the AC participants as being supportive and constructive regarding their own growth and development. If the participants perceive the feedback as an opportunity to learn about improving their own competence in the work situation, they might be more open to the feedback and more willing to implement the development recommendations.

(d) Practical

Feedback recipients after an AC for selection purposes need practical advice on how to develop the identified development areas. This information might be used to draw up a development plan for the successful candidate(s), or to give guidance to the unsuccessful candidates.

The DC and DAC participants should be given ideas on how to develop the various identified areas needing further development. It is recommended that not only attending training programmes be identified as learning opportunities, but also practical, day-to-day actions that the participants can implement.

(e) Positive

The AC participants cannot change what has happened in the past, but they can change what will happen in the future. It is therefore recommended that the feedback not focus on what the participant did not do during the AC, but rather on what the participant can do in future similar situations. This does not mean that the participants will not get the message concerning their actual performance during the AC, but the focus is rather on the future. For example, rather state, "It is recommended that Ms Flint involve other people in problem solving during interactive situations by asking for their solutions to the problems", instead of stating, "Ms Flint did not involve any other person in the process of solving problems during interactive situations". The participant will probably experience it as more motivating when the feedback is focused on future actions; it can be demotivating to continuously hear what should have been done.

The choice of words is also important. Instead of referring to "weaknesses", rather refer to "development areas". "Development area" sounds to most people that something can be done to change the area, while a "weakness" sounds as though it is a permanent state.

(f) Open, honest and balanced

The feedback giver should be open and honest in the process of giving feedback. Since the feedback process is not a popularity contest, the feedback giver should not create a perception that the participant's behaviour will lead to effective outcomes in the work situation when in fact it will not. A clear picture of the participant's behaviour, as well as of the consequences of the behaviour, needs to be provided, irrespective of whether the consequences will be positive or negative, or whether the feedback giver will be liked.

The feedback should be balanced. Positive feedback, as well as feedback on development opportunities, should be provided. It seldom, if ever, happens that only development opportunities per competency are identified. Usually, current areas of strength (behavioural elements already in place) are also identified. Feedback on those elements already in place should also be given.

2.1.4 Written feedback

The line manager and human capital practitioner who requested the AC for selection purposes should receive a written report for reference purposes, while each DC and DAC participant should receive a written report. These two different types of recipient (DC and DAC versus AC feedback recipients) have unique needs that will dictate the format and content of the written report.

We will now discuss the various feedback reports and provide some practical hints on writing reports.

(a) Written feedback after an AC for selection purposes

Probably the most pressing need of the recipient of the report (line manager(s) and human capital practitioners) is to have an overview of all participants' performance relative to the AC norm, as well as to one another.

To satisfy this need, a combined report can be written. A combined report indicates all the final ratings per focal construct, per participant, in a matrix. The report should perhaps also provide a brief description of each participant's performance per simulation, per focal construct. In the report, the final ratings and/or the overall assessment rating, per participant, are also given in ranked order.

(b) Written feedback after a DAC

The purpose of the written report after a DC or DAC is to serve as a reference for the participants in the months to come when they are unsure of a development area or area of strength, or of any other aspect related to the DC or DAC.

The participants themselves, or the AC administrator or an AC observer who attended the particular DC or DAC, can write the report. When the participants have attended a collaborative DAC, the participants will be writing their own final report with the assistance of a facilitator.[17] The facilitator will guide the participant so as to ensure that the report is comprehensive and covers all the focal construct elements.

---

17 Goodge, 1994

When the AC administrator or an AC observer writes the report, they will use the simulation observer report forms to guide them. They need to comment on every focal construct element mentioned in the observer report form. The report also usually includes an overview of how the participant approached each simulation.

The format of the report can either be in the form of comments per simulation, per focal construct, or per focal construct, per simulation. It is also recommended that summary tables be included in the report. A summary table allows an overview of all the focal construct elements at a glance.

The format in which feedback is given in a report is usually to first comment on the current areas of strength, and thereafter on the development areas.

(c) Hints on writing reports

The report should provide appropriate feedback on the simulations used, on the focal constructs and focal construct elements evaluated during the DC or DAC, on the participant's performance and current areas of strength, and on current areas needing further development. Development recommendations should be given in the report.

Positive words should be used. Rather recommend future behaviour instead of writing about what the person did not do during a simulation. Use the word "could" instead of "should". Refer to "areas needing further development" and not to "weaknesses" (as indicated earlier).

Another recommendation is to adhere to the principles of clear writing. This is especially important as English (the preferred business language and probably the language in which the report will be written) is not the home language of most South Africans. It is therefore the responsibility of the person who writes the report to use language that is easy to understand.

(d) Principles of clear writing

Adherence to the following principles by the author of a report will assist the reader of the report to easily understand it:[18]
- *Use simple words.* A simple word is a word with only one meaning. It is also a word in general use. For example, rather use the word "help" instead of "facilitate" if you mean that assistance should be given. Moreover, rather say, "It will worsen the situation" than writing, "It will exacerbate the situation".
- *Use short and simple sentences.* A simple sentence is a sentence containing only one major idea. A short sentence is about 20 words in length. On average, the sentences in the report should each comprise about 20 words. The longer and more complex a sentence, the greater the risk of the reader not understanding the message.
- *Use paragraphs.* A paragraph is a group of sentences containing related ideas. A report should be structured into paragraphs, however a paragraph should not be too long.

---

18 Joseph, 1977

- *Give preference to the active voice, not the passive voice.* When writing in the active voice, fewer words are used to convey the message. Text in the active voice is also easier to read. However, there will be situations where it is advisable to use the passive voice, for example when the message is very negative, it is easier to soften the message by conveying it in the passive voice.
- *Use a clarity or readability index to determine the ease of reading the report.* The Gunning-Fog Index is an example of such an index.

2.1.5   The feedback discussion after a DC and DAC

As stated earlier, the purpose of feedback is to provide insight into the participant's behaviour during the AC. In addition, after a DC or DAC, the purpose of the feedback discussion is to agree on a development plan for the participant. The participants therefore need to accept their development areas and take ownership of their own development plan.

To assist the feedback giver to create a situation where the participant accepts and takes ownership of his or her development, certain principles, hints and techniques will be shared.[19]

(a) Principles that apply during a feedback discussion

There are certain principles that the feedback giver needs to adhere to before and during the feedback discussion. These 12 principles will be discussed below:

Principle 1: Have a healthy self-worth

The underlying principle is to model the behaviour that the participant needs to demonstrate. In addition, a healthy self-worth means that the feedback giver will not view any possible negative reaction on the part of the DC or DAC participant as a personal attack. A healthy self-worth will enable the feedback giver to respond to the participant's reaction in a mature and professional manner.

Principle 2: Belief in the DC/DAC

If the feedback giver does not believe in the DC or DAC process, he or she cannot expect the participant to attach any value to feedback from the DC or DAC. Only when the feedback giver truly believes in the DC or DAC and in the benefits that the participant can potentially enjoy from developing the identified areas, will the participant also be able to believe in the value of the DC or DAC.

Principle 3: Be clear as regards the message

Before engaging in the feedback discussion, the feedback giver should have prepared well. In addition, he or she should have clarity regarding the main message that needs to be delivered

---

19 Schlebusch & De Wet, 2007

to the participant. For example, if the participant has many areas needing development, the participant might be overwhelmed by the task that lies ahead. In such a case, the feedback giver must be able to focus the participant's attention on the most important aspect that will have the greatest impact in the work situation. For instance, it might be that if the participant just focuses on really listening to other people, his or her interpersonal sensitivity will improve greatly.

Principle 4: Be "present" during the feedback discussion

Feedback givers should not have any other conversation going on in their heads while they are conducting the feedback discussion. They should focus totally on what the participant is saying, and not saying, during the discussion. They should focus on responding to the needs of the participant so that the participant receives the most benefit from the discussion.

Principle 5: Do not defend the DC/DAC or try to impress during the feedback discussion

It sometimes happens that the participant reacts to the feedback by attacking the validity and reliability of the DC/DAC or the competence of the centre's process owners. Apart from stating that a systematic and rigorous process has been followed in the analysis and design phases, and that the process owners are all competent, do not enter into a debate with the participant regarding those aspects of the DC or DAC that are being attacked. The focus of the feedback discussion should rather be on the participant's behaviour during the DC or DAC, and what he or she can do to develop the competencies concerned.

Principle 6: Get the participant's emotions out of the way

DAC participants are unique individuals. Consequently, each participant will react differently to the DC or DAC, and to the results from the centre. The chances are that the participant will be experiencing certain emotions concerning the DC/DAC. The feedback giver should thus draw out these emotions and deal with them as soon as possible during the feedback discussion. With these emotions out of the way, the participant will be able to participate in the discussion more freely. The possibility of him or her accepting the feedback and taking ownership of the development is therefore greater.

Principle 7: Protect the self-worth of the participant

The DC or DAC participants might already feel exposed after attending the centre. The feedback discussion should therefore not make them feel even more exposed. After the discussion, the participants should feel positive and empowered so that they can influence their own development.

Also emphasise that although there are focal constructs needing development, it does not mean that the participants cannot perform their current job. Point out that the development areas only indicate opportunities for improving effectiveness.

Principle 8: Let the participant feel in control

Closely linked to the previous principle is the principle of making the participants feel that their own development is within their control. If they do not agree with a development area, and therefore do not want to develop the specific focal construct, the participants should not be forced to develop the focal construct. Forcing participants to "develop" a focal construct might be a waste of time and a waste of the organisation's money, since adults usually only learn if they themselves see the value of learning.

Principle 9: Get the "unseen" factors out of the way during the feedback discussion

It sometimes happens that the relationship between the participant and his or her immediate line manager is not as healthy as it should be, or something could have happened that impacts on the frame of mind of the participant. If the feedback giver becomes aware of any such "unseen" factors, he or she should address these as soon as possible during the discussion. Again, getting the unseen factors out of the way will allow the participants to really focus on their development.

Principle 10: Focus on practical aspects

As stated earlier, the focus during the feedback discussion should be on practical aspects that the participants can attend to. During the feedback discussion, examples of how the participants can approach issues differently, how they can perhaps handle situations differently, and how they can possibly respond differently should be discussed. The participants should be armed with practical ideas and knowledge that they can action immediately after the feedback discussion.

Principle 11: Stress what were and were not measured

The DC or DAC participant and their line manager have not been trained in the focal constructs or in any other aspect of the DC or DAC. It may therefore happen that they each have their own idea of what has been evaluated during the centre. It is thus important for the feedback giver to continuously emphasise what has and has not been assessed.

Principle 12: Focus on the future

The focus of the whole feedback discussion should be on the future. The DC or DAC is in the past. The feedback giver should assist the participants to learn from the centre (the past) in order to change their future behaviour.

(b) *Hints for use during a DC or DAC feedback discussion*[20]

The following hints can assist in conducting an effective DC or DAC feedback discussion:

20 Schlebusch & De Wet, 2007

1. *Confidential and at the appropriate time and place*

The discussion should take place in an environment in which the participant feels safe and secure, and confidentiality should be guaranteed. Care should be taken to ensure that the discussion does not coincide with another process that can influence how the centre results are perceived. For example, if the participant has applied for a promotion, it would be appropriate to wait until the decision to promote the participant has been made. This will ensure that the participant, or anyone else, does not perceive the DC or DAC results as influencing the decision.

2. *Be caring*

Those conducting feedback discussions should show participants that they care about them as human beings. The message to the participant is that they are not just another person who attended the DC or DAC, but are a person whose best interests are being considered.

The feedback giver should avoid being seen by the participant as an "expert" who is sharing cold and clinical information with the participant. The approach should rather be that the participants themselves are the "experts" in their own lives and that the feedback giver is there to assist them to be more effective in what they do.

3. *Control own emotions*

It is very important that the feedback givers control their own emotions. They should remain calm irrespective of the participant's behaviour during the discussion. This applies especially when the participants are rationalising their behaviour during the DC or DAC.

4. *Emphasise the progress already made*

Sometimes, participants improve their performance in respect of a specific focal construct while still at the DC or DAC. The debriefing session that has taken place at the end of the DC or DAC could also have led participants to change their behaviour. This progress should be acknowledged during the feedback discussion.

5. *Give specific examples*

An understanding of the focal construct, as well as an understanding of own behaviour, is enhanced when the feedback giver provides specific examples of actual and desired behaviour. For example, instead of saying to the participants that they should apply active listening skills, rather give an example. Recommend that the participant share and verify, with the other person, what the participant has noticed, for instance by asking, "Peter, I see that you are frowning; do you have a question?"

6. Give positive recognition

There will always be evidence of positive behaviour regarding most of the focal constructs, so emphasise these. Also give recognition for what the participant has already done to improve performance related to a specific focal construct.

7. Validate the participant's emotions

The participant might be experiencing various emotions; validate these by recognising them and by showing understanding concerning them. Avoid telling the participants not to feel as they do, for they are experiencing the emotions. For example, the participant might experience the feedback as negative and as meaning that s/he is not competent in anything. Validate these feelings by pointing out that people might feel this way right now.

8. Admit that it is a difficult situation

The participant might indicate that it is very difficult, if not impossible, to change behaviour. Again, admit that it is a difficult situation to learn new ways of doing things.

9. Discuss possible alternatives

This hint is linked to the previous hint and requires that one discuss possible alternative ways of dealing with the situation. Ask the participant for suggestions and explore these suggestions during the discussion.

10. State the possible benefits that may be enjoyed

Enhance understanding of the benefits that may be experienced in changing behaviour by stating some of these benefits and asking the participant to suggest possible benefits.

11. End the discussion on a positive note

A golden rule is to always end the feedback discussion positively; leave the participant feeling energised and empowered to grow.

(c) Techniques for a feedback discussion[21]

There are a few techniques that can assist the feedback giver, however the recommended approach is to guide the participant to insight by mostly asking questions. The feedback giver should therefore share the participant's performance at the DC or DAC and then use questions to lead the participant to "discover" why and how s/he can change his or her behaviour.

21 Schlebusch & de Wet, 2007

1. *Focus on the "road ahead"*

Although the participants need to understand their performance at the DC or DAC and the impact of that behaviour in the work situation, continuously focus the participants' attention on what they can do to deal with similar situations in the future. Ensure that they learn from their experience at the DC or DAC and that they can implement the learning in the future. The majority of the time during the feedback discussion should therefore be spent on drawing up a development plan.

2. *Listen, observe and follow up on cues*

The feedback discussion is the last opportunity for the DC or DAC process owners to ensure that participants and line managers buy into the DC or DAC process, and therefore the subsequent development. The feedback giver should thus be very aware of how the participant and his or her line manager react during the discussion. Any cue, whether positive or negative, should be followed up by way of active listening. The questions should be answered and the concerns addressed immediately.

3. *Ask the line manager in cases where the participant is unable to answer*

Since the feedback giver will mostly ask questions after sharing the participant's performance at the DC or DAC, it might happen that the participant cannot answer a question. The question can then be addressed to the line manager, who might be able to answer it. For example, the participant might not be able to answer the following question: "Will you be expected to deal with similar situations in the future?" The line manager might be in a better position to respond to this question.

It is necessary to involve the line manager in the discussion. S/He should actively take part in drawing up the participant's development plan. This will increase the chances of the line manager supporting the participant in developing the focal constructs concerned.

4. *Describe the focal constructs in a nutshell*

Refresh the memory of the line manager and the participant regarding the content of the focal constructs. Describe the constructs in a nutshell by highlighting the crux of each. This ensures that everyone involved in the discussion has the same frame of reference when it comes to the focal constructs under discussion.

5. *Use the development plan, but be flexible*

The focal constructs, and the elements within them, that need further development will have been identified during the DC or DAC, and will therefore have been indicated on the participant's development plan before the start of the feedback discussion. The idea is that the development approach and actions per focal construct be noted on the plan as the feedback discussion progresses.

However, other areas needing development can be added to the plan. Certain areas that require development can even be left until the follow-up discussion. Leaving development areas until the next discussion might be an effective approach if the participant has a lot of development areas.

6. Give feedback on a specific simulation

The feedback discussion should focus not only on giving feedback per focal construct evaluated during the DC or DAC, but also on the simulations used during the DC or DAC. Again, the DC or DAC is a learning opportunity that should be used to its fullest extent, therefore feedback should be given on each simulation as well.

The recommended approach to giving feedback on each simulation is to share the participant's approach to the simulation as well as his or her performance during the simulation. This knowledge can be enriched by asking the following questions:
- "Do you often find yourself in a similar situation?"
- "Do you find it easy or difficult to deal with the situation?"
- "What do you find easy/difficult about the situation?"
- "What value will be added if you do it more effectively?"
- "What can you do differently in the future to deal with the situation more effectively?"

7. Use a four-step process

A technique that can be used to enable the participants to identify the development actions themselves (instead of the feedback giver telling the participant) is the following four-step technique:
- *Step 1:* Ask: "What do you think you can do differently?"
- *Step 2:* Respond to the participant's answer by way of positive stroking regarding what he or she says. Say, for instance, "Good idea; that will work".
- *Step 3:* Ask: "What else can you do?", or, if the participant is struggling to think of something to say, ask, "What about also doing...?"
- *Step 4:* If the participant agrees to an action, tie the action down on the development plan by asking the participant to set a due date for the action. If the participant does not agree with the action, or resists it, let it go. If participants are manipulated or forced into agreeing to something on their development plan that they are not really committed to doing, they will probably not take the action concerned.

2.1.6 Receiving feedback

The feedback process is also a valuable opportunity to receive feedback from the participants and line managers on their experience of the AC and on the AC feedback process. The feedback giver should encourage this type of feedback, note the feedback, and pass the feedback on to the AC design team. The AC design team should evaluate such feedback and decide whether to implement the recommended changes.

Apart from the obvious value of receiving feedback, the feedback giver should also model the behaviour required of the participant when receiving feedback. S/He should therefore be open to the feedback and really appreciate the feedback on the AC and the subsequent feedback process.

2.2 Development plan

An important document that is drawn up during or after the DC or DAC is the participant's development plan. This document is a summary of all the development activities that will address the identified development areas. Ideally, this document should be comprehensive, indicating on-the-job activities, training programmes, books to read, videos to watch and projects to be involved in. The plan should also indicate contact people and due dates. A new approach to develop the applicable focal constructs is to break down the focal constructs into easy, doable behaviours that can be practiced daily until the behaviours become habit.[22]

An important rule is that there should be a direct link between the development plan and the participant's written report. However, it might happen that a specific focal construct has been rated as a current area of strength during the DC or DAC, but the participant still wants to develop the focal construct further. If the line manager agrees, this focal construct can be added to the development plan.

Since the participant needs to take ownership of the development plan, it is of no use including activities to develop a focal construct that the participant does not want to develop. In such cases, it might be better to leave the focal construct needing development on the plan, without any development activities indicated.

The line manager and participant should prioritise the focal constructs needing further development. This will enable the participants to focus their development energy on those focal constructs deemed most important by themselves and their line managers.

Usually it will take the participant approximately 18 months to develop all the focal constructs that have been indicated on the plan. However, the time it takes to complete a development plan depends on the number of focal constructs needing further development, on the participant's commitment to the development plan, as well as on their unique circumstances at work. For example, if the participant is seconded to another section of the organisation in another country, it will probably take the participant longer to complete his or her development plan. However, if the participants are part of an accelerated development programme, it might take them less time to complete the development plan.

2.3 Growth framework and related human capital processes

It was mentioned earlier that the development of the participant should ideally be monitored until the participant has developed all the focal constructs needing development. This monitoring takes place by means of a follow-up discussion.

---

22 Lanik, 2018

A follow-up discussion is one involving a representative of the DC or DAC process owners, the participant and the participant's current line manager. The purpose of the discussion is to review the participant's development according to the development plan. Typically, the plan is adapted during the discussion and the participant implements the new plan in the coming period. The following questions should be answered during a typical follow-up discussion: What activities from the plan were implemented? What worked well? What did not work well? What areas are the new priority areas? What else can be done to develop the focal constructs?

A follow-up discussion is most effective if it takes place every six to eight months, however the time span between the discussions is dependent on the organisation's needs. If it is a fast-paced organisation, the follow-up discussion might need to take place every four months. In an organisation that is not development-oriented, eight months between the follow-up discussions might be more appropriate.

It is recommended that, in preparation for the follow-up discussion, the participant complete a 360-degree evaluation regarding the focal constructs evaluated during the DC or DAC. The results from this evaluation will give an overview of how the participant's competence with regard to the DC or DAC focal constructs is experienced in the work situation. This feedback can then be incorporated in the new development plan drawn up during the follow-up discussion.

Figure 17.4 indicates the process of follow-up discussions. This process is called the growth framework.

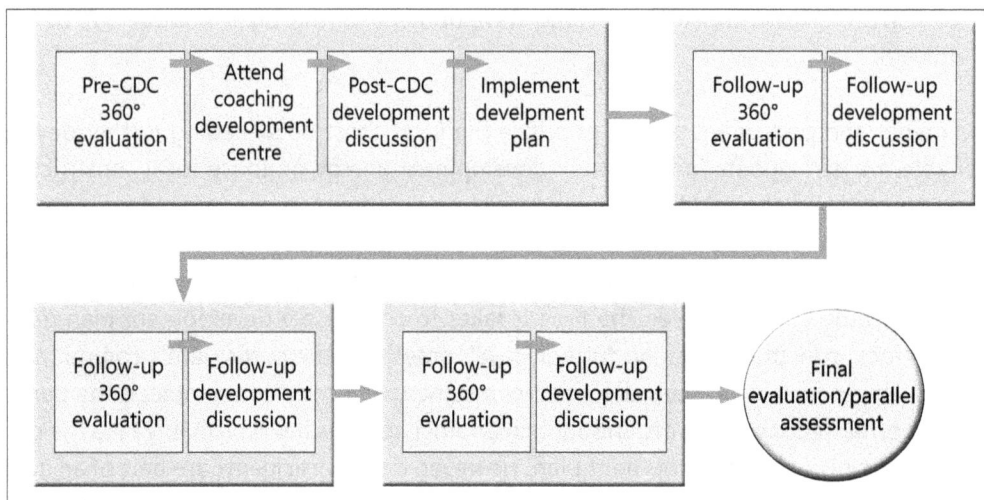

Figure 17.4: The growth framework
Source: LEMASA DAC debriefing material

The growth framework starts with the participants completing a 360-degree evaluation of their own behaviour linked to the DC or DAC focal constructs before attending the DC or DAC. Typically the participants will involve their direct line manager, subordinates and a few colleagues in completing the evaluation. The participants then attend the DC or DAC and receive feedback afterwards. During this initial feedback discussion, the original development plan is drawn up. After the discussion, the participants implement the plan (this is indicated in the first four blocks of Figure 17.4). Six to eight months after the feedback discussion, the first follow-up discussion takes place. The participants complete the 360-degree evaluation and bring the result of the evaluation to the follow-up discussion. The participants' development plans are reviewed and adapted according to the discussion. The participants again implement the development agreed upon during the discussion and indicated on their plan (the second group of blocks in Figure 17.4). The process repeats itself until the participants have completed all the development indicated on their plan, or everyone agrees that the development areas have been developed. When the development plans have been completed, the participants' plans can be closed. The participants then have the option of deciding on their next development action. They can choose between ending their development, attending another DC or DAC but at a higher level, or attending a parallel centre.

2.3.1 Parallel centre

A parallel centre is an AC at the same level of complexity as the original DC or DAC attended by the participants. The same focal constructs are evaluated as with the original DC or DAC, and similar simulations are used during the AC. The feedback after the DC or DAC is again in the form of a written report and feedback discussion. If necessary, new development plans are drawn up for the participants and they can request that follow-up discussions take place.

The purpose of a parallel AC is purely to establish whether the participant's development areas have been turned into areas of effective functioning.

The advantage of attending a parallel AC is that the participants receive objective feedback on whether the development actions implemented since they attended the original DC or DAC have been effective. The results from a parallel AC also constitute valuable feedback for the client organisation and allows the organisation to determine how effective the various development interventions were.

The results from a parallel AC can also be used during the evaluation and validation stage in the AC design model.

2.3.2 Other related human capital processes

The DC or DAC is probably most effective when the DC or DAC process forms part of other human capital processes. Earlier in this chapter reference was made to a succession development programme. It was indicated that an AC can be used to select the programme delegates, but that once delegates are on the programme, a DAC can be used to identify unique development plans for each delegate on the succession development programme.

Some progressive organisations have a framework of manager–leader development in place. As part of this framework, certain development interventions and programmes are indicated as an integral and non-negotiable part of development. Other development programmes are indicated as optional, depending on the individual's specific developmental needs. A DC or DAC will, in such a case, be a helpful instrument for identifying the unique manager-leader development needs of each manager within the organisation. The manager's DC or DAC development plan can then entail selected development programmes from the optional development programmes in the organisation's manager-leader development framework.

In some organisations, the DC or DAC process is seen as an integral part of developing effective manager-leaders. For certain vacancies advertised internally it is stated that preference will be given to employees who have successfully implemented their DC or DAC development plans or who are currently busy implementing a DC or DAC development plan.

To support the development arising from a DC or DAC, it is recommended that the client organisation has an internal library where the DC or DAC participants can borrow the various recommended books indicated on the development plans. A virtual learning centre within the organisation is also useful in addition to online resources. DC or DAC participants can register online through the virtual learning centre for various development programmes. The participants work through the training material at times convenient to them. They are thus in control of the time that they "attend" the training programme. Some organisations also offer access to appropriate apps to assist in developing the focal constructs.

It is probably the ideal situation if the participants' line managers are evaluated as part of the organisation's performance management system to determine the extent to which they support their subordinates' DC or DAC development. In addition, it would be even better if each DC or DAC participant were to be evaluated regarding the extent to which they implement their own DC or DAC development plan. These are decisions that need to be taken during the analysis stage of the design model.

Case Study:
Journeying with SAA's Succession Pool Programme[23]

Background

In 2015, SAA's executives identified that the leadership pipeline was a risk to the organisation. Potential successors for senior management positions had to be identified and readied so that the organisation could promote from within when vacancies occurred. A flexible approach, focused on a pool of people, with a balance between the needs of SAA and the development needs of individuals, would need to be created. The development focus areas should be:
- intra- and interpersonal knowledge and skills;
- management-leadership knowledge and skills;
- functional knowledge and skills;
- SAA-specific knowledge and skills; and
- aviation industry knowledge and skills.

SAA decided to implement a succession pool with accelerated, focused development over a period of three years.

---

23 Strauss, 2018; Schlebusch, 2019

SAA's Succession Pool Programme aimed at Organisational Level 2 (SPP2)

Instead of targeting one or two handpicked individuals for each executive position, the SPP2 would groom a group of high-potential individuals for executive positions in general. Being part of the SPP2 did not guarantee promotion, however the SPP2 participants would be in a better position to apply for executive positions when the positions became vacant. The SPP2 process was as follows:

Focused development		
Year 1	Year 2	Year 3
Individual development	Multi-diciplinary project work	Secondments
Focus		
Intra and interpersonal development	Business and team development	Strategic development
Coaching	Mentoring	

Selection process → Attend CDC → [Focused development table] → Attend parallel CDC → Certification

Figure 17.5: SPP2 Process

Candidates were either nominated by their direct line managers, or they could apply themselves for inclusion in the programme. Candidates who adhered to certain criteria were invited for a selection process that included a development interview and a case study. The results from the selection process were presented to the Executive Talent Review Committee (ETRC) who made the final decision to include 13 participants in the programme. The development journey started with participants attending a Coaching Development Centre (CDC). SAA decided to use a CDC so that participants could receive personal attention while in the process of assessing their current manager-leader skills. It was critical for participants to accept their assessment results and take ownership of their own development over the next three years. This required a change in mindsets that a CDC is ideally suited to enable. Participants crafted an individual development plan (IDP) based on their CDC experience that they would implement mostly during year one of the programme. In addition, participants had to follow a Learning Path mapping all the functional knowledge, skills and experience required to achieve competence at a senior management level in SAA within their specific discipline.

The CDC's focal constructs were 10 developable competencies from SAA's Leadership Framework and the following simulations:
- A Career and Self-Development Discussion.
- An In-Box.
- An Individual Role Play.
- A True-Allocated Role Group Discussion.

The CDC followed a behaviour driven approach using an adapted BOS with a PEDR approach.

The learning approach post CDC was blended learning using self, social, classroom and on-the-job learning activities. Examples of each are given in the table below:

Table 17.1: Examples of the Various Learning Activities

Self-Learning	Social Learning	Classroom Learning	On-the-job Learning
Reading	Coaching	Airline Business Models and Competitive Strategies (IATA "Mini-MBA")	Specific assignments as per Functional Learning Path
Podcasts	Quarterly Group Forums	Emotional Intelligence Training	Activities such as: chairing meetings; acting in higher positions; leading project teams
Webcasts	Power Hours	Crucial Conversations Training	
Apps		Planning, Leading, Organising, Controlling Training (PLOC)	
Videos		Courses based on individual development needs	
E-Learning Modules			

Participants also worked individually with a business coach during year one of the programme to ensure that their specific individual needs were addressed.

The learning methodology followed during year two was multi-disciplinary project work focusing on transferring industry and business knowledge and skills. Participants were divided into groups, with each group addressing an actual burning challenge within SAA. The groups had to analyse the challenge, identify possible solutions, and indicate how the solution could be implemented to the benefit of SAA. The groups had to present their project to SAA's executive team who identified the winning group. The winning solution was implemented within SAA. During year two of the programme, participants also started working with a mentor who was a senior executive within SAA.

During year three, participants were seconded for a period of six months to alternative functional business areas (out of their comfort zone) within SAA, fulfilling the role of executive. The mentorship process continued during this last year of the programme.

Throughout the three years, continuous feedback and monitoring took place to ensure accountability and development. Participants had to submit monthly reports indicating progress on implementing their IDP and Learning Path. Bi-monthly discussions with a development broker took place to support the implementation of the plans. Every six months feedback was given to the ETRC and the participants' developmental progress was discussed.

Towards the end of year three the nine remaining participants attended a parallel CDC to determine their management-leadership skills at the end of the three year programme. The table below indicates the comparison of the participants' final rating per focal construct during the original CDC and the parallel CDC. If the final rating during the parallel CDC improved, an "I" is indicated in the applicable column. When the final rating remained the same it is indicated with an "S", and if the final rating at the parallel CDC was lower than the rating received during the original CDC, it is indicated with an "L".

Table 17.2: Comparison of Final Ratings

Focal Constructs \ Participants	P1	P2	P3	P4	P5	P6	P7	P8	P9	Total Improved	Total Remaining Same	Total Lower
Competency 1	I	I	I	I	I	S	I	I	I	8	1	0
Competency 2	S	S	S	I	S	S	S	S	S	1	8	0
Competency 3	S	S	S	S	S	S	S	S	S	0	9	0
Competency 4	I	I	S	I	I	I	I	L	S	6	2	1
Competency 5	S	I	S	I	I	S	I	S	S	4	5	0
Competency 6	S	I	I	I	S	S	I	L	I	5	3	1
Competency 7	I	I	S	I	I	S	I	S	I	6	3	0
Competency 8	S	S	L	S	S	S	I	L	I	2	5	2
Competency 9	S	S	S	I	S	L	I	I	S	3	5	1
Competency 10	I	S	L	S	S	I	S	S	S	2	6	1
In-Box	I	S	S	I	S	I	I	S	S	4	5	0
Role Play	I	I	I	S	I	I	I	S	I	7	2	0
Group Meeting	I	I	I	S	I	I	I	S	I	7	2	0
Total Improved:	7	7	4	8	6	5	10	2	6			
Total Same:	6	6	7	5	7	7	3	8	7			
Total Lower:	0	0	2	0	0	1	0	3	0			

Key:
I = Improved Final Rating
S = Final Rating Remained the Same
L = Final Rating Lower

Four of the participant's final ratings on most of the focal constructs improved, while the remaining five participants' final ratings on most focal constructs remained the same. There were three participants who received lower ratings on some of the focal constructs. The speculated reasons for the ratings were that:
- personal circumstances impacted the results;
- inconsistent attention was paid to implementing the recommended personal development interventions indicated on the IDPs resulting from the CDC; and
- participants should be more exposed to situations where a section or department consisting of teams of people report to them, giving them exposure to people leadership accountabilities and situations.

Lessons Learnt

The following are some of the lessons learnt from implementing the SPP2 programme:
- Attrition will occur. Although 13 participants started the programme, one withdrew early in the programme, one participant was poached by another organisation, and two resigned to take up more senior positions at other organisations.
- A key success factor is keeping the participants accountable for implementing their own IDPs.
- Another key success factor is that the SPP2 had a dedicated, and very committed, internal custodian, as well as an external development broker who supported the implementation of the development interventions.
- Participants in specialist positions should have the opportunity to head up a section where they have full accountability for all aspects of people leadership.
- Two periods of secondment should take place – the first secondment at the beginning of the programme and the second secondment towards the end of the programme to balance out functional exposure and business acumen.

---

3. POST-AC PROCESSES RELATED TO THE FUTURE AND MAINTENANCE OF THE AC

The post-AC processes related to the future and maintenance of the AC are probably the part of ACs that are the most neglected. However, the last stage in the design model, namely the evaluation and validation stage, will be much easier to implement if proper attention is given to the post-AC processes discussed in this section. The processes referred to are data capturing after each AC, the storage of AC material and information, the reconciliation of costs, and the maintenance of ACs.

3.1 Data capturing

Directly after each AC, DC and DAC, certain data from the AC need to be captured. If the AC was a virtual assessment centre (VAC), the data are already captured electronically and stored appropriately. The purpose of capturing the data is to collect complete sets of data to be used during the evaluation and validation stage. It is recommended that the data be captured directly after each AC, and not only once a year or whenever the statistical processes need to be performed.

During the design stage, an easy-to-use spreadsheet for capturing the data should have been designed with the criterion that will be used for the AC validation in mind. Care should have been taken in the design to ensure that all the AC information is captured after the AC. This will avoid the need to later go back to stored AC data.

Accuracy is very important when the data are captured. The spreadsheet design should therefore also be such that it is easy to capture the data correctly. It is recommended that the captured data be checked to ensure accuracy.

The typical information from each AC, DC or DAC that needs to be captured is the AC number and the process owners at the AC. Per participant, the following data need to be captured: the rating per focal construct, per simulation; the final rating per focal construct; the final rating per simulation; the pre-AC 360-degree evaluation result; and performance appraisal information. During the development process following a DC or DAC, the result of each 360-degree evaluation should also be captured, as well as the participant's performance appraisal ratings.

If a participant chooses to attend a parallel centre, the result from the centre also needs to be captured.

In addition, it might be necessary to capture additional data, depending on the selected criterion for validation of the AC.

It might be useful to capture the feedback obtained from the participants in the participant reflection forms, as well as the feedback from the process owners. For example, if this information is captured, it can be determined over time how many participants addressed a specific problematic issue in the analysis exercise. Armed with this information, the AC design team may then decide to review the content of the analysis exercise simulation. The number of participants who addressed the specific problem might also indicate the orientation of the client organisation's employees who attended the AC. Perhaps the employees concerned are very financially oriented, thus leading most of them to identify a cash-flow problem, or very few may have identified the problem, indicating that the employees are possibly not financially inclined.

3.2 Storing the participants' simulations and other AC information

It is recommended that a file or folder be opened for each centre participant. The typical information placed on file or folder is the participant's background information document, the signed consent form, the participant reflection forms for each simulation, the final written report, the 360-degree evaluation result, as well as the resulting development plan. This file or folder is updated after every follow-up discussion with the new development plan as well as the 360-degree evaluation result. The file or folder is closed when the participant has completed his or her development plan, however it is recommended that it be stored in a safe place for five more years.

The report and other information from each AC for selection purposes should also be placed on file or folder and stored for a minimum of five years.

Each AC, DC and DAC participant's simulation responses need to be stored in a safe place[24], as it might be necessary to refer to the original simulation responses for whatever reason. The simulation responses should be easily retrievable. It is further recommended that the simulation responses also be stored for a minimum of five years.

If the AC participants provided permission for their AC data to be used in further research, the data need to be made anonymous before being entered into any research protocol or programme.

---

24 Protection of Personal Information Act, (Act 4 of 2013)

Every client organisation should have a professional person who is accountable for the safekeeping of the AC documentation. When this person resigns from the organisation, he or she needs to ensure that this accountability is transferred to another person who accepts the necessary professional accountability. The accountability includes the safekeeping of the AC results, research data and information, as well as ensuring the appropriate use of AC results within the client organisation.

3.3 Reconciliation of all costs

Careful book-keeping is required to keep track of all the direct and indirect costs of an AC. Not only must the invoices be paid as soon as possible, but each AC's costs (direct and indirect) need to be reconciled with the original budget for the AC. Any deviation from the budget needs to be substantiated and a decision taken as to whether the deviation will occur in future as well.

Not only will the client organisation's finance and internal audit departments expect careful control over the AC budget, but this information will also be useful during the evaluation and validation stage to show the net value of the AC.

3.4 Maintaining the AC

All instruments and machines need to be maintained to ensure optimal functioning. The same applies to ACs. As with the maintenance of machines, the maintenance of ACs includes minor actions from time to time, as well as a scheduled, large-scale action. The minor actions relate to the continuous improvements made to the AC, while the scheduled, large-scale action relates to a complete review of the entire AC.

In Chapter 15, we discussed the continued training of all the process owners. This is part of the required maintenance carried out in respect of an AC, however the process at the AC, as well as the content of the simulations, also requires maintenance.

The process at the AC and the content of the simulations are maintained through small, continuous changes, as well as the large-scale review. The continuous improvement refers to the small improvements that are made to the AC based on the feedback received from the participants, their line managers and the AC process owners. For example, the wording of the instructions of a simulation could be changed to be more effective, or perhaps the content of a debriefing session might change. However, care should be taken not to substantially change a simulation, for this will have an impact on the validation research pertaining to the AC. The changes and the date of the changes should be noted in the AC's technical manual.

The large-scale AC review should take place every three to five years. Since organisations function in dynamic environments, the needs of the organisation will change over time. To ensure that the AC remains relevant, the AC design team needs to completely review the AC. This entails reviewing the outcomes of the analysis stage, the design and development stage, and perhaps even the implementation stage. Typical questions that need to be asked include: Are the focal constructs still the critical focal constructs of the organisation? Are the organisational trends, simulated in the fictitious AC organisation, still important, or have they changed? Is the level of technology integration in the AC still appropriate? After the complete review of the AC, new data sets need to be collected to again determine the reliability and validity of the reviewed AC.

4. CRITICAL DECISIONS RELATING TO THIS STEP, AND THE OUTCOMES THEREOF

The following are the critical decisions relating to this step, and the outcomes thereof:

4.1 Insight into participants' AC performance

The first outcome of this step is that the participants, their line managers or the people who requested the AC have insight into the AC, DC and DAC participants' behaviour. They need to understand what has happened during the AC and how each person performed on the focal construct, relative to the norm. All the questions that they might have needed to be answered, and buy-in into the AC results, must be achieved. Each DC or DAC participant should have a feedback discussion as well as a written report. A feedback discussion with the people who requested the AC for selection purposes should have taken place, and they should be in possession of a written report.

4.2 Comprehensive development plans

The second outcome is that all DC or DAC participants have development plans that they are committed to. The development plans should be comprehensive and cover a wide spectrum of development actions to develop the focal constructs needing development. The plans should be the "roadmap" for their development over the next few months.

4.3 Supportive processes

The DC or DAC participants' development plans should be supported by other human capital processes. Ideally, the participants' development should be followed up on every few months to ensure that the development is taking place according to what was agreed during the feedback discussion. The participants should have access to development support in the form of books, videos and training programmes, social media groups, and perhaps even collaborative software to enable group work.

Other human capital processes such as a performance management process and a 360-degree evaluation process should be in place to support the continued development of the participants.

A process for timeously and accurately capturing the required AC, DC and DAC data should be functioning effectively. This data will be used during the next stage of the design model – the evaluation and validation stage.

All the AC information should be safely stored and should be easily retrievable for future use.

4.4 An AC that is relevant to the current needs of the organisation

The AC should be maintained so as to ensure that, over time, it remains relevant to the needs of the client organisation. The maintenance of the AC includes the small, continuous improvements made based on the feedback received after every AC, as well as the three or five yearly total overhaul of the AC.

IMPLEMENTATION

1.   PURPOSE OF THE IMPLEMENTATION STAGE

The purpose of this stage is to implement a functional AC in the client organisation. The objective is fourfold:

1.1   Train process owners and prepare for the AC

The first objective is to select and train all the AC process owners. The training includes both theoretical input and practical training. The appropriate people have to be selected according to specific criteria; once they have been declared competent, continued training needs to take place to ensure continued competence.

All the logistical and other arrangements have to be made to ensure that the AC is conducted effectively. The process of selecting and training the process owners, as well as all the preparatory tasks, was described in Chapter 15.

1.2   Conduct ACs

The second objective is to conduct ACs according to the AC Manual. Each and every AC should be conducted according to the instructions and procedures indicated therein, as this will ensure consistent, reliable results. This was discussed in Chapter 16.

1.3   Give post-AC feedback

After every AC, feedback is given to either the DC or DAC participants or to the people who requested the AC for selection purposes. The third objective is thus to implement an effective feedback process. This was discussed in Chapter 17.

1.4   Implement processes to ensure future ACs

The fourth objective is to implement processes that will ensure that the necessary research on the AC can be conducted. These processes entail the electronic capture of data, the safe storage of AC results and materials, budget-cost reconciliations, and maintaining the AC. All these processes were described in Chapter 17.

2. CRITICAL DELIVERABLES OF THIS STAGE

This stage should yield the following key deliverables:

2.1 A pool of competent AC process owners

The ACs can be conducted only if enough competent AC process owners are available. More process owners should be available than the number used during an AC. This will ensure that people are available in situations where a specific process owner cannot fulfil his or her duties at short notice. A pool of process owners will also minimise the possibility of a scheduled AC not having enough process owners to conduct the AC.

2.2 ACs conducted in a consistent manner

Conducting each AC according to the AC Manual will ensure that, over time, ACs are conducted in a consistent manner and therefore deliver comparable results.

2.3 AC results accepted by the various stakeholders

Only when the various stakeholders accept the AC results will they implement the AC recommendations. An important process in ensuring the buy-in of all the stakeholders is the process of giving feedback. Both the feedback discussion and the written report are critical for establishing buy-in.

2.4 DC and DAC participants actively developing the identified development areas

The purpose of a DC and DAC is to identify current areas of strength and areas needing further development. As a result, the DC or DAC participant should implement development actions to develop the identified areas. Processes should be in place to support the DC or DAC participant in his or her development.

2.5 Data sets for research purposes

Complete and accurate data sets should be captured electronically for use during the evaluation and validation stage. The capturing starts directly after every AC, but the data sets are updated after every follow-up discussion. In addition, a paper trail of the budget–cost reconciliations should be created.

2.6 AC information and material safely stored

The AC results, reports, development plans, simulations and other assessment results should be safely stored. The material should be regularly updated and should also be easily retrievable when it is needed.

2.7 The AC maintained

The AC should be maintained by implementing continuous improvement actions based on the feedback received from the various stakeholders. In addition, the AC should be completely reviewed every three to five years. This will ensure that the AC remains relevant to the organisation's needs.

3. THE FINAL OUTCOME OF THIS STAGE

The final outcome of this stage yields a fully operational AC, that is, an AC that is conducted effectively over time within the client organisation. This is achieved through competent process owners following the AC Manual and effectively implementing all the post-AC processes that will ensure the continued future of the AC within the client organisation.

After completing the *implementation stage*, can you confirm the following?

> - That you have the right quality and quantity of observers to conduct an AC effectively.
> - That you have the right quality and quantity of role players to conduct an AC effectively.
> - That you have selected the correct number of participants suited to the particular level of assessment to be conducted.
> - That the observers have received the correct training and are suitably qualified to conduct the observation.
> - That the physical facilities and resources are appropriate for conducting the AC.
> - That all the practices, procedures and policies (programmes, documentation, rating forms, feedback forms, etc.) for conducting the AC are in place.
> - That you have successfully conducted an AC on a specified level.
> - That you have conducted consecutive ACs in a consistent manner.
> - That you have identified all the different feedback versions and formats.
> - That you have a clear, post-centre feedback process in place for participants and for observers.
> - That you have a clear format for capturing feedback from both participants and observers.
> - That you have a post-centre debriefing process in place.

If you can respond positively to all of the above statements, you will have successfully completed the implementation stage.

INTRODUCTION TO STAGE FOUR

EVALUATION AND VALIDATION

1. WHAT THE EVALUATION AND VALIDATION STAGE IS ALL ABOUT

With reference to the design model that was introduced in the first chapter, the following section of the book will focus on the evaluation and validation stage highlighted in Figure S4.1.

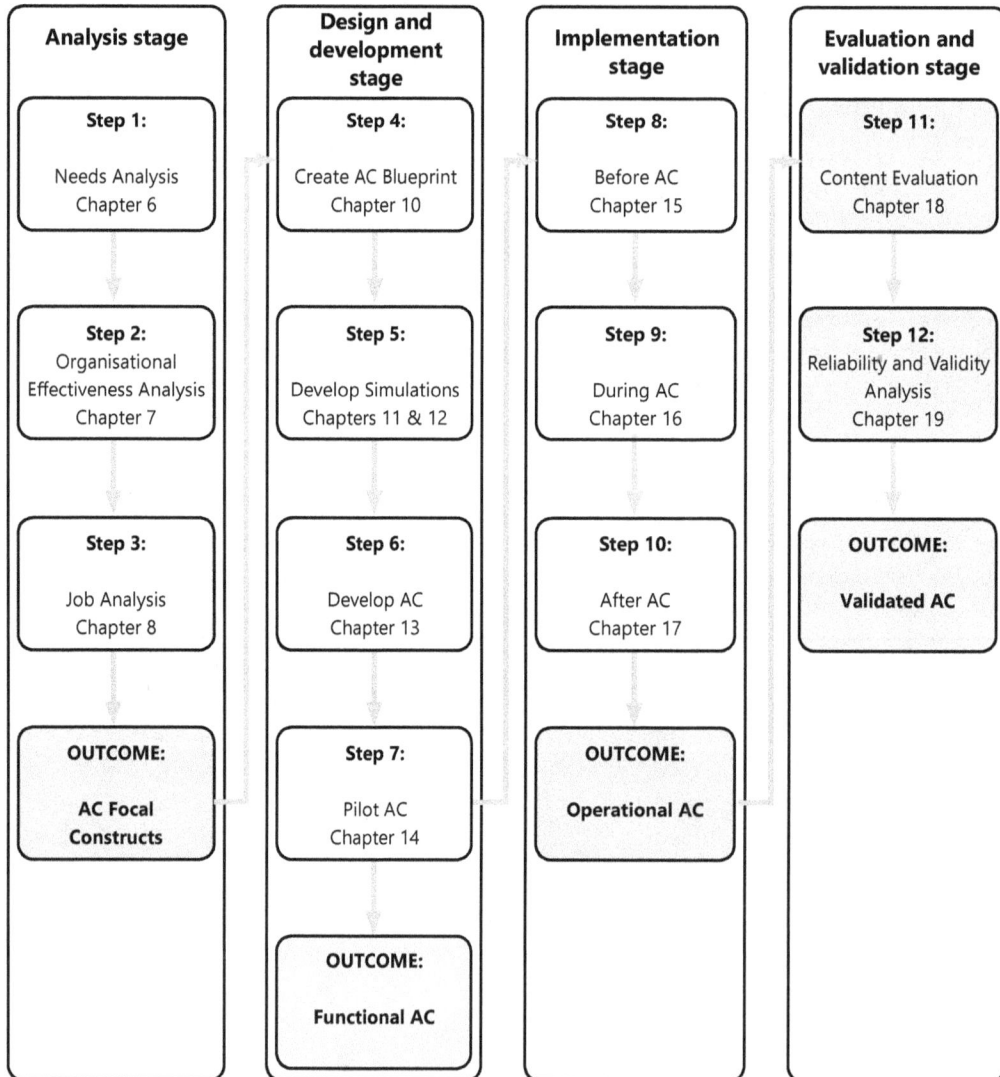

Figure S4.1: The steps in, and stages of, the AC Design Model

The fourth and last stage of the design model focuses on the evaluation and validation stage. This stage includes two steps in the design model, the first of which is the content evaluation of an AC (covered in Chapter 18) and the second of which is the validity and reliability analysis of an AC (covered in Chapter 19). The critical outcome of this stage will be a systematically evaluated and validated AC.

1.1 The content-evaluation step

Chapter 18 deals specifically with the descriptive and content evaluation of an AC and the exercises within an AC. The chapter focuses on how the perspectives of key stakeholders (such as observers, participants, subordinates, line managers and the Human Capital function of a company) are sourced so as to determine how they perceive and/or experience the content (different exercises) and the process (presentation, administration, evaluation) of the AC. This step also entails reflecting on the outcome of the different needs analyses (covered in Chapters 6, 7 and 8) in order to ensure the content relevance of the AC.

1.2 The reliability and validity evaluation step

Chapter 19 deals with the reliability and validity of ACs. The chapter first introduces a number of basic statistical concepts. Thereafter, the concept of reliability is introduced and different methods of assessing ACs or AC dimensions are discussed. The next section then deals with the validity of ACs. Different methods of capturing the validity of ACs are discussed in this section. Then, the ratings generated in ACs are discussed with special reference to raw ratings, compiled (integrated) ratings and standardised ratings. The last section deals with special cases and issues relating to the determination of the reliability and validity of AC ratings. Amongst others, special reference is made to cross-cultural and fairness issues.

2. CRITICAL DELIVERABLES OF THIS STAGE

The rationale for this stage is twofold. First, the AC and the AC dimensions need to be evaluated in terms of content relevance. Secondly, the AC programme as a whole needs to be assessed in terms of reliability and validity principles.

2.1 A content-valid AC programme and process

A systematic evaluation by the key stakeholders of the overall AC content and process, as well as of the content and processes of the different focal constructs assessments, will provide the content validity information. Key stakeholders will not only evaluate the operational reliability and validity of the overall AC process, but will also provide valuable information on the face validity and the perceived fairness of the AC programme. Key stakeholders' evaluations are conducted from different perspectives, thereby ensuring that a range of content evaluation issues, as well as the content relevance of the AC and focal constructs assessments, procedural fairness, equitability, and relevance in terms of different needs, are systematically addressed. The key deliverable of this step will be a valid AC programme from a content and a process perspective.

2.2 A reliable and valid AC programme and process

Determining the reliability and validity of the AC programme entails systematically collecting reliability and validity data. The reliability of the overall AC programme, as well as of the different focal construct assessments, will be systematically evaluated by applying different statistical procedures. Thereafter, the construct and predictive validity will be systematically investigated (assuming content validity) by applying different statistical procedures. The key deliverable of this step will be a reliable AC programme, as well as a construct- and predictive-valid AC programme.

3. INTENDED OUTCOME OF THIS STAGE

The successful completion of this stage should yield a validated AC programme. The programme should not only be operationally reliable and valid, but also reliable and valid based on statistical evaluation evidence. According to programme evaluation principles, the AC programme should be able to demonstrate its impact on the target job's effectiveness and on overall performance.

CHAPTER 18

DESCRIPTIVE (CONTENT) ANALYSIS

Gert Roodt

1. INTRODUCTION – THE PURPOSE OF A CONTENT ANALYSIS

Against the background of Stage Three of our design model, where the outcome was an operational AC, the purpose of the fourth stage will be to evaluate and validate the AC against the specific objectives and criteria it was designed for. The first step in this final stage is to conduct a content analysis of the AC and of AC focal constructs. This step is highlighted in Figure 18.1.

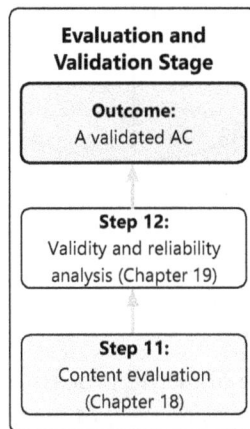

```
┌─────────────────────────────┐
│  Evaluation and             │
│  Validation Stage           │
│  ┌───────────────────────┐  │
│  │  Outcome:             │  │
│  │  A validated AC       │  │
│  └───────────────────────┘  │
│            ▲                │
│  ┌───────────────────────┐  │
│  │  Step 12:             │  │
│  │  Validity and reliability│  │
│  │  analysis (Chapter 19)│  │
│  └───────────────────────┘  │
│            ▲                │
│  ┌───────────────────────┐  │
│  │  Step 11:             │  │
│  │  Content evaluation   │  │
│  │  (Chapter 18)         │  │
│  └───────────────────────┘  │
└─────────────────────────────┘
```

Figure 18.1: The steps in, and stages of, the design model

This chapter will focus on different stakeholders' perceptions of the content relevance of the AC, on the respective competencies, on the accompanying behavioural elements/indicators, and on the stakeholders' evaluation of the process rigour of the AC and its related processes. Content validity involves determining whether the content of the measure covers a representative sample of the behaviour domain/aspect to be measured.[1] It is a non-statistical type of validity that rather refers to a specific procedure in constructing a psychological measure. In the AC context, this would entail a systematic process whereby it is determined whether the AC covers the required competencies (for example a focal construct) to be assessed. The different stakeholders identified for the content and the process evaluation are the AC process owners (in brief, the observers, role players and the Administrators), the AC participants, their subordinates, the managers of the appropriate level in the client organisation, and Human Capital specialists in the organisation. Based on the assumption that they all have a clear understanding of the purpose of ACs, these stakeholders can potentially provide a 360-degree perspective on the content relevance and the process rigour (reliability) of the overall AC process. Although there is no specific statistical procedure to evaluate the content validity of an AC

---

1   Wolfaardt & Roodt, 2005: 33

programme or process, a systematic 360-degree evaluation of the content and the process will yield useful data on the content validity.

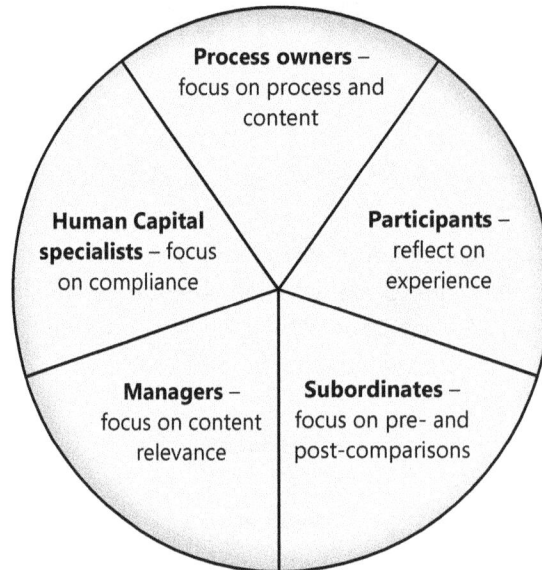

Figure 18.2: Prominent stakeholders in the AC process

Each section in the chapter will focus on a stakeholder group, as well as on its specific focus and its contribution to the content evaluation process.

The first section will cover the perspective of the AC process owners, who are primarily responsible for conducting the AC process. Their specific evaluation of content relevance and of process rigour will provide valuable feedback on the overall AC process.

The second section will cover the perspectives of the participants, who are primarily on the receiving end of the process, and the content of the AC process. Their views and comments on the content relevance and the process rigour will provide important feedback from a potential "client" perspective.

The third section will briefly deal with the direct subordinates of those managers who are being assessed (if the target level of the AC is management). Their pre- and post-AC observations and comments can provide valuable information regarding the behavioural changes of the managers who participated in the assessment.

The fourth section will deal with the relevant manager groups' evaluations. These groups can also provide valuable information on the content relevance and the process rigour of the overall AC process.

The fifth section of the chapter deals with the Human Capital specialist-stakeholder group's content evaluation in the organisation. Human Capital has (or is supposed to have) an overall picture of the current competency profile in the organisation, as well as of the future competency profile. It is in a key position to evaluate whether the AC addresses the future competency needs of the organisation.

The penultimate section of the chapter will focus on other important sources of information generated from the different needs and job analyses. The focus will be on whether the AC exercises address these needs or job analyses outcomes.

The chapter concludes by focusing on the critical outcomes of, and decisions relating to, this step in the design model. The content evaluation process will focus on a number of different issues. Before commencing with the different stakeholder perspectives on the AC process and content, a few important considerations have to be kept in mind. The following questions will typically trigger a number of different content validity-related issues:[2]

- Can you document the job-relatedness of the competencies (or other focal constructs) upon which your AC is based?
- Can you document the job-relatedness of the exercises used in your AC?
- Are the exercises appropriate to the target job?
- Are your observers fully trained?
- Are you sure that all observers are qualified?
- Are observers recording and rating behaviour?
- Is your assessor discussion operating successfully?
- Is the Administrator doing his/her job in the data integration discussion?
- Do participants understand the purpose of the AC, how the results will be used, who will see the results, and their rights if they disagree with the findings?

With these questions and considerations in mind, the AC design team can now proceed with the content evaluation step in the overall design process. The respective stakeholders provide a unique perspective on the content validity issues presented below.

Introductory case study: Generic competencies or context-specific competencies?

Organisation CD wishes to develop a DAC for middle level managers. The top management has appointed a design team which started to engage with other important stakeholder groups in the organisation in order to get clarity on what the exact focus and content of the AC should be. It soon became evident that there were disparate views on these; in brief, the views taken by the two most important stakeholder groups were as follows:

- The management stakeholder team was of the opinion that generic management competencies should be included in the AC and to design simulations around these competencies. Their view was very much based on 'get the basics right' and everything else will follow.
- The Human Capital stakeholder group, on the other hand, took the view that the AC should focus more on future competencies as well as on technology and computer skills. They argued that the company's strategic direction dictates the development of these future skills and competencies.

---

2   Byham, 1978: 4-6

The design team carefully listened to all the different views, and urged the different groups to engage in more rigorous debates on their different perspectives and to 'hear the other group out' in an attempt to resolve their conflicting views. It seemed that the two groups only became more entrenched in their views, however, and they took an even firmer stance. How can the design team resolve this impasse and what should they do to get movement on this issue?

The hypothetical case sketches a scenario of internal group dynamics that often play out in the work of a design team. Let's see if your knowledge of what you have learned so far, and what you will learn in this chapter, can help you to resolve this matter.

The next section of this chapter will take a closer look at the perspectives of the AC process owners.

2. THE AC PROCESS OWNERS' EVALUATIONS AND INPUT

The AC process owners' evaluation of an AC, or an AC exercise, serves two separate purposes. The first is to evaluate the appropriateness of the content of the exercise or the AC as a whole, and the second is to evaluate the rigour of the process by which the exercises are presented, the observations conducted, the scores collated and interpreted, and the reports and feedback provided. Overall, these two factors comment on the content validity of an AC.

2.1 Ensuring content relevance

AC process owners are directly involved in conducting the AC. In short, does the AC serve its purpose? The above questions[3] need to be carefully revisited to be able to address this question. AC process owners are thus best suited to make a judgement on whether the AC exercises assess the appropriate competencies on their respective level of complexity, that is, on the issue of content relevance. Their focus is therefore more on the structure of the content. The following aspects need to be considered:

2.1.1 Structure according to organisational level

The AC should be designed in such a way that it addresses the appropriate level in terms of required competencies for that specific level. In Chapter 7, we alluded to the fact that employees function on different levels and that ACs should therefore focus on a specific organisational level and its accompanying competencies. The AC process owners should ensure that the to-be-designed AC addresses the competencies on this specific level.

2.1.2 Structure according to competency

The AC should be designed in such a manner that it addresses the correct competencies for the specific organisational level. In this instance, the AC process owners have to ensure that the AC is designed so that it addresses the specific competencies (or other focal constructs) and needs identified in the needs and the job analyses (see Chapters 6, 7 and 8).

---

3   Byham, 1978

2.1.3 Structure of competency assessment exercises

It is also the role of the AC process owners to ensure that the different competency assessment exercises are precisely aligned with the required competency content on the specific organisational level.

2.1.4 Grouping of appropriate behavioural elements/indicators

Flowing from the previous point is the fact that the AC process owners also have to ensure that the different behavioural elements/indicators are identified and clearly defined. AC process owners have to ensure that the whole range of relevant behavioural examples is visible and included in each assessment exercise. The observers specifically need to know what the appropriate behaviours in each exercise are.

2.2 Ensuring process rigour

AC process owners are primarily responsible for executing the AC process. They can thus provide valuable comments on the following aspects of the overall AC process:

2.2.1 Purpose of the AC programme

The AC process owners should ensure that all participants have a clear picture of the overall AC programme and process. Above all, participants should have a clear picture of the specific objectives of the AC programme.

2.2.2 Structure of the AC process and exercises

The AC process owners need to ensure, first, that the overall AC programme is well structured and executed. Secondly, they also have to clearly explain the AC structure and process to all the AC participants. A knowledge and understanding of the process will greatly enhance the likelihood that participants will perceive the process as fair.

2.2.3 The rating process and forms

The AC process owners have to ensure that there is a clear and consistent rating process and procedure in place. Observers should be trained to act as assessors. Standardised forms for capturing assessment ratings (observer report forms) will be very helpful in this regard and will also enable AC process owners to leave a clear "audit trail" of the whole process for each separate AC and participant. The rating process and procedure also need to be explained to all participants. This aspect has a bearing on participants' perceptions of fairness.

2.2.4 Collating observer ratings

The AC process owners (and, specifically, the Administrators) should have a clearly developed and consistent procedure for collating the assessment ratings of the different observers. This will also contribute to decreased error variance in assessment ratings. The process of how the ratings obtained will be treated and collated also needs to be explained to the participants. Again, this will enhance participants' perceptions of fairness.

2.2.5   Report writing and report format

The AC reports need to be presented, in the agreed-upon format (see Chapters 5 and 10), to the participant and the organisation (i.e. to the managers or to the Human Capital division). Participants should have clarity regarding the format and purpose of the report and should also know who else will receive a copy of the report. This aspect relates specifically to informed consent, confidentiality and procedural fairness, all of which are important facets of fairness.[4]

2.2.6   Providing feedback and feedback format

The AC process owners should also have a clearly established procedure and process for providing feedback on the outcomes of the assessment process. The participants should be clearly informed about this process and about who else will be informed of the outcomes of the process. Furthermore, participants should know in what specific format the feedback will be provided.

2.3   In conclusion

The AC process owners' function is to scrutinise the overall AC content and to provide feedback on two critical aspects, namely the overall AC content and the AC process:

- First, from the perspective of the relevance of the programme content, it is necessary to determine whether the programme will address those competencies (or other focal constructs) and needs as specified by the needs and/or the job analyses (Byham and Temlock[5] refer to this facet of an AC as *operational validity*).
- Secondly, from a process rigour perspective, it is necessary to determine whether the programme participants will have a clear understanding of the broad assessment process and practices, the programme outcomes, and the degree of consistency in the application of this process. A new concept can be coined here, namely that of *operational reliability*. This concept refers to the overall consistency of application of all operational practices, processes and procedures. This type of reliability is a prerequisite for operational validity. After all, an AC can only be as valid as the operational (consistency) reliability allows it to be. Process owners also have to ensure that the assessment programme does not infringe any participant's personal rights (see Chapter 6). Where such infringement is avoided, this can also contribute largely to participants' positive evaluation of the programme and its fairness.

The AC process owners should also be careful not to fall into the trap of inflated self-assessments or self-ratings (i.e. a positive self-rating bias), thereby making them feel complacent. It is against this background that the other stakeholders can provide valuable feedback on the AC process and content, but from a different perspective.

---

4   SA Assessment Centre Study Group, 2018

5   Byham & Temlock, 1972

The next section deals with the evaluations and inputs of participants.

3. PARTICIPANTS' EVALUATIONS AND INPUT

The AC participants (and especially those involved in the AC pilot) are literally on the receiving end of an AC. They are thus best equipped to provide comments on the content and process of the AC. These two aspects will be discussed separately in the two sections below.

3.1 Experience of the content

Participants can provide valuable feedback on how they experienced the content of the overall AC and the content of the specific exercises. Although they may not be experts in the respective organisation levels, they may still be able to provide useful comments on the relevance of the content, but especially on how they experienced the content. This feedback is probably the most important evaluation of the face validity (an important facet of content validity) of the AC. If participants experience the content as positive, fair and valid, the AC will receive a positive rating in respect of face validity.

3.1.1 Content relevance

Participants can provide valuable feedback on their perceptions of the content relevance of the AC programme. They can provide their subjective assessment of the content of each assessment exercise and of the authenticity of the content. This information will be crucial for the AC design team, as it will allow the team to assess whether the content is aligned with the competency in question.

3.1.2 Experience of the AC content

A related aspect is how participants 'experienced' the AC content. It can probably be considered an AC best practice to afford participants the opportunity to provide feedback on their AC experience. Content-related aspects can be addressed in the feedback session or on the feedback form.

3.1.3 Face validity

This aspect needs to be mentioned separately. Because of the importance of face validity, special cognisance should be taken of participants' experience of the authenticity of the content of the AC simulations and overall programme. This feedback on the content is a direct reflection of their "face validity" assessment, which, again, is an important facet of content validity.

3.1.4 Related fairness perceptions

The perceived content validity of the overall AC, or of a particular aspect of the AC, is directly related to, and can most probably not be separated from, participants' perceptions of the fairness (or consistency) of the overall AC content.

3.2 Experience of the process

Participants are in a good position to provide comments on how they experienced the overall AC process and the individual exercises. Fairness is an important perception when people reflect on their experiences of processes, policies and procedures during staff selection processes. Employers should therefore take such factors into consideration when designing selection procedures.[6] Different kinds of perceived fairness, also termed "distributive justice, procedural justice, informational justice and interpersonal justice"[7] are identified. The AC practices, processes and procedures should be experienced by all participants as equitable and fair. It is argued that ACs can be used to grow and develop workplace fairness.[8] The feedback of participants thus serves as an important source of information regarding the fairness of the AC process. Participants' different sources of fairness perceptions will be discussed below.

3.2.1 Distributive justice

Distributive justice refers to perceptions of how an outcome or a decision affects us.[9] If participants assess a process, procedure or policy to be non-discriminatory, the distributive justice of such a process, procedure or policy will be viewed as fair.

3.2.2 Procedural justice

Procedural justice can be described as the beliefs about the process used to arrive at a decision.[10] If, for instance, the process used to collate the observer ratings were to be considered unfair, the procedural justice of that whole process would be considered to be unfair. It is therefore important to provide participants with the opportunity to comment on the process. If participants disagree, they should also be allowed the opportunity to appeal against the outcome of a process.

3.2.3 Informational justice

Informational justice can be defined as the adequacy and the truthfulness of explanations provided for an outcome.[11] If AC owners have a clearly established procedure and a specific format for recording and collating observer scores, the "paper trail" in respect of this process will provide sufficient evidence of the informational justice pertaining to how the assessments ratings were calculated.

---

6   Fodchuk & Sidebotham, 2005

7   Thornton & Rupp, 2006: 199

8   Rupp et al., 2006

9   Thornton & Rupp, 2006: 199

10 Thornton & Rupp, 2006: 199

11 Thornton & Rupp, 2006: 199

3.2.4   Interpersonal justice

"Interpersonal justice" refers to the general degree of dignity and respect with which individuals are treated.[12] If AC observers or Administrators do not treat all participants with the same degree of interpersonal dignity and respect, this will compromise the interpersonal justice of the AC programme.[13]

3.2.5   Overall fairness perceptions

All the fairness facets referred to above play an equally important role in the overall fairness assessment of the AC programme or process. It is therefore important that the AC process owners carefully consider all facets of fairness in the execution of the AC programme.

3.3   In conclusion

AC participants give feedback on the overall AC content and process with two different perspectives in mind:

- First, they provide feedback on their own perceptions of the content of the overall AC programme and individual exercises in terms of relevance and the perceived validity of the programme.
- Secondly, they provide valuable feedback on a number of different process issues that will, in the end, provide a summative assessment of the programme's face validity and overall fairness.

The next stakeholder group is the subordinates.

4.   SUBORDINATES' PRE- AND POST-AC OBSERVATIONS

Subordinates in the organisation as a stakeholder group are in the best position to provide an evaluation of the participant managers' behaviour before and after the AC process. Subordinates can therefore be good judges of whether the AC has succeeded in transforming management behaviour, provided that they are sufficiently informed about the AC process and content.

4.1   Pre- and post-evaluations of manager behaviours in respect of content

One can assume that managers do exhibit some management competencies and skills while performing their management function. It is common knowledge that the management process consists of different subprocesses and stages. Subordinates are on the receiving end of their respective managers' management skills and can therefore provide valid feedback on their managers' knowledge content. The only precondition is that they (the subordinates) should be capable of making these judgements.

---

12 Thornton & Rupp, 2006: 199

13 SA Assessment Centre Study Group, 2018

4.1.1 Managers' knowledge content

Subordinates can make a valid judgement on their managers' knowledge content of the management process. More specifically, they can evaluate their manager's planning, organising, leadership and controlling abilities. They can also pass judgement on whether the manager's management knowledge improved from the pre- to the post-AC period.

4.1.2 Competency content

The second aspect that subordinates can evaluate is the manager's actual management competence. In this case, some of the most critical behavioural elements before and after the AC process can be evaluated in order to determine whether the manager succeeded in making some critical behavioural changes.

4.2 Pre- and post-evaluations of managers' behaviours in respect of process

As stated previously, management can also be viewed as a process. The question in this case would be: To what extent is the approach to the management process integrated and coherent?

4.2.1 Management process

Subordinates can pass a judgement on whether the manager follows a logical and integrated approach to managing a specific task or project. Furthermore, the manager's ability to separate and sequence the stages correctly in the management process will provide good feedback on their ability to deal systematically with complexity.

4.2.2 Management process content

Subordinates are also suitably positioned to judge on the manager's actual management competence from a process perspective. Managers' own view of time, planning and so forth may provide valuable information from a process content perspective.

4.3 In conclusion

Suitably briefed or trained subordinates (those earmarked for management training, perhaps) can provide valuable feedback on how managers have succeeded in changing their management behaviours and applying their management skills from the period before to the period after the AC process. This information, if systematically captured, can provide valuable validity information on the AC programme's impact. More specifically, subordinates can pass a judgement on:
- the shift in managers' knowledge content as well as in the content of their competencies over the said period; and
- the shift in managers' process-management competence over the said period.

The next stakeholder group is the participants' immediate managers.

5. MANAGERS' EVALUATIONS AND INPUT

Competent managers in the organisation are probably best suited to provide comments on the content of the management function, because this is their job. One could therefore assume that such managers are knowledgeable about the content of their jobs and also have appropriate insights into what behaviours are required to perform their jobs well. The respective managers for the different management levels will therefore be the best persons to comment on the content and the process of the AC, as opposed to the AC process owners who will focus on the programme structure and process.

5.1 Strategic relevance of the content

One would assume that competent managers also have a clear understanding of the competencies needed to perform a current management job well, however managers should also have a better understanding of the competencies needed to fulfil future management needs and roles. This, therefore, puts managers in the best position to provide comments on the content of the AC from a management-content perspective. Managers can thus provide excellent feedback on aspects such as the use of technology, financial and budgeting skills, business acumen, the management of diverse groups, or any other management-specific needs.

5.1.1 Management level

Competent managers are in the best position to assess whether the overall AC is "pitched" at their specific management level and whether the exercises typically reflect the management issues at this level.

5.1.2 Management competencies

Competent managers are furthermore in a position to determine whether the specific competencies (or other focal constructs) at a particular level are the ones actually needed on that level. The focus is thus on relevance or on identifying alternatives in terms of future needs.

5.1.3 Future management competencies

Competent managers are also best suited to determine whether the future management competencies needed for achieving the company's strategic objectives are indeed in place, or have been sufficiently addressed.

5.1.4 Specific behavioural elements

Managers are furthermore in the best position to determine whether the actual behaviours to be observed are indeed the correct ones. They can thus provide valuable feedback on issues such as content and the range of behavioural elements/indicators.

5.2 Strategic relevance of the process

Competent managers in the organisation are suitably qualified to provide comments on the rigour of the AC process. The aspects that managers will be focusing on will have a specific bearing on the specific management competencies and on the context of the execution of the AC process. Does the AC as a whole or the individual simulations sufficiently reflect the management pressures, stresses and strains, and does the AC context reflect these well? The managers will therefore not only focus on the content relevance, but also on the contextual relevance of the AC exercises.

5.2.1 Strategic relevance of the overall AC process

The issue that managers will be focusing on in this instance is whether the overall AC process supports the company's strategy of management development and the development of future management competencies.

5.2.2 Strategic relevance of the overall AC context

The issue here is whether the AC succeeds in creating a management context that realistically reflects the management context and the culture of the organisation. Managers can give valuable feedback on how well the AC process captures this company-specific context and culture.

5.2.3 Strategic relevance of the specific AC competency assessment process

Managers should determine, and give feedback on, whether a specific competency assessment exercise succeeds in creating a strategically relevant process; in other words, is this how the problem will typically surface or present itself in the organisation?

5.2.4 Strategic relevance of the specific behavioural elements/indicators

Managers also have to ascertain whether the process of eliciting the required behaviours is relevant and appropriate for the specific competency exercise. Does the problem present itself in similar ways in practice, and will the resulting behaviours be predictive of management success?

5.3 In conclusion

Competent managers provide feedback on the AC content and process in order that the following aspects may be assessed:

- They provide feedback on the strategic relevance of the AC content in terms of the management level, the different competencies required at that level, and the different behavioural elements within a specific competency.
- They also provide feedback on the strategic relevance of the overall AC process, on the management culture and context, and on the presence of critical behavioural elements.

The next section deals with the feedback of Human Capital specialists.

6. HUMAN CAPITAL SPECIALISTS' EVALUATIONS AND INPUT

Human Capital specialists/professionals (such as Human Capital planning, learning and development, talent management, or management-leadership development specialists) play a key role in providing a perspective on the current and future management-leadership competency needs in an organisation. These specialists can therefore provide valid feedback on the content and process of the AC programme.

6.1 A critical competency perspective on content

Human Capital specialists are best suited, in view of the overall Human Capital strategy and plan, to provide comments on the critical future needs in respect of management-leadership competencies and skills. They can thus comment on how well the AC addresses these competencies and needs. If the AC does not address these competencies and needs, these respective specialists can make useful suggestions as to how the AC should be adapted or changed so that these needs are in fact addressed. Specific aspects to be addressed in their feedback are the following:

6.1.1 Current management-leadership competency profile

Human Capital managers and Human Capital professionals are best equipped to comment on the relevance of the competencies currently present in the organisation. They can make a valid assessment as to whether these competencies support the execution of the strategic, business or operational objectives in the organisation. If these existing competencies do not support the execution of the objectives, a thorough needs and/or job analysis will be required.

6.1.2 A competency needs analysis and job analyses

Human Capital managers and Human Capital professionals can decide to conduct a proper needs analysis first. This needs analysis and an organisational effectiveness analysis can provide guidance on which specific competencies or competency elements are required to effectively execute a specific job. This can be followed by a thorough job analysis, or an analysis of a job family. This process will enable the Human Capital managers and Human Capital professionals to assess whether there is a gap between the current competencies and the competencies that emerged from the needs or job analyses. The content of the latter competencies needs to be included in the assessment exercises, if there does, in fact, appear to be a gap.

6.1.3 Future management-leadership competency profile

Most Human Capital managers have a management-leadership strategy or a plan that projects future human capital needs. This strategy or plan will indicate which specific skills or competencies are needed, the number of competencies, and also at what point they will be needed.

6.1.4   Current management-leadership behaviour elements/indicators

Human Capital managers and/or Human Capital professionals can provide the AC design team with useful comments on the behavioural elements/indicators to be assessed within each competency assessment exercise. Given their knowledge of the outcome of the different job or job family analyses, they are ideally positioned to comment on these required behavioural elements.

6.1.5   Future management-leadership behavioural elements/indicators

As a result of Human Capital skills audits and projections, Human Capital managers and/or Human Capital professionals are normally also knowledgeable about future management-leadership training needs. This knowledge can be usefully applied to project which management-leadership behavioural elements will be needed in future. Management-competency assessment exercises can then be adapted or redesigned to address these specific elements.

6.2   A critical compliance perspective on the process

Human Capital specialists (assessment specialists or employment relations specialists) can also provide useful comments on the AC process as such. In this instance, their focus will be on how well the AC process and procedures comply with principles of fairness. These specialists will reflect on whether the AC process has an adverse impact on specific groups of people. In terms of the legislation referred to in Chapter 6, no person may be discriminated against on the grounds mentioned in the different Acts.

6.2.1   ACs should be non-discriminatory

Human Capital specialists (such as assessment specialists or employment relations specialists) and the AC process owners have a responsibility to ensure that the overall AC assessment process and procedures are non-discriminatory in nature. They should be able to provide evidence that the AC programme is not discriminating against any group or any individual on the basis of any of the grounds referred to in Chapter 6.

6.2.2   Equitable and fair

The Human Capital specialists mentioned in the aforementioned point should also ensure that the overall AC programme and process, and all the AC procedures and practices, are equitable and fair. "Fairness" here refers to the subjective perceptions of participants that the overall AC programme or process and the individual assessment exercises are equitable and just (refer to the SIOP[14] Guidelines for a discussion on fairness). Fairness is about participants' perceptions. The feedback and comments of participants should be scrutinised for clues or hints indicating that anything in the programme, process, procedures or practices was perceived by participants as being unjust or unfair.

---

14 Society for Industrial and Organisational Psychology (SIOP), 2018, 2005

6.2.3   Unbiased

Bias is an inherent characteristic of an assessment measure or an assessment exercise if a particular test or assessment systematically discriminates against a particular group. Measurement bias thus refers to the systematic discrimination of a test or an assessment that can be statistically calculated (refer to SIOP[15]). Human Capital specialists and the AC process owners are therefore responsible for collecting data and evidence to show that their assessment process does not reflect any kind of systematic bias against any group mentioned in the different Acts referred to in Chapter 6.

6.2.4   Adverse impact

If an assessment systematically discriminates against any particular group mentioned in Chapter 6, it will show adverse impact on that group. It is thus the responsibility of the Human Capital specialists mentioned and of the AC process owners to prevent any adverse impact on any group.

6.3   In conclusion

Human Capital professionals (Human Capital managers and specialists) look at AC programmes, processes, procedures and practices from a different perspective, in that they take a critical look at the content and process of the AC programme in order to determine whether:
*   the content addresses the critical competencies in respect of current and future needs; and
*   the process is equitable and fair and does not discriminate against a particular group, i.e. that it complies with all aspects of legislation.

Information from other sources is also necessary in order to make an informed decision on the content validity of ACs.

Example of Determining the Content Validity of an AC

Müller and Roodt[16] determined the content validity of a virtual assessment centre (VAC) during a research project. They started by identifying the groups of stakeholders to be involved in the process. A questionnaire was compiled that each person in the stakeholder groups had to complete independently after observing the VAC as a 'fly on the wall'. The questionnaire used a 7-point Likert type scale (1= strongly disagree; 7 = strongly agree) and covered seven dimensions. The inter-rater agreement was determined by applying the Intra-Class Correlation Coefficient (ICC).

The results indicated that the stakeholders scored the dimensions highly and there was a high degree of consistency between the stakeholders. There was also an indication that the stakeholders observed the same process. The conclusion from this research was that the specific VAC was content valid.

---

15 SIOP, 2005

16 Müller & Roodt, 2013

7.   OTHER SOURCES OF INFORMATION

Two specific sources of information will be referred to under this heading, namely the outcome of the company context and needs analysis, and the outcome of the specific job analysis. These aspects will be referred to only briefly, since they have already been discussed in Chapters 6, 7 and 8.

7.1   Contextual and company needs analyses

A proper analysis of the social and legal context in which a company is functioning will provide a clear picture of the social and legal demands that the industry (or company) has to comply with. This information is useful not only from a compliance perspective, but also from the perspective of a management-leadership competency needs analysis. The latter will provide information on which specific management-leadership competencies are needed to deal with these social and legal demands.

A specific company needs analysis will, in turn, yield valuable information on the required competencies at different organisational levels, as well as on the different behavioural elements/indicators within each specific competency. First, different sources of information outside the company may also provide useful information on competency demands (such as image in the media and national policy priorities). Secondly, a number of different company planning processes (strategic planning, Human Capital planning, succession planning), information systems (MIS, HRIS) and other record systems (safety records, performance management records) can be successfully utilised to generate information on specific competency needs.

7.2   Job and job family analyses

Specific jobs or job families can be analysed on different organisational levels in order to provide information on current required competencies or on future competency needs. The outcome of this process is of the utmost importance in providing a competency profile of the job or job level that the AC is targeting. This aspect was fully covered in Chapter 8.

8.   CRITICAL DECISIONS RELATING TO THIS STEP, AND THE OUTCOMES THEREOF

The following are the outcomes of, and critical decisions relating to, this step:

The first, and probably the most important, outcome of this step is to provide a systematic analysis of the content validity of the overall AC programme.

In order to achieve systematic feedback on the overall picture of the AC content and process, the AC design team needs to systematically collect information from different key stakeholders in the AC process. Different key decisions have to be taken in this respect:
- The design team has to identify who the key stakeholders are.

- The design team has to specify what the key focus of a specific stakeholder group should be.
- The design team then has to determine the feedback format and the focus on process and content aspects.

The systematic collection of information on process and content matters from different stakeholders will enable the design team to make informed judgements on a range of different process- and content-specific aspects. The most important content matters will relate to the relevance (appropriateness) of the programme content so that the programme can address the needs identified in the different company needs or job analyses. This is to ensure that the assessment dimensions are perfectly aligned with the specified competencies. The most important process matters are probably the AC's bias, fairness and adverse impact. This is to ensure that the AC participants have a clear picture of the overall programme and process, and, in particular, that none of their rights will be infringed.

Only with a more holistic picture of the process (operational reliability and validity) as well as the content (content validity) of the AC programme can a better informed decision about the overall content validity of an AC be made.

RELIABILITY AND VALIDITY ANALYSES

Gert Roodt

1. INTRODUCTION – THE PURPOSE OF RELIABILITY AND VALIDITY ANALYSES

In this stage, the focus is on the reliability and validity analyses of ACs. Assume for the moment that the outcome of the first step in the fourth stage of our design model is a content-valid AC. The second logical step of this stage would therefore be to conduct a reliability and validity analysis of the AC and the AC dimensions. This step is highlighted in the design model in Figure 19.1:

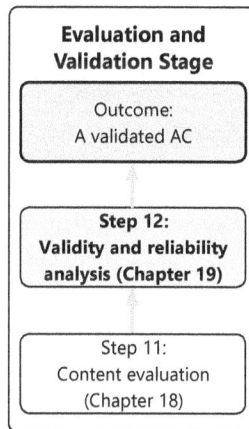

```
┌─────────────────────────────┐
│   Evaluation and            │
│   Validation Stage          │
│  ┌───────────────────────┐  │
│  │  Outcome:             │  │
│  │  A validated AC       │  │
│  └───────────────────────┘  │
│            ▲                │
│  ┌───────────────────────┐  │
│  │  Step 12:             │  │
│  │  Validity and reliability│
│  │  analysis (Chapter 19)│  │
│  └───────────────────────┘  │
│            ▲                │
│  ┌───────────────────────┐  │
│  │  Step 11:             │  │
│  │  Content evaluation   │  │
│  │  (Chapter 18)         │  │
│  └───────────────────────┘  │
└─────────────────────────────┘
```

Figure 19.1: The steps in, and stages of, the design model

This chapter will therefore focus on the "what" and "how" of reliability and validity analyses. The "what" of reliability and validity analyses will provide the necessary background for gaining a better understanding of what exactly these two terms mean. The first section of this chapter will therefore explain the concepts *reliability* and *validity*.

The second section of this chapter provides a brief overview of some basic statistical concepts that are required for understanding the meaning of reliability and validity from a statistical-equation perspective. Some measures of location, variability and association will be discussed. These should provide the reader with a workable knowledge and background for understanding the basic constructs, reliability and validity.

The third and fourth sections of the chapter will focus specifically on the "how" of reliability and validity analyses. More specifically, section three will focus on the reliability of AC ratings. Different options for calculating the reliabilities of AC ratings will be discussed. Specific attention will be given to internal-consistency reliabilities, test-retest reliabilities, alternate-form reliabilities, inter- and intra-rater reliabilities, and the standard error of measurement.

The fourth section of the chapter will provide a discussion on the validity construct. Different types of validity will be introduced and briefly discussed, with special emphasis on content (descriptive), construct (identification) and criterion (prediction) validity. A brief description of unitary validity will be provided as a concluding comment.

The fifth section of the chapter deals specifically with two types of AC rating, namely raw (assessor) ratings and standardised (integrated) ratings.

The sixth section will cover a number of special cases and issues to be considered when calculating AC ratings. Aspects such as exercise effects, the distribution of ratings and specific issues relating to fairness, bias and participant–observer mix, as well as competency redundancies, will be covered in the chapter.

The chapter concludes with a discussion on the critical outcomes of, and decisions relating to, this step. The Employment Equity Act[1] requires that all assessments, including ACs, should be reliable and valid. Let us therefore take a closer look at what exactly these two concepts mean.

Introductory case study: Different interpretations of behaviour elements

An AC service provider in the SA market is frequently conducting DACs for clients, and *post hoc* analyses of these assessment results have indicated that some competency dimensions yield lower reliabilities when compared to other competency dimensions in the same AC. What is the root cause of these low reliabilities and ultimately the poor construct validity of these dimensions?

Mainly three assessors were used for this range of DACs. Inter-correlations between these assessors have indicated that the ratings of Assessors A and B are highly correlated, but that the ratings of Assessors A and B were not highly correlated with C (specifically in respect of these problematic competency dimensions).

A descriptive (content) analysis of the three assessors' views on the competencies in question surfaced significant interpretative differences in terms of the behaviour elements between the three assessors. This resulted in frank discussions between the assessors and consequently the re-framing of the criteria for rating the behaviour elements (also termed frame-of-reference training), which resulted in significantly improved assessment results.

This chapter will introduce basic statistical tools to diagnose and address reliability problems or even associated construct validity problems.

---

1   Employment Equity Act (Act 55 of 1998)

2.   WHAT RELIABILITY AND VALIDITY ARE ALL ABOUT

Reliability and validity are two concepts that are widely used in a range of different applications, which result in a variety of different meanings and descriptions for these two terms. Measurement in the psychological context "consists of rules for assigning numbers to objects so as to (1) represent quantities of attributes numerically (scaling) or (2) define whether the objects fall in the same or different categories with respect to a given attribute (classification)".[2] In the measurement or assessment context, reliability and validity have evolved to the status of constructs – this means that validity and reliability have very specific and defined meanings when applied in the assessment context. The constructs reliability and validity are of crucial importance when specific assessment tools or techniques are scrutinised.

Reliability is defined as "the consistency with which it measures whatever it measures".[3] A measure will thus be considered reliable if it measures a particular psychological attribute such as "leadership" in a consistent manner.

Validity is about "...how well it measures what it purports to measure".[4] A measure of leadership will be considered valid if it does measure the construct *leadership* precisely.

In order to gain a better understanding of these constructs, some statistical concepts have to be explained first.

3.   BASIC STATISTICAL CONCEPTS FOR UNDERSTANDING AND INTERPRETING RELIABILITY AND VALIDITY CONSTRUCTS

The statistical concepts to be explained in the different subsections below are measures of location, measures of variability, and measures of association.

For the sake of simplicity, these concepts will be explained by means of a simple example. If you were to measure a characteristic of a random group of people (e.g. weight), the distribution of the obtained scores (their weights) would take on a particular distribution or shape, which is often referred to as the distribution curve. The distribution curve can be depicted as in Figure 19.2.

---

2   Nunnally & Bernstein, 1994: 3

3   Wolfaardt & Roodt, 2005: 28

4   Nunnally & Bernstein, 1994: 83

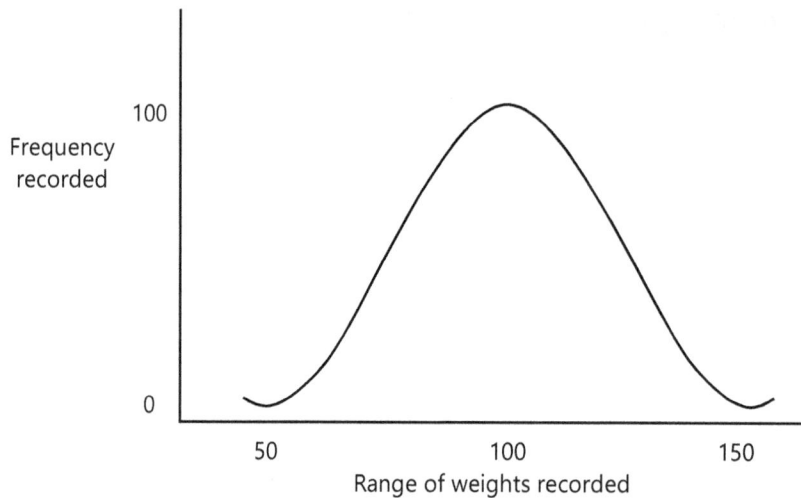

Figure 19.2: The distribution of recorded weights

Variables can be measured either as categorical variables (with ordinal and nominal scales) or as continuous variables (with interval and ratio scales). Categorical measures, as the name suggests, categorise or group people or subjects according to one or other characteristic (e.g. gender, race, marital status, etc.). Continuous measures, on the other hand, display differences between subjects in terms of measured units where these units possess equal properties (e.g. weight, height, etc.).[5] Continuous and categorical measures require different statistical treatment, respectively referred to as parametric and non-parametric statistical procedures. In the case of our example, the range of the recorded weights (continuous measures) is portrayed on the horizontal axis (X) and the frequency of the occurrence of a recorded weight on the vertical axis (Y). Let us now examine the following categories of measures more closely:

3.1 Measure of central tendency (location)

As the name suggests, measures of central tendency refer to where the measures group or are located. The mode is the score that is recorded most frequently (the one that forms the peak of the distribution in Figure 19.2) and is denoted as M_o.[6]

The median (mid-point of the distribution) represents the score where 50% of the distribution is below that point and the other 50% above that point. The formula for calculating the median (M_e) is as follows:[7]

$$M_e = N + 1 / 2$$ **Formula 19.1**

---

5   Howell, 1995

6   Howell, 1995

7   Howell, 1995

The mean ($\bar{X}$, also referred to as bar X) is the sum ($\sum$) of all the scores divided by the number (N) of the scores. The formula for calculating the mean is as follows:[8]

$$\bar{Y} = \sum X \,/\, N \qquad\qquad \textbf{Formula 19.2}$$

If the mean, the mode and the median share exactly the same value, the distribution will be normally distributed. If not, the distribution will be either negatively or positively skewed.

3.2 Measures of variability

The variability of scores gives us an indication of how the scores are distributed. If the distribution is flat and wide, the scores may cover a wide range, that is, the distance from the lowest to the highest scores.[9] The scores in the case of our example (Figure 19.2) range between about 50 and 150.

The variance gives an indication of how the scores vary about the mean or deviate from the mean (X − $\bar{X}$). Half of these scores will have negative values and the other half positive values, which leads us to the conclusion that the sum of these deviations always equals zero. To overcome this problem (of equalling zero), all the deviations are then squared (a squared minus becomes a plus) and the outcome is always a positive value. The variance is thus the sum of the squared deviations about the mean, divided by N − 1. (Please note that, for the denotation for sample parameters (a statistical term for characteristics), normal letters of the alphabet are used. In the case of population parameters, Greek letters of the alphabet are used.) The formula for the population variance is as follows[10]:

$$\sigma^2 = \sum(X - \bar{X})^2 \,/\, N - 1 \qquad\qquad \textbf{Formula 19.3}$$

The standard deviation is simply the square root of the variance. The denotation of the standard deviation (S.D.) is σ, which is also called sigma.[11]

$$\sigma = \sqrt{\sigma^2} \qquad\qquad \textbf{Formula 19.4}$$

3.3 Measures of association

Measures of association, as the name suggests, refer to the association of two measures. If we were to correlate the weights (X) of the people in our example with their height (Y), we would obtain a measure of association that is also known as a correlation coefficient. The correlation coefficient (r) is calculated as the covariance of XY divided by the product of the variances of the two moments (X and Y). This can be portrayed as follows:[12]

$$r = COV_{xy} \,/\, S_x S_y \qquad\qquad \textbf{Formula 19.5}$$

---

8   Howell, 1995
9   Howell, 1995
10 Runyon & Haber, 1980
11 Runyon & Haber, 1980
12 Howell, 1995

This formula can be simplified by replacing the variances and covariances with their computational formulae and by resolving the equation.[13] This formula is also known as the Pearson product-moment correlation.

$$r = N\sum XY - \sum X\sum Y / \sqrt{[N\sum X^2 - (\sum X)^2] \cdot [N\sum Y^2 - (\sum Y)^2]}$$ **Formula 19.6**

If a correlation coefficient shows that scores are sufficiently correlated, then we can use this information to build a prediction model. The regression coefficient is used to predict the values of an unknown set of scores by using a known set of scores. We can therefore predict a person's height (Y) by using his/her known weight (X).

Stated in AC terms, this means that we can predict people's performance ($\hat{Y}$) if we know their overall assessment rating (X) and other properties of the regression line, such as the slope (b) and the intercept (a). The regression equation (prediction model) can be formulated as follows:[14]

$$\hat{Y} = bX + a$$ **Formula 19.7**

Or, in the case of multiple predictors, the equation would look as follows:

$$\hat{Y} = b_1 X + b_1 C + a$$ **Formula 19.8**

Here, b_1 denotes the different regression weights of the predictor variables X and C, with *a* as the value of the intercept.

With a basic understanding of these descriptive statistics, we can proceed to the next section in which the reliabilities of measures will be discussed in more detail.

4. OPTIONS FOR CALCULATING THE RELIABILITY OF AC RATINGS

It is a basic technical requirement that a psychological measure meet the standards of reliability and validity. The Employment Equity Act[15] also requires that measures should be reliable and valid (see Chapter 6).

Any single measured score does not automatically accurately reflect the consistency of a measurement; a range of different reasons exists that may influence a person's "true" score. There may be different chance factors in the test room, in the measure itself, in the instructions for completing the test and, finally, in the person completing the test. All these factors are collectively referred to as error variance. Any observed score thus contains an amount of error variance. Yes, even a person's measured weight contains an amount of error variance, depending on the quality of the scale used and other measuring conditions. It then logically follows that the true score is the portion of the observed score minus the portion of the error score.

13 Howell, 1995

14 Runyon & Haber, 1980

15 Employment Equity Act (Act 55 of 1998)

Reliabilities of AC ratings may also vary in the AC context. Similar reasons can be advanced for these variations in scores, namely the variations in the AC context, in the instructions, in the role plays or exercises, in the observers and Administrators, and, finally, also within the participants of the AC (see Figure 19.3 below) (refer to Chapter 6, Section 5). These factors also contribute to error variance in AC procedures. An additional contributing factor in this instance is the error variance in the observer ratings and in the procedure for collating the final assessment ratings. For several different reasons, it is important to gain a better picture of these sources of error variance in AC ratings. The most important is obviously having a sufficiently reliable and valid AC process that will comply with the requirements of the different Acts in South Africa (as discussed in Chapter 6).

The reliability of an assessment or rating can also be formulated as an equation where the observed (total) score (O), equals the proportion of the true score (T) plus the proportion of the error score (E). The proportion of the true score (T) can be derived by subtracting the proportion of the error score (E) from the observed score (O).

$$O = T + E \qquad \text{therefore} \quad T = O - E \qquad \qquad \textbf{Formula 19.9}$$

It then follows that variance of the observed scores (S^2_O) can be expressed as the sum of the variances of the true scores (S^2_T) and the error variances (S^2_E).

$$S^2_O = S^2_T + S^2_E \qquad \qquad \textbf{Formula 19.10}$$

Reliability (R) can now be defined as the ratio of true and observed score variances that can be expressed as a coefficient:

$$R = S^2_o - S^2_e / S^2_o$$
$$R = S^2_t / S^2_o \qquad \qquad \textbf{Formula 19.11}$$

However, we can only resolve this equation if we know the value of the error scores or the true scores. Different statistical procedures have been developed for calculating the reliabilities of a measure. The following subsections will deal with different variations of reliability calculation, starting with the simpler versions first.

4.1 Test–retest reliability

The very first option for calculating the reliability of a measure is based on the definition of reliability where it refers to the degree of "consistency" of a measure. If we were to weigh a group of people and repeat this procedure within an hour, we could calculate the correlation between the first (X) and the second (Y) weight measures for this group. A Pearson product-moment correlation (Formula 19.6) can be used to calculate this relationship. However, a number of different factors may influence the relationship between the first and the second measurements, such as the time difference between the measurements, aging, learning, history, and so forth.

Applied to the AC context, this means that the ratings that people obtain for a particular competency on a first occasion can be correlated with the scores that they have obtained for the same competency on a second occasion. This would illustrate the test–retest reliability of the competency rating. It is not always practical to put the same group of people through repeated measuring sessions in respect of the same measure, however also as indicated, a number of different factors (such as learning) may occur between the pre- and the post-measurement.

4.2 Equivalent-form reliability

In the case of this method, two equivalent (alternate) forms of the same measure can be applied. The correlation between the two sets of scores obtained on the different measures will yield a reliability coefficient, which is also known as the coefficient of equivalence. This type of reliability calculation is based on the conditions that the two forms of the test should be equivalent in all respects, that is, as regards time to complete, difficulty of the items, same number of items, and the same scoring procedure.

It will be difficult in the AC context to develop an equivalent assessment exercise that will tap into exactly the same competencies and competency elements, however it is of utmost importance that the assessment procedure remain consistent across different groups in respect of time to complete, difficulty of the exercise, number of competencies observed, and scoring procedure. Operational reliability is applicable here, that is, the overall consistency with which all operational practices, processes and procedures are applied.

4.3 Split-half reliabilities

The items of a psychological measure can be randomly split into two equal halves after the completion of the test. The test can, for example, be split according to the odd- and even-numbered items. The two "equivalent" halves can then be correlated. The coefficient that is obtained is also referred to as the coefficient of internal consistency. It will be difficult to apply this specific procedure in an AC context, but the underlying logic of correlating "equal" halves provides a sound platform for further developing this line of thought. A different consistency reliability of a measure or a rating is presented in the next subsection.

4.4 Kuder-Richardson and Coefficient Alpha reliabilities

Another coefficient of internal consistency is the inter-item consistency, which is also referred to as the Kuder-Richardson (KR 20) method. In this case, the consistency of the respondents' responses to all items (assessments) is calculated. In the case of the KR 20, the test items use a dichotomous or a binary response format, i.e. a 1 for correct responses and a 0 for incorrect responses. This formula can therefore not be used for AC purposes, but its underlying logic provides the basis for a formula that we can use (which is explained further down). The equation for the KR 20 formula is as follows:[16]

$$r_{tt} = (n / n - 1) . (s_t^2 - \textstyle\sum pq) / s_t^2)$$ **Formula 19.12**

---

16 Wolfaardt & Roodt, 2005

Where:

r_{tt} = reliability coefficient

n   = number of test items

s_t^2 = variance of the test total scores

p   = proportion of testees who answered item i correctly

q   = proportion of testees who answered item i incorrectly

In the case of AC ratings, the rating format on each item is a multi-option response format where the rater can make a choice between different available rating options (e.g. a choice of four options on a scale ranging from 1 to 4). The inter-item consistency formula (Cronbach's Alpha) for the multi-option response formats can thus be equated as follows:[17]

$$\alpha = (n\,/\,n-1)\,.\,(S_t^2 - \sum Si^2)\,/\,S_t^2) \qquad\qquad \textbf{Formula 19.13}$$

Where:

α = reliability coefficient

n   = number of test items (i.e. the number of elements observed and rated)

S_t^2 = variance of the test total scores

$\sum Si^2$ = sum of the variances of individual item scores.

An example of this type of reliability analysis was applied to 14 competency ratings that were assessed through a process of structured, competency-rating interviews.[18] The reliability coefficients obtained for the different individual competency ratings and for the overall procedure are reported in Table 19.1.

Table 19.1: Reliabilities of 14 interpersonal competency ratings obtained by means of structured, competency-rating interviews

Competency-total ratings statistics				
Competencies	**Scale mean if competency deleted**	**Scale variance if competency deleted**	**Corrected competency-total correlation**	**Squared multiple correlation**	**Cronbach's Alpha if competency deleted**
Integrating	43,5059	40,112	0,774	0,785	0,937
Insight	43,5529	39,462	0,786	0,785	0,937
Environmental sensitivity	43,3382	40,321	0,757	0,647	0,938
Adaptability	43,5735	40,446	0,730	0,603	0,938
Independence	43,5147	39,670	0,707	0,658	0,939
Resilience	43,4176	41,191	0,588	0,507	0,942

---

17 Howell, 1995; Foxcroft & Roodt, 2004

18 Roodt, 2007

Competency-total ratings statistics

Competencies	Scale mean if competency deleted	Scale variance if competency deleted	Corrected competency-total correlation	Squared multiple correlation	Cronbach's Alpha if competency deleted
Empathy	43,2529	41,329	0,628	0,689	0,941
Oral communication	43,2029	41,735	0,669	0,491	0,940
Interpersonal sensitivity	43,2912	40,952	0,657	0,723	0,940
Impact	43,5412	40,199	0,709	0,581	0,939
Rapport building	43,2235	41,133	0,765	0,661	0,938
Conflict resolution	43,6176	39,584	0,804	0,714	0,936
Customer focus	43,0588	41,269	0,765	0,692	0,938
Enthusiasm	43,0471	41,137	0,699	0,610	0,939

Cronbach's Alpha	Cronbach's Alpha based on standardised items	No of competencies
0,943	0,944	14

It can be inferred from Table 19.1 that a process of structured, competency-rating interviews can still yield reliable results, as reflected by the overall Cronbach's Alpha of 0,94, despite the fact that the data was generated by means of a 'subjective' rating process. A clear and consistent rating process and procedure were developed; AC ratings are obtained by means of a similar structured process.

This particular formula is used when calculating the internal consistencies of individual competency ratings or for individual exercise ratings in an AC. A matrix of associations (Kendall's Tau-B for categorical measurements) can thus be created that will reflect the competency inter-correlations across exercises in each row, or the exercise inter-correlations across different competencies in each column. This format creates a useful framework for assessing two different types of AC reliabilities, namely for individual competencies and for individual exercises. This information enables one to detect a "weak link" in the overall rating reliabilities. Such a matrix is displayed in Table 19.2.

Table 19.2: Correlation matrix between exercise ratings and final competency ratings, including competency and exercise reliability coefficients

Competency	In-Box	Counselling discussion	Group meeting	Analysis exercise	Competency Reliability
Initiative	0,620		0,416	0,441	0,583 N = 191
Information gathering	0,536	0,291	0,215	0,514	0,645 N = 189
Judgement	0,559	0,432	0,496	0,496	0,732 N = 192
Providing direction	0,522	0,374	0,447		0,630 N = 297
Empowering	0,501	0,465	0,373		0,616 N = 295
Interpersonal sensitivity		0,802	0,635		0,844 N = 299
Persuasiveness		0,696	0,677		0,810 N = 153
Oral communication		0,818	0,798		0,895 N = 257
Written communication			0,255	0,93	0,601 N = 35
Management control	0,389	0,250	0,226	0,394	0,484 N = 191
Motivating others		0,894	0,650		0,892 N = 41
Exercise reliability	0,XX	0,XX	0,XX	0,XX	0,XX

Source: Adapted from Schlebusch, Odendaal and Roodt[19]

The correlations between a specific competency and the final ratings in Table 19.2 provide an indication of which assessment method yielded the highest correlation with the final competency rating. In this instance, the initiative rating of the in-basket exercise correlated (r = 0,620) the highest with the final rating. The rating for motivating others was best correlated (r = 0,894) with the final rating in the counselling discussion. It is also evident that initiative (α = 0,583) and management control (α = 0,484) yielded the lowest competency reliabilities. These low reliabilities suggest that something is 'wrong' with the operational reliability (consistency) or with how the construct is defined.

This type of information is helpful in selecting the most appropriate exercise for capturing a particular competency if a shortened AC needs to be designed. The last row in the table provides the illustrative reliabilities (0,XX) for the different exercises. Owing to the fact that different groups were used to calculate the reliabilities for different competencies, the data could not be integrated to calculate the reliabilities of the different exercises in this case.

---

19 Schlebusch et al., 2003; Roodt et al., 2003

The internal consistency reliabilities for the different competency ratings in Table 19.2 vary between 0,484 and 0,895. In some cases, the competency ratings still include a large proportion of error variance, which can be systematically addressed. It should be noted that the varying sample sizes reflect three different management samples for these calculated reliabilities.

4.5   Inter-rater and intra-rater reliabilities

The consistency with which raters/observers apply their ratings during the AC process is of crucial importance. Rating errors such as leniency, stringency or even central-tendency errors may have serious repercussions for the overall reliabilities of AC ratings. Further investigation into inter- and intra-rater reliabilities is therefore warranted. In the case of inter- and intra-rater reliabilities, the Cronbach's Alpha formula is applied slightly differently, with the consistency of ratings between (inter-) or within (intra-) raters being calculated.

Inter-rater consistency reliability can be calculated by either correlating the ratings of two different raters or by applying the Cronbach's Alpha formula. This formula will enable one to determine the degree of consistency between different raters. The formula can be applied for specific competencies or for the overall AC. The same formula as above is applicable here, with the only differences being that:

S_t^2 = the variance on all the raters' final ratings
$\sum S_i^2$ = the sum of raters' variances across different competency ratings

Intra-rater consistency reliability can be calculated in a similar way, except that the values of the variances are obtained from different sources. This formula will enable one to determine the degree of consistency within a particular rater. In this case, the same formula as above applies, with the only difference being in the meaning of the variances:

S_t^2 = the variance of a rater on different individual's final ratings
$\sum S_i^2$ = the sum of a rater's variances on each competency for different individuals
being rated

Another form of reliability is the Standard Error of Measurement.

4.6   The Standard Error of Measurement (SEM)

The Standard Error of Measurement can be used to interpret individual test scores in terms of probability limits within which they are likely to vary as a function of measurement error. The reliability coefficient of a test can be used for the computation of the SEM.

$$SEM = S_t\sqrt{1 - r_{tt}}$$ **Formula 19.14**

Where:
S_t = standard deviation of the total test score
r_{tt} = reliability coefficient of the test

If a person obtains a SEM of 1 on a rating score, there will be a 68% chance (the portion of the normal distribution curve covered by one S.D. below and above the mean) that a person's true score will vary by 1 point above or below his/her measured score (2,5). The ratings will thus vary between 1,5 and 3,5. The same computational principles apply here as for calculating the S.D. for the standardised normal distribution (Z-scores) (see Wolfaardt & Roodt).[20]

4.7 Potential sources of error variance

In Figure 19.3, a graphical illustration of a potential number of different sources of error variance is presented. These sources are linked to the uncontrolled variances in all the policies, practices and procedures, such as in the instructions to participants, the observer ratings, the role plays, the collation of scores by Administrators, the reactions of participants, and the different assessment exercises (simulations). Finally, variations in the context of the management competency being assessed may also contribute to error variances. (The control of these sources of error variance and the steps for ensuring the consistency of all these procedures, practices and policies are collectively labelled as operational reliability.)

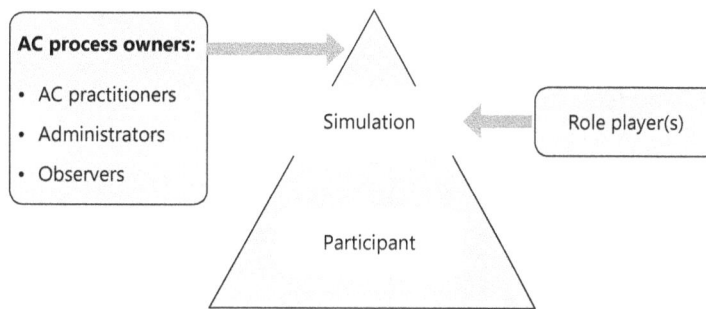

Figure 19.3: Potential sources of error variance that may affect operational reliability

Operational reliability is therefore a prerequisite AC condition for the operational validity that was discussed in Chapter 18. Guilford[21] identified a number of different, but specific, aspects related to the above-mentioned factors that may influence the reliability of measures; some of the most frequent threats are discussed below.

Researchers specifically caution about the effects of range restrictions[22], which occur when a sample is pre-selected from a larger population, i.e. managers with a qualification in business management would yield a pre-selected group of the management population in a company. Development ACs in a similar way pre-select candidates on the grounds that they do not have any management experience or knowledge. The restriction of range effects on the reliability coefficients of two Development AC dimension ratings are illustrated in Figures 19.4 and 19.5.[23] Note how the slight shift in frequency distributions results in a visible change in consistency reliability coefficients.

---

20 Wolfaardt & Roodt, 2005

21 Guilford, 1936

22 Wolfaardt & Roodt, 2005

23 Roodt & Schlebusch, 2006

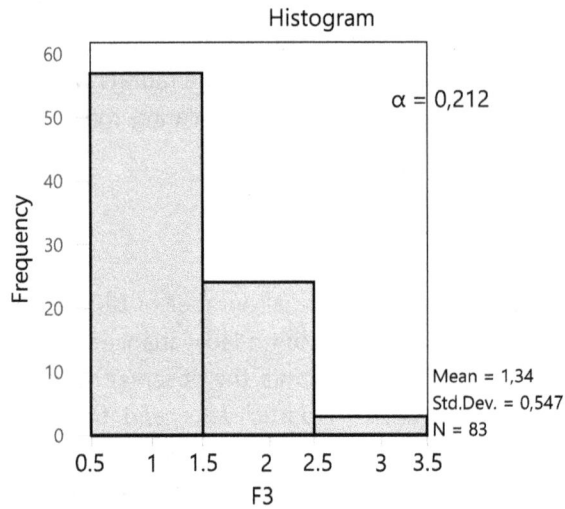

Figure 19.4: Skewed competency rating and internal consistency reliability

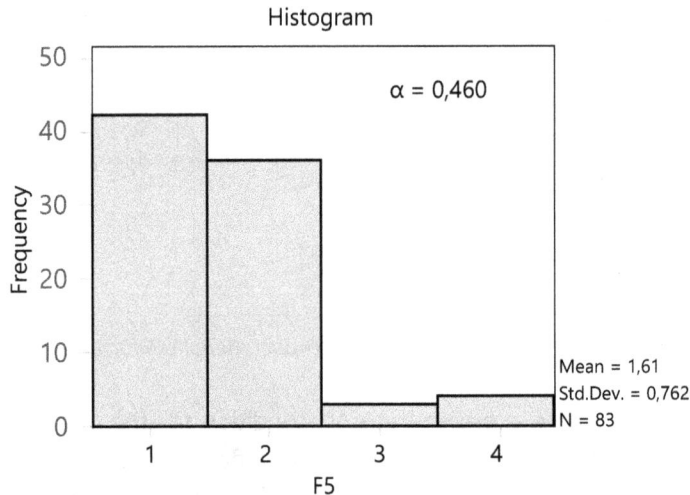

Figure 19.5: Less skewed competency rating and internal consistency reliability

Typically, Development ACs, as opposed to normal ACs, would yield lower reliabilities based on restriction-of-range reasons, because participants do not have any management experience or knowledge on the particular level. One can therefore expect their ratings to be lower. This finding also potentially illustrates the differential validity of the AC where it yields different results for non-experienced candidates as opposed to experienced candidates.

Other factors that may contribute to increased error variance are time pressure or time restrictions and ability level. Time pressure may result in rushed results or outcomes that may not reflect the true ability of a person. Ability levels should be taken into consideration so that assessment exercises are not too easy or too difficult for the targeted population. Both these aspects should be taken into consideration by the AC design team when developing exercises and determining time frames for each exercise.

The following section deals with different options for determining the validity of AC ratings.

5. OPTIONS FOR CALCULATING THE VALIDITY OF AC RATINGS

The Employment Equity Act (Act 55 of 1998) (see Chapter 6) also requires that assessments, measures or tests be valid. There are three types of validity, namely content (description), construct (identification) and criterion (prediction) validity. The first type of validity (content validity) will be discussed next.

5.1 Content (description) validity

Establishing the content validity of a measure is a process rather than a specific statistical procedure. A measure is considered to be content valid when it systematically covers the behaviours within the different domains which it is supposed to measure. A content validity analysis will therefore provide an overall picture (impression) of the content domain of the area to be measured. Within an AC context, this means that the ratings should systematically cover the different behavioural elements in a particular competency, or that the different exercises should systematically cover all the different management competencies on a specific management level. In the end, all the exercises should reflect the content of the different competencies to be assessed.

A comprehensive procedure for establishing the content validity of ACs was suggested in Chapter 18. In that chapter, the perspectives of key stakeholders were discussed, with specific emphasis on their particular focus. Three important facets of content validity came to the fore in Chapter 18, namely operational validity (a term coined by Byham & Temlock[24]), face validity, and the bias and perceived fairness of the process. For an AC programme to be operationally valid, it also needs to be operationally reliable. Face validity is an important subjective evaluation of the content and process from the perspective of the AC participants. Bias and fairness specifically relate to operational reliability and validity facets. Bias "refers to any construct-irrelevant sources of variance that result in systematically higher or lower scores for identifiable groups of examinees" (or AC participants).[25] Fairness, according to the Industrial Psychology (SIOP) guidelines, is a social rather than a psychometric concept. Four different kinds of fairness are noted:

- The first meaning of fairness requires equal outcomes and they (citing Standards for educational and psychological testing) then explain why this is not a workable definition.[26]
- The second meaning views fairness in terms of the equitable treatment of all examinees.
- The third meaning views fairness as requiring that examinees have a comparable opportunity to learn the subject matter covered by the test. (This definition would be applicable in the organisational assessment context in as far it refers to purposefully restricting a person's access to information sources.)
- The fourth meaning views fairness as a lack of predictive bias. (Subgroup differences would, in this instance, be reflected in differences of regression slopes or intercepts.)

---

24 Byham & Temlock, 1972

25 Society for Industrial and Organisational Psychology, 2018: 22-23

26 American Educational Research Association, American Psychological Association, & National Council on Measurement in Education, 2014

The next type of validity, which flows from the above content (description) validity, is construct validity.

5.2 Construct (identification) validity

Although ACs can validly predict performance, the issue of construct-related validity remains mainly unresolved.[27] According to Chen and Naquin,[28] this results in an unmet research challenge. Others argue that the purpose of construct validation is to determine the accuracy of assessments.[29] The construct (identification) validity of a measure refers to the extent to which a measure succeeds in measuring a theoretical construct that it is supposed to measure.[30] On the surface, this definition appears to be very similar to that in respect of content validity. In this instance, several statistical procedures can be applied to calculate the construct validity of a measure that would inform us about the content validity of the assessment as a whole or of specific dimensions of the AC. Several well-executed studies were reported that could not support the overall construct validity of ACs.[31] On the other hand, the same authors found that other studies that applied the same methodology reported that ACs yielded construct validity evidence for measuring intended constructs. Such findings would enable the AC design team to give construct status to competencies such as leadership, communication and other competencies, because they are precisely defined and have a specific operational content. The following procedures can be applied to establish construct validity:

First, the measure can be correlated with other similar instruments that measure the same trait or behaviour. The correlation coefficient obtained will reflect the construct validity coefficient of that instrument. AC leadership ratings that are obtained should, for instance, also correlate fairly high with scores obtained by way of a psychometric measure on leadership.

Second, a factor analytical procedure can be used to determine the construct validity of an instrument. The purpose of a factor analysis is to determine the underlying factor structure or dimensions of a set of related variables. The larger number of dimensions can be reduced by a factor analysis to a smaller number of interpretable factors or dimensions.[32] A factor analysis of management competencies can provide some understanding of the underlying management competency structure. In a similar vein, researchers[33] reported two underlying dimensions for a group of competencies for middle managers (N = 153), namely *interpersonal competencies* (Cronbach's Alpha = 0,787) and *strategic/business competencies* (Cronbach's Alpha = 0,688), consisting of six management competencies each.

Third, convergent and discriminate validity refers to the statistical procedure where the intercorrelations of a measure with other similar and different measures are portrayed in a matrix that is also known as the multi-trait–multi-method matrix. The convergent validity evidence would emerge from high

---

27 Chen & Naquin, 2006

28 Chen & Naquin, 2006

29 Rupp, et al., 2006

30 Cronbach & Meehl, 1955

31 Thornton et al., 2015

32 Allen & Yen, 1979

33 Schlebusch et al., 2003

relationships with other similar measures and discriminant validity from the low relationships with other dissimilar measures.[34] The convergent and discriminate validity of AC competency assessments can also be tested by using other measures of the same constructs. Researchers report that studies are inconclusive in this instance, but signal improved results if the methods of assessment are altered.[35]

Fourthly, the differential validity of a measure refers to its ability to successfully discriminate between groups or individuals.[36] Competent and less competent managers can be grouped on a priori grounds, that is, based on performance ratings. A managerial competency assessment should be able to successfully discriminate between competent and less competent managers. This aspect of validity can be better explored in AC validation research by comparing, for instance, the ratings of experienced and non-experienced managers and supervisors.

In the last instance, the incremental validity of a measure refers to its ability to explain, numerically, additional variance, compared with a set of other measures, in the prediction of a dependent variable.[37] This measure would be applicable in the AC context if a specific, newly developed competency assessment would explain additional variance, compared with other existing competency assessments, in the prediction of management performance. This type of validity can be productively explored when new competency assessments are developed. Researchers have reported a single study where an AC exhibited slight incremental validity over a cognitive ability test, as well as several other studies where ACs have shown significant incremental validity over cognitive ability tests, supervisory ratings, personality tests, biographical data (biodata), and a behavioural description interview.[38]

5.3 Criterion (prediction) validity

The prediction or predictive validity of a measure can be calculated by correlating the predictor and the criterion scores. A competency assessment has predictive validity if the rating obtained on the measure (leadership rating) is sufficiently correlated with a criterion measure (360° assessment of leadership competence). In this instance, variables with established construct validity (such as leadership competency) can now be used to predict a criterion measure of management behaviour (leadership effectiveness) or performance (management performance). Researchers have also reported positive evidence of the predictive validity of ACs.[39] In this instance, they reported that the prediction on a dimension level explained 43% more variance than on the overall assessment rating. This trend of dimensional "firmness" was further confirmed in a different longitudinal study over a seven-year period. Dutch researchers[40] have further reported AC predictive validity in respect of career success over a 17-year period.

---

34 Campbell & Fiske, 1959

35 Thornton & Rupp, 2006

36 Wolfaardt & Roodt, 2005: 36

37 Wolfaardt & Roodt, 2005: 36

38 Wolfaardt & Roodt 2005: 36

39 Thornton & Rupp, 2006

40 Jansen & Vinkenburg, n.d.

Two types of criteria for predictive validity are found.[41] In each case, the correlation between the predictor and the criterion can be calculated.

- Concurrent validity refers to the accuracy with which a measure can identify or diagnose the current behaviour of an individual. Can a rating on communication competency predict a manager's actual communication skills in practice as rated by subordinates? Such a relationship would prove the concurrent validity of a manager's communication competency.
- Predictive validity refers to the accuracy with which a measure can predict the future behaviour of an individual. Can a manager's overall competency rating predict the performance outcome of a manager? Such a relationship would prove the predictive validity of a manager's overall managerial competence.

Wolfaardt and Roodt[42] caution that one should ensure that the criterion is "uncontaminated", that is, it is free of any form of bias or other influences that would compromise the quality of the criterion.

It is evident from the above explanation that AC scores can be correlated with a range of different criterion scores in order to test for different kinds of validity. Earlier in Chapter 1, different types of ACs were identified, amongst which the traditional AC, the diagnostic AC, and the Development AC are the most familiar versions. Different criterion variables are therefore applicable for each of these types of ACs. Prominent authors[43] in the field of ACs have discussed this aspect of validating different types of ACs and the associated selection of appropriate criterion variables in more detail. AC process owners should therefore take care in identifying and selecting the correct criterion variables in the validation of their ACs.

The next type of validity is unitary validity.

5.4 Unitary validity

Unitary validity refers to an ongoing process of collecting all types of validity evidence. Validity is "not a singular event, but rather a process that evolves over a period of time".[44] This view is shared by other authors[45] who are also of the opinion that establishing validity is an ongoing process. The purpose of unitary validity is to collect validity evidence over a period of time in order to establish a "body of evidence" on the emerging pattern of the validity information. In an AC context, this means that all information and records on assessments and ratings should be kept and safely stored for possible future use if the validity of the AC is challenged and/or contested.

---

41 Wolfaardt & Roodt, 2005

42 Wolfaardt & Roodt, 2005

43 Thornton et al., 2015

44 Wolfaardt & Roodt, 2005: 36

45 Allen & Yen, 1979

5.5   Threats to the validity of a measure

Different aspects may influence the validities of measures.[46] If the sample is heterogeneous, with a wide range of possible scores, the scores obtained will be more normally distributed and will therefore yield higher validity coefficients.

This will only be the case if there are no significant subgroup differences. Although the group is heterogeneous, it should yield ratings that are also consistent across different subgroups, such as gender, age, race or educational level. If significant subgroup differences exist, the measure can be perceived as being biased (discriminatory) and not valid for all groups (see Chapter 6 in this regard).

It should also be established whether the relationship between the predictor and the criterion is not moderated by any moderating variables such as gender, age, race or educational level. In this case, the slopes or intercepts of the regression equations would be different for the subgroups.

The validity of a measure is directly proportional to its reliability. The reliability of a measure can place a ceiling on the validity of a measure, therefore it is no use trying to validate an unreliable measure.

6.   AC RATINGS

Certain things need to be said about the format of AC ratings. Assessors or observers record their own subjective ratings in a "raw" format, however the ratings obtained through an integrative process are referred to as the final ratings. These two rating formats will be discussed in more detail.

6.1   Raw ratings

Observers or assessors make use of categorical rating scales where a competency receives a particular label such as ND (needs development), R (rounding off), E (effective) and HE (highly effective). In some extraordinary cases, a split rating is also used such as R/E (rounding off/effective), which means that some behavioural elements need rounding off while others are on level E (effective). It is therefore quite easy to transform these categories into numerical scores where ND = 1, R = 2, E = 3 and HE = 4. These scores are viewed as categorical types of measures and should be analysed with non-parametric statistical procedures.

These raw ratings are at this point highly subjective and not validated. At no point may these raw ratings be divulged or shared with the participants or their immediate managers. These ratings only present the judgement and opinion of one particular rater at this point, which makes them unreliable and therefore invalid.

---

46 Wolfaardt & Roodt, 2005

6.2 Final (integrated) ratings

It is only after a structured process and procedure are followed to collate the different observer (assessor) scores that a final rating is awarded per competency. Two different procedures are available for integrating observer ratings.[47] The first is a plain statistical procedure where a mean score is calculated for a competency by awarding weights to the different elements in a competency. In such a case, the behavioural elements and the corresponding weights have been identified beforehand, as well as the procedure for calculating the final rating. The second is a judgemental consensus exercise where the different ratings and observations are shared and discussed until consensus is achieved through a process of mutual agreement. They[48] are of the opinion that the first yields more consistent and reliable results, mainly because a clear and consistent procedure exists.

A number of special cases and issues need to be considered when awarding and/or interpreting AC ratings.

7. **SPECIAL CASES AND ISSUES**

The AC practitioner has to take cognisance of the following aspects in conducting an AC, and also in the interpretation of AC ratings.

7.1 Exercise effects

It should be pointed out that participants who have been exposed to an AC programme before may have an unfair disadvantage over those who are participating in such a programme for the first time. The reason is that repetition accelerates learning, that is, a person who has participated and received feedback once knows more about the content and the process than those who have not participated and have not received feedback. Careful records should be kept of all the participants in a company who have gone through such a process, and also of the level of the AC process. Participants also have to indicate if they have been through such an assessment procedure.

7.2 Rating distributions

The objectives of the AC should also be kept in mind during the interpretation of overall AC results. If it is a diagnostic or a selection AC, the rating distributions' ranges should be wide and less skew. If the purpose of the Development AC is development, one can expect the distributions to be far more positively skewed. It was pointed out earlier in this chapter that truncation effects may seriously influence the reliabilities of assessment ratings. The low reliabilities obtained would in this instance not have an effect on the predictive validity of a Development AC applied to a normal population of experienced managers and non-experienced manager candidates. One should in this case rather refer to the differential validity of the Development AC, that is, to the ability of the Development AC to correctly distinguish the development candidates from the competent managers.

---

47 Thornton & Rupp, 2006

48 Thornton & Rupp, 2006

7.3 Cross-cultural issues

In Chapters 3, 6 and 18, a number of cross-cultural issues regarding bias and fairness were raised, i.e. the overall AC process should be equitable and fair for all AC participants. This means that all candidates should experience the procedure and process as fair and as non-discriminatory.

The research hypotheses that AC familiarity and utilisation are significantly higher among European managers than US managers were confirmed by their research data[49], and may be even more so between other cultural groups. Cultural, linguistic and economic fragmentation are, according to Cook and Herche[50], the main reasons for this finding in the application of AC technology in sales force selection.

The AC practitioner also needs to ensure that the overall AC process, or any individual assessment exercise, is not exhibiting any measurement bias, that is, a systematic bias towards a particular group of people. It would be fairly easy for any experienced researcher to determine whether any group (race, gender, age, language, etc.) is adversely impacted by any of the assessment exercises or by the overall AC process.

Thus far, no substantive evidence has been found against the use of ACs, however in a few court cases, the judges concerned have requested AC practitioners to reasonably accommodate deaf persons, to be more consistent in their exercises and in their role plays (by not using different role players), and to take into account other aspects relating to consistency in procedures.[51]

In a South African study it was found that the In-Basket exercise consistently produced a high general performance factor (GPF) and that cognitively loaded dimensions seem to produce the largest ethnic group differences.[52] These findings indicate that careful consideration should be given to the decision about what type of simulation exercises and focal constructs to include in an AC. The researchers recommended that more simulation exercises be included in an AC based on the specific tasks that job incumbents have to perform, while unnecessary cognitively loaded simulation exercises and focal constructs should be eliminated. The study's findings stress the importance of doing a thorough job analysis to ensure that the AC is really based on inherent job requirements.

It is thus important to keep all assessment data for validation and research purposes. A clear process or procedure should therefore be established that will enable the AC practitioner to capture and store the data in a safe and retrievable manner.

7.4 Competency redundancies

It may happen that competencies initially included in an AC programme will become redundant later on in the AC's life cycle. There are a number of reasons for this phenomenon, including:

---

49 Cook & Herche, 1994

50 Cook & Herche, 1994

51 Thornton & Rupp, 2006.

52 Buckett et al., 2017

- changes in the external or internal environment of a company;
- changes in the nature and use of technology; and
- changes in company strategy or strategic objectives.

All of these may result in changes in the nature of the job.

The changes in the nature of jobs will have an effect on the current competencies being assessed. A number of such new competencies can be, fairness (being fair), cultural adaptability, emotion management, and readiness to develop.[53]

AC design teams and practitioners should therefore always be alert to such changes. The competency profiles (and also the AC content) should also be changed accordingly to prevent any competency redundancies.

8. CRITICAL OUTCOMES OF, AND DECISIONS RELATING TO, THIS STEP

The following critical outcomes are produced by this step and are supported by different critical decisions:

8.1 A reliable AC

The AC practitioner has to ensure that the overall AC programme and the individual competency assessments are reliable (internally consistent). The practitioner has to ensure that the overall process is conducted in a consistent manner (a type of reliability for which we have coined the term, "operational validity"); that it is perceived as being procedurally fair; and that it is not biased against any group of participants. In order to comply with all these reliability requirements, the AC practitioner needs, first, to capture all assessment data, and secondly, to safely store such data. Different statistical procedures are available for calculating the reliabilities of the programme or the assessment dimensions on these data sets. The deliverable of this step is a reliable AC process and competency assessments.

8.2 A content-valid AC

The AC design team has to ensure that the different assessment exercises and the overall AC process reflect the company-specific needs as well as the competency requirements obtained through the job analyses. In other words, the competency profiles for the different management levels should reflect the current as well as the future competency needs of the organisation and the job. Not only should they reflect the broad competencies, but also the range of relevant behavioural elements within the different competencies. Only then will the competency profiles and their respective assessments be deemed to be content valid. The AC practitioner also has to ensure that the overall AC process is presented in a consistent manner (referred to as operational reliability) as a prerequisite for the

---

53 Gibbons et al., 2006

operational validity of the AC process. Operationally valid ACs are those that cover the content domain by way of logically structured and consistent practices, procedures and policies. The outcome of this step is a content-valid AC and competency assessment.

8.3   A construct-valid AC

Only after the data for the different competency assessments have been captured can the AC practitioner commence with construct-validity research. The practitioner can determine whether the competency assessments are clearly defined and cover a specific behavioural domain, and whether the assessment ratings support the structure of the construct. Different statistical procedures can also be applied in this case, all of which will yield evidence on the construct validity of the competency assessments or of the overall AC programme. The key deliverable at this stage would be a construct-valid competency assessment and a construct-valid AC programme.

8.4   A predictive-valid AC

It is unlikely that one will have a predictive-valid AC programme without having construct-valid competency assessments. Predictive validity can be attained only with construct-valid building blocks. The challenge, in this case, is to identify, develop and collect valid criterion information for the respective competency assessments, but also for the AC programme as a whole. Practitioners have to ensure that the selected criteria meet the requirements of a sound criterion. Only then can the different statistical procedures be applied to determine the predictive validity of the competency assessments and of the overall AC programme. The key deliverable is a prediction-valid competency assessment and an overall AC programme.

Case Study: Why is the Assessment Centre not Valid?

Background

Organisation A, a large South African organisation's corporate office, published a new competency framework for senior management within the organisation. The competency framework consisted of 26 competencies organised into five categories. A policy was issued that all appointments to senior management positions need to be supported by evidence from a competency assessment process.

About three years ago, the organisational support unit decided that the organisation's needs would be better served if an AC was developed that could eventually be insourced. Since Organisation A did not have any AC-related competence, the decision was taken to enlist the services of an external service provider to design the AC. The agreement was that after the AC has been designed, this service provider would conduct ACs on behalf of Organisation A, while they assisted Organisation A to create internal AC capacity. It was envisioned that within a year, the internal capacity would exist for Organisation A to professionally execute ACs.

The service provider designed three variations of the senior level AC, aimed at the different levels of complexity within Organisation A's senior level management. One-day ACs were designed, measuring 10 competencies. Each AC consisted of the following:

- A personality questionnaire completed online prior to attending the AC.
- A career interview.
- A leaderless group discussion.
- A case study.

The output of attending these ACs was a combined report per vacancy, summarising details about the candidates who applied for the position's performance. These ACs were implemented within the organisation.

The challenge

Although each business unit had relative freedom about their internal people processes, all appointments to senior management positions had to be approved by the corporate office. The corporate office started to question the relevancy of the AC and began to reject the appointment of preferred candidates. The process followed to evaluate the competence of the candidates was rejected and the business units were instructed to find an alternative process.

The organisational support unit decided, as a reaction to the corporate office rejecting the results of the AC, to employ another service provider to validate the AC as the preferred AC to use within Organisation A, and to indicate that using the results from the AC was limiting the legal risks involved in employment decisions made by Organisation A.

The process of validation

An important question to ask is "Valid for what"? Since Organisation A used the AC to select people to appoint into senior management positions, the answer to the question in this case was: "Valid to reliably predict successful job performance at a senior management level within Organisation A." This implies reliability *and* predictive validity. However, there are other types of validity that also need to be determined.

The new service provider followed a unitarian approach to validation, believing that a body of evidence needs to be built and kept up-to-date over time. Validation is not based on a single approach, but on multiple and varied sources of information and evidence. To build the body of evidence, the service provider attempted to determine the following about the AC:
- *Face validity* (does the content of the AC appear to be related to what is expected of a senior manager within Organisation A – this is not a statistical process);
- *Content validity* (does the AC systematically measure a representative sample of what is expected of a successful senior manager within Organisation A – this is also mostly a non-statistical type of validity, referring to the procedure of developing the AC);
- *Reliability* (both operational – the standardised implementation of the AC, and statistical – the consistency with which the AC measures what it measures);
- *Construct validity* (the extent to which the AC measures the competencies and other focal constructs it claims to measure); and
- *Predictive validity* (the accuracy with which the AC predicts successful job performance at the senior management level within Organisation A).

The service provider followed the logic of the AC Design Model in the process of determining validity. They investigated what the original service provider did during Stage 1 of the Design Model – Analysis Stage, to determine the competencies and other focal constructs to use during the AC. The current service provider researched how Stage 2 – the Design and Development Stage was implemented, specifically investigating the AC Blueprint, the simulation pre-pilots, the AC pilots, as well as the logic and comprehensiveness of the documentation and the developed ACs. During Stage 3 – the Implementation Stage, the observer training, the consistency with which the ACs were conducted, and how the AC results were used were investigated. Stage 4 – the Evaluation and Validation Stage, was the stage when all the researched information was combined to reach a decision about the current validity of the new AC.

The current service provider used the following documents as guidelines during the process of validation:
- *Guidelines and Ethical Considerations for Assessment Center Operations* (International Task Force on Assessment Center Guidelines, 2015).
- *Best Practice Guidelines For The Use Of The Assessment Centre Method in South Africa* (5th ed) (Meiring & Buckett, 2016).
- *Code of Ethics for Assessment Centres in South Africa* (ACSG, 2018).
- *Employment Equity Act*, Act 55 of 1998 (EEA). (Republic of South Africa, 1998).
- *Protection of Personal Information Act*, Act 4 of 2013. (Republic of South Africa, 2013).
- *Access to Personal Information Act*, Act 2 of 2007. (Republic of South Africa, 2017).

Over a period of several months, the service provider interviewed the original service provider, scrutinised various organisational documents as well as all the ACs' documents, made unannounced site-visits to operational ACs, and conducted a survey and interviews with various users of the AC results.

The findings

The current service provider's findings are summarised in the table below:

Finding	Applicable Guiding Documents	Implications	Proposed Remedy
Stage in the AC Design Model: Stage 1 – Analysis Stage			
1 No AC Business Case: • There is no document clearly indicating the business need for the new AC, or indicating what alternatives were considered before deciding on developing a new AC.		Since the new AC was not strategically positioned, the requirement for the AC can be challenged.	Confirm the need for the new AC, position the AC strategically and embed in other people processes.
2 AC focal constructs decided upon after: • conducting computer research; • conducting an interview with an IO psychologist employed by Organisation A; • reviewing organisation A's vision and values; and • reviewing Organisation A's Competency Framework.	• EEA – Inherent job requirements.	The link with the current job requirements of senior managers within Organisation A was not established. The focal constructs are based on an idealised future. The AC results can be legally challenged.	• Analyse the job descriptions of a representative sample of senior management positions within Organisation A. • Supplement the conclusions from the above analysis with conclusions from focus groups with a representative sample of SMEs and/or Critical Incident information (build evidence that the AC is measuring inherent job requirements).

	Finding	Applicable Guiding Documents	Implications	Proposed Remedy
Stage in the AC Design Model: Stage 2 – Design and Develop Stage				
3	There is no signed-off AC Blueprint.		Difficult to show that the design and development of the AC are based on the results of the analysis. Difficult to show that the SMEs agree with the findings of the analysis.	None.
4	No Competency-Simulation Matrix.	• SA Best Practice Guidelines • International Guidelines In both documents it is part of the essential elements of a process to be called an AC that focal constructs are measured more than once and that there is a clear line of sight where the competencies are assessed.	Difficult to show that competencies are evaluated more than once and in different types of assessments.	Draw-up a Competency-Simulation Matrix.
5	The various Observer Report Forms do not use a consistent rating scale. The Career Interview did not have an Observer Report Form.	• SA Best Practice Guidelines • International Guidelines Both documents emphasise standardisation.	If the same competency is measured with different rating scales in the various exercises, standardisation is compromised.	• Standardise the rating scale across simulations and adapt the Observer Report Forms. • Design an Observer Report Form for the Career Interview.
6	Too many competencies were assessed in the case study (all 10 competencies).		The cognitive load on the observers are increased; it is difficult to differentiate behaviour linked to the various competencies; the simulation does not necessarily elicit behaviour linked to all 10 competencies.	Re-conceptualise which competencies can be assessed during the case study; redesign the Observer Report Form.
7	A Leaderless Group Discussion (LGD) is used as part of the ACs.	• SA Best Practice Guidelines • International Guidelines Both documents emphasise standardisation. • EEA – an assessment needs to be applied fairly to all candidates.	An LGD cannot be standardised since the discussion participants vary.	Replace the LGD.
8	The content of the simulations are well-designed.			None – content already of a good quality.
9	Simulations were not pre-piloted.			None
10	The ACs were piloted.	• SA Best Practice Guidelines • International Guidelines Both documents emphasise piloting before roll-out		None – the ACs are already rolled-out.

	Finding	Applicable Guiding Documents	Implications	Proposed Remedy
11	Simulations have Administration and Observer Guidelines.			None – already adheres to requirements.

Stage in the AC Design Model: Stage 3 – Implementation Stage

	Finding	Applicable Guiding Documents	Implications	Proposed Remedy
12	No observer training – the original provider maintains that their observers are senior observers who do not need additional training.	• SA Best Practice Guidelines • International Guidelines Both documents emphasise comprehensive observer training, as well as refresher training.	There is no evidence that a shared frame-of-reference with regards to Organisation A's norms, values and standards exists. This impacts the inter-rater reliability of allocating ratings to competencies.	Design comprehensive observer training that includes certification and refresher training.
13	Each observer uses their own way of observing and noting behaviour during the LGD. The original service provider maintains the observers are senior observers and each has their own way of taking notes e.g. checklists; notes about behaviour; verbatim notes.	• SA Best Practice Guidelines • International Guidelines Both documents emphasise standardisation. • EEA – an assessment needs to be applied fairly to all candidates.	Since there is no standardisation of the way in which behaviour is noted, the AC's reliability is compromised and Organisation A will not be able to defend decisions taken based on the AC results, since the evidence will not be there to support the ratings allocated.	Standardise the process of observing and taking notes.
14	Only one observer administers an AC per region, including observing the LGD.	• SA Best Practice Guidelines • International Guidelines Both documents emphasise multiple observers.	There is no evidence that more than one observer ONCE candidates during different simulations.	Redesign the process of administering the AC.
15	The conditions in which the AC is administered differ from region to region – in some regions the venue is very noisy.	• SA Best Practice Guidelines • International Guidelines Both documents emphasise standardisation. • EEA – an assessment needs to be applied fairly to all candidates.	The AC results might be challenged since the AC was not applied fairly to all candidates.	Train the regional staff on creating appropriate test conditions.
16	The LGD is administered in varying ways – the number of candidates that participate per LGD varies according to the number of candidates per AC – sometimes 8, or 6, or 4, or 3. Some observers adapt the time for the LGD accordingly, other observers do not make any adaptions.	• SA Best Practice Guidelines • International Guidelines Both documents emphasise standardisation. • EEA – an assessment needs to be applied fairly to all candidates.	The LGD is not applied fairly to all candidates.	Replace the LGD with another simulation that can be applied fairly irrespective of the number of candidates.
17	Some business units make the final selection decision based solely on the AC results, some allocate weights to the different hurdles, while others do not take the AC results into consideration.	• SA Best Practice Guidelines • International Guidelines Both documents emphasise standardisation. • EEA – an assessment needs to be applied fairly to all candidates.	A strong case for unfair treatment can be made against Organisation A.	Decide on an organisation-wide way of using the AC results in the final selection decision and implement it consistently.

	Finding	Applicable Guiding Documents	Implications	Proposed Remedy
17	Some business units make the final selection decision based solely on the AC results, some allocate weights to the different hurdles, while others do not take the AC results into consideration.	• SA Best Practice Guidelines • International Guidelines Both documents emphasise standardisation. • EEA – an assessment needs to be applied fairly to all candidates.	A strong case for unfair treatment can be made against Organisation A.	Decide on an organisation-wide way of using the AC results in the final selection decision and implement it consistently.
18	Candidates are only informed whether their application has been successful or not.	• Code of Ethics • PoPI • APIA	Candidates have the right to receive detailed feedback about their performance during the AC.	Train staff on giving appropriate feedback to candidates and start giving feedback.
19	Business units deal differently with the AC Reports: some collect and destroy the reports after the decision has been made; other units email the reports to committee members with no control as to who accesses the reports; some units leave the reports with each committee member.	• SA Best Practice Guidelines • International Guidelines • Code of Ethics • PoPI • APIA	Confidentiality of AC results is breached. This leaves Organisation A open to litigation.	Train people on and enforce guidelines as to how to use and store results confidentially.
20	No AC Policy.	• SA Best Practice Guidelines • International Guidelines	Since there is no policy guiding the AC implementation, every business unit can implement the AC as they see fit. This opens the organisation to litigation for unfair treatment.	Implement an AC Policy.

Stage in the AC Design Model: Stage 3 – Implementation Stage

	Finding	Applicable Guiding Documents	Implications	Proposed Remedy
21	No raw data of any of the candidates that attended the AC are available.	• SA Best Practice Guidelines • International Guidelines • EEA – an assessment needs to reliable and valid.	No statistical procedures can be done (reliabilities; construct and predictive validity).	Obtain the raw data per candidate from the original service provider.
22	No criterion data are available.		Since there is no AC Business Case, AC Blueprint, or AC Policy, there is no agreement on what should be used to determine predictive validity of the ACs and no data were captured.	Agree on the criterion, collect data and do the statistical analysis.
23	Based on the available documentation the ACs appear to have Face Validity.			The Face Validity was determined during the piloting of the ACs. It is recommended that Organisation A designs questionnaires that can be completed by candidates and observers at the end of each AC so that Face Validity information can be collected over time.

	Finding	Applicable Guiding Documents	Implications	Proposed Remedy
24	Content Validity cannot be determined.		Since the ACs' focal constructs are not based on current job descriptions and current SMEs' input, the content validity cannot be meaningfully determined.	Implement the proposed remedy to finding number 2.

The current service provider concluded that the AC is not currently valid and reliable to predict the future job performance of senior managers within Organisation A. In addition, Organisation A is open to litigation since the organisation is in breach of the EEA, the PoPI Act and the APIA.

Lessons learnt

The following are some of the lessons that Organisation A learnt from this process:
- An AC's validity is impacted by the decision to implement the AC, the way in which the AC was designed and developed, the way in which the AC is implemented, and the way in which the AC results are used.
- To ensure that the AC will be used by the organisation, a clear business case for the AC needs to be developed and approved by all stakeholders before embarking on the process of AC design and development.
- To ensure the sustainability of an AC it is necessary to obtain and build internal AC knowledge so as to be able to embed the AC in other people processes and to be able to take professional accountability of the whole AC process.

CHAPTER 20

INTERNATIONAL PERSPECTIVE – CURRENT PRACTICES AND FUTURE CHALLENGES

Nigel Povah, Philippa Riley and Jordon Jones

1. INTRODUCTION

1.1 Setting the scene

In Chapter 15 of the first edition of this book, Diana Krause and George C. Thornton III shared the findings from their research into Assessment Centre (AC) practices across seven countries in Western Europe and two in North America, drawn from a research sample of 97 organisations. As they explained, this was the most comprehensive survey of international AC practices at that time, and they highlighted many interesting similarities and differences across a wide range of AC practices in Western Europe and North America. Their survey was focused on current practices in ACs and examined things such as: the objectives of the AC; how assessors were selected; the duration of the AC; job analysis processes and their impact on the AC; the number and types of dimensions assessed; the number and types of exercises used; other selection methods used in conjunction with the AC; the policy of sharing information about the AC; the processes of data integration; the nature and timing of feedback; and who has access to the results. Whilst this provided significant insight into the current state of play in ACs, their focus provided less information about likely future trends.

In the 11 years since the first edition of this book we have seen many changes around the world which impact the political, economic, social and environmental conditions under which organisations need to operate. These changes inevitably have implications for HR practices, including talent assessment, where the assessment centre continues to be one of the favoured tools of choice. It is therefore no surprise to find that two further significant, international AC surveys were conducted in 2008 by Povah, Crabb and McGarrigle[1] and in 2012 by Hughes, Riley, Shalfrooshan, Gibbons and Thornton[2], the latter of which is the largest survey of its type to date, with 543 respondents drawn from 53 different countries. These subsequent surveys replicated many of the topics covered by the Krause and Thornton survey and went even further, gathering additional data on topics such as: the number of times each competency is assessed; the number of participants assessed per centre; assessor to participant ratios; duration and nature of assessor training; and the use of technology within ACs and AC evaluation practices, amongst other things.

This chapter will attempt to build upon these previous surveys, referencing them where appropriate and introducing some new findings based on recent developments and some further research.

---

1   Povah et al., 2008

2   Hughes et al., 2012

1.2 Approach

As mentioned above, the world is experiencing a level of relentless change which is accelerating like never before, as highlighted by many sources (*The World is about to change even faster*, 2017[3]; *The Relentless Pace of Automation* 2017[4] ; *The Pace of Change in the VUCA World* 2015[5]). This has prompted a wave of global reports and surveys forecasting HR trends such as: *Mercer's Global Talent Trends Study*[6]; *Rewriting the rules for the digital age*; 2017 *Deloitte Global Human Capital Trends*[7]; and *CEB's Global Talent Monitor*[8], to name just a few. From these reports it was possible to identify some key Human Capital themes, such as: the need for organisations to be resilient and adaptive so they can build for an unknown future; the ongoing 'war for talent' with organisations competing to attract and retain top talent; the importance of organisations having a strong Employee Value Proposition (EVP) which provides opportunities for growth thus engaging and rewarding employees; the increasing importance of addressing issues to do with diversity, inclusion and fairness; and finally, the requirement to be able to cope with the increasing level of digital disruption driven by technology, which is supported by advances in robotics and artificial intelligence and the growth in people analytics.

With this backdrop in mind, a 'top down' approach has been adopted using these key strategic themes, and investigating how these might be impacting AC practices in different parts of the world. The research therefore differs from the previous research given its focus on future trends, in addition to current practice.

1.3 Methodology

In order to understand how current and future practices align with the key talent trends detailed above, an interview methodology was adopted. The purpose of this was to gather in-depth information about how these trends are playing out in the assessment space from experts in the field. The areas of questioning were as follows:

* The demand/popularity of ACs – is it increasing, stable or decreasing?
* How is technology being used within ACs?
* What are the primary constructs being measured on ACs? Competencies/dimensions, tasks, or a combination of the two?
* The candidate/participant experience – how is this typically addressed on ACs?
* What efforts are being made to ensure ACs address possible concerns around fairness, diversity and inclusion?
* How are AC data managed? How are they used in conjunction with wider datasets?
* What researchers (AC or otherwise) have influenced AC practices?
* What else might impact AC practices in the next 5-10 years?

---

3   Ritholtz, 2017

4   Rotman, 2017

5   Lloyd, 2015

6   Mercer, 2017

7   Deloitte, 2017

8   Gartner Talent Daily Global Talent Monitor, 2019

Having prepared this list of topics, an interview protocol was designed to capture information from a target group of interviewees. To obtain as broad a coverage as possible from a variety of territories, we identified a group of expert AC practitioners working across the world, who have experience of working with numerous clients and thus were able to provide a generalised sense of AC practices in their region. The interviewees are listed in the Acknowledgements section at the end of this chapter.

Whilst the number of interviews conducted was relatively small, and would ideally be supplemented with future quantitative research, the purpose of this qualitative approach was to gather in-depth insight from specifically identified experts, rather than broad coverage from a large volume of practitioners, as was the case in previous surveys.

The findings across each of the key topics are provided in the sections which follow.

2. DEMAND/POPULARITY OF ACs

The interviews started with a question regarding the demand and popularity of ACs across the interviewees' region(s) of focus. The purpose of this question was to explore how the popularity of ACs has been impacted by the growth of interest in other forms of assessment, such as online psychometrics (including personality questionnaires, cognitive ability tests and situational judgement tests), and the recent interest in more innovative assessment approaches, such as games-based assessments. The 13 respondents provided a mixed picture, with six suggesting AC demand is increasing, five believing it is decreasing, and two providing a balanced response with both quoting examples of increased and decreased interest. There was a notably emphatic tone from the five respondents who claimed that interest in ACs is decreasing, and it was interesting to note that three of those five respondents came from arguably more mature assessment territories, namely the US and the UK, where there is a great deal of assessment activity, with a particular fascination for some of the newer techniques. Indeed, none other than Bill Byham (often referred to as the inventor of the modern assessment centre) said: "There was no question that interest in ACs was decreasing, as it is now seen as old and slow and people have a big fixation for the new, less time-consuming solutions."

If this sample provides a true reflection of the broader AC market, then this is probably the first time that we've seen a hint of evidence of a decline in the interest of ACs, given that the previously mentioned Hughes et al.[9] survey reported that 45% of 480 respondents expected the use of Assessment and/or Development Centres to increase within their organisation/business unit over the next three years, with only 10% forecasting a decrease, 40% forecasting stability, and 5% being unsure.

At least half of the interviewees confirmed that where ACs are still being employed, there is a general wish to see them shortened, with clients wanting ACs to be less time-consuming for participants and assessors and with quicker access to the results.

---

9   Hughes et al., 2012

It was also noted that DACs were still seen as useful development tools due to the richness of the data, although they too were having to be shortened, with 2-3 day developmental ACs becoming much less common.

3. TECHNOLOGY

The use of technology has radically changed the world of recruitment and assessment over the last couple of decades. Deloitte[10] described HR's 'new' role as "leading the digital transformation" of organisations, with its goal being to both reflect, and help to create, new working environments facilitated by technology. This has put an onus on HR to use technology to demonstrate innovative practices across all parts of the employee lifecycle. Other drivers of technology adoption in HR processes have included the impact of globalisation and new generations of employees entering the workforce with different expectations of, and experience with, technology.[11]

Although it is notable that much of the technology adoption and innovation within assessment has been in the high-volume screening and psychometric space, ACs have certainly not been isolated from this development. In Hughes et al.'s *Global Survey of Assessment Centre Practices*[12], 57% of the 394 participants surveyed indicated that they were using technology within their centres. Respondents were asked to indicate what technology features they were currently using within their centres, divided into 'front-end' participant-facing features, and 'back-end' assessor-, centre manager-, or Administrator-facing ones. Usage figures are shown below for the different features described. It is notable that each of the 'back-end' features were being used more often than the 'front-end' ones, with the exception of 'real time interactions with participants via phone'. This pattern of usage was also reflected in the perceived benefits of such features, which more strongly emphasised efficiency and time-saving than they did benefits from a candidate experience perspective.

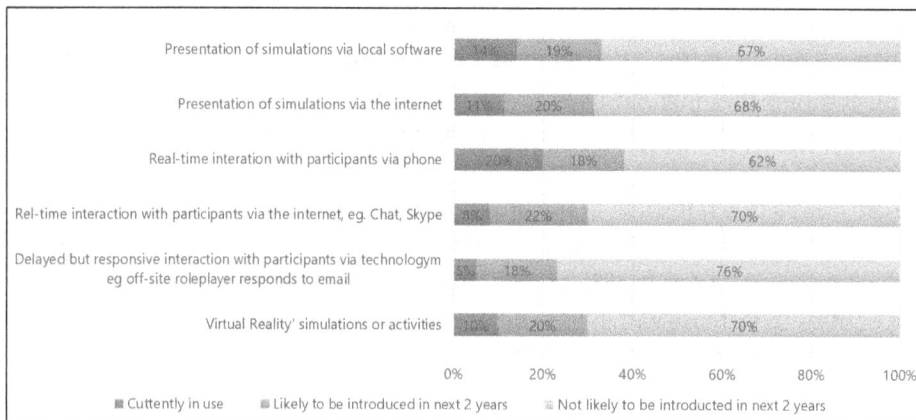

Figure 20.1: To what extent are different participant-facing technology features currently being used, and which features are likely to be introduced in the next two years?

---

10 Deloitte, 2017

11 O'Reilly, 2016

12 Hughes et al., 2012

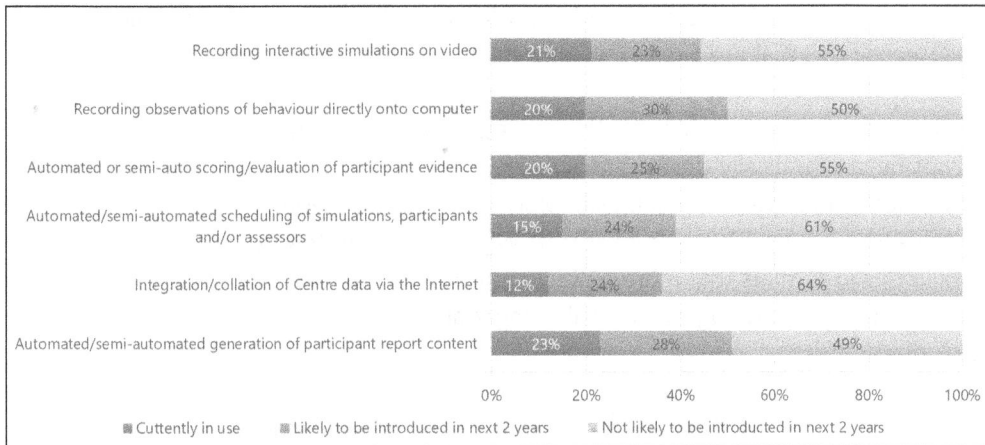

Figure 20.2: To what extent are different assessor, AC manager and Administrator technology features currently being used, and which features are likely to be introduced in the next two years?

In the interviews that were undertaken to inform this chapter, a richer picture emerged around the drivers and nature of technology usage within ACs. Whilst the discussions focused primarily on technology use within the centres themselves, it was also clear that technology use outside of ACs is having a profound impact on the conduct of centres. Specifically, with more upfront assessment being undertaken using online, automated assessments, there has been both a knock-on impact on the volumes of ACs being run, and also the expectations of the format of the centres themselves, to ensure they reflect the speed and efficiency of the earlier stages of the process.

Interviewees were asked to provide information on the types of technology being used in their centres, and their expectations for future technology use. In relation to technologies currently being used, Virtual Assessment Centres were mentioned most frequently, including both participant- and assessor-facing elements. Also listed were 'back-end' tools to support assessors, such as speech-to-text conversion (to remove the requirement for manual note-taking, and increase the accuracy of exercise recording), marking tools to help automate some of the elements of report writing (for example through the use of predetermined feedback text), and platforms to allow for the integration of non-AC activities, such as psychometrics, into single reports. Scheduling tools were also mentioned as a means of helping to reduce the effort involved in coordinating the centres themselves.

At the 'front-end', namely the participant-facing side of the AC, gamification (the use of game elements/technology to increase participant immersion and engagement) was mentioned as a development with potential impact on ACs. It was notable, however, that all the interviewees who mentioned gamification also described potential limitations on its relevance, for example to specific job role levels (notably junior roles) and certain industries. Indeed, one interviewee, working within the leadership assessment and development space, saw gamification having a very limited impact on their future practice with clients. Although it was not currently being used by any of the interviewees, the use of Virtual Reality (VR) within ACs was a topic that had been noted as a potential direction for this area of practice, with some examples being provided of use of VR within an AC context (for example Lloyds Banking

Group[13]). Other future developments included artificial intelligence/machine learning for text mining and analysis, techniques that are already gaining traction in the video interviewing arena.[14]

Several interviewees referred to supporting their centres with pre-existing, publicly available technologies, which had not been specifically developed for use in this context. These included the speech-to-text programme described above, video-call technology (specifically Skype) to facilitate interviews and role plays, and office programmes such as Microsoft Word, Excel and PowerPoint to allow participants to complete exercises in formats that more closely replicate the real working environment. Additionally, e-learning and related technologies for facilitating training delivery were detailed in the context of assessor skill development.

From the Hughes et al.[15] survey it was evident that there are differences in technology use and adoption across world regions. Whilst the numbers within each region were relatively small in this survey, there was an indication (consistent with previous surveys) that technology use in ACs was higher in Africa and Oceania than other regions, at 71% and 69% of respondents respectively. Perhaps somewhat surprisingly, the region with the lowest usage was Europe at 49%. Differences across geographical regions were noted by some of the interviewees, for example, limited demand for virtual delivery of assessment centres was noted in Turkey, and challenges around server locations due to data protection policies in Russia and China, were mentioned as a potential limitation to AC technology adoption in those countries.

4. CONSTRUCTS

The term 'constructs' refers to the behaviours measured that represent successful performance in a target job role. Recent academic publications have challenged the well-established practice of using competencies/dimensions as the traditional construct measurement in assessment centres. For example, research by Jackson, Michaelides, Dewberry and Kim[16] suggested only 1.11% of variance in AC scores is attributable to dimensions. This supports research which has observed the 'exercise effect' in AC scores, for example, Hoffman[17] and Thornton and Gibbons.[18] Furthermore, trait activation theory suggests that an environmental or interpersonal stimulus may cue the activation of specific competencies in a certain way, causing people to behave inconsistently across distinct types of workplace situations.[19] Due to these emerging themes, calls for task-based assessment centres (TBACs) have been made. A TBAC would remove the measurement of competencies/dimensions, and focus solely on measuring indicators of task-specific performance.

---

13 Lloyd's Banking Group, 2016

14 Cheeseman, 2016.

15 Hughes et al., 2012

16 Jackson et al., 2016

17 Hoffman et al., 2008

18 Thornton & Gibbons, 2009

19 Lievens et al., 2015

We were therefore keen to explore which measurement constructs were most commonly used according to our interviewees. Interestingly, all 13 of them unanimously reported that they measure competencies/dimensions, not tasks. Three of our interviewees were not at all familiar with the emerging research base on TBACs. Perhaps the task-based approach requires significantly more validation and years of marketing before international practitioners will be picking up on these recommendations. Additionally, interviewees who were familiar with the TBAC approach felt there is limited and often confusing practical advice from current research conclusions. For example, Bill Byham, Founder and Executive Chairman of DDI, suggested that if a TBAC approach were adopted, the indicators for specific tasks would more than likely be a combination of behaviours that can be categorised under competency labels. Consequently, in practice, a TBAC approach is inevitably going to reflect the language of competencies in defining what 'good performance' on a particular task looks like.

The definition of dimensions/competencies has also been refined over time. Many writers refer to them as *"observable* behaviours contributing to effective or superior job performance".[20, 21, 22] By perceiving competencies as what we can clearly see or hear someone doing/saying at work, organisations have been able to commission the design of bespoke competency frameworks, measuring performance in a way that truly reflects their world. This means that construct measurement across the employee lifecycle can reflect the way their industry operates, the way their organisation is structured vertically and laterally, and the degree of expectation set on people at distinct levels of seniority, which is helpful for assessment, development and talent pipelining. This is one of the reasons why competencies are likely to continue being measured instead of tasks, and is reflected in what our interviewees said. The majority explained that they work with organisations that currently have a competency framework already in place, and it is rare to see an absence of a competency-based approach. Indeed, six of the interviewees made comments like "this is very unlikely to change drastically" in the future, because competencies are well-established in workplace culture.

Interviewees were asked to provide specific information about the competencies that their clients are currently assessing in their centres. This topic was also covered in the Hughes et al.[23] survey, the results of which are shown in Figure 19.3 below. The competency categories covered in the survey were those identified by Arthur et al.[24]

---

20 Klein, 1996

21 Tett et al., 2000

22 Brophy & Kiely, 2002

23 Hughes et al., 2012

24 Arthur et al., 2003

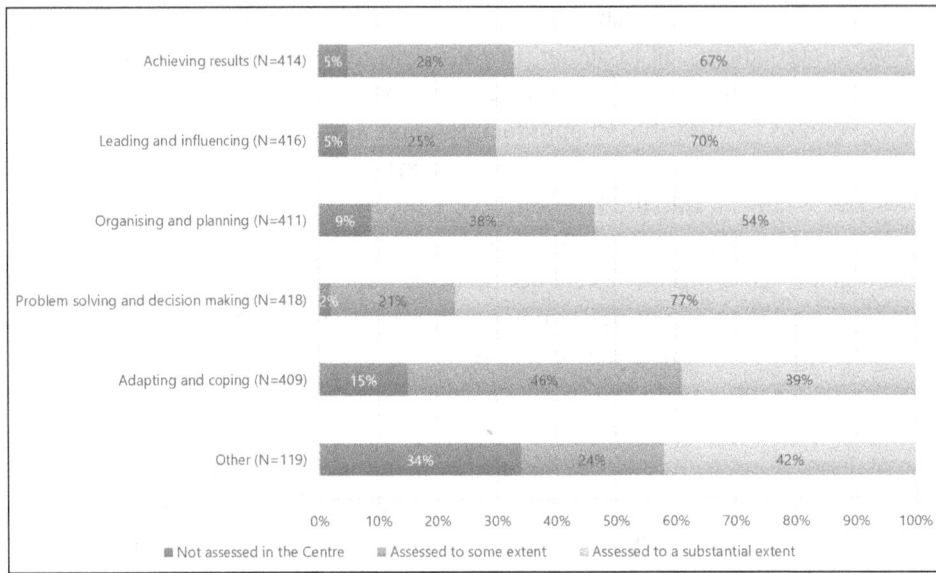

Figure 20.3: To what extent are each of these competencies assessed?

The competencies most likely to be 'Assessed to a substantial extent' in the Hughes et al.[25] survey were: 'Relating to others', 'Problem solving and decision making' and 'Leading and influencing'. These competencies were also frequently mentioned as a key focus across our interviews.

Interviewees were also asked about recent and future changes to the competencies measured. 'Agility' was mentioned by seven respondents, and there were several references to: 'Learning'; 'Innovation'; 'Drive'; and 'Motivation'. The focus on agility and learning reflects an increased organisational awareness of concepts like VUCA and the accelerating pace of change, which prompts the growing requirement for flexibility in the modern workplace.[26] These findings also reflect the increased interest in the assessment of potential within organisations. A number of our interviewees reported clients' increasing desire to measure how participants focus on continuous improvement, how engaged they are, and how they aspire to progress in the organisation. This focus seems to align with research findings, for example, Guillén and Saris[27] demonstrated that combining assessments of personality and motivation with competencies has an incrementally higher effect on predicting workplace performance above competencies alone. They conceived these as "motive-based dimensions", which in practice are sometimes marketed as 'strengths-based assessments'.

In conclusion, it would appear that despite the growing body of research evidence recommending a focus on task-, rather than competency-, based centres, the competency-based approach still remains, and is likely to remain, the primary measurement focus for ACs. However, there is likely to be an increasing focus on competencies relating to flexibility, agility and potential due to the changing context in which organisations are operating.

---

25 Hughes et al., 2012

26 Lloyd, 2015

27 Guillén & Saris, 2013

5. CANDIDATE/PARTICIPANT EXPERIENCE

Candidate experience and candidate engagement are increasingly important topics within assessment. Forming part of the drive and focus around 'employee experience', this is being reflected in the merging of assessment and marketing practices in the design of tools and processes. Deloitte's *Global Human Capital Trend Survey*[28] identified employee experience as a priority for organisations, noting regional differences as illustrated in Figure 19.4 below:

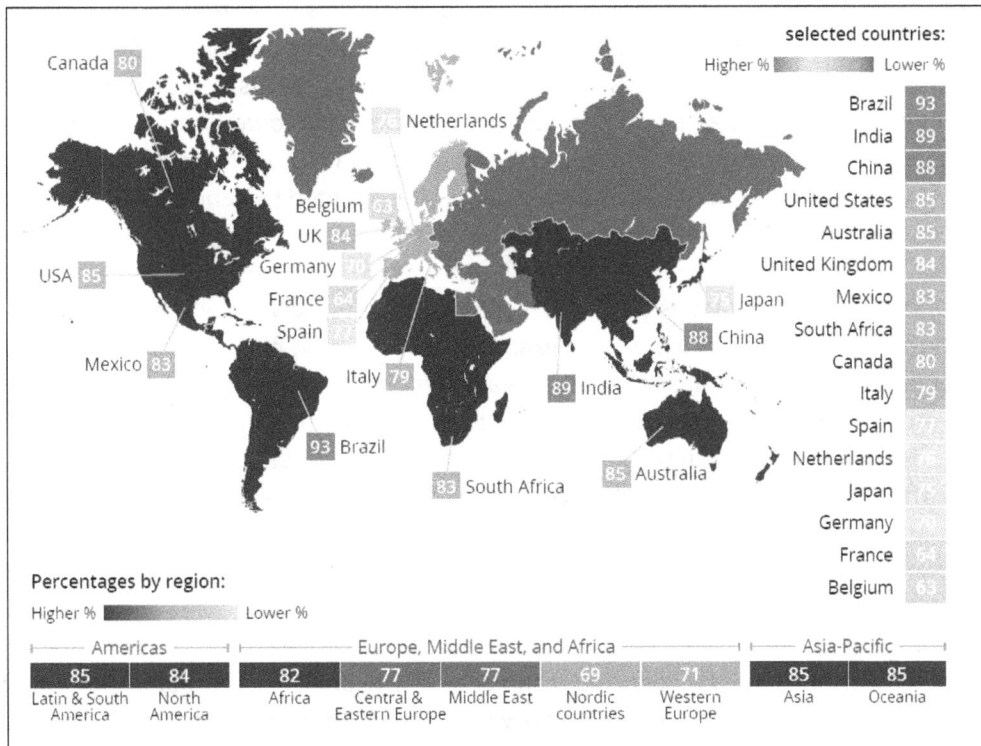

Figure 20.4: Ratings of the importance of 'employee experience' across regions.

Candidate experience was not directly a topic of the Hughes et al.[29] survey, however the questions regarding technology touched on the importance of candidate experience and some of the technologies that were being used to optimise this (see Figure 19.4 above), such as simulations delivered through software or the internet, and phone-based simulations. All interviewees indicated that candidate experience and brand were important considerations for their clients, with half indicating they were 'Extremely important', and that the focus has increased in recent years. The drivers for a focus on candidate engagement within an AC context fell into three broad categories: maximising the chances of successful participants accepting job offers; making participants (either internal or external) advocates of the process or organisation; and 'role modelling' customer service orientation for organisations

---

28 Deloitte, 2017

29 Hughes et al., 2012

where this is a key value. The focus on candidate experience was defined as more important for certain groups, such as younger candidates, and in certain sectors where 'experience' is more of a factor, such as retail.

Interviewees were asked to describe how they addressed candidate experience factors in their ACs. A key theme for a number of interviewees was around ensuring candidate convenience, i.e. moving away from the requirement for candidates to physically attend centres at a central location, and shortening the duration of the centres themselves. The content of exercises was also deemed to be important, with bespoke exercises and 'day in the life' centres providing a means to ensure candidate engagement, inform candidates about the organisation and role, and increase the perceived relevance of content and the associated fairness of decisions based on this. The constructs assessed in ACs were also mentioned by one interviewee as a potential factor influencing candidate experience, specifically the move from competency-based assessment to centres incorporating a 'strengths' and 'values' focus (mentioned in the previous section), which are arguably more oriented to 'candidate fit' and supporting candidates' decision making, rather than the organisations' decision making.

Broader candidate experience factors were also mentioned by interviewees, which are more associated with process than the specifics of the AC. For example, issues around communication were described, including the need to provide candidates with detailed information about what to expect at centres, being clear on next steps, and transparency about how assessment is undertaken and decisions are being made. Feedback was also described as a key element of candidate experience, a point which is often made when discussing the needs of millennials within the workplace.[30]

One interviewee highlighted the potential implications of some of the recent technology developments from a candidate perspective, suggesting that virtual assessment centres could have a positive impact on candidate experience in some respects, such as convenience and realism, but a potentially negative impact in others, for example by reducing 'candidate touch points'. The danger of 'uninformed' improvements to candidate experience, based on what is perceived to be cutting edge and novel rather than what genuinely drives candidate engagement, was also raised as a concern.

6. DIVERSITY AND INCLUSION

The focus on candidate immersion can also be linked to an increasing focus on ensuring ACs provide a fair experience for all involved. As shown by Harris, Paese and Greising[31], participants in an assessment centre will "compare the outcome they receive with the outcome they expected", linking primarily to theories of distributive and procedural justice.[32] A participant at an AC is likely to create an expectation of performance based on previous experiences in similar situations, therefore the realism of a set of workplace simulations leads to greater feelings of fairness because it reduces the gap between

---

30 Willyerd, 2015

31 Harris et al., 2008

32 Gilliland, 1994

expectation and outcome, even when self-awareness is accounted for.[33] This suggests that ACs need to be designed with realism in mind.

In our experiences of international practice, the issue of fairness in assessment has been raised by many clients because both diversity and inclusion are high on their agendas. Additionally, the benefits of diversity and inclusion in the workplace have been well-researched in recent times. For example, a global publication by McKinsey[34] strongly demonstrated that more diverse workplaces (in terms of age, gender, race, socio-economic background etc.) in the world's largest organisations are statistically more likely to financially outperform their competitors in their industries. They looked at companies listed in the major stock market indices such as the Dow Jones, FTSE and S&P Asia to gather data and draw these conclusions. Naturally, clients regularly express a desire to ensure fairness and objectivity is instilled in their assessment processes as a result of these commercial conclusions.

As a result, we asked our interviewees: "*How do you ensure your ACs address any concerns around diversity and inclusion, and that they are fair to all?*" The responses to this question included "reviewing data" and "getting feedback from candidates as soon as possible after the AC", implying that a simple tactic is to consistently monitor and update AC content for the next assessment initiative. From our interviewees in emerging AC markets, such as Trinidad, East Africa and South Korea, the need to "challenge clients' views" was mentioned several times. This applied to the concept of adopting best practice in ACs in general, rather than exclusively on the topic of ensuring fairness and diversity. Regardless, the conclusion reached by our AC practitioners in those areas of the world was that their ACs are not adjusted for diversity as much as they would like, but this may change once the methodology becomes more well-established. In other words, this may happen once their priority shifts away from convincing organisations to incorporate ACs in their talent management processes.

In more mature AC markets, such as the US, the UK and Australia, where clients are generally more familiar with ACs, stakeholders were more committed to taking steps to ensure their ACs were fair. These steps frequently included "training assessors to reduce cognitive bias" and "looking at selection of assessors in a way that seeks to create a diverse assessor pool". These methods are strongly advised by both the *International Taskforce on Assessment Centre Guidelines*[35] and the British Psychological Society's AC guidelines[36], and are based on past research informing us that assessor training strategies do have a significant impact on the accuracy, objectivity and fairness in assessors' evaluations. More specifically, it enhances the inter-rater reliability and discriminant validity in AC scoring.[37]

Some interviewees also explained that the context of AC exercises is sometimes tailored to suit a more diverse audience. One of our interviewees described a virtual AC project used for developing the skills of sales managers in a global pharmaceutical company. The exercise content, which had originated from their HQ in the United States, was tailored to suit the local context every time the AC was rolled

---

33 Harris et al., 2008

34 McKinsey, 2018

35 International Taskforce on Assessment Center Guidelines, 2015

36 The British Psychological Society, 2015

37 Lievens, 2001

out in a new market. Factors that were changed included character names, locations, currencies, scale of market data included in the exercise, types of products to be discussed, and even organisational structure in some cases. Additionally, the content and the virtual platform were also often translated to reflect the local language. These updates reflected the cultural differences experienced between markets like Sweden, Japan, South Africa, Germany, Spain and North America, even though they all operated in the same global organisation. However, the benchmarking of constructs being scored remained the same, so that comparisons could be made for organisational insights. In terms of perceived fairness, this approach consistently yielded highly positive reactions from participants throughout the process. Future trends concerning the focus on fairness, diversity and inclusion are therefore subject to the maturity of the market in question. Only in recent times has concrete, longitudinal evidence come to light regarding the commercial rationale for diversity in the workplace, but the effects of procedural and distributional justice have long been known in AC research. In the coming years, we might expect emerging markets to follow precedent, as set by organisations currently employing techniques to improve fairness in decision making at ACs.

7. DATA MANAGEMENT

Our interest in this particular topic, i.e. how AC data are managed and used in conjunction with wider datasets, was sparked by two relatively recent developments, namely the growing focus on issues relating to data protection, and the growing interest in the area of people analytics.

7.1 Data Protection

Although the importance of how assessment centre data should be used, its longevity and who should have access to it, has long been acknowledged, it is only due to the increasing involvement of technology since 2000 that attention is starting to turn to data security and the wider ramifications of data protection. For example, the current (6th edition) of the *Guidelines and Ethical Considerations for Assessment Center Operations*[38] provides relatively little coverage, citing in Section X. Technology:

> 2. (c) International laws and policies involving data privacy:
>
> i. If an assessment center uses remote assessment and receives data from assessees in other countries, the program must comply with any data protection laws that might exist in those countries, as data have crossed international boundaries in this case. For example, see the European Union Directive on Data Protection and the U.S. Safe Harbor Privacy Principles.

And in Section X1. Ethics, Legal Compliance, and Social Responsibility:

> 4. Data Protection. The assessment center program must also comply with any relevant data protection laws governing the regions in which assessment is being carried out (e.g., the U.K. Data Protection Act, the U.S. Freedom of Information Act, the European Union Directive on Data Protection, South Africa's Protection of Personal Information Bill, the U.S. Safe Harbor Privacy Principles). See also Section X.

---

38 International Taskforce on Assessment Center Guidelines, 2015

In 2015, the British Psychological Society (BPS) published an Assessment Centre Standard,[39] which was designed to align with the International Standard on Assessment Delivery, ISO 10667.[40] The BPS Standard goes into more detail on Data Protection within Section 5: Preparing for Centre Delivery (see pages 27-28), and in keeping with its intended approach states, amongst other things, that the service provider shall: ensure that the data from the centre are managed in accordance with all professional, legal and regulatory requirements; only use the data for the agreed purpose of the centre; maintain the necessary level of security for personal data; ensure there are clear guidelines as to how long identifiable personal data are to be kept on file, with access limited to those with a right to know and the relevant consent being obtained before releasing data; and remove names and other personal identifiers from the centre results to make them anonymous for research or statistical analysis purposes when no longer needed.

Although the BPS Standard is mainly targeted at the UK, it clearly has relevance to the international environment, given its alignment to ISO 10667. Despite the fact that it probably is not that well known as yet, and certainly is not enforceable, we were keen to explore if and how our interviewees handled these data protection issues within their territories.

Unsurprisingly, all of our interviewees reported that they always captured the data from their ACs and used them to produce reports showing things such as: individual overall assessment ratings; average competency scores; average exercise scores; group trends by job function, etc. Some of them mentioned that they would occasionally review assessor scores to check for internal consistency and the majority indicated that they would undertake validation analyses whenever the opportunity arose, but disappointingly, clients rarely showed much enthusiasm or commitment for conducting such a process.

Despite the fact that they all referred to storing the data either in paper form, or more usually in digital form and even occasionally within the cloud, very few of them made any reference to issues relating to data protection. Both US interviewees were notable exceptions, stressing that they complied with US legislative requirements for ensuring data are managed carefully. Interestingly, however, as both operated globally, they acknowledged that they were adhering to the even more demanding EU Data Protection standards, including the EU's General Data Protection Regulation (GDPR)[41] which took effect on 25 May 2018, as it affects not only EU-based organisations, but also data controllers and processors around the world. One of the three UK interviewees also highlighted sensitivity to this issue, stating that they "worked closely with client's legal teams to ensure data was managed properly" and that "anonymising data at every stage was crucial". The only other reference that could be linked to data protection came from our East African interviewee, who stated that "Clients were very hesitant to share their data due to data privacy concerns".

It therefore appears that in general our interviewees did not have data protection at the forefront of their minds when we asked them 'How is AC data managed?', although to be fair, we did not explicitly

---

39 The British Psychological Society, 2015

40 International Standard on Assessment Delivery (ISO), 2011

41 General Data Protection Regulation (GDPR), 2018

ask what they did about data protection, which might well have generated a different response. There were some references to the need to store data within their territories (China and Russia) in order to comply with local data protection legislation, which was cited earlier in the technology section. However, it is notable that the 3 respondents from our sample of 13, who made significant, unsolicited references to data protection, were from the US and the UK, where psychometric assessment practices are better established and data protection concerns are therefore more evident. It is probably fair to conclude from this that the issue of data protection is something that AC practitioners will need to be better tuned into in the future.

7.2 People Analytics

Our second question relating to data management was: 'How does the AC data you collect fit into wider datasets captured through the selection process, and/or how is it integrated with other datasets held on the participants?' This was prompted by our wish to see if there was any evidence of the growing interest in the area of people analytics.

People analytics, also known as talent or workforce analytics, is, according to Josh Bersin, who is probably the leading expert in this area, "the use of employee data to help optimise business and management decisions".[42] In short, it is all about collecting a wide variety of data about people that can be used to provide various business insights, which can then be actioned as required. For example, by using what is referred to as 'predictive analytics', it is possible to identify who are the most likely people to leave an organisation and why, enabling the organisation to take remedial or preventative action if it chooses to do so. The key to people analytics is capturing a wide range of data points and determining how to use this data in a meaningful and productive way. For many years the obvious people data held by organisations included biographical information from employee records, coupled with details about their remuneration, holidays, sickness and absenteeism, further supplemented by training and development records, assessment profiles, performance appraisal data, etc. Today further data are available in the hitherto inaccessible form of real-time behaviour, such as email habits and time spent on the phone, as well as social and professional networking behaviour using Twitter, Facebook and LinkedIn, and even physiological measures such as heart rates, and much, much more.

It should therefore be self-evident that the richness of behavioural AC data lends itself to being a useful component amongst the assessment datasets gathered on individuals; the challenge is how to integrate these data with other datasets, hence our question.

Our interviewees reported that AC data were often used in conjunction with other data, such as psychometric test data and/or performance appraisal data, in order to address a specific requirement linked to the purpose of the centre. For example, it was sometimes used to make selection/promotion decisions or to identify those with high-potential (HiPos), and on other occasions to identify development needs. It was occasionally linked to tools like the 9-box grid for succession planning purposes.[43]

---

42 Bersin, 2017

43 SHRM, 2012

However, while most of our interviewees indicated an awareness of the opportunity to use AC data with other datasets in a wider general context, such as undertaking people analytics, none of them were doing so. One of our UK interviewees explained that clients would nearly always ask about benchmarking, as they were keen to see how their people compared with others, but this interest did not extend to people analytics. Indeed, none of our interviewees' clients had requested their involvement in this area, even though several of our interviewees said they would welcome the opportunity. Furthermore, our Turkish interviewee said that only 1 of his 200 clients was attempting to undertake any people analytics using dedicated software, and that it was a challenge for most HR departments to start doing this. As several of our interviewees reported, the problem for many organisations is that they do not have the systems to enable them to collect and store the data appropriately. As mentioned earlier, even if they did, they are often reluctant to share their data due to privacy concerns.

These findings are not particularly surprising, as recent research by Bersin[44] indicates that very few organisations (only 17%) are beginning to use people analytics effectively, although he pointed out that 69% are now starting to build the necessary systems to enable them to do so. As referenced earlier, he claims the rewards will be significant when they manage to implement those systems.

From our interviews we can conclude that our AC practitioners are generally aware of the growing interest in people analytics and would welcome the opportunity of using their AC data to contribute to the process, but the biggest obstacle is client readiness to go down this path and the need to ensure that the data privacy aspects of people analytics are properly managed. It was encouraging to hear that one of our US interviewees was reviewing how AC data can be integrated with other types of data such as facial recognition data. Although they had not started doing anything with this as yet, they were at least starting to explore the possibilities.

We recognise that people analytics is still in its infancy, but we believe that AC practitioners must start to think about how their uniquely valuable behavioural data can play a part amongst all of the other datasets that are starting to be captured, otherwise ACs run the risk of being marginalised and left behind. This could lead to a reduction in AC practice, which we are sure none of us would like to see.

8. SUMMARY/CONCLUSIONS

The assessment centre is a well-established assessment methodology which has been used widely by HR departments for many years to support their various talent management activities. However, as this chapter has highlighted, the world of HR, and of talent management in particular, is now being subjected to a level of relentless change that is constantly creating new challenges. One of the primary driving forces for much of this change is the advances being made with technology, which directly impacts the ways in which ACs are run, as well as impacting other stages within the assessment process, with the obvious indirect impact on AC practices.

---

44 Bersin, 2017a; Bersin 2017b

One of the key observations from our research was the feedback from a number of the interviewees that the demand for ACs is decreasing, which was put down to a combination of pre-centre assessment activities reducing candidate numbers, and clients wanting to implement quicker and cheaper assessment methods. Although the sample is small, given the level of experience amongst this group of practitioners, they are well qualified to highlight a probable trend. It would, of course, be helpful to verify if this trend reflects reality, but whatever the case, AC practitioners need to be alert to this possibility and take steps to ensure that ACs remain relevant and valid. Given that the focus of this chapter is on international perspectives, it is also important to recognise that this particular trend probably is not universal, as it would appear that the decrease in AC demand is more likely taking place in those territories where assessment practices are better established. However, it would be reasonable to assume that this pattern will be repeated in other territories as their assessment markets mature.

Another notable finding from our survey was the interviewees unanimously reporting that competencies/dimensions is the measurement construct that they always work with, despite recent academic research advocating that tasks are a more valid focal measurement. It would seem that practitioners and their clients either are not aware of this research, or have chosen to disregard it. The interviewees often highlighted that they were working with their clients' competency frameworks, so it is little surprise that this was the chosen basis of measurement. The conclusion is that academics will need to make a much stronger case if they wish to encourage a departure from competency-/dimension-based assessments in favour of task-based assessments. It was also interesting that our interviewees confirmed the growing popularity in recent years of competencies relating to change, with the majority citing 'Agility', 'Coping with Change' and 'Innovation' as important competencies associated with tackling the challenges of the VUCA world.

All of our interviewees confirmed the growing importance of ensuring a positive candidate/participant experience on their ACs, with 9 of the 13 rating it as either 'Extremely important' or 'Very important'. This is perhaps not surprising, given that there has been strong focus in recent years on ensuring 'employee engagement'. This concept clearly extends to the attraction and selection stages of the recruitment process, where organisations are still having to compete for scarce resources, fuelling the 'war for talent'.

We were also keen to explore how well diversity and inclusion were considered within different regions, and it was interesting to find that it was considered highly important in the more mature assessment markets such as the US, UK and Australia, where stakeholders were eager to give it priority, in keeping with local 'equal opportunity legislation'. Conversely, some interviewees from the less mature assessment markets, such as Trinidad, East Africa and South Korea, pointed out that diversity and inclusion were much less likely to be high amongst their clients' priorities when discussing AC matters.

The interviews concluded with the question: "Are there any factors not covered that you think are likely to impact AC practice over the next 5-10 years?" By far the most significant responses related to technology, where things like the use of artificial intelligence to support ACs was mentioned, for example, to replace assessors, to design simulations, or to supplement the data captured with facial recognition software, etc. Quite a number of our interviewees highlighted the ongoing need for ACs to be shortened, as clients demand quicker, cheaper processes generating faster results. This led many to suggest that they anticipated a greater demand for virtual assessment centres. Further technology comments included considerations such as the need to be able to run ACs using mobiles, incorporating virtual reality into our ACs, and linking them to the concept of games-based assessment. Several of our interviewees also acknowledged that ACs will need to generate data that can be integrated with other datasets, supporting the growing interest in the topic of 'people/talent analytics'. One of the interviewees made the interesting comment that there will be "a growing expectation for us to be able to create more insight from less data".

Finally, several of our interviewees acknowledged that amongst the many changes in this fast-paced world is the continuing trend of globalisation, where organisations want to adopt standardised global assessment processes so they can move talent around as required. However, this strategy also needs to take account of the various factors impacting local working environments, such as cultural differences, changing working practices with increasing levels of remote working, virtual teams with different leadership practices, and of course new technologies including robotics, all of which means that ACs must be able to adapt and evolve if they are to survive and thrive.

9.   ACKNOWLEDGEMENTS

We would like to thank the following people who were most generous with their time and for providing us with their valuable insights into the AC practices in their regions: Bill Byham, Founder and Executive Chairman at DDI (US); Lyanne Coley, Associate Consultant at Evolve Intelligence (Australia); Heather Coop, Associate Principal at Korn Ferry Hay Group (UK); Madeleine Dunford, Founder and Managing Director at Career Connections (East Africa); Jeremy Francis, Founder and Managing Director at Beyond Consulting (Trinidad & Tobago); Marco Kim, Founder and CEO of Assesta (South Korea); Maria Leske, Senior Leader at Evolve Intelligence (Australia); Rachel Mellors, Talent & Leadership Development Consultant at Cubiks (UK); Fleur Scott, Director of Consulting (UK) at Propel International (Global); Levent Sevinc, Founder and CEO of Assessment Systems (Turkey); Svetlana Simonenko, Managing Partner at Detech (Russia); Frank Washenitz, Head of Global & North America Sales Enhancement at Mylan (US); and Louis Yang, Managing Consultant, Business Psychologist at i-Select (China).

We would also like to thank Tom Parker at PSI/a&dc for helping us with our research.

EPILOGUE

THE FUTURE OF ACs IN SA

by Sandra Schlebusch and Gert Roodt

1. INTRODUCTION

Despite the initial positive expectations for a turnaround in the South African economy when President Cyril Ramaphosa was elected, the gross domestic product (GDP) dipped to 3.2% during the first quarter of 2019.[1] Add to this the unemployment statistic of 27.6% and the loss of 126,000 jobs during the first quarter of 2019[2], and a bleak picture of the current state in South Africa emerges. So what does this mean for ACs in South Africa?

2. ACs in an emerging market economy

We need to take cognisance of the fact that South Africa is not a developed economy, but rather an emerging market economy. This means that we have organisations in South Africa that compete globally with the best in class, but we also have organisations that are not yet at that level of proficiency. The implication is that the ACs' focal constructs of these differing organisations must be relevant to their current situation, as well as to their envisioned future. For this reason, using competencies from an existing international competency framework might not be relevant to all South African organisations, i.e. the competencies used must be relevant to the specific context of the organisation.

The South African infrastructure is not in all instances comparable to the infrastructure of developed economies. We still suffer from electricity outages, breaks in internet connectivity, and challenges in public transportation, education and health care. This means that we cannot assume that a VAC would be equally accessible to all the target employees of an organisation with offices throughout the country. The need to do a thorough analysis during the first stage of the design model cannot be stressed enough. The AC design team must obtain a clear and realistic picture of the client organisation's IT infrastructure before embarking on the design of a TEAC or VAC. It might be that a traditional pen-and-paper AC would be fairer to all target employees in the client organisation.

In the Buckett, Becker and Roodt[3] study on South African AC data, results were found that contradicted similar research in developed economies. This leads to the question: How valid is it to assume that the published research findings based on data obtained from ACs conducted in developed economies are true for an emerging economy like South Africa? An urgent call is made to conduct more research studies on South African ACs and to publish these results so that a solid base of AC research in an emerging economy is built.

---

1   Trading Economics, 2019

2   Statistics SA, 2019

3   Buckett et al., 2017

3.   ACs in a country with diversity

In Chapter 3, Nkomo and Badalani stated that "the population of South Africa has been described as one of the most complicated and diversified in the world. Capturing South Africa's diversity requires recognition of ethnicity, race and culture. That is, South Africa's population contains both ethnic and race groups". They built a case for research about the impact of South Africa's multiculturism during the 10 essential characteristics of an AC. This field is largely under scrutinised and should be more prominent in AC research.

What are the implications for ACs given South Africa's multiculturism, in the context of an emerging market economy that is not growing?

Since South African organisations are already using ACs as part of their talent management, the results of these ACs should be captured and analysed to interrogate any possible adverse impact. The recommendations made in Chapter 3 should be implemented when a new AC is designed.

4.   4IR

The fourth industrial revolution is on us, which will potentially impact all economic sectors. Some jobs will be transformed with automation taking over tasks, new jobs will emerge, and some jobs will be lost. The potential role of ACs is to assist the economy in transitioning into the new era, as well as to use the new technology to design and execute ACs. The 4IR will impact what we measure during ACs, as well as how we measure it.

Over half (54%) of today's employees will have to be reskilled.[4] Here, DACs can play a potentially important role by assessing participants' current skills and affording them the opportunity to learn new skills and practice them while at the DAC.

Although the impact of the 4IR on the human being is not yet evident, typical human-oriented skill sets will become more important.[5] This includes management-leadership skills and customer service skills, both areas that ACs have been active in. The implication is that ACs will have to be updated to measure the competencies and tasks that are important in the 4IR organisation.

The AC participant experience will be more important and experiences that mimic the participant's world of work will be more prominent. Including the "new" technology at the front end of the AC (the participant's experience), as well as at the back end, will be important. Virtual reality (VR), Artificial Intelligence (AI) and machine learning will all contribute to the AC of the future. The enhanced computing ability will allow more in-depth analysis of data that can direct future developments (also see Chapter 2).

---

4   Deloitte, 2019

5   World Economic Forum, 2018

5. 21st century organisations

The current 21st century organisation is already using the enhanced workforce by including contract workers as employees, and more and more teamwork is being encouraged with the breakdown of silos.[6] Inclusion, fairness, transparency, collaboration, social responsibility, ethics and the ability to engage internally as well as externally are all critical competencies in the 4IR organisation. In addition, manager-leaders need to work with greater ambiguity, rapid change and complexity, thus future ACs need to portray these realities.

Since the future manager-leader needs to respond quickly and accurately, the ACs must be properly embedded in other people processes and the employment life-cycle so as not to demand additional effort from the side of management-leadership.

6. **Management-leadership**

More and more, the option to develop manager-leaders from within the organisation is a cost-effective option.[7] Future leaders need to lead remotely, i.e. they must lead with technology as teams will be dispersed around the globe. Perhaps the future manager-leader needs to develop the "traditional" manager-leader skill set alongside the new competencies that the 4IR organisation demands. The new competencies might be: leading a very diverse team of employees, anticipating customer and market change, ability to create purpose, etc.

However, we are still caught in a situation where appointments are made and promotions are given to friends and family who do not necessarily have the required competence. Despite the best intentions of a few, and some notable, exceptions, all three tiers of South African government are plagued by inefficiencies, maladministration and poor governance, as evidenced by the fact that in the 2017/2018 financial year, "Only 18 municipalities managed to produce good-quality financial statements and performance reports, as well as comply with key legislation, thereby receiving a clean audit".[8]

The state owned enterprises are struggling to emerge from financial woes caused by corruption and years of maladministration, but the challenges are also in the private sector. We are shocked to learn about big scale unethical management practices where stakeholders were led to believe lies and half-truths, audit companies "looked the other way", and a few people benefitted from the situation.

The South African challenge is therefore to position the traditional ethical manager-leader skill set, as well as the new skill set required by the 4IR, in an economy that is not growing and where companies are financially restricted.   ACs should, and must, play a crucial role in not only selecting manager-leaders with these competencies, but must also develop these competencies themselves.

---

6   Deloitte, 2019

7   Deloitte, 2019

8   Auditor General Kimi Makwetu, 2017/2018

7. Conclusion

In the introduction we asked what the bleak picture in South Africa means for ACs. The answer is: ACs can play a major role in assisting with the appropriate selection of individuals into critical positions, and in developing the appropriate skills within organisations. This means that AC providers need to ensure that the AC adds value to the client organisation and that they are able to show this value to the organisation through evidence collected throughout the analysis, development and execution stages of the AC.

GLOSSARY

Administrator – The person who is responsible for overseeing the observers during an assessment centre process. He/she is also responsible for collating the assessment ratings and for providing a final (integrated) rating.

Aggregation (principle of) – Implies that a measure which includes an increasing number of questions or observations will provide a more stable measurement.

Assessment centre – A simulation-based process employing multiple assessment exercises, assessment techniques and multiple assessors to produce judgements regarding the extent to which participants display appropriate competencies. Assessment centres are usually employed for either selection or for development purposes. Several variations exist within these two broad categories.

Assessment data – Information generated by the assessment process, normally in a raw-rating format as well as in a final-rating format, that can be recorded on a spreadsheet or any other record system.

Assessor – Also see **Observer** or **Rater**.

Behavioural Anchored Rating Scale (BARS) – Refers to a rating scale format that uses behaviour statements to illustrate the rating scale levels. A description of behaviour for each rating per competency element/indicator is provided. The observer ticks a behaviour statement that best describes the participant's observed behaviour.

Behavioural element – A term also referred to as a competency element or indicator. An element is a subdimension of a competency that describes a pre-specified unit of observable behaviour. A group of behavioural elements constitutes a competency.

Behavioural Observation Scale (BOS) – Refers to a rating scale format where the observer indicates the frequency at which the participant displayed the specific behavioural statement (competency element/indicator) during the simulation.

Bias – Refers to the systematic discrimination a measure exhibits against a specific group (such as age, race, gender, language, etc.). Different statistical procedures can be applied to test for bias.

Candidate – Refers to the participant in a selection assessment centre, also called a delegate in a development assessment centre. See **Participant**.

Checklist – Refers to a list of activities (behaviours) that a participant should perform in order to complete a task successfully. The observer ticks the applicable behaviour in the checklist when it is observed.

Clinical data integration – see **Judgemental data integration**.

Coefficient of equivalence – The correlation between the two sets of scores obtained on different (alternate) measures that would yield a reliability coefficient, also known as the coefficient of equivalence.

Coefficient of internal consistency – A test can, for example, be split according to the odd- and the even-numbered items. The two "equivalent" halves can then be correlated. This obtained coefficient is also referred to as the coefficient of internal consistency.

Competency – A constellation or a group of behaviours related to job success that are specific, observable and verifiable, and can be reliably and logically classified together.

Competency assessment – The process of systematically observing and recording relevant behaviours within a competency area against predetermined standards or criteria.

Competency profile – Refers to a group or a constellation of competencies that describe the unique requirements of a specific job. Candidates are selected if they sufficiently match the profile.

Criterion – A variable often referred to as the dependent variable that acts as a standard or a benchmark that a test or an assessment is supposed to be measuring. Such a variable can thus be used to investigate the empirical validity of a test.

Delegate – A participant in a development assessment centre, also called a candidate in a selection assessment centre. See **Participant**.

Deliverable – A specific, intended outcome or consequence of a particular action. In the case of the design model described in this book, it refers to a specific consequence at the end of each step in a phase.

Design model – A systematic process applied in the development of an assessment centre programme that involves distinct and distinguishable phases of analysis, design, implementation and evaluation. This model is generally encountered in the training and development literature.

Design team – A team of experts responsible for the development of the assessment centre or the simulations and the competency assessments.

Development Assessment Centre (DAC) – Refers to an assessment centre used for the purpose of determining areas of strength, development needs and to provide the opportunity to learn while at the DAC itself. An important aspect is that the participant has the opportunity to receive feedback, to learn, and to apply learning while at the DAC.

Diagnostic Centre (DC) – An assessment centre used for the purpose of identifying a profile of strengths and development areas so that a tailored development plan can be devised.

Differential validity – Refers to a measure's ability to successfully discriminate between groups or individuals on one or other predetermined criterion.

Dimension – See **Competency**.

Error variance – A proportion of the total variance that can be ascribed to unaccounted or unsystematic variance.

Ethnocultural diversity – Refers to the diverse cultural and ethnic groups within society.

Ethnocentrism - A basic attitude expressing the belief that one's own ethnic group or one's own culture is superior to other ethnic groups or cultures, and that one's cultural standards can be applied in a universal manner.

Evaluation – A systematic measurement (rating, assessment, evaluation) against a predetermined standard or content.

Exercise – See **Simulation**.

Fairness – A general, subjective perception of the overall assessment process. Specific fairness perceptions relate to different justice perceptions, such as distributive, procedural, informational and interpersonal justice.

Feedback – Information in an oral or a written format comparing actual performance with a standard or a desired level of performance, or, alternatively, providing a narrative explanation of a lived experience.

Feedback discussion – A specific event where the observer provides either the participant or the direct manager with oral feedback on the feedback report.

Fidelity – Fidelity is related to the realism of the simulation as compared with an actual job situation, task, etc. High- or low-fidelity simulations refer to the extent to which an assessment centre simulation requires the participant to display behaviours related to one or more selected competencies.

Focal construct – Refers to the behavioural construct that is evaluated during the assessment centre, for example dimensions, competencies, tasks, roles, strategies, etc.

Gamification – Refers to applying game mechanics and dynamics to non-game situations for the purpose of enhancing participant motivation and engagement.

Implicit bias – ors do not always have conscious, intentional control over the processes of social perception, impression formation, and judgment that motivate their behaviours.

Incremental validity – Refers to a measure's ability to explain additional numerical variance compared with another measure, or a set of other measures, in the prediction of a dependent variable.

Informed consent – Refers to an ethical requirement that a participant agrees to participate in an assessment centre with a clear knowledge of the purpose, process and content of the assessment centre. The participant has the right to refuse to participate.

Interactionist Theory – States that behaviour is a function of both the person and environment. The assumption is that behaviour will be affected by both person variables (that is, there are individual differences in performance levels) and characteristics of the environment.

Inter-item consistency – Also referred to as the Kuder-Richardson (KR 20) method. In this case, the consistency of the raters' ratings of all items is calculated.

Inter-rater consistency reliability – This type of reliability can be calculated by either correlating the ratings of two different raters or by applying an adapted version of the Cronbach's Alpha formula.

Intra-rater consistency reliability – The same Cronbach's Alpha formula is used as with the inter-rater reliability, but, in this instance, the variances are obtained from different sources.

Job analysis – The process used to determine the competencies linked to success or failure in a job, job role or job grouping. Different techniques of job analyses exist, such as interviews with incumbents, observations of incumbents, check lists, etc.

Judgemental data integration – Observers conduct some portion of the assessment process and then enter into a discussion where they share observations, possibly provide preliminary ratings on performance dimensions, and come to an agreement on ratings.

Leader – Also see **Manager**.

Leadership – Also see **Management**.

Management – Refers to a generic process of planning, organising, leading and controlling.

Management level – Refers to a specific tier in the management hierarchy. Normally three levels are identified, namely lower, middle and top management.

Manager – A person with a designated management function who is responsible for planning, organising, leading and controlling a specific function.

Multiple assessments – The assessment centre process applies the principle of multiple measurements, that is, the same competency is assessed in different settings or simulations. Multiple assessments provide the context for determining the consistency of behaviours across different settings or simulations.

Multiculturism – Generally described as a value system which emphasises the acceptance of different cultural groups, along with practices that give equal attention to such groups in a particular setting.

Needs analysis – A systematic investigation to determine a particular group's salient needs.

Observer – An individual who is trained and declared competent to observe, note, classify and make reliable judgements about the behaviour of participants. Observers should be representative of different groups such as race, age, gender and language.

Operational reliability – Refers to the degree of consistency and standardisation of practices, procedures and policies within the execution of the overall assessment centre process. Operational reliability is a prerequisite for operational validity.

Operational validity – Refers to the degree to which the overall assessment centre process meets the competency content requirements emerging from the different needs and job analyses. The term "operational validity" was coined by Byham and Temlock (1972).

Participant – The general term describing the individual participating in an assessment centre and whose competencies are being assessed. The terms "delegate" or "candidate" are respectively used for development and selection assessment centres.

Pilot – Refers to the experimental execution (dummy run) of an assessment centre programme in order to test the content and/or process for obvious limitations.

Practitioners – A collective term for describing the professionally qualified individuals or persons involved in executing the overall assessment centre process.

Pre-pilot – Refers to a limited experimental execution on a simulation level to ensure that the simulation will elicit the required range of behavioural elements.

Process owners – A term for collectively describing the observers, administrators and role players who jointly own or manage the overall assessment centre process. Also see **Practitioners**.

Professional accountability – Refers to an ethical requirement that a suitably trained and qualified person should accept final responsibility for safekeeping assessment data or records and their use.

Professional competence – An ethical requirement that all assessment practitioners are well trained and possess the required competency levels to professionally conduct an assessment centre.

Programme evaluation – A systematic process of reviewing or evaluating a programme for effectiveness (evaluating the fitness of purpose – doing the right things) or for efficiency (evaluating the fitness for purpose – doing things right). The programme evaluation considers different stages of the process, namely analysis, design, implementation and evaluation.

Realistic Accuracy Model (RAM) – This theory describes what must happen for a perceiver to provide accurate judgments about a person's traits. The process includes four steps: 1) The person must show in some way behaviour **relevant** to the trait being judged; 2) behaviours relevant to the trait must be **available**/observable to the perceiver; 3) the perceiver must **detect**/know what behaviours are relevant to the trait; and 4) the perceiver must **utilize** and interpret the behaviours correctly.

Range restriction – Also referred to as the truncation effect or pre-selection effects. This occurs when a significant part of a normal distribution of scores is lost or truncated owing to pre-selection or biased sampling procedures.

Rater – See **Observer**.

Rating – The recorded outcome of an assessment process. Different ratings are recorded, such as ratings per competency, final competency rating, final rating per simulation, management performance rating, etc.

Rating distributions – Refers to the range and frequency of scores within that range. The shape of the distribution normally takes on the form of a bell-shaped curve, also referred to as the normal distribution curve.

Reliability – The extent to which a measure succeeds in measuring what it is supposed to measure in a consistent manner, that is, a process of measurement that yields the same results over repeated measures.

Rigour – A term referring to the systematic and consistent manner in which a task is executed. A rigorous assessment centre process will be characterised by a high degree of consistency in the execution of a simulation and competency assessments. Rigour is a prerequisite for operational reliability and validity.

Role player – A trained person who plays a particular role against a standardised script.

Score – See **Rating**.

Simulation – An exercise or technique designed to elicit behaviours or behavioural elements that are job-related and require the participants to respond behaviourally to situational stimuli.

Stage – A distinct phase of the design model.

Stakeholder – Refers to an important party in the development and administration of an assessment centre. Different stakeholders can be identified, such as process owners (observers, administrators, role players), participants, subordinates, managers and HR specialists.

Standardisation – Refers to the consistency of administration and scoring.

Standard Error of Measurement (SEM) – Standardised scores are used to interpret individual test scores in terms of probability limits within which they are likely to vary as a function of their measurement error.

Step – An identifiable substage within a specific phase of the design model.

Trait ivation Theory (TAT) – Addresses how individual traits come to be expressed as behaviour in response to trait-relevant situational demands.

Unitary validity – Refers to an ongoing process of collecting all types of validity evidence.

Validity – Refers to the extent to which a measurement tool or process, such as an assessment centre, measures the content that it is supposed to be measuring. Different kinds of validity exist (such as content, construct and predictive validity) that each describe a facet of the overall validity of a measure, depending on the type of validity in question or the type of statistical procedure applied.

VUCA – VUCA means Volatility, Uncertainty, Complexity, and Ambiguity. It originated in US military educational settings to describe military challenges and is now being used to provide a description of the general business environment.

Wash-up session – see **Judgemental data integration.**

CHAPTER 1 REFERENCES

Camp, R. R., Blanchard, P. N. & Huszczo, G. E. (1986). *Toward a more organisationally effective training strategy and practice.* Englewood Cliffs, NJ: Prentice-Hall.

Dewbury, C. & Jackson, D. J. R. (2016). The Perceived Nature and Incidence of dysfunctional Assessment Center Features and Processes. *International Journal of Selection and Assessment, 24*(2): 189-196. Doi.org/10.1111/ijsa.12140.

Edwards, J. E., Scott, J. C. & Raju, N. S. (2003). *The human resources program-evaluation handbook.* Thousand Oaks, CA: Sage Publications.

Employment Equity Act. (1998). Act No. 55. (South Africa). Government Gazette, No 19370.

Griffiths, P. & Allen, B. (1987). Assessment Centres: Breaking with tradition. *Journal of Management Development,* 6(1): 18 – 29. doi.org/10.1108/eb051632

Highouse, S. & Nolan, K. P. (2011). One History of the Assessment Center. In D. J. R. Jackson, C. E. Lance, & B. J. Hoffman (Eds.). *The Psychology of Assessment Centers* (pp 25 – 44). New York: Routledge.

International Taskforce on Assesment Center Guidelines. (2015). Guidelines and ethical considerations for assessment center operations. *Journal of Management, 41*: 1244-1273. http://dx.doi.org/10.1177/0149206314567780.

Lipsey, M. W. (2005). *The basics of program evaluation: step by step.* Nashville, TN: Vanderbilt Institute for Public Policy Studies.

Mager, R. F. & Pipe, P. (1979). *Criterion-referenced instruction: analysis, design, and implementation.* Los Altos Hills, CA: Mager Associates.

Meiring, D. & Buckett, A. (2016). Best Practice Guidelines for the Use of the Assessment Centre Method in South Africa (5th ed.). *SA Journal of Industrial Psychology/SA Tydskrif vir Bedryfsielkunde, 42*(1), a1298. http://dx.doi.org/10.4102/sajip.v42i1.1298

Michalak, D. F. & Yager, E. G. (1979). *Making the training process work.* New York: Harper & Row.

Rossi, P. H., Lipsey, M. W. & Freeman, H. E. (2004). *Evaluation: a systematic approach.* Thousand Oaks, CA: Sage Publications.

Rupp, D. E., Gibbons, A. M., Baldwin, A. M., Snyder, L. A., Spain, S. M., Woo, S. E., Brummel, B. J., Sims, C. S. & Kim, M. (2006). An initial validation of developmental assessment centers as accurate assessments and effective training interventions. *The Psychologist–Manager, 9*(2): 171-200.

SA Assessment Centre Study Group. (2018). *Code of Ethics for Assessment Centres in South-Africa.* Retrieved from: https://www.acsg.co.za/sites/default/files/Code-of-Ethics-for-ACs-inSA-15-March-2018-ACSG.pdf. Accessed 1 December 2018.

Skills Development Levies Act. (1999). Act No. 9. (South Africa).

Thornton, G. C., Rupp, D. E. & Hoffman, B. J. (2015). *Assessment Center Perspective for Talent Management Strategies* (2nd ed.). New York: Routledge.

CHAPTER 2 REFERENCES

Dewberry, C. & Jackson, D. J. R. (2016). The perceived nature and incidence of dysfunctional assessment center features and processes. *International Journal of Selection and Assessment, 24*(2): 189-196. https://doi.org/10.1111/ijsa.12140.

Howard, A. (2006). New directions for assessment centers: a commentary by Ann Howard. *The Psychologist–Management Journal, 9*(2): 201-205.

Meiring D. & Buckett A. (2016). Best Practice Guidelines for the use of the Assessment Centre Method in South Africa (5th ed.). *SA Journal of Industrial Psychology/SA Tydskrif vir Bedryfsielkunde, 42*(1), Art. #1298. pages. http://dx.doi.org/10.4102/sajip.v42i1.1298

Meiring, D., Schlebusch, S., Lowman, R. & Muleya, V. (2016). *Code of Ethics for Assessment Center Practice in South Africa.* Plenary session at the 36thAnnual SA Assessment Centre Study Group (ACSG) conference April 2016, NH Lord Charles, Somerset West, South Africa

Meiring, D., Schlebusch, S., Lowman, R. & Muleya, V. (2017). *Code of Ethics for Assessment Center Practice in South Africa*. Plenary session at the 37th Annual Assessment Centre Study Group (ACSG) conference, 3 - 7 April 20017, NH Lord Charles , Somerset-West, South Africa

Meiring, D., Schlebusch, S., Lowman, R. & Muleya, V. (2018). *Code of Ethics for Assessment Center Practice in South Africa*. Plenary session at the 38th Annual SA Assessment Centre Study Group (ACSG) conference, 14-16 April 2018, Hilton Hotel, Johannesburg, South Africa.

Meiring, D. & Van der Westhuizen, J. H. (2011). Using computer-based simulation technology within an ADC: A South African case study. In N. Povah, & G. C. Thornton (Eds.). *Assessment centres and global talent management* (pp. 77-96). Surrey, England: Gower Publishing Limited.

Muleya, V. R., Fourie, L. & Schlebusch, S. (2017). Ethical challenges in assessment centres in South Africa. *SA Journal of Industrial Psychology/SA Tydskrif vir Bedryfsielkunde, 43*(0), a1324. https://doi. org/10.4102/sajip. v43. i0.1324

SA Assessment Centre Study Group. (2018). *Code of Ethics for Assessment Centres in South-Africa*. Retrieved from: https://www.acsg.co.za/sites/default/files/Code-of-Ethics-for-ACs-inSA-15-March-2018-ACSG.pdf. Accessed 1 December 2018.

Schlebusch, S. (2018). *Adapting to disruption: Assessment centres in the future*. Retrieved from: http://www.acsg. co.za/adapting-disruption-assessment-centres-future Accessed 16 September 2018.

Spangenberg, H. (2018). *History of the ACSG*. Retrieved from: http://www.acsg.co.za/history Accessed 11 August 2018

Taylor, N. (2018). *Beware the shiny stuff*. Retrieved from: http://www.acsg.co.za/adapting-disruption-beware-shiny-stuff Accessed 16 September 2018.

Thornton, G. C. III. (2011). Fifty years and counting: The ongoing reciprocal impact of science and practice of the assessment center method. In N. Povah & G.C. Thornton III (Eds.). *Assessment and Development Centres: Strategies for Global Talent Management*. London: Gower.

CHAPTER 3 REFERENCES

Adams, B. G., Van de Vijver, F. J. & De Bruin, G. P. (2012). Identity in South Africa: Examining self-descriptions across ethnic groups. *International Journal of Intercultural Relations, 36*(3): 377-388.

Allik, J. & McCrae, R. R. (2004). Toward a geography of personality traits patterns of profiles across 36 cultures. *Journal of Cross-Cultural Psychology, 35*, 13-28. doi:10.1177/0022022103260382

Arasaratnam, L. A. (2013). A review of articles on multiculturalism in 35 years of IJIR. *International Journal of Intercultural Relations, 37*(6), 676-685.

Association of Test Publishers of South Africa v President of the Republic of South Africa and Others (89564/14) [2017] ZAGPPHC 144; [2017] 8 BLLR 850 (GP); (2017) 38 ILJ 2253 (GP) (3 May 2017)

Barth, F. (1969). *Ethnic groups and boundaries: The social organization of cultural difference*. Oslo: Universitetsforlaget.

Booysen, L. (2001). The duality of South African leadership: afrocentric or eurocentric. *South African Journal of Labour Relations*, Spring/Summer: 36-63.

Booysen, L. A. E. (2016). The two faces of Ubuntu – an inclusive positive or exclusive parochial leadership perspective? In L. Morgan-Robert, L., L. Wooten, & M. Davidson, M. (Eds.). *Positive organizing in a global society: Understanding and engaging differences for capacity-building and inclusion*. New York: Taylor & Francis Group.

Booysen, L. & Van Wyk, M. (2007). Culture and leadership in South Africa. In J. Chhokar, F. C. Brodbeck & R. House (Eds.). *Culture and leadership, across the world: The GLOBE Book of In-Depth Studies of 25 Societies*. Mahwah, NJ: Lawrence Erlbaum Associates.

Brief, A. P., Dietz, J., Cohen, R. R., Pugh, S. D. & Vaslow, J. B. (2000). Just doing business: Modern racism and obedience to authority as explanations for employment discrimination. *Organizational behavior and human decision processes, 81*(1), 72-97.

Brouwers, S. A. & Van de Vijver, F. J. (2015). Contextualizing intelligence in assessment: the next step. *Human Resource Management Review, 25*(1), 38-46.

Buckett, A., Becker, J. R. & Roodt, G. (2017). General performance factors and group differences in assessment center ratings. *Journal of Managerial Psychology, 32*(4), 298-313.

Carrim, N. M. H. & Nkomo, S. M. (2016). Wedding intersectionality theory and identity work in organizations: South African Indian women negotiating managerial identity. *Gender, Work and Organization, 23*(3): 261-277.

Cox, T. (1993). Problems with research by organizational scholars on issues of race and ethnicity. *Journal of Applied Behavioral Sciences, 26*(1), 5–23.

Department of Labour. (2017*). Commission for Employment Equity Report 2016-2017*. Pretoria, South Africa.

Dean, M. A., Roth, P. L. & Bobko, P. (2008). Ethnic and gender subgroup differences in assessment center ratings: a meta-analysis. *Journal of Applied Psychology, 93*(3), 685-691.

Donald, F., Thatcher, A. & Milner, K. (2014). Psychological assessment for redress in South African organisations: is it just? *South African Journal of Psychology, 44*(3), 333-349.

Dunne, I. & Bosch, A. (2015). Graduate identity development in South Africa: misaligned warranting and the independent mediator. *Journal of Managerial Psychology, 30*(3), 304-319.

Durrheim, K., Tredoux, C., Foster, D. & Dixon, J. (2011). Historical trends in South African race attitudes. *South African Journal of Psychology, 41*(3), 263-278.

Eaton, L. & Louw, J. (2000). Culture and self in South Africa: individualism-collectivism predictions. *The Journal of Social Psychology, 140*(2): 210-217.

Employment Equity Act. (1998). Act No. 55. (South Africa). Government Gazette, No 19370.

Employment Equity Amendment. (2013). Act No. 47. (South Africa).

Falk, A. & Fox, S. (2014). Gender and ethnic composition of assessment centers and its relationship to participants' success. *Journal of Personnel Psychology, 13*(1): 11-20.

Fetvadjiev, V. H., Meiring, D., van de Vijver, F. J., Nel, J. A. & Hill, C. (2015). The South African Personality Inventory (SAPI): A culture-informed instrument for the country's main ethnocultural groups. *Psychological Assessment, 27*(3), 827.

Fetvadjiev, V. H., Meiring, D., Nel, J. A., Hill, C., van de Vijver, F. J. & Church, A. T. (2017). Indigenous Personality Structure and Measurement in South Africa. *The Praeger handbook of personality across cultures. Vol. 1: Trait psychology across cultures*, 137-160.

Fetvadjiev, V. H., Meiring, D., Van de Vijver, F. J., Nel, J. A., Sekaja, L., & Laher, S. (2018). Personality and behavior prediction and consistency across cultures: A multimethod study of Blacks and Whites in South Africa. *Journal of personality and social psychology, 114*(3), 465.

Franchi, V. (2003). The racialization of affirmative action in organizational discourses: A case study of symbolic racism in post-apartheid South Africa. *International Journal of Intercultural Relations, 27*(2), 157-187.

Frederikse, J. (1990). *The unbreakable thread: non-racialism in South Africa.* Bloomington: Indiana University Press.

Gade, C. B. (2012). What is Ubuntu? Different interpretations among South Africans of African descent. *South African Journal of Philosophy, 31*(3), 484-503.

Gatewood, R. D. & Field, H. S. (2001). *Human resource selection* (5th ed.). Stamford, CT: Thomson Learning.

Goldstein, H. W., Yusko, K. P. & Nicolopoulos, V. (2001). Exploring black-white subgroup differences of managerial competencies. *Personnel Psychology, 54*(4), 783-807.

Greenwald, A. G. & Krieger, L. H. (2006). Implicit bias: scientific foundations. *California Law Review, 94*(4): 945-967.

Habib, A. & Bentley, K. (2008). *Racial Redress and Citizenship in South Africa.* Pretoria: HRSC Press.

Hall, E. T. (1989). *Beyond culture.* New York: Anchor Books.

Hermelin, E., Lievens, F. & Robertson, I. T. (2007). The validity of assessment centres for the prediction of supervisory performance ratings: A meta-analysis. *International Journal of Selection and Assessment, 15*(4), 405-411.

Hewstone, M. & Ward, C. (1985). Ethnocentrism and causal attribution in Southeast Asia. *Journal of Personality and Social Psychology, 48*(3), 614.

Hofstede, G. (1991). *Cultures and organizations: software of the mind.* London: McGraw-Hill.

Hooghe, M. (2008). Ethnocentrism. In W.A. Darity (Ed.). *International encyclopedia of the social sciences. Volume 3: Ethnic – Gender.* Detroit: Gale.

Hough, L. M., Oswald, F. L. & Ployhart, R. E. (2001). Determinants, detection and amelioration of adverse impact in personnel selection procedures: Issues, evidence and lessons learned. *International Journal of Selection and Assessment, 9*(1-2), 152-194.

House, R. J., Hanges, P. J., Javidan, M., Dorfman, P. & Gupta, V. (Eds.). (2004). *Leadership, culture, and organizations: The globe study of 62 societies.* Thousand Oaks, CA: Sage Publications, Inc.

Hurst, D. N. & Charoux, J. A. E. (1994). The assessment centre: Testing the fairness hypothesis. *South African Journal of Industrial Psychology, 20*(2), 21-25.

Jackson, L.T.B., Van de Vijver, F.J.R. & Molokoane, D.H. (2013). A dual-process model of diversity outcomes: The case South African police service in the Pretoria area. *South African Journal of Human Resource Management, 11*(1), Art#504, 13 pages. http://dx.doi.org/10.4102/ sajhrm.v11i1.504

Karsten, L. & Illa, H. (2005) *Ubuntu* as a key African management concept: contextual background and practical insights for knowledge application. *Journal of Managerial Psychology, 20*(7): 607-620.

Khoza, R. (2006). *Let Africa lead: African transformational leadership for 21st century business.* Johannesburg: Vezubuntu.

Kleinmann, M. & Ingold, P. V. (2019). Towards a better understanding of assessment centers: a conceptual review. *Annual Review of Organizational Psychology and Organizational Behavior, 6*: 349-72.

Krause, D. E., Rossberger, R. J., Dowdeswell, K., Venter, N. & Joubert, T. (2011). Assessment center practices in South Africa. *International Journal of Selection and Assessment, 19*(3), 262-275.

Krause, D. E. (2011). Assessment center practices in South Africa, Western Europe and North America. In N. Povah & G. C. Thornton III (Eds.). *Assessment centres and global talent management.* Famham, England: Gower Publishing Ltd.

Kuncel, N. R. & Highhouse, S. (2011). Complex predictions and assessor mystique. *Industrial and Organizational Psychology, 4*(3), 302-306.

Lievens, F. & Thornton, G. C. III. (2005). Assessment centers: recent developments in practice and research. In A. Evers, O. Smit-Voskuijl, & N. Anderson (Eds.). *Handbook of Selection.* Hoboken, NJ: Blackwell Publishing

Littrell, R. F., Wu, N. H., Nkomo, S. M., Wanasika, I. & Howell, J. (2013). Pan-sub-Saharan African managerial leadership and the values of *Ubuntu*. In T. Lituchy, B J Punnett, & B. Puplampu (Eds.). *Management in Africa: Macro and Micro Perspectives.* New York: Routledge Publishers.

Maharaj, P. (1995). *The social identities of Indians in a changing South Africa.* M.Social Science dissertation. Durban: University of Natal.

Mangaliso, M. P. (2001). Building Competitive Advantage from Ubuntu: Management Lessons from South Africa. *Academy of Management Executive, 15*(3): 23-32.

Mbigi, L. & Maree, J. (1995). *Ubuntu: the spirit of African transformation management.* Johannesburg: Knowledge Resources.

McConahay, J. B. (1986). Modern racism, ambivalence, and the modern racism scale. In J. Dovidio & S. Gaertner (Eds.). *Prejudice, discrimination, and racism.* New York: Academic Press.

Meiring, D. & Buckett, A. (2016). Best practice guidelines for the use of the assessment centre method in South Africa. *South African Journal of Industrial Psychology, 42*(1), 1-15.

Meriac, J.P., Hoffman, B.J., Woehr, D.J. & Fleisher, M.S. (2008). Further evidence for the validity of assessment center dimensions: A meta-analysis of the incremental criterion-related validity of dimension ratings. *Journal of Applied Psychology,* 93: 1042–1052. https://doi.org/10.1037/0021-9010.93.5.1042

Mulder, G. & Taylor, N. (2015). *Validity of assessment centres (ACs) as a selection development measure.* Nari: JvR Psychometrics.

Muleya, V. R., Fourie, L. & Schlebusch, S. (2017). Ethical challenges in assessment centres in South Africa. *South African Journal of Industrial Psychology, 43*(1), 1-20.

Nel, J. A., Valchev, V. H., Rothmann, S., van de Vijver, F. J. R., Meiring, D. & de Bruin, G. P. (2012). Exploring the personality structure in the 11 languages of South Africa. *Journal of Personality, 80,* 915–948.

Neuliep, J. W., Hintz, S. M. & McCroskey, J. C. (2005). The influence of ethnocentrism in organizational contexts: Perceptions of interviewee and managerial attractiveness, credibility, and effectiveness. *Communication Quarterly, 53*(1), 41-56.

Ployhart, R. E. & Holtz, B. C. (2008). The diversity–validity dilemma: strategies for reducing racioethnic and sex subgroup differences and adverse impact in selection. *Personnel Psychology, 61*(1), 153-172.

Port Elizabeth Municipality v Various Occupiers (CCT 53/03) [2004] ZACC 7; 2005(1) SA 217 (CC); 2004 (12) BCLR 1268 (CC) (1 October 2004).

Povah, N. (2011). A review of recent international surveys into Assessment Centre practices. In N. Povah & G. C. Thornton III (Eds.). *Assessment centres and global talent management.* Famham, England: Gower Publishing Ltd.

News 24. (29 February 2016). *Half of South Africans say Race Relations have Improved.* Retrieved from: https://www. news24.com/SouthAfrica/News/half-of-south-africans-say-race-relations-have-improved-survey-20160229. Accessed 2/1/2018.

Nkomo, S. M. (2011). The Challenge of Moving from the letter of the law to the spirit of the law: The challenges of realising the intent of employment equity and affirmative action. *Transformation: Critical Perspectives on Southern Africa,* 77: 132-146.

Povah, N. & Thornton, G. C. (Eds.). (2011). *Assessment centres and global talent management.* Farnham, England: Gower Publishing, Ltd.

Radhakrishnan, S. (2005). Time to show our true colors: the gendered politics of "Indianness" in post-Apartheid South Africa. *Gender and Society,* 19(2): 262–281.

Rosette, A. S., Leonardelli, G. J. & Phillips, K. W. (2008). The white standard: racial bias in leader categorization. *Journal of Applied Psychology,* 93: 758-777.

Rossier, J., Dahourou, D. & McCrae, R. R. (2005). Structural and mean-level analyses of the five-factor model and locus of control: Further evidence from Africa. *Journal of Cross-Cultural Psychology,* 36(2), 227-246

Schlebusch, S. & Roodt, G. (Eds) (2008). *Assessment centres: unlocking potential for growth.* Johannesburg: Knowledge Resources.

Sharma, S., Shimp, T. A. & Shin, J. (1994). Consumer ethnocentrism: A test of antecedents and moderators. *Journal of the Academy of Marketing Science, 23*(1), 26-37.

Statistics South Africa. (2017). *Mid-year Population Estimates 2017.* Pretoria, South Africa.

The Constitution of the Republic of South Africa. (1996). Act No. 108. (South Africa). Government Gazette, No 17678.

Thomas, A. & Bendixen, M. (2000). Management implications of ethnicity in South Africa. *Journal of International Business Studies,* 31(3): 507-519.

Thornton, G. C., Rupp, D. E. & Hoffman, B. J. (2015). *Assessment Center Perspective for Talent Management Strategies* (2nd ed.). New York: Routledge.

Thornton III, G. C., Rupp, D. E., Gibbons, A. M., & Vanhove, A. J. (2019). Same-gender and same-race bias in assessment center ratings: A rating error approach to understanding subgroup differences. *International Journal of Selection and Assessment,* 27(1), 54-71.

Valchev, V. H., Nel, J. A., van de Vijver, F. J. R., Meiring, D., De Bruin, G. P. & Rothmann, S. (2013). Similarities and differences in implicit personality concepts across ethno-cultural groups in South Africa. *Journal of Cross-Cultural Psychology,* 44: 365–388.

Van den Heuvel, H. (2008) *Between optimism and opportunism: Deconstructing 'African management' discourse in South Africa.* Unpublished doctoral dissertation. Vrije Universiteit, Netherlands.

Van Dyk, G. A. J. & De Kock, F. S. (2004). The relevance of the individualism-collectivism (IC) factor for the management of diversity in the South African national defence force. *South African Journal of Industrial Psychology,* 30(2): 90-95.

Van Eeden, R., Taylor, N. & Prinsloo, C. H. (2013). The sixteen personality factor questionnaire in South Africa. In S. Laher & K. Cockcroft (Eds.). *Psychological assessment in South Africa: research and applications.* Johannesburg: Wits University Press.

Van de Vijver, A. J. R. & Rothmann, S. (2004). Assessment in multicultural groups: The South African case. *South African Journal of Industrial Psychology,* 30(4):1-7.

Woodruffe, C. (2011). Whiter than white: The diversity credentials of assessment and development centres. In Povah, N. and Thornton G. C. (Eds.). *Assessment centres and global talent management.* Farnham, England: Gower.

CHAPTER 4 REFERENCES

American Educational Research Association (AERA), American Psychological Association (APA), & National Council on Measurement in Education (NCME). (2014). *Standards for Educational and Psychological Testing.* Washington, DC: American Educational Research Association.

American Psychological Association (APA). (2017). *Ethical principles of psychologists and code of conduct.* Washington, DC: American Psychological Association. Retrieved from: www.apa.org/ethics.

BrainyQuote. (n.d.). *Nelson Mandela quote.* Retrieved from: https://www.brainyquote.com/quotes/nelson_mandela_378967

Employment Equity Act. (1998). Act No. 55. (South Africa). Government Gazette, No 19370.

General Data Protection Regulation. (GDPR). Retrieved from: https://www.eugdpr.org/.

International Taskforce on Assessment Center Guidelines. (2015). Guidelines and ethical considerations for assessment center operations. *Journal of Management, 41*(4): 1244-1273.DOI: 10.1177/0149206314567780

Krause, D. E., Rossberger, R. J., Dowdeswell, K., Venter, N. & Joubert, T. (2011). Assessment center practices in South Africa. *International Journal of Selection & Assessment, 19*(3): 262-275. doi:10.1111/j.1468-2389.2011.00555.x

Lefkowitz, J. (2017). *Ethics and values in industrial-organizational psychology* (2nd ed.). New York: Routledge Taylor and Francis Group.

Lefkowitz, J. & Lowman, R. L. (2017). Ethics of employee selection. In J. L. Farr, & N. Tippins (Eds.). *Handbook of employee selection* (2nd ed.). pp. 575-598. New York: Psychology Press (Taylor & Francis).

Lowman, R. L. (April 2016). *Ethical practice of ACs in the workplace.* Invited plenary address, 36th annual South African AC Study Group (ACSG) conference, 7 April, Somerset West, South Africa.

Lowman, R. L. (2018a). Ethical and legal concerns in internet-based testing. In J. Scott, D. Bartram, D. Reynolds and D. Foster (Eds.). *Next generation technology-enhanced assessment. Global perspectives on occupational and workplace testing.* (pp. 350-374) Cambridge, UK: Cambridge University Press.

Lowman, R. L. (2018b). Ethical issues and standards in research and applications of industrial, work, and organizational psychology. In D. S. Ones, N. Anderson & H. Kepir Singagil, *SAGE Handbook of Industrial, Work & Organizational Psychology, 2e, V1.* Thousand Oaks, CA: Sage Publications.

Meiring, D. & Buckett, A. (2016). Best practice guidelines for the use of the AC method in South Africa (5th ed.). *SAJIP: South African Journal Of Industrial Psychology, 42*(1):1-15.

Muleya, V. R., Fourie, L. & Schlebusch, S. (2017). Ethical challenges in assessment centres in South Africa. *SA Journal of Industrial Psychology/SA Tydskrif vir Bedryfsielkunde, 43*(0), a1324. https://doi. org/10.4102/sajip. v43. i0.1324

Newman, J. L., Robinson-Kurpiue, S. E. & Fuqua, D. R. (2002). Issues in the ethical practice of consulting psychology. In R. L. Lowman (Ed.). *Handbook of organizational consulting psychology: A comprehensive guide to theory, skills and techniques* (pp. 733-758). San Francisco, CA: Jossey-Bass.

Professional Board for Psychology, Health Professions Council of South Africa (2010, January). *Frequently asked questions.* Retrieved from: https://www.ufs.ac.za/docs/librariesprovider25/cpd-documents/cpd-psychology-frequent-asked-questions-1015-eng.pdf?sfvrsn=0

SA Assessment Centre Study Group. (2018). *Code of Ethics for Assessment Centres in South Africa.* 38th Annual South African Assessment Centre Study Group (ACSG) conference, Somerset West, South Africa.

Viswesvaran, C. & Ones, C. (2018). Non-test methods and techniques used in employee selection. In D. S. Ones, N. Anderson, C. Viswesvaran, & H. K. Sinangil. *The Sage handbook of industrial, work and organizational psychology* (pp. 451-473). Thousand Oaks, CA: Sage.

CHAPTER 5 REFERENCES

International Taskforce on Assesment Center Guidelines. (2015). Guidelines and ethical considerations for assessment center operations. *Journal of Management, 41,* 1244-1273. http://dx.doi. org/10.1177/0149206314567780.

Meiring, D. & Buckett, A. (2016). Best practice guidelines for the use of the assessment centre method in South Africa (5th edition). *SA Journal of Industrial Psychology/SA Tydskrif vir Bedryfsielkunde, 42*(1), p. a1298. http://dx.doi.org/10.4102/sajip.v42i1.1298.

Pritchard, S. & Riley, P. (2011). Fit for Purpose? Considerations when using 'off-the-shelf' versus 'customized' simulation exercises. In: *Assessment Centres and Global Talent Management*. Farnham, England: Gower Publishing Limited, pp. 61-76.

SA Assessment Centre Study Group. (2018). *Code of Ethics for Assessment Centres in South Africa*. Retrieved from: https://www.acsg.co.za. Accessed: 1 December 2018.

The British Psychological Society. (2015). *The Design and Delivery of Assessment Centres: A Standard Produced by the British Psychological Society's Division of Occupational Psychology*. Retrieved from: https://www1.bps.org.uk/networks-and-communities/member-microsite/division-occupational-psychology/assessment-centre-standards. Accessed: 16 January 2019.

CHAPTER 6 REFERENCES

Abraham, J. D., Morrison, J. D. & Burnett, D. D. (2006). Feedback-seeking among developmental assessment center participants. *Journal of Business and Psychology, 20*(3), 383-394.

Anderson, N. & Goltsi, V. (2006). Negative psychological effects of selection methods: construct formulation and an empirical investigation into an assessment center. *International Journal of Selection and Assessment, 14*(3), 236-255.

Basic Conditions of Employment Act. (1997). Act No. 75. (South African). Government Gazette, No 18491.

Cascio, W. F. (1982). *Applied psychology in personnel management*. Reston, VA: Reston Publishing Company.

Cascio, W. F. (1989). *Managing human resources: productivity, quality of work life, profits*. New York: McGraw-Hill Book Company.

Cascio, W. F. & Aguinis, H. (2019a). *Applied psychology in human resource management*. New Jersey: Pearson Prentice-Hall.

The Constitution of the Republic of South Africa. (1996). Act No. 108. (South Africa). Government Gazette, No 17678.

Employment Equity Act. (1998). Act No. 55. (South Africa). Government Gazette, No 19370.

Foxcroft, C., Roodt, G. & Abrahams, F. (2005). The practice of psychological assessment: controlling the use of measures, competing values, and ethical practice standards. In C. Foxcroft & G. Roodt (Eds.). 2005. *An introduction to psychological assessment in the South African context*. Cape Town: Oxford University Press.

Gerber, P. D., Nel, P. S. & Van Dyk, P. S. (1987). *Human resource management*. Johannesburg: Thomson International.

Gibson, E. (27 May 2017). Ervare reserviste 'nie reg' vir polisie (Experienced reservists 'not right' for police). *Rapport*.

Grieve, K. W. (2005). Interpreting and reporting assessment results. In C. Foxcroft & G. Roodt (Eds.). (2005). *An introduction to psychological assessment in the South African context*. Cape Town: Oxford University Press.

Hatch, M. J. (1997). *Organization theory: modern symbolic and postmodern perspectives*. New York: Oxford University Press.

Hellriegel, D., Slocum, J. W. & Woodman, R. W. (1998). *Organizational behavior*. Cincinnati, OH: International Thomson Publishing.

International Taskforce on Assessment Center Guidelines. (2015). Guidelines and Ethical Considerations for Assessment Center Operations. *Journal of Management, 20*(10): 1 – 30. DOI: 10.1177/0149206314567780.

Ivancevich, J. M. & Matteson, M. T. (2002). *Organizational behavior and management*. Boston: McGraw-Hill Irwin.

Jacques, E. (1996). *Requisite organization: a total system for effective management leadership for the 21st century*. Gloucester, MA: Cason Hall.

Labour Relations Act. (1995). Act No. 66. (South Africa). Government Gazette, No 16861.

Litwin, G. & Stringer, R. A. (1968). *Motivation and organizational climate*. Boston: Harvard University.

Lopes, A., Roodt, G. & Mauer, R. (2001). The predictive validity of the APIL-B in a financial institution. *Journal of Industrial Psychology, 27*(1), 61-69.

Maldé, B. (2006). Do ACs really care about the candidate? *British Journal of Guidance & Counselling, 34*(4), 539-549.

Miles, R. E. & Snow, C. C. (1984). Fit, failure and the hall of fame. *California Management Review,* Spring, 21.

Promotion of Equality and Prevention of Unfair Discrimination Act. (2000). Act No. 4. (South Africa). Government Gazette, No 20876.

Robbins, S. P. (1990). *Organisation theory: structure, design, and application.* Englewood Cliffs, NJ: Prentice-Hall.

Robbins, S. P., Judge, T. A., Odendaal, A. & Roodt, G. (2016). *Organisational behaviour: global and Southern African perspectives.* Cape Town: Pearson Education.

Roodt, G. & Van Tonder, C. (2008). Central features: change, process, values and systemic health. In C. van Tonder & G. Roodt (Eds). *Organisation development: theory and practice.* Pretoria: Van Schaik.

SA Assessment Centre Study Group. (2018). *Code of Ethics for Assessment Centres in South-Africa.* Retrieved from: https://www.acsg.co.za/sites/default/files/Code-of-Ethics-for-ACs-inSA-15-March-2018-ACSG.pdf. Accessed 7 January 2019.

Skills Development Act. (1998). Act No. 97. (South Africa). Government Gazette, No 19420.

Skills Development Levies Act. (1999). Act No. 9. (South Africa). Government Gazette, No 19984.

Statistics South Africa. (2016). *Mid-year population estimates 2016.* Retrieved from www.statssa.gov.za. Accessed 28 July 2017.

Theron, C. (2007). Confessions, scapegoats and flying pigs: psychometric testing and the law. *SA Journal of Industrial Psychology, 33*(1), 102-117.

Thornton, G. C. & Rupp, D. E. (2006). *Assessment centers in human resource management: strategies for prediction, diagnosis and development.* Mahwah, New Jersey: Lawrence Erlbaum Associates Publishers.

Thornton, G. C., Rupp, D. E. & Hoffman, B. J. (2015). *Assessment Center Perspective for Talent Management Strategies* (2nd ed.). New York: Routledge.

Van Tonder, C. & Roodt, G. (Eds.). (2008). *Organisation development: theory and practice.* Pretoria: Van Schaik.

CHAPTER 7 REFERENCES

Astley, G. (1984). Subjectivity, sophistry and symbolism in management science. *Journal of Management Studies, 21*(3), 259-271.

Byham, W. C. (1981). Applying a systems approach to personnel activities (Part I). *Training and Development Journal, 35*(12), 60-65.

Byham, W. C. (1982a). Applying a systems approach to personnel activities (Part II). *Training and Development Journal, 36*(1), 70-75.

Byham, W. C. (1982b). Applying a systems approach to personnel activities (Part III). *Training and Development Journal, 36*(2), 86-90.

Carroll, S. J. & Gillen, D. J. (1996). Are the classical management functions useful in describing managerial work? In M. T. Matteson & J. M. Ivancevich (Eds.). *Management and organizational behavior classics.* Chicago: Irwin.

Invancevich, J. M. & Matteson, M. T. (2002). *Organizational behavior and management.* New York: McGraw-Hill Irwin.

Kaplan, R. S. & Norton, D. P. (1992). The balanced scorecard – measures that drive performance. *Harvard Business Review, 70*(1), 71-79.

Koontz, H. (1996). The management theory jungle. In M. T. Matteson & J. M. Ivancevich (Eds.). *Management and organizational behavior classics.* Chicago: Irwin.

Muchinksy, P. M., Kriek, H. J. & Schreuder, A. M. G. (1998). *Personnel psychology.* Johannesburg: International Thomson Publishing.

Reed, M. I. (1984). Management as a social practice. *Journal of Management Studies, 21*(3), 273-285.

Robertson, I. T., Callinan, M. & Bartram, D. (2002). *Organizational effectiveness: the role of psychology.* New York: John Wiley & Sons.

Roodt, G. (1999). *Bedryfsielkundigemeting as bestuurshulpmiddel* (Industrial psychological measurement as a management tool). Professorial inaugural address to the Rand Afrikaans University on 11 August.

Roodt, G. (2006). *Management education and training – a South African perspective*. Unpublished paper based on a contribution in a panel discussion on perspectives on management training at the Pan Pacific Conference from 29-31 May 2006 in Busan, Korea.

Rupp, D. E., Gibbons, A. M., Runnels, T., Anderson, L. & Thornton, G. C. (2003). *What should developmental assessment centers be assessing?* Paper presented at the 63rd Annual Meeting of the Academy of Management, Seattle, Washington.

Schutte, F. G. (1991). *Integrated management systems*. Durban: Butterworths.

SHL. (2004). *Universal Competency Framework* (UCF20™), © SHL Group.

Steers, R. M. (1975). Problems in the measurement of organizational effectiveness. *Administrative Science Quarterly, 20*(4), 546-558.

Stewart, R. (1984). The nature of management? A problem for management education. *Journal of Management Studies, 21*(3), 323-330.

Stewart, R. (1989). Studies of managerial jobs and behaviour: the ways forward. *Journal of Management Studies, 26*(1), 1-10.

Townley, B. (1993). Performance appraisal and the emergence of management. *Journal of Management Studies, 30*(2), 221-238.

Willmott, H. C. (1984). Images and ideals of managerial work: a critical examination of conceptual and empirical accounts. *Journal of Management Studies, 21*(3), 349-368.

Zey-Ferrell, M. (1979). *Dimensions of organizations – environment, context, structure, process and performance*. Santa Monica, CA: Goodyear Publishing.

CHAPTER 8 REFERENCES

Bergh, Z. C. & Theron, A. L. (Eds) (2003). *Psychology in the work context* (2nd ed.). Cape Town: Oxford University Press.

Campion, M. A., Fink, A. A., Ruggeberg, B. J., Carr, L., Phillips, G. M., & Odman, R. B. (2011). Doing competencies well: Best practices in competency modelling. *Personnel Psychology, 64*: 225-262.

Cascio, W. F. & Aguinis, H. (2005). *Applied psychology in human resource management*. New Jersey: Pearson Prentice Hall.

Cascio, W. F., & Aguinis, H. (2019). *Applied psychology in talent management management*. Los Angeles: Sage Publications.

Cillié-Schmidt, L. (2018). *Incorporating Business Processes, Rules, and Policies in the Design of Simulations for an Assessment Centre for Private Bankers.* 10 October International Congress on Assessment Center Methods (ICACM), London, United Kingdom.

Employment Equity Act. (1998). Act No. 55. (South Africa). Government Gazette, No 19370.

Foxcroft, C. & Roodt, G. (2004). *An Introduction to psychological assessment in the South African context*. Cape Town, SA: Oxford University Press.

Hogan Assessment Systems. (2009). *The Job Evaluation Tool (JET)*. Tulsa, OK: Hogan Press.

Jacka, J. M. & Keller, P. J. (2002). *Business process mapping – improving customer satisfaction*. New York: John Wiley & Sons.

JvR Africa Group. (2018). *JvR Africa Role Competency Survey*. Johannesburg: JvR Africa Group

Koch, A., Strobel, A., Miller, R., Garten, C. C. & Westhoff, K. (2012). Never use one when two will do: The effects of a multi-perspective approach on the outcome of job analyses using the critical incident technique. *Journal of Psychology, 11*(2): 95-102. DOI: 10.1027/1866-5888/a00060.

Lievens, F. (1998). Factors which improve the construct validity of assessment centers: A review. *International Journal of Selection and Assessment, 6*: 141– 152.

Markus, L. H., Cooper-Thomas, H. D. & Allpress, K. N. (2005). Confounded by competencies? An evaluation of the evolution and use of competency models. *New Zealand Journal of Psychology, 34*(2): 117-126.

Morgeson, F. P. (2017). Job analysis methods. In S. G. Rogelberg, *The SAGE Encyclopedia of Industrial and Organisational Psychology*, (2nd ed.). Thousand Oaks, CA: SAGE Publications. DOI: http//dx.doi.org/10.4135/9781483386874.n264.

Morgeson, F. P., Brannick, M. T. & Levine, E. L. (2019). *Job and Work Analysis: Methods, Research and Applications for Human Resource Management* (3rd Ed.). Los Angeles: Sage Publications.

Mouton, J. (2008). *How to succeed in your master's and doctoral studies: A South-African guide and resource book.* Pretoria: Van-Schaik Publishers.

Myslicki, B., Berry, J. & Klammer, J. (2018). *Development of the Canadian Army Officer Selection Assessment Center.* 9 October. International Congress on Assessment Center Methods (ICACM), London, United Kingdom.

O*NET. (2013). *The O*NET content model at O*NET resource center.* Retrieved from: https://www.onecenter.org/content.html. Accessed 19 December 2018.

Robinson-Morral, E. J., Hendrickson, C., Gilbert, S., Myers, T., Simpson, K. & Loignon, A.C. (2018). Practical considerations for conducting job analysis linkage exercises. *Journal of Personnel Psychology, 17*(2): 12-21. https://doi.org/10.1027/1866-5888/a000191.

SA Assessment Centre Study Group. (2018). *Code of ethics for assessment centres in South-Africa.* Retrieved from: https://www.acsg.co.za/sites/default/files/Code-of-Ethics-for-ACs-inSA-15-March-2018-ACSG.pdf. Accessed 7 January 2019

Sanchez, J. I., & Levine, E. L. (2009). What is (or should be) the difference between competency modelling and traditional job analysis? *Human Resource Management Review, 19*: 53-63. Doi:10.1016/j.hrmr.2008.10.002.

Sanchez, J. I., & Levine, E. L. (2012). The rise and fall of job analysis and the future of work analysis. *Annual Review of Psychology, 63*: 397-425. DOi 10.1146/annurev-psych-12710-100401.

Stetz, T. A., & Chmielewsla, T. L. (2015). *Competency Modelling Documentation.* SHRM-SIOP Science of HR White Paper.

SurveyMonkey. (2019). [Online] Available: https://www.google.com/search?ei=kkTaXZT2IbG61fAP6bmTwAs&q=-SurveyMonkey&oq=SurveyMonkey&gs_l=psy-ab.3..0l10.18860936.18866905..18868612...0.2..0.397.3744.2-5j7......0....1..gws-wiz.......0i71j0i131j0i273j0i67.-QTaaQnjUUc&ved=0ahUKEwiUh9WGvILmAhUxXRUIHenc-BLgQ4dUDCAs&uact=5

Thoresen, C. J., & Thoresen, J. D. (2012). How to design and implement a task-based assessment center. In D. J. R. Jackson, C. B. Lance & B. J. Hoffman (Eds). *The psychology of assessment centers.* New York: Routledge.

Thornton, G. C., III., Rupp, D. E. & Hoffman, B. J. (2015). *Assessment center perspectives for talent management strategies.* (2nd ed.). New York: Routledge.

Venter, B. C. (2017). *The competencies of coaches in a coaching development centre.* M.Com thesis (Industrial and Organisational Psychology) (Unpublished). University of Johannesburg. Retrieved from: https://ujcontent.uj.ac.za/vital/access/manager/Index?site=REsearch%200utput. Accessed 20 December 2018.

CHAPTER 9 REFERENCES

Allport, G. W. (1951). *Personality- A psychological interpretation.* London: Constable.

Arthur, W. Jr., Day, E. A., McNelly, T. L. & Edens, P. S. (2003). A meta-analysis of the criterion-related validity of assessment center dimensions, *Personnel Psychology, 56*(1): 125-154.

Bedwell, W. L., Pavlas, D., Heyne, K., Lazzara, E. H., & Salas, E. (2012). Toward a taxonomy linking game attributes to learning: An empirical study. *Simulation and Gaming: An Interdisciplinary Journal, 43*(6): 729-760.

Bennett, N. & Lemoine, G. J. (2014). What VUCA really means for you. *Harvard Business Review, 92*(1/2): 27.

Bowler, M.C., & Woehr, D. J. (2006). A meta-analytical evaluation of the impact of dimension and exercise factors on assessment center ratings. *Journal of Applied Psychology.* 91(5): 1114–1124. DOI: 10.1037/0021-9010.91.5.1114

Bowler, M. C., & Woehr, D. J. (2008). Evaluating assessment center construct-related validity via variance partitioning. In B. J. Hoffman (Ed.), *Reexamining assessment centers: Alternate approaches.* Paper presented at the 23rd annual meeting of the Society for Industrial and Organisational Psychology, San Francisco, CA.

Bray, D. W. & Grant, D. L. (1966). The assessment center in the measurement of potential for business management. *Psychological Monographs* Whole No. 625.

Cronbach, L. J. & Meehl, P. E. (1955). Construct validity in psychological tests, *Psychological Bulletin, 52*(4): 281-302.

Epstein, S. (1979). The stability of behaviour: I. On predicting most of the people much of the time. *Personality and Social Psychology, 37*(7): 1097-1126.

Funder, D. C. (2012). Accurate personality judgment. *Current Directions in Psychological Science, 21*(3): 177-182.

Gibbons, A. M. & Rupp, D. E. (2009). Dimension consistency as an individual difference: A new (old) perspective on the assessment center construct validity debate. *Journal of Management, 35*(5): 1154-1180.

Ghiselli, E. E., Campbell, J. P. & Zedeck, S. (1981). *Measurement theory for the behavioural sciences.* San Francisco, CA: Freeman.

Hoffman, B. J., Kennedy, C. L., LoPilato, A. C., Monahan, E. L. & Lance, C. E. (2015). A review of the content, criterion-related, and construct-related validity of assessment center exercises. *Journal of Applied Psychology, 100*(4): 1143-1168.

International Taskforce on Assesment Center Guidelines. (2015). Guidelines and ethical considerations for assessment center operations. *Journal of Management, 41*: 1244-1273. http://dx.doi. org/10.1177/0149206314567780

Joseph, D. L., Jin, J., Newman, D. A. & O'Boyle, E. H. (2015). Why does self-reported emotional intelligence predict job performance? A meta-analytic investigation of mixed EI. *Journal of Applied Psychology, 100*(2): 298-342.

Kleinmann, M., Kuptsch, C. & Koller, O. (1996). Transparency: A necessary requirement for the construct validity of assessment centers. *Journal of Applied Psychology, 45*(1): 67-84.

Kuncel, N. R., Klieger, D. M., Connelly, B. S. & Ones, D. S. (2013). Mechanical versus clinical data combination in selection and admissions decisions: A meta-analysis. *Journal of Applied Psychology, 98*(6): 1060-1072.

Kunnanatt, J. T. (2004). Emotional intelligence: The new science of interpersonal effectiveness, *Human Resource Development Quarterly, 15*, 489-495.

Landers, R. N., Bauer, K. N., Callan, R. C. & Armstrong, M. B. (2015). Psychological theory and the gamification of learning. In T. Reiners & L. C. Wood (Eds.). *Gamification in education and business.* New York, NY: Springer. Pp 165–186.

Lewin, K. (1951). *Field theory in social science.* New York, NY: Harper.

Lievens, F. (2001). Observer training strategies and their effects on accuracy, inter-rater reliability, and discriminant validity. *Journal of Applied Psychology, 86*(2): 255-264.

Lievens, F., De Corte, W. & Westerveld, L. (2015). Understanding the building blocks of selection procedures: Effects of response fidelity on performance and validity. *Journal of Management, 41*(6): 1604-1627.

Lievens, F., Schollaert, E. & Keen, G. (2015). The interplay of elicitation and evaluation of trait-expressive behaviour: Evidence in assessment center exercises. *Journal of Applied Psychology, 100*(4): 1169–1188.

Lievens, F., Tett, R. P. & Schleicher, D. J. (2009). Assessment centers at the crossroads: Toward a reconceptualization of assessment center exercises. In J. J. Martocchio & H. Liao (Eds.). *Research in personnel and human resources management.* Bingley: JAI Press. Pp. 99-152.

Meriac, J. P., Hoffman, B. J. & Woehr, D. J. (2014). A conceptual and empirical review of the structure of assessment center dimensions. *Journal of Management, 40*(5): 1269-1296.

Mischel, W. (1973). Toward a cognitive social learning reconceptulization of personality. *Psychological Review, 80*(4): 252-283.

Mischel, W. & Shoda, Y. (1995). A cognitive-affective system theory of personality: Reconsidering situations, dispositions, dynamics, and invariance in personality structure. *Psychological Review, 102*(2): 246-268.

Murray, H. (1938). *Explorations in personality.* New York: Oxford University Press.

Nunnally, J. C. & Bernstein, I. H. (1994). *Psychometric theory* (3rd ed.). New York, NY: McGraw-Hill.

Oliver, T., Hausdorf, P., Lievens, F. & Conlon, P. (2016). Interpersonal dynamics in assessment center exercises: Effects of role player portrayed disposition. *Journal of Management, 42*(7): 992-2017.

Office of Strategic Services Assessment Staff (OSS). (1948). *Assessment of men: Selection of personnel for the Office of Strategic Services.* . New York, NY: Rinehart.

Parrigon, S., Woo, S. E., Tay, L. & Wang, T. (2017). CAPTION-ing the situation: A lexically-derived taxonomy of psychological situation characteristics. *Journal of Social and Personality Psychology, 112*(4): 642-681.

Rauthmann, J. F., Gallardo-Pjol, D., Guillaume, E. M., Todd, E., Nave, C. S., Sherman, R. A., Ziegler, M., Jones, A. B. & Funder, D. C. (2014). The situational eight DIAMONDS: A taxonomy of major dimensions of situational characteristics. *Journal of Personality and Social Psychology, 107*(4): 677-718.

Schleicher, D. J., Day, D. V., Mayes, B. T. & Riggio, R. E. (2002). A new frame for frame-of-reference training: Enhancing the construct validity of assessment centers. *Journal of Applied Psychology, 87*(4): 735-746.

Schmitt, N. & Ostrof, C. (1986). Operationalizing the "behavioural consistency" approach: Selection test development based on a content-oriented strategy. *Personnel Psychology, 39*(1): 91-108.

Schollaert, E. & Lievens, F. (2012). Building situational stimuli in assessment center exercises: Do specific exercise instructions and role player prompts increase the observability of behaviour? *Human Performance, 25*(3): 255-271.

Shore, T. H., Thornton, G. C. III. & Shore, L. (1990). Construct validity of two categories of assessment center dimension ratings. *Personnel Psychology, 43*(1): 101-116.

Steihm, J. H. & Townsend, N. W. (2002). *The U.S. Army War College: Military education in a democracy.* Philadelphia, PA: Temple University Press.

Tett, R. P. & Burnett, D. D. (2003). A personality trait-based interactionist model of job performance. *Journal of Applied Psychology, 88*(3): 500-517.

Tett, R. P. & Guterman, H. A. (2000). Situation trait relevance, trait expression, and cross-situational consistency: Testing a principle of trait activation. *Journal of Research in Personality, 34*(4): 397-423.

Thornton, G. C. III. & Byham, W. C. (1982). *Assessment centers and managerial performance.* New York: Academic Press.

Thornton, G. C. III. & Potemra, M. J. (2010). Utility of assessment center for promotion of police sergeants. *Public personnel management, 39*(1): 59–69.

Thornton, G. C. III., Johnson, S. K. & Church, A. H. (2017). Selecting leaders: Executives and high potentials. In J. L. Farr & N. Tippins (Eds.). *Handbook of employee selection* (2nd ed.). New York, NY: Erlbaum. Pp. 833-852.

Thornton, G. C. III. & Kedharnath, U. (2013). Work sample tests. In K. F. Geisinger (Ed.). *APA handbook of testing and assessment in psychology: Vol. 1 Test theory and testing and assessment in industrial and organizational psychology.* Washington, DC: American Psychological Association.

Thornton, G. C. III. & Rupp, D. R. (2006). *Assessment centers in human resource management: Strategies for prediction, diagnosis, and development.* Mahwah, NJ: Lawrence Erlbaum.

Thornton, G. C. III., Rupp D. R., Gibbons, A. & Vanhove, A. (2019). Same-gender and same-race bias in assessment center ratings: A rating error approach to understanding subgroup differences. *International Journal of Selection and Assessment,* 1-18. DOI: 10.1111/ijsa.12229

Thornton, G. C. III., Mueller-Hanson, R. A. & Rupp, D. E. (2017). *Developing organizational simulations: A guide for practitioners, students, and researchers* (2nd ed.). New York, NY: Routledge.

Thornton, G. C. III., Rupp, D. E. & Hoffman, B. J. (2015). *Assessment center perspectives for talent management strategies* (2nd ed.). New York, NY: Routledge.

Wernimont, P. F. & Campbell, J. P. (1968). Signs, samples, and criteria. *Journal of Applied Psychology, 52*(5): 372-376.

Whiteman, W. E. (1998). *Training and educating army officers for the 21st century: Implications for the United States Military Academy.* Fort Belvoir, VA: Defense Technical Information Center.

CHAPTER 10 REFERENCES

Buckett, A., Becker, J. R. & Roodt, G. (2017). General performance factors and group differences in assessment center ratings. *Journal of Managerial Psychology, 32*(4): 298-313. Doi.org/10.1108/JMP-08-2016-0264.

Cascio, W. F. & Aguinis, H. (2019). *Applied psychology in talent management.* (8th ed.). Los Angeles: Sage Publishing.

Gibbons, A. M. & Rupp, D. E. (2009). Dimension consistency as an individual difference: A new (old) perspective on the assessment center construct validity perspective. *Journal of Management, 35*: 1154-1180.

International Taskforce on Assesment Center Guidelines. (2015). Guidelines and ethical considerations for assessment center operations. *Journal of Management, 41:* 1244-1273. http://dx.doi.org/10.1177/0149206314567780.

Melchers, K. G., Kleinmann, M. & Prinz, M. A. (2010). Do assessors have too much on their plates? The effects of simultaneously rating multiple assessment center candidates on rating quality. *International Journal of Selection and Assessment, 18*(3): 329-341.

Rupp, D. E., Snyder, L. A., Gibbons, A. M. & Thornton, G. C. (2006). What should development assessment centers be developing? *The Psychologist-Manager Journal, 9*(2): 75-98.

SA Assessment Centre Study Group. (2018). *Code of ethics for assessment centres in South-Africa.* Retrieved from: https://www.acsg.co.za/sites/default/files/Code-of-Ethics-for-ACs-inSA-15-March-2018-ACSG.pdf. Accessed 7 January 2019.

Scott, J. C., Bartram, D. & Reynolds, D. H. (2018). *Next Generation Technology-Enhanced Assessment: Global Perspectives on Occupational and Workplace Testing.* Cambridge, UK: Cambridge University Press.

The British Psychological Society's Division of Occupational Psychology. (2015). *The Design and Delivery of Assessment Centres.* Leicester, UK: The British Psychological Society.

Thornton, G. C., Mueller-Hanson, R. A. & Rupp, D. E. (2017). *Developing organizational simulations: A guide for practitioners, students, and researchers (2*nd ed.). New York: Routledge.

Thornton, G. C., Rupp, D. E. & Hoffman, B. J. (2015). *Assessment center perspectives for talent management strategies* (2nd ed.). New York: Routledge.

Woo, S. E., Sims, C. S., Rupp, D. E. & Gibbons, A. M. (2008). Development engagement within and following developmental assessment centers: considering feedback favorability and self–assessor agreement. *Personnel Psychology, 61*: 727-759.

CHAPTER 11 REFERENCES

Blume, B. D., Dreher, G. F. & Baldwin, T. T. (2010). Examining the effects of communication apprehension within assessment centres. *Journal of Occupational and Organizational Psychology, 83*: 663–671.

Buckett, A., Becker, J. R. & Roodt, G. (2017). General performance factors and group differences in assessment center ratings. *Journal of Managerial Psychology, 32*(4): 298-313. Doi.org/10.1108/JMP-08-2016-0264.

Cascio, W. F. & Aguinis, H. (2019). *Applied psychology in talent management* (8th ed.). Los Angeles: Sage Publishing.

De Beer, E. (2012). *The influence of introversion/extraversion bias on leadership assessment with behaviour observation.* Unpublished dissertation submitted in partial fulfilment of the requirements for the degree Magister Commercii. University of Pretoria, Pretoria.

Employment Equity Act. (1998). Act No. 55. (South Africa). Government Gazette, No 19370.

Georganta, E. & Brodbeck, F. C. (2018). Capturing the Four-Phase Team Adaptation Process with Behaviourally Anchored Rating Scale (BARS). *European Journal of Psychological Assessment.* Advance online publication. http://dx.doi.org/10.1027/1015-5759/a000503.

Howland, A. C., Rembisz, R., Wang-Jones, T. S., Heise, S. R. & Brown. S. (2015). Developing a Virtual Assessment Center. *Counselling Psychology Journal: Practice and Research, 67*(2): 110-126.

International Taskforce on Assesment Center Guidelines. (2015). Guidelines and ethical considerations for assessment center operations. *Journal of Management, 41*: 1244-1273. http://dx.doi.org/10.1177/0149206314567780.

Kleinmann, M. & Ingold, P. V. (2019). Toward a Better Understanding of Assessment Centers: A Conceptual Overview. *Annual Reviews of Organisational Psychology and Organisational Behaviour, 6*: 349-372.

Latham, G. P. & Wexley, K. N. (1994). *Increasing Productivity through Performance Appraisal* (2nd ed.). New York: Addison-Wesley Publishing Company.

Lievens, F., Schollart, E. & Keen, G. (2015). The Interplay of Elicitation and Evaluation of Trait-Expressive Behaviour: Evidence in Assessment Center Exercises. *Journal of Applied Psychology, 100*(4): 1169-1188.

Manji, Z. & Dunford, M. (2011). Eating the Elephant: Tackling the Challenges of Introducing Assessment and Development Centres in East Africa. In N. Povah & G.C. Thornton (Eds.). *Assessment Centres and Global Talent Management.* (pp 403 – 413). Surrey: Gower Publishing Limited.

Meiring, D. & Buckett, A. (2016). Best practice guidelines for the use of the assessment centre method in South Africa (5th ed.). *SA Journal of Industrial Psychology/SA Tydskrif vir Bedryfsielkunde, 42*(1), a1298. http://dx.doi.org/10.4102/sajip.v42i1.1298

The British Psychological Society's Division of Occupational Psychology. (2015). *The Design and Delivery of Assessment Centres.* Leicester, UK: The British Psychological Society.

Thornton, G. C. & Mueller-Hanson, R. A. (2004). *Developing Organisational Simulations: A guide for practitioners and students*. New York: Lawrence Erlbaum Associates.

Thornton, G. C., Mueller-Hanson, R. A. & Rupp, D. E. (2017). *Developing organizational simulations: A guide for practitioners, students, and researchers* (2nd ed.). New York: Routledge.

Thornton, G. C., Rupp, D. E. & Hoffman, B. J. (2015). *Assessment center perspectives for talent management strategies* (2nd ed.). New York: Routledge.

Tziner, A., Joanis, C. & Murphy, K. R. (2000). A comparison of three methods of performance appraisal with regard to goal properties, goal perception, and rate satisfaction. *Group and Organization Management, 25*(2): 175-190.

Weijters, B., Cabooter, E. & Schillewaert, N. (2010). The effect of rating scale format on response styles: The number of response categories and response category labels. *International Journal of Research in Marketing, 27*: 236-247.

CHAPTER 12 REFERENCES

Brummel, B. J., Rupp, D. E. & Spain, S. M. (2009). Constructing Parallel Simulation Exercises for Assessment Centers and other Forms of Behavioral Assessment. *Personnel Psychology, 62*: 137-170.

Caldwell, C., Thornton, G. C. & Gruys, M. L. (2003). Ten classic assessment center errors: challenge to selection validity. *Public Personnel Management, 32*(1): 73-88.

Cascio, W. F. & Aguinis, H. (2019). *Applied psychology in talent management* (8th ed.). Los Angeles: Sage Publishing.

Electronic Communications and Transactions . (2002). Act No. 25 (South Africa). General Data Protection Regulation. (2018). *Official Journal of the European Union*. Retrieved from: http//www.Eur-lex.europa.eu/eli/reg/2016/679/pj.

International Taskforce on Assesment Center Guidelines. (2015). Guidelines and ethical considerations for assessment center operations. *Journal of Management, 41*: 1244-1273. http://dx.doi.org/10.1177/0149206314567780.

Jackson, D. J. R., Atkins, S. G., Fletcher, R. B. & Stillman, J. A. (2005). Frame of reference training for assessment centers: effects on interrater reliability when rating behaviors and ability traits. *Public Personnel Management, 34*(1): 17-30.

McNamara, J., Handler, C. & Fetzer, M. (2014). *Get your Game On! How to use gaming and simulations to revolutionise your hiring / training process*. Workshop presented at the Society for Occupational Psychologist annual conference, Honolulu, Hawaii, US.

Meiring, D. & Buckett, A. (2016). Best practice guidelines for the use of the assessment centre method in South Africa (5th ed.). *SA Journal of Industrial Psychology/SA Tydskrif vir Bedryfsielkunde, 42*(1), a1298. http://dx.doi.org/10.4102/sajip.v42i1.1298

Naglieri, J. A., Drasgow, F., Schmit, M., Handler, L., Prifitera, A., Margolis, A. & Velasquez, R. (2004). Psychological testing on the Internet: New problems, old issues. *American Psychologist, 59*(3), 150-162.

Promotion of Access to Information. (2000). Act No. 2. (South Africa).

Protection of Personal Information. (2013). Act No. 4. (South Africa).

SA Assessment Centre Study Group. (2018). *Code of ethics for assessment centres in South-Africa*. Retrieved from: https://www.acsg.co.za/sites/default/files/Code-of-Ethics-for-ACs-inSA-15-March-2018-ACSG.pdf. Accessed 7 January 2019.

Scott, J. C., Bartram, D. & Reynolds, D. H. (2018). *Next Generation Technology-Enhanced Assessment: Global Perspectives on Occupational and Workplace Testing*. Cambridge, UK: Cambridge University Press.

The British Psychological Society's Division of Occupational Psychology. (2015). *The Design and Delivery of Assessment Centres*. Leicester, UK: The British Psychological Society.

Thornton, G. C., Mueller-Hanson, R. A. & Rupp, D. E. (2017). *Developing organizational simulations: A guide for practitioners, students, and researchers* (2nd ed.). New York: Routledge.

Thornton, G. C., Rupp, D. E. & Hoffman, B. J. (2015). *Assessment center perspectives for talent management strategies* (2nd ed.). New York: Routledge.

CHAPTER 13 REFERENCES

Brummel, B. J., Rupp, D. E. & Spain, S. M. (2009). Constructing Parallel Simulation Exercises for Assessment Centers and Other Forms of Behavioural Assessment. *Personnel Psychology, 62*: 137-170.

Dewberry, C. & Jackson, D. J. R. (2016). The perceived nature and incidence of dysfunctional assessment center features and processes. *International Journal of Selection and Assessment*, (24): 189-196. Doi.org/10.1111/ijsa.12140.

Fletcher, C., Lovatt, C. & Baldry, C. (1997). A Study of State, Trait, and Test Anxiety and their Relationship to Assessment Center Performance. *Journal of Social Behaviour and Personality, 12*(2): 205-2014.

Goodge, P. (1994). Development Centres: Design Generation and Effectiveness. *Journal of Management Development, 13*(4): 16-22. doi.org/10.1108/02621719410057041.

Goodge, P. (1995). Design options and outcomes. *Journal of Management Development, 14*(8): 55-59. doi.org/10.1108/02621719510097424

Griffiths, P. & Allen, B. (1987). Assessment Centres: Breaking with Tradition. *Journal of Management Development, 6*(1): 18-29. doi.org/10.1108/eb051632.

Ingold, P. V., Kleinmann, M., König, C. J. & Melchers, K. G. M. (2016). Transparency of assessment centers: Lower criterion-related validity but greater opportunity to perform. *Personnel Psychology, 69*: 467-497. Doi: 10.1111/peps.12105

International Taskforce on Assessment Center Guidelines. (2015). Guidelines and Ethical Considerations for Assessment Center Operations. *Journal of Management, 20*(10): 1-30 doi: 10.1177/0149206314567780.

Jansen, A., Melchers, K. G., Lievens, F., Kleinmann, M., Brändli, M., Fraefel, L. & König, C. J. (2013). Situation assessment as an ignored factor in the behavioural consistency paradigm underlying the validity of personnel selection procedures. *Journal of Applied Psychology, 98*(2): 326-341. Doi: 10.1037/a0031257.

Kleinmann, M. & Ingold, P. V. (2019). Toward a better understanding of assessment centers: A conceptual review. *Annual Review of Organisational Psychology and Organisational Behavior, 6*: 349-372. Doi.org/10.1146/annurev-orgpsych-012218-014955.

Kolk, N. J., Born, M. & van der Vliet, H. (2003). The Transparent Assessment Centre: The Effects of Revealing Dimensions to Candidates. *Applied Psychology: An International Review, 52*(4): 648-668.

Meiring, D. & Buckett, A. (2016). Best practice guidelines for the use of the assessment centre method in South Africa (5th ed.). *SA Journal of Industrial Psychology/SA Tydskrif vir Bedryfsielkunde, 42*(1): a1298. http://dx.doi.org/10.4102/sajip.v42i1.1298

Melchers, K. G., Kleinmann, M. & Prinz, M. A. (2010). Do Assessors Have Too Much on their Plates? The Effects of Simultaneously Rating Multiple Assessment Center Candidates on Rating Quality. *International Journal of Selection and Assessment, 18*(3): 329-341.

Pollock, R. V. H., Jefferson, A. & Wick, C. (2015). *The Six Disciplines of Breakthrough Learning: How to Turn Training and Development into Business Results*. Hoboken, NJ: John Wiley & Sons Inc.

Protection of Personal Information. (2013). Act No. 4. (South Africa).

SA Assessment Centre Study Group. (2018). *Code of ethics for assessment centres in South-Africa*. Retrieved from: https://www.acsg.co.za/sites/default/files/Code-of-Ethics-for-ACs-inSA-15-March-2018-ACSG.pdf. Accessed 7 January 2019.

Schlebusch, S. & Gouws, A. (2013*). The Design and Implementation of a Collaborative Development Centre for Training Professionals – A Case Study*. Paper presented at the annual Assessment Centre and Study Group conference combined with the International Congress on Assessment Centre Method, Stellenbosch, South Africa.

Schlebusch, S. & Hoole, C. (2018). *A comparison between the impact of Coaching Development Centres, Development Assessment Centres, Diagnostic Centres and Training Programmes on participants' cognitive change*. Paper presented at the annual Assessment Centre and Study Group conference, Sandton, South Africa.

The British Psychological Society. (2015). *The Design and Delivery of Assessment Centres: A Standard produced by the British Psychological Society's Division of Occupational Psychology*. Leicester, UK: The British Psychological Society.

Thornton, G. C., Rupp, D. E., Gibbons, A. M. & Vanhove, A. J. (2019). Same-gender and same-race bias in assessment center ratings: A rating error approach to understanding subgroup differences. *International Journal of Selection and Assessment*, 1-18, doi: 10.1111/ijsa.12229.

Thornton, G. C., Rupp, D. E. & Hoffman, B. J. (2015). *Assessment center perspectives for talent management strategies* (2nd ed.). New York, NY: Routledge.

Woodruffe, C. (1993). *Assessment Centres: Identifying and Developing Competence* (2nd ed.). London: Institute of Personnel Management.

CHAPTER 14 REFERENCES

Meiring, D. & Buckett, A. (2016). Best practice guidelines for the use of the assessment centre method in South Africa (5th ed.). *SA Journal of Industrial Psychology/SA Tydskrif vir Bedryfsielkunde, 42*(1): a1298. http://dx.doi.org/10.4102/sajip.v42i1.1298

The British Psychological Society. (2015). *The Design and Delivery of Assessment Centres: A Standard produced by the British Psychological Society's Division of Occupational Psychology.* Leicester, UK: The British Psychological Society.

CHAPTER 15 REFERENCES

Caldwell, C., Thornton, G. C. & Gruys, M. L. (2003). Ten Classic Errors: Challenges to Selction Validity. *Public Personnel Management, 32*(1): 73-88.

Campbell, D. T. (1958). Systematic Error on the Part of Human Links in Communication Systems. *Information and Control,* 1: 334-369.

Cascio, W. F. & Aguinis, H. (2019). *Applied Psychology in Talent Management* (8th ed.). Los Angeles: Sage Publishing Inc.

Employment Equity Act. (1998). Act No. 55. (South Africa). Government Gazette, No 19370.

Gorman, C. A. & Rentsch, J. R. (2017). Retention of Assessment Center Rater Training: Improving Performance Schema Accuracy Using Frame-of-Reference Training. *Journal of Personnel Psychology, 16*(1): 1-11. DOI: 10.1027/1866-5888/a000167.

Hall, L. (March, 2019). *Assessor Training.* IGNITE presentation at the annual Assessment Centre Study Group Conference, Somerset West, South Africa.

International Taskforce on Assesment Center Guidelines. (2015). Guidelines and ethical considerations for assessment center operations. *Journal of Management, 41*: 1244-1273. http://dx.doi.org/10.1177/0149206314567780.

Lievens, F. (2001). Assessor Training Strategies and their Effects on Accuracy, Inter-Rater Reliability and Discriminant Validity. *Journal of Applied Psychology, 86*(2): 255-264. DOI:10.1037///002-9010.86.2.255.

Lievens, F. & Thornton, G. C. (2005). Assessment Centres: Recent Developments in Practice and Research. In A. Evers, O. Smit-Voskuijl, & N. Anderson (Eds.). *Handbook of Selection* (pp 243-264). Blackwell Publishing.

Macon, T., Mehner, K., Havill, L., Meriac, J. P., Roberts, L. & Heft, L. (2011). Two for the Price of One: Assessment Center Training to Focus on Behaviors Can Transfer to Performance Appraisals. *Human Performance, 24*:443-457. DOI: 10.1080/08959285.2011.614664.

Meiring, D. & Buckett, A. (2016). Best Practice Guidelines for the Use of the Assessment Centre Method in South Africa (5th ed.). *SA Journal of Industrial Psychology/SA Tydskrif vir Bedryfsielkunde, 42*(1), a1298. http://dx.doi.org/10.4102/sajip.v42i1.1298

Noonan, L. E. & Sulsky, L. M. (2001). Impact of Frame-of-Reference and Behavioral Observation Training on Alternative Training Effectiveness Criteria in a Canadian Military Sample. *Human Performance, 14*(1): 3-26.

Patterson, F., Zibarras, L., Kerrin, M., Lopes, S. & Price, R. (2014). Development of Competency Models for Assessors and Simulators in High-stakes Selection Processes. *Medical Teacher, 36*: 1082-1085. DOI: 10.3109/0142159X.2014.930112.

Protection of Personal Information . (2013). No. 4 (South Africa).

Roch, S. G., Woehr, D. J., Mishra, V. & Kieszczynska, U. (2012). Rater Training Revisited: An Updated Meta-Analytic Review of Frame-of-Reference Training. *Journal of Occupational and Organizational Psychology, 85*: 370-395.

Rossouw, D. & Van Vuuren, L. J. (2014). *Business ethics*. (5th ed.). Cape Town, South Africa: Oxford University Press.

SA Assessment Centre Study Group. (2018). *Code of Ethics for Assessment Centres in South-Africa*. Retrieved from: https://www.acsg.co.za/sites/default/files/Code-of-Ethics-for-ACs-inSA-15-March-2018-ACSG.pdf. Accessed 7 January 2019.

The British Psychological Society's Division of Occupational Psychology. (2015). *The Design and Delivery of Assessment Centres*. Leicester, UK: The British Psychological Society.

Thornton, G. C., Mueller-Hanson, R. A (2004). *Developing organisational simulations - a guide to for practitioners and students*. New Jersey: Lawrence Erbaum Associates.

Thornton, G. C., Mueller-Hanson, R. A. & Rupp, D. E. (2017). *Developing Organizational Simulations: A Guide for Practitioners, Students, and Researchers* (2nd ed.). New York, NY: Routledge.

Thornton, G. C., Rupp, D. E. & Hoffman, B.J. (2015). *Assessment Center Perspectives for Talent Management Strategies* (2nd ed.). New York, NY: Routledge.

Thornton, G. C. & Zorich, S. (1980). Training to Improve Observer Accuracy. *Journal of Applied Psychology, 65*(3): 351-354.

Venter, C. B. (2017). *The Competencies of Coaches in a Coaching Development Centre (CDC)*. MCom (IO Psychology) (Unpublished): University of Johannesburg. These should be Retrieved from https://ujcontent.uj.ac.za/vital/access/manager/Index?site_name=Research%20Output Accessed 12 December 2018.

Wirz, A., Melchers, K. G., Lievens, F., De Corte, W. & Kleinmann, M. (2013). Trade-Offs Between Assessor Team Size and Assessor Expertise in Affecting Rating Accuracy in Assessment Centers. *Journal of Work and Organizational Psychology, 29*: 13-20. DOI: http://dx.doi.org/10.5093/tr2013a3.

CHAPTER 16 REFERENCES

Caldwell, C., Thornton, G. S. & Gruys, M. L. (2003). Ten Classic Assessment Center Errors: Challenges to Selection Validity. *Public Personnel Management, 32*(1): 73- 88.

Dewberry, C. (2011). Integrating Candidate Data: Consensus or Arithmetic? In N. G. Povah & G. C. Thornton (Eds.). *Assessment Centres and Global Talent Management* (pp. 33-46). Surrey, UK: Gower Publishing Press.

Dewberry, C. & Jackson, D. (2016). The Perceived Nature and Incidence of Dysfunctional Assessment Center Features and Processes. *International Journal of Selection and Assessment, 24*(2): 189-196.

International Taskforce on Assesment Center Guidelines. (2015). Guidelines and ethical considerations for assessment center operations. *Journal of Management, 41*: 1244-1273. http://dx.doi.org/10.1177/0149206314567780.

Kuncel, N. R., Klieger, D. M., Connelly, B. S. & Ones, D. S. (2013). Mechanical Versus Clinical Data Combination in Selection and Admissions Decisions: A Meta-Analysis. *Journal of Applied Psychology, 98*(6): 1060-1072. DOI:10.1037//a0034156.

Meiring, D. & Buckett, A. (2016). Best practice guidelines for the use of the assessment centre method in South Africa (5th ed.). *SA Journal of Industrial Psychology/SA Tydskrif vir Bedryfsielkunde, 42*(1): a1298. http://dx.doi.org/10.4102/sajip.v42i1.1298

SA Assessment Centre Study Group. (2018). *Code of Ethics for Assessment Centres in South-Africa*. Retrieved from https://www.acsg.co.za/sites/default/files/Code-of-Ethics-for-ACs-inSA-15-March-2018-ACSG.pdf. Accessed 7 January 2019.

Thornton, G. C. (2011). Fifty Years on: The Ongoing Reciprocal Impact of Science and Practice on the Assessment Center Method. In N. Povah & G. C. Thornton (Eds.). *Assessment Centres and Global Talent Management* (pp.163 – 171). Surrey, UK: Gower Publishing Limited.

Thornton, G. C., Rupp, D. E. & Hoffman, B. J. (2015). *Assessment Center Perspectives for Talent Management Strategies* (2nd ed.). New York, NY: Routledge.

Woodruffe, C. (1993). *Assessment Centres: Identifying and developing competence* (2nd ed.). London, UK: Institute of Personnel Management.

CHAPTER 17 REFERENCES

Abraham, J. D., Morrison, J. D. & Burnett, D. D. (2006). Feedback Seeking Among Developmental Assessment Center Participants. *Journal of Business and Psychology, 20*(3): 383-394. DOI: 10.1007/s10869-005-9008-z.

Blume, B. D., Ford, J. K., Baldwin, T. T. & Huang, J. L. (2010). Transfer of Training: A Meta-Analytic Review. *Journal of Management, 36*(4): 1065-1105. DOI: 10.1177/0149206309352880.

Dewberry, C. & Jackson, D. (2016). The Perceived Nature and Incidence of Dysfunctional Assessment Center Features and Processes. *International Journal of Selection and Assessment, 24*(2): 189-196.

Goodge, P. (1994). Development Centres: Design Generation and Effectiveness. *Journal of Management Development, 13*(4): 16-22.

Hughes, D., Riley, P., Shalfrooshan, A., Gibbons, A. & Thornton, G. C. (2012). *A Global Survey of Assessment Centre Practices.* A Research Report by a&dc and Colorado State University.

Joseph, A. (1977). *Put it in writing.* New York: McGraw-Hill.

Lanik, M. (2018). *The Leader Habit: Master the Skills you Need to Lead in Just Minutes a Day.* New York, NY: American Management Association.

McCarthy, A. & Garavan, T. (2006). Post feedback Development Perceptions: Applying the Theory of Planned Behavior. *Human Resource Development Quarterly, 17*(3): 245-267. DOI: 10.1002/hrdq.1173.

Meiring, D. & Buckett, A. (2016). Best practice guidelines for the use of the assessment centre method in South Africa (5th ed.). *SA Journal of Industrial Psychology/SA Tydskrif vir Bedryfsielkunde, 42*(1): a1298. http://dx.doi.org/10.4102/sajip.v42i1.1298

Protection of Personal Information. (2013). Act No. 4. (South Africa).

SA Assessment Centre Study Group. (2018). *Code of Ethics for Assessment Centres in South-Africa.* Retrieved from: https://www.acsg.co.za/sites/default/files/Code-of-Ethics-for-ACs-inSA-15-March-2018-ACSG.pdf. Accessed 7 January 2019.

Schlebusch, S. & De Wet, C. (March 2007). *Giving feedback after the centre.* Workshop presented at the 27th Annual Conference of the AC Study Group, 14 March, Protea Hotel, Stellenbosch.

Schlebusch, S. (March 2019). *Creating Behaviour Change = Creating Mobility.* IGNITE presentation at the annual Assessment Centre Study Group's conference, Somerset-West, South Africa.

Strauss, R. (March 2018). *Making Future Talent Work Through Coaching Development Centres.* Paper presented at the annual Assessment Centre Study Group's conference, Sandton, South Africa

The British Psychological Society's Division of Occupational Psychology. (2015). *The Design and Delivery of Assessment Centres.* Leicester, UK: The British Psychological Society.

Thornton, G. C., Rupp, D. E. & Hoffman, B. J. (2015). *Assessment Center Perspectives for Talent Management Strategies* (2nd ed.). New York, NY: Routledge.

Thornton, G. C., Mueller-Hanson, R. A., & Rupp, D. E. (2017). *Developing Organizational Simulations: A Guide for Practitioners, Students, and Researchers* (2nd ed.). New York, NY: Routledge.

CHAPTER 18 REFERENCES

Byham, W. C. (1978). How to improve the validity of an assessment center. *Training and Development Journal, 31*(11): 4-6.

Byham, W. C. & Temlock, S. (1972). Operational validity – a new concept in personnel testing. *Personnel Journal, 51*: 639-647, 654.

Fodchuk, K. M. & Sidebotham, E. J. (2005). Procedural justice in the selection process: a review of research and suggestions for practical applications. *The Psychologist–Manager Journal, 8*(2): 105-120.

Müller, K.-P., & Roodt, G. (2013). Content validation: The forgotten step-child or a crucial step in assessment centre validation? *SA Journal of Industrial Psychology/SA Tydskrif vir Bedryfsielkunde, 39*(1): Art. #1153, 15 pages. http://dx.doi.org/10.4102/ sajip.v39i1.1153.

Rupp, D. E., Baldwin, A. & Bashshur, M. (2006). Using developmental assessment centers to foster workplace fairness. *The Psychologist–Manager Journal, 9*(2): 145-170.

SA Assessment Centre Study Group. (2018). *Code of Ethics for Assessment Centres in South-Africa.* Retrieved from: https://www.acsg.co.za/sites/default/files/Code-of-Ethics-for-ACs-inSA-15-March-2018-ACSG.pdf. Accessed 7 January 2019.

Society for Industrial and Organisational Psychology (SIOP). (2018). *Principles for the validation and use of personnel selection procedures.* OH: American Psychological Society.

Thornton, G. C. & Rupp, D. E. (2006). *Assessment centers in human resource management: strategies for prediction, diagnosis and development.* Mahwah, New Jersey: Lawrence Erlbaum Associates.

Wolfaardt, J. B. & Roodt, G. (2005). Basic concepts. In C. Foxcroft & G. Roodt (Eds.). *An introduction to psychological assessment in the South African context.* Cape Town: Oxford University Press.

CHAPTER 19 REFERENCES

Allen, M. J. & Yen, W. M. (1979). *Introduction to measurement theory.* Belmont, CA: Brooks/Cole Publishing Company.

American Educational Research Association (AERA), American Psychological Association (APA), & National Council on Measurement in Education (NCME). (2014). *Standards for Educational and Psychological Testing.* Washington, DC: American Educational Research Association.

Buckett, A., Becker, J. R. & Roodt, G. (2017). General performance factors and group differences in assessment center ratings. *Journal of Managerial Psychology, 32*(4): 298-313, https://doi.org/10.1108/JMP-08-2016-0264.

Byham, W.C. & Temlock, S. (1972). Operational validity – a new concept in personnel testing. *Personnel Journal, 51*: 639-647, 654.

Campbell, D.T. & Fiske, D.W. (1959). Convergent and discriminant validation by the multitrait–multimethod matrix. *Psychological Bulletin, 56,* 81-105.

Chen, H.-C. & Naquin, S. S. (2006). An integrative model of competency development, training design, assessment center, and multi-rater assessment. *Advances in Developing Human Resources, 8*(2): 265-282.

Cook, R. A. & Herche, J. (1994). Assessment centers: a contrast of usage in diverse environments. *The International Executive, 36*(5), 645-656.

Cronbach, L. J. & Meehl, P. E. (1955). Construct validity in psychological tests. *Psychological Bulletin, 52*: 281-302.

Employment Equity Act. (1998). Act No. 55. (South Africa). Government Gazette, No 19370.

Foxcroft, C. & Roodt, G. (2004). *An introduction to psychological assessment in the South African context.* Cape Town, SA: Oxford University Press.

Gibbons, A. M., Rupp, D. E., Snyder, L. A., Holub, A. S. & Woo, S. E. (2006). A preliminary investigation of developable dimensions. *The Psychologist–Manager Journal, 9*(2): 99-123.

Guilford, J. P. (1936). *Psychometric methods.* New York: McGraw-Hill Book Company.

Howell, D. C. (1995). *Fundamental statistics for the behavioral sciences.* Belmont, CA: Wadsworth Publishing.

Jansen, P. & Vinkenburg, C. (n.d.). *Predicting objective career success from assessment center data: dynamic predictor effects.* (Unpublished document)

Nunnally, J. C. & Bernstein I. H. (1994). *Psychometric theory.* New York: McGraw-Hill Book Company.

Roodt, G. (2007). *The reliability of structured interviews: competency rating interviews as a case in point.* Paper presented at the 27th Annual Conference of the AC Study Group, 14-16 March 2007, Protea Hotel, Stellenbosch.

Roodt, G. & Schlebusch, S. (2006). *Validation research on a collaborative development centre.* Paper presented at the 26th Annual Conference of the AC Study Group, 23-24 March, Spier Estate, Stellenbosch.

Roodt, G., Odendaal, A. & Schlebusch, S. (2003). *Lessons learnt from research on a centre.* Paper presented at the AC Study Group, 13-14 March Spier Estate, Stellenbosch.

Runyon, R. P. & Haber, A. (1980). *Fundamentals of behavioral statistics.* Reading, MA: Addison-Wesley Publishing Company.

Rupp, D. E., Gibbons, A. M., Baldwin, A. M., Snyder, L. A., Spain, S. M., Woo, S.E., Brummel, B. J., Sims, C. S. & Kim, M. (2006). An initial validation of developmental assessment centers as accurate assessments and effective training interventions. *The Psychologist–Manager, 9*(2): 171-200.

Schlebusch, S., Odendaal, A. & Roodt, G. (June 2003). *On the reliability of AC scores.* Paper presented at the Sixth Annual Industrial Psychology Conference, 25-27 June, Sandton Convention Centre, Johannesburg.

Society for Industrial and Organisational Psychology (SIOP). (2018). *Principles for the validation and use of personnel selection procedures.* OH: American Psychological Society.

Thornton, G. C. & Rupp, D. E. (2006). *Assessment centers in human resource management: strategies for prediction, diagnosis and development.* Mahwah, New Jersey: Lawrence Erlbaum Associates.

Thornton, G. C., Rupp, D. E., & Hoffman, B. J. (2015). *Assessment Center Perspectives for Talent Management Strategies.* New York: Routledge.

Wolfaardt, J. B. & Roodt, G. (2005). Basic concepts. In C. Foxcroft & G. Roodt (Eds.). *An introduction to psychological assessment in the South African context.* Cape Town: Oxford University Press.

CHAPTER 20 REFERENCES

Arthur, W. Jr., Day, E. A., McNelly, T. L. & Edens, P. S. (2003). A meta-analysis of the criterion-related validity of assessment center dimensions. *Personnel Psychology, 56: 125-154.*

Bersin, J. (2017a). *Effective Use of People Analytics is Strongly Related to Improved Talent and Business Outcomes.* Retrieved from: https://home.bersin.com/deloittes-bersin-finds-effective-use-people-analytics-strongly-related-improved-talent-business-outcomes/

Bersin, J. (2017b). *People Analytics: Here with a Vengeance.* Retrieved from: https://www.forbes.com/sites/joshbersin/2017/12/16/people-analytics-here-with-a-vengeance/1/

Brophy, M. & Kiely, T. (2002). Competencies: A New Sector. *Journal of European Industrial Training, 26: 165–176.*

Cheeseman, J. (2016). *HireVue Goes Beyond Video Interviews to Tackle Artificial Intelligence.* Retrieved from: http://recruitingtools.com/hireview-digital-assessment/ Accessed 22 December 2017.

Deloitte. (2017). *Rewriting the rules for the digital age: 2017 Deloitte Global Human Capital Trends.* Retrieved from: https://www2.deloitte.com/za/en/pages/human-capital/articles/introduction-human-capital-trends.html

Gartner Talent Daily Global Talent Monitor. (2019). *With Brexit Uncertainty Looming, UK Businesses and Employees Lose Confidence in Economy.* Retrieved from: https://www.cebglobal.com/talentdaily/tag/global-talent-monitor/

General Data Protection Regulation (GDPR). (2018). *The EU General Data Protection Regulation (GDPR) is the most important change in data privacy regulation in 20 years.* Retrieved from: https://www.eugdpr.org/

Gilliland, S. (1994). Effects of procedural and distributive justice on reactions to a selection system. *Journal of Applied Psychology, 79: 691-701.*

Guillén, L. & Saris, W. E. (2013). Competencies, personality traits, and organizational rewards of middle managers: A motive-based approach. *Human Performance, 26: 66-92.*

Harris, M. M., Paese, M. & Greising, L. (2008). A Field Study of Participant Reactions to a Developmental Assessment Centre: Testing an organisational justice model. *Psychologica Belgica, 48*(2-3): 177–195. DOI: http://doi.org/10.5334/pb-48-2-3-177

Hoffman, B. J. (Chair), Arthur, W., Lance, C. E., Lievens, F., Russell, C. J. & Woehr, D. J. (2008). *Assessment center validity: Where do we go from here?* Paper presented at the 23rd annual meeting of the Society for Industrial and Organizational Psychology. San Francisco, CA.

Hughes, D., Riley, P., Shalfrooshan, A., Gibbons, A. & Thornton, G. C (2012). *A Global Survey of Assessment Centre Practices.* A Research Report by a&dc and Colorado State University

International Standard on Assessment Delivery (ISO 10667). (2011). *ISO 10667-1: 2011 Assessment service delivery: Procedures and methods to assess people in work and organizational settings – Part 1: Requirements for the client.* Retrieved from: https://www.iso.org/standard/56441.html

International Taskforce on Assessment Center Guidelines. (2015). Guidelines and Ethical Considerations for Assessment Center Operations. *Journal of Management, 41*(4): 1244-1273.

Jackson, D. J. R., Michaelides, G., Dewberry, C. & Kim, Y.-J. (2016). Everything that you have ever been told about assessment center ratings is confounded. *Journal of Applied Psychology, 101*(7): 976-994.

Klein, A. L. (1996). Validity and Reliability for Competency-Based Systems: Reducing Litigation Risks. *Compensation and Benefits Review,* Jul/Aug: 31–39. http://dx.doi.org/10.1177/08863687960 2800405

Lievens, F. (2001). Assessor training strategies and their effects on accuracy, interrater reliability, and discriminant validity. *Journal of Applied Psychology, 86*(2): 255-264. Retrieved from: http://dx.doi.org/10.1037/0021-9010.86.2.255

Lievens, F., Schollaert, E. & Keen, G. (2015). The interplay of elicitation and evaluation of trait-expressive behavior: Evidence in assessment center exercises. *Journal of Applied Psychology, 100*(4): 1169-1188.

Lloyd, T. (2015). *The Pace of Change in the VUCA World.* Retrieved from: http://vucabook.com/the-pace-of-change-in-the-vuca-world/ Accessed 22 December 2017.

Lloyd's Banking Group. (2016). *Introducing Virtual Reality to attract the best Digital and IT talent. Retrieved from:* http://lloydsbankinggroupdigital.com/introducing-virtual-reality-to-attract-the-best-digital-talent/ Accessed 25 January 2018.

McKinsey (2018). *Why diversity matters.* Retrieved from: https://www.mckinsey.com/business-functions/organization/our-insights/why-diversity-matters Accessed February 5, 2018.

Mercer. (2017). Mercer Talent Trends Study: 2017 Global Study Empowerment in a Disrupted World. Retrieved from: https://qtxasset.com/cfoinnovation/field/field_p_files/white_paper/mercer-global-talent-trends-study-report_2017.pdf

O'Reilly, C. (2016). *The key to recruiting millennials.* Retrieved from https://www.personneltoday.com/hr/key-recruiting-millennials/ Accessed 25 January 2018.

Povah, N., Crabb, S. & McGarrigle, R. M. (2008). *The Global Research Report: An International Survey of Assessment Centre Practices.* A Research Report by a&dc.

Ritholtz, B. (2017). *The World Is About To Change Even Faster.* Retrieved from: https://www.bloomberg.com/view/articles/2017-07-06/the-world-is-about-to-change-even-faster Accessed 22 December 2017.

Rotman, D. (2017) *The Relentless Pace of Automation.* Retrieved from: https://www.technologyreview.com/s/603465/the-relentless-pace-of-automation/ Accessed 22 December 2017.

Society for Human Resource Management (SHRM). (2012). *Succession Planning: What is a 9-box grid?* Retrieved from: https://www.shrm.org/resourcesandtools/tools-and-samples/hr-qa/pages/whatsa9boxgridandhow-cananhrdepartmentuseit.aspx

Tett, R. P., Guterman, H. A., Bleier, A. & Murphy, P. J. (2000). Development and content validation of a 'hyperdimensional' taxonomy of managerial competence. *Human Relations, 13:* 205–251. http://dx.doi.org/10.1207/s15327043hup1303_1

The British Psychological Society. (2015). *The Design and Delivery of Assessment Centres: A Standard produced by the British Psychological Society's Division of Occupational Psychology. Retrieved from:* https://www1.bps.org.uk/networks-and-communities/member-microsite/division-occupational-psychology/news/publication-launch-design-and-delivery-assessment-centres. Accessed 22 December 2017.

Thornton, G. C. & Gibbons, A. M. (2009). Validity of assessment centers for personnel selection. *Human Resource Management Review,* 19: 169-187.

Willyerd, K. (2015). *Millennials Want to Be Coached at Work.* Retrieved from: https://hbr.org/2015/02/millennials-want-to-be-coached-at-work Accessed 20 January 2018.

EPILOGUE REFERENCES

Buckett, A., Becker, J. R. & Roodt, G. (2017). General performance factors and group differences in assessment center ratings. *Journal of Managerial Psychology, 32*(4): 298-313. Doi.org/10.1108/JMP-08-2016-0264.

Deloitte. (2019). *Leading the social enterprise: Reinvent with a human focus*. Retrieved from: https://www2.deloitte.com/content/dam/Deloitte/us/Documents/human-capital/us-human-capital-leading-the-social-enterprise-reinvent-with-a-human-focus.PDF

Statistics South Africa. (2019). *Quarterly Labour Force Survey Quarter 1*. Retrieved from: http://www.statssa.gov.za/publications/P0211/P02111stQuarter2019.pdf#page=7

Trading Economics. (2019). *South Africa Economic Indicators*. Retrieved from: https://tradingeconomics.com/

World Economic Forum. (2018). *The Future of Jobs Report*. Retrieved from: http://www3.weforum.org/docs/WEF_Future_of_Jobs_2018.pdf

INDEX

A

Adverse impact, 417
Aggregation, 184, 195, 352, 472
Agreement, 116
  project scope, 116
  time frame, 116
Analysis, 17–18, 93, 117, 119, 143–145, 154–156, 175,
    212–213, 257, 280–282, 291–292, 306, 362–363,
    400, 444–445
  broad business context, 117
  business case, 78, 445
  exercise, 212–213, 226, 280–282, 291–292, 362, 431
  information, 78, 144, 154–155, 213, 257, 280, 282, 362,
    431
  job, 17–18, 93, 97, 119, 139, 143–145, 154–156, 175,
    306, 330, 400
  options, 112
  stage, 17–18, 93–94, 97, 119, 139, 175–176, 306, 330,
    400–401, 444–445
Analytics, 464
Annual, 25, 30–32, 34, 38
  conference, 31–32, 34, 38
Assessment, 6–8, 20–33, 35–36, 41–44, 51–54, 61–62,
    64–65, 74–75, 78–79, 214–216, 260, 330–334, 367–
    369, 445, 461–463
  centre guidelines, 32
  development, 3, 10–11, 22–25, 27, 30, 79, 197–198,
    218–219, 270, 273, 316, 331, 367–368, 372, 472–473
Assessment Centre, 10–11, 20–26, 28–29, 32–33, 35–36,
    62, 64–65, 70–71, 74–75, 78–79, 83–84, 87–88,
    197–198, 214, 367–369
  administrator, 23, 246, 267, 333, 350, 362, 454
  applications, 78
  Blueprint, 87, 197–199, 214, 219, 267, 295
  coaching, 273, 316
  collaborative, 23
  constitution, 29
  design hints, 267–268
  development, 10–11, 20, 22–25, 75, 79, 83, 197–199,
    206, 267, 270, 273, 316, 362, 367–369, 473
  diagnostic, 78, 270, 367–368, 473
  features, 6, 454
  functional, 6, 197, 219, 267, 295
  guidelines, 6, 28, 32–33, 53, 64, 70, 79, 225, 260, 262,
    445, 461–462
  learning, 21–23, 79, 316, 473
  manual, 350
  objectives, 29
  performance, 24, 84, 205, 333, 368
  policy, 78–79, 443
  purpose, 21, 65, 79, 91, 201, 270, 295, 350, 367, 369, 473
  stakeholders, 12, 87, 408, 461
  system, 79
  technical, 198
  traditional, 23, 309
  types, 219–220

B

Behaviour Observation Scale (BOS), 217, 238
Behavioural consistency, 180
Behavioural observation, 8
Budget, 250
Building, 118, 189, 291–292
  business case, 118
  project plan, 118
Business, 27, 36–37, 78–79, 128, 130, 170, 228, 389–390,
    445, 448, 467
  analysis, 445, 448
  game, 228–229

C

Career path, 344
Checklists, 201, 241, 243
Classifying behaviour, 327
Client organisation, 330
Coaching Development Centre (CDC), 389
Company, 29, 170, 214
  strategy, 170
Competency, 131, 133–134, 143–144, 152–153, 214–216,
    241–242, 281–282, 313–314, 317–318, 334–335,
    358–359, 391, 429–431, 445–446, 473–474
  designing, 95
  elements, 95, 134, 143, 161, 174, 299, 412, 446
  levels, 130, 144, 161, 314, 335
  modelling, 143–144
  profile instruments, 152
  profiles, 95, 159, 161, 174
  redundancies, 441
  representative sample, 445
  summary form, 281–282, 299

Competent, 7, 291, 347, 413–414, 437
  observers, 7, 347
  process owners, 347
Comprehensive, 263, 395
  development plans, 395
Conclusion, 41, 75, 471
Conduct ACs, 397
Considerations, 30, 62–63, 70–71, 74–75, 84, 114, 260,
    324, 445, 462
Constitution, 43, 46–47, 49, 99–100, 115
Construct (identification) validity, 436
Content, 18, 41, 81, 93, 175, 319, 323–324, 400, 403, 409,
    417, 421, 435, 444, 449
  description, 324, 435
  evaluation, 18, 93, 175, 306, 400, 403–404, 409, 421
  relevance, 403, 409
Continued training, 332
Corporate, 117
  climate, 117
  culture, 117
Covariance, 137
Critical, 110, 112, 134, 138, 151–152, 445
  incidents, 110, 151–152
Cross-cultural issues, 441
Cutting time, 359

D

DAC participant final report, 283
Data capturing, 392
Data integration, 8, 57, 206, 272–273, 341, 352
  process, 272, 352
Debriefing sessions, 299, 341
Demarcation of terminology, 2
Deon Meiring, 21, 24, 29
Design, 17–18, 169, 175, 195–197, 232, 253, 255, 257,
    290–291, 293, 295, 306, 400, 444–448, 473
  centre, 197, 219, 260, 267, 295, 473
  evaluation, 18, 175, 306, 400–401, 473
  model, 144, 175, 182, 291, 293, 306, 330, 400–401,
    444–448, 473
  objectives, 17, 196
  process, 69, 144, 255, 257, 267, 306, 444, 473
  purpose, 17, 138, 169–170, 232, 473
  simulations, 18, 93, 169–170, 175, 197, 219, 253, 255,
    267, 293, 295, 306, 400, 446–447, 473
  stage, 17–18, 93, 175–176, 197, 219, 267, 295, 306,
    330, 400–401, 444–448
  team, 17, 169, 257, 290–291, 295, 306, 473
  validation, 175, 306, 400–401

Development plans, 11, 287, 368
Diagnostic, 2–3, 16, 23, 270, 272, 341, 352, 367–368,
    473
  assessment centre, 270, 367–368, 473
  purposes, 2, 16, 270, 367–368
Different, 2, 126, 128, 135, 159, 401, 410, 418, 421–
    422, 427, 438–439, 442–443, 472, 475, 477–478
  management levels, 126, 128, 135, 173
  organisational effectiveness, 173
  outcome levels, 135
  views, 173
Diversity, 41, 47, 53, 56–57, 66
Document everything, 167

E

Economical, 137
Effectiveness, 18, 93, 121, 135, 158, 175, 183, 306, 400
  analysis, 18, 93, 175, 306, 400
  criteria model, 121
Equitable and fair, 416
Error variance, 136, 474
Ethical, 30, 37, 39, 61–63, 66–72, 74–75, 104–105, 260,
    324, 445, 462
  conduct, 104–105
Ethnocultural diversity, 59, 474
Exercise effects, 440
Experience, 141, 409–410
  content, 409
  process, 409–410
External, 310–311, 316
  observers, 310–311, 316
  specialists, 310, 316

F

Face validity, 409, 435, 444
Facilitating, 279
Feedback, 2–3, 9–10, 79, 112, 215, 218, 272–273, 286,
    296–300, 338, 341, 368–371, 374–376, 379, 474
  discussions, 10, 341
  process, 79, 272, 296–297, 300, 368, 474
  training, 79, 112, 338
Fidelity, 189, 191–192, 196, 201, 217, 474
Figures, 284, 433
Filip Lievens, 27–28
Final, 116, 155–156, 241, 280–284, 288, 352, 391, 440
  approval from the top, 116
  report, 241, 281–283
Focus-group discussions, 150
Functional ACs, 2, 6

G

Gamification, 186, 195, 474
Gender neutral names, 232
General Data Protection Regulations (GDPR), 64
Gert Roodt, 1, 26, 97, 119, 403, 421
Growth framework, 385

H

Hand-outs, 288, 299
Human capital department, 14, 315

I

Identify and develop evaluation criteria, 138
Image in the media, 111
Implement, 17, 368, 386, 397, 448–449
   processes, 17, 397
   stage, 17–18, 448
Important validity considerations, 253
Inclusion, 470
Insourcing, 84–85
Interactionist Theory, 195, 231, 263–264, 475
Internal, 123, 129, 311, 315
   human capital specialists, 310, 315
   versus external observers, 311
Inter-rater, 338, 432, 475
Interview, 215–216, 357, 362, 446
Intra-rater, 432, 475

J

Job analysis, 6, 95, 97, 111, 119, 139–140, 475
   competencies, 6, 120, 140, 475
   competency profiles, 95
   purpose, 140
   target, 140
   techniques, 475
Job and job family analyses, 418

L

Learning ACs, 2, 4
Line managers as observers, 314

M

Maintaining the AC, 394
Management, 22, 25, 31, 110, 125–130, 287, 363, 412–413, 416, 431, 470, 475
   behavioural elements, 416
   competency profiles, 110
   functions, 125, 127, 129
   generic, 126, 130, 475
   information systems (MIS), 110
   key functions, 127
   levels, 110, 127–130, 475
   strategic, 127–128, 130
   top, 22, 25, 127–128, 130, 475
Maximum or typical performance, 210
Measure, 113, 424
   central tendency, 424
Model, 144, 175, 182–183, 195, 202, 291, 293, 306, 318, 330, 400, 444–448, 477
Multiple, 7, 56, 58, 112–113, 121, 154, 187, 196, 475
   observers, 7, 112, 187

N

National government policy priorities, 108
Needs analysis, 97, 119, 139, 476
   specific, 97
Nigel Povah, 451
North America, 42, 451, 462, 467

O

Observer, 216–217, 236–237, 242, 244–246, 272–273, 276–277, 280, 298–299, 310–311, 313, 318–319, 337–340, 363–364, 446–447, 476–477
   content, 59, 298, 319, 339
   guidelines, 245–246, 298, 319, 446–447
   process, 236, 244, 299, 310, 313, 319, 322, 338, 350, 472, 477
   purpose, 236, 245
   report form, 216, 236, 242, 244, 255, 298, 446
   selection criteria, 313
   selection criteria and competencies, 313
   training, 56, 59, 263, 318–319, 322, 338–340, 447
One-to-one interaction simulation, 222
Oral, 42, 159, 183, 212, 227–228, 291–292, 430–431
   fact-finding exercise, 228
   presentation, 212, 227–228, 291
Organisational, 18, 31, 77, 87, 93, 97, 119–120, 122, 139, 163, 170, 175, 306, 369, 371
   context, 18
   effectiveness analysis, 18, 93, 97, 119, 139, 175, 306, 400
Outsourcing, 84–85
Overall fairness perceptions, 411

P

Parallel centre, 387
Participant, 64–67, 73–75, 199, 217, 234–235, 237, 239, 269, 274–277, 280, 282, 297–299, 327–328, 472–473, 476
  experience, 299, 350
  instructions, 199, 234–235, 254, 298
  report form, 235, 298
  role, 199, 217, 234, 255, 274, 298–299, 327, 433
Performance management systems, 110
Philippa Riley, 451
Point of assessment, 204
Post-AC processes, 308
Potential sources, 433
Practical and accessible, 137
Pre-AC, 288
  documents, 288
Pre-pilot, 232, 254, 476
Principles, 64, 194, 260, 377–378, 462
Process, 87, 125, 147, 171, 201, 232, 271–275, 322, 335, 363, 389, 404, 408, 476
  mapping, 147
  owners, 271, 404, 408, 476
Programme, 11, 16, 24, 88, 277, 389, 476
  observer, 277
  participant, 277
  process, 16, 476
Project, 115–117, 129–130, 165, 246, 344
  ambassadors, 115, 117
  communication plan, 116
  leader, 115, 344
  sponsor, 115
  steering committee, 115
Promotion, 38, 99, 260
  equality, 99
  prevention, 99
Psychometric theories, 183
Purpose, 79, 143, 201, 319, 370, 407
  observer training, 319

Q

Questionnaires, 150

R

Rating, 155–156, 201, 205–206, 216, 218, 237, 239, 242, 244, 281, 391, 432, 440, 472, 477
  distributions, 440, 477
  final, 155, 281–282, 363, 391, 472, 477

integrated, 201, 218
  raw, 237, 239, 242, 472
  selection purposes, 201, 205–206
Realistic Accuracy Model (RAM), 318, 477
Reconciliation of all costs, 394
Related fairness perceptions, 409
Reliabilities, 427, 429
Reliability, 18, 72, 93, 175, 264, 306, 400, 423, 427, 431, 444, 477
Republic of South Africa, 43–44, 260, 445
Research, 38, 41, 48, 50, 54–55, 60, 63, 107, 156, 179, 191
  purposes, 63
Resource, 116, 121, 145–146
  approval, 116
  plan, 115–116
Role-player, 248, 255, 277, 477

S

Sandra Schlebusch, 1, 29, 139, 197, 219, 253, 267, 295, 309, 349, 367
Security, 259–260, 319
Selecting, 15, 310
Senior managers, 15
Service provider, 291
Shelf information, 146
Simulation, 56, 58, 80–83, 171, 209, 243–244, 246, 254, 265–266, 268, 272–273, 298–299, 338, 358–359, 446
  approach, 358–359
  design, 199, 209, 265, 268, 446, 477
  documentation, 251, 265
  duration, 216
  interaction, 299
  modularity, 231
  specifications, 199, 340
  types, 209
Sources of information, 108
Spreadsheets, 289, 299
Stakeholder, 38, 477
Stella Nkomo, 41
Steps and stages, 17
Strategic relevance, 413–414
Study group *See* Assessment Centre Study Group
Success and Competency Profiling Software Platform, 153
Succession planning, 110
Supportive processes, 395
Survey, 122, 153, 454

T

Taxonomy, 145, 187–188, 191, 196
  of aspects of fidelity, 191, 196
  competencies, 187, 196
  simulations, 191, 196
Technology, 201, 207–208, 217, 222, 229, 260–261,
    314, 335, 462
Test the AC, 296
Threats, 439
Time pressure, 434
Traditional ACs, 2–3
Training, 2, 11, 246, 250, 290, 293, 299, 318, 322, 324,
    330–331, 335, 338–340, 342, 390
  content, 59, 299, 324, 335, 339, 341
  process, 322, 331, 335, 340, 342
Trait ivation Theory (TAT), 189, 230, 330, 478

U

Unbiased, 417
Understanding, 95, 98, 169, 173, 187, 230, 246
  diverse context, 98
  dynamics, 95, 173
  organisational trends, 169
  specific needs, 95, 173
  target job context, 169
Unions, 15, 122
Unitary validity, 438, 478

V

Validity, 18, 42, 93, 175, 264, 306, 400, 403, 417, 421,
    423, 438, 448–449, 478
  constructs, 423, 449
Various, 7, 12, 28, 31, 49, 145, 164, 218, 224, 263, 291,
    390
  matrices, 218
  simulations, 7, 218
Virtual Assessment Centre (VAC), 207
VUCA, 188, 452, 458, 466, 478

W

Walk the talk, 361
Work-profiling system (WPS), 153